FOOD & WINE

ANNUAL COOKBOOK 2016

FOOD & WINE
ANNUAL COOKBOOK 2016
EDITOR IN CHIEF **Dana Cowin**
EXECUTIVE EDITOR **Kate Heddings**
EDITOR **Susan Choung**
DESIGNER **Alisha Petro**
DEPUTY WINE EDITOR **Megan Krigbaum**
COPY EDITOR **Lisa Leventer**
PRODUCTION DIRECTOR
Joseph Colucci
PRODUCTION MANAGERS
Stephanie Thompson, David Richey
EDITORIAL ASSISTANT **Kate Malczewski**

FRONT COVER

Pork Chop with Fennel and Juniper
(recipe, p. 172)
PHOTOGRAPHER **Con Poulos**
FOOD STYLIST **Simon Andrews**
STYLE EDITOR **Suzie Myers**

BACK COVER

PHOTOGRAPHER (CHICKEN AND SALAD)
Con Poulos
PHOTOGRAPHER (PUDDING) **John Kernick**

ISBN 0-8487-4838-7

ISSN 1097-1564

Manufactured in
the United States of America

FOOD & WINE MAGAZINE
SVP/EDITOR IN CHIEF **Dana Cowin**
CREATIVE DIRECTOR **Fredrika Stjärne**
EXECUTIVE MANAGING EDITOR **Mary Ellen Ward**
EXECUTIVE EDITOR **Pamela Kaufman**
DEPUTY EDITOR **Christine Quinlan**
EXECUTIVE FOOD EDITOR **Tina Ujlaki**
EXECUTIVE WINE EDITOR **Ray Isle**
DIGITAL DIRECTOR **Alex Vallis**

FOOD
FOOD DIRECTOR **Kate Heddings**
TEST KITCHEN SENIOR EDITORS **Justin Chapple,
Kay Chun**
TEST KITCHEN ASSOCIATE EDITOR **Anna Painter**
ASSISTANT EDITOR **Julia Heffelfinger**
TEST KITCHEN ASSISTANT **Emily Tylman**

FEATURES
RESTAURANT EDITOR **Kate Krader**
DEPUTY WINE EDITOR **Megan Krigbaum**
DEPUTY DIGITAL EDITOR
Lawrence Marcus
SENIOR EDITORS **Lucy Madison,
Justine Sterling**
STYLE EDITOR **Suzie Myers**
ASSOCIATE EDITORS **Noah Kaufman,
Chelsea Morse**
ASSISTANT EDITOR **Brianna Wippman**
EDITORIAL ASSISTANT **Morgan Goldberg**

ART
ART DIRECTOR **James Maikowski**
ASSOCIATE ART DIRECTOR **Kelly McGuire**
DESIGNER **Mark Romero**

PHOTO
PHOTO EDITOR **Sara Parks**
PHOTO ASSISTANT **Rebecca Delman**

COPY & RESEARCH
COPY CHIEF **Elizabeth Herr**
SENIOR EDITOR **Amanda Woytus**
ASSOCIATE RESEARCH EDITOR **Erin Laverty Healy**

PRODUCTION
Joseph Colucci (Director), **Patrick Sheehan,
Nestor Cervantes, David Richey, Elsa Säätelä**
(Associate Digital Producer)

ASSOCIATE MANAGING EDITOR **Kerianne Hansen**
ASSISTANT TO THE EDITOR IN CHIEF **Annie P. Quigley**

FOOD&WINE

ANNUAL COOKBOOK 2016

AN ENTIRE YEAR OF COOKING

FOOD&WINE
BOOKS
Time Inc. Affluent Media Group

CONTENTS

LINGUINE WITH
CLAMS AND FENNEL
Recipe, page 94

PORK TENDERLOIN
WITH SAGE, GARLIC
AND HONEY
Recipe, page 173

FOREWORD

THE RISE OF THE GLOBAL NOMAD was a huge new trend FOOD & WINE noted in 2015. These food adventurers travel the world in search of new flavors, often documenting their adventures on social media. They've brought FOOD & WINE with them to familiar places like Rome (the inspiration for expat author Rachel Roddy's ingenious Buffalo Mozzarella with Neat and Messy Roasted Tomatoes; page 19) and more remote spots like Kabul, Afghanistan (where Berlin-based blogger Malin Elmlid learned to make Leek-and-Scallion Fry Bread; page 266).

Chefs with a passion for travel also brought their international perspective to FOOD & WINE: Mexican master Enrique Olvera introduced the classic Mexico City cooking that influenced his brilliant New York City restaurant, Cosme; TV chef Scott Conant explored Turkish home cooking on a family vacation to the Aegean resort town of Bodrum.

This year FOOD & WINE investigated global flavors in our beloved Gastronaut Files column, a DIY cook's dream with step-by-step photographs that make it easy to understand complex recipes. You'll find lessons and photos for dishes as diverse as Chinese dumplings (using a small rolling pin for the wrappers is key) and croissants (start with butter and dough at the same temperature).

The world's best cooking is becoming ever more accessible. We hope you will use this book to try new dishes, find new favorites and expand your own horizons.

Editor in Chief
FOOD & WINE

Executive Editor
FOOD & WINE Cookbooks

Blogger Mimi Thorisson runs a small pop-up restaurant in her Bordeaux villa. She cooks the rustic, seasonal food she loves, like a crisp, rich ham and cheese tart (recipe, p. 34).

STARTERS

CAMEMBERT
BAKED IN THE BOX
Recipe, page 20

WHIPPED CORN DIP
WITH CHILE OIL

Herbed Potato Chips

⏲ Total **45 min**; Serves **10 to 12**

- **3** large baking potatoes, scrubbed and patted dry
  Grapeseed oil, for frying
- **4** sage sprigs
- **3** rosemary sprigs
- **3** thyme sprigs
- **2** parsley sprigs
  Kosher salt

1. Using a mandoline, very thinly slice the potatoes crosswise into a large bowl. Cover with cold water and swish to rinse off the starch; drain. Repeat the rinsing until the water is clear. Transfer the potato slices to a paper towel–lined baking sheet and pat thoroughly dry.

2. In a large pot, heat 3 inches of oil to 360°. Add the sage, rosemary, thyme and parsley sprigs to the hot oil and fry, stirring, until crisp, 1 to 2 minutes. Using a slotted spoon, transfer the herbs to paper towels to drain.

3. Working in small batches, fry the potato slices at 350°, stirring occasionally, until golden, 3 to 5 minutes. Using a slotted spoon, transfer the potato chips to paper towels to drain. Generously sprinkle the chips and herbs with salt and serve.
—*Tyler Florence*

MAKE AHEAD The chips and herbs can be made early in the day and stored uncovered at room temperature.

Marinated Olives with Orange

⏲ Total **15 min**; Makes **1 quart**

- **2** Tbsp. extra-virgin olive oil
- **1** Tbsp. thinly sliced garlic
- **1½** tsp. finely grated orange zest
- **1** tsp. crushed red pepper
- **1** quart mixed olives
- **⅓** cup fresh orange juice

In a large skillet, heat the oil. Add the garlic, orange zest and crushed red pepper and cook over moderate heat, stirring, until the garlic is softened, about 2 minutes. Add the olives and cook, stirring, until hot, about 5 minutes. Remove from the heat and stir in the orange juice. Let cool completely, stirring occasionally. Serve at room temperature. —*Martha Wiggins*

Mixed Radishes with Yogurt Butter

⏲ Total **10 min**; Serves **8**

- **5** Tbsp. salted cultured butter, at room temperature
- **¼** cup plain whole-milk yogurt
  Coarse sea salt, for garnish
- **3** bunches of mixed radishes with their greens (about 2¼ lbs.)

In a small bowl, using a hand mixer, beat the butter with the yogurt at medium speed until well blended and fluffy, about 3 minutes. (Don't beat at high speed or the mixture will separate.) Transfer the yogurt butter to a serving bowl and garnish with sea salt. Serve with the radishes.
—*Zakary Pelaccio*

Roasted Onion Dip

Active **45 min**; Total **2 hr 45 min**
Serves **10 to 12**

- **2** medium unpeeled red onions
- **2** medium unpeeled Spanish onions
- **2** medium unpeeled sweet onions
- **½** cup mayonnaise
- **½** cup sour cream
- **½** tsp. onion powder
  Kosher salt and pepper
  Salmon, trout and sturgeon caviar, for serving
  Fennel fronds, for garnish
  Herbed Potato Chips (recipe at left), for serving

1. Preheat the oven to 350°. Using a paring knife, trim the bottoms of the onions and stand them in a baking dish. Bake until very soft, 1 hour and 30 minutes. Let cool.

2. Using a paring knife, carefully cut ½ inch off the top of the onions. Using a small spoon, scoop out all but 2 or 3 layers of the roasted onions to form cups; you should have 2½ cups of pulp. Finely chop the onion pulp and transfer to a medium bowl. Stir in the mayonnaise, sour cream and onion powder and season the dip generously with salt and pepper. Cover and refrigerate until chilled, about 30 minutes. Keep the onion cups at room temperature.

3. Spoon the onion dip into the onion cups and transfer to a platter. Top the dip with salmon, trout and sturgeon caviar and garnish with fennel fronds. Serve with Herbed Potato Chips. —*Tyler Florence*

Baby Kale and Cool Ranch Dip

⏲ Total **15 min**; Makes **3 cups**

This healthy, fast and supertasty dip features kale, buttermilk and the thick, creamy fresh cheese called lebneh.

- **10** oz. baby kale (12 cups)
- **2** cups lebneh (about 12 oz.)
- **¼** cup buttermilk
- **¼** cup chopped chives
- **1** Tbsp. granulated garlic
- **1** Tbsp. granulated onion
- **¾** tsp. dried dill
- **¾** tsp. dried parsley
  Kosher salt and pepper
  Crudités, for serving

In a medium saucepan of salted boiling water, blanch the kale until wilted, about 30 seconds. Drain well. Squeeze out any excess water and coarsely chop. Transfer to a medium bowl. Add the next 7 ingredients, season with salt and pepper and mix well. Serve with crudités.
—*Kay Chun*

Whipped Corn Dip with Chile Oil

⏲ Total **30 min**; Serves **6**

- **3** Tbsp. unsalted butter
- **2** cups fresh corn kernels (from about 3 ears)
- **1** large shallot, minced
- **1** garlic clove, minced
- **½** cup fresh ricotta cheese
- **1½** Tbsp. fresh lemon juice
  Kosher salt and white pepper
  Chile oil, for garnish
  Crudités or pita chips, for serving

In a large skillet, melt the butter. Add the corn, shallot and garlic and cook over moderate heat until the corn is crisp-tender, about 7 minutes. Scrape into a food processor and let cool slightly. Add the ricotta, lemon juice and 1 tablespoon of water and puree until very smooth. Season with salt and white pepper. Transfer the dip to a bowl and drizzle with chile oil. Serve with crudités or pita chips. —*Justin Chapple*

MAKE AHEAD The dip can be refrigerated overnight. Serve at room temperature.

Lemony Tofu-Herb Dip

⊙ Total **20 min;** Makes **about 1 cup**

Kristen Kish, winner of *Top Chef* Season 10, uses silken tofu to give her healthy dip a thick, creamy texture. Fresh herbs and briny anchovies add terrific flavor.

- **4** oz. drained silken tofu
- **½** cup full-fat Greek yogurt
- **1** cup parsley leaves
- **¼** cup chopped chives
- **3** drained boquerones (white anchovies) or oil-packed anchovies, drained and rinsed
- **½** tsp. finely grated fresh garlic
- **½** tsp. finely grated lemon zest plus 1 Tbsp. fresh lemon juice

  Kosher salt and pepper

  Radishes and cucumber sticks, for serving

In a blender, combine the tofu, yogurt and 2 tablespoons of water and puree until smooth, scraping down the side. Add the parsley, chives, boquerones, garlic and lemon zest and juice and puree until smooth and well blended. Season with salt and pepper. Serve the dip with radishes and cucumber sticks. —*Kristen Kish*

MAKE AHEAD The dip can be refrigerated for up to 3 days.

Carrot-Cardamom Dip

⊙ Total **15 min;** Makes **2 cups**

- **1** Tbsp. extra-virgin olive oil, plus more for serving
- **2** garlic cloves, minced
- **½** tsp. ground cardamom
- **1** cup coarsely grated carrot
- **1** cup lebneh or plain Greek yogurt

  Kosher salt and pepper

  Toasted sesame seeds, for garnish

  Toasted pita triangles, for serving

1. In a small skillet, heat the 1 tablespoon of olive oil. Add the garlic and cook over low heat, stirring, until fragrant. Remove from the heat.

2. Stir the cardamom into the garlic oil, then scrape into a bowl and let cool. Add the carrot and lebneh and season with salt and pepper. Drizzle with olive oil, top with toasted sesame seeds and serve with pita triangles. —*Charleen Badman*

Lemony Tuna and Artichoke Dip

⊙ Total **30 min;** Serves **4 to 6**

- **10** oz. frozen artichoke quarters, thawed and patted dry
- **7½** oz. tuna in olive oil, drained
- **¾** cup mayonnaise
- **2** tsp. fresh lemon juice
- **1** tsp. hot sauce
- **1** garlic clove, finely grated
- **¼** cup freshly grated Parmigiano-Reggiano cheese

  Kosher salt and pepper

Preheat the oven to 375°. In a medium bowl, mix the artichokes with the tuna, mayonnaise, lemon juice, hot sauce, garlic and cheese; season with salt and pepper. Scrape the dip into a small ovenproof skillet and bake for 15 minutes, until hot. Turn on the broiler and broil 8 inches from the heat until browned, 1 to 2 minutes. —*Justin Chapple*

SERVE WITH Crudités and chips.

Coconut-Curried Red Lentil Dip

Active **20 min;** Total **45 min plus cooling** Makes **4 cups**

Red lentils cook down to a puree quickly. Combined with coconut milk and vibrant Indian spices like garam masala, they become a luscious dip.

- **2** Tbsp. extra-virgin olive oil
- **1** cup finely chopped onion
- **½** cup finely chopped carrot
- **½** cup finely chopped celery

  Kosher salt
- **½** tsp. curry powder
- **½** tsp. garam masala
- **½** tsp. ground cumin
- **½** tsp. ground cinnamon
- **8** oz. red lentils, picked over
- **2** cups chicken stock or low-sodium broth

  One 15-oz. can unsweetened coconut milk

  Hot sauce, chips and crudités, for serving

1. In a medium saucepan, heat the olive oil. Add the onion, carrot, celery and a pinch of salt and cook over moderate heat, stirring occasionally, until softened and just starting to brown, 8 to 10 minutes. Stir in the curry powder, garam masala, cumin and cinnamon and cook until fragrant, about 30 seconds.

2. Add the lentils, chicken stock and coconut milk to the saucepan and bring to a boil over moderately high heat. Cover and simmer over moderately low heat, stirring frequently, until the lentils have cooked down to a thickened puree, 20 to 25 minutes. Let cool completely, then season with salt. Serve at room temperature with hot sauce, chips and crudités. —*Courtney McBroom*

Three-Queso Dip

⊙ Total **40 min;** Makes **6 cups**

To achieve ultimate creaminess and flavor in her silky queso, L.A. chef Courtney McBroom uses three cheeses plus a blend of heavy cream, skim milk and buttermilk. "I made it my personal mission to come up with a great queso," says McBroom, who couldn't find any amazing versions outside her native Texas.

- **¾** cup heavy cream
- **½** cup skim milk
- **1¾** lbs. white American cheese, sliced ⅓ inch thick and diced
- **1** cup coarsely shredded Manchego cheese (3½ oz.)
- **1** cup coarsely shredded sharp white cheddar cheese (3½ oz.)
- **¼** tsp. garlic powder
- **1¾** cups buttermilk

  Tortilla chips, chopped cilantro and fresh salsa, for serving

In a small saucepan, combine the heavy cream and skim milk and bring just to a simmer. Transfer to a large heatproof bowl set over a saucepan of simmering water. Add the three cheeses and heat, whisking occasionally, until completely melted, 7 to 10 minutes. Add the garlic powder and gradually whisk in the buttermilk; heat until thoroughly incorporated and the queso is very smooth, about 5 minutes. Keep warm over very low heat and serve with tortilla chips, cilantro and fresh salsa. —*Courtney McBroom*

THREE-QUESO DIP

CRISPY SUMMER
SQUASH PANCAKES

Crispy Summer Squash Pancakes

Total **25 min**; Makes **6**

2 medium summer squash, grated on the medium holes of a box grater and squeezed dry

2 scallions, thinly sliced

1 jalapeño, thinly sliced

1 large egg, beaten

½ cup all-purpose flour

2 tsp. baking powder

Kosher salt and pepper

6 Tbsp. canola oil

Lemon wedges and sour cream, for serving

1. In a medium bowl, combine the squash with the scallions, jalapeño, egg, flour and baking powder and season with salt and pepper. Mix gently just to combine.

2. In a large nonstick skillet, heat 2 tablespoons of the oil. Spoon 3 heaping ⅓-cup mounds of the batter into the skillet and press lightly to flatten them. Cook over moderate heat until golden, about 3 minutes. Flip the pancakes, add 1 tablespoon of the oil and cook until golden and crisp, 2 minutes longer. Drain on paper towels. Repeat with the remaining oil and batter. Serve the pancakes hot, with lemon wedges and sour cream. —*Kay Chun*

Country Ham with Okra and Cheddar

Total **15 min**; Serves **4**

California chef Jeremy Fox created this no-cook hors d'oeuvres platter. Be sure to use superfresh okra because you'll be serving it raw and sliced paper-thin over the ham.

8 oz. dry-cured smoked country ham, such as Benton's or Edwards, very thinly sliced

8 small okra, thinly sliced lengthwise

4 scallions, thinly sliced

¼ cup extra-virgin olive oil

1 Tbsp. fresh lemon juice

One ¼-lb. piece of best-quality cheddar, such as Cabot clothbound

Arrange the sliced ham on plates and top with the sliced okra and scallions. Drizzle evenly with the olive oil and lemon juice. Shave the cheddar on top; you probably won't need to use the whole piece. —*Jeremy Fox*

Salt Cod Fritters with Curry Aioli

Active **1 hr**; Total **1 hr 45 min plus 2 days soaking**; Makes **about 3 dozen**

Chef Adam Schop puts his spin on these classic Caribbean fritters by increasing the amount of fish, onion, bell pepper and black pepper in the batter.

¾ lb. skinless, boneless center-cut salt cod fillet

1½ tsp. unsalted butter

½ cup minced onion

¼ cup minced green bell pepper

¼ cup minced red bell pepper

1 tsp. freshly ground black pepper

1¾ cups all-purpose flour

¼ cup cornstarch

2 tsp. sugar

1½ tsp. baking powder

Kosher salt

1 large egg, beaten

1¼ cups ice-cold sparkling water

Vegetable oil, for frying

Curry Aioli (recipe follows) and lime wedges, for serving

1. In a medium bowl, cover the salt cod with 3 inches of cold water and soak in the refrigerator for 2 days, changing the water at least 3 times each day.

2. Drain the salt cod, transfer to a medium saucepan and add enough cold water to cover the fish by 2 inches. Bring to a boil. Reduce the heat to low and simmer the fish until it just flakes with a fork, about 20 minutes. Using a slotted spoon, transfer the fish to a plate and let cool. Flake the fish and discard any bones or bits of skin.

3. Meanwhile, in a small saucepan, melt the butter. Add the onion, bell peppers and black pepper and cook over moderate heat, stirring, until the vegetables are softened, about 10 minutes. Scrape the vegetables into a small bowl and let cool.

4. In a large bowl, whisk the flour with the cornstarch, sugar, baking powder and 1 tablespoon of salt. Mix in the egg and chilled sparkling water with a fork until almost combined. Stir in the flaked salt cod and the cooked vegetables.

5. In a large saucepan, heat 2 inches of oil to 350°. Carefully scoop eight 1-tablespoon balls of batter into the hot oil and fry, turning occasionally, until richly browned, about 4 minutes. Using a slotted spoon, transfer the fritters to a paper towel–lined plate to drain and season with salt. Repeat with the remaining batter. Serve the fritters hot with Curry Aioli and lime wedges.
—*Adam Schop*

BEER Light, crisp, hoppy American pilsner: Firestone Walker Pivo.

CURRY AIOLI

Total **15 min**; Makes **1¼ cups**

2 Tbsp. vegetable oil

3 scallions, white and light green parts only, minced

One ½-inch piece of fresh ginger, peeled and minced

1 garlic clove, minced

Kosher salt and pepper

1 Tbsp. West Indian curry powder (see Note)

1 cup mayonnaise

⅓ cup minced cilantro

In a small skillet, heat the oil. Add the scallions, ginger and garlic, season with a pinch each of salt and pepper and cook over moderately low heat, stirring, until the aromatics are softened, about 5 minutes. Add the curry powder and cook until fragrant and lightly toasted, about 1 minute. Scrape the seasonings into a small bowl and stir in the mayonnaise and cilantro. Season with salt and pepper and serve. —*AS*

NOTE West Indian curry powder usually contains allspice, which Indian blends often don't, and it's usually quite yellow thanks to a large amount of turmeric. It's available at spice shops and online from kalustyans.com.

MAKE AHEAD The curry aioli can be refrigerated for up to 4 days. Bring to room temperature before serving.

Gruyère Queso with Tuna and Wheat Berries

Active **15 min**; Total **1 hr 35 min**
Serves **8 to 10**

- 1 cup wheat berries
- 4 Tbsp. unsalted butter
- ¼ cup all-purpose flour
- 2 cups whole milk
- Kosher salt and pepper
- 2 cups grated Gruyère cheese (5 oz.)
- Two 6-oz. cans tuna, drained and flaked
- ½ cup snipped chives, plus more for garnish
- Crackers, for serving

1. In a medium saucepan, cook the wheat berries in boiling water until tender, about 1 hour. Drain.

2. Preheat the oven to 375°. In a large cast-iron skillet, melt the butter. Whisk in the flour and cook over moderate heat until golden, about 2 minutes. Whisk in the milk and cook until thickened, about 3 minutes; season with salt and pepper. Stir in the wheat berries, cheese, tuna and the ½ cup of chives. Bake for 20 minutes, until golden and bubbly. Garnish with more chives and serve with crackers. —*Kay Chun*

El Original Queso

Total **35 min**; Serves **10 to 12**

PICO DE GALLO

- 1 cup chopped cherry tomatoes
- 2 Tbsp. chopped sweet onion
- 1 jalapeño, seeded and chopped
- 1 Tbsp. chopped cilantro
- 1 Tbsp. fresh lime juice
- Pinch of kosher salt

QUESO

- 2 lbs. Velveeta, cubed
- 1 cup whole milk
- 1 Tbsp. unsalted butter
- 9 jalapeños, seeded and chopped (about ¾ cup)
- ¼ cup chopped sweet onion
- 1 tsp. ground cumin
- ½ tsp. kosher salt
- Tortilla chips and lime wedges, for serving

1. Make the pico de gallo In a bowl, mix the tomatoes with the onion, jalapeño, cilantro, lime juice and salt.

2. Make the queso In a medium enameled cast-iron casserole, melt the cheese with the milk over low heat, stirring often, until smooth, 7 minutes.

3. Meanwhile, melt the butter in a medium skillet. Add the jalapeños and onion and cook over moderately high heat until softened, 7 minutes. Stir in the cumin and salt.

4. Stir the jalapeño mixture into the melted cheese. Off the heat, stir in the pico de gallo. Serve hot with tortilla chips and lime wedges. —*Morgan Robinson*

Spicy Pea Guacamole

Total **20 min**; Serves **4**

Green peas add lovely sweetness to this guacamole from New York and Mexico City chef Enrique Olvera. Olvera doesn't use lime juice—he prefers to show off the subtle acidity of the avocado—but you can add a squeeze if you like.

- 1 serrano chile, chopped
- ½ cup chopped cilantro
- ½ cup thawed frozen peas
- 2 medium Hass avocados— peeled, pitted and chopped
- Kosher salt
- Tortilla chips, for serving

In a mortar, mash the chile with the cilantro. Add the peas and avocados and mash until well blended but chunky. Season with salt and serve with chips. —*Enrique Olvera*

Pumpkin Hummus

Total **15 min**; Makes **3 cups**

- Two 15-oz. cans chickpeas, drained and rinsed
- 1 cup pumpkin puree
- ¼ cup fresh lemon juice
- 2 small garlic cloves
- ¼ tsp. cayenne
- Kosher salt and pepper
- Pita chips or crudités, for serving

In a food processor, combine the chickpeas, pumpkin, lemon juice, garlic, cayenne and ⅓ cup of water; puree until smooth. Season with salt and pepper and serve with pita chips or crudités. —*Justin Chapple*

Shrimp and Avocado Dip with Chiles and Lime

Total **30 min**; Serves **8 to 10**

L.A. chef Courtney McBroom makes her shrimp dip extra-creamy and indulgent with a mix of sour cream, cream cheese and avocado.

- 1 Tbsp. grapeseed oil
- ½ lb. shelled and deveined shrimp, finely chopped
- 2 garlic cloves, minced
- Kosher salt
- ⅓ cup sour cream
- ¼ cup cream cheese, at room temperature
- 1½ tsp. chili powder
- 1 tsp. garlic powder
- 1 tsp. onion powder
- 1 tsp. finely grated lime zest plus 2 Tbsp. fresh lime juice
- 1 Hass avocado—peeled, pitted and finely diced
- 2 Tbsp. finely chopped cilantro, plus more for garnish
- Thinly sliced scallions and jalapeños, for garnish
- Hot sauce, chips and crudités, for serving

1. In a large skillet, heat the oil. Add the shrimp, garlic and a pinch of salt and cook over high heat, stirring, until the shrimp are white throughout, about 2 minutes. Let the shrimp cool.

2. In a medium bowl, mix the sour cream with the cream cheese, chili powder, garlic powder, onion powder, lime zest and lime juice. Fold in the shrimp, avocado and 2 tablespoons of cilantro and season the dip with salt. Garnish with cilantro, scallions and jalapeños. Serve with hot sauce, chips and crudités. —*Courtney McBroom*

MAKE AHEAD The shrimp and avocado dip can be refrigerated overnight.

DIY MOZZARELLA

Warm, tender, milky mozzarella is easier to make than you might think. Plus, it takes just 30 minutes. **SAL LAMBOGLIA,** chef-partner at Bar Primi in New York City, needs just three ingredients: water, salt and high-quality curds.

Fresh Mozzarella

⏱ Total **30 min**; Makes **2 pounds**

- 2 **lbs. mozzarella cheese curd (see Note), cut into ½-inch-pieces**
- 2 **Tbsp. kosher salt**
  Extra-virgin olive oil and sea salt, for serving

1. In a large heatproof bowl, soak the cheese curds in lukewarm water for 10 minutes to bring them to room temperature. Pour off the water. Toss the cheese curds with the kosher salt.

2. Heat 2 quarts of water to 170° (measured on a candy thermometer). Slowly pour the water around the edge of the bowl until the cheese curds are completely submerged; be sure not to pour the water directly on the curds. Let the curds stand until they begin to melt together into a mass, about 1 minute.

3. Using 2 wooden spoons or spatulas, pull the curd up from the bottom and fold it over onto itself until it's smooth and silky and forms tender strands, about 3 minutes.

4. Fill a large bowl with cold water. Pull a fist-size piece of the warm curd and form it into a ball by stretching and tucking it under and into itself. Pinch off the ball and drop it into the cold water. Repeat with the remaining curd.

5. To serve, slice the mozzarella, drizzle with olive oil and sprinkle with sea salt. Or wrap in plastic and refrigerate for up to 3 days.

NOTE Mozzarella curd is available in many large stores that make their own mozzarella, or by mail from saxelbycheese.com and caputobrotherscreamery.com.

STEP-BY-STEP CHEESEMAKING

1

SOAK & SEASON Soak mozzarella curds in lukewarm water. Drain, season the curds with kosher salt and toss.

2

WARM Pour hot water around the edge of the bowl (not directly on the curds) until the curds are submerged.

3

MELT Let the curds soften in the hot water until they melt together. The water will become cloudy.

4

STRETCH Pull the curd up from the bottom. Fold it over onto itself until smooth and silky.

5

FORM Stretch the pieces like taffy. Fold them over and around to form balls as taut as balloons.

6

SERVE Slice the mozzarella for caprese salad or use in your favorite dish. "Eat it within the hour," Lamboglia says.

BUFFALO MOZZARELLA
WITH NEAT AND MESSY
ROASTED TOMATOES

Buffalo Mozzarella with Neat and Messy Roasted Tomatoes

Active **20 min**; Total **3 hr 30 min**
Serves **6 to 8**

- 2 lbs. cherry tomatoes, halved
- 2 lbs. cherry tomatoes on the vine
  Kosher salt and pepper
- ¼ cup extra-virgin olive oil
  Two 8-oz. balls of buffalo mozzarella cheese, sliced
  Crusty bread, for serving

1. Preheat the oven to 300°. Arrange the halved cherry tomatoes cut side up on a parchment paper–lined baking sheet. Roast for 2 to 2½ hours, until the tomatoes are shriveled and half-dried. Remove from the oven.

2. Increase the oven temperature to 350°. Arrange the cherry tomatoes on the vine on a parchment paper–lined baking sheet. Season with salt and drizzle with the olive oil. Roast for about 1 hour, until the tomatoes soften and start to split open. Using a spatula, carefully transfer the tomatoes to a large platter. Arrange the dried tomatoes on the platter along with the mozzarella. Season with pepper and serve with crusty bread. —*Rachel Roddy*

Pan con Tomate with Garrotxa Cheese

Total **20 min**; Serves **8**

Garrotxa is a semi-firm, delicately flavored Catalan goat cheese that's perfect for grating over crunchy, garlicky, tomato-rubbed toast.

- Eight ½-inch-thick slices of ciabatta
- Extra-virgin olive oil, for brushing and drizzling
- 2 garlic cloves, halved crosswise
- 4 tomatoes, halved crosswise
  Kosher salt and pepper
  Shaved Garrotxa cheese, for topping

Preheat the oven to 375°. Brush one side of each bread slice with oil and arrange oiled side up on a baking sheet. Bake for 10 minutes, until golden. Rub the toasts with the garlic cloves, then rub with the tomato halves until all of the flesh is gone; discard the tomato skins. Season the toasts with salt and pepper. Top with cheese, drizzle with olive oil and serve. —*Kay Chun*

Curried Onion and Cauliflower Hummus

Total **1 hr 30 min** plus overnight soaking
Makes **about 5 cups**

Cooking soaked dried chickpeas in baking soda softens them, making this hummus extra-silky.

- 1 lb. dried chickpeas (2½ cups), soaked overnight and drained
- 8 garlic cloves, peeled
- 1 tsp. baking soda
- ½ cup tahini
- ½ cup fresh lemon juice
- ⅓ cup extra-virgin olive oil, plus more for drizzling
- ½ tsp. ground cumin
  Kosher salt
  Canola oil, for frying
- ½ lb. cauliflower, cut into ½-inch florets
- 2 tsp. curry powder
- 1 large onion, halved and thinly sliced
- 1½ tsp. finely crushed pink peppercorns
  Chopped parsley, for garnish

1. In a medium saucepan, cover the chickpeas, garlic and baking soda with 2 inches of water and bring to a boil. Cover and simmer over moderately low heat, stirring every 15 minutes, until the chickpeas are tender, 50 minutes; if necessary, add water to keep them covered.

2. Drain the chickpeas and garlic and transfer to a food processor; puree until very smooth. With the machine on, gradually add the tahini, lemon juice, ⅓ cup of olive oil and the cumin; season the hummus with salt.

3. In a medium skillet, heat ¼ inch of canola oil. Add the cauliflower and fry over moderately high heat, stirring, until tender and deeply browned, 8 to 10 minutes. Drain in a paper towel–lined bowl. Add 1 teaspoon of the curry powder and toss well. Season with salt and toss again.

4. Pour off all but ¼ cup of the oil from the skillet. Add the onion and a big pinch of salt and cook over moderately high heat, stirring, until just starting to soften and brown in spots, about 5 minutes. Add the pink peppercorns and the remaining 1 teaspoon of curry powder and cook, stirring, until fragrant, 3 minutes. Season with salt.

5. Spoon the hummus into a bowl and top with the onion and cauliflower. Drizzle with olive oil, garnish with parsley and serve. —*Alon Shaya*

SERVE WITH Warm pita or naan.

Bruschetta with Peperonata

Total **30 min**; Serves **6 to 8**

Star chef Mario Batali says that the Italian way to cook with peppers often starts with a basic pepper "stew," to which he adds serranos and anchovies.

- 2 Tbsp. extra-virgin olive oil, plus more for brushing
- ½ Spanish onion, thinly sliced
- 2 small red bell peppers, cut into thin strips
- 2 small yellow bell peppers, cut into thin strips
- 2 serrano chiles, seeded and cut into thin strips
- 2 tsp. anchovy paste
  Kosher salt and pepper
- 2 Tbsp. sherry vinegar
- 1 tsp. finely chopped oregano
  Six ¾-inch-thick slices from a round rustic loaf
- 1 garlic clove, peeled

1. In a large skillet, heat the 2 tablespoons of olive oil until shimmering. Add the onion, bell peppers, serranos, anchovy paste and a generous pinch each of salt and pepper. Cook over high heat, stirring occasionally, until the vegetables start to soften and brown on the edges, about 4 minutes. Add the vinegar and cook over moderate heat, stirring occasionally, until the peppers are tender, 5 to 7 minutes. Stir in the oregano and season the peperonata with salt and pepper; keep warm.

2. Heat a grill pan. Brush the bread slices on both sides with olive oil. Grill over moderately high heat, turning once, until nicely toasted, about 2 minutes. Transfer the grilled bread to a plate and rub with the garlic clove. Spoon the peperonata on top and serve warm. —*Mario Batali*

White Anchovy Toasts with Parsnip Butter

Active **1 hr**; Total **1 hr 30 min**; Makes **24**

PARSNIP BUTTER

1¼ **lbs. parsnips, peeled and cut into 1-inch chunks**

2 **Tbsp. unsalted butter**

⅓ **cup half-and-half**

Kosher salt and pepper

BASIL OIL

½ **cup lightly packed basil**

¼ **cup lightly packed parsley**

1 **small garlic clove**

¼ **cup plus 2 Tbsp. extra-virgin olive oil**

Kosher salt and pepper

TOASTS

24 **baguette slices, cut on the diagonal ⅓ inch thick (from 1 baguette)**

Extra-virgin olive oil, for brushing

24 **white anchovy fillets (alici or boquerones)**

1. Make the parsnip butter In a large saucepan of salted boiling water, cook the parsnips until tender, 8 to 10 minutes. Drain well and transfer to a food processor. Add the butter and half-and-half and puree until smooth. Scrape the puree into a medium saucepan and cook over moderately low heat, stirring frequently, until thick, 15 minutes. Season with salt and pepper. Transfer to a medium bowl and press a sheet of plastic wrap directly on the butter. Let cool completely, then refrigerate until chilled, 30 minutes.

2. Meanwhile, make the basil oil In a mini food processor, combine the basil, parsley and garlic and pulse until finely chopped. With the machine on, stream in the olive oil until smooth. Season the basil oil with salt and pepper.

3. Make the toasts Preheat the oven to 400°. Arrange the baguette slices on a baking sheet and brush both sides with olive oil. Toast for 8 to 10 minutes, until golden; let cool.

4. Spread the toasts with the parsnip butter and arrange on a platter. Top with the anchovies, drizzle with the basil oil and serve. —*Matt Jennings*

MAKE AHEAD The parsnip butter can be covered and refrigerated for up to 2 days.

New England–Style Crab Dip with Brown-Butter Crumbs

Active **30 min**; Total **1 hr 45 min**; Serves **12**

Chef Matt Jennings of Townsman in Boston elevates his crab dip with jumbo lump crabmeat. He adds wonderful texture to the warm, creamy dip with a crisp topping of breadcrumbs tossed in browned butter.

1 **cup mayonnaise**

¼ **cup minced celery**

¼ **cup minced green bell pepper**

2 **Tbsp. finely grated sweet onion**

2 **Tbsp. finely chopped parsley**

1 **tsp. finely grated lemon zest plus 1 Tbsp. fresh lemon juice**

½ **tsp. hot sauce, preferably Tabasco**

⅛ **tsp. cayenne**

1 **lb. jumbo lump crabmeat, picked over**

Kosher salt and pepper

4 **oz. day-old rustic white bread, torn into 1-inch pieces (4 cups)**

4 **Tbsp. unsalted butter**

Crostini, chips or radicchio leaves, for serving

1. In a large bowl, blend the mayonnaise with the celery, green pepper, onion, parsley, lemon zest, lemon juice, hot sauce and cayenne. Fold in the crab and season with salt and pepper. Refrigerate for 1 hour.

2. Meanwhile, preheat the oven to 400°. In a food processor, pulse the bread until fine crumbs form. Spread the breadcrumbs on a rimmed baking sheet and toast for about 8 minutes, until crisp.

3. In a large skillet, cook the butter over moderate heat until the milk solids turn dark golden, about 4 minutes. Stir in the toasted breadcrumbs and season with salt.

4. Scrape the crab mixture into a 10-inch round baking dish or skillet. Sprinkle the brown-butter crumbs evenly on top. Bake for 20 to 25 minutes, until golden on top and bubbling at the edge. Let cool for 5 minutes before serving with crostini, chips or radicchio leaves. —*Matt Jennings*

MAKE AHEAD The crab dip can be prepared through Step 3 and refrigerated overnight.

Open-Face Cheese Toasts with Broccoli Rabe Relish

Total **30 min**; Serves **6**

2 **Tbsp. canola oil, plus more for brushing**

½ **lb. broccoli rabe, trimmed and cut into ¾-inch pieces**

1 **cup thinly sliced red onion**

2 **Tbsp. Asian fish sauce**

2 **Tbsp. malt vinegar**

Kosher salt and pepper

Six ½-inch-thick slices cut from a sourdough boule

½ **lb. sharp cheddar cheese, sliced**

1. In a large skillet, heat the 2 tablespoons of oil until shimmering. Add the broccoli rabe and cook over high heat, tossing, until just starting to wilt, about 2 minutes. Add the onion and cook, stirring, until softened, about 3 minutes longer. Stir in the fish sauce and vinegar and season with salt and pepper. Let cool slightly.

2. Light a grill or heat a grill pan. Lightly brush both sides of the bread with oil, then grill over moderate heat until lightly charred on the bottom, about 1 minute. Flip the bread and top with the sliced cheese and broccoli rabe relish. Close the grill and cook until the cheese is melted and the bread is browned and crisp, about 2 minutes. Transfer to a platter, cut in half and serve right away. —*Stephanie Izard*

CIDER Funky, dry cider: Virtue Nichols Farm & Orchard.

Camembert Baked in the Box

PAGE 9

Total **20 min**; Serves **4 to 6**

Baking Camembert in its box keeps it from collapsing. Be sure the cheese comes in a box that's stapled, not glued.

One 8-oz. wheel of Camembert, unwrapped

Crackers and apple slices, for serving

Preheat the oven to 375°. Set the box of cheese in a baking dish and bake, uncovered, until just melted, 15 minutes. Slice off the top rind and serve immediately, with crackers and apple slices. —*Eric Ripert*

WINE Rich, green apple–scented Champagne: NV Charles Heidsieck Brut Réserve.

Herbed Chickpea Bruschetta

Active **45 min**; Total **3 hr 40 min plus overnight soaking**; Makes **about 30**

- 1 cup dried chickpeas, soaked overnight and drained
- 14 garlic cloves, 4 cloves halved
- 1 oz. pancetta or prosciutto, diced
- ½ medium yellow onion, halved lengthwise
- ½ medium carrot, halved lengthwise
- ½ celery rib, halved lengthwise
- 3 sage leaves
- 1 small rosemary sprig plus ½ tsp. finely chopped leaves
- 1 bay leaf
- 1 dried chile de árbol
- 2 Tbsp. kosher salt
- ¾ cup extra-virgin olive oil, plus more for brushing and drizzling
  About 30 baguette slices (½ inch thick)
- ½ tsp. minced thyme
  Flaky sea salt, for garnish

1. Preheat the oven to 350°. In a medium Dutch oven, combine the soaked chickpeas with the 10 whole garlic cloves, the pancetta, onion, carrot, celery, sage, rosemary sprig, bay leaf, chile, salt, ¼ cup of the olive oil and 8 cups of water. Bring to a boil over high heat and stir. Cover and bake for about 2 hours, until the chickpeas are tender. Remove from the oven, uncover and let the chickpeas cool in the liquid for 1 hour.

2. Meanwhile, lightly brush the baguette slices with olive oil and arrange on a rimmed baking sheet. Bake until lightly toasted, about 15 minutes. Rub the cut halves of garlic on one side of each toast.

3. Drain the chickpeas, reserving ½ cup of the cooking liquid; discard all the aromatics except the garlic. Transfer the chickpeas and garlic to a blender. Add the remaining ½ cup of olive oil and the reserved cooking liquid and puree until smooth.

4. Arrange the toasts on a platter. Dollop the chickpea puree on top and use a small spoon to form a little well in each dollop. Drizzle the bruschetta with olive oil, sprinkle with the chopped rosemary, minced thyme and sea salt and serve.
—*Nancy Silverton*

Olive, Chile and White Bean Crostini

Total **25 min**; Serves **4**

- Four ½-inch-thick slices from a sourdough boule
- ¼ cup plus 2 Tbsp. extra-virgin olive oil, plus more for brushing or drizzling
- ¾ cup pitted oil-cured black olives, coarsely chopped
- 2½ Tbsp. Champagne vinegar
- 2 Tbsp. finely chopped seeded oil-packed Calabrian chiles or other hot chiles
  Kosher salt
  One 15-oz. can cannellini beans, rinsed and drained
  Torn mint, for garnish

1. Light a grill or heat a grill pan. Brush or drizzle the bread with olive oil and grill over moderate heat, turning once, until lightly charred, 1 to 2 minutes total. Transfer to a work surface to cool slightly, then cut each slice into thirds.

2. In a medium bowl, mix the olives with the vinegar, chiles and the ¼ cup plus 2 tablespoons of olive oil; season lightly with salt and gently mix in the beans. Spoon the bean-and-olive topping on the crostini, garnish with mint and serve. —*Greg Denton and Gabrielle Quiñónez Denton*

WINE Fruit-forward sparkling rosé: 2014 Domaine La Grange Tiphaine Rosa, Rosé, Rosam.

Apricot and Ricotta Tartines

Total **30 min**; Serves **4**

- 4 slices of sourdough bread
- 1 Tbsp. extra-virgin olive oil, plus more for brushing
- 4 apricots, halved and pitted
  Kosher salt and pepper
- 1 cup cherry tomatoes, halved
- 3 Tbsp. Champagne vinegar
- 1½ Tbsp. chopped tarragon
- 1 cup fresh ricotta cheese

1. Light a grill or heat a grill pan. Brush the bread with olive oil and grill over high heat until toasted and charred in spots, about 1 minute per side. Transfer to a work surface.

2. Brush the apricot halves with olive oil and season with salt and pepper. Grill cut side down over high heat until charred on the bottom, about 3 minutes. Transfer to a work surface and let cool slightly, then cut into ½-inch wedges.

3. In a medium bowl, toss the apricots with the tomatoes, vinegar, tarragon and the 1 tablespoon of olive oil. Season the salad with salt and pepper. Spread the ricotta on the grilled bread and spoon the apricot salad on top. Serve right away.
—*Justin Chapple*

Grilled Escarole Toasts with Trout Roe

Total **45 min**; Serves **6**

- Two 10- to 12-oz. heads of escarole
  Extra-virgin olive oil
- 1 Tbsp. chopped thyme
- 2 garlic cloves, minced
  Kosher salt and pepper
  Eighteen ½-inch-thick baguette slices cut on a wide diagonal
  Crème fraîche and trout roe, for serving

1. Light a grill. Fill a large bowl with cold water. Holding the escarole by the root end, dip the heads in the water to release any dirt between the leaves. Shake off the excess water.

2. In a small bowl, whisk ½ cup of olive oil with the thyme and garlic. Brush the escarole with garlic oil and season with salt and pepper. Grill over moderate heat until charred outside and tender within, about 20 minutes; brush a few times with garlic oil during grilling. Transfer to a work surface and let cool, then coarsely chop.

3. Brush the baguette slices with olive oil and season with salt and pepper. Grill until lightly charred on both sides, about 2 minutes.

4. In a large bowl, toss the escarole with any remaining garlic oil; season with salt and pepper. Top the toasts with the escarole, crème fraîche and trout roe and serve.
—*Maggie Harrison*

Smoked Trout–Caraway Rillettes

Total **15 min**; Makes **2½ cups**

Lebneh is a thick, creamy fresh cheese made by straining yogurt to remove the whey. Here, it provides the base for a light and tangy smoked trout spread.

1½ cups lebneh

2 Tbsp. minced shallot

3 Tbsp. extra-virgin olive oil

2 tsp. caraway seeds

3 thinly sliced scallions, plus more for garnish

Kosher salt and pepper

4 smoked trout fillets (12 oz.), skinned, meat flaked into large pieces

Spicy Quick-Pickled Radishes (p. 362) and rye crackers, for serving

In a medium bowl, combine the lebneh, shallot, olive oil, caraway seeds and the 3 sliced scallions; season with salt and pepper and mix well. Gently fold in the flaked trout. Garnish the rillettes with scallions and serve at room temperature with pickled radishes and rye crackers. —*Kay Chun*

MAKE AHEAD The rillettes can be refrigerated for 2 to 3 days and brought to room temperature before serving.

Warm Tofu with Soy-Ginger Sauce

Total **15 min**; Serves **4**

1 Tbsp. soy sauce

½ Tbsp. finely grated peeled fresh ginger

1 tsp. toasted sesame oil

Kosher salt

One 12-oz. package silken firm tofu, drained and cut into 4 equal pieces

Thinly sliced scallion, white sesame seeds and togarashi, for garnish

In a small bowl, whisk the soy sauce with the ginger and oil; season with salt. In a medium saucepan of gently simmering water, heat the tofu just until warmed through, about 5 minutes. Using a slotted spoon, transfer the tofu to paper towels to drain briefly. Arrange the tofu on plates and drizzle with the soy-ginger sauce. Garnish with sliced scallion, sesame seeds and togarashi. —*Kuniko Yagi*

Chicken Liver Pâté with Green Peppercorns

Total **40 min plus overnight soaking** Makes **2½ cups**

F&W's Kay Chun balances the richness of this velvety pâté with tart green peppercorns. The pâté is even better the day after it's prepared, making it a convenient starter for dinner parties.

1 lb. chicken livers, well trimmed

2 cups whole milk

3 Tbsp. extra-virgin olive oil

1 small onion, thinly sliced

Small sage leaves

2 garlic cloves, thinly sliced

Kosher salt and pepper

2 Tbsp. bourbon

3 Tbsp. fresh lemon juice

2 sticks unsalted butter, at room temperature

2 Tbsp. chopped brined green peppercorns, plus 1 Tbsp. brine from the jar

Rye crackers, for serving

1. In a medium bowl, refrigerate the livers in the milk overnight.

2. Drain and rinse the livers; pat dry. In a large nonstick skillet, heat 2 tablespoons of the olive oil. Add the onion and 5 sage leaves and cook over moderate heat until deep golden, about 8 minutes. Stir in the garlic and cook for 1 minute. Scrape the mixture into a food processor.

3. In the same skillet, heat the remaining 1 tablespoon of oil. Season the livers with salt and pepper and cook over moderately high heat, turning once, until golden, 2 minutes. Add the bourbon; cook until almost evaporated and the livers are barely pink inside, 1 minute.

4. Add the livers to the food processor along with the lemon juice; pulse to finely chop. With the machine on, add the butter, 1 tablespoon at a time, until the pâté is very smooth. Stir in the green peppercorns and brine. Season with salt and pepper.

5. Transfer the pâté to 2 bowls. Cover and refrigerate until chilled. Garnish with sage and serve with rye crackers. —*Kay Chun*

Grilled Kale Toasts

Total **25 min**; Makes **4**

"Grilled toasts in the backyard are one of my absolute summer favorites," says New York City chef Camille Becerra. "They're extremely adaptable and let me use whatever I find at the market that day."

½ cup Greek yogurt

6 Tbsp. extra-virgin olive oil, plus more for brushing

1 tsp. fresh lemon juice

1 tsp. whole-grain mustard

Kosher salt and pepper

1 bunch of Tuscan kale (12 oz.)

Four 1-inch-thick slices of ciabatta bread

1 garlic clove, halved lengthwise

½ cup pecorino cheese shavings

1. Heat a cast-iron grill pan. In a large bowl, whisk the yogurt with the 6 tablespoons of olive oil, the lemon juice and mustard. Season with salt and pepper.

2. Working in 2 batches, grill the kale over moderate heat, turning, until lightly charred, about 3 minutes per batch. Transfer to a work surface. Discard the ribs and chop the kale. Add to the yogurt dressing and toss to coat evenly.

3. Brush one side of each bread slice with oil and grill oil side down until golden, about 5 minutes. Rub the grilled sides with the cut garlic. Top with the kale and cheese and arrange on a platter. Serve warm. —*Camille Becerra*

MAKE AHEAD The dressing can be refrigerated overnight.

WINE Crisp and peppery Austrian white: 2013 Glatzer Grüner Veltliner.

MINI SPINACH-
AND-HERB PIES

Mini Spinach-and-Herb Pies

Active **45 min**; Total **1 hr 45 min**
Makes **12 mini pies**

These terrific little pastries, stuffed with spinach and two cheeses, are made throughout the town of Chaniá on the Greek island of Crete.

DOUGH

- **2 cups all-purpose flour, plus more for dusting**
- **1½ tsp. kosher salt**
- **2 Tbsp. extra-virgin olive oil**

FILLING

- **5 oz. curly spinach, stemmed and finely chopped**
- **¼ lb. Greek feta cheese, finely crumbled**
- **¼ lb. manouri or mild feta cheese, finely crumbled**
- **½ small onion, finely grated**
- **½ cup finely chopped parsley**
- **½ cup finely chopped mint**
- **½ cup finely chopped fennel fronds or dill**
- **2 Tbsp. extra-virgin olive oil**
   Kosher salt and pepper
- **1 large egg beaten with 1 tsp. water**
   Sesame seeds, for sprinkling

1. Make the dough In a large bowl, whisk the 2 cups of flour with the salt. Make a well in the center and pour in ½ cup of water and the oil, using a wooden spoon to gradually incorporate them into the flour until a shaggy dough starts to form. Turn the dough out onto a lightly floured work surface and knead until a soft dough forms, about 2 minutes. Wrap the dough in plastic and let rest at room temperature for 30 minutes.

2. Make the filling In another large bowl, combine all of the ingredients except the egg wash and sesame seeds and mix well.

3. Preheat the oven to 450°. On a lightly floured surface, roll out the dough to a 12-by-16-inch rectangle, a scant ¼ inch thick. Cut the dough into twelve 4-inch squares. Spoon 2 tablespoons of the filling into the center of each square; bring up the 4 corners to meet in the center, then pinch together to seal. Arrange the pies on a parchment paper–lined baking sheet. Brush with the egg wash and sprinkle with sesame seeds.

4. Bake the pies for about 30 minutes, until lightly browned and the filling is hot. Let cool for at least 5 minutes, then serve warm or at room temperature. —*Evelina Makrinaki*

WINE Vibrant, orange peel–scented Greek white: 2012 Alexakis Vidiano.

Carbonara Arancini

Active **1 hr 15 min**; Total **2 hr 30 min**
Makes **twelve 3-inch arancini**

To make these rich, Sicilian-style snacks, star chef Mario Batali wraps cheesy rice around a filling of onion-and-pancetta béchamel, shaping the mixture into balls. Breaded and fried, they get supercrispy.

- **1 Tbsp. extra-virgin olive oil**
- **2 oz. pancetta, cut into ¼-inch dice**
- **½ small onion, finely chopped**
   Kosher salt
- **1 cup plus 1 Tbsp. all-purpose flour**
- **½ cup milk**
- **¼ cup finely chopped parsley**
- **1 cup plus 2 Tbsp. grated pecorino cheese, plus more for sprinkling**
   Pinch of crushed red pepper
- **3 cups cooled cooked white rice**
- **3 large eggs, 1 beaten and 2 separated**
- **1 cup plain dry breadcrumbs**
   Canola oil, for frying
   Chopped mint and coarse sea salt, for garnish

1. In a medium saucepan, heat the olive oil. Add the pancetta and cook over moderately high heat, stirring occasionally, until browned and nearly crisp, about 5 minutes. Using a slotted spoon, transfer the pancetta to paper towels to drain.

2. Add the onion and a generous pinch of salt to the saucepan and cook over moderate heat, stirring occasionally, until the onion is softened and well browned, about 12 minutes. Stir in 1 tablespoon of the flour and cook until a paste forms. Gradually whisk in the milk and bring to a simmer, then cook over moderately low heat, whisking, until thickened and no floury taste remains, 5 to 7 minutes. Scrape the onion béchamel into a medium bowl and stir in the pancetta, parsley, 2 tablespoons of the cheese, ½ teaspoon of salt and the crushed red pepper. Let the filling cool completely.

3. In a large bowl, mix the cooked rice with the beaten egg and the 2 egg yolks until evenly coated. Stir in the remaining 1 cup of pecorino cheese until the rice becomes sticky.

4. Line a large baking sheet with wax paper. Scoop 3 packed tablespoons of the rice mixture into one moistened hand and press it into a 3½-inch round. Scoop 2 teaspoons of the cooled filling into the center and wrap the rice around it, pressing to form a tight ball. Transfer to the baking sheet. Repeat with the remaining rice mixture and filling to make 12 arancini.

5. Place the breadcrumbs and the remaining 1 cup of flour in 2 separate shallow bowls. In another shallow bowl, beat the egg whites until frothy. Dust the arancini with flour, tapping off the excess. Roll them in the beaten egg whites and then in the breadcrumbs. Transfer the arancini to the baking sheet and refrigerate, uncovered, until firm, about 1 hour.

6. In a large saucepan, heat 2 inches of canola oil to 350°. Add half of the arancini to the hot oil and fry over moderate heat, turning occasionally, until golden and heated through, about 4 minutes. Using a slotted spoon, transfer to paper towels to drain. Repeat with the remaining arancini. Pile the arancini on plates or a platter, garnish with chopped mint, grated cheese and coarse sea salt and serve. —*Mario Batali*

MAKE AHEAD The arancini can be prepared through Step 5 and refrigerated overnight.

WINE Lively, full-bodied Chardonnay: 2012 Starmont Carneros.

Pink Peppercorn and Fennel Gravlax

Active **30 min**; Total **3 days**; Serves **10 to 12**

- ½ cup plus 2 Tbsp. kosher salt
- One 2-lb. skin-on center-cut salmon fillet, pinbones removed
- 2 Tbsp. pink peppercorns
- 2 Tbsp. caraway seeds
- 2 Tbsp. coriander seeds
- 2 Tbsp. fennel pollen
- 1 tsp. freshly ground white pepper
- ¼ cup sugar
- 1 large bunch of dill
- Rye crackers, sour cream, sliced onions and drained capers, for serving

1. Fill a large bowl or baking dish with water, add 2 tablespoons of the salt and stir until dissolved. Submerge the salmon in the water and let stand for 10 minutes. Drain the fish and pat dry with paper towels.

2. Meanwhile, in a small skillet, toast the pink peppercorns, caraway and coriander over moderate heat, stirring, until very fragrant, about 2 minutes. Cool slightly, then coarsely grind in a mortar or spice grinder. Transfer the spice mixture to a small bowl and stir in the fennel pollen, white pepper, sugar and the remaining ½ cup of salt.

3. Line a rimmed baking sheet with plastic wrap. Arrange half of the dill down the center of the baking sheet. Sprinkle half of the spice mixture evenly over the dill, then top with the salmon, skin side down. Sprinkle the remaining spice mixture over the top and sides of the salmon in an even layer. Top with the remaining dill. Wrap the salmon tightly in the plastic wrap and place skin side down on the baking sheet. Top with a second baking sheet and heavy canned goods to weigh it down. Refrigerate for 1 day.

4. Unwrap the fish and pat dry. Rewrap the fish and seasonings in a clean sheet of plastic, leaving behind any released liquid and squeezing out excess liquid from the dill. Place the freshly wrapped salmon skin side up on the baking sheet. Top with the baking sheet and weights; refrigerate for 2 days, until the flesh feels firm in the center.

5. Rinse off the fish, pat it dry and thinly slice. Serve with rye crackers, sour cream, sliced onions and capers. —*Matt Jennings*

Smoked Whitefish Tartare with Herb Oil

Total **30 min**; Serves **4**

Chef Amélie Darvas, who learned her technique in grand Paris kitchens like Le Meurice, makes a point of using inexpensive ingredients. At her Paris restaurant Haï Kaï, her light, bright, citrusy "tartare" features smoked whitefish instead of sushi-grade tuna. The dish can also be made with smoked bluefish.

- ½ lb. fava beans, shelled (½ cup), or ½ cup frozen baby peas
- ¼ cup extra-virgin olive oil
- ¼ cup loosely packed flat-leaf parsley, chopped
- 2 Tbsp. chopped chives
- Kosher salt and pepper
- ½ lb. smoked whitefish, skinned and cut into ¼-inch pieces
- ½ cup loosely packed microgreens
- 2 Tbsp. fresh lime juice
- ¼ tsp. piment d'Espelette (see Note)
- ¼ cup crème fraîche
- 1 Tbsp. fresh Meyer lemon or lemon juice

1. In a saucepan of salted boiling water, blanch the fava beans or peas for 1 minute. Drain and cool in a bowl of ice water for 1 minute. Drain well; if using favas, slip off and discard the tough outer skins. Transfer the beans or peas to a bowl.

2. In a small bowl, whisk the olive oil with the parsley and chives and season with salt and pepper. Add 2 tablespoons of the herb oil to the favas in the bowl along with the smoked fish, microgreens and lime juice. Toss gently to coat. Season with salt, pepper and the piment d'Espelette.

3. In another bowl, whisk the crème fraîche and lemon juice. Spoon the tartare onto plates and dollop the lemon cream alongside. Drizzle the remaining herb oil on top and serve. —*Amélie Darvas*

NOTE The mildly spicy Basque chile powder piment d'Espelette is available at specialty food stores and from amazon.com.

WINE Brisk, savory Muscadet: 2014 Domaine du Haut Bourg Côtes de Grandlieu.

Quick-Cured Salmon with Salmon Cracklings

Active **40 min**; Total **1 hr 30 min**; Serves **6**

This starter from Seattle chef Tom Douglas is an almost-instant gravlax. While the sliced fillet gets a 30-minute cure, the skin is baked until it's as crisp as a potato chip.

- ¾ lb. center-cut skin-on salmon fillet
- ¾ cup sugar
- 3 Tbsp. Aleppo pepper
- ½ cup kosher salt, plus more for seasoning
- Togarashi, for sprinkling
- ½ cup whole-milk yogurt
- ¼ cup chopped mint
- Salmon roe, for serving

1. Line a large rimmed baking sheet with parchment paper. Using a sharp knife, carefully remove the salmon skin from the fillet and reserve. Thinly slice the salmon across the grain a scant ¼ inch thick.

2. In a medium bowl, whisk the sugar with the Aleppo pepper and the ½ cup of kosher salt. Spread half of the sugar mixture on the prepared baking sheet and arrange the salmon slices on top. Sprinkle the remaining sugar mixture evenly over the salmon and refrigerate until the fish is slightly firm, about 30 minutes.

3. Meanwhile, preheat the oven to 325°. Spread the salmon skin on a parchment paper–lined baking sheet, silvery side up, and sprinkle with togarashi. Cover with a sheet of parchment paper and another baking sheet to keep the skin flat. Bake for 30 minutes, until crisp. Remove the top baking sheet and parchment paper and let the salmon crackling cool completely, then break into bite-size pieces.

4. Fill a large bowl with cold water. Rinse the cured salmon in the water, rubbing off the sugar mixture. Transfer the salmon to paper towels to drain; pat thoroughly dry.

5. In a small bowl, whisk the yogurt with the mint and season with salt. Arrange the salmon slices on plates or a platter and garnish with the cracklings and roe. Serve with the mint yogurt. —*Tom Douglas*

MAKE AHEAD The salmon can be prepared through Step 4 and refrigerated overnight.

WINE Bright, dry Oregon Riesling: 2011 Brooks Willamette Valley.

QUICK-CURED
SALMON WITH
SALMON CRACKLINGS

Oyster Mushroom and Truffle Croquettes

Active **1 hr 15 min**; Total **2 hr**; Makes **18**

New York City chef David Waltuck fills his fried croquettes with sautéed oyster mushrooms suspended in a cheesy béchamel sauce.

- 1 Tbsp. extra-virgin olive oil
- 1½ tsp. white truffle oil
- ¾ lb. oyster mushrooms, trimmed and torn into large pieces
  Kosher salt and pepper
- 2 cups whole milk
- 1 stick unsalted butter
- 1 cup plus 1 Tbsp. all-purpose flour
- ¼ cup freshly grated Grana Padano cheese
- 2 large eggs
- ½ cup plain dry breadcrumbs
  Canola oil, for frying
  Truffle salt, for sprinkling
  Lemon wedges, for serving

1. In a large skillet, heat the olive oil with 1 teaspoon of the truffle oil. Add the mushrooms, season with salt and pepper and cook over moderate heat, stirring occasionally, until golden and tender, 5 to 7 minutes. Transfer to a plate. Finely chop the mushrooms and transfer to a small bowl. Stir in the remaining ½ teaspoon of truffle oil.

2. In a small saucepan, bring the milk to a simmer. In a medium saucepan, melt the butter. Add ½ cup plus 1 tablespoon of the flour and whisk until smooth. Cook over low heat, whisking frequently, for 5 minutes. While whisking constantly, slowly drizzle in the hot milk. Cook over low heat, whisking frequently, until the béchamel is very thick and smooth, about 20 minutes. Remove from the heat and fold in the mushrooms and cheese. Season with salt and pepper. Transfer the mixture to a bowl and press plastic wrap directly onto the surface. Refrigerate until firm, about 1 hour.

3. Spread the remaining ½ cup of flour in a shallow bowl. In another shallow bowl, whisk the eggs. Spread the breadcrumbs in a third shallow bowl. Roll the mushroom mixture into eighteen 1½-inch balls. Dredge them in the flour, then coat with the egg and dredge in the breadcrumbs. Transfer to a plate.

4. In a medium enameled cast-iron casserole, heat 2 inches of canola oil to 350°. Line a large plate with paper towels. Working in 2 batches, fry the croquettes until golden brown, about 4 minutes. Transfer to the paper towels to drain. Arrange on a platter and sprinkle with truffle salt. Serve with lemon wedges. —*David Waltuck*

MAKE AHEAD The breaded croquettes can be refrigerated for 4 to 6 hours.

WINE Fresh, lemony sparkling wine: J. Laurens Crémant de Limoux.

Cheese Sables with Rosemary Salt

Active **20 min**; Total **1 hr 45 min**; Makes **32**

These buttery cheese crackers are a great party snack because they come together quickly and can be made in advance.

- ½ cup plus 2 Tbsp. self-rising flour, plus more for dusting
- 7 Tbsp. unsalted butter, softened
- ½ cup freshly grated Parmigiano-Reggiano cheese
- ⅓ cup shredded sharp cheddar cheese
  Pinch of cayenne
- 1 Tbsp. chopped rosemary
- ½ tsp. kosher salt

1. In a food processor, combine the flour, butter, cheeses and cayenne. Pulse until a crumbly dough forms. On a lightly floured surface, form the dough into a log 1½ inches in diameter. Wrap in plastic and chill until firm, about 1 hour.

2. Meanwhile, preheat the oven to 350°. Line 2 baking sheets with parchment paper. In a mortar, pound the rosemary with the salt until blended.

3. Using a thin, sharp knife, slice the dough into ⅛-inch-thick rounds. Arrange the sables 2 inches apart on the baking sheets. Bake in the middle and lower thirds of the oven for 12 to 15 minutes, until golden; shift the pans from top to bottom and front to back halfway through baking. Sprinkle the hot sables with the rosemary salt and let cool on the sheets for 5 minutes. Transfer the sables to a rack to cool completely. —*Anna May*

MAKE AHEAD The sables can be stored in an airtight container for up to 3 days.

Quinoa Balls with Cauliflower and Cheese

Active **25 min**; Total **1 hr 30 min plus overnight soaking**; Makes **26**

Quinoa, grated cauliflower, salty halloumi cheese and chickpea flour become crisp, fluffy little balls that are wonderful as an hors d'oeuvre or with tomato sauce as a main course. Soaking the quinoa overnight before cooking makes it more digestible.

- ⅔ cup quinoa (4½ oz.)
- 1 large egg, beaten
- 8 oz. cauliflower florets, grated on the medium holes of a box grater (1½ cups)
- 6 oz. halloumi cheese, grated (1½ cups)
- 2 scallions, thinly sliced
- 3 Tbsp. chickpea or buckwheat flour
- 1 garlic clove, minced
- ½ tsp. sea salt
- ⅛ tsp. pepper
  Pinch of freshly grated nutmeg (optional)
- ½ tsp. baking soda
- 1½ tsp. fresh lemon juice

1. In a bowl, cover the quinoa with 2 inches of water and soak overnight. Drain well.

2. In a medium saucepan of boiling water, cook the quinoa until tender, about 10 minutes. Drain well, then return the quinoa to the hot saucepan. Cover and let stand for 10 minutes. Fluff the quinoa and scrape out onto a baking sheet to cool slightly.

3. Preheat the oven to 375°. Line a baking sheet with parchment paper. In a large bowl, combine the egg, cauliflower, cheese, scallions, chickpea flour, garlic, salt, pepper, nutmeg and quinoa; mix well. In a small bowl, mix the baking soda with the lemon juice and stir into the quinoa mixture. Scoop out 2 tablespoons of the mixture and press together to form a ball. Place on the prepared baking sheet. Repeat to make 26 balls.

4. Bake the quinoa balls for about 30 minutes, until golden and firm. Serve hot. —*Jasmine and Melissa Hemsley*

WINE Toasty, apple-scented sparkling wine: NV Lucien Albrecht Crémant d'Alsace Brut.

Jamaican Greens-Stuffed Patties

Active **1 hr**; Total **2 hr**; Makes **24**

Acclaimed Jamaican singer and caterer Suzanne Couch is the culinary adviser and muse for the Miss Lily's restaurants in New York City. She fills her phyllo dough patties with the popular Jamaican greens called callaloo. The adaptation here uses Swiss chard.

½ **each green, red and yellow bell pepper, chopped**

5 **scallions, coarsely chopped**

4 **garlic cloves, crushed**

1 **medium onion, coarsely chopped**

1 **Scotch bonnet or habanero chile, stemmed and halved**

¼ **cup extra-virgin olive oil**
   Kosher salt and pepper

2 **lbs. Swiss chard, stems removed and leaves coarsely chopped (21 lightly packed cups)**

4 **oz. cream cheese, softened**

30 **sheets of phyllo dough, from 2 packages (see Note)**

1 **stick unsalted butter, melted**

1 **large egg beaten with 1 Tbsp. water**

1. In a food processor, combine the bell peppers with the scallions, garlic, onion and Scotch bonnet. Pulse until very finely chopped.

2. In a large, deep skillet, heat the olive oil until shimmering. Add the chopped vegetable mixture and a generous pinch each of salt and pepper. Cook over moderately high heat, stirring occasionally, until the vegetables are softened and just starting to brown, about 8 minutes. Stir in one-third of the Swiss chard at a time; cover and cook over moderate heat until the greens are tender and any liquid has evaporated, about 5 minutes per batch. Remove from the heat and stir in the cream cheese until incorporated. Season the filling with salt and pepper. Scrape the filling into a bowl and let cool completely, then refrigerate until chilled, about 30 minutes.

3. Preheat the oven to 350°. Line 2 baking sheets with parchment paper. Lay 1 sheet of the phyllo on a work surface with a long side facing you. Lightly brush the phyllo with melted butter and lay another sheet on top. Repeat the brushing and stacking until you have a stack of 5 buttered sheets. Using a sharp knife, cut the phyllo crosswise into four 4-by-12-inch strips. Cover the remaining phyllo with a damp towel.

4. Spoon 2 tablespoons of the filling in a corner of 1 phyllo strip, ½ inch from the top; fold the opposite corner over the filling to form a triangle. Continue folding the triangle down and over itself until you reach the end of the strip. Transfer the patty to a prepared baking sheet and brush with melted butter. Repeat Steps 3 and 4 with the remaining phyllo dough and filling.

5. Brush the patties with the egg wash. Using a paring knife, make slits ½ inch apart across the top of each patty; be careful not to cut through to the filling. Bake for about 25 minutes, until browned, shifting the pans halfway through baking. Let cool for 5 minutes before serving.
—*Suzanne Couch*

NOTE If necessary, stack and trim your phyllo sheets to 12-by-16 inches.

BEER Spiced, citrusy wheat beer: Allagash White.

Sea Scallop Lollipops

Total **20 min**; Makes **12**

Meaty sea scallops make the perfect party skewer, great for dipping into this sweet-spicy sauce from Boston chef Matt Jennings.

½ **cup mayonnaise**

2 **Tbsp. gochujang**

2 **Tbsp. minced dill pickle**
   Kosher salt and pepper

2 **Tbsp. canola oil**

12 **large sea scallops (1 lb.)**
   Lollipop sticks or small skewers, for serving

1. In a small bowl, stir the mayo with the gochujang and pickle; season with salt.

2. In a large cast-iron skillet, heat the oil. Season the scallops with salt and pepper and cook over moderately high heat, turning once, until golden and just cooked through, about 3 minutes. Skewer the scallops on lollipop sticks and arrange on a platter. Serve with the gochujang mayo.
—*Matt Jennings*

Tuna Briks

Total **30 min**; Makes **8 small pies**

Briks are small, triangular, savory pastries prepared throughout Tunisia with fillings that range from meat and egg to mashed potato. One constant: the Tunisian chile paste harissa. This version is phyllo-based and filled with tuna, scallions, capers and parsley. The pastries are shallow-fried, so there's no need to brush butter between the phyllo layers as you would if you were baking them.

   Two 7-oz. cans tuna packed in water, drained well and flaked

¼ **cup finely chopped scallions**

¼ **cup chopped drained capers**

¼ **cup chopped parsley**

¼ **cup extra-virgin olive oil**

2 **Tbsp. harissa**
   Kosher salt and pepper

6 **sheets of phyllo dough**

1 **large egg, beaten**
   Canola oil, for frying

1. In a medium bowl, combine the tuna, scallions, capers, parsley, olive oil and harissa. Season with salt and pepper and mix gently.

2. On a work surface, make 2 stacks of 3 phyllo sheets each. Cut each stack crosswise into four 4-by-12-inch strips. Keep the phyllo dough covered with a damp kitchen towel. Place a heaping ¼ cup of the tuna filling at the end of a strip closest to you. Brush the edge of the other end with the beaten egg. Fold the corner of the phyllo over the filling to form a triangle. Continue folding the triangle up and over itself until you reach the end of the phyllo strip; press to adhere. Repeat with the remaining phyllo strips, filling and beaten egg.

3. In a large cast-iron skillet, heat ¼ inch of canola oil until it shimmers. Fry 4 of the phyllo triangles over moderately low heat, turning occasionally, until golden and crisp, 3 to 4 minutes. Transfer the briks to a paper towel–lined plate to drain. Repeat with the 4 remaining phyllo triangles. Serve hot.
—*Kay Chun*

MAKE AHEAD The filled phyllo triangles can be refrigerated for 3 hours before frying.

WINE Lively, fruit-forward sparkling wine: 2010 Juvé y Camps Brut Nature.

FILIPINO SALAD
CRÊPES

Filipino Salad Crêpes

Total **1 hr**; Makes **8**

- 1 **large egg**
- **Fine salt**
- 1 **cup all-purpose flour**
- 1 **Tbsp. grapeseed oil, plus more for brushing**
- ½ **cup creamy peanut butter**
- ½ **cup unsweetened coconut milk**
- 1 **Tbsp. tamari or soy sauce**
- 1 **garlic clove, finely grated**
- 1 **green (unripe) mango, peeled and julienned**
- 1 **cup julienned carrot**
- 1 **cup julienned daikon**
- 1 **cup julienned English cucumber**
- ½ **cup torn mint leaves**
- ½ **cup lightly packed chopped cilantro**
- **Small butter lettuce leaves, chopped roasted peanuts and coconut vinegar (see Note), for serving**

1. In a medium bowl, beat the egg with ½ teaspoon of salt and 1½ cups of water. Gradually whisk in the flour just until a batter forms (it's OK if there are lumps), then whisk in the 1 tablespoon of grapeseed oil.

2. Heat an 8-inch nonstick skillet and brush with grapeseed oil. Add ¼ cup of the batter and tilt the skillet to distribute the batter evenly. Cook over moderate heat until bubbles start to form around the edge of the crêpe, about 1 minute. Flip, then cook until lightly browned on the bottom, about 45 seconds longer. Transfer the crêpe to a baking sheet and top with a piece of wax or parchment paper. Repeat with the remaining batter, brushing the skillet with oil as needed; layer paper between each crêpe.

3. In a small bowl, whisk the peanut butter with the coconut milk, tamari, garlic and 3 tablespoons of water; season with salt. In a medium bowl, toss the mango with the carrot, daikon, cucumber, mint and cilantro.

4. Arrange the crêpes on plates. Top each with a lettuce leaf and some of the salad; drizzle with the peanut dressing. Sprinkle with peanuts and coconut vinegar and serve, passing additional vinegar and dressing at the table. —*Paul Qui*

NOTE If you can't find coconut vinegar, use white vinegar.

Roasted Shrimp Skewers with Fennel and Mustard Chimichurri

Total **45 min**; Makes **24 small skewers**

- 2 **cups lightly packed parsley**
- 1 **cup snipped chives**
- 2½ **Tbsp. sherry vinegar**
- 1½ **Tbsp. fresh lemon juice**
- 1 **Tbsp. finely grated peeled fresh horseradish**
- 2 **garlic cloves, finely chopped**
- 1 **tsp. crushed red pepper**
- 1 **tsp. honey**
- ¼ **cup plus 3 Tbsp. extra-virgin olive oil, plus more for brushing**
- 1½ **Tbsp. whole-grain mustard**
- **Kosher salt and black pepper**
- 2 **medium fennel bulbs—halved lengthwise, cored and cut into thin wedges**
- 24 **large shrimp, shelled and deveined**

1. Preheat the oven to 375°. In a food processor, combine the parsley with the chives, vinegar, lemon juice, horseradish, garlic, crushed red pepper, honey, ¼ cup plus 2 tablespoons of the olive oil and ¼ cup of water and pulse until the herbs are finely chopped. Scrape the chimichurri into a bowl, stir in the mustard and season with salt and black pepper.

2. Arrange the fennel pieces on one half of a large rimmed baking sheet, keeping the wedges intact. Brush with olive oil and season with salt and pepper. Roast for 25 to 30 minutes, until tender.

3. In a medium bowl, toss the shrimp with the remaining 1 tablespoon of olive oil and season with salt and black pepper. Spread the shrimp on the other half of the baking sheet and roast for 5 minutes, until just cooked through.

4. Thread the shrimp onto twenty-four 6-inch skewers and arrange on a platter with the fennel wedges. Serve with the mustard chimichurri. —*Matt Jennings*

MAKE AHEAD The chimichurri can be made early in the day and refrigerated. Bring to room temperature before serving.

Shrimp and Avocado Summer Rolls

Total **45 min**; Makes **6**

Blogger Shu Han Lee calls these fresh, herb-packed Vietnamese summer rolls "salad inside rice paper." Avocado adds creamy lushness to the raw vegetables.

- 2 **oz. rice vermicelli**
- **Boiling water**
- 18 **medium shrimp, shelled and deveined**
- **Six 8-inch round rice paper wrappers**
- 1 **Hass avocado—peeled, pitted and thinly sliced**
- ⅓ **cup cilantro leaves**
- ⅓ **cup mint leaves**
- ⅓ **cup snipped chives**
- ¼ **cup sugar**
- 1 **Fresno chile, seeded and minced**
- 1 **small garlic clove, minced**
- **Kosher salt**
- **Asian chile-garlic sauce, for serving**

1. In a large heatproof bowl, cover the vermicelli with boiling water and let stand until softened, about 10 minutes. Drain and cool under running water, then drain again and pat dry.

2. Meanwhile, in a medium saucepan of salted boiling water, cook the shrimp until just white throughout, about 2 minutes. Drain and run under cold water to cool completely, then drain again and pat dry.

3. Fill a medium skillet with hot water. Soak 1 rice paper wrapper in the water for 30 seconds, until just pliable. Transfer the wrapper to a work surface and top with some noodles, avocado, herbs and shrimp. Tightly roll up the wrapper around the filling, tucking in the sides as you roll. Repeat with the remaining wrappers and fillings.

4. In a small bowl, whisk the sugar with ¼ cup of warm water until dissolved. Stir in the chile and garlic and season with salt. Serve the summer rolls with the dipping sauce, passing chile-garlic sauce at the table. —*Shu Han Lee*

WINE Zippy, citrusy Albariño: 2013 Fefiñanes.

Venezuelan Fresh Corn Cakes with Cheese

Total **30 min**; Serves **6**

Blogger Sasha Martin uses a mix of fresh (or frozen) corn and masa harina (corn flour) to make her crispy cakes, called cachapas in Venezuela. They develop a delicious charred-corn flavor as they cook on the griddle. Serve them steaming hot and folded around a generous amount of melted cheese.

- **1 lb. fresh or thawed frozen corn kernels (3 cups)**
- **½ cup masa harina**
- **1 tsp. kosher salt**
- **¼ tsp. pepper**
- **2 Tbsp. canola oil**
- **¾ cup shredded mozzarella cheese**
- **¼ cup chopped cilantro**

1. In a food processor, pulse the corn until coarsely ground. Add the masa harina, salt and pepper. Pulse until a stiff batter forms; scrape down the side of the bowl. Form the batter into 6 equal balls, about ⅓ cup each.

2. Preheat a griddle and brush with 1 tablespoon of the oil. Set the balls on the griddle and, using a spatula, flatten them into ¼-inch-thick rounds. Cook over moderate heat until golden brown, 4 to 5 minutes. Flip the cakes and add the remaining tablespoon of oil to the griddle. Flatten the cakes until they're ⅛ inch thick and about 5 inches in diameter and cook until golden brown on the bottom, 4 to 5 minutes longer. Sprinkle with the cheese and cook until melted, 1 to 2 minutes. Transfer to a platter, sprinkle with the cilantro, fold in half and serve. —*Sasha Martin*

WINE Ripe, fruit-forward Chardonnay: 2013 Joel Gott Monterey.

Baked Sweet Potato and Tempeh Empanadas

Active **1 hr 15 min**; Total **3 hr 15 min**
Makes **20 mini empanadas**

Tempeh has a long way to go before it becomes as popular as other soy products, but its wonderfully firm texture and versatility make it an excellent protein source. Here, it stands in for ground meat in a vegan baked empanada that gets great flavor from a sweet potato dough.

DOUGH

- **One 1-lb. sweet potato**
- **1 cup all-purpose flour**
- **½ cup whole-wheat flour**
- **½ cup fine cornmeal**
- **¼ tsp. kosher salt**
- **2 Tbsp. coconut oil, at room temperature**

FILLING

- **2 Tbsp. extra-virgin olive oil**
- **1 small onion, finely chopped**
- **One 8-oz. package tempeh, crumbled**
- **3 garlic cloves, minced**
- **1 Tbsp. cumin seeds**
- **1 cup tomato puree**
- **1 Tbsp. adobo sauce from a can of chipotles in adobo**
- **1 tsp. dried oregano**
- **Kosher salt**
- **Avocado Chimichurri (recipe follows), for serving**

1. Make the dough Line the bottom of the oven with a sheet of foil and preheat to 350°. Prick the sweet potato all over with a fork and roast directly on the oven rack for about 1 hour, until tender. Let cool slightly. Scrape the flesh into a bowl and mash well with a fork.

2. In a medium bowl, whisk both flours with the cornmeal and salt. In a stand mixer fitted with the paddle, beat 1½ cups of the sweet potato puree (save the rest for another use) with the coconut oil until smooth. Gradually beat in the dry ingredients until a smooth dough forms.

3. Scrape the dough onto a work surface and gather into a ball; divide in half and pat into 6-inch disks. Wrap in plastic and refrigerate for 1 hour.

4. Meanwhile, make the filling In a large skillet, heat the olive oil. Add the onion and cook over moderate heat, stirring occasionally, until just starting to brown, about 7 minutes. Add the tempeh, garlic and cumin seeds and cook, stirring, until fragrant and heated through, 3 to 5 minutes. Stir in the tomato puree, adobo sauce, oregano and 2 tablespoons of water and cook for 2 minutes. Season with salt and let the filling cool completely.

5. Preheat the oven to 350° and line 2 large baking sheets with parchment paper. On a lightly floured surface, working with 1 disk at a time, roll out the dough ¼ inch thick. Using a 4-inch round cutter, stamp out 10 rounds of dough. Moisten the edges with water and mound a scant 2 tablespoons of the filling on one half of each round; fold the dough over to form half-moons. Press the edges to seal and pleat at intervals or crimp with a fork. Transfer the empanadas to the prepared baking sheets. Repeat with the remaining dough and filling.

6. Bake the empanadas in the upper and lower thirds of the oven for about 25 minutes, until browned; shift the pans halfway through baking. Serve warm, with the Avocado Chimichurri. —*Alexa Weitzman*

MAKE AHEAD The unbaked empanadas can be frozen for 2 months; bake from frozen.

WINE Fragrant Argentinean white: 2014 Hermanos Torrontés.

AVOCADO CHIMICHURRI

Active **10 min**; Total **40 min**
Makes **1¼ cups**

- **⅓ cup extra-virgin olive oil**
- **¼ cup fresh lime juice**
- **1 garlic clove, minced**
- **Kosher salt**
- **1 cup finely chopped parsley**
- **1 Tbsp. finely chopped oregano**
- **1 Hass avocado—peeled, pitted and diced**

In a medium bowl, whisk the olive oil with the lime juice, garlic and a pinch of salt. Stir in the parsley and oregano and let stand at room temperature for 30 minutes. Fold in the avocado and season with salt. —*AW*

MAKE AHEAD The chimichurri can be refrigerated for up to 4 hours.

BAKED SWEET
POTATO AND TEMPEH
EMPANADAS

Ham-and-Cheese Puff Pastry Tart

📷 PAGE 8

Active **40 min**; Total **1 hr 45 min**; Serves **4**

    3 Tbsp. unsalted butter
    1 large shallot, thinly sliced
    3 Tbsp. all-purpose flour
    1 cup milk
    2 tsp. whole-grain mustard
       Pinch of freshly grated nutmeg
       Kosher salt and pepper
    ½ lb. all-butter puff pasty, cut in half
    2 oz. Comté cheese, shredded (⅔ cup)
    ½ lb. thinly sliced baked ham
    1 large egg yolk mixed with
       1 tsp. water

1. In a medium saucepan, melt the butter. Add the shallot and cook over moderate heat until softened and lightly browned, 3 to 5 minutes. Stir in the flour and cook until bubbling, about 1 minute. Gradually whisk in the milk and bring to a boil, whisking. Cook over moderate heat, whisking frequently, until the sauce is thickened and no floury taste remains, 5 to 7 minutes. Stir in the mustard and nutmeg. Season the béchamel with salt and pepper. Let cool.

2. Line a large rimmed baking sheet with parchment paper. On a lightly floured work surface, roll out each piece of puff pastry to a 10-by-6-inch rectangle. Slide 1 pastry rectangle onto the prepared baking sheet. Spread one-third of the cooled béchamel on the first pastry, leaving a 1-inch border all around. Sprinkle half of the cheese on top and cover with half of the ham. Repeat the layering with another third of the béchamel and the remaining cheese and ham. End with a final layer of béchamel. Cover the tart with the remaining pastry and press all around the edge to seal. Crimp the edge decoratively. Using a paring knife, cut four 1-inch slits in the top of the tart, then brush all over with the egg wash. Refrigerate until chilled, about 20 minutes.

3. Preheat the oven to 450°. Bake the tart for 20 to 25 minutes, until puffed and golden brown. Let cool for 10 minutes before serving. —*Mimi Thorisson*

WINE Fruit-forward French Chardonnay: 2009 Domaine Rolet Côtes du Jura.

Free-Form Autumn Vegetable Tart with Bacon Marmalade

Active **1 hr 15 min**; Total **2 hr 15 min** Serves **4**

For this beautiful tart, L.A. chef Timothy Hollingsworth tops a sturdy crust with savory-sweet bacon marmalade and a spectacular pile of roasted and raw vegetables.

BACON MARMALADE

    12 slices of bacon, finely chopped
     ¼ cup canola oil
     3 medium shallots, minced
     ½ cup red wine vinegar
     ½ cup packed light brown sugar
     1 cup chicken stock or
        low-sodium broth
        Kosher salt and pepper

CRUST

     1 cup all-purpose flour
     1 Tbsp. sugar
        Kosher salt
     4 Tbsp. melted butter
     1 large egg, beaten
     1 large egg beaten with 1 Tbsp. milk

TOPPING

     ¾ lb. chopped mixed mushrooms, such
        as chanterelle, oyster and cremini
     ½ lb. small brussels sprouts, halved
     4 oz. pearl onions, peeled
     2 Tbsp. canola oil
        Kosher salt and pepper
     1 cup torn tender escarole leaves
     1 cup torn Swiss chard leaves
     1 cup shaved carrot
        (from 1 medium carrot)
     1 cup torn radicchio

1. Make the marmalade In a large skillet, cook the bacon in the oil over moderately high heat, stirring occasionally, until browned and crisp, about 8 minutes. Using a slotted spoon, transfer to a paper towel–lined plate to drain.

2. Pour all but 2 tablespoons of the fat from the skillet into a heatproof bowl. Add the shallots to the skillet and cook over moderately low heat, stirring, until softened but not browned, about 3 minutes. Add the vinegar and brown sugar and cook over moderately high heat, stirring occasionally, until the vinegar is reduced by half, about 2 minutes. Whisk in the chicken stock and cook until reduced to a thick syrup, about 5 minutes. Stir in the bacon and whisk in ⅓ cup of the reserved bacon fat. Let cool until thickened slightly, then season with salt and pepper.

3. Make the crust Preheat the oven to 350°. In a stand mixer fitted with the paddle, combine the flour, sugar and a generous pinch of salt. At medium speed, gradually add the melted butter and the egg until a dough forms. Turn the dough out onto a lightly floured work surface, gather up any crumbs and press the dough into a disk. Working on a sheet of parchment paper, roll out the dough to a 12-by-10-inch oval, about ⅛ inch thick. Slide the dough on the parchment onto a large baking sheet; brush with the egg wash and top with another sheet of parchment paper and another baking sheet. Bake for about 10 minutes, until just set. Remove the top baking sheet and parchment paper and bake the crust for 10 minutes more, until browned and crisp. Transfer to a rack to cool.

4. Meanwhile, make the topping On a large rimmed baking sheet, toss the mushrooms with the brussels sprouts, pearl onions and oil. Season generously with salt and pepper. Bake for about 35 minutes, until the vegetables are tender and lightly browned. Let cool slightly.

5. Transfer the crust to a platter and spread half of the bacon marmalade on top. In a large bowl, toss the roasted vegetables with the escarole, Swiss chard, shaved carrot and radicchio; season with salt and pepper. Pile the vegetables on the crust and serve with the remaining bacon marmalade on the side. —*Timothy Hollingsworth*

WINE Berry-rich Santa Barbara Pinot Noir: 2013 Foxen Santa Maria Valley.

Bacony Tortillas with Melted Cheese and Crispy Mushrooms

Active **1 hr**; Total **2 hr**; Serves **4**

BACONY TORTILLAS

- 1 cup all-purpose flour, plus more if needed
- ¾ tsp. kosher salt
- 2 Tbsp. cold rendered bacon fat, from 4 oz. bacon (see Note)
- 2 Tbsp. vegetable shortening

MELTED CHEESE

- 2 Tbsp. unsalted butter
- 6 oz. chanterelle, hen-of-the-woods or black trumpet mushrooms, cut into large pieces
- 2 thyme sprigs
  Kosher salt
- 8 oz. Chihuahua or Fontina cheese, shredded
- 1 serrano chile, thinly sliced
- ¼ cup cilantro leaves

1. Make the tortillas In a stand mixer, combine the 1 cup of flour and the salt. Using your hands, rub the bacon fat and vegetable shortening into the flour until the mixture is crumbly. Using the dough hook, slowly mix in ½ cup of warm water at medium speed until a ball forms, adding more flour if necessary; the dough will be moist but should start to pull away from the side of the bowl. Continue kneading until the dough is smooth, shiny and elastic, about 10 minutes. Cover the bowl with plastic wrap; let rest for 45 minutes.

2. Scoop slightly rounded tablespoonfuls of the dough and roll between pieces of parchment paper into 4-inch rounds. Heat a cast-iron skillet and cook the tortillas in batches over moderately high heat, turning once, until lightly browned, about 1 minute total. Transfer to a kitchen towel and keep warm.

3. Make the melted cheese In a medium skillet, melt the butter. Add the mushrooms and thyme and cook over moderately high heat, undisturbed, until lightly browned, about 2 minutes. Season the mushrooms with salt and cook, tossing occasionally, until browned and crisp, about 6 minutes. Transfer to a paper towel–lined plate; discard the thyme sprigs.

4. Preheat the broiler. In a small cast-iron skillet or ovenproof dish, broil the cheese 8 inches from the heat until just melted, about 1 minute. Top the cheese with the mushrooms, chile and cilantro and serve immediately with the warm tortillas.
—*Ford Fry*

NOTE If bacon fat is unavailable, double the amount of vegetable shortening.

Tomatoes Two Ways with Crab and Soppressata

Total **50 min**; Serves **4**

- 1 lb. ripe tomatoes
- 2 Tbsp. extra-virgin olive oil
- ¼ cup minced white onion
- 2 garlic cloves, minced
  Pinch of crushed red pepper
  Pinch of sweet paprika
  Kosher salt and black pepper
- ½ cup dry white wine
- 1 large purple or green basil sprig, plus basil sprigs and flowers (optional) for garnish
- 2 oz. uncured soppressata or hot Italian sausage, crumbled
- 1½ lbs. heirloom tomatoes, cut into ½-inch slices
- 4 oz. lump crabmeat (about ¾ cup)

1. Halve the tomatoes crosswise. Working over a bowl, grate them on a box grater, discarding the skin; you should have 1½ cups of pulp.

2. In a medium saucepan, heat the oil. Add the onion and garlic and season with the red pepper, paprika, salt and black pepper. Cook over moderate heat, stirring occasionally, until the onion is softened, about 5 minutes. Add the wine and simmer until just evaporated, 3 minutes. Add the grated tomatoes and basil sprig and cook, stirring occasionally, until the sauce thickens, 20 to 25 minutes. Discard the basil sprig.

3. Add the soppressata to the sauce and cook, stirring, until cooked through, about 5 minutes. Spoon the sauce into shallow bowls and cover with the sliced tomatoes. Season with salt and pepper. Top with the crab, garnish with basil and serve.
—*James Henry*

WINE Full-bodied, minerally Jura white: 2011 Domaine Badoz Côtes du Jura Chardonnay.

Stuffed Grape Leaves

Active **30 min**; Total **1 hr 30 min**; Serves **6**

New York City chef Scott Conant learned to make these stuffed grape leaves from his Turkish mother-in-law. She sweetens the rice filling with sautéed onions, tomato paste and dried mint. "They're best eaten warm, with your hands," says Conant's wife, Meltem.

- ½ cup extra-virgin olive oil
- 1 large onion, minced
- 1 Tbsp. tomato paste
- 1 cup long-grain white rice
- ½ cup chopped parsley leaves plus 12 stems
- 2 tsp. dried mint
- ½ tsp. sugar
  Kosher salt and pepper
- 18 large brined grape leaves, rinsed and patted dry

1. In a medium saucepan, heat 2 tablespoons of the oil. Add the onion and cook over moderate heat, stirring occasionally, until translucent, 5 minutes. Stir in the tomato paste and cook, stirring, until lightly caramelized, about 3 minutes. Add the rice and 1 cup of water; bring to a simmer. Cover and cook over low heat until the water is absorbed, about 5 minutes. Remove the saucepan from the heat. Stir in the chopped parsley, mint and sugar and season with salt and pepper. (The rice will not be fully cooked yet.)

2. Spread the grape leaves on a work surface. Spoon 2 tablespoons of the filling down the center of each leaf, leaving a 1-inch border on each side. For each stuffed grape leaf, fold the sides over the rice, then roll up the leaf into a log.

3. Scatter the parsley stems in a large skillet. Set the stuffed grape leaves on top in a single layer. Season with salt and add enough water to just cover the rolls. Bring to a simmer and cook over moderately low heat, uncovered, until the rice is tender, about 25 minutes. Transfer the stuffed grape leaves to a platter, drizzle the remaining oil on top and let stand until cooled to room temperature. Serve.
—*Scott Conant*

DIY CHINESE DUMPLINGS

At Bao Bao Dumpling House in Portland, Maine, chef **CARA STADLER** offers traditional dumplings like pork-and-shrimp alongside original versions, such as mapo tofu and chicken with cashew. Here, she shares her recipes for all three fillings plus her delicately chewy homemade wrappers.

PLEATING TUTORIAL

1

LAY a wrapper in one hand. Using your finger, brush the outer edge with water. Spoon filling in the center. Fold the wrapper over; pinch at the top to adhere.

2

FOLD a pleat in the dough on the top left, angling back toward the center. Press with your fingers to adhere.

3

MAKE a second pleat. Repeat on the top right to meet the first pleat in the center. Transfer to a parchment-lined baking sheet and cover with plastic wrap.

MAKE THE DUMPLING WRAPPERS

Active **30 min**; Total **1 hr 30 min**
Makes **about 3 dozen wrappers**

A small rolling pin (available at amazon .com) makes it easier to prep the wrappers. However, if pressed for time, you could also use store-bought wrappers.

1. Put 1¼ cups of all-purpose flour into a medium bowl. Slowly drizzle in ¾ cup of boiling water and mix with a wooden spoon until the mixture just comes together. Turn it out onto a lightly floured work surface and knead until a smooth dough forms, 5 minutes. Return the dough to the bowl and cover with plastic wrap. Let rest at room temperature for at least 1 hour or up to 4 hours.

2. Turn the dough out onto a lightly floured work surface and, using a sharp knife, cut it into 36 equal pieces (9 to 10 grams each). Roll each piece into a ball. Using a small, lightly floured rolling pin, roll out 1 ball of dough to a ⅛-inch-thick round, then roll out just the outer edge until it is ¹⁄₁₆ inch thick and the wrapper is 3½ inches in diameter. (To hold the filling properly, the wrapper should be slightly thicker in the center than at the edge.)

3. Transfer the wrapper to a parchment paper–lined baking sheet and cover with a damp kitchen towel. Repeat with the remaining balls of dough.

MAKE AHEAD The dough can be refrigerated for up to 2 days. Bring to room temperature before rolling out.

CHOOSE A FILLING

Total **40 min**; Makes **about 3 cups (for 3 dozen dumplings)**

Spoon 1 heaping tablespoon into each wrapper, then pleat according to the directions at far left.

Chicken and Cashew

- ¾ lb. skin-on, boneless chicken thighs
- ¾ oz. dried shiitake mushroom caps
- ⅓ cup diced canned water chestnuts
- ½ cup chopped cilantro
- ½ cup thinly sliced scallions
- ⅓ cup chopped salted cashews
- 1½ Tbsp. minced peeled fresh ginger
- 1½ Tbsp. soy sauce
- 1½ Tbsp. hoisin sauce
- 2 tsp. Shaoxing wine
- 1 tsp. Sriracha
- 1 tsp. toasted sesame oil
- 1 large egg white
- ¾ tsp. kosher salt
- 2 tsp. cornstarch

1. Cut the chicken into ¼-inch pieces and spread on a baking sheet. Freeze until firm but not frozen, 40 minutes.

2. In a food processor, in 2 batches, pulse the chicken until coarsely ground.

3. In a heatproof bowl, cover the mushrooms with boiling water; let stand, stirring occasionally, until softened, 15 minutes. Drain well, then squeeze out any excess water. Finely chop the mushrooms.

4. In a large bowl, combine the ground chicken with the mushrooms and all the remaining ingredients except the cornstarch; fold gently to combine. Fold in the cornstarch just until incorporated.

Spicy Mapo Tofu

- 7 oz. firm tofu, drained
- 4 dried chiles de árbol, stemmed
- 1 tsp. Sichuan peppercorns
- ½ lb. fatty ground pork, preferably pork butt
- 2 garlic cloves, minced
- 1 scallion, thinly sliced
- ½ cup finely chopped flowering chives
- ¼ cup minced peeled fresh ginger
- ¼ cup black bean paste with chile
- 1 Tbsp. ground bean sauce
- 1 Tbsp. tobanjan (fermented broad-bean paste)
- 3 Tbsp. Shaoxing wine
- 1 large egg white
- ½ tsp. kosher salt
- 2 Tbsp. cornstarch

1. Cut the tofu into ¼-inch-thick slices; put them on a paper towel–lined plate and press dry with paper towels. Finely chop the tofu and transfer to a large bowl.

2. In a spice grinder, combine the chiles and Sichuan peppercorns and finely grind. Add to the tofu in the bowl along with all of the remaining ingredients except the cornstarch. Fold gently until well blended. Fold in the cornstarch just until incorporated.

Pork and Shrimp

- ¾ oz. dried shiitake mushroom caps
- ½ lb. fatty ground pork, preferably pork butt
- ½ lb. shelled and deveined large shrimp, finely chopped
- 2 scallions, thinly sliced
- ⅓ cup finely chopped canned water chestnuts (about 5)
- 2 Tbsp. minced peeled fresh ginger
- 1½ Tbsp. soy sauce
- 1½ Tbsp. Shaoxing wine
- ½ Tbsp. toasted sesame oil
- ½ Tbsp. sugar
- 1½ tsp. kosher salt
- 1 large egg white
- 1 Tbsp. cornstarch

1. In a heatproof bowl, cover the mushrooms with boiling water; let stand, stirring occasionally, until softened, 15 minutes. Drain well, then squeeze out any excess water. Finely chop the mushrooms.

2. In a large bowl, combine the mushrooms with all of the remaining ingredients except the cornstarch and fold gently until well blended. Fold in the cornstarch.

CRISP-BOTTOMED DUMPLINGS
The simple shape of these dumplings provides a lot of surface area for them to crisp in the pan.

COOK THE DUMPLINGS
Total **20 min**; Makes **about 3 dozen**

Stadler's favorite method for perfectly cooked, crisp-bottomed dumplings is fry-steam-fry. It's the classic way to prepare pot stickers.

1. Pour enough canola oil into a large non-stick skillet to cover the bottom. Arrange some of the dumplings in the skillet with a non-pleated side down (you will need to work in batches). Cook over low heat until golden on the bottom, about 3 minutes.

2. Carefully pour in enough water to reach halfway up the dumplings. Cover and cook until almost all of the water is absorbed and the filling is cooked through, 4 minutes. Uncover and cook until all of the liquid has evaporated and the dumplings are crispy on the bottom, 2 minutes longer. Carefully invert onto a plate. Repeat the process with the remaining dumplings. Serve warm.

MAKE AHEAD The fillings can be refrigerated overnight. The assembled, uncooked dumplings can be frozen for up to 1 month and cooked from frozen. Just add 2 minutes to the covered cooking time in Step 2. Alternatively, you can boil or steam the frozen dumplings for about 8 minutes.

Ellen Bennett, founder of Hedley & Bennett handmade aprons, hosts a party at her L.A. home. Friends, including actor Jesse Tyler Ferguson, helped prep dishes, like a Mexican grilled-corn salad (recipe, p. 63).

SALADS

TOMATO-FETA SALAD
WITH LIME AND MINT
Recipe, page 49

SUMMER SALAD
WITH HERBS
AND PITA CRISPS

Summer Salad with Herbs and Pita Crisps

⏱ Total **40 min;** Serves **4 to 6**

F&W's Kay Chun cleverly rubs the inside of a wooden salad bowl with a mint sprig, then makes the dressing right in the bowl. This lets the dressing absorb the natural mint oils.

- 6 **Tbsp. extra-virgin olive oil, plus more for brushing**
- 1 **tsp. finely grated garlic**
- 2 **pita breads, each split into 2 rounds**
  Kosher salt and pepper
- ½ **lb. haricots verts, green beans or wax beans, trimmed**
- 1 **mint sprig plus 2 cups chopped mint**
- 2 **Tbsp. fresh lemon juice**
- 1 **shallot, minced**
- 1 **Kirby cucumber, chopped**
- 6 **cups packed chopped baby romaine (6 oz.)**
- 2 **cups parsley leaves**
- 12 **multicolored cherry tomatoes, halved**
- 1 **cup sunflower sprouts or chopped purslane**

1. Preheat the oven to 375°. In a small bowl, mix the 6 tablespoons of olive oil with the garlic. Brush the pita with 2 tablespoons of the garlic oil. Toast in the oven for 5 to 7 minutes, until crisp and golden. Transfer the pita to a plate; season with salt and pepper. Let cool, then break into big crisps.

2. Meanwhile, in a medium saucepan of salted boiling water, blanch the beans until crisp-tender, about 2 minutes. Drain and chill in a bowl of ice water. Drain and pat dry; halve the beans crosswise.

3. Rub the mint sprig all over the inside of a large wooden bowl; discard the sprig. In the bowl, mix the remaining 4 tablespoons of garlic oil with the lemon juice and shallot; season with salt and pepper. Add the chopped mint, beans, cucumber, romaine, parsley, tomatoes, sprouts and pita crisps. Toss to coat, then serve. —*Kay Chun*

WINE Spritzy, citrusy Portuguese Vinho Verde: 2014 Vera.

Gem Lettuce Salad with Chile Dressing and Breadcrumbs

⏱ Total **40 min;** Serves **4**

L.A. chefs Jon Shook and Vinny Dotolo flavor the dressing for this Caesar salad riff with fruity Calabrian chiles.

DRESSING

- 2 **large egg yolks**
- 2 **oil-packed Calabrian chiles, drained and chopped**
- 1 **oil-packed anchovy fillet, drained**
- 2 **Tbsp. fresh lemon juice**
- 1½ **Tbsp. red wine vinegar**
- 1 **Tbsp. sour cream**
- ½ **Tbsp. balsamic vinegar**
- ½ **Tbsp. Worcestershire sauce**
- 1 **tsp. Dijon mustard**
- ½ **tsp. minced garlic**
  A few dashes of Tabasco
- ½ **cup grapeseed oil**
- ¼ **cup extra-virgin olive oil**
- ¼ **cup freshly grated Parmigiano-Reggiano cheese**
- 2 **Tbsp. minced shallot**
  Kosher salt and pepper

BREADCRUMBS

- 2 **Tbsp. unsalted butter**
- 2 **Tbsp. extra-virgin olive oil**
- 1 **cup panko**
- ½ **tsp. chopped oregano**
  A few pinches of garlic powder
  Kosher salt

SALAD

- 4 **heads of Little Gem lettuce (1 lb.), leaves pulled apart**
  Kosher salt and pepper
  Freshly grated Parmigiano-Reggiano cheese and chopped parsley, for garnish

1. Make the dressing In a food processor, combine the first 11 ingredients and puree until blended. With the machine on, slowly drizzle in both oils. Scrape the dressing into a medium bowl and stir in the cheese and shallot. Season with salt and pepper.

2. Make the breadcrumbs In a large non-stick skillet, melt the butter in the oil. Add the panko and cook over moderately low heat, stirring, until golden, about 5 minutes. Remove the skillet from the heat. Stir in the oregano and garlic powder and season with salt. Transfer to a paper towel–lined plate to drain.

3. Make the salad In a large bowl, toss the lettuce leaves with ½ cup of the dressing and season with salt and pepper. Toss to evenly coat. Layer the lettuce on plates and top with the breadcrumbs. Garnish with grated cheese and parsley and serve, passing the remaining dressing at the table. —*Jon Shook and Vinny Dotolo*

MAKE AHEAD The dressing can be refrigerated for 3 days. The breadcrumbs can be stored in an airtight container overnight.

WINE Fruity sparkling rosé: NV Château de Brézé Crémant de Loire Brut Rosé.

Little Gem Lettuce with Roasted Beets and Feta Dressing

📷 BACK COVER

Active **20 min**; Total **1 hr 20 min**
Serves **4 to 6**

"Moroccan dishes can be heavy; I'm always looking for ways to make them lighter and brighter," says chef Tara Stevens, who teaches cooking classes at The Courtyard Kitchen at Dar Namir in Fez. She uses Little Gem lettuce and lots of fresh herbs in this modern take on a traditional roasted beet salad.

- 1 **Tbsp. cumin seeds**
- 1 **tsp. flaky sea salt**
- 4 **beets (2 lbs.), peeled and cut into wedges**
- 2 **medium red onions, cut into wedges**
- 3 **Tbsp. extra-virgin olive oil**
- 2 **Tbsp. fresh lemon juice**
- 2 **tsp. honey**
- ¾ **cup crumbled feta cheese**
- 2 **Tbsp. plain Greek yogurt**
- ½ **tsp. grated lemon zest**
  Pepper
- 2 **heads of Little Gem or baby romaine lettuce (10 oz.)**
  Chopped cilantro and mint, for garnish

1. Preheat the oven to 375°. In a small skillet, toast the cumin seeds over low heat until fragrant, 2 minutes; let cool.

2. In a mortar, coarsely grind the cumin seeds with the salt. Transfer to a bowl and add the beets, onions and olive oil; toss to coat. Scrape the vegetables onto a rimmed baking sheet and roast for about 1 hour, stirring occasionally, until tender. Let cool to room temperature.

3. In a bowl, whisk the lemon juice and honey. In another bowl, mix the feta, yogurt and lemon zest so it remains a bit chunky. Season with pepper.

4. Arrange the lettuce on plates. Top with the beets and onions and drizzle the lemon honey on top. Dollop with the feta dressing and season with pepper. Garnish with cilantro and mint and serve. —*Tara Stevens*

Garden Herb Salad with Crab and Harissa Vinaigrette

Total **1 hr**; Serves **6**

HARISSA VINAIGRETTE

- ½ **tsp. coriander seeds**
- ½ **tsp. cumin seeds**
- ½ **tsp. fennel seeds**
- 1 **small red bell pepper**
- 1 **small jalapeño**
- 1 **garlic clove**
- 3 **Tbsp. sherry vinegar**
- ¼ **cup canola oil**
- ¼ **cup extra-virgin olive oil**
  Kosher salt and pepper

SALAD

- 1 **lb. crabmeat, preferably Dungeness, picked over**
- 2 **Tbsp. minced shallot**
- 1 **Tbsp. fresh lemon juice**
- 1 **Tbsp. extra-virgin olive oil**
  Kosher salt and pepper
- 3 **heads of Little Gem lettuce or 1 medium head of romaine lettuce, torn into bite-size pieces (8 cups)**
- ½ **cup parsley leaves**
- ½ **cup mint leaves**
- ½ **cup basil leaves**
- ½ **cup chopped dill**
- ¼ **cup snipped chives**

1. Make the vinaigrette In a small skillet, toast the coriander, cumin and fennel seeds over low heat, stirring frequently, until very fragrant, about 2 minutes. Transfer to a spice grinder and let cool slightly. Grind the spices to a powder and transfer to a food processor.

2. Roast the red pepper and jalapeño directly over a gas flame or under the broiler, turning, until charred all over, about 10 minutes. Transfer to a large bowl, cover tightly with plastic wrap and let cool for about 15 minutes. Peel, stem and seed the red pepper and jalapeño and transfer to the food processor with the toasted spices. Add the garlic and vinegar and pulse until the red pepper and jalapeño are finely chopped. With the machine on, drizzle in both oils. Season the harissa vinaigrette with salt and pepper.

3. Make the salad In a small bowl, combine the crabmeat with the shallot, lemon juice and olive oil. Season with salt and pepper and toss to coat. In a large bowl, toss the lettuce and herbs with ½ cup of the vinaigrette and season with salt and pepper. Gently fold in the crab mixture. Transfer the salad to plates and serve, passing the remaining vinaigrette at the table. —*Sarah Schafer*

MAKE AHEAD The vinaigrette can be refrigerated for up to 2 days.

WINE Minerally Corsican Vermentino: 2013 Clos Alivu Patrimonio Blanc.

Swazi Salad

Active **20 min**; Total **1 hr 20 min**; Serves **6**

- 3 **medium beets (12 oz.), scrubbed**
- ¼ **cup canola oil**
- 2 **Tbsp. fresh lemon juice**
- 2 **tsp. minced peeled fresh ginger**
  Kosher salt and pepper
- 1 **head of romaine lettuce (1 lb.), coarsely chopped**
- 3 **radishes, thinly sliced**
- 1 **Hass avocado, peeled and coarsely chopped**
- ¼ **cup crushed roasted peanuts**

1. Preheat the oven to 450°. Wrap the beets in foil and place them on a baking sheet. Roast for about 1 hour, until tender. Unwrap and let cool. Slip off the skins and cut the beets into wedges.

2. Meanwhile, in a small bowl, whisk the oil with the lemon juice and ginger and season with salt and pepper.

3. In a large bowl, toss the romaine, radishes, beets and all but 2 tablespoons of the dressing. Transfer to a bowl. Top with the avocado and drizzle with the remaining dressing. Scatter the peanuts on top and serve. —*Sasha Martin*

MAKE AHEAD The roasted beets can be refrigerated for up to 3 days.

Frenchie Salad

Active **30 min**; Total **1 hr**; Serves **4 to 6**

PICKLED MUSTARD SEEDS

- **2 Tbsp. yellow mustard seeds**
- **¼ cup distilled white vinegar**

DRESSING

- **4 oz. cherry tomatoes**
- **¾ cup plus 1 Tbsp. extra-virgin olive oil**
- **1 Tbsp. red wine vinegar**
- **1 Tbsp. Dijon mustard**
- **1 Tbsp. fresh orange juice**
- **Kosher salt and pepper**

SALAD

- **4 slices of thick-cut bacon (4 oz.), cut into 1-inch dice or strips**
- **2 oz. blue cheese, crumbled (⅓ cup)**
- **¼ cup crème fraîche**
- **4 heads of Little Gem or baby romaine lettuce (1 lb.), leaves separated**
- **Kosher salt and pepper**
- **Chopped chives, for garnish**

1. Pickle the mustard seeds In a small saucepan, bring the mustard seeds and vinegar to a boil. Remove the saucepan from the heat and let stand for 1 hour.

2. Make the dressing Preheat the oven to 450°. In a small ovenproof skillet or baking dish, toss the tomatoes with 1 tablespoon of the oil. Roast for 30 minutes, until the tomatoes have popped and are browned in spots. Transfer to a blender. Add the remaining ingredients; puree until smooth.

3. Make the salad In a small skillet, cook the bacon over moderate heat until browned and crisp, 5 to 7 minutes. Transfer to paper towels to drain. In a small bowl, blend the blue cheese with the crème fraîche until smooth. Dollop the mixture onto plates and spread slightly. In a large bowl, toss the lettuce with half of the dressing and season with salt and pepper. Arrange the lettuce on top of the blue cheese mixture. Garnish with the pickled mustard seeds, the bacon and chives. Serve the remaining dressing on the side. —*Ryan Angulo*

MAKE AHEAD The dressing can be refrigerated for up to 3 days.

Butter Lettuce Salad with Fresh Cranberry Vinaigrette

Total **30 min**; Serves **12**

TV chef Carla Hall loves to feature cranberries during the holidays. She uses the berries two ways here, tossing dried ones into the salad and adding minced fresh cranberries to the sweet-tart vinaigrette.

VINAIGRETTE

- **½ cup fresh cranberries**
- **1 Tbsp. sugar**
- **1 tsp. finely grated lemon zest plus 2 Tbsp. fresh lemon juice**
- **¼ cup extra-virgin olive oil**
- **Kosher salt and pepper**

SALAD

- **2 heads of butter lettuce**
- **2 oz. goat cheese, crumbled (½ cup)**
- **¼ cup sliced dried apricots**
- **¼ cup dried cranberries**
- **½ cup pecans, toasted and chopped**

1. Make the vinaigrette In a food processor, pulse the cranberries and sugar until finely chopped. Transfer half of the cranberries to a bowl. Add the lemon zest and juice to the processor and pulse to combine. With the machine on, slowly drizzle in the olive oil until combined. Add the vinaigrette to the bowl with the cranberries, season with salt and pepper and mix well.

2. Make the salad Arrange the lettuce, goat cheese, dried apricots, dried cranberries and pecans on a platter. Drizzle with the vinaigrette and serve. —*Carla Hall*

MAKE AHEAD The vinaigrette can be refrigerated overnight.

Wedge Salad with Sunflower Tahini and Ranch Dressing

Total **1 hr 10 min**; Serves **8 to 10**

DRESSING

- **½ cup Japanese Kewpie mayonnaise**
- **⅓ cup buttermilk**
- **⅓ cup sour cream**
- **½ tsp. garlic powder**
- **1½ tsp. finely chopped dill**
- **1½ tsp. finely chopped thyme**
- **1½ tsp. finely chopped marjoram**
- **1½ Tbsp. minced shallot**
- **1 Tbsp. rice wine vinegar**
- **1 tsp. Asian fish sauce**
- **Kosher salt and pepper**

SUNFLOWER TAHINI

- **½ cup salted roasted sunflower seeds**
- **2 Tbsp. fresh lemon juice**
- **2 Tbsp. grapeseed oil**
- **Kosher salt**

SALAD

- **1 large head of iceberg lettuce, quartered through the core and cut crosswise into 2-inch wedges**
- **½ English cucumber, thinly sliced**
- **3½ oz. enoki mushrooms, trimmed**
- **Salted roasted sunflower seeds and chile oil, for garnish**

1. Make the dressing In a bowl, whisk together the first 10 ingredients; season with salt and pepper. Cover and refrigerate the dressing until well chilled, about 1 hour.

2. Make the tahini In a blender, combine the sunflower seeds with ¼ cup of water and puree until nearly smooth. With the machine on, gradually add the lemon juice and grapeseed oil until the tahini is smooth. Scrape into a bowl and season with salt.

3. Make the salad Arrange the iceberg wedges on a platter. Dollop ½ teaspoon of the tahini onto each wedge and top with a cucumber slice and a small amount of enoki; secure the toppings with toothpicks. Drizzle some of the ranch dressing on the wedges and garnish with sunflower seeds and chile oil. Serve with additional dressing and tahini. —*Courtney McBroom*

Shaved Baby Artichoke and Marinated Mushroom Salad

⏱ Total **45 min**; Serves **6**

This fresh and crunchy salad is from Julia Sherman, an artist, photographer, writer, editor and cook who shares her excellent garden-centric recipes on the blog Salad for President. Here, she features baby artichokes, celery and raw mushrooms tossed in an herb-packed vinaigrette and topped with shavings of Parmigiano cheese.

- 1½ Tbsp. fresh lemon juice plus 1 lemon half
- 2 Tbsp. red wine vinegar
- 6 Tbsp. extra-virgin olive oil
- 3 Tbsp. coarsely chopped parsley
- 1 tsp. coarsely chopped oregano
- 1 garlic clove, smashed
- 6 oz. white mushrooms, trimmed and sliced
- 6 oz. oyster mushrooms, trimmed and torn into small pieces
  - Kosher salt and pepper
- 1 lb. firm, superfresh baby artichokes
- 4 celery ribs, thinly sliced
  - Parmigiano-Reggiano cheese shavings, for garnish

1. In a medium bowl, combine the lemon juice with the vinegar. Whisk in the olive oil until well blended. Add the parsley, oregano, garlic and mushrooms, season with salt and pepper and toss to coat. Let stand at room temperature for 15 minutes. Discard the garlic clove.

2. Meanwhile, squeeze the lemon half into a medium bowl of water; add the lemon to the bowl. Working with 1 artichoke at a time, cut off and discard the stems. Pull off the dark outer leaves until you reach the tender yellow leaves. Using a serrated knife, cut 1 inch off the top of each artichoke, then slice very thinly and add to the lemon water.

3. Drain the artichokes and pat dry. Add the artichokes and celery to the mushrooms, season with salt and pepper and toss. Transfer to plates and top with cheese shavings. —*Julia Sherman*

Escarole Salad with Red Quinoa and Hazelnuts

📷 PAGE 378

⏱ Total **40 min**; Serves **4 to 6**

- ¼ cup red quinoa, rinsed and drained
- ¼ cup plus 2 Tbsp. extra-virgin olive oil
- 3 Tbsp. apple cider vinegar
- 1 Tbsp. plus 1 tsp. honey
  - Fine sea salt and pepper
- 1 head of escarole, chopped into bite-size pieces
- 1 Granny Smith apple—halved, cored and thinly sliced on a mandoline
- ½ cup toasted hazelnuts, chopped

1. In a medium saucepan of boiling water, cook the quinoa just until tender, about 10 minutes. Drain well and spread out on a baking sheet to cool.

BUILD YOUR OWN SALAD

Watercress Salad

TOSS WATERCRESS WITH ONE FLAVOR COMBINATION

1. Roasted beets, oranges, hummus	**4.** Pickled onions, avocado, pepitas, queso fresco
2. Seared tofu, roasted carrots, sesame seeds	**5.** Watermelon, pistachios, jalapeños
3. Cherries, sautéed shallots, feta cheese	**6.** Shaved mushrooms, grated Parmigiano-Reggiano, parsley

DRESS WITH
Chive Vinaigrette
Makes ½ cup

In a bowl, combine 2 Tbsp. **fresh lemon juice**, 2 Tbsp. chopped **chives**, 1 Tbsp. **balsamic vinegar** and 1 tsp. **Dijon mustard**. Gradually whisk in ¼ cup **extra-virgin olive oil** until blended. Season with **kosher salt** and **pepper**. —*Michelle Bernstein*

---

2. In a large bowl, whisk the oil with the vinegar and honey. Season with salt and pepper. Add the escarole, apple, hazelnuts and quinoa and toss to coat. Season with salt and pepper and serve. —*Marco Canora*

Escarole and Golden Beet Salad with Toasted Hazelnuts

⏱ Total **45 min**; Serves **12**

Escarole is one of the best greens to use in make-ahead salads; it's hardy and doesn't wilt as soon as it's dressed.

- 1 cup hazelnuts
- 1 medium shallot, minced
- ¼ cup Champagne vinegar
- 2 tsp. honey
- 2 tsp. Dijon mustard
- ⅓ cup extra-virgin olive oil
  - Kosher salt and pepper
  - Two 1¼-lb. heads of escarole, white and light green leaves only, torn
- ½ lb. small golden beets, peeled and very thinly sliced or julienned
- ¾ cup snipped chives

1. Preheat the oven to 375°. Spread the hazelnuts in a pie plate and bake for 10 to 12 minutes, until fragrant and lightly browned. Transfer the hazelnuts to a kitchen towel and rub them together in the towel to release the skins. Let the hazelnuts cool, then coarsely chop.

2. In a serving bowl, whisk the shallot with the vinegar, honey and mustard. Gradually whisk in the olive oil and season the dressing with salt and pepper. Add the escarole, beets, chives and toasted hazelnuts and toss well. Season with salt and pepper, toss again and serve. —*Justin Chapple*

DIY Salad
» Romaine

Chef and cookbook author **JOANNE WEIR** shares her six fantastic variations and an easy citrus vinaigrette.

ROASTED BUTTERNUT SQUASH
+
RICOTTA SALATA
+
TOASTED PEPITAS

GRILLED SHRIMP
+
AVOCADO
+
MANGO
+
MACADAMIA NUTS

ROTISSERIE CHICKEN
+
BELL PEPPERS
+
JICAMA
+
CORN

ROASTED BEETS
+
GOAT CHEESE
+
SPICED PECANS
+
TOASTED QUINOA

GREEN OLIVES
+
MINT
+
CILANTRO
+
BASIL
+
ARUGULA

DRIED FIGS
+
PROSCIUTTO
+
PARMESAN CRISPS
+
SHAVED FENNEL

Toss this zippy vinaigrette with romaine and any of the ingredient combinations here.

Citrus Vinaigrette
Makes 1 cup

In a small bowl, combine ½ tsp. finely grated **orange zest**, 6 Tbsp. **fresh orange juice** and 2 Tbsp. **white balsamic vinegar**. Whisk in ½ cup **extra-virgin olive oil** and season with **kosher salt** and **pepper**.

FALL SALAD WITH
SHERRY VINAIGRETTE

Fall Salad with Sherry Vinaigrette
⏱ Total **30 min**; Serves **10 to 12**

¾ cup pecans
½ cup sherry vinegar
¼ cup Dijon mustard
2 Tbsp. honey
1 tsp. thyme leaves
1½ cups extra-virgin olive oil
   Sea salt and black pepper
1 head of red leaf lettuce, leaves torn
2 heads of Treviso or radicchio, cored and leaves torn
1 head of frisée (4 oz.), white and light green leaves only
2 Fuyu persimmons, cored and very thinly sliced crosswise on a mandoline
1 Pink Lady apple, cored and very thinly sliced on a mandoline
1 medium fennel bulb, cored and very thinly sliced on a mandoline
   Nasturtium leaves, for garnish (optional)

1. Preheat the oven to 375°. Spread the pecans in a pie plate and toast for about 7 minutes, until golden. Let cool, then coarsely chop.

2. In a medium bowl, whisk the vinegar with the mustard, honey and thyme. Gradually whisk in the olive oil and season the dressing with sea salt and pepper.

3. In a very large serving bowl, toss the lettuce, Treviso and frisée. Scatter the persimmons, apple, fennel and pecans on top and garnish with nasturtium leaves. Serve the salad, passing the dressing at the table. —*Tyler Florence*

MAKE AHEAD The nuts can be stored in an airtight container for up to 2 days. The dressing can be refrigerated overnight.

Frisée-and-Potato Salad
Active **40 min**; Total **1 hr 30 min**; Serves **4**

1 large baking potato
2 Tbsp. mustard seeds
½ cup extra-virgin olive oil
2 Tbsp. minced shallots
2 tsp. minced garlic
2 Tbsp. sherry vinegar
1 tsp. Dijon mustard
   Kosher salt and pepper
2 tsp. nutritional yeast
6 oz. frisée, white and light green parts only, torn into bite-size pieces (8 cups)
2 Tbsp. chopped chives
½ cup finely grated cauliflower

1. Preheat the oven to 425°. Wrap the potato in foil and bake for about 1 hour, until tender. Let the potato cool, then cut into ½-inch dice.

2. Meanwhile, in a medium saucepan of boiling water, cook the mustard seeds for 5 minutes. Remove from the heat and let stand for 5 minutes. Drain well.

3. Wipe out the saucepan and heat 2 tablespoons of the olive oil in it. Add the shallots and garlic and cook over moderately high heat, stirring, until lightly browned, about 3 minutes. Remove from the heat and whisk in ¼ cup of the olive oil, then whisk in the vinegar, mustard and mustard seeds. Season with salt and pepper.

4. In a large nonstick skillet, heat the remaining 2 tablespoons of olive oil. Add the diced potato and cook over moderately high heat, stirring occasionally, until browned and crisp in spots, about 7 minutes. Season with salt and pepper and sprinkle with the nutritional yeast.

5. In a large bowl, toss the potato with the frisée, chives and half of the dressing; season with salt and pepper. Transfer the salad to a platter and sprinkle the cauliflower on top. Serve the remaining dressing on the side. —*Richard Landau*

Dark Green Thai Escarole Salad
⏱ Total **40 min**; Serves **6**

The tougher outer leaves of a head of escarole are too often discarded or just reserved for the soup pot. Here, they become the base of a salad, their robust flavor complemented by lots of cilantro and basil, crisp vegetables and a tangy, spicy Thai chile–spiked dressing.

¼ cup canola oil
3 Tbsp. fresh lime juice
2 Tbsp. Asian fish sauce
1 tsp. turbinado sugar
2 Thai chiles, thinly sliced
1 Kirby or Persian cucumber, halved lengthwise and cut into 1-inch pieces
2 carrots, thinly sliced
2 oz. green beans, thinly sliced on the diagonal (1 cup)
   Kosher salt and pepper
12 oz. outer escarole leaves, chopped (10 cups)
2 cups chopped mixed herbs, such as cilantro and basil

In a large bowl, whisk the oil with the lime juice, fish sauce, sugar and chiles. Add the cucumber, carrots and green beans and season with salt and pepper. Mix well and let stand for 10 minutes. Add the escarole and herbs, season with salt and pepper, toss well and serve. —*Kay Chun*

MAKE AHEAD The dressing can be refrigerated overnight.

Endive Salad with Pears and Pumpkin Seeds

⏱ Total **30 min**; Serves **6**

VINAIGRETTE

- **3** Tbsp. red wine vinegar
- **1** Tbsp. fresh lemon juice
- **2** tsp. Dijon mustard
- **2** tsp. honey
- **½** cup extra-virgin olive oil
  Kosher salt

SALAD

- **1** Tbsp. extra-virgin olive oil
- **½** cup pumpkin seeds
  Kosher salt
- **3** Belgian endives (1 lb.), cored and sliced 1 inch thick
- **1** head of frisée (8 oz.), core and dark green leaves discarded, white and light green leaves chopped into 2-inch pieces (8 cups)
- **1** large red d'Anjou pear—cored, quartered and thinly sliced
- **3** scallions, thinly sliced on the diagonal

1. Make the vinaigrette In a medium bowl, combine the vinegar, lemon juice, mustard and honey. While whisking constantly, slowly drizzle in the oil until well emulsified. Season with salt.

2. Make the salad In a small skillet, heat the olive oil. Toast the pumpkin seeds over moderate heat, stirring, until golden, 2 to 3 minutes. Transfer to a paper towel–lined plate to drain; season with salt.

3. In a large bowl, toss the endives, frisée, pear and scallions with half of the vinaigrette and season with salt. Transfer the salad to plates and top with the pumpkin seeds. Serve the remaining vinaigrette on the side. —*Daniel Holzman*

MAKE AHEAD The vinaigrette can be refrigerated overnight. The toasted pumpkin seeds can be stored in an airtight container overnight.

WINE Ripe Oregon Pinot Gris: 2014 Erath.

Endive and Manchego Salad with Smoked Cocoa Walnuts

⏱ Total **40 min**; Serves **4**

"Not everyone pairs salad with wine, but if it's a thoughtful, hearty salad, it deserves a wine," says Jordon Sipperley, beverage director at Next in Chicago. Next chef Dave Beran created this dish, which represents all the flavors of a typical New Zealand Sauvignon Blanc, to have with that wine.

COCOA WALNUTS

- **1** cup grapeseed oil
- **1½** cups walnut halves (5 oz.)
- **1** Tbsp. smoked salt
- **1** Tbsp. unsweetened cocoa powder
- **1½** tsp. sugar
  Freshly ground pepper

SALAD

- **1** large pink grapefruit
- **1** large egg yolk
- **1** Tbsp. fresh lemon juice
- **⅛** tsp. vanilla bean paste or ¼ tsp. pure vanilla extract
  Kosher salt and pepper
- **1½** lbs. Belgian and red endives, cored, leaves separated (8 cups)
- **3** oz. Manchego cheese, shaved
  Tarragon, for garnish

1. Make the cocoa walnuts In a saucepan, combine the grapeseed oil and walnuts; cook over low heat, stirring, until the oil reaches 300° on a candy thermometer and the walnuts are deep golden brown, 8 to 10 minutes. Strain the walnuts over a bowl, then spread on a paper towel–lined platter and let cool. Set aside ½ cup of the frying oil; reserve the rest for another use.

2. In a mortar, crush the smoked salt to a powder. Stir in the cocoa powder and sugar and season with pepper. In a bowl, toss the walnuts with the smoked cocoa seasoning.

3. Make the salad Using a sharp knife, peel the grapefruit, removing all of the bitter white pith. Working over a small bowl, cut in between the membranes to release the sections. Reserve 1 tablespoon of juice.

4. In a food processor, pulse the egg yolk, reserved grapefruit juice, lemon juice and vanilla bean paste. With the machine on, slowly drizzle in the reserved ½ cup of frying oil until emulsified. Season the dressing with salt and pepper.

5. In a large bowl, toss the endives with three-fourths of the dressing and season with salt and pepper. Arrange the endives on plates and top with the grapefruit sections, Manchego and cocoa walnuts. Garnish with tarragon and serve, passing the remaining dressing at the table.
—*Dave Beran*

MAKE AHEAD The cocoa walnuts can be stored in an airtight container for 1 week.

WINE New Zealand Sauvignon Blanc: 2014 Mt. Difficulty.

Endive and Citrus Salad with Bacon Vinaigrette

⏱ Total **30 min**; Serves **8**

- **1** small shallot, finely chopped
- **2** Tbsp. seasoned rice vinegar
- **¼** cup extra-virgin olive oil
  Kosher salt and pepper
- **2** Ruby Red grapefruits
- **2** blood oranges
- **1** navel orange
- **1** tangerine
- **6** Belgian endives, leaves separated
- **4** slices cooked bacon, coarsely chopped
- **2** tsp. chopped tarragon
  Mesclun greens, for garnish (optional)

1. In a small saucepan, combine the shallot and vinegar and let stand for 10 minutes. Whisk in the olive oil and season with salt and pepper.

2. Meanwhile, using a very sharp knife, peel the grapefruits, oranges and tangerine, being sure to remove all of the bitter white pith. Working over a large bowl to catch the juices, cut the navel orange and tangerine in between the membranes to release the sections. Slice the grapefruits and blood oranges into rounds, then cut into quarters. Arrange the endives and the citrus on a large platter.

3. Bring the dressing to a simmer over moderate heat. Remove from the heat and add the bacon. Drizzle the dressing over the salad and top with the tarragon and mesclun, if using. —*Erin French*

Spinach Salad with Pork Rinds

⏱ Total **25 min**; Serves **10 to 12**

¼ cup extra-virgin olive oil
3 Tbsp. fresh lime juice
1 cup thinly sliced scallions
1 cup cilantro leaves
10 oz. curly spinach, stemmed (16 cups)
8 oz. radishes, thinly sliced (2 cups)
Kosher salt and pepper
Crumbled pork rinds, for garnish

In a large bowl, whisk the olive oil with the lime juice, scallions and cilantro. Add the spinach and radishes, season with salt and pepper and toss to coat. Transfer to a platter, top with crumbled pork rinds and serve immediately. —*Kay Chun*

BUILD YOUR OWN SALAD

Tomato Salad

TOSS CHOPPED TOMATOES WITH ONE FLAVOR COMBINATION

1.	**3.**
Soppressata, garlic croutons, ricotta, basil	Avocado, dill, tarragon
2.	**4.**
Snow peas, scallions, lemongrass, mint	Watermelon, mint, fried capers

DRESS WITH

Charred Tomato Vinaigrette
Makes 1¼ cups

Light a grill to medium or heat a grill pan. In a bowl, toss ½ lb. **tomatoes,** halved, with 1 Tbsp. **olive oil.** Grill, turning, until blistered and lightly charred, 5 to 7 minutes. Let cool slightly. In a food processor, combine the grilled tomatoes with 1 Tbsp. **sherry vinegar,** 1 Tbsp. **fresh lemon juice** and ½ Tbsp. **Dijon mustard;** pulse to blend. With the machine on, slowly drizzle in ½ cup **olive oil.** Transfer the vinaigrette to a bowl, stir in 1 Tbsp. chopped **parsley, cilantro** or **basil** and season with **kosher salt** and **pepper.** —*Jennifer Toomey*

Mustard Greens with Apple Cider–Dijon Dressing

⏱ Total **20 min**; Serves **10 to 12**

¼ cup apple cider vinegar
½ cup canola oil
2 Tbsp. stone-ground mustard
2 Tbsp. fresh lemon juice
2 bunches of mustard greens, stemmed, leaves shredded (16 cups)
2 Granny Smith apples, peeled and sliced
½ cup chopped dill
Kosher salt and pepper

In a large bowl, whisk the vinegar with the oil, mustard and lemon juice. Add the mustard greens, apples and dill, season with salt and pepper and toss well. Transfer to a platter and serve. —*Kay Chun*

Tomato-Feta Salad with Lime and Mint

📷 PAGE 39

⏱ Total **20 min**; Serves **4 to 6**

3 large heirloom tomatoes (2¼ lbs.), each cut into 1-inch wedges
1 small red onion, halved and thinly sliced
¼ cup extra-virgin olive oil
½ tsp. finely grated lime zest plus 3 Tbsp. fresh lime juice
1 small garlic clove, minced
4 oz. feta cheese, crumbled
½ cup lightly packed mint leaves
Kosher salt and pepper

In a large bowl, toss the tomatoes with the onion, olive oil, lime zest, lime juice and garlic. Gently fold in the feta and mint. Season with salt and pepper and fold again. Serve right away. —*April Bloomfield*

WINE Vibrant, medium-bodied Spanish Albariño: 2014 Condes de Albarei.

Kale Salad with Garlicky Panko

⏱ Total **30 min**; Serves **6**

Rubbing curly kale leaves with a rice vinegar dressing and salt makes them surprisingly tender. The technique also works with shaved brussels sprouts and cabbage.

½ cup plus 2 Tbsp. extra-virgin olive oil
1 garlic clove, thinly sliced
½ cup panko
Kosher salt and pepper
1 bunch of curly kale
¼ cup rice vinegar
3 oz. feta cheese, crumbled
6 fried eggs (optional)

1. In a large nonstick skillet, heat 2 tablespoons of the olive oil. Add the garlic and cook over moderate heat, stirring, until fragrant, 30 seconds. Stir in the panko and cook, stirring, until golden and crisp, 3 minutes. Season the garlic panko with salt and pepper and transfer to a plate to cool.

2. Cut the stems from the kale and tear the leaves into pieces. In a large bowl, whisk the vinegar with the remaining ½ cup of oil and season with salt and pepper. Add the kale and massage the leaves with the dressing using your fingers. Season with salt and pepper and toss. Transfer to a platter, top with the feta, garlic panko and fried eggs, if using, and serve.
—*Margaret, Irene and Andy Li*

Grilled Tomato Salad with Mozzarella and Unagi Sauce

Total **45 min**; Serves **6**

Chicago chef Stephanie Izard dresses the ultimate summer salad with a creamy version of unagi tare, a sweet-salty Japanese sauce typically brushed over eel.

¼ cup soy sauce

¼ cup mirin

¼ cup sugar

2 Tbsp. soju or sake

⅓ cup mayonnaise

1 Tbsp. fresh lime juice

Kosher salt

2 green (unripe) tomatoes, sliced ¼ inch thick

1 Tbsp. canola oil, plus more for brushing

2 cups yellow grape tomatoes, 1 cup halved

1 lb. fresh mozzarella cheese, sliced and torn into bite-size pieces

3 Tbsp. thinly sliced basil

3 Tbsp. chopped mint

1. In a small saucepan, combine the soy sauce with the mirin, sugar and soju; bring to a boil. Simmer over moderate heat, stirring, until reduced to ¼ cup, 12 minutes. Let cool, then whisk in the mayonnaise and lime juice and season with salt.

2. Light a grill or heat a grill pan. Brush the green tomatoes with oil and season with salt. Grill over high heat, turning once, until lightly charred, 4 minutes. Transfer to a plate to cool, then cut into quarters.

3. In a perforated grill pan, toss the whole grape tomatoes with the 1 tablespoon of oil and season with salt. Grill over high heat, tossing occasionally, until lightly charred, about 2 minutes. Let cool slightly.

4. On a platter, toss the mozzarella with all of the tomatoes. Drizzle with ½ cup of the unagi sauce and scatter the basil and mint on top. Serve, passing the remaining sauce at the table. —*Stephanie Izard*

MAKE AHEAD The unagi sauce can be refrigerated for up to 3 days. Bring to room temperature before serving.

BEER Malty ale: Off Color Brewing Scurry Dark Honey Ale.

Tomato-and-Mozzarella Salad with Orange Oil

Total **25 min**; Serves **6**

At The Hubb at Angéline's in Canada's Prince Edward County, chef Elliot Reynolds updates caprese salad by combining more than half a dozen different heirloom tomatoes, four types of basil, buffalo mozzarella and orange-scented olive oil.

½ baguette, cut into 1-inch pieces (4 cups)

5 Tbsp. extra-virgin olive oil

Kosher salt and pepper

2 lbs. heirloom tomatoes, halved or cut into ½-inch wedges

1 lb. buffalo mozzarella cheese, cut into large pieces

1 Tbsp. orange-flavored olive oil

Basil leaves, for garnish

1. Preheat the oven to 350°. On a large baking sheet, toss the baguette pieces with 2 tablespoons of the extra-virgin olive oil and season with salt and pepper. Bake, tossing occasionally, until crisp and golden, 10 to 12 minutes. Let cool.

2. In a large bowl, gently toss the tomatoes with the remaining 3 tablespoons of extra-virgin olive oil. Season with salt and pepper. Arrange the tomatoes and mozzarella on a platter. Top with the croutons and drizzle with the orange oil. Garnish with basil and serve. —*Elliot Reynolds*

WINE Fruit-forward French sparkling rosé: NV Parigot Crémant de Bourgogne Rosé.

Tomato Salad with Tomato Water Granita

Active **45 min**; Total **4 hr 45 min** plus overnight draining; Serves **6**

F&W Best New Chefs 2015 Michael Fojtasek and Grae Nonas, the duo behind Olamaie in Austin, explore every dimension of the tomato in this ingenious mix of flavors, temperatures and textures.

GRANITA

5 large tomatoes, chopped (2¼ lbs.)

1½ Tbsp. honey

1½ Tbsp. red wine vinegar

Sea salt

SALAD

2½ lbs. multicolored heirloom tomatoes, cut into different sizes

2 cups multicolored cherry tomatoes, halved (10 oz.)

3 Tbsp. extra-virgin olive oil, plus more for drizzling

Sea salt and black pepper

Chervil sprigs, for garnish

1. Make the granita In a blender or food processor, puree the chopped tomatoes until nearly smooth. Line a strainer with a double layer of cheesecloth and set over a medium bowl. Pour the tomato puree into the strainer and let drain in the refrigerator overnight. You should have about 1 cup of tomato water; reserve the solids for making soup or sauce. Whisk the honey and vinegar into the tomato water and season lightly with salt.

2. Pour the tomato water into an 8-inch-square glass or stainless steel baking pan. Freeze for 1 hour. Scrape the frozen edges into the center with a fork. Freeze for about 3 hours longer, scraping hourly, until the granita is uniformly icy and flaky.

3. Make the salad In a large bowl, toss all of the tomatoes with the 3 tablespoons of olive oil and season with salt and pepper. Transfer to shallow bowls and spoon the granita on top. Garnish with chervil sprigs, drizzle with olive oil and serve. —*Michael Fojtasek and Grae Nonas*

MAKE AHEAD The granita can be frozen for up to 3 days. Fluff before serving.

WINE Zesty California Sauvignon Blanc: 2013 Elizabeth Spencer.

TOMATO SALAD
WITH TOMATO
WATER GRANITA

DIY Salad » Spinach

Seattle chef **ETHAN STOWELL** of Staple & Fancy created four outstanding variations on the ultimate spinach salad, featuring a mustardy red wine vinaigrette.

HARICOTS VERTS + CRAB + AVOCADO

RADISHES + ORANGE + GOAT CHEESE

Toss this tangy dressing with spinach leaves and any of the ingredient combinations here.

FARRO + MARINATED ARTICHOKES + OLIVES

GOLDEN RAISINS + PINE NUTS + CHICKPEAS

Red Wine–Dijon Vinaigrette
Makes ¾ cup

In a small saucepan, bring ½ cup **dry red wine** to a simmer. Cook over moderate heat until reduced to 2 Tbsp., about 8 minutes. Transfer to a medium bowl to cool. Whisk in ¼ cup **red wine vinegar** and 1 Tbsp. **Dijon mustard**. Whisking constantly, slowly drizzle in ¼ cup **grapeseed** or **canola oil** until well emulsified. Season with **salt** and **pepper**.

Snow Pea Salad

⏱ Total **35 min;** Serves **6**

Matthew DeMille, chef at the Drake Devonshire Inn in Canada's Prince Edward County, uses just a bit of local maple syrup to add a sweet, slightly smoky note to this bright green pea salad.

- **4** tsp. apple cider vinegar
- **2** tsp. fresh lemon juice
- **1** garlic clove, minced
- **1** Tbsp. pure maple syrup
- **½** tsp. Dijon mustard
- **¼** cup canola oil
  Kosher salt and pepper
- **½** tsp. black sesame seeds
- **½** tsp. white sesame seeds
- **¾** lb. snow peas, trimmed
- **2** cups shelled fresh English peas
- **½** cup mixed sprouts, such as radish and alfalfa
- **1** radish, thinly sliced
- **¼** cup torn mint leaves

1. In a small bowl, whisk the cider vinegar with the lemon juice and garlic; let stand for 5 minutes. Whisk in the maple syrup and mustard, then gradually whisk in the oil. Season with salt and pepper.

2. In a small skillet, toast the sesame seeds over high heat, tossing occasionally, until lightly browned, 2 to 3 minutes.

3. Halve one-third of the snow peas crosswise on the diagonal and julienne the rest. In a saucepan of salted boiling water, blanch the snow peas and English peas until crisp-tender, 30 seconds. Drain and rinse under cold water; pat dry.

4. In a bowl, toss the peas with the sprouts, radish, half of the mint and some of the vinaigrette. Transfer to a platter and top with the remaining mint and the toasted sesame seeds. Serve the remaining vinaigrette at the table. —*Matthew DeMille*

Snap Pea and Radish Salad with Tahini Dressing

⏱ Total **20 min;** Serves **4 to 6**

- **⅓** cup extra-virgin olive oil
- **⅓** cup tahini
- **2** Tbsp. fresh lemon juice
- **1** Tbsp. toasted sesame seeds
- **½** lb. snap peas, thinly sliced
- **½** lb. radishes, thinly sliced
- **2** cups mixed chopped herbs, such as parsley, mint and chives
  Kosher salt and pepper

In a large bowl, whisk the olive oil with the tahini, lemon juice, sesame seeds and 2 tablespoons of water. Add the snap peas, radishes and herbs and season with salt and pepper. Mix well and serve. —*Kay Chun*

Stir-Fried Snow Peas and Romaine

⏱ Total **25 min;** Serves **4 to 6**

Everyday ingredients—snow peas, romaine, capers and egg—come together brilliantly in this flavorful warm salad from cookbook author Tara Duggan.

- **1** large egg
- **2** Tbsp. capers, drained
- **¼** cup canola oil
- **1** garlic clove, thinly sliced
- **1** lb. snow peas, trimmed
  Kosher salt and pepper
- **1** head of romaine lettuce (1 lb.), large leaves chopped
- **1½** Tbsp. fresh lemon juice

1. In a small saucepan, submerge the egg in water and bring to a full boil. Remove from the heat, cover and let stand for 10 minutes. Drain the egg and cool under cold water. Peel and chop the egg.

2. Meanwhile, pat the capers thoroughly dry with paper towels.

3. In a large skillet, heat 1 tablespoon of the oil. Add the capers and cook over moderate heat, stirring, until they pop and are crispy, about 2 minutes. Using a slotted spoon, transfer the capers to paper towels to drain.

4. In the same skillet, heat 2 tablespoons of the oil. Add the garlic and cook over moderate heat, stirring, until fragrant, 30 seconds. Add the snow peas and season with salt and pepper. Cook until the snow peas are crisp-tender, 2 minutes; transfer to a medium bowl. Add the remaining 1 tablespoon of oil and the romaine to the skillet. Stir-fry just until the lettuce is wilted, 2 minutes. Stir in the lemon juice and snow peas. Season with salt and pepper and toss well. Transfer the salad to plates. Top with the chopped egg and crispy capers and serve. —*Tara Duggan*

Crunchy Asparagus Salad

⏱ Total **20 min;** Serves **4**

- **1** Tbsp. soy sauce
- **1** tsp. toasted sesame oil
- **1** tsp. distilled white vinegar
- **1** bunch of thin asparagus (about 1 lb.), trimmed
  One 4-oz. piece of daikon radish, peeled and thinly sliced (1 cup)
  Kosher salt and pepper
  Toasted sesame seeds and togarashi, for sprinkling

1. In a large bowl, whisk the soy sauce with the sesame oil and vinegar.

2. Fill a medium bowl with ice water. In a steamer basket set in a large saucepan of simmering water, steam the asparagus until crisp-tender, 2 to 3 minutes. Transfer to the ice bath to cool. Drain and pat dry, then chop the asparagus into 2-inch lengths. Add the asparagus and daikon to the soy sauce dressing, season with salt and pepper and toss to coat. Transfer to plates, sprinkle with sesame seeds and togarashi and serve. —*Kuniko Yagi*

Sliced Cauliflower Salad with Chickpea Dressing

⏱ Total **40 min**; Serves **6**

CHICKPEA DRESSING

- ¼ cup canned chickpeas, rinsed
- 1 Tbsp. seasoned rice vinegar
- 1 garlic clove, crushed
- 3 Tbsp. fresh lemon juice
- 2 Tbsp. tahini
- ½ cup parsley leaves
- ½ cup mint leaves
- 1 cup canola oil
- ½ tsp. sumac (optional)
- ½ tsp. Aleppo pepper flakes
  Kosher salt and pepper

SALAD

- 1 medium head of cauliflower, cut into large florets and thinly sliced (4 cups)
- 1 small head of romaine, chopped (about 6 cups)
- ½ cup canned chickpeas, rinsed
- ½ cup parsley leaves
- ½ cup mint leaves
  Kosher salt
- 1 medium tomatillo—husked, rinsed and cut into ¼-inch dice
  Toasted sesame seeds, finely grated orange zest and cracked black pepper, for garnish

1. Make the dressing In a blender, combine the chickpeas, rice vinegar, garlic, lemon juice, tahini, parsley and mint. With the machine on, slowly drizzle in the oil and blend until a smooth, thick dressing forms. Add the sumac, if using, and Aleppo pepper and season with salt and pepper.

2. Make the salad In a large bowl, toss the cauliflower, romaine, chickpeas, parsley and mint with the chickpea dressing. Season with salt and toss again. Transfer the salad to a platter and top with the tomatillo. Garnish with toasted sesame seeds, grated orange zest and cracked black pepper and serve. —*Gerardo Gonzalez*

MAKE AHEAD The dressing can be refrigerated overnight.

Broccoli Coleslaw with Bacon and Raisins

⏱ Total **30 min**; Serves **6**

- 6 slices of bacon (4 oz.)
- ½ cup mayonnaise
- 3 Tbsp. apple cider vinegar
- 1 tsp. sugar
  Kosher salt and pepper
- 1 large head of broccoli (1¼ lbs.), cut into bite-size florets and thinly sliced lengthwise
- ½ cup raisins
- ½ small red onion, finely chopped
- ⅓ cup roasted unsalted sunflower seeds

1. Preheat the oven to 375°. Set a rack over a baking sheet. Arrange the bacon slices on the rack in a single layer. Bake for about 25 minutes, until browned and crisp. Drain on paper towels, then coarsely chop.

2. In a large bowl, whisk the mayonnaise with the vinegar and sugar; season with salt and pepper. Add the broccoli, raisins, onion, sunflower seeds and bacon and toss to coat evenly. Transfer the coleslaw to a serving bowl. —*Timothy Hollingsworth*

MAKE AHEAD The slaw (without the bacon and sunflower seeds) can be refrigerated for 1 day. Bring to room temperature and add the bacon and sunflower seeds right before serving.

Radicchio Salad with Manchego Vinaigrette

Active **20 min**; Total **1 hr 20 min**
Serves **8 to 10**

This salad is a favorite of the Food52 online community because it tastes like it takes much more work than it really does. The secret: Soaking an onion in vinegar results in a deeply flavorful vinaigrette, with none of the harshness that can often come from raw onion. The idea was adapted from a recipe in the *Toro Bravo* cookbook by John Gorham and Liz Crain.

- ¼ cup balsamic vinegar
- ¼ cup sherry vinegar
- 1 red onion, chopped
- 3 heads of radicchio (2 lbs.)— halved, cored and chopped into 1-inch pieces
- 1 Tbsp. honey
- ¾ cup extra-virgin olive oil
- 6 oz. Manchego cheese, shredded (1½ cups)
  Kosher salt and pepper

1. In a large bowl, combine the balsamic vinegar, sherry vinegar and onion. Let stand at room temperature for 1 hour.

2. In another large bowl, cover the radicchio with ice water and let stand for 15 minutes. Drain and dry well.

3. Remove the onion from the vinegar; discard the onion. Whisk the honey and olive oil into the vinegar and add the radicchio and 1 cup of the Manchego. Season with salt and pepper and toss to coat. Mound the radicchio on a serving platter, top with the remaining Manchego and serve. —*Kristen Miglore*

WINE High-acid northern Italian Pinot Grigio: 2013 Tiefenbrunner.

RADICCHIO SALAD WITH
MANCHEGO VINAIGRETTE

THAI BRUSSELS
SPROUT SALAD

Leeks Vinaigrette with Soft-Boiled Eggs and Leek Ash

Total **1 hr**; Serves **4 to 6**

This outstanding salad from chef Daniel Eddy of Rebelle in Manhattan features tender leeks with an egg sauce, a parsley puree and a punchy mustard vinaigrette.

- **9 medium leeks (about 2½ lbs.), white and light green parts only**
- **½ cup plus 2 Tbsp. extra-virgin olive oil**
- **3 Tbsp. plus 1 tsp. Banyuls vinegar or sherry vinegar**
- **¼ cup fresh orange juice**
- **½ tsp. finely grated orange zest**
- **Kosher salt and pepper**
- **4 large eggs**
- **2 Tbsp. minced shallot**
- **1 tsp. finely chopped mint**
- **1 Tbsp. grainy mustard**
- **1 Tbsp. Dijon mustard**
- **1 cup packed parsley leaves**

1. Preheat the broiler and set a rack 6 inches from the heat. Cut 1 leek in half lengthwise. Separate the layers and arrange on a foil-lined baking sheet. Broil, turning occasionally, until burnt and crisp, 10 to 15 minutes; transfer the pieces to a plate as they char. Let cool, then crumble the pieces to make the leek ash.

2. Meanwhile, tie the remaining leeks into 2 bundles of 4 with kitchen twine. Cook in a pot of unsalted boiling water until tender, 8 to 10 minutes. Cool the leeks in a bowl of ice water. Discard the twine and pat the leeks dry. Cut the leeks into ½-inch rounds and blot dry.

3. In a large bowl, combine 3 tablespoons of the olive oil, 2 tablespoons each of the vinegar and orange juice and the orange zest. Add the leeks and turn to coat; season with salt and pepper.

4. Cook the eggs in a pot of boiling water for 6 minutes, then transfer them to a bowl of ice water to cool, about 3 minutes. Peel the eggs and carefully separate the whites from the runny yolks. Chop the egg whites and transfer to a small bowl. Stir in the shallot, mint and 1 teaspoon of the vinegar and season with salt and pepper.

5. In a small bowl, combine the egg yolks with 1 tablespoon of the oil and the remaining 2 tablespoons of orange juice. Season with salt and whisk until smooth. Strain into a small bowl. In another bowl, combine both of the mustards with 2 tablespoons of the oil and the remaining 1 tablespoon of vinegar; season with salt and pepper.

6. In a blender, puree the parsley with the remaining ¼ cup of oil until smooth.

7. Spread some of the mustard vinaigrette, parsley puree and egg yolk sauce on plates. Top with the leeks vinaigrette and the egg whites. Garnish with leek ash and serve. —*Daniel Eddy*

MAKE AHEAD The leek ash, mustard vinaigrette and parsley puree can refrigerated separately overnight.

Thai Brussels Sprout Salad

Total **25 min**; Serves **6**

- **⅓ cup fresh lime juice**
- **3 Tbsp. Asian fish sauce**
- **3 red Thai chiles, minced**
- **1 Tbsp. turbinado sugar**
- **¾ lb. brussels sprouts, thinly sliced (about 5 cups)**
- **2 Honeycrisp apples, cored and chopped**
- **1 cup chopped mixed cilantro and basil**
- **Kosher salt and pepper**

In a large bowl, stir the lime juice with the fish sauce, chiles and sugar until the sugar dissolves. Add the brussels sprouts, apples and herbs and season with salt and pepper. Toss to coat, then serve. —*Kay Chun*

Leeks with Tomato Vinaigrette

Total **30 min**; Serves **4**

Master chef Jacques Pépin reinvigorates classic leeks vinaigrette with fresh tomato and a little Worcestershire sauce.

- **4 medium leeks (1¼ lbs.), white and light green parts only, halved lengthwise**
- **1 large tomato**
- **3 Tbsp. extra-virgin olive oil**
- **1 Tbsp. red wine vinegar**
- **1 Tbsp. Dijon mustard**
- **1 tsp. Worcestershire sauce**
- **Kosher salt and pepper**

1. In a large saucepan, bring 2 cups of water to a boil over high heat. Add the leeks to the pan cut side down, cover and reduce the heat to low. Cook until the leeks are tender when pierced with a paring knife, about 15 minutes. Transfer the leeks to a paper towel–lined plate to drain, then arrange cut side up on a platter.

2. Meanwhile, bring a small saucepan of water to a boil. Fill a medium bowl with ice and water. Using a sharp paring knife, mark an X on the bottom of the tomato. Add it to the saucepan and blanch just until the skin starts to peel, about 30 seconds. Transfer the tomato to the ice bath to cool. Peel, halve and seed the tomato; cut it into ¼-inch dice.

3. In a small bowl, toss the tomato with the olive oil, vinegar, mustard and Worcestershire sauce and season with salt and pepper. Spoon the tomato dressing over the leeks and serve. —*Jacques Pépin*

Peas with Ricotta and Spring Onion Kimchi

Active 40 min; Total 2 hr 30 min; Serves 8

Chef Zakary Pelaccio of Fish & Game in Hudson, New York, likes using spring onions (or ramps) to make a quick kimchi. He serves it alongside creamy ricotta—an unusual but compelling combo.

KIMCHI

- 2 lbs. small spring onions, scallions or ramps, cut into 2-inch pieces, bulbs quartered if large
- ¼ cup Asian fish sauce
- ½ cup gochugaru (Korean red chile flakes)
- 1 Tbsp. minced peeled fresh ginger
- 1 Tbsp. sesame seeds
- 1 Tbsp. anise seeds

SALAD

- 1½ lbs. sugar snap peas, trimmed
- 1½ lbs. snow peas, trimmed
- 1 Belgian endive, quartered lengthwise and sliced crosswise ¼ inch thick
  Kosher salt and pepper
- 1 lb. fresh ricotta cheese

1. Make the kimchi Bring a large saucepan of water to a boil. Blanch the onions until tender, about 1 minute, then drain well. Transfer to a large heatproof jar.

2. In a small saucepan, combine the fish sauce, gochugaru and ginger with 1 cup of water and bring to a boil. Pour the hot mixture over the onions. Stir in the sesame seeds and anise seeds. Close the jar and let stand for 2 hours.

3. Meanwhile, make the salad Fill a large bowl with ice water. In a large saucepan of boiling water, blanch the snap peas until bright green and crisp-tender, about 3 minutes. Using a slotted spoon, transfer to the ice bath to cool. Blanch the snow peas until bright green and crisp-tender, about 1 minute. Drain and transfer to the ice bath. Drain all of the peas and pat dry, then cut in half lengthwise and transfer to a large bowl. Add the endive and ¼ cup of the kimchi pickling liquid, season with salt and pepper and toss to coat.

4. Spoon the ricotta onto plates and top with the pea salad. Garnish with some of the kimchi and serve. —*Zakary Pelaccio*

Persimmon and Burrata Salad with Sesame Candy

Total 35 min; Serves 8

The Fuyu persimmon called for here is light orange and shaped like a tomato; don't confuse it with the Hachiya variety, which is heart-shaped.

- ½ cup sugar
- ⅔ cup toasted sesame seeds
  Kosher salt and pepper
- ⅓ cup extra-virgin olive oil
- ¼ cup balsamic vinegar
- 3 Tbsp. pure maple syrup
- 2 Tbsp. minced shallot
- 5 oz. baby arugula
- ½ lb. burrata cheese (2 small balls), drained and cut into ¾-inch pieces
- 2 firm Fuyu persimmons, cut into ¾-inch wedges
- ½ cup pomegranate seeds

1. In a medium saucepan, cook the sugar over moderate heat, undisturbed, until melted and light golden, about 3 minutes. Stir in the sesame seeds and a pinch of salt and immediately scrape onto a parchment paper–lined plate. Let cool completely, then break the candy into small pieces.

2. In a medium bowl, whisk the olive oil with the vinegar, maple syrup and shallot; season with salt and pepper. Mound the arugula on a platter and scatter the burrata, persimmons, sesame candy and pomegranate seeds on top. Drizzle some of the dressing over the salad and serve, passing the remaining dressing at the table. —*Helene Henderson*

MAKE AHEAD The sesame candy can be stored in an airtight container for 5 days.

WINE Tropical-fruit-inflected California Sauvignon Blanc: 2014 Star Lane Vineyard.

Burrata Salad with Peaches, Pickled Pepper and Pea Tendrils

Active 30 min; Total 1 hr 45 min; Serves 4

PICKLED PEPPER

- 1 banana pepper or cubanelle pepper, seeded and thinly sliced into rings
- ⅔ cup Champagne vinegar
- 2 tsp. kosher salt

DRESSING

- 2 Tbsp. red wine vinegar
- 2 Tbsp. minced shallot
- 2 Tbsp. extra-virgin olive oil
- 2 Tbsp. grapeseed oil
  Kosher salt and pepper

SALAD

- Two 6-oz. balls of burrata cheese, patted dry and halved
- ½ cup small mint leaves
- 8 cups pea tendrils (4½ oz.)
- 1 cup small purslane sprigs
  Kosher salt and pepper
- 1 large, ripe yellow peach, pitted and cut into 12 wedges

1. Make the pickled pepper Place the pepper rings in a small heatproof bowl. In a small saucepan, boil the vinegar and salt, stirring, until the salt dissolves; pour over the pepper rings. Let stand at room temperature for 90 minutes. Drain.

2. Meanwhile, make the dressing In a small bowl, combine the vinegar and shallot and let stand for 30 minutes. Slowly whisk in both oils until incorporated. Season with salt and pepper.

3. Make the salad In a food processor, puree 1 ball of burrata until smooth and spreadable. Spread the burrata puree in shallow bowls. In a medium bowl, toss the mint, pea tendrils, purslane and pickled pepper rings with the dressing. Season with salt and pepper and toss to coat. Mound the salad in the bowls. Tear the remaining burrata into small pieces and arrange in the salads along with the peach wedges. —*Ori Menashe*

MAKE AHEAD The drained pickled pepper rings can be refrigerated for 1 week.

WINE Minerally, strawberry-scented rosé: 2014 Tenuta delle Terre Nere Etna Rosato.

Watermelon, Feta and Almond Salad

⏱ Total **20 min**; Serves **6**

½ cup raw almonds (3 oz.)

½ small seedless watermelon (4½ lbs.), flesh cut into 1-inch pieces (8 cups)

Kosher salt

½ lb. Greek feta cheese, broken into ½-inch pieces (1 cup)

1. Preheat the oven to 375°. Spread the almonds in a pie plate and toast for about 10 minutes, until golden. Let cool.

2. Mound the watermelon in a large bowl and season with salt. Top with the cheese and toasted almonds and serve. —*Scott Conant*

BUILD YOUR OWN SALAD
Squash Salad

TOSS ROASTED BUTTERNUT SQUASH CUBES WITH ONE FLAVOR COMBINATION

1. Black kale, Spanish Manchego, roasted beets, corn nuts	**3.** Frisée, crispy bacon, dates, toasted pepitas
2. Baby mustard greens, Cabrales cheese, pomegranate seeds, candied pecans	**4.** Feta, chickpeas, roasted fennel, lemon zest

DRESS WITH
Coriander Vinaigrette
Makes 1¼ cups

In a small skillet, toast 1½ Tbsp. crushed **coriander seeds** until very fragrant, about 2 minutes. Transfer the seeds to a medium bowl and add 6 Tbsp. **white wine vinegar**, 1 finely chopped **shallot**, 2 minced **garlic cloves** and ½ cup chopped **cilantro**. While whisking constantly, slowly drizzle in ¾ cup **extra-virgin olive oil** until well blended. Season with **kosher salt** and **pepper**. —*Susan Feniger*

Fresh Cherries with Spring Onions and Cilantro

⏱ Total **40 min**; Serves **8**

3¼ lbs. fresh cherries, pitted and halved (about 8 cups)

3 spring onions, bulbs only, thinly sliced (greens reserved for another use)

1 cup coarsely chopped cilantro, plus leaves for garnish

1 Tbsp. white wine vinegar, plus more for seasoning

1 Tbsp. Asian fish sauce, plus more for seasoning

In a large bowl, toss all of the ingredients. Season with more vinegar and fish sauce, if desired. Transfer to a platter, garnish with cilantro and serve. —*Zakary Pelaccio*

Fennel, Apple and Avocado Crudo

⏱ Total **30 min**; Serves **4**

Pink peppercorns (berries unrelated to true peppercorns) are slightly spicy and fruity, with a mild citrus taste. They're used here to flavor a salt mix sprinkled on a supereasy vegetable crudo.

1 Tbsp. crushed pink peppercorns

1 Tbsp. chopped drained capers

½ tsp. flaky sea salt

½ tsp. finely grated Ruby Red grapefruit zest

6 Tbsp. fresh grapefruit juice

3 Tbsp. extra-virgin olive oil

1 Tbsp. chopped dill

2 firm, ripe Hass avocados—halved, pitted and cut into very thin wedges

1 fennel bulb—halved, cored and very thinly sliced lengthwise (2 cups)

1 medium Granny Smith apple, cored and thinly sliced

1. In a small bowl, mix the pink peppercorns with the capers and salt. In another small bowl, whisk the grapefruit zest with the juice, oil and dill.

2. On a platter, layer the avocados, fennel and apple, overlapping them slightly. Drizzle the grapefruit vinaigrette over the crudo and sprinkle with some of the pink peppercorn–caper salt. Serve immediately, passing the remaining salt at the table. —*Kay Chun*

Fig and Arugula Salad with Grated Frozen Gorgonzola Piccante

⏱ Active **20 min**; Total **45 min**; Serves **6**

F&W Best New Chef 2015 Ori Menashe makes amazingly creative salads at Bestia in L.A. Here, he dresses arugula, fresh Black Mission figs and pistachios with a spicy, lemony vinaigrette and a drizzle of crème fraîche.

VINAIGRETTE

2 Tbsp. fresh lemon juice

2 Tbsp. minced shallot

¼ tsp. kosher salt

⅛ tsp. crushed red pepper

2 Tbsp. extra-virgin olive oil

2 Tbsp. canola oil

SALAD

½ cup unsalted pistachios

5 oz. baby arugula (8 packed cups)

Kosher salt and pepper

9 fresh Black Mission figs, quartered

¼ cup crème fraîche

One 3-oz. wedge of Gorgonzola piccante, frozen overnight

1. Make the vinaigrette In a medium bowl, mix the lemon juice with the shallot, salt and crushed red pepper. Let stand for 30 minutes. While whisking constantly, slowly drizzle in both oils until incorporated.

2. Make the salad Preheat the oven to 425°. Spread the pistachios in a pie plate and toast for about 5 minutes, until golden. Let cool, then coarsely chop.

3. In a large bowl, toss the arugula with half of the pistachios and the vinaigrette; season with salt and pepper. Transfer to plates and arrange the figs around the salad. In a small bowl, stir the crème fraîche with 1 tablespoon of water until smooth; drizzle over the salad. Grate the frozen Gorgonzola over the salad, top with the remaining pistachios and serve. —*Ori Menashe*

WINE Citrus- and herb-scented Italian white: 2013 Pieropan Soave Classico.

Grilled Vegetables and Summer Greens with Shallot Vinaigrette

⏱ Total **40 min**; Serves **6 to 8**

Curtis Stone, the chef at L.A.'s Maude, grills everything in the summer, even avocados (keeping the skins on makes them easier to grill). He adds chunks of them to this hearty knife-and-fork salad.

VINAIGRETTE

- 6 Tbsp. extra-virgin olive oil
- 3 Tbsp. sherry vinegar
- 2 Tbsp. chopped tarragon
- 2 Tbsp. minced shallot
- 1½ Tbsp. grainy mustard
  Kosher salt and pepper

SALAD

- 1 lb. thin asparagus
- 4 heirloom tomatoes, quartered lengthwise
- 2 medium zucchini, halved lengthwise
- 2 unpeeled Hass avocados—washed, quartered and pitted
- 2 Tbsp. extra-virgin olive oil
  Kosher salt and pepper
- 5 oz. mixed baby greens, such as baby kale and mustard greens (8 cups)
- ¼ cup toasted hazelnuts, chopped

1. Make the vinaigrette In a medium bowl, whisk all of the ingredients until well blended. Season with salt and pepper.

2. Make the salad Light a grill. In a large bowl, toss the asparagus, tomatoes, zucchini, avocados and oil; season with salt and pepper. Grill over moderately high heat until tender, 2 minutes for the asparagus and avocados and about 5 minutes for the tomatoes and zucchini. Let cool.

3. Arrange the greens on a platter. Drizzle with 3 tablespoons of the vinaigrette and top with the hazelnuts. Serve with the grilled vegetables and the remaining vinaigrette. —*Curtis Stone*

WINE Fragrant, pear-scented Pinot Grigio: 2014 Erste + Neue.

Corn-and-Barley Salad

Active **25 min**; Total **50 min**; Serves **4 to 6**

- ½ cup pearled barley
- ¾ cup walnuts
- 3 cups fresh corn kernels (from about 4 ears)
- ¼ cup chopped dill
- ¼ cup snipped chives
- ¾ cup chopped pitted mild green olives
- 3 Tbsp. fresh lemon juice
- ¼ cup extra-virgin olive oil
  Kosher salt and pepper

1. Preheat the oven to 375°. In a medium saucepan of salted boiling water, cook the barley until just tender, about 25 minutes. Drain well and spread out on a plate to cool completely.

2. Meanwhile, spread the walnuts in a pie plate and toast for about 12 minutes, until golden. Let cool, then coarsely chop.

3. In a large bowl, toss the barley with the corn, walnuts and all of the remaining ingredients. Season with salt and pepper and serve. —*Justin Chapple*

MAKE AHEAD The salad can be made up to 6 hours ahead and refrigerated. Serve at room temperature.

Homestyle Cucumber Salad with Garlic

Active **5 min**; Total **25 min**; Serves **4**

- 1 large hothouse cucumber (1 lb.)— quartered lengthwise, seeded and cut into 2-inch lengths
- 1 Tbsp. minced garlic
- ½ tsp. kosher salt
- 1 Tbsp. toasted sesame oil

1. In a medium bowl, toss the cucumber with the garlic and salt. Cover and refrigerate for 20 minutes.

2. Drain the cucumber and transfer to a serving bowl. Drizzle with the sesame oil and serve cold. —*Kian Lam Kho*

MAKE AHEAD The cucumber salad can be refrigerated overnight.

Honey-Roasted Carrots with Lemon-Ginger Vinaigrette, Mâche and Crispy Prosciutto

⏱ Total **45 min**; Serves **6 to 8**

This roasted carrot salad with prosciutto is a master class in how to use hardy vegetables like sunchokes, parsnips, cauliflower or carrots. It would make a fine starter or a light main course for four people.

- 1½ lbs. small carrots, scrubbed but not peeled
- 4 Tbsp. melted unsalted butter
  Kosher salt and pepper
- 3 Tbsp. honey
- 1 Tbsp. canola oil
- 4 thin slices of prosciutto (2 oz.)
- 1½ Tbsp. fresh lemon juice
- 1 tsp. finely grated peeled fresh ginger
- ¼ tsp. finely grated lemon zest
- ¼ tsp. finely grated lime zest
- ¼ cup extra-virgin olive oil
- 4 oz. mâche

1. Set a large heavy rimmed baking sheet in the oven and preheat to 500°. In a large bowl, toss the carrots with the melted butter and season with salt and pepper. Spread on the preheated baking sheet and roast for about 10 minutes, until just softened. Drizzle the honey over the carrots and roast for 5 minutes longer, until caramelized. Transfer the carrots to a platter.

2. Meanwhile, in a large skillet, heat the canola oil. Add the prosciutto in a single layer and cook over moderate heat, turning once, until browned and crisp, about 4 minutes. Transfer to a paper towel–lined plate to cool, then break into large pieces.

3. In a medium bowl, whisk the lemon juice with the ginger and lemon and lime zests. Gradually whisk in the olive oil and season the dressing with salt and pepper.

4. In a bowl, lightly toss the mâche and prosciutto with half of the dressing. Mound the salad on top of the carrots and serve right away, passing the remaining dressing at the table. —*Brandi Henderson*

Mexican Grilled-Corn Salad with Citrus Aioli

Total **30 min;** Serves **8**

This sweet, salty salad inspired by elote (Mexican street corn) is the perfect picnic side. Bonus: You can make the aioli the night before and fold it in right before serving.

10 **ears of corn, shucked**
Kosher salt and pepper
½ **cup mayonnaise**
½ **tsp. finely grated lime zest plus 3 Tbsp. fresh lime juice**
½ **tsp. finely grated lemon zest plus 1 Tbsp. fresh lemon juice**
1 **Tbsp. extra-virgin olive oil, plus more for brushing**
½ **tsp. Dijon mustard**
1 **garlic clove, finely grated**
⅛ **tsp. cayenne**
4 **Tbsp. unsalted butter, softened**
2 **oz. queso fresco, crumbled (½ cup)**
2 **oz. Cotija cheese, finely crumbled (½ cup)**
¼ **cup chopped parsley**
¼ **cup chopped cilantro**

1. Bring a large pot of water to a boil. Add the corn and a generous pinch of salt and return to a boil. Remove from the heat, cover and let stand for 5 minutes. Drain the corn and let cool slightly.

2. Meanwhile, in a small bowl, whisk the mayonnaise with the lime and lemon zests and juices along with the 1 tablespoon of olive oil, the mustard, garlic and cayenne. Season the citrus aioli with salt.

3. Light a grill or heat a grill pan. Brush the corn with olive oil and season with salt. Grill over high heat, turning occasionally, until lightly charred all over, about 5 minutes. Transfer to a plate and let cool slightly, then cut the kernels off the cobs; discard the cobs.

4. In a large bowl, toss the corn with the softened butter. Stir in the citrus aioli. Add the queso fresco, Cotija, parsley and cilantro. Season with salt and pepper and serve warm. —*Ellen Bennett*

MAKE AHEAD The citrus aioli can be refrigerated overnight.

Sweet Corn Salad with Pancetta and Mushrooms

Total **50 min;** Serves **6**

6 **large ears of corn, shucked**
8 **scallions**
4 **oz. pancetta, cut into ¼-inch dice**
½ **cup extra-virgin olive oil**
12 **oz. cremini mushrooms, halved or quartered if large**
Kosher salt and pepper
1 **tsp. finely grated lemon zest plus ¼ cup fresh lemon juice**
½ **tsp. honey**
1 **tsp. apple cider vinegar**
4 **oz. frisée, white and light green parts only (4 cups), torn into bite-size pieces**
2 **Tbsp. snipped chives**
Shaved Gruyère cheese, for serving

1. In a pot of salted boiling water, cook the corn until crisp-tender, 5 minutes. Let cool, then cut the kernels off the cobs.

2. Meanwhile, in a large cast-iron skillet, cook the scallions over high heat until charred on the bottom, about 3 minutes. Cut into 2-inch lengths.

3. In the same skillet, cook the pancetta over moderate heat, stirring occasionally, until browned, about 5 minutes. Using a slotted spoon, transfer to a paper towel–lined plate to drain. Pour off all but 1 tablespoon of fat from the skillet.

4. Heat 2 tablespoons of the oil in the skillet. Add the mushrooms and season with salt and pepper. Cook over moderately high heat, stirring occasionally, until browned, 5 to 7 minutes.

5. In a large bowl, whisk the lemon zest and juice with the honey, vinegar and remaining ¼ cup plus 2 tablespoons of olive oil. Season the dressing with salt and pepper. Add the corn, scallions, pancetta, mushrooms, frisée and chives and toss to coat; season with salt and pepper. Top the salad with shaved Gruyère and serve. —*Shea Gallante*

Cucumber Salad with Buttermilk Dressing and Pickled Onion

Total **45 min;** Serves **4 to 6**

PICKLED ONION

1 **cup red wine vinegar**
¼ **cup sugar**
¼ **tsp. sea salt**
1 **red onion, thinly sliced**

DRESSING

½ **cup crème fraîche**
¼ **cup buttermilk**
¼ **cup mayonnaise**
2 **Tbsp. fresh lemon juice**
1 **Tbsp. minced tarragon**
1 **Tbsp. minced chives**
1 **Tbsp. minced parsley**
1 **garlic clove, finely grated**
Sea salt and black pepper

SALAD

3 **Persian cucumbers, thinly sliced lengthwise**
3 **Kirby cucumbers, cut into thin wedges**
2 **Tbsp. red wine vinegar**
2 **Tbsp. extra-virgin olive oil, plus more for drizzling**
Sea salt and black pepper
Sunflower sprouts, roasted sunflower seeds and tarragon leaves, for garnish

1. Pickle the onion In a small saucepan, combine the vinegar, sugar and salt with ¼ cup water and bring just to a boil, stirring to dissolve the sugar. Remove from the heat; add the onion. Let cool, then refrigerate until chilled.

2. Make the dressing In a small bowl, whisk all of the ingredients together and season with salt and pepper.

3. Make the salad In a medium bowl, toss all of the cucumbers with the vinegar and the 2 tablespoons of olive oil. Season with salt and pepper; let stand for 5 minutes.

4. Spoon the dressing into shallow bowls and top with the cucumber salad. Drain the onion and scatter over the salad. Garnish with sunflower sprouts and seeds, tarragon and a drizzle of olive oil. Serve. —*Michael Fojtasek and Grae Nonas*

Greek Bread Salad with Spinach and Tomatoes

⏱ Total **30 min;** Serves **6 to 8**

Ntounias restaurant on the island of Crete serves this excellent version of a classic Greek salad. It calls for the large, store-bought toasts called rusks. If you can't find them, use extra-large plain croutons or torn and toasted pieces of sourdough.

- **2 lbs. tomatoes, cut into 1-inch pieces**
- **2 oz. curly spinach, stemmed and sliced**
- **1 cup thinly sliced white onion**
- **¼ cup sliced scallions**
- **6 oz. manouri or mild feta cheese, crumbled**
- **3 oz. rusks, broken into large pieces, or plain large croutons**
- **⅓ cup extra-virgin olive oil**
- **3 Tbsp. fresh lemon juice**
- **Kosher salt and pepper**

In a large bowl, combine all of the ingredients, season with salt and pepper and toss thoroughly. Let stand at room temperature until the rusks soften slightly, about 15 minutes, then serve. —*Stelios Trilyrakis*

WINE Lemony, medium-bodied Greek white: 2014 Argyros Assyrtiko.

Fried Eggplant Salad with Feta

⏱ Total **45 min;** Serves **4**

This warm salad is all about the tender fried eggplant. Leaving some of its skin on makes the dish pleasantly chewy.

- **One 1½-lb. eggplant**
- **Vegetable oil, for frying**
- **Kosher salt and pepper**
- **3 Tbsp. red wine vinegar**
- **1 Tbsp. extra-virgin olive oil**
- **1 small garlic clove, minced**
- **4 large scallions, thinly sliced**
- **1 medium green bell pepper, cut into ¼-inch dice**
- **1 medium red bell pepper, cut into ¼-inch dice**
- **2 oz. Greek feta cheese, crumbled**

1. Using a vegetable peeler, peel half of the eggplant; cut into ½-inch dice.

2. In a large saucepan, heat 1 inch of vegetable oil to 350°. Add half of the eggplant and fry over moderately high heat, stirring, until lightly browned, 5 to 7 minutes. Transfer the eggplant to a paper towel–lined baking sheet to drain; season with salt and pepper. Fry the remaining eggplant.

3. In a large bowl, whisk the vinegar with the olive oil and garlic. Add the eggplant, scallions and bell peppers and toss well. Season with salt and pepper and toss again. Sprinkle the feta on top and serve.
—*Yiannis Tsivourakis*

WINE Zesty, herb-scented Greek white: 2014 Domaine Skouras Salto Moscofilero.

Sausage and Heirloom Tomato Salad

⏱ Total **30 min;** Serves **8**

L.A. chef-turned-apron-designer Ellen Bennet combines her favorite American and Argentinean salads into one giant bowl of tomatoes, spicy sausages, hearts of palm, olives and cilantro.

- **Five 4-oz. Calabrese or fresh chorizo sausages**
- **1½ lbs. heirloom tomatoes, cut into chunks**
- **One 15-oz. can hearts of palm, drained and sliced**
- **⅓ cup pitted kalamata olives, halved**
- **¼ cup extra-virgin olive oil**
- **⅓ cup chopped cilantro**
- **3 Tbsp. fresh lime juice**
- **Kosher salt**

1. Light a grill or heat a grill pan. Grill the sausages over moderate heat, turning occasionally, until lightly charred and an instant-read thermometer inserted in each sausage registers 165°, about 10 minutes. Transfer to a carving board; let rest for 5 minutes, then slice ½ inch thick.

2. In a large bowl, toss the sausages with the remaining ingredients. Season with salt and serve. —*Ellen Bennett*

WINE Vibrant, robustly fruity Spanish rosé: 2014 Armas de Guerra.

Grilled Chicken Thigh and Cucumber Salad

⏱ Total **30 min;** Serves **4**

"I'm a thigh guy," says star chef Michael Symon, co-host of *The Chew*. "It has the deepest flavor of all chicken cuts."

- **6 skin-on, boneless chicken thighs (2 lbs.), pounded ½ inch thick**
- **¼ cup plus 2 Tbsp. extra-virgin olive oil**
- **Kosher salt and pepper**
- **3 Tbsp. red wine vinegar**
- **1 Tbsp. minced shallot**
- **1 tsp. minced garlic**
- **1 English cucumber, thinly sliced**
- **¼ cup thinly sliced red onion**
- **1 small Fresno or red jalapeño chile, thinly sliced**
- **2 Tbsp. chopped mint, plus whole leaves for garnish**
- **3 Tbsp. chopped roasted unsalted almonds**

1. Light a grill. Rub the chicken thighs with 2 tablespoons of the olive oil and season with salt and pepper. Arrange the chicken skin side down on the grill and top with a sheet of foil and a weighted heavy baking sheet. Grill the chicken over moderate heat until the skin is golden brown, about 5 minutes. Turn the chicken skin side up, top with the foil and weighted baking sheet and grill for 3 minutes longer. Remove the baking sheet. Turn the chicken skin side down once more and grill until the skin is crispy and the chicken is cooked through, about 2 minutes longer. Transfer the chicken to a cutting board.

2. Meanwhile, in a large bowl, combine the vinegar, shallot and garlic; gradually whisk in the remaining ¼ cup of olive oil until well blended. Add the cucumber, onion, chile and chopped mint and season with salt and pepper. Toss to coat.

3. Slice the chicken and toss with the cucumber salad. Garnish with the nuts and mint leaves and serve. —*Michael Symon*

WINE Juicy, ripe-apple-scented Spanish white: 2013 Finca Antigua Viura.

GRILLED CHICKEN
THIGH AND
CUCUMBER SALAD

Erin French cooked pop-up dinners in a 1965 Airstream before opening The Lost Kitchen in Freedom, Maine. She specializes in unfussy, satisfying dishes like duck confit stew (recipe, p. 85).

SOUPS & STEWS

CELERY SOUP WITH
BACONY CROUTONS
Recipe, page 72

LEMONY ROASTED
ASPARAGUS SOUP

Lemony Roasted Asparagus Soup

Active **1 hr**; Total **2 hr**; Serves **4**

- 2 lbs. jumbo asparagus
- 1 onion, coarsely chopped
- ½ cup dry white wine
- 2 Tbsp. unsalted butter
- 2 Tbsp. all-purpose flour
- 4 large egg yolks
- ¼ cup fresh lemon juice
- Kosher salt and freshly ground pepper
- 5 Tbsp. extra-virgin olive oil
- 1 lb. oyster mushrooms, torn into small pieces
- Chopped dill and dried oregano, for garnish

1. Peel and trim the asparagus. Slice the stalks diagonally ¼ inch thick; reserve the stems and peelings. In a large saucepan, combine the asparagus trimmings, onion, wine and 6 cups of water. Bring to a boil, then simmer, covered, over moderately low heat until the asparagus trimmings are soft, about 1 hour. Transfer the contents of the pan to a blender and puree until as smooth as possible. Strain the broth through a fine sieve, pressing on the solids. Wipe out the saucepan.

2. Preheat the oven to 450°. Melt the butter in the saucepan over moderate heat. Whisk in the flour until golden brown and nutty-smelling, about 3 minutes. Whisk in the asparagus broth until smooth and bring to a gentle simmer. In a medium bowl, whisk the egg yolks with the lemon juice. Gradually whisk in ¼ cup of the hot broth, then whisk in half of the remaining broth. Return this mixture to the broth in the saucepan and simmer, whisking frequently, until hot. Season with salt.

3. On a rimmed baking sheet, toss the sliced asparagus with 2 tablespoons of the oil and season with salt and pepper. Roast for about 8 minutes, stirring, until the asparagus is golden but still slightly firm.

4. In a nonstick skillet, heat the remaining 3 tablespoons of oil. Add the mushrooms and cook over moderately high heat until golden and crisp, 8 minutes.

5. Transfer the roasted asparagus to shallow bowls. Ladle the soup over the asparagus and top with the mushrooms. Garnish with dill and oregano and serve.
—*Cassie Piuma*

Cold Tomato Soup with Ham and Hard-Boiled Eggs

Active **20 min**; Total **1 hr 20 min**; Serves **4**

Blender blades can heat up the soup if they're working really hard, so chef José Andrés throws in a few ice cubes to keep the temperature cool.

- 2 lbs. ripe plum tomatoes, cored and quartered
- 2 garlic cloves, crushed
- 3 Tbsp. sherry vinegar
- ¾ cup extra-virgin olive oil, preferably Spanish, plus more for drizzling
- 1 cup cubed stale rustic white bread (1 oz.)
- ½ cup large ice cubes
- Kosher salt
- 2 large eggs
- 4 thin slices of serrano ham (1½ oz.)

1. In a blender, combine the tomatoes, garlic and vinegar with ¼ cup of cold water and the ¾ cup of olive oil; puree until nearly smooth. With the machine on, gradually add the bread and ice cubes and puree until very smooth, 1 to 2 minutes. Scrape the soup into a medium bowl and season with salt. Refrigerate until cold, about 1 hour.

2. Meanwhile, in a small saucepan, cover the eggs with water and bring to a boil. Remove the pan from the heat, cover and let stand for 10 minutes. Drain the eggs and run them under cold water until cooled, then peel and cut in half. Separate the yolks from the whites. Separately press the whites and yolks through a fine sieve.

3. Ladle the soup into bowls. Garnish with the ham and sieved egg whites and yolks. Drizzle with olive oil and serve.
—*José Andrés*

Chunky Artichoke and Sunchoke Soup

Active **45 min**; Total **2 hr**; Serves **6 to 8**

This creamy soup simmers with a layer of prosciutto on top, which adds marvelous flavor.

- 1 lemon, halved
- 9 medium artichokes
- ¼ cup extra-virgin olive oil
- 2 medium onions, cut into ½-inch pieces
- 3 garlic cloves, minced
- Kosher salt
- 1¼ lbs. sunchokes, peeled and cut into ½-inch pieces
- ¾ cup dry white wine
- 4 oz. thinly sliced prosciutto
- 1 cup heavy cream
- 4 scallions, thinly sliced

1. Squeeze the juice from 1 lemon half into a large bowl of water. Snap off the dark green outer leaves of 1 of the artichokes. Cut 1 inch off the top, then peel the bottom and stem. Halve the artichoke lengthwise and scoop out the furry choke. Cut each half in half lengthwise, then rub the quarters with the remaining lemon half and add them to the lemon water. Repeat the process with the remaining 8 artichokes.

2. In a large enameled cast-iron casserole, heat the oil. Add the onions, garlic and 2 teaspoons of salt and cook over moderate heat, stirring, until softened and light golden, about 15 minutes. Scatter the sunchokes over the onions in an even layer. Drain the artichokes and arrange on top. Pour in the wine and 2 cups of water. Completely cover the vegetables with the prosciutto.

3. Cover the casserole and cook over low heat for 30 minutes. Stir in the cream and sprinkle the scallions on top. Cover and cook until all of the vegetables are tender and the soup has thickened slightly, about 30 minutes longer. Remove from the heat and let stand for 10 minutes. Season with salt and serve. —*April Bloomfield*

MAKE AHEAD The soup can be refrigerated for up to 2 days.

Green Gazpacho with Fennel and Blueberries

Active **40 min**; Total **2 hr 45 min**
Serves **4 to 6**

BLUEBERRIES

- 1 cup dried blueberries (4 oz.)
- 1 Tbsp. plus 1 tsp. sugar
- 2 tsp. Champagne vinegar

SOUP

- 1 lb. ripe green melon, such as honeydew, peeled and cut into 1-inch pieces (3 cups)
- 4 Persian cucumbers—peeled, seeded and chopped
- 2 Hass avocados (12 oz.)—peeled, pitted and chopped
- ½ tsp. fresh lemon juice
- ½ cup crème fraîche
  Kosher salt

SWEET HERB OIL

- ½ cup mild, fruity extra-virgin olive oil or grapeseed oil, chilled
- 1 cup packed fennel fronds, anise hyssop or lemon balm (1 oz.)

GARNISH

- 1 small fennel bulb, inner core only, halved and very thinly sliced lengthwise
- 1 Persian cucumber—peeled, halved lengthwise and thinly sliced crosswise on the diagonal
- ½ tsp. Champagne vinegar
  Pinch of sugar
  Pinch of kosher salt
  Fennel pollen and mint or anise hyssop flowers, for garnish

1. Make the blueberries In a medium bowl, mix the blueberries with the sugar and vinegar. Let macerate at room temperature for 1 hour, stirring occasionally.

2. Preheat the oven to 200°. Spread the blueberries on a parchment paper–lined baking sheet and bake for 1 hour and 30 minutes, stirring occasionally, until thickened but still moist. Let cool.

3. Meanwhile, make the soup In a blender, combine all of the ingredients, season with salt and puree until smooth. Strain the soup through a fine sieve into a large bowl. Cover and refrigerate for about 2 hours, until cold.

4. Make the sweet herb oil In a blender, combine the oil and herbs and puree until smooth. In a sieve set over a small bowl, strain the oil through a coffee filter or a double layer of cheesecloth.

5. Make the garnish In a medium bowl, toss the fennel and cucumber with the vinegar, sugar and salt. Let stand for 3 minutes. Add 1 tablespoon of the sweet herb oil; toss to coat.

6. Spoon the blueberries into bowls and top with the fennel-cucumber garnish. Pour the soup around the berries. Drizzle with some of the remaining herb oil, top with fennel pollen and mint or anise hyssop flowers and serve. —*Carlos Salgado*

Chilled Beet and Green Apple Bisque

Active **40 min**; Total **1 hr 15 min** plus chilling
Serves **4 to 6**

Shredding the beets and apples for this deep fuchsia soup cuts down on the cooking time and keeps the sweet-tart flavors fresh.

- 1½ lbs. medium beets, peeled and cut into wedges
- 2 Granny Smith apples—peeled, cored and cut into wedges
- 2 Tbsp. extra-virgin olive oil
- 2 shallots, thinly sliced
- 2 garlic cloves, thinly sliced
- 2 cups chicken stock or low-sodium broth
- ¼ cup apple juice
  Kosher salt
- ½ cup sour cream mixed with 1 Tbsp. water
  Shaved or julienned beets and small beet greens, for garnish

1. In a food processor fitted with the shredding disk or using a box grater, shred the beets and apples.

2. In a large saucepan, heat the oil. Add the shallots and garlic and cook over moderately high heat, stirring occasionally, until softened, 3 minutes. Add the shredded beets and apples and cook, stirring occasionally, until just starting to soften, 5 minutes. Add the stock and 3½ cups of water; bring to a boil. Simmer over moderate heat, stirring occasionally, until the beets are tender, 25 to 30 minutes.

3. In a blender, puree the soup with the apple juice until very smooth. Transfer to a bowl; refrigerate until chilled, 45 minutes.

4. Stir tablespoons of water into the soup if it gets too thick, then season with salt. Ladle the soup into bowls and swirl in the sour cream. Garnish with shaved or julienned beets and beet greens and serve. —*Justin Chapple*

MAKE AHEAD The soup can be refrigerated for up to 3 days.

Chunky Red Beet and Tomato Soup

Active **25 min**; Total **2 hr**; Serves **6**

- 1 Tbsp. extra-virgin olive oil
- 1 medium onion, cut into ½-inch dice
- 2 garlic cloves, minced
  One 28-oz. can whole peeled Italian tomatoes, crushed by hand, juices reserved
- 2 large beets (1½ lbs.), peeled and cut into ½-inch pieces
- 2 medium carrots, cut into ½-inch pieces
- ¾ tsp. ground cumin, plus more for serving
- ¼ tsp. cayenne, plus more for seasoning
  Sea salt
  Whole-milk plain Greek yogurt, for serving

1. In a large pot, heat the olive oil. Add the onion and garlic and cook over moderate heat, stirring occasionally, until softened, 8 minutes. Add the tomatoes and their juices, the beets, carrots, ¾ teaspoon of cumin and ¼ teaspoon of cayenne. Season with salt and add enough water to cover the vegetables by 1 inch. Bring to a boil, cover partially and simmer over low heat until the vegetables are very tender, about 1 hour. Remove from the heat and let stand for at least 30 minutes to allow the flavors to develop.

2. Reheat the soup and season with salt, cumin and cayenne. Serve topped with a dollop of yogurt and a pinch of cumin. —*Michael Stebner*

MAKE AHEAD The soup can be refrigerated for up to 3 days.

Broccoli Soup with Raisin Sauce and Pine Nuts

Total **1 hr**; Serves **6 to 8**

- ⅓ cup pine nuts
- 2 Tbsp. unsalted butter
- 3 garlic cloves, crushed
- 1 leek, split lengthwise and thinly sliced crosswise
- ¼ tsp. crushed red pepper
  Kosher salt and black pepper
- 6 cups chicken stock or low-sodium broth
  One 1-lb. head of broccoli, florets and stem coarsely chopped
- 2 small shallots, finely chopped
- ½ cup apple cider
- ¼ cup apple cider vinegar
- ⅓ cup raisins
- 2 Tbsp. cream cheese, softened
- ½ cup freshly grated Parmigiano-Reggiano cheese
- ¼ cup extra-virgin olive oil

1. Preheat the oven to 350°. Spread the pine nuts in a pie plate and toast for about 8 minutes, until golden brown.

2. In a large saucepan, melt 1 tablespoon of the butter. Add the garlic, leek, crushed red pepper and 2 teaspoons of salt and cook over moderate heat until the leek begins to soften, 5 minutes. Add the stock and broccoli and bring to a boil over high heat. Reduce the heat to a simmer and cook until the broccoli is tender and the soup is slightly reduced, about 20 minutes.

3. Meanwhile, heat the remaining 1 table-spoon of butter in a small saucepan. Add the shallots and cook over moderate heat until softened, about 5 minutes. Pour in the cider and vinegar and bring to a boil over high heat. Stir in the raisins and ½ tea-spoon of salt. Remove from the heat and let stand for 10 minutes. Pour the raisins and their liquid into a blender. Add the cream cheese and blend to a smooth sauce. Pour into a small bowl.

4. In a blender, working in batches, puree the soup with the Parmigiano-Reggiano and olive oil. Season with pepper. Ladle the soup into shallow serving bowls, drizzle with some of the raisin sauce and sprinkle with the pine nuts. Serve immediately.
—*Vivian Howard*

Cauliflower Soup with Herbed Goat Cheese

Total **50 min**; Serves **4 to 6**

- One 2½-lb. head of cauliflower, cored
- ¼ cup extra-virgin olive oil
- 1 medium leek, white and light green parts only, coarsely chopped
- 1 large garlic clove, minced
  Kosher salt
- 1 large baking potato, peeled and cut into 1-inch pieces
- ¾ cup dry white wine
- 1 quart chicken stock or low-sodium broth
- 3 thyme sprigs tied in a bundle plus 1 tsp. chopped leaves
- 8 brussels sprouts (6 oz.), trimmed and separated into leaves
- 4 oz. cold fresh goat cheese, crumbled
- 2 Tbsp. snipped chives
- ¼ cup heavy cream

1. Preheat the oven to 375°. On a work surface, cut one-fourth of the cauliflower into ½-inch florets. Coarsely chop the remaining cauliflower.

2. In a large saucepan, heat 2 tablespoons of the olive oil. Add the leek, garlic and a generous pinch of salt and cook over moderate heat, stirring occasionally, until softened, 5 minutes. Stir in the potato and the chopped cauliflower, then add the wine and cook over high heat until reduced by half, 4 minutes. Add the stock and the thyme bundle and bring to a boil. Reduce the heat to moderately low and simmer, stirring occasionally, until the vegetables are very tender, about 30 minutes. Discard the thyme bundle.

3. Meanwhile, at either end of a large rimmed baking sheet, separately toss the cauliflower florets and brussels sprout leaves each with 1 tablespoon of olive oil and season with salt. Roast for 15 to 18 minutes, stirring each halfway through, until lightly browned and tender. In a small bowl, mix the goat cheese with the chives and chopped thyme.

4. In a blender, puree the soup in 2 batches until very smooth. Return the soup to the saucepan and stir in the cream. Rewarm over moderate heat, adding water if the soup seems too thick; season with salt.

Ladle into bowls and top with the roasted brussels sprout leaves and cauliflower florets. Sprinkle the herbed goat cheese on top and serve hot. —*Anne Burrell*

Cauliflower and Cashew Soup with Apple

Active **15 min**; Total **1 hr**; Serves **6**

This vegan soup gets a hint of fruity sweetness from apple and a double dose of creaminess from almond milk and pureed raw cashews.

- 1 head of cauliflower (2¼ lbs.), bottom trimmed and leaves removed
- 1 medium onion, chopped
- 1 small Pink Lady apple—peeled, cored and chopped
- ½ cup raw cashews
- 1 Tbsp. minced peeled fresh ginger
- ½ tsp. ground cinnamon
- ½ tsp. ground cardamom
- ¼ tsp. cayenne
  Salt
- 1 cup plain unsweetened almond milk
  Chopped roasted cashews, for garnish

1. Chop the cauliflower into large pieces, including the stem. In a large pot, combine all of the ingredients except the salt, almond milk and garnish. Add enough water to cover the vegetables, season with salt and bring to a boil. Simmer over low heat until the cauliflower is very tender, about 30 minutes. Let cool slightly.

2. Working in batches, puree the soup in a blender until smooth. Transfer to a clean pot and stir in the almond milk. Rewarm over moderate heat, adding more water or almond milk for a thinner consistency, if desired. Season the soup with salt, garnish with chopped cashews and serve.
—*Michael Stebner*

MAKE AHEAD The soup can be refrigerated for up to 3 days.

Celery Soup with Bacony Croutons

📷 PAGE 67

Active **1 hr**; Total **1 hr 30 min**; Serves **8**

This elegant soup gets a surprising amount of flavor from sautéed celery. It has great garnishes, too: bacon, croutons cooked in bacon fat and a drizzle of lemon olive oil. Be sure to buy extra-virgin olive oil infused with pure lemon extract.

- 6 **Tbsp. unsalted butter**
- 3 **medium leeks, halved and thinly sliced**
- 2 **medium onions, finely chopped**
- 3 **large garlic cloves, thinly sliced**
  Kosher salt and pepper
- 12 **large celery ribs (2 lbs.), trimmed and thinly sliced**
- 4 **oz. bacon, finely diced**
  Three ½-inch-thick slices of country bread, cut into ½-inch dice
- ½ **cup crème fraîche or sour cream**
  Lemon olive oil, for drizzling

1. In a large saucepan, melt 4 tablespoons of the butter. Add the leeks, onions, garlic and a generous pinch each of salt and pepper and cook over moderately high heat, stirring, until softened but not browned, about 12 minutes. Add the celery and cook, stirring, until just starting to soften, about 3 minutes. Add 8 cups of water and bring to a boil, then reduce the heat to moderate. Simmer, stirring occasionally, until the vegetables are very tender, 35 to 40 minutes.

2. Meanwhile, in a large skillet, cook the bacon over moderate heat, stirring occasionally, until browned and crisp, 8 minutes. Using a slotted spoon, transfer the bacon to half of a paper towel–lined baking sheet to drain. Melt the remaining 2 tablespoons of butter in the bacon fat. Add the bread and cook over moderately high heat, stirring, until browned and crisp, 8 minutes. Transfer the croutons to the other side of the prepared baking sheet; season with salt and pepper.

3. Working in batches, puree the soup in a blender until smooth. Return the soup to the saucepan, whisk in the crème fraîche and season with salt and pepper. Serve hot, topped with the bacon, the croutons and a drizzle of lemon olive oil.
—*Naomi Pomeroy*

Farro and White Bean Soup with Swiss Chard and Herb Oil

Active **1 hr**; Total **2 hr plus overnight soaking**; Serves **18**

Chef Dan Kluger's vegetarian soup is perfect for feeding a crowd. It was inspired by events like the annual Social Soup Experiment at New York City's High Line park. The "experiment" involves hundreds of people seated at long tables sharing soup and reveling in communal spirit.

SOUP

- 2 **cups Great Northern beans—picked over, soaked overnight and drained**
  Kosher salt and pepper
- 1½ **cups farro (9 oz.)**
- ½ **cup extra-virgin olive oil**
- 1 **large Spanish onion, halved and thinly sliced**
- 1¼ **cups thinly sliced carrots**
- 1¼ **cups thinly sliced celery root**
- ⅓ **cup thinly sliced garlic**
  Two 28-oz. cans fire-roasted diced tomatoes
- 1 **lb. red Swiss chard, stemmed and leaves chopped**

HERB OIL

- 2 **Tbsp. minced parsley**
- 1 **Tbsp. minced rosemary**
- 1 **Tbsp. minced thyme**
- 1 **Tbsp. minced oregano**
- ½ **jalapeño, seeded and minced**
- 1½ **tsp. finely grated lemon zest**
- 1 **cup extra-virgin olive oil**
  Kosher salt
  Freshly grated Parmigiano-Reggiano cheese, for serving

1. Make the soup In a large pot, cover the soaked beans with at least 4 inches of water and bring to a boil. Simmer over moderately low heat until the beans are tender, about 1 hour and 15 minutes. Add 1 tablespoon of salt and let stand for 5 minutes. Drain, reserving 6 cups of the cooking liquid.

2. Meanwhile, in a medium saucepan of salted boiling water, cook the farro until al dente, about 20 minutes. Drain.

3. Wipe out the large pot and heat the olive oil in it. Add the onion and a generous pinch of salt and cook over moderate heat, stirring occasionally, until softened but not browned, about 7 minutes. Add the carrots, celery root and garlic and cook, stirring occasionally, until the vegetables just start to soften, about 5 minutes. Add the tomatoes with their juices and cook over moderately high heat, stirring occasionally, until the juices have reduced by half, 8 to 10 minutes.

4. Add the reserved bean cooking liquid and 14 cups of water to the pot and bring to a simmer. Stir in the beans, farro and Swiss chard and simmer over moderate heat until the chard is wilted and the soup is hot, about 5 minutes. Season with salt and pepper.

5. Make the herb oil In a medium bowl, whisk the herbs with the jalapeño, lemon zest and olive oil; season with salt.

6. To serve, ladle the soup into bowls and top with the herb oil and grated cheese.
—*Dan Kluger*

MAKE AHEAD The soup can be refrigerated for up to 3 days. Reheat gently before serving. The herb oil can be refrigerated overnight; serve at room temperature.

FARRO AND WHITE
BEAN SOUP WITH SWISS
CHARD AND HERB OIL

WINTER SQUASH
SOUP WITH KALE
AND FIDEOS

Winter Squash Soup with Kale and Fideos

Active **30 min**; Total **1 hr 50 min**; Serves **4**

- 1 **yellow onion, halved**
- 2 **Tbsp. plus 1 tsp. extra-virgin olive oil**
- One 2½-lb. **Red Kuri squash— scrubbed, peeled, seeded and cut into 1-inch pieces, skin and seeds reserved**
- 8 **cups Rooster Soup Co. Broth (recipe follows) or water**
- 1 **cup canned crushed tomatoes**
- One 2-inch piece of fresh **ginger, thinly sliced**
- 2 **whole cloves**
- 1 **cinnamon stick**
- **Kosher salt and pepper**
- 2½ oz. **fideos or angel hair pasta, broken into 1-inch pieces (about 1 cup)**
- 1 **small bunch of kale, stemmed and coarsely chopped (3 cups)**
- 1 **cup thawed frozen pearl onions, halved**

1. Heat a cast-iron skillet until smoking, 3 minutes. Add the yellow onion cut side down and cook over high heat, without turning, until completely charred, 5 minutes. Transfer the onion halves to a plate.

2. In a large saucepan, heat 1 tablespoon of the olive oil. Add the reserved squash skins and seeds and cook over moderate heat, stirring occasionally, until lightly browned, about 5 minutes. Add the broth, charred onion, tomatoes, ginger, cloves, cinnamon stick and 2 teaspoons of salt and bring to a simmer over moderately high heat. Reduce the heat to low and cook until the broth is a deep golden brown, about 1 hour. Strain the squash broth and return it to the saucepan; keep warm.

3. Meanwhile, preheat the oven to 400°. On a rimmed baking sheet, toss the fideos with 1 teaspoon of the olive oil. Toast in the oven until golden, about 4 minutes. Transfer to a bowl.

4. On the rimmed baking sheet, toss the squash cubes with the remaining 1 tablespoon of olive oil and season with salt and pepper. Roast the squash until beginning to brown but still slightly firm, about 12 minutes.

5. Bring the broth to a simmer. Add the kale and pearl onions and cook over moderately high heat until the onions start to soften, 5 minutes. Add the squash and fideos and cook until the fideos are al dente, 8 minutes longer. Season with salt and pepper and serve. —*Michael Solomonov*

ROOSTER SOUP CO. BROTH
Active **10 min;** Total **6 hr 30 min**
Makes **5 quarts**

- 5 **lbs. chicken carcasses, backs, wings and/or legs**
- 1 **yellow onion, halved**
- 1 **carrot, halved**
- 1 **celery rib, halved**
- 2 **garlic cloves**
- 1 **bay leaf**
- 1 **Tbsp. kosher salt**

In a large stockpot, cover the chicken bones with 6 quarts of water and bring to a boil over moderately high heat, skimming as necessary. Add the remaining ingredients and reduce the heat to a simmer. Cover and cook over moderately low heat until the broth is a light golden color and slightly reduced, about 6 hours. Strain the broth and let cool. —*MS*

Herbed Yogurt Soup with Rice

⏲ Total **45 min;** Serves **4**

- 1 **large egg**
- 2 **Tbsp. all-purpose flour**
- ½ **cup arborio rice, rinsed and drained**
- 1 **quart full-fat plain yogurt**
- ½ **cup each finely chopped mint, cilantro, parsley, and watercress or basil**
- **Kosher salt**
- **Ground cinnamon, for sprinkling**

In a large saucepan, beat the egg with the flour and rice. Whisk in the yogurt and 3 cups of water and cook over moderate heat, stirring frequently, until thickened slightly and the rice is tender, about 30 minutes. Stir in the herbs and cook for 2 minutes. Season the soup with salt. Ladle into wide bowls, sprinkle with cinnamon and serve. —*Naomi Duguid*

Amaranth in Brodo with Egg and Spinach

Active **20 min;** Total **4 hr;** Serves **4 to 6**

Tiny whole-grain amaranth stands in for pastina, the smallest pasta shape. The rich, deep broth is fantastic with the nutty pop of the amaranth.

- 8 **whole chicken legs (4½ lbs.)**
- 1 **lb. beef stew meat, cut into 1-inch pieces**
- 2 **turkey wings**
- 1 **onion, chopped**
- 4 **celery ribs, chopped**
- 2 **carrots, chopped**
- One 12-oz. can **whole tomatoes**
- 1 **tsp. black peppercorns**
- 12 **parsley sprigs plus 1 Tbsp. chopped parsley**
- ½ **cup amaranth**
- 4 **cups baby spinach (4 oz.)**
- 3 **large eggs**
- 2 **Tbsp. freshly grated Parmigiano-Reggiano, plus more for garnish**
- **Pinch of grated nutmeg**
- **Fine sea salt and pepper**

1. In a large pot, combine the chicken, beef and turkey. Fill the pot with 4½ quarts of water and bring to a boil. Cover partially and simmer over moderate heat, skimming off the fat and foam that rise to the surface, until the broth looks clear, about 30 minutes. Add the onion, celery, carrots, tomatoes, peppercorns and parsley sprigs. Simmer until the broth is very flavorful and reduced to 5 cups, about 2½ hours. Strain the broth through a sieve; discard the solids.

2. In a large saucepan, bring the broth to a boil. Add the amaranth, cover and cook over moderately low heat until tender, about 30 minutes. Stir in the spinach.

3. In a small bowl, beat the eggs with the cheese, chopped parsley, nutmeg and ½ teaspoon each of sea salt and pepper. Remove the saucepan from the heat and drizzle in the eggs. Cover the soup and let stand, without stirring, for 8 minutes. Gently stir the eggs to break them into strands. Season the soup with salt and pepper and serve garnished with cheese. —*Marco Canora*

French Onion Soup

Active **1 hr**; Total **2 hr**; Serves **6**

Chef Matt Conroy of Little Prince in New York City makes a hearty beef broth for his richly flavored classic French onion soup. If you make the broth a day in advance and refrigerate it, it's supereasy to skim off the cold solidified fat, and you'll have a soup with a clearer onion flavor.

BEEF BROTH

- **5 lbs. beef neck and shinbones**
- **2 onions, halved**
- **2 leeks, white and light green parts only, chopped**
- **1 carrot, chopped**
- **1 head of garlic, halved**
- **3 thyme sprigs**
- **6 parsley sprigs**
- **2 bay leaves**
- **½ tsp. whole black peppercorns**

SOUP

- **2 Tbsp. canola oil**
- **8 large onions (4 lbs.), thinly sliced**
   Kosher salt and pepper
- **2 Tbsp. unsalted butter**
- **2 Tbsp. all-purpose flour**
   Bouquet garni made with 2 bay leaves, 4 thyme sprigs and 1 tsp. whole black peppercorns
- **1 Tbsp. Cognac**
- **2 Tbsp. apple cider vinegar**

FOR SERVING

- **Toasted baguette slices**
- **4 oz. cave-aged Gruyère, shredded (1½ cups)**
- **4 oz. Emmental cheese, shredded (1½ cups)**
   Chopped chives and cracked black pepper

1. Make the beef broth Preheat the oven to 450°. Arrange the bones on a baking sheet and roast for about 30 minutes, until browned. Transfer to a very large pot and add all of the remaining ingredients. Add 7 quarts of water and bring to a boil. Cook over moderately high heat, skimming as necessary, until reduced by half (to 3½ quarts), about 1 hour. Strain the broth into a large bowl and skim off the fat.

2. Meanwhile, start the soup In a large pot, heat the oil. Add the onions and cook over moderately low heat, stirring frequently, until deep golden, about 1 hour. Season with salt.

3. Stir the butter into the onions until melted. Add the flour and cook over moderate heat, stirring, until the flour is incorporated and the onions are sizzling, 2 to 3 minutes. Add the 3½ quarts of beef broth and bouquet garni and bring to a simmer. Cook until reduced to 10 cups, about 35 minutes. Discard the bouquet garni. Stir in the Cognac and vinegar and season the soup with salt and pepper.

4. Preheat the broiler. Ladle the soup into 6 ovenproof bowls set on a baking sheet. Top with toasted baguette slices. Toss the cheeses together and sprinkle over the bread. Broil 6 inches from the heat for 7 to 8 minutes, until the cheese is melted and golden. Garnish with chives and pepper and serve. —*Matt Conroy*

Chicken-Chile Soup

Total **30 min**; Serves **6 to 8**

- **3 Tbsp. extra-virgin olive oil**
- **2 poblano chiles—stemmed, seeded and thinly sliced**
- **1 onion, chopped**
- **2 garlic cloves, sliced**
- **1½ tsp. ground coriander**
   Kosher salt
- **2 quarts chicken stock or low-sodium broth**
- **4 cups shredded cooked chicken (1¼ lbs.)**
   Two 15-oz. cans hominy, rinsed and drained
   Chopped cilantro and thinly sliced radishes, for garnish
   Lime wedges, for serving

In a large saucepan, heat the olive oil until shimmering. Add the chiles, onion, garlic, coriander and a generous pinch of salt and cook over moderate heat, stirring occasionally, until the chiles are softened, about 8 minutes. Add the stock and bring to a boil. Stir in the chicken and hominy and simmer over moderate heat for 5 minutes. Season with salt. Ladle the soup into shallow bowls, garnish with cilantro and sliced radishes and serve with lime wedges.
—*Justin Chapple*

Stracciatella Soup

Total **15 min**; Serves **4**

Stracciatella means "little rag," which is exactly what the beaten eggs look like once they're cooked in the soup. Jenn Louis, the chef at Lincoln Restaurant in Portland, Oregon, amps up her tasty version of the classic Roman chicken soup by adding peas, carrots and spinach.

- **4 cups chicken stock or low-sodium broth**
- **2 medium carrots, thinly sliced**
- **½ cup thawed frozen peas**
- **3 oz. curly spinach (4 cups)**
- **3 large eggs**
- **2 Tbsp. freshly grated Parmigiano-Reggiano cheese, plus more for garnish**
   Kosher salt and pepper
   Extra-virgin olive oil, for drizzling
   Crusty bread, for serving

In a medium saucepan, bring the chicken stock to a boil. Add the carrots and peas and cook over moderate heat until just tender, about 3 minutes. Add the spinach and cook until wilted, 1 minute. In a small bowl, beat the eggs with the 2 tablespoons of cheese. Slowly drizzle the egg mixture into the soup and cook over moderate heat, stirring, until ribbons form, about 1 minute. Season with salt and pepper. Ladle the soup into bowls, drizzle with olive oil and garnish with grated cheese. Serve with crusty bread. —*Jenn Louis*

Moroccan Split Pea Soup with Sweet-Spiced Pickles

Active **20 min**; Total **1 hr 30 min**
Serves **4 to 6**

- 2 Tbsp. extra-virgin olive oil
- 1 large onion, finely chopped
- 6 garlic cloves, thinly sliced
- 2 tsp. ground cumin
- 2 tsp. sweet paprika
  Kosher salt
- 2 cups green split peas (14 oz.)
- ½ cup finely chopped cilantro, plus leaves for garnish
  Sweet-Spiced Pickles (recipe follows), for garnish
  Warm crusty bread, for serving

1. In a large saucepan, heat the oil. Add the onion and garlic and cook over moderately low heat, stirring, until softened and translucent, about 10 minutes. Stir in the cumin and paprika, season with salt and cook, stirring, until the spices are fragrant, about 2 minutes. Add the split peas and 8 cups of water and bring to a boil. Simmer, stirring, until the peas just start to soften, 20 minutes.

2. Add the chopped cilantro to the saucepan. Cover and cook over moderately low heat, stirring occasionally, until the peas are broken down and the soup is thick, about 40 minutes longer. Season with salt, garnish with pickles and cilantro and serve with crusty bread. —*Tara Stevens*

SWEET-SPICED PICKLES

Total **15 min**; Makes **about 2 cups**

- 3 carrots, peeled and shaved into ribbons with a vegetable peeler
- 4 radishes, thinly sliced
- ½ Fresno or red jalapeño chile, thinly sliced
- 6 Tbsp. sherry vinegar
- 1 Tbsp. sugar
- 1 tsp. salt

In a heatproof bowl, combine the carrots, radishes and chile. In a small saucepan, cook the vinegar, sugar and salt over low heat, stirring, until the sugar and salt dissolve. Let cool for 5 minutes. Pour the brine over the vegetables and serve. —*TS*

MAKE AHEAD The pickles can be refrigerated for up to 2 weeks.

Caldo Verde

Active **30 min**; Total **1 hr**; Serves **4**

Beth Kirby, the blogger behind Local Milk, was inspired to make this potato-and-kale soup after hosting a food photography workshop in Portugal. She gives the soup a savory lift with chorizo and a bit of tang with a splash of sherry vinegar.

- 2 Tbsp. extra-virgin olive oil, plus more for drizzling
- 1 medium onion, finely chopped
- 3 garlic cloves, minced
  Kosher salt
- 1 lb. baking potatoes, peeled and cut into ½-inch pieces
  Two 4-oz. fresh chorizo sausages
  One 8-oz. bunch of Tuscan kale, stems discarded and leaves thinly sliced
- 1 Tbsp. sherry vinegar
- 1 tsp. sugar

1. Preheat the oven to 400°. In a large saucepan, heat the 2 tablespoons of olive oil. Add the onion, garlic and a generous pinch of salt and cook over moderate heat, stirring occasionally, until just starting to soften, about 5 minutes. Add 6 cups of water and the potatoes and bring to a boil. Cover and simmer over moderately low heat, stirring occasionally, until the potatoes are very tender, about 25 minutes.

2. Meanwhile, on a rimmed baking sheet, roast the sausages for about 20 minutes, until an instant-read thermometer inserted in each one registers 165°. Transfer to a carving board and let rest for 5 minutes, then slice crosswise ½ inch thick.

3. Working in batches, puree the soup in a blender until very smooth. Return the soup to the saucepan and bring just to a simmer over moderate heat. Add the kale and simmer until softened, about 3 minutes. Stir in the vinegar and sugar, then season with salt. Ladle the soup into bowls, top with the sliced chorizo and a drizzle of olive oil and serve. —*Beth Kirby*

Hot-and-Sour Soup

Active **25 min**; Total **50 min**; Serves **4**

In *Lucky Peach Presents 101 Easy Asian Recipes*, co-author Peter Meehan champions this lighter, thinner and intensely delicious version of hot-and-sour soup. "We're reclaiming the goopy, satisfying stuff we eat from takeout cartons at home on the couch," Meehan says.

- 1 oz. dried wood ear mushrooms (½ cup)
  Boiling water
- 2 Tbsp. canola oil
- ½ lb. lean pork shoulder, sliced ⅛ inch thick and cut into 1-by-¼-inch strips
- 1 Tbsp. finely chopped garlic
- 1 Tbsp. finely chopped peeled fresh ginger
- ½ cup chopped scallions
- 4 cups chicken stock or low-sodium broth
- ½ lb. soft tofu, cut into ½-inch dice
- ⅓ cup unseasoned rice vinegar, plus more for serving
- 3 Tbsp. soy sauce
- 1 tsp. sugar
- 1 tsp. black pepper
- 1 tsp. toasted sesame oil
- 1 Tbsp. Sriracha, plus more for serving
  Kosher salt
- 2 large eggs, beaten

1. In a small heatproof bowl, cover the mushrooms with boiling water and let stand until softened, about 30 minutes. Drain and coarsely chop the mushrooms; discard the soaking water.

2. In a large saucepan, heat the canola oil. Add the pork, garlic, ginger and scallions and cook over moderately high heat, stirring occasionally, until the pork is golden brown, about 3 minutes. Stir in the stock and add the tofu, ⅓ cup of vinegar, the soy sauce, sugar, pepper, sesame oil, mushrooms and 1 tablespoon of Sriracha. Bring the soup to a simmer and season with salt. While stirring constantly, drizzle in the eggs and cook until strands form, 1 minute. Serve hot, passing rice vinegar and Sriracha at the table. —*Peter Meehan*

Crab Omelet–and–Tomato Soup

Total **1 hr**; Serves **4**

In her unfussy version of the Vietnamese soup *bun rieu cua*, blogger Shu Han Lee skips the traditional method of pounding crab shells and simmering them with pork bones and tomatoes; instead, she prepares a quick broth with chicken stock, fermented shrimp paste and cherry tomatoes. At the end, she swirls in beaten eggs mixed with crabmeat and ground pork to make an omelet right in the fragrant soup.

- 2 Tbsp. vegetable oil
- 4 shallots, minced
- 2 garlic cloves, minced
- 2 tsp. fermented shrimp paste (see Note)
- 1 Tbsp. tomato paste
- 1 quart chicken stock or low-sodium broth
- ½ lb. cherry tomatoes
- 1 Tbsp. Asian fish sauce
- Kosher salt
- 4 large eggs
- 2 Tbsp. Asian chile-garlic paste
- 6 oz. lump crabmeat, picked over for shells
- 4 oz. ground pork
- 6 oz. rice vermicelli
- Boiling water
- 6 oz. mung bean sprouts
- Lime wedges and mint, cilantro and basil leaves, for serving

1. In a large saucepan, heat the oil. Add the shallots and garlic and cook over moderately high heat, stirring occasionally, until golden, 3 to 5 minutes. Stir in the shrimp paste and tomato paste and cook, stirring, until fragrant, about 30 seconds. Add the chicken stock and 1 cup of water and bring to a boil. Reduce the heat to moderate, add the tomatoes and simmer until just starting to pop, about 8 minutes. Using a wooden spoon, lightly crush some of the tomatoes against the side of the pan. Stir in the fish sauce and season the soup lightly with salt.

2. In a medium bowl, beat the eggs with the chile-garlic paste and a generous pinch of salt. Add the crab and pork and, using a fork, stir the mixture well to break up the meat.

3. Bring the soup to a rolling boil over high heat. Stir in a circular motion and pour the egg mixture into the center of the swirl. Stop stirring and simmer the omelet in the soup over moderate heat for 6 minutes, then turn off the heat and stir to distribute the omelet throughout the soup.

4. In a large heatproof bowl, cover the vermicelli with boiling water and let stand until softened, about 10 minutes. Drain well. Divide the vermicelli and bean sprouts among 4 bowls. Ladle the soup on top and serve with lime wedges and mint, cilantro and basil leaves. —*Shu Han Lee*

NOTE Fermented shrimp paste is available at Asian markets and from amazon.com.

Tuscan White Bean and Escarole Soup with Tuna

Total **30 min**; Serves **4**

- ¼ cup extra-virgin olive oil
- 1 onion, chopped
- 3 garlic cloves, chopped
- 10 oz. escarole, chopped
- 2 tsp. minced rosemary
- 6 cups chicken stock or low-sodium broth
- One 15-oz. can cannellini beans, rinsed
- 15 oz. tuna in olive oil, drained
- Kosher salt and pepper
- Shredded Parmesan cheese and crusty bread, for serving

Heat the oil in a pot. Add the onion and garlic and cook over moderate heat, stirring occasionally, until softened, about 10 minutes. Add the escarole and rosemary and cook until the escarole is wilted, 3 minutes. Add the stock, beans and tuna and bring to a boil. Simmer over low heat for 5 minutes. Season with salt and pepper. Serve the soup with shredded Parmesan and crusty bread. —*Justin Chapple*

Shrimp Bisque with Muscadet and Tarragon

Active **30 min**; Total **1 hr**; Serves **4**

This simple, superlight bisque from the heart of France's Muscadet country has a surprisingly deep shrimp flavor.

- 2 Tbsp. unsalted butter
- 1 Tbsp. canola oil
- 1 lb. medium shrimp, shelled and deveined, shells reserved
- 1 small onion, thinly sliced
- 1 garlic clove, crushed
- 1 Tbsp. tomato paste
- ½ cup Muscadet
- ¼ cup heavy cream
- Kosher salt and pepper
- Coarsely chopped tarragon, for garnish

1. In a large saucepan, melt the butter in the oil. Add the shrimp and cook over moderate heat, stirring, until light golden and just white throughout, about 2 minutes. Transfer 8 of the shrimp to a plate to cool; finely chop and reserve them for adding to the finished bisque.

2. Add the reserved shrimp shells, the onion and garlic to the remaining shrimp in the saucepan. Cook over moderate heat, stirring occasionally, until the onion is softened, about 3 minutes. Add the tomato paste and cook, stirring, until lightly caramelized, about 2 minutes. Stir in the wine and cook until almost evaporated, about 1 minute. Stir in 6 cups of water and bring to a simmer. Cook over low heat for 25 minutes.

3. Working in 2 batches, puree the soup in a blender. Strain through a fine sieve set over a medium saucepan, pressing on the solids. Bring the soup to a simmer and stir in the cream. Add the reserved chopped shrimp and season with salt and pepper. Ladle the bisque into bowls and garnish with chopped tarragon. —*Thibaut Clochet*

MAKE AHEAD The bisque can be refrigerated for up to 2 days; rewarm and add the shrimp just before serving.

SHRIMP BISQUE
WITH MUSCADET
AND TARRAGON

MONKFISH STEW WITH
SAFFRON BROTH

Ajo Blanco with Crab and Green Grapes

Active **40 min**; Total **4 hr 40 min plus overnight soaking**; Serves **6**

Making almond milk is supersimple, and crucial for this recipe from F&W Best New Chef 2015 Katie Button of Cúrate in Asheville, North Carolina. Just soak almonds overnight in water, puree in a blender, then strain. Be sure to use skin-on raw almonds for the most flavor.

1¼ lbs. raw almonds (3½ cups)
1   packed cup cubed (1 inch) crustless country bread
2   garlic cloves
2   Tbsp. sherry vinegar, plus more for seasoning
2   tsp. kosher salt, plus more for seasoning
¾   cup extra-virgin olive oil
8   oz. lump crabmeat
18 green grapes, halved

1. In a food processor, pulse the almonds until finely chopped. Transfer to a large bowl and add 7 cups of cold water. Mix well, cover and refrigerate overnight.

2. Working in 2 batches, puree the almonds with their soaking liquid in a blender until smooth. Strain the almond puree through a fine sieve, pressing on the solids. Discard the solids. You should have about 6 cups of almond milk. (If you don't have enough, add cold water to make 6 cups.)

3. In a blender, combine 3 cups of the almond milk with ½ cup of the bread cubes, 1 garlic clove, 1 tablespoon of the vinegar and 1 teaspoon of the salt. Puree until smooth. With the machine on, slowly drizzle in half of the olive oil. Transfer the soup to the large bowl. Repeat with the remaining almond milk, bread, garlic, vinegar, salt and olive oil. Strain the soup through a fine sieve into another large bowl, pressing gently on the solids. Cover and refrigerate until very cold, about 4 hours.

4. Season the soup with salt and vinegar. Spoon the crab and grapes into 6 bowls, add the soup and serve. —*Katie Button*

MAKE AHEAD The soup can be refrigerated for up to 3 days.

WINE Briny, creamy fino sherry: El Maestro Sierra.

Smoky Mussel Stew

Active **40 min**; Total **1 hr**
Serves **12 as an hors d'oeuvre**

¾   lb. Yukon Gold potatoes, peeled and cut into ½-inch pieces
3   Tbsp. extra-virgin olive oil
    Kosher salt and pepper
½   lb. brussels sprouts, quartered
1   lb. fresh mussels, scrubbed and debearded
1   cup dry white wine
1   medium white onion, quartered through the core and peeled
2   medium shallots, chopped
2   Tbsp. unsalted butter
2   parsley sprigs, plus chopped parsley for garnish
2   thyme sprigs
1   bay leaf
    Pinch of cayenne
2   cups heavy cream
1   large egg yolk
½   lb. smoked mussels
2   Tbsp. fresh lemon juice

1. Preheat the oven to 375°. On one side of a large rimmed baking sheet, toss the potatoes with 2 tablespoons of the olive oil and season with salt and pepper. On the other side of the baking sheet, toss the brussels sprouts with the remaining 1 tablespoon of olive oil and season with salt and pepper. Roast for about 25 minutes, until the vegetables are tender and charred in spots.

2. Meanwhile, in a large saucepan, combine the fresh mussels with the wine, onion, shallots, butter, parsley sprigs, thyme, bay leaf and cayenne and bring to a boil over high heat. Cover and cook over moderately high heat until the mussels open, 6 to 8 minutes. Using a slotted spoon, transfer the mussels to a bowl. Remove the mussels from their shells; discard the shells and any mussels that do not open. Strain the broth through a fine sieve.

3. Wipe out the saucepan. Add the strained broth along with any accumulated mussel broth from the bowl and bring to a boil. Add the cream and bring just to a boil.

4. In a small bowl, beat the egg yolk with 2 tablespoons of the hot cream, then gradually whisk the mixture into the saucepan. Simmer the soup over moderate heat, whisking, until thickened slightly, 3 to 5 minutes. Stir in the brussels sprouts, potatoes and the cooked mussels and smoked mussels and simmer until hot, about 3 minutes. Stir in the lemon juice and season with salt and pepper. Serve the stew in small ramekins, garnished with chopped parsley. —*Matt Jennings*

WINE Vivid, briny Muscadet: 2014 Domaine de la Louvetrie Sur Lie.

Monkfish Stew with Saffron Broth

⏲ Total **35 min**; Serves **4**

¼   cup extra-virgin olive oil
1½ lbs. monkfish fillet, trimmed and sliced crosswise 1 inch thick
    Kosher salt and pepper
2   shallots, thinly sliced
2   carrots, sliced into ½-inch rounds
1   tsp. fresh thyme leaves
    Pinch of saffron threads
⅓   cup dry white wine
    Basil leaves, for garnish
    Steamed or mashed potatoes, for serving

1. In an enameled cast-iron casserole, heat 2 tablespoons of the olive oil. Season the monkfish with salt and pepper and cook over moderate heat, turning, until light golden, 3 minutes. Using a slotted spoon or tongs, transfer the monkfish to a plate.

2. Add the remaining 2 tablespoons of oil and the shallots to the casserole and cook over moderate heat, stirring occasionally, until softened, about 2 minutes. Add the carrots and cook, stirring occasionally, until light golden, about 5 minutes. Stir in the thyme, saffron and wine and cook until reduced by half, about 1 minute. Add ½ cup of water along with the monkfish and any accumulated juices. Bring just to a simmer, cover and cook over low heat until the vegetables are tender and the fish is cooked through, about 15 minutes. Spoon the stew into shallow bowls, garnish with basil and serve with potatoes. —*Mimi Thorisson*

WINE Orange-scented, medium-bodied white Bordeaux: 2013 Château Graville-Lacoste.

DIY SEAFOOD GUMBO

Chef **SLADE RUSHING** of the legendary Brennan's restaurant in New Orleans shares his secret to great gumbo: It's all about taking the roux "where it needs to go," from a pale beige to a dark, toasty mahogany brown.

Seafood Gumbo

Active **1 hr 20 min**; Total **3 hr 50 min**
Serves **8**

This superlative gumbo is loaded with Louisiana seafood, but you can substitute your local fish and shellfish.

CRAB STOCK

- 1 **onion, quartered**
- 1 **head of garlic, halved**
- 2 **bay leaves**
- 1 **Tbsp. whole black peppercorns**
- 2 **gallons water**
- 6 **live blue crabs**

GUMBO

- 1 **cup canola oil**
- ½ **cup all-purpose flour**
- ¾ **lb. andouille sausage, finely chopped (2 cups)**
- 1 **large onion, finely chopped**
- 2 **celery ribs, finely chopped**
- 1 **red bell pepper, finely chopped**
- 1 **green bell pepper, finely chopped**
- ½ **cup finely chopped garlic (12 large cloves)**
- ½ **lb. okra, thickly sliced**
- 1 **lb. tomatoes, finely chopped**
- ½ **tsp. filé powder (see Note)**
- ⅛ **tsp. Creole seasoning, such as Zatarain's**
- 2 **thyme sprigs**
- 1 **bay leaf**
- 1 **Tbsp. kosher salt**
- 1 **lb. jumbo lump crabmeat, picked over**
- 1 **lb. large shrimp, shelled and deveined**
- 2 **dozen freshly shucked oysters**
- 2 **Tbsp. hot sauce, such as Crystal or Tabasco, plus more for serving**
  Basmati rice and sliced scallions, for serving

MAKE THE CRAB STOCK

1. In a large pot, combine all of the ingredients except the crabs and bring to a boil. Add the crabs and simmer briskly over moderate heat for 1 hour, skimming as necessary. Strain the stock into a pot. You should have about 12 cups; add water if necessary, and reserve any extra stock for another use. Discard the crabs.

MAKE THE GUMBO

2. In a large pot, heat the oil. Whisk in the flour and cook over moderately low heat, whisking constantly, until the roux is deep mahogany brown with a nutty aroma, about 40 minutes.

3. Stir in the andouille, onion, celery, red and green bell peppers, garlic and okra and cook, stirring occasionally, until the vegetables soften, about 10 minutes. Add the tomatoes, filé powder, Creole seasoning, thyme, bay leaf, salt and the 12 cups of crab stock. Simmer over moderate heat for 1 hour and 30 minutes, stirring occasionally.

4. Stir in the crabmeat, shrimp, oysters and 2 tablespoons of hot sauce and cook until the shrimp are white throughout, about 3 minutes. Discard the thyme sprigs and bay leaf. Ladle the gumbo into bowls and top with rice. Garnish with scallions; serve with hot sauce.

NOTE Filé powder is made from ground, dried sassafras leaves. It is available from cajungrocer.com.

MAKE AHEAD The gumbo can be prepared 3 days ahead through Step 3. Reheat gently and cook the seafood just before serving.

WINE Fragrant, honeyed Loire Valley Chenin Blanc: 2011 Domaine des Baumard Savennières.

ROUX LESSON

The roux is only done when "it smells like a roomful of toasted hazelnuts," says Rushing.

1

START Heat the oil until hot, add the flour and whisk over moderately low heat until it is thoroughly incorporated.

2

WHISK Cook the roux, whisking constantly; it will turn light brown after about 15 minutes.

3

FINISH The roux is done when it is a deep, dark mahogany color and has a toasty aroma.

FINISHING THE DISH
Rushing tops each bowl of his seafood gumbo with just a small scoop of basmati rice and sliced scallions.

HUNTER'S
CHICKEN STEW

Hunter's Chicken Stew

Active **40 min**; Total **1 hr 15 min**; Serves **4**

- 4 Tbsp. unsalted butter
  One 4-lb. chicken, cut into 8 pieces
  Kosher salt and pepper
  All-purpose flour, for dusting
- 1 large onion, thinly sliced
- 2 large shallots, sliced
- 2 large garlic cloves, sliced
- ¾ cup dry white wine
- 1 Tbsp. tomato paste
  One 15-oz. can diced tomatoes
- ½ cup chicken stock
- ½ oz. dried porcini mushrooms, rinsed
- 2 thyme sprigs
- 1 bay leaf
- ½ lb. cremini mushrooms, halved
  Chopped parsley, for garnish

1. In a large enameled cast-iron casserole, melt 2 tablespoons of the butter. Season the chicken with salt and pepper and dust with flour. Add half of the chicken to the casserole and cook over moderately high heat, turning occasionally, until browned all over, about 7 minutes. Transfer to a plate. Repeat with the remaining butter and chicken.

2. Add the onion, shallots, garlic and a generous pinch each of salt and pepper to the casserole and cook over moderately high heat, stirring occasionally, until softened, about 5 minutes. Add the wine and tomato paste and simmer until slightly reduced, 2 minutes. Add the tomatoes, stock, porcini, thyme and bay leaf and bring to a boil. Nestle the chicken in the sauce, cover and simmer over moderately low heat until nearly cooked, about 25 minutes. Stir in the cremini mushrooms and cook, uncovered, until the chicken is cooked through, about 12 minutes. Discard the thyme sprigs and bay leaf. Transfer the stew to plates, garnish with parsley and serve. —*Mimi Thorisson*

SERVE WITH Roasted potatoes.

WINE Earthy, red-berried red Burgundy: 2010 Joseph Faiveley.

Chunky Snapper and Root Vegetable Chowder

Total **1 hr 30 min**; Serves **8**

- 1 Tbsp. canola oil
- 4 oz. thick-cut bacon, cut into ¼-inch dice
- 1 yellow onion, chopped
- ½ cup all-purpose flour
- 5 cups fish stock, clam juice or chicken broth, warmed
- 3 baking potatoes (1¾ lbs.), peeled and cut into 1-inch pieces
- 3 turnips (10 oz.), peeled and cut into 1-inch pieces
- 2 parsnips (10 oz.), peeled and cut into 1-inch pieces
- 1 celery root (1 lb.), peeled and cut into 1-inch pieces
- 1½ tsp. chopped thyme
- 3 cups whole milk
- 1½ lbs. skinless red snapper fillet, cut into 1½-inch pieces
- ¼ cup fresh lemon juice
- 1 tsp. Worcestershire sauce
  Hot sauce
- 2 Tbsp. chopped parsley
  Kosher salt and pepper
  Chopped dill, for garnish

1. In a large enameled cast-iron casserole, heat the oil. Add the bacon and cook over moderate heat until crisp. Add the onion and cook until beginning to brown, about 5 minutes. Whisk in the flour and cook until lightly browned, about 2 minutes. Whisk in the fish stock and bring to a simmer. Add the potatoes, turnips, parsnips, celery root and thyme and simmer over moderate heat until tender, about 20 minutes.

2. Add the milk and cook, stirring occasionally, until the soup is thickened, about 10 minutes. Stir in the snapper, lemon juice, Worcestershire and a dash of hot sauce and cook until the fish is just white throughout, about 5 minutes. Stir in the parsley and season with salt and pepper. Transfer the chowder to bowls and garnish with dill. Serve, passing more hot sauce at the table. —*Mike Lata*

WINE Vivid, full-bodied dry German Riesling: 2013 Leitz Eins Zwei Dry.

Duck Confit and White Bean Stew

Active **45 min**; Total **1 hr 45 min** plus overnight soaking; Serves **8**

This easy take on the laborious French classic cassoulet has just three steps.

- 2 quarts low-sodium chicken broth
- 2 cups dried cannellini beans (¾ lb.), soaked overnight and drained
- 2 Tbsp. extra-virgin olive oil
  Four 6-oz. whole confit duck legs
- 6 large shallots, thinly sliced
- 4 purple or orange carrots, sliced ¼ inch thick
- 2 garlic cloves, crushed
- 2 thyme sprigs, plus leaves for serving
- 1 tsp. herbes de Provence
- 1 small head of radicchio, leaves torn into bite-size pieces

1. In a large pot, combine the chicken broth and beans with 4 cups of water and bring to a boil. Simmer over moderate heat until the beans are tender, about 1 hour.

2. Meanwhile, in a large skillet, heat the olive oil. Add the duck legs and cook over moderate heat, turning occasionally, until crisp and heated through, about 15 minutes. Transfer to a plate to cool slightly, then coarsely chop or shred the meat. Set aside the crispy skin.

3. Add the shallots, carrots, garlic, thyme sprigs and herbes de Provence to the skillet and cook over moderate heat, stirring occasionally, until the shallots are caramelized and completely tender, about 20 minutes. Add 2 tablespoons of water to the skillet and stir, scraping up any browned bits. Discard the thyme sprigs. Stir the shallots and carrots into the beans, then stir in the duck and radicchio. Garnish with thyme leaves and serve topped with the crispy skin. —*Erin French*

MAKE AHEAD The stew (without the radicchio) can be refrigerated for up to 2 days. Reheat gently and add the radicchio just before serving.

WINE Spiced, berry-scented Oregon Pinot Noir: 2013 Evesham Wood Willamette Valley.

Irish Lamb and Turnip Stew

Active **45 min**; Total **3 hr**; Serves **8**

- 3 Tbsp. extra-virgin olive oil, plus more for the roux
- 3½ lbs. boneless lamb shoulder, cut into 2-inch pieces
  Kosher salt and pepper
- 2 small yellow onions, quartered
- 8 garlic cloves, crushed
- 6 Tbsp. all-purpose flour
- 1 cup dry white wine
- 4 cups chicken stock or low-sodium broth
- 3 small turnips, peeled and quartered
- ½ lb. medium carrots, cut into 2-inch pieces
- 8 fingerling potatoes (¾ lb.)
- 3 Tbsp. heavy cream
  Chopped parsley and mint, for garnish
  Crusty bread, for serving

1. In a large enameled cast-iron casserole, heat the 3 tablespoons of oil until shimmering. Season the lamb with salt and pepper. Working in 3 batches, cook the lamb over moderate heat until browned all over, about 8 minutes per batch. Transfer to a large plate. Add the onions to the casserole and cook over moderate heat, stirring, until golden, about 5 minutes. Add the garlic and cook, stirring, until golden, about 2 minutes; transfer to the plate.

2. Remove the casserole from the heat and add enough oil to make 6 tablespoons of fat. Whisk in the flour, then return the casserole to the heat. Add the wine and bring to a simmer over moderate heat, scraping the bottom of the casserole. Stir in 4 cups of water along with the stock and whisk until smooth and simmering, then add the lamb and onion mixture and bring to a simmer. Cover and cook over moderately low heat, stirring occasionally, until the lamb is tender, about 1 hour and 45 minutes.

3. Add the turnips, carrots and potatoes to the casserole and cook until tender, about 30 minutes. Stir in the heavy cream; season with salt and pepper. Ladle the stew into bowls and garnish with chopped parsley and mint. Serve with crusty bread. —*April Bloomfield*

WINE Earthy, spicy Côtes du Rhône: 2012 Domaine la Garrigue Cuvée Romaine.

Brisket and Mushroom Stew

Active **45 min**; Total **5 hr**; Serves **6 to 8**

At the Drake Devonshire Inn in Canada's Prince Edward County, chef Matthew DeMille likes to tinker with classic British recipes, as a nod to the inn's name. He serves this luscious stew with a dollop of whipped cream and a cheddar-jalapeño biscuit on the side.

- 2¼ lbs. beef brisket, trimmed and cut into 1-inch pieces
  One 750-ml bottle dry red wine, such as Pinot Noir
- 10 garlic cloves, crushed
  Sage leaves from 3 sprigs
  Rosemary leaves from 2 sprigs
- ¼ cup vegetable oil
  Kosher salt and pepper
- ½ lb. mixed mushrooms, such as stemmed shiitake, button or oyster, cut into 1-inch pieces
- 6 celery ribs, chopped
- 2 medium yellow onions, chopped
- 2 medium carrots, chopped
- 1 quart beef stock or low-sodium broth
  Whipped cream and Cheddar-Jalapeño Biscuits (p. 259), for serving

1. In a large bowl, cover the meat with the wine and add the garlic, sage and rosemary. Cover with plastic wrap and let stand at room temperature for at least 2 hours or refrigerate overnight.

2. Using tongs, transfer the meat to a paper towel–lined plate; pat dry. Strain the marinade through a fine sieve set over a bowl; reserve the wine and discard the garlic and herbs.

3. In a large enameled cast-iron casserole, heat the oil until shimmering. Season the meat generously with salt and pepper and add half of it to the casserole in a single layer. Cook over moderate heat, turning occasionally, until browned all over, 8 to 10 minutes. Using a slotted spoon, transfer to a large plate; repeat with the remaining meat.

4. Add the mushrooms, celery, onions and carrots to the casserole and cook over moderately high heat, stirring occasionally, until softened and beginning to brown, about 10 minutes. Add the reserved wine to the casserole and simmer until reduced by three-quarters, about 10 minutes. Return the meat and any accumulated juices to the casserole along with the stock and return to a simmer. Cover the casserole and cook over low heat until the meat is very tender, about 2 hours.

5. Ladle the brisket stew into bowls and top with a dollop of whipped cream. Serve immediately, passing the Cheddar-Jalapeño Biscuits at the table. —*Matthew DeMille*

WINE Dark-berried, medium-bodied Pinot Noir: 2012 Hubbs Creek.

Spring Beef Stew

Active **30 min**; Total **2 hr**; Serves **4 to 6**

- 2 Tbsp. extra-virgin olive oil
- 2 lbs. beef chuck, cut into 1½-inch pieces
  Kosher salt and pepper
- 1 qt. chicken stock or low-sodium broth
- 6 shallots, halved
- ½ lb. carrots, cut into 2-inch lengths
- 1½ cups frozen peas
- 5 oz. curly spinach
- 2 Tbsp. chopped dill
  Crusty bread, for serving

1. In a large saucepan, heat the olive oil until shimmering. Season the meat with salt and pepper and add it to the saucepan in a single layer. Cook over moderately high heat, turning occasionally, until browned all over, about 10 minutes. Add the stock and shallots and bring to a boil. Simmer over low heat until the meat is tender, about 1½ hours.

2. Add the carrots to the saucepan and simmer until tender, about 12 minutes. Add the peas, spinach and dill and cook until the spinach is wilted, about 2 minutes. Ladle the stew into bowls and serve with crusty bread. —*Justin Chapple*

Asian Beef Stew

Active **45 min**; Total **3 hr 30 min**; Serves **4**

Jasmine and Melissa Hemsley, the British sisters behind the Hemsley + Hemsley wellness blog, invigorate this stew with fish sauce, Asian spices and lemon juice. "We both just love sour flavors," says Jasmine. "It's our Filipino mum's influence."

- 2 **Tbsp. coconut oil**
- 5 **lbs. English-cut short ribs**
  Sea salt and pepper
- 1 **red onion, finely chopped**
- 3 **garlic cloves, finely chopped**
- 3 **Tbsp. finely chopped peeled fresh ginger**
- 1 **tsp. Chinese five-spice powder**
- 3 **whole star anise pods**
- 3 **large carrots, peeled and cut into 2-inch pieces**
- 2 **celery ribs, cut into 1-inch pieces**
- 3 **Tbsp. Asian fish sauce**
  One 14.5-oz. can crushed tomatoes in juice
- 2 **cups beef stock or broth**
- 4 **cups stemmed curly spinach (4 oz.)**
- 1 **Tbsp. fresh lemon juice**
  Chopped cilantro, for garnish

1. In a large enameled cast-iron casserole, heat the coconut oil. Season the ribs with salt and pepper. Working in 2 batches, brown the ribs over moderately high heat, turning, 4 to 5 minutes per batch. Transfer the ribs to a large plate. Add the onion, garlic and ginger to the casserole and cook over moderate heat, stirring, until golden, about 3 minutes. Stir in the five-spice powder, then add the star anise, carrots, celery and fish sauce and cook, stirring, for 1 minute. Add the tomatoes, stock and short ribs to the casserole and bring to a simmer. Cover and cook over moderately low heat, turning the ribs every hour, until they are very tender, about 2½ hours.

2. Discard the star anise. Stir the spinach and lemon juice into the casserole and season with salt and pepper. Ladle the stew into bowls and garnish with cilantro.
—*Jasmine and Melissa Hemsley*

WINE Peppery, fruit-dense California Syrah: 2013 McManis Family Vineyards.

Autumn Oxtail Stew

Active **45 min**; Total **3 hr 45 min plus overnight marinating**; Serves **4**

Chef Dave Beran of Next in Chicago uses warm spices—cinnamon, peppercorns and juniper—to punch up this hearty recipe. He also adds pears and apples, which give the stew a lovely fruitiness.

- 6 **sprigs each of rosemary, thyme and parsley**
- 1½ **Tbsp. black peppercorns**
  One 3-inch cinnamon stick
- ½ **Tbsp. juniper berries**
- 1 **bay leaf**
- 4 **lbs. meaty oxtails, cut into pieces**
- 2 **cups dry red wine**
- 5 **cups chicken stock or low-sodium broth**
- 6 **garlic cloves, crushed**
- 4 **small carrots, cut into 1-inch pieces**
- 4 **tomatoes, cut into 1½-inch pieces**
- 1 **celery rib, cut into 1-inch pieces**
- 1 **small onion, cut into 1-inch pieces**
- 1 **fennel bulb, cored and cut into 1-inch pieces**
- 1 **leek, light green and white parts only, sliced 1 inch thick**
- 2 **small Honeycrisp apples, peeled and cut into 1-inch pieces**
- 2 **small Anjou pears, peeled and cut into 1-inch pieces**
  Kosher salt and pepper
  Chopped parsley, for garnish

1. In a piece of cheesecloth, wrap the herbs, peppercorns, cinnamon, juniper berries and bay leaf and tie with kitchen twine. In a large enameled cast-iron casserole, combine the herb and spice bundle, the oxtails, wine and stock; add 2 cups of water. The oxtails should be completely submerged; if necessary, add more water. Cover and refrigerate overnight.

2. Preheat the oven to 350°. Transfer the oxtails to a plate. Bring the marinade to a simmer, skimming off any foam. Add the oxtails and all of the remaining ingredients except the salt, pepper and chopped parsley and bring to a boil. Press a sheet of parchment paper directly on the stew and cover tightly with foil. Braise the oxtails in the oven for about 3 hours, until the meat is very tender. Using a slotted spoon, transfer the oxtails to a plate. Transfer the vegetables to another plate. Discard the herb and spice bundle. If necessary, simmer the cooking liquid until slightly thickened.

3. Pick the oxtail meat off the bones in large pieces; discard the bones and any excess fat. Return the meat and vegetables to the casserole and bring to a simmer; cook for 5 minutes, until heated through. Season the stew with salt and pepper, garnish with chopped parsley and serve.
—*Dave Beran*

MAKE AHEAD The oxtail stew can be refrigerated for up to 3 days; reheat gently before serving.

WINE Medium-bodied, black cherry–rich Oregon Pinot Noir: 2012 Rex Hill Willamette Valley.

For this New Year's Day lunch, chef Helene Henderson of L.A.'s Malibu Farm tosses orecchiette with black-eyed peas—a "lucky" ingredient (recipe, p. 98).

PASTA & NOODLES

ANGRY SHRIMP
SPAGHETTINI
Recipe, page 97

Spaghetti with Fresh Tomato Pesto

⏱ Total **25 min**; Serves **6 to 8**

Debi Mazar and her husband, Gabriele Corcos, hosts of the Cooking Channel's show *Extra Virgin*, spend summers at their rustic villa in Tuscany. "We don't have a TV, so most of the fun happens in the garden," says Corcos. They turn their meaty plum tomatoes into a rich uncooked sauce.

1½ lbs. plum tomatoes

½ cup pine nuts (3 oz.)

3 small garlic cloves, crushed

½ cup freshly grated Parmigiano-Reggiano cheese, plus shavings for garnish

⅓ cup extra-virgin olive oil, plus more for drizzling

Kosher salt and pepper

1 lb. spaghetti

Basil leaves, for garnish

1. Bring a medium saucepan of water to a boil. Fill a large bowl with ice water. Using a sharp paring knife, mark an X on the bottom of each tomato. Add the tomatoes to the saucepan and blanch just until the skins start to peel, about 30 seconds. Transfer the tomatoes to the ice bath to cool. Peel and transfer to a blender.

2. In a small skillet, toast the pine nuts over moderately low heat, stirring, until golden, about 5 minutes. Add to the tomatoes in the blender, along with the garlic, ½ cup of grated cheese and ⅓ cup of olive oil; puree until smooth. Season with salt and pepper.

3. In a large pot of salted boiling water, cook the spaghetti until al dente; drain and transfer to a large bowl. Add the tomato sauce and toss to coat evenly. Drizzle the pasta with olive oil, garnish with cheese shavings and basil leaves and serve.
—*Debi Mazar and Gabriele Corcos*

MAKE AHEAD The sauce can be refrigerated overnight. Bring to room temperature before tossing with the spaghetti.

WINE Bright, fruity Italian red: 2013 Argiano Rosso di Montalcino.

Spaghetti with Fresh Zucchini Pesto

Total **50 min**; Serves **6**

¾ cup blanched almonds (4½ oz.)

½ cup extra-virgin olive oil

1 garlic clove, thinly sliced

Pinch of crushed red pepper

3 medium zucchini (1½ lbs.), half of 1 zucchini cut into matchsticks and the remainder chopped into ½-inch pieces

Kosher salt and black pepper

1 lb. spaghetti

2 tsp. finely grated lemon zest

1½ cups freshly grated Pecorino Romano cheese (4 oz.), plus more for serving

½ cup chopped mint, plus more for garnish

1. Preheat the oven to 375°. Spread the almonds on a baking sheet and toast for about 8 minutes, until golden. Let cool, then coarsely chop. Reserve ¼ cup for garnish.

2. In a large skillet, heat 2 tablespoons of the oil. Add the garlic and crushed red pepper and cook over moderate heat, stirring, until fragrant, 1 minute. Add the chopped zucchini, season with salt and pepper and cook, stirring occasionally, until lightly golden, about 10 minutes. Scrape the zucchini into a food processor and add the remaining ½ cup of chopped almonds; pulse to combine. With the machine on, slowly add the remaining 6 tablespoons of oil until combined but still slightly chunky. Season the pesto with salt and pepper.

3. In a large pot of salted boiling water, cook the spaghetti until al dente. Reserve 1 cup of the pasta water, then drain. Off the heat, return the pasta to the hot pot and add the reserved pasta water, the pesto, zucchini matchsticks, lemon zest, 1½ cups of cheese and ½ cup of mint. Stir until well combined and saucy. Transfer the pasta to bowls. Garnish with mint and the reserved almonds. Serve, passing cheese at the table. —*Katie Parla*

WINE Fragrant, apple-scented northern Italian white: 2014 Tiefenbrunner Pinot Bianco.

Zucchini Confetti Pasta with Dill and Walnuts

⏱ Total **25 min**; Serves **4**

Grated zucchini sautéed with anchovies and garlic makes an excellent, quick spaghetti sauce.

½ lb. spaghetti

2 Tbsp. extra-virgin olive oil

3 medium zucchini, grated on the large holes of a box grater and squeezed dry

3 anchovies packed in oil, drained

3 garlic cloves, thinly sliced

1 Tbsp. fresh lemon juice

½ cup freshly grated Parmigiano-Reggiano cheese

Kosher salt and pepper

Chopped dill and toasted chopped walnuts, for garnish

1. In a large pot of salted boiling water, cook the spaghetti until al dente. Drain.

2. Meanwhile, in a large nonstick skillet, heat the olive oil. Add the zucchini, anchovies and garlic and cook over moderate heat, stirring, until the zucchini is tender and the anchovies have dissolved, about 5 minutes. Stir in the spaghetti, lemon juice and cheese and season with salt and pepper. Serve, garnished with chopped dill and toasted chopped walnuts. —*Kay Chun*

WINE Citrusy Chilean Sauvignon Blanc: 2014 Leyda.

Spaghetti with Radish-Greens Pesto

Total **30 min**; Serves **4**

In place of the radish tops here, you can use any other slightly pungent greens, such as watercress, arugula or mustard.

- 2 **garlic cloves, crushed**
- **Greens from 1 big bunch of radishes (8 loosely packed cups), chopped**
- ¼ **cup parsley leaves**
- ¾ **cup roasted salted pumpkin seeds (3 oz.), plus more for garnish**
- ¾ **cup extra-virgin olive oil**
- 1 **cup freshly grated Parmigiano-Reggiano cheese, plus more for garnish**
- **Kosher salt and pepper**
- 12 **oz. spaghetti**
- 2 **Tbsp. fresh lemon juice**

1. In a food processor, combine the garlic, greens, parsley leaves and the ¾ cup of pumpkin seeds; pulse until finely chopped. With the machine on, slowly drizzle in the olive oil. Stir in the 1 cup of cheese. Season with salt and pepper.

2. In a pot of salted boiling water, cook the spaghetti until al dente. Drain, reserving 1 cup of the pasta water. Return the pasta to the pot. Add the pesto, lemon juice and ½ cup of the pasta water. Season with salt and pepper and toss over low heat until coated, about 2 minutes; add more pasta water if a thinner consistency is desired.

3. Transfer the pasta to bowls and garnish with pumpkin seeds and cheese.
—*Kay Chun*

WINE Lively, medium-bodied white: 2014 Frenzy Marlborough Sauvignon Blanc.

Ricotta Cavatelli with Nut Ragout

Active **1 hr 45 min**; Total **3 hr 15 min**
Serves **6**

Chef Philip Krajeck makes incredibly tender pasta at Rolf and Daughters in Nashville, but if you don't want to follow his recipe, you can substitute store-bought fresh cavatelli or gnocchi instead. Toasted Southern nuts replace meat in the richly flavored ragout.

RAGOUT

- 1¼ **cups pecans, coarsely chopped**
- ½ **cup raw peanuts, coarsely chopped**
- 2 **Tbsp. extra-virgin olive oil**
- ⅓ **cup sliced garlic**
- 2 **thyme sprigs**
- 2 **bay leaves**
- 1 **rosemary sprig**
- ¼ **cup dry white wine**
- **One 28-oz. can plus one 15-oz. can crushed tomatoes**
- 2 **Tbsp. unsalted butter**
- **Kosher salt and pepper**

CAVATELLI

- 2¼ **cups Italian 00 flour (available at specialty food stores)**
- 1 **cup fresh ricotta cheese**
- 1 **large egg**
- 1½ **tsp. kosher salt**
- **Freshly grated Parmigiano-Reggiano cheese, for serving**

1. Make the ragout Preheat the oven to 300°. Shake the nuts in a fine sieve to remove any fine crumbs. In a large oven-proof saucepan, heat the oil. Add the garlic and stir over moderate heat until fragrant, 30 seconds. Add the nuts and cook, stirring, until well toasted, about 5 minutes. Add the thyme, bay leaves, rosemary and wine and cook until the wine is evaporated, about 2 minutes. Add the 28 ounces of tomatoes and bring to a boil. Partially cover the ragout and bake for about 1½ hours, until thickened and the nuts are tender.

2. Meanwhile, make the cavatelli In a stand mixer fitted with the paddle, combine the flour with the ricotta, egg and salt and beat at medium speed until a dough just starts to form, about 1 minute. Attach the dough hook and beat at medium speed until a ball forms, 2 to 3 minutes. Scrape the dough out onto an unfloured work surface and knead until smooth. Wrap in plastic and let stand at room temperature for 1 hour.

3. Cut the dough into 4 pieces. Work with 1 piece at a time; cover the remaining pieces with plastic wrap. On an unfloured work surface, roll the dough into a ½-inch-thick rope. Cut the rope into ¼-inch pieces. Roll each piece into a 1½-inch-long strip. Using the front side of a table knife, press each strip of dough against the work surface, pulling the knife toward you to form a curling strip. Transfer to a lightly floured baking sheet. Repeat with the remaining dough and let stand at room temperature for 30 minutes.

4. Stir the 15 ounces of tomatoes into the saucepan and bring the ragout to a simmer over moderately low heat. Stir in the butter and season with salt and pepper. Discard the thyme, bay leaves and rosemary.

5. In a saucepan of salted boiling water, cook the cavatelli until al dente, 3 to 5 minutes. Drain the pasta, reserving ½ cup of the cooking water. Toss the cavatelli with the reserved cooking water and half of the nut ragout (reserve the remaining ragout for another dish). Serve with the cheese.
—*Philip Krajeck*

MAKE AHEAD The ragout can be refrigerated for 5 days or frozen for 1 month.

WINE Juicy, red-berried Sangiovese: 2012 Col d'Orcia Rosso di Montalcino.

Pappardelle with Summer Squash and Arugula-Walnut Pesto

⏱ Total **45 min;** Serves **4 to 6**

This recipe is a fantastic showcase for ultrafresh summer squash. F&W's Kay Chun cuts zucchini and yellow squash lengthwise into ribbons on a mandoline, then tosses them with hot pasta so they just barely cook.

- ¾ cup walnut halves
- 4 cups packed arugula leaves (4 oz.)
- ¾ cup extra-virgin olive oil, plus more for drizzling
- ½ tsp. finely grated garlic
- ½ cup freshly grated Parmigiano-Reggiano cheese, plus shavings for garnish

  Kosher salt and pepper
- 12 oz. pappardelle
- 3 firm, fresh medium zucchini and/or yellow squash (1¼ lbs.), very thinly sliced lengthwise on a mandoline
- 3 Tbsp. fresh lemon juice

1. In a small skillet, toast the walnuts over moderately low heat until golden, about 5 minutes. Finely chop ½ cup of the walnuts; coarsely chop the rest for garnish.

2. In a food processor, pulse 2 cups of the arugula until finely chopped; scrape into a large bowl and stir in the ¾ cup of olive oil, the garlic, grated cheese and finely chopped walnuts. Season the pesto with salt and pepper.

3. In a large pot of salted boiling water, cook the pappardelle until al dente. Drain the pasta and add to the pesto in the bowl. Add the zucchini and toss to evenly coat. Stir in the lemon juice and the remaining 2 cups of arugula and season with salt and pepper. Transfer the pasta to a platter, drizzle with olive oil and garnish with the coarsely chopped walnuts and cheese shavings. —*Kay Chun*

WINE Ripe California Chardonnay: 2013 Buehler Russian River.

Spaghetti with Brussels Sprout and Sausage Breadcrumb Topping

⏱ Total **20 min;** Serves **2**

Thinly sliced brussels sprouts are a quick-cooking alternative to broccoli rabe in this superfast pasta with sausage. The panko mixed in with the spaghetti adds a fabulous crunch.

- ½ lb. spaghetti
- ¼ cup extra-virgin olive oil, plus more for drizzling
- ½ lb. brussels sprouts, thinly sliced (about 3 cups)
- ½ lb. loose pork sausage
- 1 cup panko
- 2 Tbsp. snipped chives

  Kosher salt and pepper

  Lemon wedges, for serving

1. In a large pot of salted boiling water, cook the spaghetti until al dente.

2. Meanwhile, in a large nonstick skillet, heat the ¼ cup of olive oil. Add the brussels sprouts and sausage and cook over moderately high heat, stirring, until the sausage is browned and cooked through, about 5 minutes. Stir in the panko and cook until crisp, 3 minutes. Stir in the chives and season with salt and pepper.

3. Drain the spaghetti and transfer to a bowl. Top with the brussels sprout breadcrumbs, drizzle with olive oil and serve with lemon wedges. —*Kay Chun*

WINE Juicy, light-bodied Italian red: 2012 Bartolo Mascarello Dolcetto d'Alba.

Spaghetti with Clams and Braised Greens

⏱ Total **45 min;** Serves **4**

- ½ cup extra-virgin olive oil
- 8 garlic cloves, crushed
- 4 dozen littleneck clams
- 2 cups dry white wine
- 2 jarred roasted red peppers, drained
- 1 tsp. crushed red pepper
- 1 lb. Swiss chard or collard greens, stemmed and chopped (8 cups)

  Kosher salt and pepper
- ½ lb. spaghetti
- 2 Tbsp. unsalted butter, cubed and chilled
- 1 tsp. finely grated lemon zest plus 1 Tbsp. fresh lemon juice
- ½ cup freshly grated Parmigiano-Reggiano cheese, plus more for garnish

1. In a large pot, heat ¼ cup of the oil. Add half of the garlic and cook over moderate heat, stirring, for 1 minute. Stir in the clams. Add the wine and bring to a boil. Cover and cook over moderately high heat, stirring occasionally, 5 to 7 minutes; as the clams open, transfer them to a baking sheet. Discard any unopened clams. Strain the cooking liquid through a sieve into a blender. Add the roasted peppers and puree until smooth.

2. Wash out the pot, then heat the remaining ¼ cup of oil in it. Add the remaining garlic and cook over moderate heat, stirring, for 1 minute. Stir in the crushed red pepper and Swiss chard in batches until the chard is just wilted, about 3 minutes. Stir in the roasted pepper broth and season with salt and pepper.

3. In a large pot of salted boiling water, cook the spaghetti until al dente; drain. Add the pasta to the Swiss chard mixture along with the butter, lemon zest, lemon juice and the ½ cup of grated cheese. Add the clams and toss to heat through. Transfer the pasta and broth to shallow bowls, garnish with grated cheese and serve. —*Ashley Christensen*

WINE Ripe, lemony Sauvignon Blanc: 2014 Joel Gott.

Spicy Fideos with Mussels and Calamari

Total **50 min**; Serves **4**

Catalan cooks brown short dry noodles called fideos in oil, then simmer them with a bit of stock and fresh seafood. F&W's Kay Chun adds an untraditional topping of parsley and crunchy almonds.

¼ cup chopped parsley

¼ cup chopped marcona almonds

2 Tbsp. extra-virgin olive oil

1 shallot, finely chopped

3 garlic cloves, minced

2 dried chiles de árbol, stemmed and crumbled

7 oz. fideos or angel hair pasta, broken into 1-inch lengths (2 cups)

Kosher salt and pepper

1 small tomato, diced

1 Tbsp. tomato paste

Pinch of saffron threads

1 cup chicken stock or low-sodium broth

One 8-oz. bottle clam juice

1 lb. mussels, scrubbed and debearded

½ lb. cleaned calamari, bodies sliced ¼ inch thick

1. In a small bowl, combine the parsley and almonds.

2. In a large enameled cast-iron casserole or paella pan, heat the oil. Add the shallot, garlic, chiles and fideos, season with salt and pepper and cook over moderately low heat, stirring occasionally, until the fideos are lightly toasted, about 5 minutes. Stir in the tomato, tomato paste and saffron and cook, stirring, until the tomato paste is lightly caramelized, about 3 minutes. Stir in the stock and clam juice and bring to a simmer. Cook over moderate heat until the fideos are al dente, about 5 minutes.

3. Stir the mussels and calamari into the casserole, cover and cook over low heat until the mussels open, 8 to 10 minutes. Season with salt and pepper. Top with the parsley and almonds and serve. *—Kay Chun*

WINE Green apple–scented, dry sparkling wine: 2012 Raventós i Blanc L'Hereu.

Fettuccine with Shrimp

Total **30 min**; Serves **4**

12 oz. fettuccine

4 Tbsp. unsalted butter

8 scallions, thinly sliced

3 garlic cloves, thinly sliced

¾ cup dry white wine

⅔ cup mascarpone cheese

12 oz. cooked shrimp

6 oz. curly spinach leaves

Kosher salt and pepper

1. In a large pot of salted boiling water, cook the pasta until al dente. Drain.

2. Wipe out the pot; melt the butter in it. Add the scallions and garlic and cook over moderately high heat until softened, about 2 minutes. Add the white wine and simmer until reduced by half, about 3 minutes. Stir in the mascarpone. Add the pasta and shrimp and cook, tossing, until the pasta is coated, 3 minutes longer. Stir in the spinach and season with salt and pepper. Serve hot. *—Justin Chapple*

WINE Lemon-zesty Vermentino: 2013 Prelius Vermentino.

Linguine with Clams and Fennel

Total **40 min**; Serves **4**

½ cup extra-virgin olive oil, plus more for drizzling

3 leeks, white and light green parts only, thinly sliced crosswise (3 cups)

12 oz. linguine

½ medium fennel bulb, cored and thinly sliced (½ cup)

2 garlic cloves, minced

4 lbs. Manila clams, scrubbed

1 cup dry white wine

1 cup fish stock

4 tsp. neonata (see Note), sambal oelek or other chunky chile paste

1 Tbsp. fresh lemon juice

2 Tbsp. chopped parsley

Kosher salt and pepper

Torn basil leaves, for garnish

1. In a large pot, heat 2 tablespoons of the oil. Add the leeks and cook over moderate heat, stirring occasionally, until tender and lightly golden, about 8 minutes. Transfer the leeks to a bowl.

2. In a saucepan of salted boiling water, cook the linguine until just al dente; drain.

3. Meanwhile, in the pot, heat 2 tablespoons of the olive oil. Add the fennel and garlic and cook over moderate heat, stirring occasionally, until the fennel is softened, about 3 minutes. Add the clams, white wine and stock and bring to a simmer. Cover and cook until the clams open, 3 to 5 minutes; transfer the clams to a large bowl as they open. Remove the pot from the heat; discard any clams that don't open. Reserve 12 whole clams in their shells; shell the remaining clams.

4. Bring the juices in the pot to a boil and stir in the linguine, neonata, clams and leeks. Add the remaining ¼ cup of olive oil and toss until the pasta is coated and the juices are thickened. Stir in the lemon juice and half of the parsley; season with salt and pepper. Serve the pasta in shallow bowls garnished with basil, the remaining parsley and a drizzle of olive oil. *—Erling Wu-Bower*

NOTE Neonata is an Italian condiment made from salted fish and chiles. It's available at Italian markets and from amazon.com.

WINE Crisp, lightly herbal Italian white: 2013 Punta Crena Ca da Rena Pigato.

LINGUINE WITH
CLAMS AND FENNEL

PENNE WITH CHICKEN
AND PICKLED PEPPERS

Penne with Chicken and Pickled Peppers

Total **30 min**; Serves **4**

12 oz. penne rigate

1½ cups shredded cooked chicken

1½ cups sliced mixed pickled peppers, drained

½ cup extra-virgin olive oil

Kosher salt

1 cup basil leaves

1. In a pot of salted boiling water, cook the penne until al dente. Drain, reserving ½ cup of the cooking water.

2. Wipe out the pot; add the chicken, peppers and oil. Cook over moderate heat, stirring occasionally, until hot, 6 minutes. Add the penne and cooking water and cook, tossing, until hot, 3 minutes. Season with salt, stir in the basil and serve.
—*Justin Chapple*

WINE Fresh, juicy, pear-scented Piedmontese white: 2013 Brovia Roero Arneis.

Angry Shrimp Spaghettini

PAGE 89

Total **30 min**; Serves **4**

1 lb. spaghettini

½ cup extra-virgin olive oil

1 lb. shelled and deveined large shrimp

½ cup panko

2 tsp. crushed red pepper

2 garlic cloves, thinly sliced

1 tsp. finely grated lemon zest

Kosher salt and black pepper

Chopped parsley, for garnish

1. In a large pot of salted boiling water, cook the pasta until al dente. Drain, reserving 1 cup of the cooking water.

2. In a large saucepan, heat the oil. Add the shrimp, panko, crushed red pepper, garlic and zest. Season with salt and pepper; cook over moderately high heat, stirring, until the shrimp are just cooked through, 6 minutes.

3. Add the pasta and reserved cooking water to the saucepan and cook, tossing, until coated, about 2 minutes. Transfer to shallow bowls, garnish with chopped parsley and serve. —*Justin Chapple*

WINE Citrusy Pinot Grigio: 2014 Kris.

Spaghetti with Corn Carbonara and Crab

Total **45 min**; Serves **4**

This brilliant take on carbonara is from F&W Best New Chef 2015 Tim Maslow, of Ribelle in Boston. He uses pureed corn instead of egg or cheese to thicken the sauce and give it deep corn flavor.

7 ears of corn, shucked

1 lb. spaghetti

2 Tbsp. unsalted butter

¼ lb. guanciale, cut into ¼-inch dice

2 medium shallots, minced

2 garlic cloves, thinly sliced

1 Tbsp. fresh lemon juice, plus finely grated zest for garnish

Kosher salt and pepper

½ lb. jumbo lump crabmeat

Extra-virgin olive oil and shichimi togarashi, for serving

1. On a work surface, cut the corn kernels off of the cobs; using the sharp side of the knife, scrape the pulp off the cobs. You should have 4 cups of kernels and pulp. Transfer the kernels and pulp to a blender and puree until smooth. Strain the puree through a fine sieve, pressing on the solids.

2. In a large saucepan of salted boiling water, cook the spaghetti until al dente. Reserve 2 cups of the cooking water, then drain the pasta.

3. Wipe out the saucepan and melt the butter in it. Add the guanciale and cook over moderate heat, stirring occasionally, until the fat is rendered, about 7 minutes. Add the shallots and garlic and cook, stirring, until softened, about 3 minutes. Add the spaghetti, strained corn puree, 1¼ cups of the pasta cooking water and the lemon juice. Cook over moderate heat, tossing, until the sauce is thickened and creamy, 3 to 5 minutes; add more of the cooking water if necessary. Season the pasta with salt and pepper and very gently fold in the crab. Transfer to shallow bowls and drizzle with olive oil. Garnish with lemon zest and shichimi togarashi and serve right away.
—*Tim Maslow*

MAKE AHEAD The strained corn puree can be refrigerated overnight.

WINE Tangy Loire Valley Sauvignon Blanc: 2013 Puzelat-Bonhomme Touraine.

Spaghetti with Crab

Total **45 min**; Serves **4**

When she can, chef Nina Compton of New Orleans's The Old No. 77 Hotel swaps in local Louisiana shrimp for the crabmeat in this otherwise Italian pasta.

12 oz. spaghetti

¾ cup extra-virgin olive oil

¼ cup pine nuts

½ cup panko

Kosher salt

6 scallions, thinly sliced, plus more for garnish

5 garlic cloves, thinly sliced

½ tsp. crushed red pepper

1½ cups clam juice or fish stock

½ cup finely chopped parsley

2 tsp. finely grated lemon zest

½ lb. jumbo lump crabmeat, picked over

1. In a large saucepan of salted boiling water, cook the spaghetti until al dente. Drain the pasta well, then toss with 1 tablespoon of the olive oil. Wipe out the saucepan.

2. Meanwhile, in a small skillet, toast the pine nuts over moderate heat, stirring occasionally, until golden, about 5 minutes. Transfer to a work surface and chop.

3. In the same skillet, heat 1 tablespoon of the olive oil. Add the panko and cook over moderately high heat, stirring frequently, until golden, 3 to 5 minutes. Transfer to a small bowl and season with salt.

4. In the large saucepan, heat ¼ cup of the olive oil. Add the 6 sliced scallions, the garlic and crushed red pepper and cook over moderate heat, stirring, until the garlic is softened, about 3 minutes. Add the clam juice and bring to a boil. Add the spaghetti and cook over moderately high heat, tossing, until most of the clam juice has been absorbed, 3 to 5 minutes. Add the parsley, lemon zest, pine nuts and remaining ¼ cup plus 2 tablespoons of olive oil and season with salt. Toss well. Gently fold in the crabmeat. Transfer the pasta to shallow bowls and garnish with the panko and scallions.
—*Nina Compton*

WINE Salty, lemon-inflected French white: 2014 Domaine de la Pépière Muscadet Sèvre et Maine.

Orecchiette with Bacon, Black-Eyed Peas and Spinach

📷 PAGE 88

⏱ Total **45 min**; Serves **8**

½ lb. bacon, frozen for 15 minutes and very thinly sliced crosswise

¼ cup extra-virgin olive oil

1 large garlic clove, thinly sliced

½ tsp. crushed red pepper

1 lb. cherry tomatoes, halved

2 cups drained canned or thawed frozen black-eyed peas

2 Tbsp. balsamic vinegar

Kosher salt and black pepper

1½ lbs. orecchiette

5 oz. baby spinach

Freshly grated Parmigiano-Reggiano cheese, for serving

1. In a medium skillet, cook the bacon over moderate heat, stirring, until browned and crisp, about 7 minutes. Using a slotted spoon, transfer the bacon to paper towels to drain. Pour off all but 2 tablespoons of fat from the skillet and heat the olive oil in it. Add the garlic and crushed red pepper and cook over moderate heat, stirring, until fragrant, about 2 minutes. Scrape the garlic oil into a serving bowl. Add the tomatoes, black-eyed peas, vinegar and a generous pinch each of salt and black pepper to the bowl and toss well.

2. In a large saucepan of salted boiling water, cook the orecchiette until al dente. Drain well. Add the pasta and the spinach to the tomato mixture and toss until the spinach is just wilted. Season the pasta generously with salt and black pepper and toss again. Sprinkle the bacon on top and serve, passing cheese at the table.
—Helene Henderson

WINE Earthy, berried Santa Barbara County Pinot Noir: 2012 Brewer-Clifton Sta. Rita Hills.

Spaghetti with Bacon, Capers and Mint

⏱ Total **30 min**; Serves **4 to 6**

1 lb. spaghetti

1 Tbsp. extra-virgin olive oil, plus more for drizzling

1 onion, finely chopped

½ lb. slab bacon, cut into ¼-inch dice

2 garlic cloves, finely chopped

1 lb. cherry tomatoes, halved, seeds squeezed out

Kosher salt and pepper

⅓ cup salted capers, rinsed with hot water and drained

½ cup torn mint leaves

Shredded Parmigiano-Reggiano cheese, for serving

1. In a large saucepan of salted boiling water, cook the spaghetti until al dente. Reserve ½ cup of the cooking water, then drain the pasta.

2. Meanwhile, in a large nonstick skillet, heat the 1 tablespoon of olive oil. Add the onion and cook over moderate heat, stirring occasionally, until starting to soften, about 4 minutes. Add the bacon and cook, stirring occasionally, until the bacon and onion are browned, about 5 minutes. Stir in the garlic and cook until fragrant, about 30 seconds. Add the tomatoes and a generous pinch of salt and simmer over moderately low heat, stirring occasionally, until the tomatoes start to soften, about 6 minutes. Stir in the capers and mint and season with salt and pepper.

3. Add the pasta and the reserved cooking water to the tomato sauce and toss over moderate heat for 1 minute. Season with salt and pepper, drizzle with oil and serve, passing cheese at the table.
—Katie Quinn Davies

WINE Perfumed, light-bodied Italian red: 2013 Matteo Correggia Anthos.

Spelt Rigatoni with Chicken Livers, Leeks and Sage

⏱ Total **40 min**; Serves **4 to 6**

Marco Canora, the chef at Hearth in New York City, likes pasta made from spelt, an ancient strain of wheat, but any good-quality whole-wheat rigatoni will work. He also recommends buying livers from pastured chickens because they're more nutritious than those from factory-farmed birds.

1 lb. spelt rigatoni

3 Tbsp. unsalted butter

1 Tbsp. extra-virgin olive oil

3 scallions, thinly sliced

2 leeks, white and light green parts only, thinly sliced

1 large shallot, thinly sliced

Fine sea salt and pepper

2 Tbsp. chopped sage

1 lb. chicken livers—trimmed, patted dry and cut into ½-inch pieces

¼ cup dry white wine

1 cup freshly grated Parmigiano-Reggiano cheese

Lemon wedges, for serving

1. In a large pot of salted boiling water, cook the rigatoni until al dente, about 8 minutes. Drain, reserving ½ cup of the pasta water.

2. Meanwhile, in a large, deep skillet, melt 2 tablespoons of the butter in the olive oil. Add the scallions, leeks and shallot and season with salt and pepper. Cook over moderate heat, stirring occasionally, until softened, about 8 minutes. Stir in the sage.

3. Increase the heat to high. Season the livers with salt and pepper and add them to the skillet. Cook, stirring occasionally, until golden all over, about 2 minutes. Add the wine and cook until evaporated, 1 minute.

4. Add the pasta, ¼ cup of the reserved pasta water, ½ cup of the cheese and the remaining 1 tablespoon of butter to the livers and season with salt and pepper. Remove the skillet from the heat and toss the pasta. Add the remaining pasta water if necessary. Transfer the pasta to plates, top with the remaining ½ cup of cheese and serve with lemon wedges.
—Marco Canora

WINE Minerally, fruit-forward Sicilian red: 2012 Di Giovanna Nerello Mascalese.

SPELT RIGATONI WITH
CHICKEN LIVERS,
LEEKS AND SAGE

Pasta with Guanciale, Radicchio and Ricotta

⏲ Total **30 min**; Serves **6**

L.A. chef Nancy Silverton likes to use a little-known pasta called calamarata—which looks like thick squid rings—to catch the sauce, but any wide, tubular pasta is great.

- ½ **lb. calamarata or other short, wide tubular pasta**
- ¼ **cup extra-virgin olive oil, plus more for drizzling**
- 3 **medium red onions, cut into 8 wedges each**
  Kosher salt and freshly ground pepper
- 6 **oz. guanciale or pancetta, cut into ¼-inch dice**
- ¾ **cup freshly grated Pecorino Romano cheese**
- ¼ **small head of radicchio, torn into 2-inch pieces**
- ⅓ **cup fresh ricotta cheese**
- ¼ **cup chopped walnuts**

1. In a large pot of salted boiling water, cook the pasta until al dente, about 8 minutes. Drain the pasta, reserving ½ cup of the cooking water.

2. Meanwhile, in a large, straight-sided skillet, heat the ¼ cup of olive oil. Add the onions, season with salt and toss to coat with the oil. Cook over high heat until the onions are just beginning to soften, about 1 minute. Stir in ¾ cup of water and cook until the water is evaporated and the onions are just tender, about 6 minutes. Stir in the guanciale and cook, stirring, until the fat is rendered and the guanciale is lightly browned and crisp, about 7 minutes.

3. Carefully drain off all but 2 tablespoons of the fat from the skillet. Stir in the pasta along with the pecorino, radicchio and the reserved pasta water. Cook over high heat, stirring constantly, until hot, about 1 minute. Season the pasta with salt and pepper and top with dollops of the ricotta. Transfer the pasta to a large serving dish, sprinkle with the walnuts and top with a drizzle of olive oil. Serve immediately.
—*Nancy Silverton*

WINE Lively Sangiovese-based Montefalco Rosso: 2010 Tabarrini.

Rigatoni all'Amatriciana

⏲ Total **30 min**; Serves **6 to 8**

Star chef Mario Batali doesn't mess around with his Amatriciana, which is perfectly spicy and porky, with plenty of rich tomato flavor.

- 1 **lb. rigatoni**
- ¼ **cup extra-virgin olive oil**
- ¼ **lb. thick-cut bacon, sliced crosswise ¼ inch thick**
- 1 **medium red onion, halved and thinly sliced**
- ¼ **cup tomato paste**
- 2 **tsp. crushed red pepper**
- 1¼ **cups strained tomatoes**
- ½ **cup freshly grated pecorino cheese, plus more for serving**
- ½ **cup chopped parsley, plus more for garnish**
  Kosher salt and black pepper

1. In a large saucepan, cook the rigatoni until al dente. Drain the pasta, reserving 1 cup of the cooking water.

2. Meanwhile, in a large saucepan, heat the olive oil. Add the bacon and onion and cook over moderately high heat, stirring occasionally, until the onion is softened and the bacon is browned, 5 to 7 minutes. Add the tomato paste and crushed red pepper and cook, stirring, for 1 minute. Stir in the strained tomatoes and bring the sauce just to a simmer.

3. Add the pasta and reserved cooking water to the sauce and cook over moderate heat, tossing, until the pasta is coated. Remove from the heat and stir in the ½ cup each of cheese and parsley. Season the pasta with salt and black pepper and transfer to bowls. Garnish with chopped parsley and serve, passing more cheese at the table. —*Mario Batali*

MAKE AHEAD The sauce can be refrigerated overnight. Reheat gently before adding the pasta.

WINE Herb-scented, dark-berried red: 2013 Vallevò Montepulciano d'Abruzzo.

Rigatoni with Cabbage and Crème Fraîche

⏲ Total **45 min**; Serves **4**

- 8 **oz. pumpernickel bread, torn into pieces (3 cups)**
- 2 **Tbsp. unsalted butter**
- 3 **Tbsp. extra-virgin olive oil**
  Kosher salt and black pepper
- 4 **oz. thick-cut bacon, cut into ¼-inch dice**
- 1 **small onion, chopped**
- 3 **garlic cloves, thinly sliced**
- ½ **tsp. crushed red pepper**
- 1 **head of Savoy cabbage (1½ lbs.), shredded**
- 2 **cups chicken stock**
- 1 **lb. rigatoni**
- ½ **cup crème fraîche**
- ½ **cup grated Parmigiano-Reggiano cheese, plus more for serving**

1. In a food processor, pulse the bread until coarse crumbs form. In a skillet, melt the butter in 2 tablespoons of the olive oil. Add the breadcrumbs and cook over moderately low heat, stirring occasionally, until crisp, about 8 minutes. Season with salt.

2. In a large straight-sided skillet, heat the remaining 1 tablespoon of olive oil. Add the bacon and cook over moderate heat until crisp; transfer to paper towels to drain. Add the onion, garlic and crushed red pepper to the skillet and cook until the onion is softened, about 2 minutes. Add the cabbage and stock and bring to a simmer. Cook, stirring, until almost all of the stock has evaporated, about 8 minutes.

3. Meanwhile, in a large saucepan of salted boiling water, cook the pasta until al dente. Drain, reserving ½ cup of the pasta water. Toss the pasta with the cabbage. Stir in the crème fraîche, the ½ cup of cheese and, if necessary, the reserved pasta water; season with salt and black pepper. Transfer the pasta to bowls and garnish with the breadcrumbs, bacon and black pepper. Serve with additional cheese on the side.
—*Mike Lata*

WINE Brisk, fragrant California Pinot Grigio: 2014 Palmina.

Casarecce with Sausage, Pickled Cherries and Pistachios

⏱ Total **35 min**; Serves **6**

- 2 Tbsp. plus 2 tsp. extra-virgin olive oil
- ½ cup unsalted pistachios
  Kosher salt and black pepper
- 1 lb. casarecce pasta
- ½ lb. sweet Italian sausage, casings removed
- 1 Tbsp. thyme leaves, chopped
- 1 garlic clove, thinly sliced
- 1 tsp. Aleppo pepper
- ¾ cup pitted and chopped Pickled Cherries (recipe follows)
  Shredded Pecorino Romano cheese, for serving

1. In a small skillet, heat 1 teaspoon of the olive oil. Add the pistachios and toast over moderate heat, tossing occasionally, until lightly browned, about 3 minutes. Season with salt and let cool, then coarsely chop.

2. In a large saucepan of salted boiling water, cook the pasta until al dente. Drain, reserving 1 cup of the cooking water. Toss the pasta with 1 teaspoon of the olive oil.

3. In the same saucepan, heat the remaining 2 tablespoons of oil. Add the sausage and cook over moderate heat, breaking up the meat with a wooden spoon, until just cooked through, 5 to 7 minutes. Stir in the thyme, garlic and Aleppo pepper and cook until fragrant, about 1 minute. Add the pasta and reserved cooking water and cook, stirring, until the pasta is hot and coated in a light sauce, about 3 minutes. Stir in the pickled cherries and toasted pistachios and season with salt and black pepper. Transfer to shallow bowls, top with cheese and serve. —*Tom Colicchio*

WINE Tart, cherry-scented Austrian red: 2013 Berger Zweigelt.

PICKLED CHERRIES

Total **10 min plus overnight pickling**
Makes **about 2 cups**

Make a double batch of these pickled cherries—you'll want to put them on everything. Serve alongside pâté, tossed into a salad or on crostini smeared with fresh ricotta.

- 2 cups sherry vinegar
- 1 cup sugar
- 1 lb. sweet cherries

In a medium saucepan, combine the vinegar, sugar and ½ cup of water and bring to a boil over high heat. Add the cherries and return to a boil, then simmer over moderately high heat for 2 minutes. Remove from the heat and let cool completely. Transfer the cherries and brine to a 1-quart container and refrigerate overnight. Drain and pit before serving. —*TC*

MAKE AHEAD The pickled cherries can be refrigerated for up to 2 weeks.

Orecchiette with Sausage, Chickpeas and Mint

⏱ Total **30 min**; Serves **6**

- 1 lb. orecchiette
- ⅓ cup extra-virgin olive oil
- ¾ lb. loose sweet Italian sausage
- 1 large red onion, thinly sliced
  One 15-oz. can chickpeas, rinsed
- 1½ cups torn mint leaves
- 2 Tbsp. fresh lemon juice
  Kosher salt and pepper
  Plain yogurt, for serving

1. In a pot of salted boiling water, cook the orecchiette until al dente. Drain, reserving ¾ cup of the cooking water.

2. Wipe out the pot and heat the olive oil in it. Add the sausage and cook over moderate heat, breaking up the meat with a wooden spoon, until browned and nearly cooked through, about 7 minutes. Add the onion and cook, stirring occasionally, until softened, about 3 minutes. Add the chickpeas, orecchiette and reserved cooking water and toss over moderate heat until the pasta is hot and coated in a light sauce, about 2 minutes. Stir in the mint and lemon juice and season with salt and pepper. Spoon the pasta into bowls and serve with yogurt. —*Justin Chapple*

WINE Vibrant, spice-inflected Barbera d'Alba: 2013 Pio Cesare.

INGREDIENT TIP
Pairing Pasta Shapes and Sauces

CASARECCE "HOME-STYLE"	**ROTINI OR FUSILLI** "SPIRALS" OR "TWISTS"	**CAMPANELLE** "BELLFLOWERS"	**CONCHIGLIE** "SHELLS"	**CAVATAPPI** "CORKSCREWS"
Excellent with pesto or lighter, smoother sauces such as simple marinara.	Fabulous with carbonara, pesto or meaty ragùs or in pasta salad.	Best paired with creamy sauces, butter-and-oil sauces or ground-meat ragùs.	Perfect for soups and stews, tomato and meat sauces or mac and cheese.	Great in baked dishes or tossed with pesto or thick and hearty ragùs.

Baked Semolina Gnocchi

Active **20 min**; Total **1 hr 45 min**; Serves **6**

- **6 cups whole milk**
- **1 tsp. kosher salt**
- **2 cups fine semolina (12 oz.), sifted (see Note)**
- **1 stick salted butter, cut into tablespoons, plus more for greasing**
- **1½ cups freshly grated Parmigiano-Reggiano cheese (about 5 oz.)**
- **2 large egg yolks**

1. Line a baking sheet with parchment paper. In a large saucepan, whisk the milk with the salt and bring just to a boil. While whisking constantly, slowly add the semolina in a steady stream until smooth. Cook over moderate heat, whisking constantly, until slightly thickened, 1 to 2 minutes.

2. Remove the pan from the heat and whisk in 6 tablespoons of the butter until incorporated. Add 1 cup of the cheese and the egg yolks and stir with a wooden spoon until well blended. Scrape the semolina mixture onto the prepared baking sheet and spread in an even layer about ¾ inch thick. Refrigerate until completely cooled, about 1 hour.

3. Preheat the oven to 350°. Butter a 2½- to 3-quart baking dish.

4. Using a 2½-inch round cookie cutter or wineglass, cut the semolina dough into rounds as close together as possible. Reserve the scraps for another use. Arrange the rounds in the prepared dish, overlapping them slightly. Cube the remaining 2 tablespoons of butter and scatter over the top. Sprinkle the remaining ½ cup of cheese over the gnocchi and bake for about 30 minutes, until they are golden brown and hot throughout. Serve warm.
—*Katie Caldesi*

NOTE Fine semolina (semolina flour) is available at specialty stores and online from amazon.com.

MAKE AHEAD The unbaked gnocchi can be assembled, covered and refrigerated overnight.

Potato Gnocchi with Wild Mushroom Ragù and Hazelnuts

Active **1 hr**; Total **2 hr 15 min**
Serves **4 to 6**

This versatile mushroom-and-herb ragù is as good on rigatoni or cheese ravioli as it is on the gnocchi here.

GNOCCHI

- **Four ½-lb. baking potatoes, pierced all over with a fork**
- **2 large eggs, beaten**
- **1½ tsp. kosher salt**
- **¾ cup plus 2 Tbsp. all-purpose flour, plus more for dusting**

RAGÙ

- **4 Tbsp. unsalted butter, softened**
- **2½ Tbsp. finely chopped mixed herbs, such as parsley, chives, tarragon, thyme and chervil**
- **Kosher salt and pepper**
- **¼ cup extra-virgin olive oil**
- **1 small fennel bulb, cored and thinly sliced, fronds chopped and reserved for garnish**
- **2 shallots, thinly sliced**
- **1 lb. mixed mushrooms, such as oyster, cremini and stemmed shiitake, cut into 1-inch pieces**
- **⅓ cup dry white wine**
- **½ cup chicken stock or low-sodium broth**
- **Finely chopped skinned toasted hazelnuts and shredded pecorino cheese, for serving**

1. Make the gnocchi Preheat the oven to 400°. Bake the potatoes directly on the oven rack for about 1 hour, or until tender. Transfer to a work surface and let cool slightly. Halve the potatoes lengthwise. Scoop the flesh into a ricer and rice the potatoes. Spread the riced potatoes on a work surface and let cool completely. Discard the skins.

2. On the work surface, gather the riced potatoes into a loose mound and make a well in the center. Add the eggs and salt to the well. Sift the flour on top and, using a bench scraper, mix everything together until a dough forms. Knead gently until smooth; the dough will be slightly sticky.

3. Line a baking sheet with wax paper and dust with flour. On a floured work surface, cut the dough into 8 pieces and roll each piece into a ¾-inch-thick rope. Cut each rope into 1-inch lengths. Roll the gnocchi against the tines of a fork or a gnocchi paddle to make ridges; transfer to the prepared baking sheet.

4. Make the ragù In a small bowl, blend the butter with the mixed herbs. Season the herb butter with salt and pepper.

5. In a very large skillet, heat the olive oil. Add the sliced fennel and shallots and cook over moderately high heat, stirring, until just starting to soften, 3 to 5 minutes. Add the mushrooms and season with salt and pepper. Cook over high heat, stirring occasionally, until the mushrooms are browned and tender, about 10 minutes. Add the wine and cook, stirring, until absorbed, about 2 minutes. Add the chicken stock and cook over moderate heat, stirring, until the mushrooms are coated in a light sauce, 3 to 5 minutes. Remove from the heat and stir in the herb butter. Season the ragù with salt and pepper; keep warm.

6. In a large saucepan of salted simmering water, working in 2 batches, cook the gnocchi until they rise to the surface, then simmer until cooked through, 1 to 2 minutes longer. Using a slotted spoon, transfer to shallow bowls or a platter.

7. Spoon the ragù over the gnocchi and top with chopped hazelnuts, shredded pecorino and chopped fennel fronds. Serve right away. —*Brad Grimes*

MAKE AHEAD The uncooked gnocchi can be frozen on a baking sheet, then transferred to a sturdy plastic bag and frozen for up to 1 month. Boil from frozen.

WINE Focused, full-bodied Oregon Chardonnay: 2013 Antica Terra Aurata.

Andouille Mac and Cheese

Active **1 hr**; Total **1 hr 30 min**; Serves **4**

At The Heron in New York's Catskill Mountains, chef Paul Nanni grinds and smokes his own andouille sausage for supergenerous portions of Cajun-inspired macaroni and cheese.

- 1½ **cups whole milk**
- 1½ **cups heavy cream**
- 4 **Tbsp. unsalted butter**
- ⅓ **cup all-purpose flour**
- 1 **garlic clove, minced**
- ½ **tsp. finely chopped thyme**
  Pinch of cayenne
  Pinch of freshly grated nutmeg
  Pinch of white pepper
- 1½ **cups shredded mild white cheddar (6 oz.)**
- 1½ **cups shredded sharp cheddar (6 oz.)**
  Kosher salt and black pepper
- 3 **Tbsp. canola oil**
- 1 **cup panko**
- 6 **oz. andouille sausage, diced**
- ¾ **cup finely diced red bell pepper**
- ½ **cup finely diced onion**
- ¼ **cup thinly sliced scallions, plus more for garnish**
- ¼ **cup finely chopped cilantro, plus leaves for garnish**
- ¼ **cup finely chopped parsley**
- 1 **lb. medium pasta shells**
  Hot sauce
  Thinly sliced hot red chiles or jalapeños, for garnish

1. Preheat the oven to 450°. In a small saucepan, bring the milk and cream to a simmer. Keep warm over very low heat.

2. In a medium saucepan, melt the butter. Whisk in the flour and cook over moderate heat until bubbling, 1 to 2 minutes. Add the garlic, thyme, cayenne, nutmeg and white pepper and whisk until the roux is lightly browned, 3 to 5 minutes. Gradually whisk in the milk and cream until the sauce is smooth and bring to a boil. Simmer over moderate heat, whisking, until no floury taste remains, 5 to 7 minutes. Remove from the heat and whisk in the mild cheddar and ½ cup of the sharp cheddar. Season the cheese sauce with salt and black pepper.

3. In a large skillet, heat 1 tablespoon of the oil. Add the panko and toast over moderately high heat, stirring, until lightly browned, 3 minutes. Transfer to a plate. Wipe out the skillet.

4. Heat the remaining 2 tablespoons of oil in the skillet. Add the andouille, bell pepper and onion and cook over moderate heat until the vegetables are lightly browned, 5 minutes. Stir in the ¼ cup of sliced scallions and the chopped cilantro and parsley.

5. In a large pot of salted boiling water, cook the pasta until al dente. Drain well, then return the pasta to the pot. Stir in the cheese sauce and the andouille mixture. Season with hot sauce and salt and black pepper.

6. Spoon the pasta into four 12-ounce gratin dishes set on a baking sheet. Top with the remaining 1 cup of sharp cheddar and the toasted panko. Bake until piping hot, 15 to 20 minutes. Let stand for 5 minutes. Garnish with scallions, cilantro and red chiles and serve with hot sauce.
—*Paul Nanni*

WINE Red-berry-rich Italian red: 2011 Alberice Refosco dal Peduncolo.

Ukrainian Pasta Bake

Active **20 min**; Total **1 hr 30 min**; Serves **4**

Lokshyna are Ukrainian egg noodles, featured here in a hearty baked pasta that is rich with bacon, cottage cheese and eggs.

- 4 **Tbsp. unsalted butter, melted, plus more for greasing**
- ½ **lb. sliced bacon (about 8 slices)**
- ½ **lb. wide egg noodles**
- 2 **cups cottage cheese**
- ¼ **cup half-and-half**
- 2 **large eggs, beaten**
- 1 **tsp. kosher salt**
- ½ **tsp. pepper**
- ½ **cup plain dry breadcrumbs**

1. Preheat the oven to 350°. Butter a 2-quart ovenproof baking dish.

2. Arrange the bacon on a rack over a baking sheet. Bake for 20 minutes, until golden and cooked through. Let cool, then chop. Reserve 2 tablespoons of the bacon fat.

3. Meanwhile, in a large saucepan of salted boiling water, cook the noodles until al dente, about 8 minutes. Drain and run under cold water to cool. Drain well.

4. In a large bowl, combine the noodles, cottage cheese, half-and-half, eggs, bacon and reserved bacon fat. Season with the salt and pepper and mix well, then transfer the pasta to the prepared dish. In a small bowl, mix the breadcrumbs with the 4 tablespoons of melted butter and sprinkle on top of the pasta. Bake for about 45 minutes, until golden and crispy on top. Serve.
—*Sasha Martin*

WINE Robust Malbec: 2012 Durigutti.

DAD'S BUCATINI PIE

Dad's Bucatini Pie

Active **20 min;** Total **1 hr;** Serves **6**

This crispy, creamy skillet-baked pie has been in L.A. chef Vinny Dotolo's family for ages.

- **1 lb. bucatini, broken in half**
- **4 Tbsp. unsalted butter, melted and cooled**
- **6 large eggs, beaten**
- **1½ cups freshly grated Parmigiano-Reggiano cheese (4 oz.)**
- **¾ cup heavy cream**
- **⅓ cup chopped parsley**
- **¼ cup extra-virgin olive oil**
- **1 Tbsp. minced garlic**
- **1 Tbsp. freshly ground pepper**
- **2 tsp. kosher salt**
- **Warm marinara sauce, for serving**

1. Preheat the oven to 375°. Lightly grease a 10-inch cast-iron skillet.

2. In a large pot of salted boiling water, cook the bucatini until al dente. Drain and run under cold water to stop the cooking. Drain well.

3. In a large bowl, whisk together the butter, eggs, cheese, cream, parsley, olive oil, garlic, pepper and salt. Add the pasta and toss to coat thoroughly. Scrape into the prepared skillet and bake for about 30 minutes, until just set. Remove from the oven.

4. Preheat the broiler. Broil the bucatini pie 6 inches from the heat until golden, about 5 minutes. Transfer to a rack and let cool for 10 minutes before cutting into wedges. Serve with warm marinara sauce.
—*Vinny Dotolo*

MAKE AHEAD The pie can be kept at room temperature for 4 to 6 hours before serving.

WINE Zesty Corsican Vermentino: 2012 Antoine Arena Haut de Carco Patrimonio Blanc.

Cacio e Pepe Pasta Pie

Active **30 min;** Total **1 hr 30 min;** Serves **8**

Three types of cheese flavor this show-stopping baked spaghetti pie.

- **1 lb. spaghetti**
- **1½ cups milk**
- **¾ cup freshly grated Parmigiano-Reggiano cheese**
- **3 large eggs, lightly beaten**
- **2½ tsp. ground black pepper**
- **2 tsp. kosher salt**
- **6 oz. Fontina cheese, shredded (2 cups)**
- **6 oz. sharp white cheddar cheese, shredded (2 cups)**
- **Butter, for greasing**

1. Preheat the oven to 425°. In a large pot of salted boiling water, cook the spaghetti until al dente. Drain well.

2. In a large bowl, mix the pasta, milk, Parmigiano, eggs, pepper, salt and 1½ cups each of the Fontina and cheddar. Scrape into a buttered 9-inch springform pan, then sprinkle the remaining ½ cup each of Fontina and cheddar on top. Bake for 35 to 40 minutes, until the cheese is melted and bubbling.

3. Turn on the broiler. Broil the pie 8 inches from the heat for 2 to 3 minutes, until browned on top. Transfer to a rack and let cool for 15 minutes. Remove the ring, cut the pie into wedges and serve.
—*Justin Chapple*

WINE Silky, concentrated northern Italian red: 2012 Foradori Teroldego.

Pasta with Spicy Tofu and Pistachios

Active **50 min;** Total **1 hr 45 min;** Serves **6**

- **1 lb. firm tofu—drained, patted dry and cut into ¾-inch dice**
- **6 garlic cloves, minced**
- **1½ tsp. ground Calabrian chiles or cayenne**
- **¼ tsp. finely chopped thyme**
- **Kosher salt**
- **⅓ cup extra-virgin olive oil**
- **¾ cup finely chopped onion**
- **¾ cup dry white wine**
- **One 28-oz. can tomato puree**
- **2 Tbsp. finely chopped basil**
- **¼ cup canola oil**
- **1 lb. strozzapreti pasta**
- **Chopped pistachios, grated pecorino and dried oregano, for serving**

1. In a medium bowl, toss the tofu with half of the garlic, the chiles, thyme and 2 teaspoons of salt. Cover and refrigerate the tofu for at least 30 minutes or overnight.

2. Meanwhile, in a large saucepan, heat the olive oil until shimmering. Add the onion, the remaining garlic and a generous pinch of salt and cook over moderately high heat, stirring occasionally, until softened, about 7 minutes. Add the wine and simmer until evaporated, about 5 minutes. Add the tomato puree and basil and bring to a boil. Cover partially and simmer over moderately low heat until thickened slightly, 20 to 25 minutes; keep the sauce warm.

3. In a large skillet, heat the canola oil until shimmering. Add the tofu and cook over moderate heat until browned on the bottom, about 2 minutes. Flip the tofu and cook, stirring occasionally, until lightly browned all over, about 3 minutes longer; keep warm.

4. In a pot of salted boiling water, cook the strozzapreti until al dente. Add the pasta to the sauce and cook over moderate heat, stirring, until coated, about 2 minutes. Fold in the tofu and season with salt. Transfer to a platter and garnish with chopped pistachios, grated pecorino and dried oregano. Serve right away. —*Gerard Craft*

WINE Spicy, berried southern Italian red: 2013 Librandi Cirò.

Lemongrass Pork and Rice Noodle Bowl

Active **1 hr**; Total **2 hr 30 min**; Serves **6**

This lemongrass pork from Nhi Mundy, owner of the Bà & Me Vietnamese restaurants in New York and Pennsylvania, is based on an old family recipe.

- ¼ **cup oyster sauce**
- ¼ **cup vegetable oil**
- 2 **medium shallots, minced**
- 1 **lemongrass stalk, inner white bulb only, minced**
- 2 **Tbsp. light brown sugar**
- 2 **Tbsp. honey**
- 2 **Tbsp. Asian chile sauce, plus more for serving**
- 1 **tsp. toasted sesame oil**
- 1 **tsp. white pepper**
- ¼ **tsp. baking soda**
- 6 **garlic cloves, minced**
- **Kosher salt**
- 2 **lbs. boneless pork shoulder, sliced ¼ inch thick**
- 1½ **cups julienned carrot**
- 1 **cup julienned daikon**
- ¼ **cup distilled white vinegar**
- ¼ **cup plus 2 Tbsp. granulated sugar**
- 3 **Tbsp. fresh lime juice**
- 2 **Tbsp. Asian fish sauce**
- 1 **small jalapeño, minced**
- 8 **oz. rice vermicelli**
- **Mint, cilantro, romaine lettuce and sliced cucumber, for serving**

1. In a large bowl, whisk the oyster sauce with the vegetable oil, shallots, lemongrass, brown sugar, honey, 2 tablespoons of chile sauce, the sesame oil, white pepper, baking soda, 5 of the garlic cloves and 1 teaspoon of salt. Add the pork and turn to coat. Refrigerate for 2 hours.

2. Meanwhile, in a medium bowl, toss the carrot and daikon with the vinegar, ¼ cup of the granulated sugar and ¼ cup of water. Let stand for 30 minutes. Drain well and refrigerate until chilled.

3. In a small bowl, stir ¼ cup of water with the lime juice, fish sauce and jalapeño. Add the remaining garlic clove and 2 tablespoons of granulated sugar and stir until the sugar is dissolved.

4. In a large saucepan of salted boiling water, cook the vermicelli until al dente. Drain and rinse with cool water. Pat dry and transfer to bowls.

5. Light a grill. Remove the pork from the marinade, scraping off any excess. Grill over high heat, turning, until lightly charred and just cooked through, 3 to 5 minutes. Top the noodles with the pork and some of the pickled vegetables. Serve with mint, cilantro, romaine, cucumber and the chile-lime sauce. —*Nhi Mundy*

WINE White-peach-scented, full-bodied Rhône white: 2014 Château L'Ermitage Blanc.

Udon with Preserved Mustard Greens and Chile Sauce

Active **45 min**; Total **4 hr 30 min**; Serves **4**

At the forthcoming San Francisco restaurant Fat Noodle, chef Josh Skenes will make his rich broth with fresh kelp. Home cooks may want to use store-bought kombu, a readily available dried kelp.

- 12 **oz. mustard greens, stems discarded and leaves torn**
- **Kosher salt**
- **One 3-lb. chicken, cut into 12 pieces**
- **One 4-inch piece of kelp or kombu, rinsed**
- 2 **Fresno chiles—stemmed, seeded and thinly sliced**
- 1 **Tbsp. Asian fish sauce**
- 1 **Tbsp. fresh lime juice**
- 1 **Tbsp. mala sauce or other preserved chile flakes in oil (see Note)**
- **Two 8-oz. packages frozen udon noodles**

1. In a large bowl, toss the mustard greens with 1 teaspoon of salt. Gently massage the greens until just starting to wilt. Let stand at room temperature for 20 minutes, tossing occasionally. Gently squeeze the excess water from the mustard greens and drain well. Transfer the greens to a 1-pint glass jar, cover and let stand at room temperature for at least 4 hours or overnight.

2. Meanwhile, in a large saucepan, cover the chicken and kelp with 12 cups of water. Add a generous pinch of salt and bring to a boil. Simmer over low heat until the broth is richly flavored, about 2½ hours, skimming off the foam as it rises to the surface. Strain the broth through a fine sieve into a heatproof bowl; you should have about 4 cups. Reserve the chicken for another use. Return the broth to the saucepan, cover and keep hot.

3. In a small bowl, whisk the Fresno chiles with the fish sauce, lime juice and mala sauce. Season lightly with salt.

4. In a large saucepan of boiling water, cook the udon until tender, about 2 minutes. Drain well and transfer to 4 warm bowls. Ladle the hot broth over the udon and top with some of the preserved mustard greens. Serve hot, passing the chile sauce at the table. —*Joshua Skenes*

NOTE Mala sauce is a Chinese chile sauce with Sichuan peppercorns and spices. It is available at Asian markets or online.

MAKE AHEAD The preserved mustard greens, rich broth and pickled chile sauce can be refrigerated separately for up to 3 days.

Hansen & Lydersen in London smokes salmon over juniper-infused hay. The recipe has been handed down through generations of Norwegian fishmongers.

SEAFOOD

SPICY COCONUT
SHRIMP
Recipe, page 132

CARAWAY SALMON
WITH RYE BERRY
AND BEET SALAD

Caraway Salmon with Rye Berry and Beet Salad

Active **40 min**; Total **1 hr 40 min**; Serves **4**

SAUCE

- ½ cup full-fat plain Greek yogurt or sour cream
- 1 Tbsp. chopped dill
- 2 tsp. drained prepared horseradish
- 1 Tbsp. apple cider vinegar
  Fine sea salt and pepper

SALAD

- 1 bunch of beets (1½ lbs.)—scrubbed, greens trimmed and reserved, beets sliced ½ inch thick
- 5 Tbsp. extra-virgin olive oil
  Fine sea salt and pepper
- 1 cup rye berries
- 2 Tbsp. apple cider vinegar
- 1 Tbsp. drained prepared horseradish

SALMON

- 2 Tbsp. extra-virgin olive oil
  Four 6-oz. skin-on wild salmon fillets
  Fine sea salt
- 2 Tbsp. unsalted butter
- 1 tsp. caraway seeds

1. Make the sauce In a small bowl, combine all of the ingredients, season with salt and pepper and mix well.

2. Make the salad Preheat the oven to 300°. On a rimmed baking sheet lined with aluminum foil, toss the sliced beets with 2 tablespoons of the olive oil; season with salt and pepper. Arrange the beets in a single layer and roast until tender, flipping the slices halfway through, about 1 hour. Chop the beets and transfer to a large bowl.

3. Meanwhile, bring a medium saucepan of salted water to a boil. Add the rye berries and cook over moderate heat, stirring occasionally, until al dente, about 1 hour.

4. Drain the rye berries and add them to the bowl with the beets. Add the vinegar, horseradish and the remaining 3 tablespoons of olive oil, season with salt and pepper and toss to coat evenly. Keep warm.

5. In a small saucepan of boiling water, blanch the beet greens for 2 minutes. Drain and cool under cold water; pat dry. Chop the greens and toss with the beets and rye berries.

6. Cook the salmon In a large cast-iron or nonstick skillet, heat the oil. Season the salmon with salt and cook skin side down over moderately high heat until golden and crisp, 4 minutes. Flip the fish and cook for 2 minutes. Add the butter and caraway seeds to the skillet and cook, basting with the caraway butter, until the salmon is just cooked through, 1 minute longer.

7. Mound the rye berry salad on plates and spoon some dill sauce alongside. Top with the salmon, skin side up. Serve, passing the remaining dill sauce at the table.
—Marco Canora

MAKE AHEAD The dill sauce and cooked rye berries can be refrigerated in separate containers overnight.

WINE Boldly fruity California Sauvignon Blanc: 2013 Brander.

Salmon and Citrus Salad with Poppy Seed Dressing

Total **45 min**; Serves **4 to 6**

- 1 lb. salmon fillet
  Kosher salt and pepper
- ½ cup buttermilk
- 2 Tbsp. extra-virgin olive oil
- 1½ tsp. poppy seeds
- 2 medium navel oranges, such as Cara Cara, peeled and sliced ½ inch thick or separated into sections
- 1 medium grapefruit, peeled, sections cut into thirds
- 1 Hass avocado, sliced into wedges
  Snipped chives, for garnish

1. Preheat the oven to 375°. Lay the salmon fillet skin side down on a rimmed baking sheet and season with salt and pepper. Bake for about 20 minutes, until just cooked through. Let cool, then flake into large chunks; discard the skin.

2. Meanwhile, in a small bowl, whisk the buttermilk with the olive oil and poppy seeds. Season the dressing with salt and pepper.

3. Arrange the salmon, oranges, grapefruit and avocado on a platter or plates. Drizzle some of the dressing on top. Garnish with snipped chives and serve, passing additional dressing at the table.
—Justin Chapple

WINE Vibrant, medium-bodied Spanish white: 2013 Shaya Verdejo.

Seared Salmon with Anise-Cucumber Salad

Active **30 min**; Total **50 min**; Serves **4**

At The Durham Hotel in Durham, North Carolina, chef Andrea Reusing's menu is built around sustainable foods. Here, she pairs rich sockeye salmon with a creamy cucumber salad that mimics the cooling anise flavors of her favorite Thai dishes.

- Four 6-oz. skin-on sockeye salmon fillets
  Kosher salt and pepper
- 4 Persian cucumbers, thinly sliced
- 1 red onion, thinly sliced
- 1 Tbsp. anise seeds
- ⅓ cup crème fraîche
- 3 Tbsp. fresh lemon juice
- 20 basil leaves, torn
- 2 Tbsp. extra-virgin olive oil

1. Season the salmon with salt and pepper and let stand for 30 minutes.

2. Meanwhile, in a colander, toss the cucumbers, onion, anise seeds and 2 teaspoons of salt. Let stand for 30 minutes.

3. Gently squeeze the cucumbers dry. In a medium bowl, whisk the crème fraîche with the lemon juice. Add the cucumbers and onion and mix well, then gently stir in the basil.

4. In a large cast-iron skillet, heat the oil until shimmering. Add the salmon, skin side down, and flatten gently with a spatula. Cook over moderate heat until the skin is crisp, 4 minutes. Flip and cook until opaque throughout, 3 minutes longer. Serve with the salad. *—Andrea Reusing*

WINE Dry German Riesling: 2013 Dr. Bürklin-Wolf Estate.

Roast Salmon with Miso Butter and Radish Salad

🕐 Total **35 min**; Serves **4**

Chef Jenn Louis of Lincoln Restaurant in Portland, Oregon, creates an umami-rich glaze for salmon using miso and butter.

- **2 Tbsp. unsalted butter, at room temperature**
- **2 Tbsp. red miso paste**
- **Four 6-oz. center-cut salmon fillets**
- **¼ cup canola oil**
- **Kosher salt and pepper**
- **2 tsp. toasted sesame oil**
- **2 Tbsp. unseasoned rice vinegar**
- **6 radishes, thinly sliced**
- **½ English cucumber, coarsely chopped**
- **2 scallions, thinly sliced**
- **1 small jalapeño, sliced**
- **1 garlic clove, minced**
- **1 tsp. minced fresh ginger**
- **2 Tbsp. chopped mint**
- **1 tsp. togarashi**

1. Preheat the oven to 425°. In a small bowl, mash the butter with the miso until blended. Rub the salmon all over with 2 tablespoons of the canola oil, season with salt and pepper and arrange in a baking dish. Spread the miso butter over the top of the fillets and roast until just opaque throughout, about 15 minutes. Transfer to a platter.

2. Meanwhile, in a large bowl, whisk the remaining 2 tablespoons of canola oil with the sesame oil and vinegar; reserve 1 tablespoon of the dressing. Add all of the remaining ingredients to the dressing, season with salt and pepper and toss well.

3. Drizzle the reserved tablespoon of dressing over the salmon and serve with the radish salad. —*Jenn Louis*

WINE Juicy Oregon Chardonnay: 2013 Mouton Noir Knock on Wood.

Crisp Salmon with Sesame-Cumin Eggplant Panzanella

Active **25 min**; Total **1 hr 20 min**; Serves **4**

- **½ cup plus 2 Tbsp. extra-virgin olive oil**
- **3 Tbsp. tahini**
- **2 Tbsp. fresh lemon juice**
- **2 garlic cloves, minced**
- **Kosher salt and pepper**
- **2 medium eggplants, cut into 1-inch pieces**
- **1 hothouse cucumber, sliced**
- **1 red onion, halved and thinly sliced**
- **2 tsp. white sesame seeds, plus more for garnish**
- **1½ tsp. ground cumin**
- **3 oz. sesame bread, torn into small pieces**
- **Four 6-oz. skin-on salmon fillets**
- **2 Tbsp. unsalted butter**
- **Chopped dill, for garnish**

1. Preheat the oven to 425°. In a small bowl, whisk 6 tablespoons of the olive oil with the tahini, lemon juice and garlic and season with salt and pepper.

2. Place the eggplant and cucumber in 2 separate medium bowls. Add 2 teaspoons of salt to the eggplant and 1 teaspoon of salt to the cucumber. Toss to coat and let stand for 15 minutes. Rinse and gently squeeze the eggplant and cucumber to remove the excess water; pat dry.

3. Transfer the eggplant to a rimmed baking sheet and the cucumber to a small bowl. Add all but ¼ cup of the tahini dressing to the eggplant along with the onion, 2 teaspoons of sesame seeds and the cumin; season with salt and pepper and toss to coat. Roast the eggplant for 30 minutes, stirring occasionally.

4. In a medium bowl, toss the bread with 2 tablespoons of the oil, then toss with the eggplant on the baking sheet. Bake for 5 to 7 minutes, until the bread and eggplant are golden brown. Toss with the cucumber. Spoon the salad onto plates and drizzle with half of the remaining tahini dressing.

5. In a large nonstick skillet, heat the remaining 2 tablespoons of olive oil. Season the salmon with salt and pepper, add to the skillet skin side down and cook over moderately high heat until the skin is golden and crisp, about 5 minutes. Flip the fish, add the butter to the skillet and baste until just cooked through, 2 to 3 minutes longer. Set the salmon on the eggplant and drizzle with the remaining dressing. Garnish with dill and sesame seeds and serve. —*Kay Chun*

WINE Fragrant, light-bodied red: 2013 Arnot-Roberts Trousseau.

Salmon and Cherry Tomato Skewers with Rosemary Vinaigrette

🕐 Total **40 min**; Serves **4**

- **¼ cup extra-virgin olive oil, plus more for brushing**
- **3 Tbsp. fresh lemon juice**
- **2 tsp. Dijon mustard**
- **2 tsp. finely chopped rosemary**
- **Kosher salt and pepper**
- **1½ lbs. skinless salmon fillet, cut into 1½-inch cubes**
- **16 cherry tomatoes**
- **4 long metal skewers, or wooden skewers soaked in water for 1 hour**

1. In a small bowl, whisk the ¼ cup of olive oil with the lemon juice, mustard and rosemary. Season the vinaigrette with salt and pepper.

2. Light a grill or heat a grill pan. Thread the salmon and cherry tomatoes onto the skewers, brush with olive oil and season all over with salt and pepper. Grill over moderately high heat, turning once, until the salmon is just cooked through, about 6 minutes. Transfer the skewers to a platter and drizzle with some of the vinaigrette. Serve right away, passing additional vinaigrette at the table.
Justin Chapple

WINE Berry-scented Provençal rosé: 2014 Chêne Bleu.

SALMON AND CHERRY
TOMATO SKEWERS WITH
ROSEMARY VINAIGRETTE

Grilled Salmon and Lentil Tacos with Spicy Pickled Onions

Active **45 min;** Total **1 hr 15 min;** Serves **6**

For chef Camille Becerra, a perfect summer day means a trip to New York City's Rockaway Beach, a surfers' hangout. This recipe is an ode to the former Rockaway Taco, which Becerra still dreams about.

PICKLED ONIONS

- 3 **red onions (1 lb.), thinly sliced**
- 1 **cup apple cider vinegar**
- ½ **cup sugar**
- 4 **dried chiles de árbol, lightly crushed**
- 1 **tsp. kosher salt**

TACOS

- 1 **cup green (du Puy) lentils, picked over**
- 4 **garlic cloves, crushed**
- 1 **tsp. kosher salt**
- 1 **dried chile de árbol**
- ¼ **cup extra-virgin olive oil**
  Kosher salt and pepper
- 3 **Hass avocados, pitted and peeled**
- 2 **Tbsp. fresh lemon juice**
  Canola oil, for brushing
- 1½ **lbs. skin-on center-cut salmon fillet**
  Warm corn tortillas and hot sauce, for serving

1. Pickle the onions Put the onions in a medium heatproof bowl. In a medium saucepan, combine the vinegar with the sugar, chiles, salt and 1½ cups of water and bring to a simmer over moderate heat, stirring, until the sugar dissolves, about 2 minutes. Pour the brine over the onions, cover and let stand for 1 hour. Discard the chiles.

2. Meanwhile, make the tacos In a medium saucepan, combine the lentils with the garlic, salt and chile and cover with 2 inches of water. Bring to a simmer and cook over moderate heat until the lentils are tender, about 15 minutes. Drain the lentils; discard the chile and garlic. Transfer the lentils to a bowl. Add 2 tablespoons of the olive oil, season with salt and pepper and toss to coat.

3. In a medium bowl, mash the avocados with the lemon juice and season with salt.

4. Light a grill or heat a grill pan and brush with canola oil. Rub the salmon with the remaining 2 tablespoons of olive oil and season with salt and pepper. Grill over moderate heat, turning once, until just opaque throughout, 6 to 8 minutes per side; transfer to a platter.

5. Serve the salmon and lentils with the mashed avocado, pickled red onions, warm corn tortillas and hot sauce. —*Camille Becerra*

MAKE AHEAD The pickled onions can be refrigerated for up to 2 weeks.

BEER Lively summer beer: Blue Point Summer Ale.

Salmon, Broccolini and Fresh Red Chile Papillotes

Active **15 min;** Total **30 min;** Serves **4**

These impressive-looking salmon fillets baked in parchment are quick and easy, and there's almost no cleanup involved.

- 1 **lb. Broccolini**
  Four 6-oz. skinless center-cut salmon fillets
- 8 **thin slices of lemon**
- 1 **Fresno chile, thinly sliced into rings**
- 6 **Tbsp. extra-virgin olive oil**
  Kosher salt and pepper

1. Preheat the oven to 425°. Lay 4 large sheets of parchment paper on a work surface. Divide the Broccolini among the parchment sheets and top each mound with a salmon fillet, 2 lemon slices and some chile rings; drizzle each fillet with 1½ tablespoons of olive oil and season with salt and pepper. Fold the parchment paper over the fish, then fold the edge over itself in small pleats to seal the papillotes.

2. Transfer the papillotes to a large baking sheet and bake for 15 minutes, until slightly puffed. Carefully snip the packets open with scissors and serve. —*Justin Chapple*

WINE Crisp, white peach–scented northern Italian white: 2014 Alois Lageder Dolomiti Müller Thurgau.

Miso-Cured Salmon with Asparagus and Black Garlic Sauce

Total **1 hr plus overnight curing;** Serves **4**

Rubbing salmon with miso and letting it sit overnight imparts a huge amount of flavor; plus, it gives the pan-fried fillets a lovely burnished look. The simple, creamy black garlic sauce is subtle, delicious and striking-looking.

- **Four 5-oz. skin-on salmon fillets**
- ¼ **cup white miso**
- 1 **lb. medium asparagus**
- ¼ **cup extra-virgin olive oil**
- 1 **shallot, thinly sliced**
- 8 **black garlic cloves (see Note), peeled**
- 1 **cup fish stock**
- 1 **cup heavy cream**
  Kosher salt and pepper

1. On a large plate, coat the salmon fillets with the miso. Wrap the fillets in plastic and refrigerate overnight.

2. Fill a large bowl with ice water. Cook the asparagus in a skillet of salted boiling water until crisp-tender, about 3 minutes. Transfer the asparagus to the ice bath to cool, then drain and pat dry.

3. In a small saucepan, heat 1 tablespoon of the olive oil. Add the shallot and cook over moderate heat, stirring, until softened, about 2 minutes. Add the black garlic and fish stock and cook over moderate heat until the stock is reduced to ⅓ cup, 7 to 8 minutes. Stir in the cream and cook over moderately low heat, stirring occasionally, until the sauce is thickened, about 10 minutes. Transfer the sauce to a blender and puree until smooth, then strain through a fine sieve set over a small saucepan, pressing on the solids. Season with salt and pepper and keep warm.

4. Wipe the miso off the salmon fillets and rinse them; pat thoroughly dry. In a large nonstick skillet, heat 2 tablespoons of the olive oil. Cook the salmon skin side down over moderate heat until the skin is golden brown and crisp, 3 to 4 minutes. Turn the fillets and cook over moderately low heat until just opaque throughout, 3 to 4 minutes longer. Transfer the salmon to a plate to drain briefly.

5. Wipe out the skillet and add the remaining 1 tablespoon of olive oil. Add the asparagus, season with salt and pepper and cook over moderate heat, stirring, until warmed through, 2 minutes. Transfer the asparagus to plates. Top with the salmon fillets; drizzle with some of the black garlic sauce. Serve the remaining sauce on the side. —*Dominic Quirke*

NOTE Black garlic is prized for its sweet and savory, deep molasses-like flavor; its jelly-like texture makes it perfect for adding to sauces because it dissolves so easily. It's available at specialty shops and from blackgarlic.com.

MAKE AHEAD The sauce can be refrigerated for 3 days; rewarm before serving.

WINE Lively, minerally Muscadet: 2012 Michel Brégeon Muscadet Sur Lie.

Tuna Conserva with Grilled Shishito and Bean Salad

Total **30 min plus 4 hr marinating; Serves 8**

L.A. chef Jon Shook's wife, actress Shiri Appleby, is a huge fan of this light and tangy salad. "She asks me to make it for her and her friends every week," he says.

TUNA CONSERVA

- **1 cup extra-virgin olive oil**
- **¾ cup fresh lemon juice**
- **½ cup distilled white vinegar**
- **3 Tbsp. kosher salt**
- **1 Tbsp. sugar**
- **1 tsp. grated garlic**
- **Four 7-oz. cans water-packed best-quality tuna, drained**
- **One 14½-oz. can chickpeas, rinsed and drained**
- **2 carrots, sliced crosswise ⅛ inch thick**
- **2 celery ribs, sliced crosswise ⅛ inch thick**
- **½ small red onion, thinly sliced**
- **¼ cup coarsely chopped parsley**
- **2 Tbsp. coarsely chopped oregano**

SALAD

- **½ lb. shishito peppers**
- **½ lb. green beans, trimmed**
- **2 Tbsp. extra-virgin olive oil**
- **Kosher salt and pepper**

1. Make the tuna conserva In a large bowl, whisk the oil with the lemon juice, vinegar, salt, sugar and garlic. Add all the remaining ingredients and gently toss until well combined. Cover and let stand at room temperature for at least 4 hours, stirring every hour.

2. Make the salad Light a grill. In a large bowl, toss the shishito peppers and green beans with the olive oil and season with salt and pepper. Using a grill pan, grill over moderate heat, turning, until the shishitos and beans are lightly charred, 3 to 4 minutes. Transfer the vegetables to a platter, top with the tuna conserva and serve. —*Jon Shook*

MAKE AHEAD The tuna conserva can be refrigerated for up to 3 days.

WINE Crisp northern Italian Riesling: 2012 Kuenhof Kaiton.

INGREDIENT TIP
The New School of Fish

Chefs are cooking with unpopular seafood as a way to support sustainability. In New York City, chef **Michael Anthony** works with community-supported fishery Dock to Dish to source native bycatch and lesser-known fish. L.A. chef **Michael Cimarusti** champions delicious oddball West Coast varieties at his market, Cape Seafood and Provisions. Here, some of the fish that inspire them.

THE FISH	ATLANTIC BUTTERFISH	THORNYHEAD	BLUEFISH	VERMILION SNAPPER	SEA ROBIN
HOW IT TASTES	Flaky, with rich, oily flesh	Firm, sweet and nutty	Dense, strongly flavored dark flesh	Medium-firm, flaky and mild	Firm and sweet
HOW TO USE IT	Fillet and serve in a light broth.	Dredge in seasoned flour and fry whole.	Smoke or grill.	Grill or use in a seafood stew.	Grill the small fillets and serve on salad.

TUNA ESCABECHE
TOSTADAS

Tuna Escabeche Tostadas

⏱ Total **30 min**; Serves **4 to 6**

Canola oil, for frying

6 corn tortillas

Kosher salt

15 oz. tuna in olive oil, drained

¼ cup chopped pickled Mexican jalapeños and carrots from a can plus ¼ cup of the brine

Cilantro leaves, sliced radishes and toasted pumpkin seeds, for serving

1. In a medium skillet, heat ¼ inch of oil. Add 1 tortilla to the hot oil and fry over moderate heat, turning, until browned and crisp, 2 to 3 minutes. Transfer to paper towels to drain; season lightly with salt. Repeat with the remaining tortillas.

2. In a medium bowl, mix the tuna with the jalapeños and carrots and their brine. Spoon the tuna onto the tostadas and top with cilantro, radishes and toasted pumpkin seeds. Serve. —*Justin Chapple*

BEER Lightly hoppy, crisp lager: Victory Prima Pils.

Pan-Seared Tuna Steaks with Ginger Vinaigrette

⏱ Total **30 min**; Serves **4**

5 Tbsp. low-sodium soy sauce

5 Tbsp. sake

2½ Tbsp. mirin

3 Tbsp. minced shallot

½ Tbsp. finely grated peeled fresh ginger

¼ cup plus 2 Tbsp. extra-virgin olive oil

Kosher salt and pepper

1 bunch of Broccolini, trimmed

Two 1-inch-thick yellowfin tuna steaks

2 tsp. toasted white sesame seeds

Lemon wedges, for serving

1. In a small saucepan, simmer the soy sauce, sake, mirin and shallot until the liquid is slightly reduced, 3 minutes. Remove from the heat; stir in the ginger. Slowly whisk in ¼ cup of the oil. Season the vinaigrette with salt and pepper.

2. In a steamer basket set in a large saucepan of simmering water, steam the Broccolini until tender, about 6 minutes. Transfer to plates.

3. Meanwhile, in a nonstick skillet, heat the remaining oil. Season the tuna with salt and pepper. Sear over high heat until golden brown but still rare within, 30 seconds per side. Transfer to a paper towel–lined plate to drain. Slice against the grain and transfer to the plates. Drizzle with some of the vinaigrette and sprinkle with the sesame seeds. Serve with lemon and the remaining vinaigrette. —*Kuniko Yagi*

WINE Lively, fruit-forward California Chenin Blanc: 2013 Vinum Cellars.

Grilled Tuna with Red Wine Sauce

Total **50 min**; Serves **6**

2 Tbsp. unsalted butter

2 medium shallots, halved

¾ cup Pinot Noir

½ cup fish stock or clam juice

½ cup drained oil-packed sun-dried tomatoes

1 garlic clove

¼ cup pitted oil-cured olives

2 Tbsp. extra-virgin olive oil, plus more for brushing

Kosher salt

Six 6-oz. tuna steaks, 1 inch thick

1. In a small saucepan, melt the butter. Add the shallots and cook over moderate heat, stirring occasionally, until just starting to soften and brown, 3 minutes. Add the wine and bring to a boil, then simmer over moderately high heat until reduced to ½ cup, 5 minutes. Add the fish stock and simmer over moderately low heat until reduced to ½ cup, 10 minutes; discard the shallots.

2. In a food processor, puree the sun-dried tomatoes and garlic until nearly smooth. Add the olives and pulse until a coarse paste forms. Add the 2 tablespoons of olive oil and pulse to incorporate. Scrape into a medium bowl and whisk in the wine reduction. Season the sauce with salt.

3. Heat a large cast-iron skillet or griddle over high heat. Brush the tuna steaks with oil and season generously with salt. Cook over high heat, turning once, until lightly browned outside and rare within, about 2 minutes total. Transfer to plates and serve with the sauce. —*Nate Ready*

WINE Dark-berried Oregon Pinot Noir: 2012 Hiyu.

Hake with Walnut Tahini and Carrot Tabbouleh

⏱ Total **40 min**; Serves **4**

Chef Ana Sortun of Oleana in Cambridge, Massachusetts, tops hake with a rich, spicy walnut tahini inspired by Lebanese tarator sauce. The fresh carrot tabbouleh served alongside adds more bright flavor.

2 carrots, chopped

1 cup parsley leaves

¼ cup chopped dill

¼ cup plus 3 Tbsp. extra-virgin olive oil

3 Tbsp. fresh lemon juice

Kosher salt

3 garlic cloves, crushed

¼ cup walnuts (1 oz.)

¼ cup tahini

½ jalapeño, chopped

½ cup cilantro leaves

1 tsp. ground cumin

1 tsp. ground coriander

Four 6-oz. skinless hake or cod fillets

1. Preheat the oven to 425°. In a food processor, pulse the carrots until finely chopped. Add ½ cup of the parsley and the dill and pulse until minced. Scrape into a bowl and stir in 1 tablespoon each of oil and lemon juice. Season the carrot tabbouleh with salt.

2. Wipe out the processor. Add the garlic and walnuts; pulse until chopped. Add the tahini, jalapeño, cilantro, cumin, coriander, ¼ cup of the oil and the remaining ½ cup of parsley and 2 tablespoons of lemon juice. Pulse until smooth. Scrape the walnut tahini into a bowl; season with salt.

3. Arrange the fish in a medium baking dish. Drizzle with the remaining 2 tablespoons of oil, season with salt and turn to coat. Roast for 8 to 10 minutes, until the fish is cooked through. Transfer to plates. Spread some of the walnut tahini on the fillets and spoon the carrot tabbouleh alongside. Serve the remaining tahini at the table. —*Ana Sortun*

WINE Robust, full-bodied California Chardonnay: 2012 Bacchus.

Hake, Clams and Chorizo in Broth with Paella Rice

⟳ Total **45 min**; Serves **4**

BROTH

- **2** Tbsp. extra-virgin olive oil
- **1** small shallot, thinly sliced
- **1** bay leaf
- **1** tsp. crushed fennel seeds
  Pinch of saffron threads
- **2** cups chicken stock or low-sodium broth
- **24** manila clams or cockles, scrubbed
- **3** oz. Spanish chorizo, cut into ¼-inch dice
- **1½** Tbsp. minced garlic
  Kosher salt and pepper

FISH

- Four 5-oz. skinless hake fillets
  Kosher salt and pepper
  Smoked sweet paprika
  All-purpose flour, for dusting
- **¼** cup extra-virgin olive oil
  Paella Rice (recipe follows), for serving

1. Make the broth In a large saucepan, heat the olive oil. Add the shallot, bay leaf, fennel seeds and saffron and cook until fragrant, about 20 seconds. Add the stock and bring to a boil. Cover, remove from the heat and let steep for 10 minutes.

2. Return the broth to a boil and add the clams, chorizo and garlic. Season with salt and pepper, cover and cook over high heat, shaking the pan occasionally, until the clams just open, about 5 minutes. Discard the bay leaf and keep the broth warm.

3. Meanwhile, cook the fish Season the hake fillets with salt, pepper and smoked paprika and dust with flour. In a large skillet, heat the olive oil until shimmering. Add the fish and cook over moderately high heat, turning once, until golden and just cooked through, about 6 minutes.

4. Transfer the fish to shallow bowls. Spoon the clams, chorizo and broth around the fish and serve with Paella Rice. —*Sandy D'Amato*

WINE Citrusy, full-bodied Spanish white: 2013 Finca Os Cobatos Godello.

PAELLA RICE

Active **30 min**; Total **1 hr 5 min**
Serves **4 to 6**

The success of this ham-, chorizo- and pepper-studded side dish depends on the rice. For the best texture, use a short-grain Spanish variety such as Bomba or Calasparra, or a short-grain Japanese rice.

- **4** cups chicken stock or low-sodium broth
  Pinch of saffron threads
  Kosher salt and pepper
- **¼** cup extra-virgin olive oil
- **1** medium onion, finely chopped
- **⅓** cup finely diced Spanish chorizo
- **⅓** cup finely diced ham
- **⅓** cup finely diced red bell pepper
- **⅓** cup finely diced green bell pepper
- **2** bay leaves
- **1½** tsp. minced garlic
- **1½** cups short-grain rice, such as Bomba

1. In a medium saucepan, combine the stock with the saffron and a generous pinch each of salt and pepper and bring just to a boil. Remove from the heat.

2. Meanwhile, in a large, deep skillet, heat the olive oil. Add the onion and cook over moderate heat, stirring occasionally, until just starting to soften, about 7 minutes. Add the chorizo, ham, red and green peppers, bay leaves and garlic. Cook over moderately high heat, stirring occasionally, until the vegetables are softened, about 5 minutes. Add the rice and cook, stirring, until coated, about 1 minute.

3. Add the chicken stock to the skillet and bring to a boil over high heat. Cover and cook over moderately low heat until the rice is tender and the liquid is absorbed, about 20 minutes. Let stand for 15 minutes, then fluff with a fork. Discard the bay leaves. Season the rice with salt and pepper and serve. —*SD*

Grilled Snapper with Pink Chile Salt

⟳ Total **40 min**; Serves **4**

Once you make the pink chile salt that seasons both the fish and the salad here, you'll want to have it on everything from raw and cooked summer vegetables to grilled bread, melons, mangoes and margaritas.

- **1** fresh hot red chile, stemmed and chopped
- **1¼** cups kosher salt
- **2** Tbsp. grapeseed or canola oil, plus more for brushing
  Four 6-oz. skin-on red snapper fillets
- **¼** cup minced red onion
- **2** Tbsp. Champagne vinegar
- **12** multicolored radishes, half thinly sliced and half cut into thin wedges
- **1** small kohlrabi, peeled and thinly sliced
  Radish sprouts, for garnish

1. In a food processor, puree the red chile with the kosher salt until the salt is pink with flecks of chile. Transfer the pink chile salt to an airtight container.

2. Light a grill or heat a nonstick grill pan. Oil the grate or the pan. Brush the fish with grapeseed oil and season with pink chile salt. Grill over moderate heat, turning once, until just cooked through, about 5 minutes.

3. Meanwhile, in a large bowl, cover the onion with the vinegar and let stand for 5 minutes. Add the radishes, kohlrabi and the 2 tablespoons of grapeseed oil and toss well. Season the salad with pink chile salt and toss again.

4. Transfer the snapper fillets to plates and serve the radish salad alongside, garnished with radish sprouts. —*Justin Chapple*

MAKE AHEAD The pink chile salt can be kept in an airtight container for up to 1 month.

WINE Fruit-forward dry rosé: 2014 Muga.

EASY PERSIAN
FRIED FISH

Easy Persian Fried Fish

Total **20 min**; Serves **4**

Cookbook author Naomi Duguid learned this recipe by spending time in the kitchen with a woman from Bushehr, a port city in Iran that's famous for its fish dishes. Turmeric imparts a vibrant color; the mild, nutty fenugreek leaves have a distinctive maple flavor.

¼ cup all-purpose flour

1 Tbsp. crumbled fenugreek leaves (see Note)

½ Tbsp. each dried mint, dried dill and dried thyme

½ tsp. cayenne

¼ tsp. ground turmeric

Four 6-oz. skin-on red snapper fillets

Kosher salt and pepper

¼ cup vegetable oil

Lemon wedges and greens, for serving

1. In a shallow bowl, whisk the flour with the fenugreek, mint, dill, thyme, cayenne and turmeric. Season the fish with salt and pepper; dredge in the flour.

2. In a large cast-iron skillet, heat the oil until shimmering. Add the fish skin side down and press with a spatula to flatten. Cook over moderately high heat until the skin is browned, 4 minutes. Turn the fish and cook until white throughout, 2 minutes longer. Serve with lemon wedges and greens. —*Naomi Duguid*

NOTE Fenugreek leaves are available at Indian markets and from kalustyans.com.

WINE Crisp but full-bodied Chardonnay: 2013 Vincent Mothe Chablis.

Fish Tacos with Tomatillo-Jalapeño Salsa

Total **45 min**; Serves **4**

These light yet satisfying tacos are from chef Deborah Schneider of Sol Cocina in Newport Beach, California. She fills warm corn tortillas with meaty charred halibut and a spicy, tart salsa verde.

SALSA

4 medium tomatillos—husked, rinsed and quartered

½ cup lightly packed cilantro

2 small jalapeños, chopped

1½ Tbsp. fresh lime juice

1 tsp. vegetable oil

Kosher salt

TACOS

2 Tbsp. fresh lemon juice

1 Tbsp. extra-virgin olive oil

1 Tbsp. minced cilantro

1 small garlic clove, minced

1 lb. skinless halibut fillet, about ¾ inch thick

Kosher salt

Warm corn tortillas, chopped avocado and sliced red onion and cucumber, for serving

1. Make the salsa In a blender, combine all of the ingredients except the salt and puree until nearly smooth. Season with salt and transfer to a small bowl.

2. Make the tacos Heat a grill pan. In a large baking dish, whisk the lemon juice with the olive oil, cilantro and garlic. Add the fish and turn to coat. Season the fish all over with salt and grill over moderately high heat, turning once, until white throughout, 6 to 8 minutes. Transfer the fish to a platter and flake into large pieces with a fork. Serve the fish in warm corn tortillas with the salsa, avocado, red onion and cucumber. —*Deborah Schneider*

MAKE AHEAD The salsa can be refrigerated for up to 3 days.

BEER Hoppy American pale ale: Evil Twin Brewing Hipster Ale.

Red Snapper with Grilled Radicchio Salad

Active **45 min**; Total **1 hr 30 min**; Serves **6**

Star chef Michael Symon makes this recipe when he wants to cook an entire meal on the grill—including the salad.

3 Tbsp. fresh lemon juice

2 Tbsp. finely chopped fresh oregano

⅓ cup plus 2 Tbsp. extra-virgin olive oil, plus more for drizzling

Two 2-lb. whole red snappers, cleaned

Kosher salt and pepper

Canola oil, for brushing

2 heads of radicchio (1 lb.), quartered through the core

½ tsp. finely grated orange zest plus ¼ cup fresh orange juice

1 Tbsp. balsamic vinegar

1. In a roasting pan or large baking dish, whisk the lemon juice with the oregano and ⅓ cup of the olive oil. Using a sharp knife, make 3 diagonal slits ½ inch deep on both sides of each fish. Season the fish inside and out with salt and pepper and add to the marinade; turn to coat. Let stand at room temperature for 30 minutes, turning once.

2. Light a grill and brush the grate with canola oil. Grill the fish over moderate heat, turning once, until cooked through, 13 to 15 minutes per side. Transfer to a platter.

3. In a medium bowl, toss the radicchio with the remaining 2 tablespoons of olive oil and season with salt and pepper. Grill over moderate heat, turning, until lightly charred and crisp-tender, about 3 minutes. Arrange on the platter. Drizzle the fish and radicchio with the orange juice, vinegar and olive oil. Sprinkle with the orange zest and serve. —*Michael Symon*

WINE Juicy California rosé: 2014 Edmunds St. John Bone-Jolly.

Steamed Sea Bass with Potatoes and Avocado-Tarragon Salsa

⏱ Total **45 min;** Serves **4**

Fresh grapefruit juice flavors the sea bass and potatoes while they steam; a little of it also goes into the tasty salsa.

- **1** lb. small Yukon Gold potatoes, sliced ¼ inch thick
- **2** Tbsp. drained capers
- **2** Tbsp. extra-virgin olive oil
  Kosher salt and pepper
  Four 5- to 6-oz. skin-on sea bass fillets
- **3** Tbsp. fresh grapefruit juice
- **1** Hass avocado—peeled, pitted and chopped
- **2** Tbsp. chopped tarragon

1. In a medium bowl, combine the potatoes, capers and 1 tablespoon of the olive oil; season with salt and pepper and toss to coat. On a heatproof plate that fits inside a large enameled cast-iron casserole, arrange the potatoes in a slightly overlapping layer. Place a small heatproof bowl upside down in the center of the casserole and place the plate with the potatoes on top. Add enough water to reach 1 inch up the side of the casserole. Bring the water to a simmer, cover the casserole and steam the potatoes over moderate heat until almost tender, about 15 minutes.

2. Rub the fish with the remaining 1 tablespoon of olive oil and season with salt and pepper. Arrange the fillets on top of the potatoes, skin side up, in a single layer and drizzle with 2 tablespoons of the grapefruit juice. Cover and steam until the potatoes are tender and the fish is just opaque throughout, about 8 minutes longer.

3. Meanwhile, in a small bowl, toss the avocado with the tarragon and the remaining 1 tablespoon of grapefruit juice; season with salt and pepper.

4. Transfer the potatoes and fish to plates. Top with any juices from the plate and the avocado salsa and serve. —*Kay Chun*

WINE Zesty, peppery New Zealand Sauvignon Blanc: 2014 Astrolabe.

Sea Bass with Prosciutto and Sage

⏱ Total **20 min;** Serves **4**

Cookbook author Katie Caldesi makes this buttery, fragrant, decadent riff on classic saltimbocca in just minutes.

- **Four 6-oz. skin-on sea bass fillets**
  Kosher salt and pepper
- **4** thin slices of prosciutto (2 oz.)
- **4** large sage leaves
- **½** cup all-purpose flour
- **2** Tbsp. extra-virgin olive oil
- **¼** cup dry white wine
- **3** Tbsp. unsalted butter

1. Season the fish with salt and pepper. Arrange 1 slice of prosciutto and 1 sage leaf on the flesh side of each fillet, then secure with toothpicks.

2. In a medium bowl, stir the flour with ¼ teaspoon each of salt and pepper.

3. In a large nonstick skillet, heat the olive oil. Dredge the fish in the flour mixture, shaking off the excess. Add the fish to the skillet, prosciutto side down, and cook over moderate heat until golden, about 3 minutes. Flip the fish and cook until golden outside and just opaque throughout, 3 to 4 minutes longer. Transfer the fish to plates and remove the toothpicks.

4. Add the wine to the skillet and cook until reduced by half, 1 to 2 minutes. Whisk in the butter and season with salt and pepper. Spoon the sauce over the fish and serve warm. —*Katie Caldesi*

WINE Floral, medium-bodied Piedmontese white: 2014 Bruno Giacosa Arneis.

Halibut in Parchment with Corn and Tomatoes

Active **20 min;** Total **1 hr;** Serves **4**

- **One 1½-lb. center-cut skinless halibut fillet, 1 inch thick**
- **1** Tbsp. sugar
- **2** tsp. fennel seeds
- **1** tsp. whole black peppercorns, plus ground pepper for seasoning
- **1** tsp. whole coriander seeds
  Kosher salt
- **4** ears of corn, kernels cut off 3, 1 cob reserved
- **6** oz. wax or green beans, trimmed
- **15** small cherry tomatoes (about 8 oz.), preferably on the vine
- **2** Tbsp. extra-virgin olive oil
- **½** Tbsp. white wine vinegar
- **3** tarragon sprigs
- **2** thyme sprigs
- **4** Tbsp. unsalted butter, cubed

1. Place the halibut in a shallow baking dish. In a medium saucepan, combine 1 cup of water with the sugar, fennel seeds, peppercorns, coriander seeds and 2½ tablespoons of kosher salt and bring to a simmer. Cook, stirring, until the salt and sugar dissolve. Remove the pan from the heat and stir in 3 cups of ice water. Pour the cold brine over the halibut and let stand at room temperature for 25 minutes. Remove the halibut from the brine and pat it dry; discard the brine. Season the halibut lightly on one side with salt and pepper.

2. Preheat the oven to 400°. Arrange a 12-by-32-inch piece of parchment paper on a baking sheet. Mound the corn kernels on one half of the parchment and top with the fish, skinless side up, leaving a 3-inch border on 3 sides. Top with the beans and tomatoes, then drizzle with the oil and vinegar. Scatter the herbs on top. Set the reserved corn cob next to the fish. Top the fish with the butter. Fold the parchment over the fish and pleat, fold and crimp the edges to seal; add 3 tablespoons of water before completely sealing the packet.

3. Roast for 20 minutes, until the halibut is just opaque throughout. Transfer the packet to a serving platter, open and serve. —*Kristen Kish*

WINE Vibrant, lemon-scented Spanish white: 2013 Martínsancho Verdejo.

HALIBUT IN PARCHMENT
WITH CORN
AND TOMATOES

Steamed Sea Bass with Carrots Three Ways

Total **50 min**; Serves **4**

In this bright and delicate dish, chef Ludovic Pouzelgues of Lulu Rouget in Nantes, France, features carrots three ways: He purees some until silky, slices some into thin ribbons and marinates them, and frizzles the frilly green tops to serve as a garnish.

- **6** medium carrots with very fresh tops, carrots peeled and ¼ cup carrot tops reserved
- **2** Tbsp. unsalted butter
- **2** tsp. toasted sesame oil
  Kosher salt and pepper
- **2** tsp. black sesame seeds
- **1** Tbsp. extra-virgin olive oil
- **1** Tbsp. fresh lemon juice
- **¼** tsp. finely grated peeled fresh ginger
  Four 5-oz. skinless sea bass fillets
  Canola oil, for frying
- **1** scallion, thinly sliced
  One 2-inch strip of orange zest, julienned
  Fleur de sel, for garnish

1. Chop 4 of the carrots into ½-inch pieces. In a medium saucepan of salted boiling water, cook the chopped carrots until tender, about 15 minutes. Drain well. Transfer the carrots to a blender, add the butter and sesame oil and puree until smooth; season with salt and pepper and keep warm.

2. Meanwhile, in a small skillet, toast the sesame seeds over low heat, stirring, until fragrant, 2 minutes. Transfer to a plate.

3. Using a vegetable peeler, shave the remaining 2 carrots lengthwise into ribbons. In a medium bowl, toss the carrot ribbons with the olive oil, lemon juice and ginger and season with salt and pepper.

4. Season the sea bass with salt and pepper and arrange in a steamer basket set over a saucepan of simmering water. Cover and steam until just white throughout, 4 to 5 minutes.

5. Meanwhile, in a small skillet, heat ⅛ inch of canola oil. Add the carrot tops and fry over moderate heat until deep green, 1 to 2 minutes. Transfer to a paper towel–lined plate to drain; the carrot tops will crisp as they cool.

6. Spread the carrot puree on plates; top with the steamed fish and carrot salad. Garnish with the sesame seeds, fried carrot tops, scallion and orange zest. Sprinkle with fleur de sel and pepper and serve. —*Ludovic Pouzelgues*

MAKE AHEAD The carrot puree can be refrigerated overnight and rewarmed before serving.

WINE Brisk, minerally Muscadet: 2013 Luneau-Papin La Grange.

Grilled Sea Bream

Active **30 min**; Total **1 hr 30 min**; Serves **6**

Chef Scott Conant, a judge on Food Network's *Chopped,* employs what he calls "a boat owner's trick" for whole fish: He soaks it in salted water for an hour before grilling to keep the flesh moist and to ensure crispy skin.

- Two 1½-lb. cleaned whole sea bream (orata)
  Kosher salt
  Canola oil, for brushing
- **4** Tbsp. extra-virgin olive oil

1. In a large bowl, cover the fish with cool water. Generously salt the water and let stand for 1 hour at room temperature. Drain the fish and pat dry.

2. Light a grill to medium and oil the grate. Rub the fish with 2 tablespoons of the olive oil and season lightly with salt. Grill, turning once, until cooked through, about 20 minutes. Transfer to a platter, drizzle with the remaining olive oil and serve. —*Scott Conant*

WINE Crisp, lemony Greek white: 2013 Semeli Mountain Sun Moschofilero.

Grilled Branzino with Skordalia and Ladolemono

Active **30 min**; Total **50 min**; Serves **4 to 6**

F&W Best New Chef 2015 Zoi Antonitsas of Westward in Seattle tops flaky grilled fish with a super-lemony Greek ladolemono sauce. She serves it with the tangy, garlicky potato puree called skordalia.

SKORDALIA

- **2½** lbs. baking potatoes, peeled and cut into chunks
  Kosher salt
- **¾** cup extra-virgin olive oil
- **⅓** cup Champagne vinegar
- **¼** cup fresh lemon juice
- **1** Tbsp. finely grated garlic

FISH

- **1** tsp. finely grated lemon zest plus ¼ cup fresh lemon juice
- **1** tsp. Dijon mustard
- **1** tsp. dried oregano
- **1** tsp. chopped marjoram
- **½** cup extra-virgin olive oil, plus more for brushing
  Kosher salt and pepper
  Four 1- to 1¼-lb. whole branzino, cleaned

1. Make the skordalia In a medium saucepan, cover the potatoes with water and bring to a boil. Season with salt and simmer over moderate heat until tender, about 15 minutes. Drain well. Press the potatoes through a ricer into the saucepan. Stir in the olive oil, vinegar, lemon juice and garlic and season with salt. Keep warm.

2. Meanwhile, prepare the fish In a small bowl, whisk the lemon zest and lemon juice with the Dijon, oregano and marjoram. Gradually whisk in the ½ cup of olive oil until incorporated. Season the ladolemono with salt and pepper.

3. Light a grill and oil the grate. Season the fish with salt and pepper and grill over moderately high heat, turning once, until white throughout, about 15 minutes. Transfer the fish to plates and serve with the ladolemono and skordalia. —*Zoi Antonitsas*

WINE Citrusy, medium-bodied Greek white: 2013 Hatzidakis Santorini Assyrtiko.

Cornmeal-Crusted Trout with Caper–Cherry Pepper Pan Sauce

⏱ Total **40 min**; Serves **4**

- 2 Tbsp. extra-virgin olive oil
- 2 medium shallots, minced
- 1 garlic clove, minced
- ¾ cup dry white wine
- 2½ Tbsp. fresh lemon juice
- 3 Tbsp. unsalted butter, cut into tablespoons
- 4 small jarred hot cherry peppers, seeded and chopped
- 1 Tbsp. finely chopped parsley, plus more for garnish
- 2 tsp. salt-packed capers, rinsed and chopped
- ½ tsp. finely grated lemon zest, plus lemon wedges for serving
  Kosher salt and pepper
- ½ cup all-purpose flour
- 2 large eggs
- 1½ cups fine cornmeal
  Four 6-oz. skin-on trout fillets
- ¼ cup vegetable oil

1. In a saucepan, heat the olive oil. Add the shallots and garlic and cook over moderate heat, stirring, until softened, 2 minutes. Add the wine and lemon juice; bring to a boil, then simmer over moderate heat until reduced to ½ cup, 3 minutes. Remove from the heat and whisk in the butter, 1 tablespoon at a time, until incorporated. Stir in the hot peppers, 1 tablespoon of parsley, the capers and lemon zest; season with salt and pepper. Keep warm over very low heat.

2. Spread the flour in a shallow bowl. In another shallow bowl, beat the eggs. In a third shallow bowl, spread the cornmeal. Season the trout with salt and pepper. Coat in the flour; dip in the egg, letting the excess drip off; then dredge in the cornmeal.

3. In a large cast-iron skillet, heat the vegetable oil until shimmering. Working in batches if necessary, add the trout fillets and cook over moderately high heat, turning once, until browned and crisp, about 4 minutes total. Drain on paper towels, then transfer to a platter. Spoon the sauce on top, garnish with parsley and serve with lemon wedges. —*Colby Garrelts*

WINE Zesty, herb-scented Vermentino: 2012 Rocca delle Macìe Occhio a Vento.

Sole Fillets with Herbed Wine Sauce

⏱ Total **45 min**; Serves **4**

- 2 medium tomatoes, cored and scored on the bottoms with an X
- 3 Tbsp. unsalted butter
- 2 large shallots, thinly sliced
- ½ cup dry white wine
- ⅓ cup fish stock or clam juice
- ¾ cup heavy cream
- ⅓ cup chopped mixed herbs, like parsley, basil, chives and chervil
- 2 Tbsp. dry vermouth
  Pinch of freshly grated nutmeg
  Kosher salt and pepper
- 1¼ lbs. sole fillets
  Crusty bread, for serving

1. In a saucepan of boiling water, blanch the tomatoes until the skins just wrinkle, 30 seconds. Drain and cool under running water, then peel and cut into ¼-inch dice.

2. Wipe out the saucepan and melt the butter in it. Add the shallots and cook over moderate heat, stirring, until softened, about 2 minutes. Add the wine and simmer over moderately high heat until reduced by half, about 3 minutes. Add the fish stock and simmer until the liquid is reduced to ½ cup, about 3 minutes. Add the heavy cream and simmer until thickened, about 3 minutes. Stir in the diced tomatoes, herbs, vermouth and nutmeg. Season the sauce with salt and pepper.

3. Preheat the broiler and position the rack 8 inches from the heat. Season the sole lightly with salt and pepper and transfer to a 2-quart flameproof baking dish. Spoon the sauce on top and broil for 8 to 10 minutes, until the sauce is bubbling and the fish is just cooked through. Let stand for 5 minutes before serving with crusty bread. —*Mimi Thorisson*

WINE Orange rind–scented white Bordeaux: 2012 Château Villa Bel-Air Graves.

Sesame Trout Meunière with Dried Apricots

⏱ Total **40 min**; Serves **4**

For the dried apricots here, be sure to use a good-quality sweet and tart variety like Blenheims; they make a wonderful accent to the sesame-crusted fish.

- ¾ cup toasted sesame seeds
  Four 5-oz. skin-on trout fillets, pinbones removed
- 6 Tbsp. canola oil
  Kosher salt and pepper
- 1 stick unsalted butter, cut into tablespoons
- ¼ cup minced shallots
- 1 garlic clove, minced
- 2 Tbsp. apricot preserves
- 2 Tbsp. chopped dried apricots
- 1 Tbsp. fresh lemon juice
- 1 tsp. toasted sesame oil
- 2 Tbsp. chopped parsley
  Lemon wedges, for serving

1. Spread the sesame seeds on a plate. Rub the trout fillets with 2 tablespoons of the canola oil and season with salt and pepper. Coat the flesh side of each fillet with sesame seeds, pressing gently to help them adhere.

2. Preheat the broiler. In a large nonstick skillet, heat 2 tablespoons of the canola oil. Place 2 fillets skin side down in the skillet and cook over moderate heat until the skin is crisp and the fish is almost cooked through, about 5 minutes. Transfer the fillets skin side down to a rack set over a baking sheet. Wipe out the skillet and cook the remaining 2 fillets in the remaining 2 tablespoons of canola oil. Broil 8 inches from the heat until the seeds are golden and the fish is cooked through, 3 minutes. Transfer to plates.

3. Melt the butter in the skillet. Add the shallots and garlic; cook over moderate heat, stirring occasionally, until the butter is golden brown, about 3 minutes. Off the heat, stir in the apricot preserves, dried apricots, lemon juice, sesame oil and parsley. Season with salt and pepper, spoon the sauce over the fish and serve with lemon wedges. —*Rich Torrisi*

WINE Dry, stone fruit–inflected Alsace Riesling: 2012 Marcel Deiss.

THAI COOKING TUTORIAL

Chef **ANDY RICKER** of the Pok Pok restaurants in New York City and Portland, Oregon, shows how to use authentic ingredients to prepare a signature recipe from Thailand's Isan region: grilled catfish with sticky rice and an intense, fragrant dipping sauce.

Isan-Style Catfish with Sticky Rice and Jaew Dipping Sauce

Active **1 hr 15 min**; Total **2 hr 30 min plus overnight soaking**; Serves **4**

- **4** cups plus 2 Tbsp. Thai sweet (sticky) rice (30 oz.)
- **2** dried guajillo chiles, stemmed and seeded
- **4** chiles de árbol, stemmed and seeded
- **3** Tbsp. packed finely chopped Thai palm sugar or light brown sugar
- **2½** Tbsp. boiling water
- **8** lemongrass stalks, outer leaves removed, inner cores thinly sliced
- **7** Tbsp. lime juice
- **¼** cup Thai fish sauce
- **3** Tbsp. Thai "thin" soy sauce
- **1½** tsp. Thai seasoning sauce
- **½** cup coarsely chopped garlic (15 large cloves)
- **¼** cup kosher salt
    Two 2-lb. whole domestic-farmed catfish, cleaned
- **2** Tbsp. coarsely chopped cilantro

1. In a large bowl, cover the rice with 2 inches of cold water and let soak for at least 8 hours or overnight.

2. Meanwhile, make the jaew Heat a large wok or nonstick skillet over high heat. Add the guajillo chiles, reduce the heat to low and cook, stirring, for 2 minutes. Add the chiles de árbol and cook, stirring, until the chiles are very dark, about 3 minutes longer. Transfer the chiles to a spice grinder and let cool, then grind coarsely. Transfer to a medium bowl. In a small bowl, stir the palm sugar with the boiling water until the sugar dissolves. Stir 3 tablespoons of the syrup into the ground chiles; discard any remaining syrup.

3. In a mortar or food processor, pound or pulse the lemongrass to a coarse puree. Add half of the lemongrass to the chile mixture along with the lime juice, fish sauce, soy sauce and Thai seasoning sauce. Let

stand at room temperature for at least 1 hour or refrigerate for up to 2 days. Bring to room temperature before serving.

4. Make the toasted rice powder Preheat the oven to 325°. Drain 2 tablespoons of the rice and spread out on a small foil-lined baking pan. Bake, stirring occasionally, until light golden brown, 10 to 12 minutes. Let cool, then process in a spice grinder until finely ground.

5. Make the fish Add the garlic and salt to the remaining lemongrass in the mortar or food processor and pound or pulse to a chunky paste. Set the catfish on a baking sheet and score down to the bone at 1-inch intervals. Rub the lemongrass paste all over the fish, inside and out.

6. Light a hardwood charcoal fire and rake the coals to one side. Grill the fish over indirect heat (opposite the coals), covered, until cooked through, 45 minutes to 1 hour; you may need to add hot coals periodically to maintain the heat. Alternatively, roast the fish in a 350° oven for about 35 minutes, until it is cooked all the way through and flakes easily.

7. Meanwhile, make the sticky rice In a wok, bring 3 inches of water to a boil. Line a bamboo steamer with a double thickness of cheesecloth. Drain the remaining rice in a colander and set the colander in a large bowl. Fill the bowl with cold water and gently stir the rice; the water will become cloudy. Lift the colander from the bowl and pour out the water. Repeat this process until the water runs clear. Spread the rice in the steamer in an even layer and fold the overhanging cheesecloth over it. Cover the steamer and set it in the wok. Steam the rice until tender, about 15 minutes; halfway through steaming, using 2 tongs, carefully flip the rice over in the cheesecloth. It should be tender but chewy when done. Transfer the rice to a bowl, cover and let stand for 15 minutes.

8. To serve Transfer the catfish to a platter. Stir the toasted rice powder and cilantro into the jaew sauce and serve with the fish and sticky rice.

WINE Juicy, watermelon-inflected Spanish rosé: 2014 Campos de Luz.

TWO KEY STEPS

1

GRIND Toasted, finely ground uncooked rice thickens the dipping sauce and adds a nutty flavor.

2

RUB A chunky lemongrass paste rubbed all over the fish, inside and out, permeates it with bright flavor as it grills.

GRILLED LOBSTER WITH
MISO-CHILE BUTTER

Grilled Lobsters with Miso-Chile Butter

⏲ Total **40 min**; Serves **4**

"If we're grilling for a big group, we get our lobsters halved and cleaned at the fishmonger," says F&W's Gail Simmons. "It really cuts down on work and mess."

- 1 **stick unsalted butter, cubed**
- 2 **Tbsp. white miso**
- 1 **Tbsp. Sriracha**
- 2 **Tbsp. fresh lemon juice, plus wedges for serving**
- 2 **bunches of scallions**
- 1 **Tbsp. canola oil**
  Kosher salt and pepper
- 8 **long metal skewers**
  Four 1½-lb. lobsters, halved lengthwise, claws detached and reserved

1. In a small saucepan, melt the butter. Whisk in the miso, Sriracha and lemon juice. Reserve ¼ cup of the miso-chile butter for serving.

2. Light a grill. In a large bowl, toss the scallions with the oil and season with salt and pepper. Grill the scallions over moderate heat, turning, until lightly charred and tender, 5 minutes. Chop the scallions and toss with 1 tablespoon of the miso-chile butter.

3. Skewer the lobster bodies from the tail to the head to keep them straight. Brush the lobster meat with 2 tablespoons of the miso-chile butter. Grill the lobster bodies and claws over moderate heat, turning and basting the meat with the remaining miso-chile butter, until the shells are bright red, 7 to 8 minutes for the tails and 12 to 15 minutes for the claws. Remove the skewers.

4. Arrange the lobsters on a platter or plates and scatter the scallions on top. Serve with lemon wedges and the reserved ¼ cup of miso-chile butter. —*Gail Simmons*

WINE Herb-scented, full-bodied Italian white: 2013 Garofoli Macrina Verdicchio.

Crab Salad with Corn Pudding and Carolina Gold Rice

Active **1 hr**; Total **1 hr 45 min**; Serves **6**

This composed salad elegantly combines three Southern favorites—buttery corn, tangy crab salad and nutty heirloom rice.

CORN PUDDING

- 3 **ears of corn, shucked**
- 1 **tsp. unflavored powdered gelatin**
- 1 **stick unsalted butter, cut into tablespoons**
- 1 **small shallot, minced**
  Kosher salt
- ¼ **cup heavy cream**

RICE

- 2 **cups Carolina Gold rice**
- 1 **bay leaf**
- 5 **Tbsp. unsalted butter**
  Kosher salt

SALAD

- ¼ **cup extra-virgin olive oil**
- 2 **Tbsp. finely chopped parsley**
- 3 **Tbsp. fresh lemon juice**
- 1 **Tbsp. minced jalapeño**
  Kosher salt
- 1 **lb. jumbo lump crabmeat, picked over**
  Thinly sliced jalapeños and popped sorghum (see Note), for garnish
  Hot sauce, for serving

1. Make the pudding Using the large holes of a box grater, grate the corn into a medium bowl; discard the cobs. In a small bowl, sprinkle the gelatin over 2 tablespoons of cold water. In a large skillet, melt 2 tablespoons of the butter. Add the shallot and cook over moderate heat, stirring, until softened, about 3 minutes. Add the corn and cook, stirring frequently, until thickened and the corn is tender, about 5 minutes.

2. Scrape the corn into a blender. Add the gelatin and puree until smooth. With the blender on, gradually add the remaining 6 tablespoons of butter until incorporated. Strain the corn mixture through a fine sieve into a medium bowl and season the puree with salt. Let cool slightly.

3. In a medium bowl, whip the cream until firm. Fold into the corn puree and let cool completely. Refrigerate until chilled and set, about 45 minutes.

4. Meanwhile, make the rice In a medium saucepan, bring 3¼ cups of water to a boil. Add the rice, bay leaf, 1 tablespoon of the butter and a generous pinch of salt and return to a boil. Cover and simmer over low heat until the rice is tender and the water is absorbed, about 20 minutes. Remove from the heat and let stand, covered, for 20 minutes. Fluff with a fork. Fold in the remaining 4 tablespoons of butter and season with salt.

5. Make the salad In a medium bowl, mix the olive oil with the parsley, lemon juice and minced jalapeño and season with salt. Gently fold in the crab. Spoon the rice into shallow bowls and top with the crab salad and corn pudding. Garnish with sliced jalapeños and popped sorghum and serve with hot sauce.
—*Michael Fojtasek and Grae Nonas*

NOTE Popped sorghum is available at health food stores.

MAKE AHEAD The corn pudding can be refrigerated overnight.

WINE Ripe, full-bodied Oregon Chardonnay: 2013 Argyle.

Pan-Seared Pickerel on Mixed Vegetable and Crab Panzanella

Total **1 hr 15 min**; Serves **4**

Matthew DeMille, chef at Drake Devonshire Inn in Canada's Prince Edward County, makes this dish with pickerel, a flaky white fish that comes right from Lake Ontario. If pickerel isn't available, flounder or perch would also be delicious.

- 1 cup cubed ciabatta (1-inch pieces)
- ¼ cup plus 3 Tbsp. extra-virgin olive oil
- ¼ cup sherry vinegar
- 2 garlic cloves, minced
- 2 red bell peppers
- 2 yellow bell peppers
  Canola oil, for brushing
- 1 small red onion, sliced crosswise ½ inch thick
- 1 ear of corn, shucked
  Kosher salt and pepper
- ½ fennel bulb—halved, cored and thinly sliced
- 12 cherry tomatoes, halved
- 4 oz. jumbo lump crabmeat, picked over (½ cup)
  Four 6-oz. skin-on pickerel, flounder or perch fillets
- ¼ cup lightly packed parsley leaves
- ¼ cup lightly packed mint leaves

1. Preheat the oven to 400°. On a rimmed baking sheet, toss the ciabatta cubes with 1 tablespoon of the olive oil and bake, tossing occasionally, until crisp and golden, 8 to 10 minutes. In a large bowl, whisk the vinegar with the garlic and let stand for 10 minutes.

2. Roast the red and yellow peppers directly over a gas flame or under the broiler, turning, until charred all over. Transfer the peppers to a bowl, cover tightly with plastic wrap and let cool, about 15 minutes. Peel, stem and seed the peppers, then cut them into 1½-inch pieces. Add to the vinegar in the bowl.

3. Light a grill or heat a grill pan and oil the grate. Season the onion and corn with salt and pepper and grill over high heat, turning as necessary, until tender and nicely charred, about 6 minutes. Cut the kernels off the cob. Add the corn, onion, croutons, fennel, tomatoes, crabmeat and ¼ cup of the olive oil to the bowl with the peppers and toss well. Season the panzanella with salt and pepper.

4. In a large nonstick skillet, heat the remaining 2 tablespoons of olive oil until shimmering. Season the fish with salt and pepper and add to the skillet skin side down. Cook over moderately high heat, gently pressing with a spatula, until the skin is browned and crisp, 3 to 4 minutes. Flip the fillets and cook until the fish is white throughout, 2 to 3 minutes longer.

5. Toss three-quarters each of the parsley and mint leaves with the panzanella and mound on plates or a platter. Top with the fish, garnish with the remaining parsley and mint and serve immediately. —*Matthew DeMille*

WINE Creamy, full-bodied Chardonnay: 2013 Closson Chase Vineyards.

Seared Sea Scallops with Ricotta and Spring Pea Mash and Chive Oil

Total **1 hr**; Serves **4**

There are three simple parts to this dish from star chef Emeril Lagasse. The ricotta and pea mash and the chive oil can be made well in advance, so the only last-minute task is cooking the scallops.

CHIVE OIL

- 2 cups chopped chives (4 oz.)
- ½ cup canola oil
  Kosher salt

RICOTTA AND SPRING PEA MASH

- 1½ cups baby peas
- 3 Tbsp. extra-virgin olive oil
- 3 Tbsp. finely chopped fresh mint
- 2 Tbsp. freshly grated Parmigiano-Reggiano cheese
- 1 Tbsp. finely chopped basil
- 1 Tbsp. minced shallot
- 1 Tbsp. fresh lemon juice
- 1 tsp. minced garlic
- 1 cup fresh ricotta cheese
  Kosher salt and pepper

SCALLOPS

- ¼ cup extra-virgin olive oil
- 12 extra-large sea scallops (about 2 lbs.)
  Kosher salt and pepper
  Lemon wedges, for serving

1. Make the chive oil Fill a medium bowl with ice water. In a medium saucepan of boiling water, blanch the chives for 10 seconds. Drain, then transfer the chives to the ice bath to cool. Drain well. Squeeze out as much water from the chives as possible and pat dry.

2. In a blender, puree the chives with the canola oil until smooth. Strain the chive oil through a fine sieve into a bowl, pressing on the solids. Season the chive oil with salt.

3. Make the mash In a medium saucepan of salted boiling water, cook the peas just until tender, 2 to 3 minutes; drain well and pat dry. Using a fork, mash the peas until chunky. Stir in the olive oil, mint, Parmigiano, basil, shallot, lemon juice and garlic. Fold in the ricotta and season with salt and pepper.

4. Cook the scallops In a large nonstick skillet, heat 2 tablespoons of the olive oil. Season the scallops with salt and pepper, add 6 to the skillet and cook over moderate heat, turning once, until golden and just opaque throughout, about 5 minutes per side. Transfer to a large plate. Wipe out the skillet and repeat with the remaining olive oil and scallops.

5. Spoon the mash onto plates and arrange the scallops around it. Drizzle with the chive oil and serve with lemon wedges. —*Emeril Lagasse*

WINE Vibrant, medium-bodied Grüner Veltliner: 2013 Bründlmayer Berg Vogelsang.

Garlicky Clams with Confited Potatoes

Active **1 hr**; Total **1 hr 40 min**; Serves **4 to 6**

At The Perennial in San Francisco, chef Chris Kiyuna confits potatoes by cooking them in a good amount of olive oil; Kiyuna reserves the oil for braising the clams and for shallow-frying other ingredients.

POTATOES

- 1 **lb. fingerling potatoes, halved lengthwise**
- 4 **garlic cloves**
- 2 **tsp. black peppercorns**
- 1 **tsp. kosher salt**
- 1 **cup extra-virgin olive oil**

CLAMS

- 2 **garlic cloves, minced**
- 2 **medium shallots, minced**
- 4 **thyme sprigs plus ½ tsp. finely chopped thyme**
- 1 **Tbsp. crushed red pepper**
- 2 **lbs. littleneck clams, scrubbed and rinsed**
- 1 **cup dry white wine**
  Kosher salt and freshly ground black pepper
- 2 **Tbsp. Champagne vinegar**
- 1 **Tbsp. chopped walnuts**
- 1 **Tbsp. minced chervil**
- 8 **radishes with greens, radishes halved and greens torn**
- ¼ **cup snipped dill**

1. Confit the potatoes In a 10-inch skillet, combine all of the ingredients and bring just to a simmer. Cook over moderately low heat until the potatoes are just tender, about 15 minutes. Let cool. Drain the potatoes, discarding the garlic and peppercorns; reserve the oil.

2. Prepare the clams In a large saucepan, heat ⅓ cup of the reserved potato oil. Add the garlic and half the shallots and cook over moderate heat, stirring occasionally, until softened, 5 minutes. Add the thyme sprigs and crushed pepper and cook until fragrant, about 30 seconds. Add the clams, wine and a pinch each of salt and black pepper. Cover and cook over high heat, shaking the pan, until the clams open, 5 minutes. Remove the clams and discard the shells. Discard any unopened clams. Finely chop ⅓ cup of the clams. Strain the broth; reserve for another use.

3. In a medium bowl, whisk the vinegar with the chopped clams, walnuts, chervil and thyme and the remaining shallot; let stand for 15 minutes. Season the dressing with salt.

4. In a large skillet, heat 2 tablespoons of the reserved potato oil until shimmering. Add the potatoes cut side down and cook over moderately high heat, turning once, until lightly browned, 3 to 5 minutes. Transfer to a platter. Add the radishes to the skillet cut side down and cook until browned on the bottom, about 3 minutes. Transfer to the platter, fold in the radish greens and season with salt.

5. Add the dressing and the whole clams to the skillet and warm over moderately low heat, about 3 minutes. Spoon over the potatoes and radishes, top with the dill and serve. —*Chris Kiyuna*

WINE Lightly fruity sparkling rosé: NV Joseph Cattin Crémant d'Alsace Brut.

Cockles with Beans and Cherry Tomatoes in Garlic Broth

Active **30 min**; Total **1 hr 15 min**; Serves **4**

Cockles are among the smallest bivalves, but they deliver loads of flavor. F&W's Kay Chun combines them with just a few simple ingredients for a rich, hearty stew. If you can't find cockles, use scrubbed and debearded mussels or littleneck clams.

- 1 **cup dried cranberry or borlotti beans (6 oz.)**
- 2 **Tbsp. extra-virgin olive oil**
- 7 **garlic cloves, thinly sliced**
- 2 **shallots, finely chopped**
- ½ **lb. yellow cherry tomatoes, halved**
  Kosher salt and pepper
- ½ **cup dry white wine**
- 1 **cup low-sodium chicken broth**
- 3 **lbs. cockles, rinsed**
- ½ **cup coarsely chopped parsley**
- ½ **cup coarsely chopped tarragon**
  Grilled bread, for serving

1. In a large saucepan, cover the beans with 3 inches of water and bring to a boil. Simmer, stirring occasionally, until the beans are tender, about 45 minutes. Drain.

2. In a large enameled cast-iron casserole, heat the olive oil. Add the garlic and shallots and cook over moderate heat, stirring, until fragrant and golden, about 3 minutes. Add the beans and tomatoes and season with salt and pepper. Cook, stirring occasionally, until the tomatoes soften, about 3 minutes. Stir in the wine and cook until almost evaporated, about 1 minute. Add the broth and cockles and bring to a simmer. Cover and cook over low heat until the cockles open, about 3 minutes. Discard any unopened cockles. Stir in the parsley and tarragon and serve with grilled bread. —*Kay Chun*

MAKE AHEAD The cooked beans can be refrigerated for up to 2 days.

WINE Fresh and minerally Languedoc white: 2014 Julie Benau Picpoul de Pinet.

Mussels with Caramelized Fennel and Leeks

Total **1 hr**; Serves **6 to 8**

A simple mussel broth, caramelized vegetables and crème fraîche pump up the flavor of these steamed mussels from Shane McBride and Daniel Parilla of Cherche Midi in New York City.

MUSSEL BROTH

- ½ lb. mussels, scrubbed and debearded
- 1 shallot, thinly sliced
- 4 tarragon sprigs
- 2 cups dry white wine
- ¼ cup Pernod

CARAMELIZED FENNEL AND LEEKS

- 2 Tbsp. unsalted butter
- 2 fennel bulbs, trimmed and cut into ½-inch dice
- 2 leeks, light green and white parts only, sliced ½ inch thick

MUSSELS

- 2 Tbsp. unsalted butter
- 2 shallots, thinly sliced
- 5 lbs. mussels, scrubbed and debearded
- ¼ cup Pernod
- ¾ cup crème fraîche
  Kosher salt
  Small tarragon leaves, for garnish
  Toasted or grilled baguettes, for serving

1. Make the mussel broth Combine all of the ingredients in a saucepan. Cover, bring to a simmer and cook until the mussels open, about 3 minutes. Strain the broth and reserve the mussels. Discard any unopened mussels.

2. Make the caramelized fennel and leeks In a large skillet, melt the butter. Add the fennel and cook over moderately low heat, stirring occasionally, until tender and golden, about 15 minutes. Add the leeks and cook, stirring occasionally, until tender and the fennel is lightly caramelized, about 8 minutes more. Remove from the heat.

3. Prepare the mussels In a pot, melt the butter. Add the shallots and cook over moderate heat until softened, 2 minutes. Add the mussels and Pernod and cook, stirring, for 1 minute. Add the mussel broth and the fennel mixture. Cover and cook until the mussels open, about 5 minutes; using a slotted spoon, transfer the mussels to a large bowl as they open. Discard any that don't open.

4. Bring the broth to a simmer. Whisk in the crème fraîche and season with salt. Add all of the mussels and cook until hot. Transfer the mussels and broth to bowls, garnish with tarragon and serve with toasted or grilled baguettes. —*Shane McBride and Daniel Parilla*

MAKE AHEAD The caramelized fennel mixture can be refrigerated for 2 days.

WINE Full-bodied Loire Valley Chenin Blanc: 2013 Champalou Vouvray.

Butterflied Shrimp with Pistachios and Orange-Saffron Vinaigrette

Active **30 min**; Total **50 min**
Serves **4 as a first course**

VINAIGRETTE

- 1 cup fresh orange juice
- 1 Tbsp. minced shallot
- ¼ tsp. saffron threads
- 2 Tbsp. Champagne vinegar
- ¼ cup extra-virgin olive oil
  Kosher salt

SHRIMP

- ¼ cup unsalted pistachios
- 8 head-on shrimp (1 lb.), butterflied through the shells
  Kosher salt and pepper
- ¼ cup extra-virgin olive oil
- 8 large scallions, cut into 2-inch pieces (2 cups)
  Pistachio oil, for drizzling

1. Make the vinaigrette In a small saucepan, combine the orange juice, shallot and saffron. Bring to a simmer and cook over moderate heat until reduced to ¼ cup, about 25 minutes. Transfer to a small bowl and let cool completely. Whisk in the vinegar and oil and season with salt.

2. Meanwhile, prepare the shrimp Preheat the oven to 375°. Spread 2 tablespoons of the pistachios in a pie plate and toast for 5 minutes, or until golden; coarsely chop. In a spice grinder, finely grind the remaining 2 tablespoons of pistachios. Season the flesh side of the shrimp with salt and pepper and coat with the finely ground pistachios.

3. In a large nonstick skillet, heat 2 tablespoons of the olive oil. Add the scallions and cook over moderately high heat, stirring, until lightly charred and just tender, about 3 minutes. Transfer to a plate.

4. Wipe out the skillet and heat the remaining 2 tablespoons of olive oil in it. Add the shrimp, flesh side down, and cook over moderate heat, turning once, until just white throughout, about 3 minutes. Transfer the shrimp to plates. Spoon some of the vinaigrette over the shrimp and top with the scallions, a drizzle of pistachio oil and the chopped pistachios. Serve the remaining vinaigrette on the side. —*Ori Menashe*

WINE Fruit-forward, floral Piedmontese white: 2013 Brovia Roero Arneis.

Spicy Coconut Shrimp

📷 PAGE 109

🕐 Total **40 min**; Serves **4**

- ⅓ cup all-purpose flour
- 1 tsp. cayenne
  Kosher salt
- ½ cup panko
- ⅓ cup unsweetened shredded coconut
- ⅓ cup unsweetened coconut milk
- 1 lb. large shrimp, shelled and deveined
  Canola oil, for frying
  Lemon wedges, for serving

1. In a shallow dish, whisk the flour with the cayenne and ½ teaspoon of salt. In a second shallow dish, mix the panko with the shredded coconut. Pour the coconut milk into a small bowl.

2. Season the shrimp with salt. Working with 1 shrimp at a time, dredge it in the flour mixture, then dip it in the coconut milk, letting the excess drip off. Coat the shrimp in the panko mixture. Transfer to a plate. Repeat to coat the remaining shrimp.

3. In a large cast-iron skillet, heat ¼ inch of oil until shimmering. In 2 batches, fry the shrimp over moderate heat, turning, until golden and crisp and cooked through, about 3 minutes. Drain briefly on paper towels and serve hot with lemon wedges. —*Sasha Martin*

WINE Zippy, lightly sparkling Vinho Verde: NV Broadbent.

MUSSELS WITH
CARAMELIZED
FENNEL AND LEEKS

JALAPEÑO-PICKLED
SHRIMP AND VEGETABLES

Jalapeño-Pickled Shrimp and Vegetables

Total **30 min** plus **4 hr** pickling
Makes **1 pound**

PICKLE

- **3** cups water
- **1** cup red wine vinegar
- **½** cup diced carrot
- **½** cup diced trimmed shiitake mushrooms
- **½** cup diced turnip
- **1** jalapeño, thinly sliced crosswise
- **2** Tbsp. sugar
- **1** Tbsp. kosher salt
- **1** Tbsp. dried oregano
- **1** tsp. ground fennel
- **1** tsp. crushed red pepper
- **1** tsp. black pepper

SHRIMP

- **8** cups water
- **1** lemon, halved
- **5** bay leaves
- **1** Tbsp. kosher salt
- **2** tsp. cayenne
- **1** lb. shell-on large shrimp

1. Make the pickle In a medium saucepan, combine all of the ingredients and bring just to a boil, stirring to dissolve the sugar and salt. Transfer the pickling mixture to a large bowl and let cool completely.

2. Meanwhile, prepare the shrimp Wipe out the saucepan. Add all of the ingredients except the shrimp and bring to a boil for 2 minutes. Add the shrimp and cook over moderately high heat until just white throughout, 2 to 3 minutes. Drain and transfer the shrimp to an ice bath to cool. Add the shrimp to the pickle, cover and refrigerate for 4 to 5 hours. Drain and peel the shrimp and serve with the pickled vegetables. —*Donald Link*

SERVE WITH Jalapeño-spiked mayonnaise.

MAKE AHEAD The drained pickled shrimp can be refrigerated for up to 3 days.

WINE Tangy, citrusy Sauvignon Blanc: 2013 Pascal Jolivet Sancerre.

Pickled Shrimp

Total **40 min** plus **12 hr** marinating
Makes **1 pound**; Serves **6**

These tangy, make-ahead shrimp are from F&W's People's Best New Chef 2015, Cory Bahr, of Cotton in Monroe, Louisiana. At the restaurant, Bahr serves the pickled shrimp with microgreens over a simple tomato-corn salad. "Many Southern cooks use Wishbone Italian dressing," he says, "but we 'church it up' with good oil and vinegar."

- **¼** cup plus 2 Tbsp. kosher salt
- **1** lb. large shrimp, shelled and deveined
- **2** cups extra-virgin olive oil
- **6** lemons, halved and juiced (1 cup), lemons reserved
- **4** garlic cloves, thinly sliced
- **1** medium Vidalia onion, halved and thinly sliced
- **18** bay leaves
- **½** cup flat-leaf parsley
- **3** oz. crab boil seasoning

1. In a medium saucepan, boil 8 cups of water with ¼ cup of the salt. Add the shrimp and boil until cooked, 2 minutes. Drain and chill in an ice bath; drain again.

2. In a medium bowl, whisk the olive oil with the lemon juice and the remaining 2 tablespoons of salt. In two 1-quart glass jars, layer the shrimp, garlic, onion, bay leaves, parsley and 6 of the lemon halves. Add the crab boil seasoning and the lemon dressing and cover. Marinate the shrimp in the fridge for 12 to 24 hours before serving. —*Cory Bahr*

Masala Prawns

Total **1 hr**; Makes **24 shrimp**

- **⅓** cup fresh lime juice
- **2** small shallots, minced
- **3** Tbsp. minced peeled fresh ginger
- **2** Tbsp. canola oil, plus more for brushing
- **1** Tbsp. chaat masala (see Note)
- **2** garlic cloves, minced
- **1½** tsp. ground fenugreek
- **1½** tsp. dried mango powder (see Note)
- **1½** tsp. fine sea salt
- **¾** tsp. ground coriander
- **¾** tsp. crushed red pepper
- **24** large shrimp, shelled and deveined
  Lime wedges and cilantro leaves, for serving

1. In a medium bowl, combine all of the ingredients except the shrimp, lime wedges and cilantro. Add the shrimp and toss well. Cover and refrigerate for at least 30 minutes or up to 2 hours.

2. Heat a grill pan and brush with canola oil. Remove the shrimp from the marinade and scrape off some of the excess. Grill over moderately high heat, turning once, until just cooked through, 4 minutes. Transfer the shrimp to a platter and serve with lime wedges and cilantro. —*Akasha Richmond*

NOTE Chaat masala is an Indian spice blend made with black sea salt. Dried mango powder (amchoor) is a citrusy seasoning made from unripe green mangoes. Look for these products at Indian markets and on amazon.com.

WINE Rich, tropical-fruit-inflected Riesling: 2013 Dr. Bürklin-Wolf Bürklin Estate.

Garlic Shrimp

Total **15 min**; Serves **4**

- ¼ cup extra-virgin olive oil, preferably Spanish
- 6 garlic cloves, thinly sliced
- 1 lb. large shrimp, shelled and deveined
  Kosher salt
- 1 whole dried chile, such as árbol or guindilla
- 1 tsp. brandy
- 1 Tbsp. chopped parsley

In a large nonstick skillet, heat the olive oil. Add the garlic and cook over moderate heat, stirring, until golden, 2 minutes. Season the shrimp with salt. Add the shrimp and chile to the skillet and cook until the shrimp are golden on one side, about 2 minutes. Flip the shrimp and add the brandy; cook until the shrimp are white throughout, 1 to 2 minutes longer. Stir in the parsley, transfer to a platter and serve. —*José Andrés*

WINE Crisp, strawberry-scented Spanish rosé: 2014 Ostatu Rosado.

Hot Pepper Shrimp

Total **30 min**; Serves **4 to 6**

If you can get head-on shrimp, use them. The shells keep the shrimp tender and trap all the spices and seasonings, so the flavors permeate the shrimp.

- ¼ cup vegetable oil
- ½ cup finely chopped onion
- 4 garlic cloves, minced
- 8 scallions, 2 minced and 6 cut into 1-inch lengths
  One 2-inch piece of fresh ginger, peeled and minced
- 6 Tbsp. thyme leaves
- 2 Tbsp. sweet paprika
- 2 tsp. ground allspice
- ½ Scotch bonnet or habanero chile, stemmed and minced
  Kosher salt and pepper
- 20 extra-large shell-on shrimp, deveined (see Note)
- 2 Tbsp. white wine vinegar

1. In a large nonstick skillet, heat 2 tablespoons of the oil. Add the onion, garlic, minced scallions, ginger, thyme, paprika, allspice and chile. Season with salt and pepper and cook over high heat until the aromatics are softened and beginning to brown, about 5 minutes. Scrape into a bowl.

2. In the same skillet, heat the remaining 2 tablespoons of oil. Add the shrimp, season with salt and pepper and cook over high heat, turning once, until curled, about 4 minutes. Return the cooked aromatics to the skillet and add the remaining scallions and the vinegar. Cook, tossing, until the shrimp are evenly coated and the scallions are softened, about 3 minutes. Transfer the shrimp to a platter and serve. —*Adam Schop*

NOTE To devein shell-on shrimp, slit them down the back with kitchen shears and remove the intestinal vein, then rinse well.

WINE Citrusy, spritzy Spanish white: 2014 Ulacia Txakoli.

Tequila-Chipotle Shrimp

Total **15 min**; Serves **4**

- 2 Tbsp. canola oil
- ½ cup finely chopped red onion
- 1 chipotle chile in adobo sauce, minced
  One 15-oz. can diced tomatoes
  Kosher salt and pepper
- 1 lb. shelled and deveined large shrimp
- ¼ cup finely diced fresh pineapple
- 1 Tbsp. tequila
  Chopped cilantro, for garnish

In a large skillet, heat the oil. Add the onion and chipotle and cook over moderately high heat, stirring, until just starting to soften, 2 to 3 minutes. Add the tomatoes and bring to a simmer. Season with salt and pepper, then nestle the shrimp in the sauce and cook, turning once, until just white throughout, about 5 minutes. Stir in the pineapple and tequila, garnish with cilantro and serve right away. —*Deborah Schneider*

WINE Fruit-forward, full-bodied California Chardonnay: 2013 Talbott Logan.

Grilled Shrimp with Shrimp Butter

Total **30 min**; Serves **6**

The secret to this amazingly simple and delicious grilled shrimp recipe from Chicago chef Stephanie Izard is the onion-and-shrimp-paste butter that's spooned on just before serving.

- 6 Tbsp. unsalted butter
- ½ cup finely chopped red onion
- 1½ tsp. crushed red pepper
- 1 tsp. Malaysian shrimp paste (belacan; see Note)
- 1½ tsp. fresh lime juice
  Kosher salt and black pepper
- 24 large shrimp, shelled and deveined
- 6 long wooden skewers, soaked in water for 30 minutes
  Torn mint leaves and assorted sprouts, for garnish

1. In a small skillet, melt 3 tablespoons of the butter. Add the onion and cook over moderate heat until softened, 3 minutes. Whisk in the crushed red pepper and shrimp paste and cook, stirring, until fragrant, 2 minutes. Whisk in the lime juice and the remaining 3 tablespoons of butter and season with salt. Keep the shrimp butter warm.

2. Light a grill or heat a grill pan. Season the shrimp with salt and black pepper and thread onto the skewers (don't pack them on too tightly). Grill over high heat, turning once, until lightly charred and just cooked through, about 4 minutes total. Transfer to a platter and spoon the shrimp butter on top. Garnish with mint leaves and sprouts and serve. —*Stephanie Izard*

NOTE Belacan is a pungent seasoning made by grinding small shrimp into a paste that is fermented, dried and pressed into cakes. It's available at Southeast Asian markets or online from indomart.us.

MAKE AHEAD The shrimp butter can be refrigerated overnight. Warm gently over low heat before serving.

BEER Citrusy farmhouse ale: Prairie Artisan Ales Birra.

Shrimp Salad with Green Curry Dressing

⏱ Total **30 min**; Serves **4 to 6**

¼ cup fresh lime juice
¼ cup canola oil
2 Tbsp. green curry paste
1 lb. cooked large shrimp
8 oz. torn mixed lettuces (10 cups)
1 cup each of cilantro and mint leaves
1 cup thinly sliced carrot
½ cup thinly sliced red onion
  Kosher salt
  Chopped roasted peanuts, for garnish

In a large bowl, whisk the lime juice, oil and curry paste. Add the remaining ingredients and toss well. Season with salt and toss again. Garnish with chopped peanuts and serve. —*Justin Chapple*

Shrimp Cakes with Spicy Mayo

⏱ Total **30 min**; Serves **4**

½ cup mayonnaise
1 Tbsp. hot sauce
1 lb. shelled and deveined shrimp, chopped
¾ cup panko
2 large eggs
3 Tbsp. finely chopped scallions
1 tsp. finely grated lemon zest
¾ tsp. smoked paprika
  Kosher salt and pepper
¼ cup extra-virgin olive oil
  Lemon wedges, for serving

1. In a small bowl, whisk the mayonnaise with the hot sauce.

2. In a large bowl, mix the chopped shrimp with the panko, eggs, scallions, lemon zest, smoked paprika, 1 teaspoon of salt and ½ teaspoon of pepper. Form the mixture into eight ¾-inch-thick cakes.

3. In a large skillet, heat the olive oil. In batches, add the cakes and cook over moderately high heat, turning once, until browned and cooked through, about 4 minutes. Transfer to plates and serve with the spicy mayonnaise and lemon wedges. —*Justin Chapple*

WINE Spritzy, citrusy Portuguese white: 2014 Vera Vinho Verde.

Barbecue Shrimp

⏱ Total **30 min**; Serves **6**

This quick and easy shrimp is flavored with plenty of Worcestershire sauce.

3 Tbsp. canola oil
1 shallot, finely chopped
1 garlic clove, finely chopped
¼ cup dry white wine
½ tsp. chopped thyme
¾ cup Worcestershire sauce
½ cup low-sodium chicken broth
24 large shrimp, shelled and deveined
  Kosher salt and pepper
2 Tbsp. unsalted butter, cut into tablespoons
  Sliced scallions, for garnish

1. In a medium saucepan, heat 1 tablespoon of the canola oil. Add the shallot and garlic and cook over moderate heat, stirring occasionally, until softened, about 3 minutes. Stir in the white wine and thyme and cook until reduced by half, about 2 minutes. Add the Worcestershire sauce and chicken broth and cook until reduced to ½ cup, about 15 minutes.

2. In a large skillet, heat the remaining 2 tablespoons of canola oil. Season the shrimp with salt and pepper. Cook over moderately high heat, turning once, for 2 minutes total. Stir in the sauce and cook, stirring, until thickened, about 2 minutes. Stir in the butter until incorporated and season with salt. Transfer the shrimp to a platter, garnish with scallions and serve. —*Colby Garrelts*

WINE Fruit-forward, citrusy Chenin Blanc: 2014 Ken Forrester Petit Chenin.

Pan-Fried Shrimp with Lemony Pea Pesto

⏱ Total **45 min**; Serves **4**

This pesto, made with fresh young peas, toasted pine nuts and lots of Parmesan, would also be a great dip for crudités.

3 Tbsp. pine nuts
½ lb. shelled fresh young peas (2 cups)
¾ cup freshly grated Parmigiano-Reggiano cheese
1 garlic clove, crushed
½ cup plus 1 Tbsp. extra-virgin olive oil
1 Tbsp. plus 1 tsp. fresh lemon juice
  Kosher salt and pepper
12 jumbo shrimp (1 lb.), shelled and deveined
4 cups baby arugula (2 oz.)

1. In a small skillet, toast the pine nuts over low heat, stirring frequently, until golden, about 5 minutes. Transfer to a plate and let cool completely.

2. In a food processor, combine the toasted pine nuts, the peas, cheese, garlic, ¼ cup of the olive oil and 1 tablespoon of the lemon juice and puree until a coarse, thick pesto forms. Season the pea pesto with salt and pepper.

3. In a large nonstick skillet, heat 2 tablespoons of the olive oil. Season the shrimp with salt and pepper. Add half of the shrimp to the skillet and cook over moderately high heat for 3 minutes. Turn the shrimp over, reduce the heat to moderate and cook until golden outside and white throughout, 2 to 3 minutes longer. Repeat with another 2 tablespoons of the olive oil and the remaining shrimp.

4. Toss the arugula with the remaining 1 tablespoon of olive oil and 1 teaspoon of lemon juice; season with salt and pepper. Spread the pea pesto on plates, top with the shrimp and arugula and serve. —*Dominic Quirke*

WINE Stony, peach-inflected Muscadet: 2012 Domaine de l'Ecu Orthogneiss.

Octopus with Chorizo and Potatoes

Active **30 min**; Total **1 hr 45 min**; Serves **4**

For the most tender octopus, dip it in boiling water three times before cooking it. This allows the proteins to break down slowly.

- **1 onion, coarsely chopped**
- **3 bay leaves**
- **1¾ lbs. octopus tentacles**
- **¾ lb. potatoes, peeled and cut into ½-inch dice**
- **Kosher salt and freshly ground pepper**
- **3 Tbsp. extra-virgin olive oil, plus more for drizzling**
- **2 tsp. chopped thyme**
- **5 oz. cured Spanish chorizo, cut into ½-inch dice**
- **Shredded shiso (optional)**

1. Bring a large saucepan of salted water to a boil with the onion and bay leaves. Using tongs, carefully dip the octopus into the boiling water 3 times, then leave it in the water. Cook the octopus over moderately low heat until tender, about 1 hour. Remove from the heat and let the octopus stand in the water for 10 minutes; drain. Cut the octopus into ½-inch pieces.

2. In a medium saucepan, cover the potatoes with water and add salt. Bring to a boil and simmer over moderate heat until just tender, about 10 minutes. Drain and transfer to a bowl. Toss the potatoes with the 3 tablespoons of olive oil and the thyme; season with salt and pepper.

3. In a grill pan, cook the chorizo over moderately high heat until warmed through, 2 minutes. Transfer to a bowl. Add the potatoes and octopus to the pan and cook until hot and the potatoes are golden in spots, about 5 minutes. Add to the chorizo, season with salt and pepper and toss. Drizzle with oil, garnish with shiso, if using, and serve. —*Alex Larrea*

WINE Strawberry-scented Spanish rosé: 2014 Viña Zorzal.

Grilled Octopus with Ancho Chile Sauce

Active **1 hr**; Total **2 hr 30 min**; Serves **6**

Star chef Tom Colicchio was inspired by the flavors of Mexico while filming Season 12 of *Top Chef*. He incorporated many of those elements into menus at 1 Hotel in Miami Beach, including this smoky-sweet ancho chile glaze for grilled octopus.

OCTOPUS

- **2 Tbsp. extra-virgin olive oil**
- **One 3½- to 4-lb. cleaned octopus, head and tentacles separated**
- **3 shallots, thinly sliced**
- **3 garlic cloves, thinly sliced**
- **1 Tbsp. sweet pimentón de la Vera (smoked paprika)**
- **2 cups dry sherry**

SAUCE

- **3 ancho chiles, stemmed and seeded**
- **1 small dried chipotle chile, stemmed and seeded**
- **¾ cup apple cider vinegar**
- **3 Tbsp. honey**
- **1 garlic clove**
- **¼ cup plus 2 Tbsp. grapeseed or canola oil**
- **Kosher salt**
- **Canola oil, for brushing**
- **Jicama Salad (recipe follows), for serving**

1. Prepare the octopus Preheat the oven to 300°. In a large enameled cast-iron casserole, heat the olive oil. Add half of the octopus and cook over moderately high heat, turning, until lightly browned all over, 3 to 5 minutes. Transfer to a plate. Repeat with the remaining octopus.

2. Add the shallots and garlic to the casserole and cook over moderate heat, stirring, until lightly browned, 2 minutes. Add the pimentón and cook, stirring, until fragrant, about 20 seconds. Carefully add the sherry and bring to a boil. Return the octopus to the casserole, cover and braise in the oven until very tender, about 1½ hours. Let the octopus cool completely in the liquid.

3. Meanwhile, make the sauce In a medium saucepan, toast the chiles over moderate heat, turning, until fragrant and pliable, 2 to 3 minutes. Add the vinegar, honey and garlic and bring just to a simmer. Remove from the heat and let stand until the chiles are softened, about 20 minutes. Transfer to a blender and puree until smooth. With the machine on, gradually add the grapeseed oil until incorporated. Season the ancho chile sauce with salt.

4. Remove the octopus from the liquid. Using a paper towel, wipe the purple skin off the tentacles, leaving the suckers intact. Cut the head in half. Discard the braising liquid.

5. Light a grill or heat a grill pan and brush with canola oil. Grill the octopus over high heat, turning, until lightly charred all over, about 4 minutes. Transfer to a baking sheet and immediately brush with some of the ancho chile sauce. Serve with the jicama salad, passing the remaining sauce at the table. —*Tom Colicchio*

MAKE AHEAD The recipe can be prepared through Step 4; refrigerate the octopus and ancho chile sauce separately for up to 3 days.

WINE Dry, fruit-forward Italian rosé: 2014 Bisson Portofino.

JICAMA SALAD

Total **30 min**; Serves **6**

To keep the jicama crisp in this dish, start with a very firm root and cut the julienne a bit on the thick side.

- **One 1½-lb. jicama, peeled and julienned**
- **2 celery ribs, thinly sliced**
- **1 Fresno chile, thinly sliced**
- **⅓ cup fresh lime juice**
- **¼ cup extra-virgin olive oil**
- **½ cup torn basil leaves**
- **Kosher salt**

Combine all of the ingredients in a large bowl and let the jicama salad stand for 15 minutes. Serve. —*TC*

GRILLED OCTOPUS
WITH ANCHO
CHILE SAUCE;
JICAMA SALAD

At Thanksgiving, chef Tyler Florence serves roast turkey with polenta stuffing (recipe, p. 166) to legendary restaurateur Cecilia Chang, a family friend.

POULTRY

CHICKEN LEGS
COQ AU VIN
Recipe, page 154

Chicken Piccata with Radishes

⏱ Total **40 min;** Serves **4**

L.A. chefs Jon Shook and Vinny Dotolo have a soft spot for Italian-American classics like chicken piccata, updated here with quick-cooked radishes.

RADISHES

- **1 Tbsp. extra-virgin olive oil**
- **8 breakfast radishes**
  Kosher salt

CHICKEN

- **Four 8-oz. skinless, boneless chicken breast halves, pounded ¼ inch thick**
- **Kosher salt and pepper**
- **½ cup all-purpose flour**
- **5 Tbsp. extra-virgin olive oil**
- **1½ tsp. minced garlic**
- **⅓ cup dry white wine**
- **½ cup chicken stock or low-sodium broth**
- **4 Tbsp. unsalted butter**
- **1 Tbsp. fresh lemon juice**
- **1 Tbsp. chopped capers**
- **1 Tbsp. chopped parsley**

1. Cook the radishes In a large nonstick skillet, heat the olive oil. Add the radishes, season with salt and cook over moderately high heat, stirring occasionally, until golden and crisp-tender, about 3 minutes. Transfer to a plate and let cool slightly. Wipe out the skillet.

2. Make the chicken Season the chicken breasts with salt and pepper. Dredge in the flour; shake off the excess. Heat 2 table-spoons of the oil in the skillet. Add 2 of the chicken breasts; cook over moderately high heat until golden on the bottom, about 3 minutes. Flip the chicken and cook until golden and white throughout, 2 to 3 minutes longer. Transfer to a large plate. Repeat with 2 tablespoons of oil and the remaining chicken. Wipe out the skillet.

3. Heat the remaining 1 tablespoon of oil in the skillet. Add the garlic and cook over moderate heat, stirring, until fragrant, 30 seconds. Add the wine and cook until almost evaporated, 1 minute. Add the stock and bring to a boil. Whisk in the butter, lemon juice, capers and parsley and cook until slightly thickened, about 2 minutes. Season the sauce with salt.

4. Return the chicken to the skillet, 2 pieces at a time, and turn to coat with the sauce. Transfer the chicken to plates and spoon the remaining sauce on top. Halve the radishes, scatter over the chicken and serve. —*Jon Shook and Vinny Dotolo*

WINE Vibrant, medium-bodied Piedmon-tese red: 2010 Brovia Valmaggione Nebbiolo d'Alba.

Chicken in an Herb Garden

Active **30 min;** Total **3 hr 30 min;** Serves **4**

Cookbook author Katie Caldesi poaches rolled chicken breasts in vinegar before marinating them in olive oil with plenty of fresh herbs. It's a light, summery make-ahead dish.

- **4 skinless, boneless chicken breast halves (2 lbs.), pounded ¼ inch thick**
- **Kosher salt and pepper**
- **2½ cups white wine vinegar**
- **1 cup extra-virgin olive oil**
- **1 cup finely chopped mixed herbs, such as parsley, tarragon, basil, thyme, rosemary, sage and mint**
- **Crusty bread, for serving**

1. Season the chicken breasts with salt and pepper. Tightly roll them up lengthwise and secure with toothpicks at 1-inch intervals.

2. In a large saucepan, combine the vinegar, ¾ cup of water and a pinch of salt and bring to a gentle simmer. Add the chicken and cook over low heat until just white through-out, 10 to 12 minutes. Transfer the chicken to a work surface and let cool slightly. Dis-card the toothpicks. Slice the chicken cross-wise into 1-inch-thick rounds.

3. In a large bowl, whisk the olive oil with the mixed herbs and season with salt and pepper. Add the chicken, turning to coat in the herb oil. Let cool to room tempera-ture, about 30 minutes. Cover and refriger-ate for at least 2 hours or overnight. Bring to room temperature and serve with crusty bread. —*Katie Caldesi*

WINE Lively, zesty Italian white: 2014 Aia Vecchia Vermentino.

Green and Red Chicken Chilaquiles with Fried Eggs

Active **30 min;** Total **1 hr;** Serves **4**

In Mexico, this recipe is known as "divorced" chilaquiles because of the contrasting red and green salsa toppings.

SALSA ROJA

- **12 oz. small tomatoes, chopped**
- **½ white onion, finely chopped**
- **1 garlic clove, crushed**
- **2 serrano chiles, finely chopped**
- **¼ cup chopped epazote or 1 Tbsp. chopped oregano**
- **1 cup water**
- **Kosher salt**

CHICKEN CHILAQUILES

- **Two 8-oz. skinless, boneless chicken breast halves**
- **1 garlic clove, crushed**
- **1 bay leaf**
- **Kosher salt**
- **2 Tbsp. olive oil**
- **4 large eggs**
- **6 oz. corn tortilla chips**
- **1½ cups Salsa Verde (p. 182)**
- **Grated queso panela or queso fresco, sour cream and chopped white and red onion, for garnish**

1. Make the salsa roja In a medium sauce-pan, combine all of the ingredients, season with salt and bring to a simmer. Cook over moderately low heat, stirring occasionally, until saucy, about 25 minutes; keep warm.

2. Meanwhile, make the chicken chila-quiles In another medium saucepan, cover the chicken, garlic and bay leaf with 1 inch of water. Bring to a simmer and cook over low heat until the chicken is white throughout, about 20 minutes. Transfer the chicken to a plate to cool slightly; reserve the cooking liquid for another use. Coarsely shred the chicken and season with salt; keep warm.

3. In a large nonstick skillet, heat the olive oil. Crack the eggs into the skillet and sea-son with salt. Cover and cook over low heat until the whites are firm but the yolks are still a little runny, about 3 minutes.

4. Mound the tortilla chips on plates. Spoon some of the salsa roja over half of the chips and some salsa verde over the rest. Top with the shredded chicken and fried eggs. Garnish with cheese, sour cream and onion and serve with the remaining salsa roja and salsa verde. —*Enrique Olvera*

MAKE AHEAD The salsas and shredded chicken can be refrigerated separately for up to 3 days. Rewarm all before serving.

Chicken Caesar Skewers

Active **20 min**; Total **50 min**; Serves **4 to 6**

½ cup mayonnaise
1 Tbsp. Dijon mustard
1 Tbsp. extra-virgin olive oil
1 Tbsp. minced anchovies
1 garlic clove, minced
2 lbs. skinless, boneless chicken breasts or thighs, cut into 1-inch pieces
12 long wooden skewers, soaked in water for 1 hour
Freshly grated Parmigiano-Reggiano cheese, for garnish
Romaine lettuce and lemon wedges, for serving

1. In a large bowl, whisk the mayonnaise with the mustard, olive oil, anchovies and garlic. Add the chicken and toss to coat. Let marinate at room temperature for 20 minutes.

2. Preheat the broiler and position the rack 6 inches from the heat. Thread the chicken onto the skewers and arrange on a large baking sheet. Broil for 8 to 10 minutes, until lightly browned and cooked through. Transfer the skewers to a platter. Sprinkle with grated Parmigiano-Reggiano and serve with lettuce cups and lemon wedges. —*Justin Chapple*

WINE Lemony Sauvignon Blanc: 2014 Simi.

Ginger-Nut-Butter-Stuffed Chicken Breasts

Total **1 hr 15 min**; Serves **4**

1 stick unsalted butter, 4 Tbsp. softened
¼ cup chopped mixed herbs, such as parsley, chives, tarragon and dill
2 Tbsp. minced raw cashews, plus more for sprinkling
2 Tbsp. almond meal
1 Tbsp. finely grated fresh ginger
Kosher salt and pepper
Four 6-oz. skin-on, boneless chicken breast halves
1 Tbsp. vegetable oil
1 shallot, finely chopped
1½ cups dry white wine
1½ cups chicken stock

1. In a small bowl, mash the softened butter with the herbs, 2 tablespoons of cashews, the almond meal and ginger. Season with salt and pepper. Using your fingers, loosen the skin of each chicken breast to form a pocket, then stuff with a generous tablespoon of the ginger-nut butter. Season the chicken with salt and pepper and refrigerate until the butter is firm, about 20 minutes.

2. Preheat the oven to 400°. In a large cast-iron skillet, heat the oil. Add the chicken breasts skin side down and cook over moderately high heat until well browned, 5 minutes. Turn the breasts and cook for 3 minutes. Transfer the skillet to the oven and bake the chicken for 8 to 10 minutes, until just cooked through. Transfer to a platter and keep warm.

3. Melt 1 tablespoon of the butter in the skillet. Add the shallot and cook over moderately high heat, stirring, until softened, 1 minute. Add the wine and cook, scraping up the browned bits, until nearly evaporated, about 3 minutes. Add the stock and simmer until reduced to ½ cup, about 9 minutes. Whisk in the remaining 3 tablespoons of butter and season with salt and pepper. Strain the sauce into a bowl.

4. Spoon the sauce onto plates. Set the chicken on top, sprinkle with cashews and serve. —*Tatiana Levha*

WINE Ripe, focused Chenin Blanc: 2012 Les Vignes Herbel La Rue aux Loups.

Grilled Chicken with Cabbage Anchoïade

Active **45 min**; Total **1 hr 15 min**; Serves **4**

The Provençal anchovy dressing tossed with cabbage here would also be great drizzled over grilled vegetables or as a dip for crusty bread.

Four 6-oz. skinless, boneless chicken breast halves
Eight 2-inch-long strips of lemon zest
¼ cup loosely packed fresh oregano leaves
2 tsp. whole black peppercorns
¼ cup plus 3 Tbsp. extra-virgin olive oil
Kosher salt and pepper
1 small red bell pepper, cut into ¼-inch dice
One 1¼-lb. head of Savoy cabbage, cored and finely shredded (8 cups)
6 oil-packed anchovy fillets, drained and finely chopped
2 tsp. minced garlic
4 tsp. red wine vinegar

1. Place the chicken breasts in a medium baking dish. In a mini food processor, pulse the lemon zest with the oregano and peppercorns until finely chopped. Rub the mixture all over the chicken and drizzle with 3 tablespoons of the olive oil. Cover with plastic wrap and let marinate at room temperature for 30 minutes.

2. Light a grill. Season the chicken with salt and grill over moderately high heat, turning once, until well browned outside and white throughout, 6 to 8 minutes. Transfer the chicken to a work surface and let rest for 5 minutes.

3. Reserve 2 tablespoons of the diced red pepper for garnish. In a large bowl, toss the remaining diced red pepper with the cabbage, anchovies, garlic, vinegar and the remaining ¼ cup of olive oil. Season with salt and pepper and toss again. Mound on plates. Slice the chicken and arrange over the cabbage anchoïade. Garnish with the reserved diced red pepper and serve. —*Jacques Pépin*

WINE Slightly herbal Sauvignon Blanc: 2013 Bailly-Reverdy Cuvée Chavignol Sancerre.

WEST AFRICAN
CHICKEN KEBABS

Poached Chicken, Lentil and Watercress Salad

Active **45 min**; Total **1 hr 15 min**; Serves **4**

To make supermoist poached chicken breasts, chef Shea Gallante of the Baccarat Hotel in Manhattan recommends keeping the chicken in the cooled poaching liquid until serving time.

CHICKEN

- ¼ cup dry white wine
- 1 quart chicken stock or low-sodium broth
- 1 Tbsp. white peppercorns
- 1 bay leaf
- 1 garlic clove
  Kosher salt
  Two 8-oz. skinless, boneless chicken breast halves

LENTILS

- 2 Tbsp. extra-virgin olive oil
- 1 yellow onion, quartered
- 1 carrot, cut into large pieces
- 1 celery rib, cut into large pieces
- 2 slices of bacon, finely chopped
- ½ cup green lentils, picked over
  Kosher salt and pepper

SALAD

- 1 small shallot, minced
- 2 Tbsp. fresh lemon juice
- 2 Tbsp. Champagne vinegar
- 1 Tbsp. Dijon mustard
- ½ cup extra-virgin olive oil
  Kosher salt and pepper
- 4 oz. watercress, thick stems discarded (8 cups)
- ⅓ cup sliced almonds, toasted
- 2 Tbsp. chopped dill

1. Poach the chicken In a medium saucepan, bring the wine to a simmer and cook over moderate heat until reduced by half, about 3 minutes. Add the stock, peppercorns, bay leaf, garlic and a generous pinch of salt and return to a simmer. Add the chicken and cook over moderately low heat, turning the meat occasionally, until an instant-read thermometer inserted in the thickest part registers 160°, about 25 minutes. Transfer the chicken to a work surface and let cool completely before returning it to the cooled poaching liquid.

2. Meanwhile, cook the lentils In a medium saucepan, heat the olive oil. Add the onion, carrot and celery and cook over moderate heat, stirring occasionally, until the vegetables start to soften, about 5 minutes. Add the bacon and cook, stirring, until the fat is rendered but the bacon is not crisp, 3 to 5 minutes. Add 2½ cups of water and bring to a boil. Stir in the lentils and season generously with salt and pepper. Simmer over moderate heat, stirring occasionally, until the lentils are just tender, about 20 minutes. Let the lentils cool in the liquid; drain. Using tongs, remove the onion, carrot and celery and discard.

3. Make the salad In a small bowl, whisk the shallot with the lemon juice and vinegar and let stand for 5 minutes. Whisk in the mustard. Slowly drizzle in the olive oil and whisk until incorporated. Season the vinaigrette with salt and pepper. In a large bowl, toss the watercress with the almonds, dill and ¼ cup of the vinaigrette.

4. In another large bowl, toss the lentils with ¼ cup of the vinaigrette and season with salt and pepper. Remove the chicken from the poaching liquid and transfer to a work surface. Slice the chicken, arrange on plates and drizzle with the remaining vinaigrette. Serve the lentils and watercress alongside. —*Shea Gallante*

MAKE AHEAD The poached chicken and lentils can be refrigerated in their cooking liquids overnight. Return to room temperature before serving.

WINE Full-bodied French white: 2013 Domaine Vocoret Chablis.

Chai-Spiced Chicken Breasts

Active **15 min**; Total **55 min**; Serves **6**

- 3 Tbsp. extra-virgin olive oil
- 2 Tbsp. crushed loose chai tea (from 6 bags, if using)
- 2½ tsp. kosher salt
- ¾ tsp. pepper
  Six 8- to 10-oz. skin-on, bone-in chicken breast halves
- 1 cup chopped cilantro
  Lime wedges, for serving

Preheat the oven to 450°. In a small bowl, whisk the oil with the tea, salt and pepper. Rub the chai mixture all over the chicken breasts and under the skin. Set the chicken skin side up on a large rimmed baking sheet and roast for about 30 minutes, until browned and an instant-read thermometer inserted in the thickest part of each breast registers 160°. Let rest for 10 minutes, then transfer to a platter. Scatter the cilantro on top and serve with lime wedges. —*Justin Chapple*

WINE Rich, spiced California Chardonnay: 2012 Neyers Carneros District.

West African Chicken Kebabs

Active **30 min**; Total **1 hr**; Serves **4**

- 1 cup roasted peanuts
- 1 Tbsp. finely grated ginger
- 3 garlic cloves, crushed
- 1 chicken bouillon cube
- 2 tsp. paprika
- 1½ tsp. onion powder
- ½ tsp. cayenne
- 1 lb. skinless, boneless chicken breast, sliced crosswise ¼ inch thick
- ¼ cup canola oil
  Kosher salt and pepper
- 16 wooden skewers, soaked in water for 30 minutes

1. In a food processor, pulse the peanuts until finely chopped. Add the ginger, garlic, bouillon cube, paprika, onion powder and cayenne and pulse until a coarse and crumbly mixture forms. Spread the peanut mixture on a large plate.

2. Rub the chicken all over with 2 tablespoons of the oil and season with salt and pepper. Thread the chicken onto the skewers and press into the peanut mixture to coat both sides. Arrange the skewers on a plate. Let stand at room temperature for 30 minutes.

3. In a grill pan, heat 1 tablespoon of the oil. Cook half of the chicken over moderate heat, turning carefully, until deep golden and cooked through, about 5 minutes. Repeat with the remaining oil and chicken. Serve hot. —*Sasha Martin*

WINE Full-bodied, aromatic Alsace white: 2013 Hugel Gentil.

Grilled Chicken Wings with 9-Spice Dry Rub

Active **30 min**; Total **4 hr**; Serves **6**

BRINED WINGS

½ cup kosher salt

3 Tbsp. light brown sugar

2 garlic cloves

1 tsp. whole black peppercorns

1 bay leaf

3 lbs. chicken wings, tips discarded and wings split

DRY RUB

¼ cup dark brown sugar

¼ cup granulated sugar

¼ cup sweet paprika

1 Tbsp. granulated garlic

1 Tbsp. kosher salt

1 Tbsp. granulated onion

¾ Tbsp. black pepper

½ Tbsp. dry sage

½ Tbsp. dry mustard

½ Tbsp. ground ginger

½ Tbsp. cayenne

Canola oil, for brushing

Lime wedges, for serving

1. Brine the wings In a large saucepan, combine the salt, sugar, garlic, peppercorns and bay leaf with 2 quarts of water and bring to a boil. Cook over moderate heat, stirring, until the sugar and salt dissolve, about 3 minutes. Let the brine cool to room temperature.

2. In a large bowl, pour the brine over the chicken wings. Cover and refrigerate for 3 hours.

3. Meanwhile make the rub In a medium bowl, mix all of the ingredients except the oil and lime.

4. Light a grill and oil the grate. Drain the wings and pat dry with paper towels. In a large bowl, toss the wings with ⅓ cup of the dry rub. Grill over moderate heat, turning, until nicely charred and cooked through, about 15 minutes. Serve hot with lime wedges. —*Timothy Hollingsworth*

MAKE AHEAD The dry rub can be stored in an airtight container for up to 1 month.

WINE Red-berried, light-bodied red: 2013 Damien Coquelet Beaujolais-Villages.

Golden Chicken Thighs with Charred-Lemon Salsa Verde

Active **1 hr**; Total **3 hr 10 min**; Serves **6 to 8**

Ristorante Masolino in Panicale, Italy, has served chicken with lemon and capers for years. Famed Los Angeles chef Nancy Silverton makes the dish even better by roasting lemon slices so they're lightly charred, then stirring them into a piquant salsa verde. The sauce is an excellent accompaniment to these crisp-skinned chicken thighs; it's also great with roasted fish and vegetables.

CHICKEN

12 chicken thighs

24 sage leaves

16 garlic cloves—6 cut into 4 slices each, the rest gently smashed and peeled

4 Tbsp. unsalted butter, cut into 12 slices

Strips of zest from 2 lemons

3 Tbsp. extra-virgin olive oil

1 Tbsp. each chopped thyme, oregano and parsley

1 tsp. crushed red pepper

Kosher salt

12 fresh bay leaves (optional)

SALSA VERDE

1 lemon, cut into ½-inch slices and seeded

1 Tbsp. plus ½ cup extra-virgin olive oil

¼ cup each chopped oregano and mint

2 garlic cloves, chopped

1 anchovy fillet

½ tsp. chopped drained capers

1 tsp. kosher salt

1. Prepare the chicken Run your fingers under the skin of each chicken thigh to create a pocket. Stuff each pocket with 2 sage leaves, 2 slices of garlic and 1 slice of butter. Transfer the stuffed thighs to a large bowl. In a small bowl, stir the lemon zest strips with the smashed garlic, olive oil, chopped herbs and crushed red pepper. Pour the mixture over the chicken and turn to coat. Cover with plastic wrap and refrigerate for at least 2 hours or overnight.

2. Meanwhile, make the salsa verde Preheat the oven to 450°. On a baking sheet, toss the lemon slices with 1 tablespoon of the olive oil. Spread the lemon slices in an even layer and bake for 16 to 18 minutes, until charred on the bottom. Transfer to a cutting board and let cool for 5 minutes. Chop the slices into ¼-inch pieces. Leave the oven on.

3. In a mortar, mash the oregano and mint with the chopped garlic, anchovy, capers and the 1 teaspoon of salt until a smooth paste forms. Slowly drizzle in the remaining ½ cup of olive oil, stirring to create a sauce. Stir in the chopped lemon.

4. Finish the dish Heat a very large ovenproof skillet. Season the chicken thighs evenly with 4 teaspoons of salt; reserve the lemon zest and smashed garlic from the marinade. Arrange the chicken thighs skin side down in the skillet and cover with another large skillet or pot weighed down with a few heavy cans. Cook the chicken over moderate heat until the skin is golden brown and crisp, about 15 minutes.

5. Remove the weight and turn the chicken over. Scatter the reserved lemon zest and garlic and the bay leaves, if using, among the thighs. Roast in the oven for about 30 minutes, until the chicken is golden brown and cooked through. Discard the bay leaves. Transfer the chicken to a platter and serve with the salsa verde. —*Nancy Silverton*

MAKE AHEAD The salsa verde can be refrigerated overnight. Serve at room temperature.

WINE Juicy, brambly Italian red: 2010 Còlpetrone Montefalco Rosso.

MODERN DUCK À L'ORANGE

Chef **LUDO LEFEBVRE** of Petit Trois in L.A. modernizes this French classic. He cooks duck breast and tender leg confit separately, then serves them in a North African–inspired sauce of orange juice simmered with honey and the spice blend ras el hanout.

Spiced Duck à l'Orange

Active **1 hr**; Total **1 hr 30 min plus overnight drying**; Serves **4**

Ras el hanout is available at some grocery stores (McCormick makes a version) and from kalustyans.com.

- 5 Tbsp. dark honey, such as buckwheat
- 1 cup fresh orange juice
- ⅓ cup chicken stock or low-sodium broth
- ¼ cup apple cider vinegar
- 2 Tbsp. orange blossom water
- 1 Tbsp. ras el hanout
- 4 Tbsp. unsalted butter
  Kosher salt and white pepper
- 4 confit duck legs
  Four 8-oz. duck breasts, refrigerated uncovered on a rack overnight
- 2 blood oranges or oranges
- 2 cups amaranth leaves or baby spinach leaves
  Mint leaves, for garnish

MAKE THE SAUCE

1. In a small saucepan, bring the honey to a boil over high heat. Add the juice, stock, vinegar, orange blossom water and ras el hanout. Return to a boil and cook over moderately high heat until reduced by half (to about 1 cup), 16 to 18 minutes. Off the heat, whisk in 2 tablespoons of the butter. Season with salt and pepper; keep warm.

COOK THE DUCK

2. Meanwhile, preheat the oven to 425°. Place the duck legs on a foil-lined rimmed baking sheet and roast until heated through and browned, 14 to 16 minutes. Transfer to a plate and tent with foil to keep warm.

3. Using a paring knife, deeply score the skin of each duck breast every ½ inch in a crosshatch pattern; season with salt. In a large skillet, arrange the duck breasts skin side down. Cook over moderately low heat without turning until some of the fat has rendered and the skin is golden brown, 14 to 16 minutes. Turn the breasts over and cook until medium-rare (130° internal temperature), 2 to 3 minutes longer. Transfer to a cutting board and let rest. Drain the fat from the skillet and save for another use; reserve the skillet.

FINISH THE DISH

4. On a cutting board, trim the ends from each orange and then slice away all the peel and pith. Cut each orange crosswise into ¼-inch slices, then halve the slices.

5. Return the skillet to high heat and melt the remaining 2 tablespoons of butter. Add the amaranth leaves and swirl the skillet until they are wilted and fragrant, 20 seconds. Slice the duck breasts. Arrange the breasts and the amaranth on plates and drizzle with the sauce. Top with the duck legs and orange slices and garnish with mint leaves.

WINE Fragrant southern Rhône red: 2013 J.L. Chave Mon Coeur Côtes du Rhône.

THREE KEY STEPS

1

AIR-DRY THE DUCK Refrigerate the breasts uncovered on a rack overnight to remove moisture from the skin. It will get supercrisp and golden when cooked.

2

PREP THE ORANGES Cut the peel and pith from the blood oranges by slicing along the curves of the fruit. Then cut crosswise to make neat slices.

3

FINISH THE DISH Slice the duck breasts, drizzle with sauce and top with duck legs and orange slices.

BRAISED CHICKEN THIGHS
WITH POTATOES, PORCINI
AND DRIED CHERRIES

Braised Chicken Thighs with Potatoes, Porcini and Dried Cherries

Active **35 min**; Total **2 hr 45 min**; Serves **4**

- 1 Tbsp. plus 1 tsp. canola oil
- 11 large garlic cloves—8 whole and 3 crushed
- 1 cup sour cream or crème fraîche
- ½ cup dried porcini mushrooms (½ oz.)
  Kosher salt
- 2 lbs. large chicken thighs
- 2 medium Yukon Gold potatoes, peeled and sliced ⅛ inch thick
- ½ cup unsweetened dried sour cherries (about 2 oz.)
  Celery leaves, for garnish

1. In a medium saucepan, heat 1 teaspoon of the canola oil. Add the whole garlic cloves and cook over low heat, stirring, until golden and fragrant, about 5 minutes. Add 4 cups of water and bring to a boil. Cover and simmer over low heat until reduced to 2 cups, about 1 hour. Strain the garlic broth into a bowl.

2. In another bowl, whisk 1 cup of the garlic broth with the sour cream and porcini and season with salt; reserve the remaining garlic broth for another use.

3. Preheat the oven to 350°. In a large cast-iron skillet, heat the remaining 1 tablespoon of oil. Season the chicken with salt and cook over moderate heat until golden all over, about 10 minutes total. Transfer the chicken to a plate. Pour off all but 1 tablespoon of the oil in the skillet. Arrange the potato slices in the pan, overlapping them slightly. Set the chicken skin side down on top of the potatoes. Scatter the cherries and crushed garlic around the chicken and pour the garlic sauce with porcini on top. Roast the chicken for 20 minutes. Reduce the oven temperature to 300° and roast for about 45 minutes longer, until the potatoes are tender and the chicken is cooked through.

4. Preheat the broiler and arrange the rack 6 inches from the heat. Turn the chicken skin side up and broil until the skin is golden and crisp, about 8 minutes. Garnish with celery leaves and serve. —*Bonnie Morales*

WINE Earthy, black cherry–inflected Oregon Pinot Noir: 2013 Cloudline.

Honey-Thyme Chicken-and-Apricot Kebabs

Total **45 min**; Serves **4**

- ¼ cup honey
- 1 Tbsp. chopped thyme leaves
  Kosher salt and pepper
- 1 lb. skinless, boneless chicken thighs, cut into 1-inch pieces
- 4 apricots—halved, pitted and cut into 1-inch pieces
- 8 long wooden skewers, soaked in water for 30 minutes
  Extra-virgin olive oil, for brushing

1. In a small bowl, whisk the honey and 1 tablespoon of water with the thyme. Season with salt and pepper.

2. Light a grill or heat a grill pan. Thread the chicken and apricots onto the skewers. Brush the kebabs with olive oil and season with salt and pepper. Grill over moderate heat, turning occasionally, until the chicken is just cooked through, about 10 minutes. Transfer the kebabs to a platter, brush with the honey-thyme mixture and serve. —*Justin Chapple*

WINE Fruit-forward, lightly off-dry Washington state Riesling: 2013 Eroica.

Spicy Jerk Chicken

Active **40 min**; Total **1 hr 10 min plus 12 hr marinating**; Serves **6**

- 10 scallions, coarsely chopped
- 1 medium onion
- ⅓ cup thyme leaves
- 10 garlic cloves, peeled
- 2 to 3 Scotch bonnet or habanero chiles, stemmed
- One 4-inch piece of fresh ginger, peeled and thinly sliced
- 3 Tbsp. ground allspice
- 3 Tbsp. kosher salt
- 3 Tbsp. vegetable oil
- 12 skinless, boneless chicken thighs (about 2½ lbs.), cut into thirds
- 12 wooden skewers, soaked in water for 1 hour
  Fresh Pineapple Salsa (recipe follows), for serving

1. In a food processor, combine the scallions, onion, thyme, garlic, chiles, ginger, allspice, salt and vegetable oil and puree. Pour the puree into a large bowl, add the chicken and turn to coat. Cover and refrigerate for at least 12 hours or overnight, turning the chicken once or twice. Remove the chicken from the refrigerator 30 minutes before cooking.

2. Light a grill or heat a grill pan. Thread 3 pieces of chicken onto each skewer, wiping off as much of the marinade as possible as you go. Grill the chicken skewers over moderately high heat, turning once, until lightly charred outside and cooked through, about 8 minutes. Serve hot off the grill, with pineapple salsa. —*Suzanne Couch*

WINE Ripe, off-dry German Riesling: 2014 Christoffel Erdener Treppchen Kabinett.

FRESH PINEAPPLE SALSA

Active **15 min**; Total **45 min**
Makes **4 cups**

- 2 Tbsp. fresh lemon juice
- 1 Tbsp. sugar
- ½ tsp. kosher salt
- 1 garlic clove, finely chopped
- 1 small red onion, finely chopped
- 2 cups finely chopped fresh pineapple
- ⅓ cup finely chopped cilantro
- ¼ cup finely chopped green bell pepper
- ¼ cup finely chopped yellow bell pepper
- ¼ cup finely chopped red bell pepper
- ½ Scotch bonnet or habanero chile, stemmed and seeded

1. In a medium bowl, combine the lemon juice, sugar, salt and garlic; let stand for 10 minutes.

2. In a colander, rinse the onion under cold running water; drain well and pat dry. Add the onion and all of the remaining ingredients to the bowl with the garlic mixture and stir well. Cover and let stand at room temperature for about 30 minutes. Pick out and discard the Scotch bonnet chile before serving. —*SC*

Tunisian Chicken Skewers

Total **30 min plus 3 hr marinating**; Serves **8**

The marinade for these chicken skewers is spiked with tangy pomegranate syrup. It would also be delicious on whole chicken legs or breasts.

- **2** Tbsp. extra-virgin olive oil
- **½** small onion, thinly sliced
- **1** red bell pepper, chopped
- **½** cup drained mild Peppadew peppers, plus ¼ cup brine from the jar
- **½** cup raisins
- **¼** cup pomegranate molasses
- **¼** cup unsalted roasted peanuts
- **¼** tsp. cayenne

  Kosher salt and pepper
- **6** skinless, boneless chicken thighs (1½ lbs.), cut into 1½-inch pieces

  Eight 8-inch skewers, soaked in water for 30 minutes if wooden

1. In a large nonstick skillet, heat the olive oil. Add the onion and cook over moderately low heat, stirring occasionally, until lightly caramelized, about 10 minutes. Transfer the onion to a blender. Add the bell pepper, Peppadews and brine, raisins, pomegranate molasses, peanuts and cayenne to the blender and puree until smooth. Season the marinade with salt and pepper.

2. In a medium bowl, rub the marinade into the chicken. Cover and refrigerate for at least 3 hours or overnight.

3. Light a grill. Thread the chicken onto the skewers and season with salt and pepper. Grill over moderately high heat, turning, until lightly charred and cooked through, 10 to 12 minutes. Serve hot.
—*JohnPaul Damato*

MAKE AHEAD The marinade can be refrigerated overnight.

WINE White peach–scented, full-bodied white: 2014 Domaine de la Janasse Côtes du Rhône Blanc.

Rosemary Chicken with Rice Krispies

Total **45 min plus 1 hr marinating**; Serves **4**

Los Angeles chef Roy Choi says this crazy-crispy, cereal-topped chicken sounds a little weird, "but you're gonna love it!"

- Two 12-oz. bottles of beer, such as pale ale or lager
- **1** cup coarsely chopped rosemary sprigs plus ¼ tsp. chopped leaves
- **½** cup crushed garlic cloves plus 1 clove thinly sliced
- **½** cup apple cider vinegar

  Kosher salt and pepper
- **8** boneless skin-on chicken thighs (2 lbs.)
- **2** Tbsp. canola oil
- **1** cup Rice Krispies cereal
- **½** cup Grape-Nuts cereal
- **¼** cup chopped parsley

1. In a large bowl, combine the beer with the chopped rosemary sprigs, crushed garlic and vinegar and season with salt and pepper. Add the chicken and turn to coat. Cover and refrigerate for 1 hour.

2. Preheat the oven to 425°. Remove the chicken from the marinade and pat dry; discard the marinade. In a large cast-iron skillet, heat the oil. Season the chicken with salt and pepper. Cook half of the chicken skin side down over moderately high heat until golden and crisp, 4 to 5 minutes. Transfer to a plate. Repeat with the remaining chicken. Return all of the chicken to the skillet skin side up and bake for 15 to 20 minutes, until browned and cooked through. Transfer to a platter.

3. Pour off all but ¼ cup of the oil from the skillet. Add the chopped rosemary leaves, sliced garlic and Rice Krispies and cook over moderate heat, stirring, until the cereal is golden, about 3 minutes. Stir in the Grape-Nuts and parsley and season with salt and pepper. Sprinkle the Rice Krispies mixture on the chicken and serve.
—*Roy Choi*

MAKE AHEAD The chicken can be marinated overnight.

WINE Dark, fragrant, medium-bodied Austrian red: 2012 Moric Blaufränkisch.

Chipotle Chicken Tacos

Active **30 min**; Total **1 hr 15 min**; Serves **4**

At Empellón Al Pastor in New York City, chef Alex Stupak makes the tortillas for these spicy, saucy tacos with house-ground masa.

- **8** chicken thighs (3 lbs.)
- **2** Tbsp. vegetable oil, plus more for brushing

  Kosher salt and pepper
- **½** medium white onion, minced, plus more for serving
- **2** jalapeños—stemmed, seeded and minced
- **2** Tbsp. minced chipotle chiles plus 3 Tbsp. adobo sauce from the can or jar
- **4** plum tomatoes, finely chopped

  Warm corn tortillas, cilantro leaves, sour cream and lime wedges, for serving

1. Preheat the oven to 350°. On a large rimmed baking sheet, brush the chicken with oil and season with salt and pepper. Bake for about 45 minutes, until an instant-read thermometer inserted in the largest piece registers 165°. Let cool, then shred the meat; discard the skin and bones.

2. In a large skillet, heat the 2 tablespoons of vegetable oil until shimmering. Add the ½ onion, the jalapeños and a generous pinch of salt and cook over moderate heat, stirring occasionally, until just softened, about 5 minutes. Add the chipotles and adobo sauce and cook for 2 minutes. Add the tomatoes and cook until softened and any liquid has evaporated, about 7 minutes. Stir in the shredded chicken and cook until hot, about 3 minutes. Season with salt and pepper.

3. Spoon the chicken into warm corn tortillas and serve with cilantro, sour cream, lime wedges and minced onion.
—*Alex Stupak*

BEER Ice-cold canned Mexican lager: Mexicali.

Rosemary Chicken with Corn and Sausage Fricassee

Active **1 hr**; Total **2 hr**; Serves **6**

At her restaurant Compère Lapin, in The Old No. 77 Hotel in New Orleans, chef Nina Compton combines Italian sausage, vegetables and herbs for a Southern-style fricassee. With corn, tomatoes and basil, this is her summer version of the dish. She uses butternut squash and mushrooms in the fall, and fresh fava beans, English peas and fiddlehead ferns in the spring.

CHICKEN

- ½ cup kosher salt
- 12 chicken drumsticks
- ½ cup extra-virgin olive oil
- 4 large garlic cloves, chopped
- 2 Tbsp. finely chopped rosemary
- 1 Tbsp. finely grated lemon zest
- 1 tsp. crushed red pepper

FRICASSEE

- 6 scallions
- 3 Tbsp. extra-virgin olive oil
- 1 medium sweet onion, halved and thinly sliced lengthwise
  Kosher salt
- 4 oz. hot Italian sausage, casings removed
- 3 cups fresh corn kernels (from 4 ears)
- 2 cups cherry tomatoes (10 oz.), halved
- ¼ lb. sugar snap peas, halved lengthwise
- ½ cup torn basil leaves

1. Make the chicken In a large bowl, whisk the salt with 6 cups of cold water until dissolved. Add the chicken and refrigerate for 45 minutes. Remove the chicken and pat dry with paper towels. Wipe out the bowl.

2. In the same bowl, whisk the olive oil with the garlic, rosemary, lemon zest and crushed red pepper. Add the chicken and turn to coat, rubbing some of the marinade under the skin. Marinate the chicken at room temperature for 45 minutes.

3. Light a grill or heat a grill pan. Grill the chicken over moderate heat, turning occasionally, until the skin is lightly charred and an instant-read thermometer inserted in the thickest part of each leg registers 165°, about 25 minutes.

4. Meanwhile, make the fricassee In a large cast-iron skillet, cook the scallions over high heat until charred on the bottom, 3 minutes. Transfer to a work surface and cut into 1-inch lengths. In the same skillet, heat the olive oil. Add the onion and a generous pinch of salt and cook over moderately high heat, stirring occasionally, until softened and lightly browned, 6 minutes. Add the sausage and cook, breaking up the meat with a wooden spoon, until nearly cooked through, 6 to 8 minutes. Add the corn and tomatoes and cook, stirring occasionally, until the corn is crisp-tender and the tomatoes are softened, 5 minutes. Stir in the snap peas and cook until crisp-tender, about 2 minutes longer. Stir in the basil and scallions and season with salt. Transfer the fricassee to a platter, top with the chicken and serve. —*Nina Compton*

WINE Bright, ripe California Chardonnay: 2014 Bishop's Peak.

Herb-Basted Grilled Chicken

⏲ Total **35 min**; Serves **4**

- Kosher salt and pepper
- 2 garlic cloves, peeled and smashed
- 4 rosemary sprigs plus ½ Tbsp. chopped rosemary
- 4 thyme sprigs plus ½ Tbsp. chopped thyme
- ½ cup boiling water
- 2 lbs. skinless, boneless chicken thighs
- 2 Tbsp. extra-virgin olive oil
  Canola oil, for brushing

1. Light a grill. In a large heatproof bowl, combine 1 teaspoon of salt and ¼ teaspoon of pepper with the garlic and the chopped rosemary and thyme. Add the boiling water and stir until the salt dissolves. Tie the rosemary and thyme sprigs together with kitchen twine.

2. Rub the chicken all over with the olive oil and season with salt and pepper. Oil the grate and grill the chicken over moderate heat until nicely charred and cooked through, turning and using the herb bundle to baste the chicken with the brine as it cooks, 12 to 15 minutes. Transfer the chicken to plates and serve. —*Greg Denton and Gabrielle Quiñónez Denton*

WINE Crisp, savory Italian white: 2013 Sartarelli Verdicchio Classico.

Chicken Chile Verde

Total **1 hr**; Serves **4**

The secret to this stew from California chef Deborah Schneider is the tangy and spicy tomatillo and chile sauce. Schneider sometimes swaps pork, cubed tofu or vegetables like zucchini or mushrooms for the chicken.

- 2 poblano chiles
- 1 lb. tomatillos—husked, rinsed and quartered
- 1 large jalapeño, chopped
- 2 garlic cloves
- 1 white onion, minced
- 1 cup cilantro leaves
  Kosher salt and pepper
- 2 Tbsp. vegetable oil
- 1½ lbs. skinless, boneless chicken thighs, cut into ½-inch pieces
  Steamed rice, chopped avocado and sour cream, for serving

1. Roast the poblanos directly over a gas flame or under the broiler, turning, until charred all over. Transfer to a bowl, cover with plastic wrap and let cool. Peel, stem and seed the poblanos, then cut into ½-inch dice.

2. Meanwhile, in a medium saucepan, combine the tomatillos, jalapeño, garlic and half of the onion with 3 cups of water and bring to a boil. Simmer over moderately high heat until softened, 5 to 7 minutes. Drain the vegetables, reserving ½ cup of the cooking liquid.

3. In a blender, combine the boiled vegetables with the cilantro and reserved cooking liquid and puree until smooth. Season the sauce with salt and pepper.

4. In a large, deep skillet, heat the oil. Season the chicken with salt and pepper and cook over moderately high heat for 5 minutes, stirring occasionally. Add the remaining onion and the poblanos and cook, stirring occasionally, until the onion is just starting to brown, 5 to 7 minutes. Stir in the sauce and bring to a boil, then simmer over moderate heat until slightly thickened, about 5 minutes. Serve the chile verde with steamed rice, avocado and sour cream. —*Deborah Schneider*

WINE Zesty Sauvignon Blanc: 2013 Brander Santa Ynez Valley.

Chicken Legs Coq au Vin

📷 PAGE 141

Active **45 min**; Total **2 hr 15 min**; Serves **4**

- 8 chicken drumsticks (2 lbs.)
  Kosher salt and pepper
- 3 Tbsp. all-purpose flour
- 2 Tbsp. canola oil
- 1 slice of bacon, chopped (optional)
- ½ cup finely chopped carrot
- ½ cup finely chopped onion
- ½ cup finely chopped celery
- 1½ cups chopped mushrooms (3 oz.)
- 2 garlic cloves, thinly sliced
- ½ cup brandy
- 1 Tbsp. tomato paste
- 1 bottle dry red wine
- 1 cup chicken stock
- 2 thyme sprigs, plus chopped thyme for garnish

1. Season the chicken with salt and pepper and dust all over with 2 tablespoons of the flour. In a large cast-iron casserole, heat the oil. Add the chicken and cook over moderately high heat, turning, until golden, about 5 minutes. Transfer to a plate.

2. Add the bacon to the casserole and cook until crisp, 1 to 2 minutes. Add the carrot, onion, celery, mushrooms and garlic and cook over moderate heat, stirring, until golden, about 5 minutes. Stir in the brandy and cook until reduced by half, 1 minute. Stir in the tomato paste and the remaining 1 tablespoon of flour until incorporated. Add the wine, stock and thyme sprigs; bring to a boil. Return the chicken to the pot and bring to a simmer. Cover and cook over low heat, turning the chicken occasionally, until very tender, about 1½ hours. Transfer the chicken to a plate.

3. Simmer the sauce until thickened and reduced by half, about 10 minutes. Season with salt and pepper and discard the thyme sprigs. Return the chicken to the sauce and heat through. Garnish with chopped thyme and serve. —*Eric Ripert*

MAKE AHEAD The coq au vin can be refrigerated for up to 3 days.

WINE Fragrant, earthy red Burgundy: 2012 Bruno Clair Les Longeroies.

Chicken Legs with Honey and Aleppo

Active **20 min**; Total **1 hr plus overnight marinating**; Serves **6**

- ½ cup extra-virgin olive oil
- ⅓ cup honey
- ⅓ cup red wine vinegar
- 3 Tbsp. Aleppo pepper
- 2 Tbsp. kosher salt, plus more for sprinkling
- 6 garlic cloves, minced
- 1 Tbsp. finely chopped rosemary
- 1 Tbsp. finely chopped thyme
- 4 chicken drumsticks
- 4 chicken thighs

1. In a large bowl, combine all of the ingredients except the chicken and whisk until the honey is dissolved. Reserve 2 tablespoons of the marinade in a small bowl and refrigerate. Add the chicken to the large bowl and turn to coat. Cover and refrigerate overnight.

2. Preheat the oven to 425°. Line a large rimmed baking sheet with foil. Remove the chicken from the marinade, letting the excess drip back into the bowl. Arrange the chicken skin side up on the baking sheet. Roast for 40 to 45 minutes, until an instant-read thermometer inserted in the largest piece registers 160°. Transfer to a platter. Drizzle the chicken with the reserved marinade, sprinkle with salt and serve. —*Zoi Antonitsas*

SERVE WITH Flatbread, tzatziki and Greek salad.

WINE Spiced, brambly Sonoma Coast Pinot Noir: 2012 Red Car.

Coconut-Braised Chicken with Chorizo and Potatoes

Active **45 min**; Total **1 hr 45 min**; Serves **4**

CHICKEN

- 2 Tbsp. canola oil
- 6 whole chicken legs (2 lbs.)
  Kosher salt and pepper
- ½ lb. fresh Mexican chorizo
- 1 onion, thinly sliced
- 1 Tbsp. minced peeled fresh ginger
- 1 garlic clove, minced
- 1 dried chile de árbol, broken in half
- 3 cups unsweetened coconut milk
- 1 lb. baking potatoes, peeled and cut into 2-inch pieces
- 2 Tbsp. fresh lime juice, plus lime wedges for serving
- 1 Tbsp. unsalted butter

GREMOLATA

- ¼ cup finely chopped cilantro, plus sprigs for garnish
- 7 coffee beans, finely crushed (½ tsp.)
- 2 tsp. finely grated lime zest

1. Make the chicken Preheat the oven to 425°. In a large enameled cast-iron casserole, heat the oil. Season the chicken with salt and pepper. Working in 2 batches, brown the chicken over moderate heat, turning occasionally, about 8 minutes per batch. Transfer the chicken to a large plate. Add the chorizo and onion to the casserole and cook, stirring to break up the meat, until the onion is translucent, about 5 minutes. Stir in the ginger, garlic and chile and cook until fragrant, 1 minute. Add the coconut milk, potatoes and chicken to the casserole and bring to a simmer. Cover and braise in the oven for about 1 hour, until the chicken is cooked through. Stir in the lime juice and butter and season with salt.

2. Meanwhile, make the gremolata In a small bowl, combine all of the ingredients and mix well.

3. Spoon the braised chicken and potatoes into shallow bowls. Garnish with the gremolata and cilantro sprigs and serve with lime wedges. —*CJ Jacobson*

WINE Floral, berry-scented, light-bodied red: 2013 Castello di Verduno Pelaverga.

COCONUT-BRAISED
CHICKEN WITH CHORIZO
AND POTATOES

Grilled Chile Chicken with Saffron Potatoes

Active **40 min**; Total **1 hr 15 min plus 4 hr marinating**; Serves **4**

- 1 Tbsp. coriander seeds
- 1 tsp. cumin seeds
- ½ tsp. fenugreek seeds
- ½ tsp. mustard seeds
- 2 chiles de árbol
- 2 garlic cloves, crushed
- **One 1-inch piece of peeled fresh ginger, chopped**
- **One 2-inch piece of peeled fresh turmeric, chopped, or 1 tsp. ground turmeric**
- 2 serrano chiles, stemmed and chopped
- ½ cup canola oil, plus more for brushing
- 1½ cups chopped cilantro
- **Kosher salt**
- 4 whole chicken legs (2 lbs.)
- 1 lb. large fingerling potatoes, peeled and cut into 1-inch pieces
- 1 Tbsp. unsalted butter
- **Pinch of saffron threads**
- **Chopped mint and cilantro, for garnish**
- **Plain yogurt seasoned with salt, for serving**

1. In a small skillet, toast the coriander, cumin, fenugreek and mustard seeds and chiles de árbol over low heat, stirring, until very fragrant, about 5 minutes. Let cool slightly, then grind in a spice grinder.

2. In a blender, mince the garlic, ginger, turmeric and serranos with ¼ cup of the oil. Add the cilantro and the remaining ¼ cup of oil and puree to a coarse paste. Stir in the spice mixture and 1 teaspoon of salt.

3. In a large bowl, massage the marinade all over and under the chicken skin. Refrigerate at least 4 hours or overnight.

4. Light a grill or heat a grill pan and brush with oil. Grill the chicken over moderately low heat, turning, until golden and cooked through, about 40 minutes.

5. In a saucepan, cover the potatoes with water and add the butter and saffron. Simmer over moderate heat until tender, about 15 minutes. Drain and season with salt.

6. Arrange the chicken on the potatoes on a platter and garnish with mint and cilantro. Serve with seasoned yogurt.
—*Preeti Mistry*

WINE Perfumed, full-bodied white: 2013 Ferraton Samorëns Côtes du Rhône Blanc.

Chicken with Mole Negro

Active **1 hr**; Total **2 hr 40 min**; Serves **4**

"The process of making homemade mole negro is intense," says chef Marcela Valladolid, host of Food Network's *Mexican Made Easy*. "You dry the chiles yourself; you grind all the nuts to extract the oils. But I know that no one, including me, is going to grab a mortar." So she makes this thick, spicy sauce with store-bought nut butters instead. It's great with chicken and pork.

CHICKEN

- **One 4-lb. chicken, cut into 8 pieces, backbone reserved**
- 1 small onion, halved
- 2 garlic cloves, crushed
- 2 tsp. kosher salt

MOLE

- ¼ cup plus 2 Tbsp. lard, melted
- 2 oz. guajillo chiles—stemmed, seeded and chopped, seeds reserved
- 2 oz. pasilla chiles—stemmed, seeded and chopped, seeds reserved
- ½ lb. plum tomatoes, halved
- ½ small onion, chopped
- 3 garlic cloves, crushed
- 2 Tbsp. raisins
- ¼ tsp. dried oregano
- ⅛ tsp. cumin seeds
- ⅛ tsp. dried thyme
- 2 coriander seeds
- 2 black peppercorns
- 2 oz. tomatillos, husked and halved
- 3 Tbsp. chunky natural peanut butter
- 3 Tbsp. chunky roasted almond butter
- 3 Tbsp. tahini
- 1 Tbsp. kosher salt
- 2½ Tbsp. sugar
- 2 oz. Mexican chocolate, chopped
- **Sesame seeds, for garnish**

1. Make the chicken In a large pot, bring 2 quarts of water to a boil. Add the chicken pieces and backbone, onion, garlic and salt and return to a simmer. Cover and cook over low heat until the chicken is white throughout, about 20 minutes. Transfer the chicken to a plate and cover to keep warm. Simmer the broth to concentrate the flavor, about 30 minutes. Strain the broth; discard the solids, including the chicken backbone.

2. Make the mole In a large cast-iron skillet, heat ¼ cup of the lard. Add the chiles and cook over moderate heat, stirring, until toasted, about 2 minutes. Using a slotted spoon, transfer the chiles to a medium saucepan and cover with water. Bring to a boil and simmer until softened, 10 minutes; drain the chiles and transfer to a blender.

3. Add the tomatoes to the skillet cut side down and cook over moderate heat until lightly caramelized, about 3 minutes per side. Transfer the tomatoes to the blender. Wipe out the skillet.

4. Heat 1 tablespoon of the lard in the skillet. Add the onion and garlic and cook over moderate heat, stirring, until softened and golden, about 5 minutes. Add the chile seeds, raisins, oregano, cumin, thyme, coriander and peppercorns. Cook, stirring, until very fragrant, about 3 minutes. Scrape the mixture into the blender. Add the tomatillos, peanut butter, almond butter, tahini, salt, 1½ tablespoons of the sugar and 1½ cups of water and puree until thick and smooth. Strain the mole sauce into a large bowl.

5. Wipe out the skillet and heat the remaining 1 tablespoon of lard. Add 2 cups of the mole sauce and 2 cups of the chicken broth (reserve the remaining mole and broth for another use). Bring to a simmer over low heat, whisking constantly. Whisk in the chocolate and the remaining 1 tablespoon of sugar until melted. Cover and cook, whisking, until the mole has thickened and the flavors have melded, about 15 minutes. Add the chicken and cook until warmed through, about 5 minutes. Transfer the chicken and mole to a serving platter and garnish with sesame seeds. Serve warm. —*Marcela Valladolid*

WINE Spiced, dark-berried Oregon Pinot Noir: 2012 Cristom Mt. Jefferson Cuvée.

Double-Decker Dr Pepper Chicken Tacos

Active **2 hr**; Total **3 hr**; Serves **8 to 10**

Crazy-delicious potatoes, peppers and chiles plus chicken roasted on a can of Dr Pepper make up the filling for these flour-and-corn-tortilla tacos.

FILLING

- 1 **stick unsalted butter, softened**
- 1 **small onion, chopped, plus 1 large onion, thinly sliced**
- 2 **Tbsp. chili powder**
- 4 **garlic cloves, crushed**
- 1 **tsp. finely grated orange zest plus 2 Tbsp. fresh juice**
- 1 **tsp. finely grated lime zest plus 1 Tbsp. fresh juice**
- 1 **Tbsp. honey**
- 2 **tsp. ground cumin**
  Kosher salt and pepper
  One 4-lb. chicken
- 1 **lb. baby Yukon Gold potatoes, halved**
- 3 **poblano peppers, sliced lengthwise ½ inch thick**
- 1 **jalapeño, sliced lengthwise ¼ inch thick**
- ¼ **cup extra-virgin olive oil**
  One 12-oz. can Dr Pepper

TACOS

- **Canola oil, for frying**
- 20 **small corn tortillas**
- 20 **small flour tortillas**
- 2 **cups shredded Oaxaca cheese (½ lb.)**
  One 15-oz. can black beans, drained and rinsed
- 1¼ **cups finely chopped white onion**
- 1 **cup sour cream**
- 1 **Tbsp. fresh lime juice**
  Kosher salt
  Salsa, diced avocado, chopped cilantro and lime wedges, for serving

1. Make the filling Preheat the oven to 400°. In a food processor, combine the butter with the chopped onion, the chili powder, garlic, citrus zest and juice, honey, cumin and 1 tablespoon of salt; puree until smooth. Loosen the chicken's breast and thigh skin; spread three-fourths of the butter under the skin. Rub the remaining butter over the chicken and let stand for 30 minutes.

2. In a medium roasting pan, toss the potatoes with the poblanos, jalapeño, sliced onion and the olive oil and season with salt and pepper. Open the can of Dr Pepper and nestle it in the center of the roasting pan. Stand the chicken upright on the can and roast in the center of the oven for about 30 minutes, until lightly browned. Reduce the oven temperature to 325° and roast the chicken for about 45 minutes longer, until an instant-read thermometer inserted in the inner thigh registers 155° and the vegetables are tender. Let rest for 15 minutes, then transfer the chicken to a carving board. Discard the soda.

3. Remove the meat and skin from the chicken and shred. Add the shredded chicken and skin to the roasting pan and toss with the vegetables. Cover with foil and keep warm.

4. Make the tacos In a medium skillet, heat ¼ inch of canola oil until shimmering. Add 1 corn tortilla and cook over moderately high heat until pliable, about 20 seconds. Fold the tortilla in half and fry, using tongs to prop it open and turning occasionally, until a crisp shell forms, 1 to 2 minutes longer. Transfer to a paper towel–lined baking sheet. Repeat with the remaining corn tortillas; add more oil as necessary.

5. Heat a large cast-iron griddle over moderate heat. Place 2 or 3 flour tortillas on the griddle and scatter 2 scant tablespoons of the cheese and 1 tablespoon each of the beans and white onion on top. Cook over moderate heat until the cheese is melted, 1 to 2 minutes. Working quickly, wrap a crispy corn tortilla in a flour tortilla, pressing gently to help it adhere. Repeat with the remaining flour tortillas, cheese, beans and white onion.

6. In a bowl, whisk the sour cream with the lime juice; season with salt. Fill the double-decker taco shells with the chicken and vegetables. Serve with the lime cream, salsa, avocado, cilantro and lime wedges. —*Courtney McBroom*

MAKE AHEAD The taco filling can be refrigerated overnight. Reheat gently.

WINE Light-bodied, fruit-forward French red: 2013 Georges Descombes Beaujolais.

Apricot-Thyme-Glazed Roast Chicken

Active **20 min**; Total **1 hr 40 min**; Serves **4**

This chicken gets its sweet, slightly herbal flavor from the buttery glaze brushed on during the last 20 minutes of roasting.

- ½ **cup dried apricots**
- 3 **Tbsp. unsalted butter**
- 2 **tsp. chopped thyme**
  Kosher salt and pepper
- 5 **Tbsp. extra-virgin olive oil**
  One 4-lb. chicken
- 1 **Meyer lemon, halved**
- 3 **cups low-sodium chicken broth**

1. Preheat the oven to 450°. In a small heatproof bowl, cover the apricots with boiling water and let stand until softened, about 15 minutes. Drain the apricots; discard the water.

2. In a food processor, puree the apricots with the butter until smooth. Scrape into a small bowl, add the thyme and season with salt and pepper. Transfer ¼ cup of the apricot butter to another small bowl and whisk in 3 tablespoons of the oil to make a glaze.

3. Place the chicken on a rack set over a rimmed baking sheet. Season the cavity with salt and pepper. Squeeze the lemon halves all over the chicken, then stuff them in the cavity and tie the legs together with twine. Rub the remaining 2 tablespoons of oil all over the chicken and season with salt and pepper. Carefully pour the broth onto the baking sheet.

4. Roast the chicken for 35 minutes, until golden. Brush with half of the apricot glaze and roast for 10 minutes. Brush with the remaining glaze and roast for 5 to 10 minutes longer, until an instant-read thermometer inserted in the thigh registers 165°. Tilt the chicken to release the juices from the cavity, then transfer the chicken to a work surface and let rest for 15 minutes.

5. Strain the juices into a bowl; skim off the fat. Season with salt and pepper. Carve the chicken and serve with the pan jus and remaining apricot butter. —*Kay Chun*

WINE Ripe, full-bodied Chardonnay: 2014 Yalumba Y Series Unwooded.

SESAME-GINGER
CHICKEN MEATBALLS

Creole-Spiced Fried Chicken

Active **1 hr**; Total **13 hr**; Serves **8**

- **10** bags English Breakfast tea
- **¼** cup kosher salt
- **2** Tbsp. sugar
- **¾** cup JG Creole Spice Mix (recipe follows)
- Two 3½-lb. chickens, cut into 8 pieces each
- **2** cups buttermilk
- **¼** cup Tabasco or Crystal hot sauce
- **2** large eggs
- **2** cups all-purpose flour
- **2** cups fine cornmeal
- **¼** cup cornstarch
- Rendered pork lard or canola oil, for frying

1. In a large saucepan, combine 8 cups of water with the tea bags, salt, sugar and 2 tablespoons of the Creole spice mix. Bring just to a boil, stirring to dissolve the salt and sugar; let steep for 10 minutes. Discard the tea bags and let the brine cool completely. Submerge the chicken in the brine, cover and refrigerate for 6 hours.

2. In a large bowl, whisk the buttermilk with the hot sauce, eggs and 2 tablespoons of the Creole spice mix. Drain the chicken, discarding the brine. Add the chicken to the buttermilk mixture, turning to coat completely. Cover and refrigerate for at least 6 hours or overnight.

3. Preheat the oven to 250°. Line a large rimmed baking sheet with wax paper. In a large bowl, whisk the flour, cornmeal, cornstarch and remaining ½ cup of Creole spice mix. Remove the chicken from the buttermilk; let the excess drip into the bowl. Dredge the chicken in the flour mixture, then transfer to the prepared baking sheet.

4. In a large, heavy saucepan, heat 1½ inches of lard to 350°. Set a rack over a rimmed baking sheet. Add half of the coated chicken to the lard and fry at 300°, turning occasionally, until golden brown and an instant-read thermometer inserted in the thickest part of each piece registers 155°, 15 to 18 minutes. Transfer the fried chicken to the rack and keep warm in the oven while you fry the second batch. —*Josh Galliano*

WINE Lively, citrusy sparkling wine: NV Joseph Cattin Crémant d'Alsace Brut.

JG CREOLE SPICE MIX

Total **5 min**; Makes **1¼ cups**

- **½** cup paprika
- **¼** cup plus 2 Tbsp. kosher salt
- **2** Tbsp. garlic powder
- **2** Tbsp. onion powder
- **2** Tbsp. black pepper
- **1** Tbsp. dried thyme
- **1** Tbsp. dried oregano
- **1** Tbsp. dried basil
- **2** tsp. cayenne
- **1½** tsp. sugar
- **½** tsp. crushed red pepper

In a medium bowl, whisk together all of the ingredients until evenly combined. —*JG*

Sesame-Ginger Chicken Meatballs

Total **30 min**; Serves **4**

- Canola oil, for brushing
- **1** lb. ground chicken, preferably dark meat
- **½** cup plain dry breadcrumbs
- **⅓** cup minced scallions, plus thinly sliced scallions for garnish
- **3** Tbsp. minced peeled fresh ginger
- **1** large egg
- **2** garlic cloves, minced
- **2** tsp. toasted sesame oil
- **2** tsp. soy sauce
- **¼** tsp. kosher salt
- Asian chile sauce, for serving

Preheat the oven to 450° and brush a rimmed baking sheet with canola oil. In a large bowl, mix together all of the remaining ingredients except the sliced scallions and chile sauce. Form the chicken mixture into 1½-inch balls and arrange them on the baking sheet. Brush the meatballs with canola oil and bake for about 13 minutes, until browned and cooked through. Transfer the meatballs to a platter, garnish with sliced scallions and serve with Asian chile sauce. —*Justin Chapple*

WINE Brightly fruity, light-bodied Beaujolais: 2013 George Descombes Morgon.

Crispy Wok-Fried Chile Chicken

Total **45 min**; Serves **4**

- **1** large egg white, beaten
- **⅓** cup cornstarch
- **2** tsp. soy sauce
- **2** tsp. Shaoxing wine or dry sherry
- **1** tsp. toasted sesame oil
- **1¾** tsp. kosher salt
- **1** lb. skinless, boneless chicken thighs, cut into ¾-inch pieces
- **1** cup white rice flour
- **2** cups canola oil
- **1½** oz. Chinese dried red chiles
- **1** Tbsp. Sichuan peppercorns
- **2** tsp. minced peeled fresh ginger
- **1** tsp. minced garlic
- **8** scallions, cut into 1-inch lengths
- **1** tsp. sugar
- **1** cup lightly packed basil leaves

1. In a medium bowl, combine the egg white, cornstarch, soy sauce, wine, sesame oil and 1 teaspoon of the salt. Add the chicken and turn to coat. Let stand for 15 minutes.

2. Remove the chicken from the marinade and transfer to a large bowl. Add the rice flour and toss to coat, separating the pieces of chicken as necessary. Transfer the chicken to a colander and shake well to remove any excess rice flour.

3. In a wok, heat the canola oil to 300°. Add the chiles and fry until bright red and plump, about 15 seconds. Using a slotted spoon, transfer the chiles to another large bowl.

4. Heat the oil to 350°. Add half of the chicken and fry over high heat, stirring occasionally, until golden, crisp and cooked through, about 4 minutes. Transfer the chicken to the bowl with the chiles. Repeat with the remaining chicken.

5. Pour off all but 2 tablespoons of oil from the wok. Add the Sichuan peppercorns, ginger and garlic and stir-fry over moderate heat until softened but not browned, 30 seconds. Add the scallions and stir-fry for 15 seconds. Add the chicken, chiles, sugar and the remaining ¾ teaspoon of salt and stir-fry until hot, 2 minutes. Stir in the basil, transfer the chicken and chiles to a bowl and serve. —*Jerry Traunfeld*

WINE Fresh, lightly sweet German Riesling: 2014 Weiser-Künstler Feinherb.

Cast-Iron Roast Chicken with Lentils and Walnut Vinaigrette

Active **45 min**; Total **1 hr**; Serves **4**

LENTILS

½ cup walnuts

1 Tbsp. extra-virgin olive oil

1 small red onion, thinly sliced

1 cup black beluga lentils

1 bay leaf

½ cup balsamic vinegar

3 Tbsp. unsalted butter

1 Tbsp. Dijon mustard

Kosher salt and pepper

CHICKEN

2 Tbsp. extra-virgin olive oil

One 4-lb. chicken, backbone removed, chicken halved

Kosher salt and pepper

1 Tbsp. unsalted butter

WALNUT VINAIGRETTE

¼ cup toasted walnut oil

2 Tbsp. sherry vinegar

1 Tbsp. chopped parsley

Kosher salt and pepper

1. Make the lentils In a medium saucepan, toast the walnuts over moderate heat until lightly golden, about 5 minutes. Chop the nuts and transfer to a small bowl. In the same saucepan, heat the olive oil. Add the onion and cook over moderate heat, stirring occasionally, until golden, about 3 minutes. Add the lentils, bay leaf, balsamic vinegar and 1½ cups of water and bring to a simmer. Cover and cook over low heat for 15 minutes. Uncover and cook, stirring occasionally, until the liquid is absorbed and the lentils are just tender, 15 minutes longer. Stir in the butter and mustard and season with salt and pepper. Keep warm.

2. Meanwhile, make the chicken Preheat the oven to 400°. In a large cast-iron skillet, heat the olive oil. Season the chicken with salt and pepper and set breast side down in the skillet. Cover with foil and another large cast-iron skillet. Cook the chicken over moderate heat until golden, 8 to 10 minutes. Flip the chicken halves and roast in the oven, uncovered, until golden and an instant-read thermometer inserted in the inner thigh registers 165°, about 30 minutes. Transfer the chicken to a cutting board and let rest for 5 minutes. Whisk the butter into the pan juices and season with salt and pepper. Strain the jus; keep warm.

3. Make the vinaigrette In a small bowl, whisk the walnut oil with the sherry vinegar and parsley. Season with salt and pepper.

4. Carve the chicken. Stir the toasted walnuts into the lentils and spoon onto plates. Top with the chicken. Drizzle with the vinaigrette and serve the chicken jus on the side. —*Ryan Angulo*

MAKE AHEAD The lentils (without the walnuts) can be refrigerated overnight. Rewarm the lentils before serving.

WINE Tangy, earthy Rhône red: 2013 Saint Cosme Côtes du Rhône.

Whole Roast Chicken with 40 Brussels Sprouts

Active **10 min**; Total **1 hr 15 min**; Serves **4**

When F&W's Kay Chun roasts chicken, she adds brussels sprouts to the roasting pan so they absorb the fantastic flavor of the caraway-infused chicken juices.

One 4-lb. chicken

2 Tbsp. extra-virgin olive oil

Kosher salt and pepper

40 brussels sprouts (1½ lbs.), trimmed

2 Tbsp. unsalted butter, cubed

1 tsp. caraway seeds

2 Tbsp. fresh lemon juice, plus lemon wedges for serving

Preheat the oven to 450°. Rub the chicken with the olive oil and season with salt and pepper. Place the chicken in a roasting pan and roast for 30 minutes. Add the brussels sprouts, butter and caraway seeds to the pan and roast for 20 minutes longer, until the chicken is cooked through. Sprinkle the lemon juice over the sprouts and let the chicken rest for 15 minutes. Carve the chicken, toss the brussels sprouts and serve with lemon wedges. —*Kay Chun*

WINE Citrusy and peppery Grüner Veltliner: 2014 Hirsch Heiligenstein.

Roast Chicken Paprikash with Watercress and Dilled Sour Cream

Active **35 min**; Total **1 hr 20 min**; Serves **4**

In his fun riff on chicken paprikash, F&W's Justin Chapple rubs the bird with paprika, caraway and garlic before roasting, then serves it with sour cream mixed with dill.

One 3½-lb. chicken

2 Tbsp. extra-virgin olive oil

2 tsp. sweet paprika

2 tsp. hot paprika

2 tsp. caraway seeds

2 small garlic cloves, finely grated

Kosher salt and pepper

½ cup sour cream

2 Tbsp. minced dill

4 oz. watercress

1 Tbsp. fresh lemon juice

1. Preheat the oven to 425°. Using a small, sharp knife, make a ¾-inch slit in one side of the excess chicken skin around the cavity; carefully slip the end of the drumstick from the opposite side into the slit. Repeat on the other side of the chicken with the remaining drumstick.

2. In a small bowl, whisk 1 tablespoon of the olive oil with the sweet paprika, hot paprika, caraway, garlic, 1 tablespoon of kosher salt and ½ teaspoon of pepper. Set the chicken in a small roasting pan and rub all over with the mixture. Roast the chicken for about 45 minutes, until an instant-read thermometer inserted in the inner thigh registers 165°. Transfer the chicken to a carving board and let rest for 15 minutes.

3. Meanwhile, in a small bowl, whisk the sour cream with the dill and season with salt and pepper. On a platter, toss the watercress with the lemon juice and the remaining 1 tablespoon of olive oil and season with salt and pepper.

4. Carve the chicken and arrange the pieces on the watercress. Drizzle any pan juices over the chicken and serve right away, with the dilled sour cream. —*Justin Chapple*

WINE Ripe, fruit-forward Italian white: 2011 Sartori di Verona Ferdi Bianco.

ROAST CHICKEN
PAPRIKASH WITH
WATERCRESS
AND DILLED
SOUR CREAM

DUCK BREASTS
WITH DULCE DE
LECHE CHILE SAUCE

Duck Breasts with Dulce de Leche Chile Sauce

Total **1 hr**; Serves **6 to 8**

Dulce de leche makes a brilliant addition to the rich, spicy sauce that chef Aarón Sánchez serves alongside crispy pan-seared duck breasts. "I use dulce de leche in sauces as a substitute for honey," he says. "It adds sweetness, but because it's creamy, it also adds a stealth layer of richness."

- 4 ancho chiles, stemmed and seeded
- ½ cup fresh orange juice
- ½ cup chicken stock or low-sodium broth
- ¼ cup dulce de leche
- 3 garlic cloves, chopped
-    **Four 12-oz. Muscovy duck breast halves, excess fat removed and skin scored**
-    **Kosher salt and pepper**
- 1 chile de árbol
- 1 thyme sprig
- 3 Tbsp. unsalted butter, cut into cubes
- 2 Tbsp. fresh lemon juice
- 2 Tbsp. chopped cilantro, plus small sprigs for serving

1. In a large skillet, toast the ancho chiles over moderately high heat, turning, until fragrant and pliable, about 1 minute. Transfer to a heatproof bowl, cover with 2 cups of hot water and let stand until softened, about 20 minutes. Drain, reserving the soaking liquid.

2. In a small saucepan, simmer the orange juice over moderately high heat until reduced by half, 3 to 5 minutes. Transfer to a blender and add the stock, dulce de leche, anchos, 1 cup of the chile soaking liquid and one-third of the garlic. Puree until smooth.

3. Heat the large skillet. Season the duck breasts with salt and pepper and cook skin side down over moderate heat, spooning off the fat, until golden and crisp, about 10 minutes. Turn the duck skin side up and add the árbol chile, thyme, 2 tablespoons of the butter, the lemon juice and the remaining garlic to the skillet. Cook, basting the duck occasionally, until medium within, 8 minutes. Transfer the duck to a carving board and let rest for 5 minutes.

4. Pour off all but 2 tablespoons of fat from the skillet. Add the chile mixture and bring to a boil. Simmer over moderately high heat, stirring frequently, until just thickened, about 5 minutes. Off the heat, whisk in the remaining 1 tablespoon of butter and the chopped cilantro. Discard the árbol chile and thyme; season the sauce with salt and pepper. Thinly slice the duck across the grain and serve with the sauce and cilantro sprigs. —*Aarón Sánchez*

SERVE WITH Sautéed spinach.

WINE Lively, minerally Spanish Mencía: 2012 D. Ventura Viña do Burato.

Chicken Tagine with Herbs and Harissa Olives

Active **30 min**; Total **2 hr 15 min**; Serves **4**

This outstanding chicken dish is served in a sauce made with handfuls of herbs and plenty of spices.

- 3 mint sprigs
-    **One 4-lb. chicken, liver trimmed and chopped**
- 1 small onion, finely chopped
- 3 garlic cloves, minced
- 1½ cups parsley leaves
- 1 cup cilantro leaves
- 1 Tbsp. salted butter
- 2 tsp. ground coriander
- 1 tsp. turmeric
- 1 tsp. ground ginger
-    **Pinch of saffron threads**
-    **Kosher salt and pepper**
- ½ preserved lemon, rind only, finely chopped
- 2 Tbsp. extra-virgin olive oil
- 1 cup pitted green olives
- 1 Tbsp. harissa
-    **Crusty bread, for serving**

1. In a small saucepan, cover the mint with 1 cup of water and bring to a boil. Remove the pan from the heat and let stand for 15 minutes. Strain the tea into a small bowl and let cool.

2. In a large pot, rub the mint tea all over the chicken. Add the onion, garlic, parsley, cilantro, butter, coriander, turmeric, ginger, saffron and enough water to cover the chicken. Season with salt and pepper and bring to a simmer. Reduce the heat to

moderately low and simmer gently until the chicken is tender but not falling off the bone, 45 minutes. Transfer the chicken to a rack set over a rimmed baking sheet.

3. Strain the chicken cooking broth into a large bowl; reserve the solids. In the pot, combine the solids with 8 cups of the broth. Add the chicken liver and the preserved lemon and bring to a boil. Cook over moderate heat until thickened to a loose, sauce-like consistency, about 30 minutes. Season with salt and pepper.

4. Meanwhile, preheat the oven to 425°. Rub the chicken all over with the olive oil. Roast for about 30 minutes, until golden and crisp. Let the chicken rest for 10 minutes before carving.

5. In a bowl, toss the olives with the harissa until evenly coated. Serve the chicken with the sauce, harissa olives and crusty bread. —*Tara Stevens*

WINE Full-bodied Rhône white: 2013 Yves Cuilleron Les Vignes d'à Côté.

Chicken Roasted on Bread with Caperberries and Charred Lemons

Active **20 min**; Total **1 hr**; Serves **4**

- ½ lb. sourdough bread, torn into bite-size pieces
- 4 large shallots, quartered lengthwise
- ¾ cup drained caperberries
- 2 lemons, scrubbed and quartered lengthwise
- ¼ cup extra-virgin olive oil, plus more for brushing
-    **Kosher salt and pepper**
-    **Four 12-oz. whole chicken legs**

Preheat the oven to 400°. On a large rimmed baking sheet, toss the bread with the shallots, caperberries, lemons and the ¼ cup of olive oil; season with salt and pepper. Brush the chicken legs with oil and season with salt and pepper. Arrange the chicken on the bread and roast for about 50 minutes, until the bread is crisp and an instant-read thermometer inserted in the thighs registers 160°. Transfer the chicken, bread and vegetables to plates and serve. —*Justin Chapple*

WINE Fresh, Meyer lemon–scented Sicilian white: 2014 Graci Etna Bianco.

SELF-BASTING TURKEY

JUSTIN CHAPPLE, star of F&W's Mad Genius Tips videos, shares his method for making an effortlessly juicy bird, plus three amazing recipes. His basting trick: Soak a cheesecloth in melted flavored butter, then drape it over the turkey before roasting. The bird will become moist and rich.

STEP-BY-STEP

1

PREPARE THE CHEESECLOTH Dampen a cheesecloth with water, squeeze it dry, then soak it in melted flavored butter.

2

COVER THE TURKEY Drape the cheesecloth over the turkey breast and legs.

3

REMOVE THE CLOTH After roasting, carefully peel the cheesecloth off the turkey and discard.

Citrus-and-Butter Turkey
Active **40 min;** Total **3 hr 30 min**
Serves **10 to 12**

> One 12- to 14-lb. turkey, rinsed and patted dry
>
> Kosher salt and black pepper
>
> 1½ sticks unsalted butter
>
> 1½ Tbsp. finely grated grapefruit zest plus ¼ cup fresh grapefruit juice
>
> 1½ Tbsp. finely grated orange zest plus ¼ cup fresh orange juice
>
> 1½ Tbsp. finely grated lemon zest plus 3 Tbsp. fresh lemon juice
>
> 4 garlic cloves, finely grated
>
> 1 Tbsp. minced thyme plus 5 sprigs
>
> ½ grapefruit, cut into wedges
>
> ½ orange, cut into wedges
>
> 1 lemon, cut into wedges
>
> 3 cups chicken stock or low-sodium broth

1. Season the turkey inside and out with salt and pepper. Transfer to a rack set in a roasting pan and let the turkey come to room temperature.

2. Meanwhile, preheat the oven to 400°. In a medium saucepan, melt the butter. Whisk in the citrus zests and juices along with the garlic and minced thyme; let cool slightly. Transfer half of the citrus butter to a small bowl and refrigerate until spreadable, about 20 minutes.

3. Run your fingers under the breast and thigh skin to loosen it, then spread the chilled butter under the skin and over the breast and thighs. Stuff the turkey cavity with the thyme sprigs and the grapefruit, orange and lemon wedges. Dampen an 18-by-18-inch double-layer piece of cheesecloth with water and squeeze dry. Soak the cheesecloth in the remaining citrus butter and drape it over the breast and legs; pour any remaining butter on top.

4. Roast the turkey for about 30 minutes. Add the stock to the roasting pan and continue to roast for about 1 hour and 45 minutes longer, rotating the pan a few times, until an instant-read thermometer inserted in an inner thigh registers 165°.

5. Carefully peel the cheesecloth off the turkey. Transfer the turkey to a cutting board and let rest for 30 minutes. Skim the fat off the pan juices and transfer to a gravy bowl. Carve the turkey and serve with the pan juices.

WINE Fresh, grapefruit-scented white Bordeaux: 2014 Chateau de Fontenille.

Soy-and-Sesame Turkey
Active **40 min;** Total **3 hr 30 min**
Serves **10 to 12**

> One 12- to 14-lb. turkey, rinsed and patted dry
>
> Kosher salt and black pepper
>
> 1½ sticks unsalted butter
>
> ½ cup plus 2 Tbsp. soy sauce
>
> ½ cup plus 2 Tbsp. toasted sesame oil
>
> ½ cup minced scallions plus 6 whole scallions
>
> ¼ cup light brown sugar
>
> 3 Tbsp. finely grated peeled fresh ginger, plus one 3-inch piece, thinly sliced
>
> 1 tsp. crushed red pepper
>
> 3 cups chicken stock or low-sodium broth

1. Season the turkey inside and out with salt and pepper. Transfer to a rack set in a roasting pan and let the turkey come to room temperature.

2. Meanwhile, preheat the oven to 400°. In a medium saucepan, melt the butter. Whisk in the soy sauce, sesame oil, minced scallions, sugar, grated ginger and crushed red pepper; let cool slightly. Transfer half of the flavored butter to a small bowl and refrigerate until spreadable, about 20 minutes.

3. Run your fingers under the breast and thigh skin to loosen it, then spread the chilled butter under the skin and over the breast and thighs. Stuff the turkey cavity with the whole scallions and sliced ginger. Dampen an 18-by-18-inch double-layer piece of cheesecloth with water and squeeze dry. Soak the cheesecloth in the remaining flavored butter and drape it over the breast and legs; pour any remaining butter on top.

4. Roast the turkey for about 30 minutes. Add the stock to the roasting pan and continue to roast for about 1 hour and 45 minutes longer, rotating the pan a few times, until an instant-read thermometer inserted in an inner thigh registers 165°.

5. Carefully peel the cheesecloth off the turkey. Transfer the turkey to a cutting board and let rest for 30 minutes. Skim the fat off the pan juices and transfer to a gravy bowl. Carve the turkey and serve with the pan juices.

WINE Bold, fruit-forward Alsace Pinot Gris: 2012 Trimbach Reserve.

CITRUS-AND-BUTTER TURKEY
Citrus butter does double duty here before roasting: Some is spread under the skin and over the turkey; a cheesecloth soaked in the remaining butter gets draped over the breast and legs.

Chipotle-Butter Turkey

Active **40 min;** Total **3 hr 30 min**
Serves **10 to 12**

> One 12- to 14-lb. turkey, rinsed and patted dry
> Kosher salt and black pepper
> 2 sticks unsalted butter
> ½ cup distilled white vinegar
> ⅓ cup minced chipotle chiles in adobo
> 2 Tbsp. minced garlic, plus 1 head of garlic, halved crosswise
> 1 Tbsp. dried oregano plus 4 sprigs
> 1 Tbsp. chopped thyme plus 4 sprigs
> 1 lime, quartered
> 3 cups chicken stock or low-sodium broth

1. Season the turkey inside and out with salt and pepper. Transfer to a rack set in a roasting pan and let the turkey come to room temperature.

2. Meanwhile, preheat the oven to 400°. In a medium saucepan, melt the butter. Whisk in the vinegar, chipotles, minced garlic, dried oregano and chopped thyme; let cool slightly. Transfer half of the chipotle butter to a small bowl and refrigerate until spreadable, about 20 minutes.

3. Run your fingers under the turkey breast and thigh skin to loosen it, then spread the chilled butter under the skin and over the breast and thighs. Stuff the turkey cavity with the head of garlic, the lime wedges and the thyme and oregano sprigs. Dampen an 18-by-18-inch double-layer piece of cheesecloth with water and squeeze dry. Soak the cheesecloth in the remaining chipotle butter and drape it over the breast and legs; pour any remaining butter on top.

4. Roast the turkey for about 30 minutes. Add the stock to the roasting pan and continue to roast for about 1 hour and 45 minutes longer, rotating the pan a few times, until an instant-read thermometer inserted in an inner thigh registers 165°.

5. Carefully peel the cheesecloth off the turkey. Transfer the turkey to a cutting board and let rest for 30 minutes. Skim the fat off the pan juices and transfer to a gravy bowl. Carve the turkey and serve with the pan juices.

WINE Herb-scented, light-bodied red: 2014 Vietti Tre Vigne Dolcetto d'Alba.

Roast Turkey with Polenta Stuffing

Active **2 hr**; Total **5 hr**; Serves **10 to 12**

Instead of roasting a bird whole, star chef Tyler Florence spatchcocks turkey (removing the backbone and cracking the breastbone so the bird lies flat) to ensure that it cooks evenly. Ask your butcher to do this for you. You can gently prop up the turkey on a platter for a traditional presentation at the table.

STUFFING

- **6 cups turkey or chicken stock or low-sodium broth**
- **¼ cup extra-virgin olive oil**
- **2 lbs. sweet Italian sausage, casings removed and meat crumbled**
- **2 cups finely chopped onion (1 large onion)**
- **1 cup finely diced carrot (2 medium carrots)**
- **1 cup finely diced celery (3 celery ribs) Kosher salt and black pepper**
- **½ lb. mixed mushrooms, such as oyster and cremini, quartered**
- **3 cups fine polenta (not instant)**
- **6 thyme sprigs**
- **4 sage sprigs**
- **2 bay leaves**
- **1½ cups freshly grated Parmigiano-Reggiano cheese**

TURKEY

- **8 thyme sprigs**
- **6 sage sprigs**
  One 14- to 16-lb. turkey, butterflied
  Extra-virgin olive oil, for brushing
  Kosher salt and pepper

1. Make the stuffing In a medium saucepan, bring the stock and 6 cups of water just to a simmer over moderately high heat. Keep hot over very low heat.

2. In a large pot, heat the olive oil. Add the sausage and cook over moderately high heat, breaking up the meat with a wooden spoon, until browned and just cooked through, about 8 minutes. Using a slotted spoon, transfer the sausage to a bowl.

3. Add the onion, carrot, celery and a generous pinch of salt to the pot and cook over moderate heat, stirring occasionally, until softened and just starting to brown, about 8 minutes. Add the mushrooms and a generous pinch of salt and cook, stirring occasionally, until tender, about 8 minutes.

4. Return the sausage to the pot, then stir in the polenta, thyme, sage and bay leaves. Very gradually stir in the hot stock and bring to a boil. Simmer over moderately low heat, stirring frequently, until the polenta is tender and thick, 45 to 50 minutes. Pick out and discard the thyme, sage and bay leaves. Stir in the cheese and season the polenta with salt and pepper.

5. Spoon 3 cups of the polenta into a food processor and puree until smooth. Transfer to a bowl and let cool slightly. Scrape the remaining polenta dressing into a large baking dish, cover with foil and keep at room temperature.

6. Prepare the turkey Preheat the oven to 425°. Set a flat rack on a large rimmed baking sheet and spread the thyme and sage sprigs on it. Run your fingers under the turkey's breast and thigh skin to loosen it, then stuff the pureed polenta under the skin. Brush the turkey with olive oil and season with salt and pepper. Place on the rack breast side up and let stand at room temperature for 45 minutes.

7. Roast the turkey for about 1 hour and 40 minutes, until an instant-read thermometer inserted in the thickest part of the breast registers 155° and in the thickest part of a thigh registers 165°. Transfer to a carving board and let rest in a warm place for 30 minutes.

8. Meanwhile, in the oven, warm the polenta dressing in the baking dish for 20 minutes. Carve the turkey; serve with the dressing. —*Tyler Florence*

MAKE AHEAD The recipe can be prepared through Step 5 and refrigerated overnight. Rewarm the pureed polenta before stuffing under the skin; add water to thin it slightly if necessary. Reheat the polenta dressing before serving.

WINE Bold, brightly fruity Sonoma red: 2013 Bedrock Wine Co. The Bedrock Heritage.

Porchetta-Spiced Turkey with Pan Gravy

Active **1 hr**; Total **3 hr 15 min plus overnight drying**; Serves **12**

- **3 Tbsp. fennel seeds**
- **7 garlic cloves, minced**
- **2 Tbsp. chopped oregano plus 3 oregano sprigs**
- **1 Tbsp. chopped sage**
- **1 Tbsp. chopped rosemary**
- **1 Tbsp. chopped thyme**
- **1 tsp. coarsely ground black pepper**
- **2 tsp. finely grated lemon zest plus 1 Tbsp. fresh lemon juice**
- **½ tsp. crushed red pepper**
- **1 stick plus 3 Tbsp. unsalted butter, at room temperature**
  One 12-lb. turkey
- **2 Tbsp. extra-virgin olive oil**
  Kosher salt and pepper
- **¼ cup all-purpose flour**
- **4 cups low-sodium chicken broth**
- **2 Tbsp. chopped parsley**
  Caramelized lemon halves, for serving (see Note)

1. In a medium bowl, blend the fennel seeds, garlic, chopped oregano, sage, rosemary, thyme, coarsely ground black pepper, lemon zest and crushed red pepper with 1 stick of the butter.

2. Put the turkey on a rack set over a flameproof roasting pan. Using your fingertips and starting at the neck end of the turkey, carefully loosen the skin over the breast. Spread all but 2 tablespoons of the spiced butter under the skin in an even layer over the breast. Spread the remaining 2 tablespoons of spiced butter all over the skin. Refrigerate the turkey uncovered overnight.

3. Preheat the oven to 425°. Rub the olive oil all over the turkey and season with salt and pepper. Roast for about 1 hour and 45 minutes, until the turkey is golden and an instant-read thermometer inserted in an inner thigh registers 160°.

4. Transfer the turkey to a cutting board. Carefully tilt the turkey and pour the cavity juices into a medium bowl. Let the turkey rest for 30 minutes.

5. Meanwhile, pour off all but ¼ cup of fat from the roasting pan. Add the flour and set the roasting pan over low heat. Cook, stirring, until the flour is golden, 1 to 2 minutes. Stir in the broth, turkey cavity juices and oregano sprigs and bring to a simmer, scraping up any browned bits. Cook until thickened, 4 to 5 minutes. Whisk in the remaining 3 tablespoons of butter and the lemon juice and season with salt and pepper. Strain the gravy into a gravy boat and stir in the parsley.

6. Carve the turkey and serve with the pan gravy and caramelized lemon halves.
—*Kay Chun*

NOTE To caramelize lemon halves, sear them cut side down in a hot cast-iron skillet until browned, about 3 minutes.

WINE Earthy, fragrant Piedmontese red: 2013 Guidobono Langhe Nebbiolo.

Green Goddess Turkey Burgers
☼ Total **30 min**; Serves **4**

1½ lbs. ground turkey
⅓ cup finely chopped basil
⅓ cup finely chopped scallions
⅓ cup finely chopped parsley
 1 Tbsp. minced anchovy
   Kosher salt and pepper
⅓ cup mayonnaise, plus more
   for serving
 4 hamburger buns, split and toasted
   Sliced red onion and baby greens,
   for serving

1. In a large bowl, using a fork, gently stir the turkey with the basil, scallions, parsley, anchovy, 1 teaspoon of salt, ½ teaspoon of pepper and the ⅓ cup of mayonnaise. Using 2 plastic lids from 1-quart takeout containers, press the turkey mixture into 4 patties. Transfer to a plate.

2. Light a grill or heat a grill pan. Season the patties lightly with salt and pepper. Grill over moderately high heat, turning once, until cooked through, about 8 minutes. Transfer the burgers to the buns, top with mayonnaise, onion and greens and serve.
—*Justin Chapple*

MAKE AHEAD The patties can be refrigerated for up to 3 hours before grilling.

WINE Crisp, medium-bodied Verdicchio: 2013 Le Vaglie.

Ginger Turkey Meatballs
☼ Total **45 min**; Makes **40**

 2 lbs. 85% lean ground turkey
½ cup minced red onion
 3 Tbsp. finely grated peeled
   fresh ginger
 3 Tbsp. sambar masala (see Note)
 1 tsp. finely grated peeled
   fresh turmeric
1½ tsp. fine sea salt
 2 Tbsp. canola oil
   Cilantro leaves, for garnish

1. Preheat the oven to 400°. In a large bowl, mix the ground turkey with the onion, ginger, masala, turmeric and salt. Using a 2-tablespoon scoop, scoop and roll the meatballs and place on a large baking sheet.

2. In a very large skillet, heat 1 tablespoon of the oil. Add half of the meatballs and cook over moderate heat, turning, until browned all over, 5 to 7 minutes. Using a slotted spoon, transfer the meatballs to the baking sheet. Repeat with the remaining 1 tablespoon of oil and meatballs.

3. Bake the meatballs in the oven for about 8 minutes, until cooked through. Arrange the meatballs on a platter, garnish with cilantro and serve.
—*Akasha Richmond*

NOTE Sambar masala is a spice blend made with myriad spices, including coriander, fenugreek and cumin. Look for it at Indian markets and on amazon.com.

MAKE AHEAD The meatballs can be made up to 6 hours ahead; serve at room temperature or reheat gently.

WINE Berry-forward Beaujolais: 2013 Domaine du Clos du Fief Juliénas.

Fried Italian Turkey-and-Cheese Meatballs
Active **1 hr**; Total **2 hr 15 min**
Makes **about 2 dozen**

 1 lb. medium Yukon Gold
   potatoes, peeled
 1 lb. cooked turkey,
   shredded or chopped
½ cup freshly grated Parmigiano-
   Reggiano cheese
½ cup minced parsley
 2 garlic cloves, minced
   Pinch of freshly grated nutmeg
 4 large eggs, lightly beaten
   Kosher salt and pepper
 1 cup all-purpose flour, plus
   more for dusting
 2 cups plain breadcrumbs
   Vegetable oil, for frying
   Lemon wedges, for serving

1. In a medium saucepan, cover the potatoes with water and bring to a boil. Cook over high heat until tender, about 15 minutes. Drain the potatoes and let cool for 5 minutes, then mash.

2. In a food processor, pulse the turkey until finely chopped. Add the potatoes, cheese, parsley, garlic, nutmeg and half of the beaten eggs. Season with salt and pepper and pulse until well mixed. Scrape the mixture into a bowl, cover with plastic and refrigerate for at least 1 hour or overnight.

3. On a lightly floured work surface, knead the meat mixture into a ball. Cut the ball in half, then roll each half into a 17-inch-long rope, about 1 inch thick. Cut the ropes into 1½-inch pieces; roll each piece into a ball.

4. Put the 1 cup of flour in a shallow bowl, the remaining beaten eggs in a second bowl and the breadcrumbs in a third bowl. Dredge each turkey meatball in the flour, then dip in the egg and coat with the bread crumbs. Arrange the coated meatballs on a baking sheet.

5. In a large, deep skillet, heat 1 inch of oil to 375°. Working in 2 batches, fry the meatballs, turning, until golden and cooked through, about 4 minutes per batch. Using a slotted spoon, transfer the meatballs to paper towels to drain. Sprinkle with salt; serve with lemon. —*Anya von Bremzen*

WINE Lively Italian sparkling wine: NV Sorelle Bronca Extra Dry Prosecco.

Chef Zak Pelaccio and his wife, Jori Jayne Emde (far right), host a garden-inspired cookout in New York's Hudson Valley. On the grill: juicy pork belly slicked with a tangy rhubarb glaze (recipe, p. 182).

PORK

GLAZED
AGRODOLCE RIBS
Recipe, page 181

Citrus-Marinated Pork Chops

Total **1 hr**; Serves **4**

Seamus Mullen, chef at New York City's Tertulia, serves his citrus-glazed pork chops with a fresh, spicy slaw that's an unexpected combination of endives, cauliflower and jalapeños.

PORK

- 1 cup fresh orange juice
- 1 tsp. finely grated lemon zest plus ¼ cup fresh lemon juice
- 1 tsp. finely grated lime zest plus ¼ cup fresh lime juice
- ¼ cup honey
- 2 garlic cloves, crushed
- 1 small red onion, sliced

  Four 10-oz. bone-in pork loin chops, cut 1 inch thick
- 3 Tbsp. extra-virgin olive oil

  Kosher salt and pepper
- 4 Tbsp. unsalted butter

SLAW

- 3 Tbsp. coconut oil
- 3 Tbsp. vinegar
- 1 garlic clove, minced
- ½ tsp. finely grated orange zest plus ¼ cup fresh orange juice
- 2 endives—halved lengthwise, cored and thinly sliced
- 1 jalapeño, thinly sliced
- ½ head of cauliflower, florets thinly sliced
- ¼ cup chopped cilantro

  Kosher salt and pepper
- ⅓ cup roasted cashews, chopped
- ⅓ cup unsweetened coconut flakes

1. Prepare the pork Whisk the citrus juices and zests with the honey, garlic and onion. Add the chops and let stand at room temperature for 15 minutes.

2. Remove the chops from the marinade. Strain and reserve the marinade. In a large nonstick skillet, heat 2 tablespoons of the olive oil. Season the chops with salt and pepper, add 2 to the skillet and cook over moderately high heat until golden, about 2 minutes per side; transfer to a plate. Repeat with the remaining 1 tablespoon of olive oil and 2 chops. Clean the skillet.

3. In the same skillet, melt the butter. Add the chops and the strained marinade and cook over moderate heat, turning and basting, until the chops are cooked through, 6 to 8 minutes; an instant-read thermometer inserted in the center of each chop should register 135°. Transfer the chops to plates and spoon some of the sauce on top.

4. Meanwhile, make the slaw In a large bowl, whisk the coconut oil, vinegar, garlic and orange zest and juice. Add the endives, jalapeño, cauliflower and cilantro, season with salt and pepper and toss well.

5. Top the chops with the slaw. Scatter the cashews and coconut flakes on top and serve. —*Seamus Mullen*

WINE Juicy, raspberry-inflected Garnacha: 2012 Celler de Capçanes Mas Donís.

Crispy Pork Chops with Warm Fennel Salad

⏱ Total **45 min**; Serves **4**

Pounding bone-in pork chops schnitzel-thin before pan-frying means they cook in just 5 minutes, so the meat stays tender within the crispy panko crust. The secret ingredient in the coating here: ground fennel.

- ¾ cup all-purpose flour
- 2 tsp. ground fennel

  Kosher salt and pepper
- 1 large egg
- 2 cups panko

  Four 8-oz. bone-in pork rib chops, meat pounded ⅛ inch thick
- 2 Tbsp. unsalted butter
- 5 Tbsp. extra-virgin olive oil
- 2 fennel bulbs (1¼ lbs.), cored and thinly sliced
- 2 Tbsp. fresh lemon juice
- ⅓ cup chopped pitted oil-cured olives
- 1 Fuji apple, finely chopped

  Lemon wedges, for serving

1. In a shallow dish, mix the flour and ground fennel; season with salt and pepper. In another shallow dish, beat the egg. In a third shallow dish, spread the panko and season with salt and pepper. Dredge the pork chops in the flour, shaking off the excess. Dip them in the egg, then dredge in the panko to coat. Place the pork chops on a large plate.

2. In a large cast-iron skillet, melt ½ tablespoon of the butter in 1 tablespoon of the oil. Add 2 of the chops and cook over moderately high heat until golden, about 2 minutes. Flip the chops, add another ½ tablespoon of butter and 1 tablespoon of oil to the skillet and cook until just golden on the outside and white throughout, about 2 minutes. Transfer the chops to a paper towel–lined plate. Wipe out the skillet. Repeat the process to fry the remaining 2 pork chops.

3. Wipe out the skillet and add the remaining 1 tablespoon of oil. Add the fennel and cook over moderately high heat, stirring occasionally, until light golden and crisp-tender, about 3 minutes. Stir in the lemon juice and olives and cook until the olives are warm, about 1 minute. Stir in the apple and season with salt and pepper. Transfer the pork chops to plates and top with the fennel salad. Serve with lemon wedges. —*Kay Chun*

WINE Floral, citrus-edged Chardonnay: 2013 Varner Bee Block.

Pork Chops with Fennel and Juniper

📷 FRONT COVER

Active **30 min**; Total **3 hr 45 min**; Serves **4**

When her Roman butcher can get it, cookbook author Rachel Roddy uses pork from a revered breed of Tuscan pig, the white-belted Cinta Senese. She rubs the chops with a mix of crushed juniper, fresh fennel and fennel seeds to give them a fragrant, herbal flavor.

½ cup plus 2 Tbsp. extra-virgin olive oil

6 garlic cloves, chopped

12 juniper berries, crushed

1 Tbsp. fennel seeds, crushed

 Four 1-inch-thick bone-in pork rib chops (12 oz. each)

 Kosher salt and pepper

1 fennel bulb with fronds, bulb and fronds coarsely chopped

1. In a small bowl, mix ½ cup of the olive oil with the garlic, juniper berries and fennel seeds. Season the pork chops with salt and pepper and rub all over with the garlic-juniper oil. Arrange the pork in a baking dish or place in a resealable plastic bag. Add the chopped fennel and fronds and turn to coat. Cover and refrigerate for 3 to 4 hours. Remove the pork from the marinade; discard the marinade.

2. Preheat the oven to 425°. In a large cast-iron grill pan, heat the remaining 2 tablespoons of olive oil. Add the chops and cook over moderately high heat, turning once, until golden, about 5 minutes. Transfer the pan to the oven and roast the chops for 12 to 14 minutes, until an instant-read thermometer inserted in the center of a chop registers 140°. Transfer the chops to a cutting board and let rest for 5 minutes before serving. —*Rachel Roddy*

SERVE WITH Grilled young fennel.

WINE Cherry-rich, lightly herbal Tuscan red: 2010 Villa di Capezzana Carmignano.

Grilled Pork Chops with Malt and Burnt Onion Glaze

Active **1 hr**; Total **2 hr 10 min**; Serves **8**

4 yellow onions—2 peeled, quartered and separated into petals, and 2 peeled and chopped

2 Tbsp. grapeseed oil

1 cup barley malt syrup (see Note)

 Kosher salt and pepper

 Four 1-inch-thick meaty pork blade chops (3½ lbs.)

¼ cup canola oil

1 lb. Japanese eggplants, halved lengthwise

2 Tbsp. chopped parsley

2 Tbsp. chopped mint

2 Tbsp. chopped cilantro

½ tsp. finely grated lemon zest, plus lemon wedges for serving

¼ tsp. ground cinnamon

⅛ tsp. finely grated garlic

1. Preheat the oven to 425°. Line a baking sheet with foil. Spread the onion petals on the foil and roast for about 1 hour, until completely black. Transfer to a blender and blend until powdery black ash forms.

2. In a large skillet, heat the grapeseed oil. Add the chopped onion and cook over moderate heat, stirring, until golden, about 10 minutes. Stir in the syrup and onion ash; remove from the heat. Let stand for 5 minutes. Transfer the mixture to the blender and puree until smooth. Scrape the glaze into a medium bowl and season with salt.

3. Light a grill. Rub the pork chops with 2 tablespoons of the canola oil and season with salt and pepper. Grill over moderate heat, turning and basting occasionally with the onion glaze, until an instant-read thermometer inserted in the thickest part of a chop registers 140°, about 15 minutes. Transfer the chops to a cutting board and let rest for 10 minutes.

4. Meanwhile, in a medium bowl, toss the eggplant with the remaining 2 tablespoons of canola oil and season with salt and pepper. Grill over moderate heat, turning, until nicely charred and tender, about 8 minutes.

5. In a small bowl, mix the herbs with the lemon zest, cinnamon and garlic and season with salt. Thinly slice the chops and transfer to plates. Add the eggplant and sprinkle with the cinnamon gremolata. Serve with lemon wedges. —*Jim Christiansen*

NOTE Barley malt syrup is available at health food stores and online from kingarthurflour.com.

MAKE AHEAD The glaze can be refrigerated for up to 3 days.

WINE Earthy, red-berried Italian red: 2013 La Kiuva Arnad-Montjovet.

Chicken-Fried Pork

🕐 Total **30 min**; Serves **4**

2 large eggs

1 Tbsp. whole milk

1 cup all-purpose flour

2 cups panko (2½ oz.)

 Four 6-oz. boneless pork loin chops, pounded ⅓ inch thick

 Kosher salt and pepper

4 Tbsp. unsalted butter

2 Tbsp. extra-virgin olive oil

 Lemon wedges, for serving

1. Preheat the oven to 300°. In a shallow bowl, beat the eggs with the milk. Put the flour and panko into 2 separate shallow bowls. Season the pork with salt and pepper; dredge in the flour, then dip in the eggs and coat with the panko, pressing lightly to help it adhere.

2. Set a rack on a baking sheet. In a large skillet, melt 1 tablespoon of the butter in 1 tablespoon of the olive oil. Add 2 pieces of pork and cook over moderately high heat until golden, about 2 minutes. Flip the pork, add another tablespoon of butter to the skillet and cook until the pork is golden brown and cooked through, about 3 minutes. Transfer to the rack and keep warm in the oven. Wipe out the skillet and repeat to fry the remaining 2 pork chops. Transfer the chops to plates and serve with lemon wedges. —*Ford Fry*

WINE Ripe, full-bodied German Riesling: 2013 Hexamer Quarzit.

Pork Milanese with Dandelion Green Salad

⏱ Total **45 min**; Serves **4 to 6**

- 2 large eggs
- 1 cup all-purpose flour
- 2 cups panko
- Six 3-oz. pork loin cutlets
- Kosher salt and pepper
- 1 tsp. extra-virgin olive oil, plus more for frying
- 4 bacon slices (4 oz.), cut crosswise ¼ inch thick
- 2 Granny Smith apples, peeled and cut into ½-inch dice
- ½ small red onion, cut into thin strips
- ½ cup apple cider
- 2½ Tbsp. apple cider vinegar
- ½ lb. dandelion greens, thick stems discarded, leaves cut crosswise into 1-inch pieces

1. Preheat the oven to 200°. Line a large baking sheet with paper towels. In a shallow bowl, beat the eggs with 1 tablespoon of water. Put the flour and panko in 2 separate shallow bowls.

2. Season the pork cutlets with salt and pepper. Dredge in the flour, then dip in the egg, letting the excess drip back into the bowl. Dredge the coated pork in the panko, pressing lightly to help it adhere.

3. In a large skillet, heat ¼ inch of olive oil until shimmering. Add 3 of the cutlets and fry over moderately high heat, turning once, until browned and just cooked through, about 5 minutes; transfer to the prepared baking sheet. Repeat with the remaining cutlets. Transfer the pork to the oven to keep warm.

4. Wipe out the skillet and heat the 1 teaspoon of olive oil in it. Add the bacon and cook over moderate heat, stirring, until browned and crisp, 3 to 5 minutes. Add the apples and onion and cook over moderately high heat, stirring occasionally, until the apple just starts to soften, about 3 minutes. Add the apple cider and vinegar and cook until the liquid is reduced by half, about 3 minutes.

5. Scrape the apple mixture into a large bowl. Add the dandelion greens and toss well. Season with salt and pepper and toss again. Transfer the pork Milanese to plates, top with the salad and serve right away. —*Anne Burrell*

WINE Spiced, cherry-rich Oregon Pinot Noir: 2013 St. Innocent Temperance Hill.

Beet-and-Caraway-Roasted Pork Tenderloin

Active **15 min**; Total **1 hr 15 min**
Serves **4 to 6**

This pork roast gets its striking fuchsia color from an unexpected ingredient: beet peels. Along with the caraway seeds, they add a sweet earthiness.

- 3 oz. red beet peels (1½ cups)
- 2 Tbsp. kosher salt
- 2 tsp. caraway seeds
- Two 1-lb. pork tenderloins
- 2 Tbsp. extra-virgin olive oil, plus more for drizzling
- Pepper
- Lemon wedges, for serving

1. In a mini food processor, puree the beet peels, salt and caraway seeds until a paste forms. On a rimmed baking sheet, rub each pork tenderloin with 2 tablespoons of the beet paste. Let stand at room temperature for 30 minutes.

2. Preheat the oven to 400°. Drizzle the pork with the 2 tablespoons of olive oil and season with pepper. Roast for 25 to 30 minutes, until an instant-read thermometer inserted in the center registers 135°. Transfer to a cutting board and let rest for 10 minutes. Slice the pork ½ inch thick and transfer to a platter. Drizzle with olive oil and serve with lemon wedges. —*Justin Chapple*

WINE Dark-berried, lightly herbal Loire Valley Cabernet Franc: 2010 Olga Raffault Les Picasses Chinon.

Pork Tenderloin with Sage, Garlic and Honey

📷 PAGE 6

Active **35 min**; Total **1 hr 30 min**; Serves **4**

- ½ tsp. freshly grated nutmeg
- One 1½-lb. pork tenderloin, cut in half crosswise and tied (have your butcher do this)
- Kosher salt and pepper
- 3 large garlic cloves, thinly sliced
- 12 sage leaves
- 3 Tbsp. unsalted butter
- 3 Tbsp. extra-virgin olive oil
- ½ medium onion, thinly sliced
- 1 small carrot, sliced
- 2 thyme sprigs
- 1 bay leaf
- ½ cup dry white wine
- 1 cup chicken stock
- 2 Tbsp. honey

1. Rub the nutmeg all over the pork and season generously with salt and pepper. Tuck the garlic and sage under the strings and let the pork stand at room temperature for 30 minutes.

2. In a large, deep skillet, melt 2 tablespoons of the butter in the oil. Cook the pork over high heat, turning, until browned all over, about 7 minutes. Transfer to a plate.

3. Pour off all but 2 tablespoons of fat from the skillet. Add the onion, carrot, thyme, bay leaf and a generous pinch each of salt and pepper. Cook over moderately high heat, stirring occasionally, until the vegetables are softened and browned, 3 to 5 minutes. Add the wine and simmer for 1 minute. Add the stock and bring to a boil. Return the pork to the skillet, cover and braise over moderately low heat, turning occasionally, until an instant-read thermometer inserted in the pork registers 135°, 13 to 15 minutes. Transfer the pork to a carving board; let rest for 10 minutes.

4. Meanwhile, strain the braising liquid; discard the solids. Return the liquid to the skillet and bring to a simmer. Remove from the heat; whisk in the honey and remaining butter. Season with salt and pepper.

5. Discard the string. Slice the tenderloin. Serve with the sauce. —*Mimi Thorisson*

WINE Cabernet-forward Left Bank Bordeaux: 2011 Château de Pez.

Thyme-Basted Pork Tenderloin with Oyster Mushrooms

⏱ Total **45 min**; Serves **4**

Chef Dai Shinozuka of Les Enfants Rouges in Paris garnishes pan-roasted pork with an enticing, crunchy mix of walnuts, shallot and chives.

- 1 Tbsp. grapeseed oil
  One 1¼-lb. pork tenderloin
  Kosher salt and pepper
- 4 Tbsp. unsalted butter
- ¼ cup extra-virgin olive oil
- 1½ lbs. oyster mushrooms, trimmed and torn into 1-inch pieces
- 4 garlic cloves—2 minced and 2 crushed
- 2 Tbsp. chopped parsley
- 2 large thyme sprigs
  Toasted walnuts, chopped shallot and chives and flaky sea salt, for garnish

1. In a 12-inch ovenproof skillet, heat the grapeseed oil until shimmering. Season the pork with salt and pepper and cook over moderately high heat until browned all over, about 5 minutes. Transfer to the oven and roast the pork until an instant-read thermometer inserted in the thickest part registers 135°, 18 to 20 minutes.

2. Meanwhile, in a very large skillet, melt 1 tablespoon of the butter in the olive oil. Add the mushrooms, season with salt and pepper and cook over moderately high heat, turning occasionally, until golden, about 15 minutes. Add the minced garlic and the parsley and cook, stirring, until the garlic is fragrant, about 30 seconds. Remove from the heat.

3. Set the pork over moderate heat. Add the remaining 3 tablespoons of butter, the crushed garlic and the thyme to the skillet and cook until the butter is foamy. Baste the meat with the butter just until the butter browns, 2 to 3 minutes.

4. Transfer the pork to a cutting board and cut into thick slices. Spoon the mushrooms onto a platter, top with the pork and drizzle with the brown butter. Garnish with walnuts, shallot, chives and flaky salt and serve. —*Dai Shinozuka*

WINE Vibrant, earthy red Burgundy: 2011 Louis Jadot Nuits-Saint-Georges Les Boudots.

Curried Pork Tenderloin with Apple-Coconut Yogurt Sauce

Active **20 min**; Total **1 hr**; Serves **6**

This juicy, spice-rubbed pork tenderloin is from chef Jenn Louis of Lincoln Restaurant in Portland, Oregon. She serves it with a creamy, sweet and spicy yogurt sauce that comes together in minutes.

- 1 bay leaf, crumbled
- ¾ tsp. each ground coriander, ground cumin and mustard powder
- 1½ Tbsp. curry powder
- ¼ tsp. cayenne
- 2 tsp. light brown sugar
  Kosher salt and pepper
  Two 1-lb. pork tenderloins
- 2 Tbsp. canola oil
- 1 cup full-fat Greek yogurt
- 1 small jalapeño, seeded and minced
- 1 small carrot, finely grated
- 1 Honeycrisp apple, peeled and coarsely grated
- 2 Tbsp. unsweetened shredded coconut
- ½ tsp. finely grated lime zest plus 1 Tbsp. fresh lime juice

1. In a small bowl, combine the bay leaf, coriander, cumin, mustard powder, curry powder, cayenne, brown sugar and 1 teaspoon of salt. Rub the spice mix all over the pork and let stand at room temperature for 15 minutes.

2. Preheat the oven to 450°. In a large cast-iron skillet, heat the oil. Season the pork with salt and pepper and cook over moderate heat, turning, until golden brown, 2 minutes. Transfer to the oven and roast for 10 to 12 minutes, until an instant-read thermometer inserted in the thickest part registers 135°. Transfer the pork to a plate; let rest for 10 minutes.

3. Meanwhile, in a medium bowl, combine the remaining ingredients and season with salt and pepper.

4. Slice the pork crosswise ½ inch thick. Serve with the yogurt sauce. —*Jenn Louis*

WINE Cherry-rich, medium-bodied Oregon Pinot Noir: 2012 Erath Estate Selection.

Earl Grey–Crusted Pork Loin with Fennel and Apples

Active **30 min**; Total **2 hr 15 min**
Serves **6 to 8**

Bergamot-scented Earl Grey tea infuses this pork with a lovely citrusy flavor. If you don't have loose-leaf tea, cut open nine tea bags; each holds about 1 teaspoon.

- 3 Tbsp. finely ground Earl Grey tea
  Kosher salt and pepper
  One 3½-lb. boneless pork loin roast, tied
- 3 fennel bulbs, trimmed and cut through the core into 1-inch wedges
- 3 firm, sweet cooking apples, such as Gala, quartered lengthwise and cored
- 2 Tbsp. extra-virgin olive oil
- 1 Tbsp. thyme leaves

1. In a small bowl, whisk the tea with 1 tablespoon of salt and 1 teaspoon of pepper. Rub all over the pork and set the meat fat side up on a large rimmed baking sheet. Let stand at room temperature for 45 minutes.

2. Preheat the oven to 450°. Roast the pork for 20 minutes, until lightly browned. Meanwhile, in a large bowl, toss the fennel and apple wedges with the olive oil and thyme and season with salt and pepper.

3. Reduce the oven temperature to 400°. Scatter the fennel and apple wedges around the pork. Roast for about 35 minutes longer, until an instant-read thermometer inserted in the thickest part registers 135°. Transfer the pork to a carving board and let rest for 15 minutes. Discard the strings. Thinly slice the pork and serve with the fennel and apples.
—*Justin Chapple*

WINE Fragrant, light-bodied red: 2012 Potel-Aviron Côte de Brouilly Beaujolais.

EARL GREY–CRUSTED
PORK LOIN WITH
FENNEL AND APPLES

SLOW-COOKED
PORK SHOULDER WITH
ROASTED APPLES

Slow-Cooked Pork Shoulder with Roasted Apples

Active **45 min**; Total **8 hr 15 min**
Serves **6 to 8**

Bone-in pork shoulder takes a long time to cook, but the prep is minimal: Simply score the skin with a sharp knife and season the meat, then leave it alone to baste itself in the oven.

> **One 9-lb. skin-on, bone-in pork shoulder**
> 8 **bay leaves**
> 1 **Tbsp. juniper berries**
> **Kosher salt and pepper**
> 6 **baking apples, such as Gala, quartered and cored**
> ¼ **cup extra-virgin olive oil**
> 3 **small cinnamon sticks**

1. Preheat the oven to 400°. Using a sharp knife, score the pork skin in a crosshatch pattern. Set the pork in a large roasting pan, skin side up.

2. In a spice grinder, combine the bay leaves with the juniper berries, ¼ cup of salt and 2 teaspoons of pepper and grind into a powder. Rub the spice mixture all over the pork and into the scored skin. Roast the pork for 30 minutes, until lightly browned. Reduce the oven temperature to 325° and roast for about 6½ hours, until the pork is very tender and the skin is crisp. Transfer to a carving board and let rest for 30 minutes.

3. Meanwhile, on a large rimmed baking sheet, toss the apples with the oil and cinnamon sticks; season generously with salt and pepper. Roast for about 30 minutes, tossing once, until the apples are lightly browned and softened slightly. Discard the cinnamon sticks.

4. Remove the pork skin and coarsely chop it. Using 2 forks, pull the pork into large pieces, discarding the fat and bones. Transfer the pork to a platter and scatter the chopped skin on top. Serve with the roasted apples. —*Nate Ready*

WINE Robust, hillside Napa Cabernet Sauvignon: 2010 Abreu Howell Mountain.

Roast Pork with Acorn Squash Romesco Puree

Active **45 min**; Total **2 hr 30 min**; Serves **8**

Romesco, a Catalan sauce made with almonds and red bell pepper, is the inspiration for this winter squash puree.

PORK AND SQUASH

> **One 8-rib center-cut rack of pork, chine bone removed (8 lbs.)**
> ½ **cup plus 1 Tbsp. extra-virgin olive oil**
> 1 **Tbsp. chopped rosemary**
> 1 **Tbsp. chopped thyme**
> **Kosher salt and pepper**
> 1 **acorn squash (1¾ lbs.), quartered and seeded**
> 5 **garlic cloves**
> 1 **yellow onion, quartered**
> 1 **red bell pepper, quartered**
> 4 **oz. sourdough bread, cut into 1-inch pieces**
> ¼ **cup unsalted roasted almonds, chopped**
> 1 **Tbsp. sherry vinegar**
> ¼ **tsp. piment d'Espelette**

SALAD

> ½ **small shallot, finely diced**
> 2 **Tbsp. sherry vinegar**
> 1 **Tbsp. grated fresh horseradish, plus more for garnish**
> ½ **Tbsp. sorghum syrup**
> 1 **tsp. Dijon mustard**
> ¼ **cup extra-virgin olive oil**
> 2 **bunches of dandelion greens, coarsely chopped**
> **Kosher salt and pepper**

1. Make the pork and squash Preheat the oven to 450°. Set the pork fat side up on a rack set over a rimmed baking sheet. Rub the roast with 2 tablespoons of the oil and the rosemary and thyme; season with salt and pepper. On another rimmed baking sheet, toss the squash, garlic, onion and bell pepper with 2 tablespoons of the oil; season with salt and pepper.

2. Roast the pork in the middle third of the oven and the vegetables in the bottom third for about 40 minutes, until the squash is tender. Transfer the vegetables to a rack to cool. Turn the oven down to 375° and roast the pork for about 45 minutes longer, until an instant-read thermometer inserted in the thickest part registers 135°. Transfer the pork to a work surface and let rest for 15 minutes.

3. Meanwhile, on another baking sheet, toss the bread with 1 tablespoon of the oil and bake until golden, 12 minutes.

4. When the squash is cool, scoop the flesh into a food processor. Peel the bell pepper and discard the skin. Add the roasted pepper, garlic and onion to the processor along with the croutons, almonds, vinegar and piment d'Espelette. Puree until almost smooth. With the machine on, slowly stream in the remaining ¼ cup of olive oil. Season the puree with salt and pepper.

5. Make the salad In a medium bowl, whisk the first 6 ingredients. Add the greens and season with salt and pepper. Transfer to a serving bowl and garnish with more fresh horseradish.

6. Carve the pork and serve with the squash puree and dandelion salad. —*Mike Lata*

WINE Lively, red-berried Beaujolais: 2013 Terres Dorées Côte de Brouilly.

Tacos al Pastor

Total **1 hr 15 min plus overnight marinating**
Serves **8**

- 1 Tbsp. canola oil, plus more for brushing
- 3 garlic cloves
- 1 tsp. dried oregano
- ½ tsp. ground cumin
- ½ tsp. pepper
- ¼ tsp. ground cloves
- 4 guajillo chiles—stemmed, seeded and cut into 2-inch pieces
- ⅓ cup pineapple juice
- ¼ cup distilled white vinegar
- 2 Tbsp. achiote paste
  Sea salt
- 2 lbs. boneless pork shoulder, sliced ¼ inch thick
- ½ medium pineapple, peeled and sliced ½ inch thick
- 1 medium red onion, sliced crosswise ½ inch thick
  Warm corn tortillas, chopped cilantro and lime wedges, for serving

1. In a medium saucepan, heat the 1 tablespoon of oil. Add the garlic and cook over moderately high heat, turning occasionally, until lightly browned, about 1 minute. Stir in the oregano, cumin, pepper and cloves and cook until fragrant, about 1 minute. Add the chiles and cook, stirring, until blistered in spots, about 30 seconds. Add the pineapple juice, vinegar and achiote paste and bring to a boil. Remove from the heat and let stand for 5 minutes.

2. Transfer the chile mixture to a blender and puree until smooth. Season with salt. Scrape the marinade into a large, sturdy plastic bag. Add the pork and turn to coat. Set the bag in a small baking dish and refrigerate overnight.

3. Light a grill or heat a grill pan. Brush the pineapple and onion with oil. Grill over high heat, turning once, until lightly charred and softened, 3 to 5 minutes. Transfer to a carving board and tent with foil.

4. Remove the pork from the marinade. Grill over high heat until lightly charred and just cooked through, 2 to 4 minutes. Transfer to the carving board and let rest for 5 minutes.

5. Cut the pineapple, onion and pork into thin strips and transfer to a bowl. Season with salt. Serve with corn tortillas, chopped cilantro and lime wedges.
—*Courtney Contos*

BEER Crisp, lightly malty amber ale: Anderson Valley Brewing Company Boont Amber.

Spiced Pork Crown Roast with Roasted Vegetables

Active **45 min**; Total **4 hr 15 min**
Serves **16**

- 1½ Tbsp. whole cloves
- 1½ Tbsp. whole allspice berries
- 6 whole star anise
  One 1½-inch cinnamon stick
- 3 bay leaves
- 1 dried Thai chile, stemmed
- 1 tsp. ground mace
  One 16-rib crown roast of pork (about 10 lbs.), tied, bones frenched
  Kosher salt and pepper
- 16 torpedo onions or large shallots, peeled
- 1½ lbs. medium fingerling potatoes
- 1½ lbs. parsnips, peeled and cut into 2½-inch pieces
- 1½ lbs. medium turnips, peeled and cut into 2½-inch pieces
- 1 lb. rutabaga, peeled and cut into 2½-inch pieces
- 1 cup sage leaves
- 12 garlic cloves
- 2 Tbsp. canola oil

1. In a small skillet, combine the cloves, allspice, star anise, cinnamon stick, bay leaves and chile and toast over moderately high heat, stirring, until the spices just start to smoke, 2 to 3 minutes. Transfer to a spice grinder and let cool, then add the mace and grind to a powder.

2. Season the pork roast with salt and pepper and rub the spice mixture all over it. Let the roast stand at room temperature for 1 hour.

3. Meanwhile, preheat the oven to 325°. In a very large roasting pan, toss the onions with the potatoes, parsnips, turnips, rutabaga, sage, garlic cloves and oil. Season with salt and pepper.

4. Set the pork roast on top of the vegetables. Lightly coat 16 small squares of foil with nonstick spray and wrap each rib bone to prevent burning. Roast the pork for 2 hours, until beginning to brown. Increase the oven temperature to 450° and roast for about 40 minutes longer, until the vegetables are tender and an instant-read thermometer inserted in the thickest part of the pork registers 140°. Transfer the roast to a platter and let rest for 15 minutes. Carve the pork roast between the ribs and serve with the roasted vegetables.
—*Christina Lecki*

MAKE AHEAD The spice mix can be made up to 3 days ahead.

WINE Robust Cabernet Sauvignon: 2012 Joseph Carr Napa County.

Clove-and-Cider-Glazed Ham

Active **30 min**; Total **2 hr**; Serves **12**

- One 7- to 8-lb. spiral-cut ham
- 1 cup fresh apple cider
- ½ cup light brown sugar
- 3 Tbsp. unsalted butter
- 2 Tbsp. Dijon mustard
- 2 Tbsp. bourbon
- 1 Tbsp. apple cider vinegar
  One 3-inch cinnamon stick
- 6 whole cloves
- ½ tsp. black peppercorns
- ½ tsp. freshly grated nutmeg

1. Preheat the oven to 375°. Place the ham in a 9-by-13-inch baking dish.

2. In a small saucepan, combine all of the remaining ingredients and bring to a simmer, whisking occasionally. Cook over moderately low heat until reduced to ¾ cup, about 25 minutes. Pour the glaze over the ham, leaving the spices on the meat. Cover tightly with foil. Bake for about 1 hour and 15 minutes, basting every 15 minutes, until heated through. Transfer to a platter.

3. Strain the pan juices into a small saucepan. Bring to a boil and cook until reduced to a glaze, 8 to 10 minutes. Spoon the glaze over the ham; serve. —*Carla Hall*

WINE Spiced, red-berried, medium-bodied red: 2013 Monte La Sarda Garnacha.

TACOS AL PASTOR

DIY SMOKED RIBS

Texas pit master **TIM RATTRAY** of The Granary in San Antonio reveals how to make tender, crusty, smoky ribs using an ordinary grill, wood chips and a 20-pound bag of hardwood lump charcoal.

Smoked St. Louis–Style Ribs

Active **2 hr**; Total **7 hr 15 min**; Serves **6 to 8**

- 1 **cup packed light brown sugar**
- 1 **Tbsp. freshly ground black pepper**
- 1½ **tsp. chile powder**
- 1½ **tsp. cinnamon**
- 1½ **tsp. ground cumin**
- 1½ **tsp. ground dark-roast coffee**
- **Kosher salt**
- 2 **racks St. Louis–cut pork ribs (6 lbs.), membranes removed from the undersides**
- 7 **cups oak chips, soaked in water for 1 hour and drained**

1. In a medium bowl, whisk the sugar with the pepper, chile powder, cinnamon, cumin, coffee and ⅓ cup of salt. Season the ribs all over with salt, then rub both racks with 1 cup of the spice mix.

2. Light a hardwood charcoal fire and set up the grill for indirect cooking; you'll need to replenish the coals periodically to maintain the heat. Close the grill and, using the air vents to control the fire, bring the internal temperature to 250°.

3. Scatter 2 cups of the oak chips over the hot coals. Set the ribs meat side up on the grill opposite the coals. Close the grill and smoke the ribs at 250° to 275° for 2 hours, adding coals as necessary to maintain the heat; add another 2 cups of the oak chips to the hot coals after the first hour.

4. Transfer the ribs to a baking sheet. Layer two 36-inch sheets of heavy-duty foil on a work surface and set a rack of ribs in the center, meat side up; wrap tightly in the foil. Repeat with 2 more layers of foil and the remaining rack of ribs. Set the rib packets meat side up on the grill opposite the coals. Close the grill and cook the ribs at 250° to 275° for 2 hours longer, adding coals as necessary to maintain the heat.

5. Transfer the rib packets to a baking sheet, then unwrap the ribs, discarding the foil. Scatter 2 cups of the oak chips over the hot coals. Return the ribs meat side up to the grill opposite the coals. Close the grill and smoke the ribs at 250° to 275° until very tender, 1 hour. Add coals as necessary to maintain the heat and scatter the remaining 1 cup of oak chips on the hot coals halfway through smoking.

6. Transfer the ribs to a carving board and let rest for 15 minutes. Cut and serve.

STEP-BY-STEP

1 MAKE THE SPICE MIX Whisk brown sugar, salt, pepper, coffee and spices.

2 APPLY THE RUB Sprinkle ribs with the spice mix and rub it into the meat.

3 GET THE SMOKE GOING Lay oak chips over hot coals on one side of the grill.

4 SMOKE THE RIBS Set the ribs on the grill opposite the heat. Cover and cook.

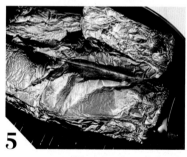

5 STEAM THE RIBS Wrap the ribs in foil and continue to cook on the grill.

6 PERFECT THE CRUST Unwrap the ribs and cook until they're crusty all over.

MAKE AHEAD The spice mix can be stored in an airtight container for up to 1 week.

WINE Smoky, bold Washington state Syrah: 2012 Owen Roe Ex Umbris.

Glazed Agrodolce Ribs

📷 PAGE 169

Active **45 min**; Total **2 hr 45 min**; Serves **8**

  Two 4-lb. racks of pork spareribs, membranes removed
1½ Tbsp. fennel seeds, crushed
1½ Tbsp. finely chopped thyme
 2 tsp. crushed red pepper
 2 tsp. finely chopped rosemary
  Kosher salt and freshly ground black pepper
 2 Tbsp. extra-virgin olive oil
 1 small red onion, coarsely grated
 3 garlic cloves, finely grated
 1 cup balsamic vinegar
 ¼ cup white distilled vinegar
 1 cup ketchup
 ¾ cup packed light brown sugar

1. Preheat the oven to 325°. Line 2 large rimmed baking sheets with foil and set the ribs on them, meaty side up. In a mortar, crush the fennel seeds with the thyme, crushed red pepper, rosemary, 1½ tablespoons salt and 2 teaspoons black pepper. Rub the spice mix all over the ribs and roast for about 2 hours, until the meat is tender.

2. Meanwhile, in a medium saucepan, heat the oil. Add the onion, garlic and a generous pinch of salt and cook over moderately high heat, stirring, until the onion is softened, 3 to 5 minutes. Add both vinegars along with the ketchup and brown sugar and bring to a boil. Simmer over moderate heat, stirring frequently, until the sauce is thick and reduced to 2 cups, 15 minutes.

3. Remove the ribs from the oven and turn on the broiler. Brush the underside of the racks with some of the sauce. Broil 1 sheet of ribs 8 inches from the heat until browned. Flip the ribs and repeat on the other side. Move the ribs to the bottom rack of the oven to keep warm while you glaze the rest.

4. Transfer the racks to a work surface. Cut in between the bones to form individual ribs and mound on a platter. Pass the remaining sauce at the table. —*Justin Chapple*

MAKE AHEAD The sauce can be refrigerated for up to 1 week.

WINE Spiced, fruit-forward Sicilian red: 2012 Manenti Nero d'Avola.

Country-Style Pork Ribs with Tomato Salad and Garlic Toast

Active **40 min**; Total **1 hr 10 min**
Serves **4 to 6**

Inspired by humble early-1900s cooking, chef Andrea Reusing of The Durham Hotel in North Carolina uses flavorful pork ribs for this weeknight dish. She's "almost wary" of telling people to cook the inexpensive cut, for fear it will become too popular and pricey.

 2 lbs. country-style boneless pork ribs (about 4 ribs)
1½ tsp. celery seeds
  Kosher salt and pepper
 ¼ cup extra-virgin olive oil, plus more for brushing
  Three 1-inch-thick slices of country bread, halved crosswise
 2 garlic cloves, 1 halved and 1 minced
 1 small Fresno or red jalapeño chile, stemmed and minced
 1 lb. tomatoes, cut into 1-inch pieces
 8 light-green celery ribs with leaves, thinly sliced on the diagonal (2 cups)

1. Season the pork with the celery seeds, salt and pepper. Let stand for 30 minutes.

2. Light a grill or heat a grill pan and brush with oil. Grill the pork over moderately high heat, turning occasionally, until lightly charred all over and an instant-read thermometer inserted in the thickest part registers 140°, about 12 minutes. Transfer to a work surface and let rest for 5 minutes, then slice the meat against the grain.

3. Meanwhile, brush the bread with oil and season with salt and pepper. Grill over moderately high heat, turning, until lightly charred on both sides, about 2 minutes. Rub with the halved garlic clove.

4. In a large bowl, whisk the ¼ cup of oil with the chile and minced garlic. Add the tomatoes and celery and toss to coat. Season the salad with salt and pepper.

5. Transfer the garlic toasts to plates, top with the tomato salad and sliced pork and serve. —*Andrea Reusing*

WINE Vibrant and medium-bodied Chianti Classico: 2012 Isole e Olena.

Sweet-and-Spicy Spareribs with Korean Barbecue Sauce

Active **30 min**; Total **2 hr 30 min**; Serves **10**

Top Chef Season 12 winner Mei Lin slow-roasts these ribs in the oven, then glazes them on the grill with a sweet and spicy sauce spiked with gochujang (Korean chile paste). She also stirs the sauce into pulled pork, serves it with french fries instead of ketchup and mixes it with melted butter to toss with fried chicken.

 1 cup gochujang (see Note)
 ½ cup hoisin sauce
 ½ cup ketchup
 ½ cup honey
 ½ cup soy sauce
 ½ cup sake
 2 Tbsp. unseasoned rice vinegar
 2 Tbsp. finely grated fresh ginger
 1 Tbsp. finely grated garlic
 2 Tbsp. ground white pepper
 3 racks pork spareribs (about 8 lbs.), membranes removed
  Kosher salt

1. Preheat the oven to 325°. In a medium bowl, whisk together all of the ingredients except the ribs and salt. Layer 2 long sheets of heavy-duty foil on a work surface and set 1 rack of ribs in the center, meaty side up. Brush with ¾ cup of the sauce and wrap tightly in the foil. Repeat with the remaining 2 racks of ribs. Transfer the foil packets to 2 large rimmed baking sheets and bake the ribs until tender, about 2 hours.

2. Unwrap the racks and transfer to a work surface. Cut them into 3- or 4-rib sections.

3. Light a grill. Season the ribs with salt and grill over high heat, brushing with the remaining sauce and turning occasionally, until glazed and lightly charred in spots, about 4 minutes. Cut into individual ribs if desired. Transfer to a platter and serve. —*Mei Lin*

NOTE Gochujang is available at Asian markets, Whole Foods and amazon.com.

MAKE AHEAD The ribs can be prepared through Step 1 and refrigerated overnight. Bring to room temperature before grilling.

WINE Dark, cherry-inflected Argentinean Malbec: 2013 BenMarco.

Pork Belly with Rhubarb Glaze

Active **30 min**; Total **4 hr 45 min plus 24 hr brining**; Serves **8**

After brining pork belly, Hudson Valley chef Zakary Pelaccio slow-roasts the meat until it's tender and crisp, brushing it with a sweet and tangy rhubarb glaze. You will need a juicer to make the glaze here.

PORK BELLY

- 1 **gallon water**
- 1 **onion, thinly sliced**
- 1 **head of garlic, halved crosswise**
- 3 **rosemary sprigs**
- 3 **Tbsp. kosher salt**
- ½ **cup coriander seeds**
- 2 **Tbsp. white peppercorns**
- 2 **Tbsp. fennel seeds**
  One 5-lb. pork belly
  Nasturtium leaves and flowers, for garnish (optional)

GLAZE

- 2 **lbs. rhubarb, juiced (2¼ cups)**
- ½ **cup pure maple syrup**
- ¼ **cup Asian fish sauce**
- 1 **Tbsp. chile powder**

1. Brine the pork belly In a large pot, combine all of the ingredients except the pork; simmer, partially covered, over low heat for 30 minutes. Let cool to room temperature. Add the pork to the brine and leave at room temperature for 1 hour, then cover and refrigerate for 24 hours. Bring to room temperature for 1 hour before cooking.

2. Make the glaze In a small saucepan, cook the rhubarb juice over moderate heat until reduced to 1 cup, 8 to 10 minutes. Add the maple syrup and cook until slightly thickened, 5 minutes. Stir in the fish sauce and chile powder; let cool.

3. Light a grill and set it up for indirect cooking. Remove the pork belly from the brine and score the skin in a crosshatch pattern. Set the pork on the grill, fat side up, opposite the heat source. Cover and grill at 325° for 2½ to 3 hours, until very tender; brush with the glaze during the last 45 minutes of grilling. Transfer the pork to a cutting board and let rest for 15 minutes. Thinly slice, garnish and serve. —*Zakary Pelaccio*

WINE Juicy, red cherry–inflected Sicilian rosé: 2014 Cornelissen Susucaru.

Salsa Verde Chicharrón Tacos

Total **30 min**; Makes **6**

Famed Mexican chef Enrique Olvera turns fried pork rinds into an unusual and delicious taco filling by simmering them in salsa verde. Pork rinds crumbled on top add crunch.

- ¼ **lb. thick, crisp chicharrones, plus crushed chicharrones for garnish (see Note)**
- 1½ **cups Salsa Verde (recipe follows)**
  Kosher salt
- 6 **warm 8-inch Corn Tortillas (recipe follows) or fresh corn tortillas**
  Sour cream and purslane or watercress, for serving

In a large skillet, combine the chicharrones with ⅓ cup water and cook over moderately high heat, stirring, until the chicharrones start to soften and the water is absorbed, 3 to 5 minutes. Add the salsa verde and cook over moderate heat, stirring, until the chicharrones are coated and the salsa is thick, about 5 minutes. Season with salt. Serve in the corn tortillas, topped with sour cream, purslane and crushed chicharrones. —*Enrique Olvera*

NOTE Look for good-quality chicharrones, preferably with a little meat attached, at Mexican markets.

WINE Bright, citrusy white: 2014 Grooner Grüner Veltliner.

SALSA VERDE

Active **10 min**; Total **30 min plus cooling** Makes **3 cups**

Olvera's garlicky tomatillo salsa is great on everything from tacos and enchiladas to seafood, roast chicken and pork.

- 1½ **lbs. tomatillos, husked and rinsed**
- 2 **cups water**
- ½ **medium white onion, chopped**
- 3 **large garlic cloves, minced**
- 2 **large scallions, chopped**
- ½ **cup chopped cilantro**
- ¼ **cup chopped epazote or 1 Tbsp. chopped oregano**
- 1 **tsp. cumin seeds**
  Fine sea salt

Combine all the ingredients except the salt in a large saucepan and bring to a boil. Add a generous pinch of salt and simmer over moderate heat until the onion is tender, about 20 minutes. Remove from the heat and coarsely mash the salsa with a potato masher. Let cool completely, season with salt and serve. —*EO*

MAKE AHEAD The salsa can be refrigerated for up to 5 days.

CORN TORTILLAS

Active **40 min**; Total **1 hr 40 min** Makes **twelve 5-inch or six 8-inch tortillas**

Homemade tortillas have exceptional corn flavor and a tender texture.

1¾ cups masa harina, preferably Bob's Red Mill

1. In a medium bowl, mix the masa with 1¼ cups of water until a dough forms. Cover and let stand for 1 hour.

2. Divide the dough into 12 equal pieces (or 6 pieces for 8-inch tortillas) and roll each piece into a ball. Line a tortilla press with parchment paper or plastic wrap and press the 12 balls of dough into 5-inch tortillas. If making 8-inch tortillas, roll them out with a rolling pin.

3. Heat a griddle or cast-iron skillet. Working in batches, cook the tortillas over moderate heat, turning, until cooked through, about 6 minutes. —*EO*

MAKE AHEAD The tortillas can be refrigerated for 2 days or frozen for 2 weeks.

PORK BELLY WITH
RHUBARB GLAZE

Crispy Pork Belly Tacos with Pico de Gallo

Active **1 hr**; Total **4 hr**; Serves **4**

BRAISED PORK BELLY

- **One 2-lb. piece of meaty pork belly**
- **1 cup extra-virgin olive oil**
- **1 cup melted lard or shortening**
- **3 garlic cloves, crushed**
- **1 white onion, coarsely chopped**
- **2 morita chiles (see Note)**
- **2 tsp. kosher salt**

PICO DE GALLO

- **½ lb. cherry tomatoes, finely chopped**
- **4 oz. tomatillos—husked, rinsed and finely chopped (about ¾ cup)**
- **½ small red onion, finely chopped**
- **1 chile de árbol, crumbled**
- **¼ cup Mexican beer, such as Corona**
- **¼ cup fresh lime juice**
- **Kosher salt**

TACOS

- **1 Tbsp. canola oil**
- **12 warm 5-inch Corn Tortillas (p. 182) or fresh corn tortillas**
- **Lime wedges, for serving**

1. Braise the pork belly Preheat the oven to 250°. In a large ovenproof saucepan, combine all of the ingredients and bring to a simmer over moderate heat. Cover, transfer to the oven and braise the pork until very tender, about 3 hours. Transfer the pork to a plate to cool slightly; discard the braising liquid.

2. Make the pico de gallo In a medium bowl, combine all of the ingredients except the salt. Season with salt and mix well.

3. Make the tacos In a large cast-iron skillet, heat the canola oil. Add the pork belly, skin side down, and weigh it down with another heavy skillet. Cook over moderately low heat until golden and crisp, about 10 minutes. Transfer the pork, skin side up, to a cutting board and let cool slightly. Slice across the grain ¼ inch thick, then halve the slices crosswise. Top each tortilla with a few pieces of pork belly and a little pico de gallo and serve warm. —*Enrique Olvera*

NOTE Morita chiles are small, dried smoked chiles; they're a little spicier than chipotles, which can be substituted here.

BEER Ice-cold Mexican lager: Bohemia.

Pork, Potato and Apple Pie

Active **1 hr 45 min**; Total **3 hr 45 min plus cooling**; Serves **8**

In her take on a traditional English pub meat pie, blogger Marte Marie Forsberg fills a flaky double crust with potatoes, apple and two kinds of pork: tender ale-braised pork shoulder and chorizo.

PASTRY

- **¼ cup plus 2 Tbsp. lard or vegetable shortening**
- **¼ cup plus 2 Tbsp. unsalted butter**
- **1 Tbsp. Dijon mustard**
- **4½ cups all-purpose flour, plus more for dusting**
- **1 Tbsp. kosher salt**

FILLING

- **2 Tbsp. unsalted butter**
- **2 Tbsp. canola oil**
- **1 lb. trimmed boneless pork shoulder, cut into 1-inch pieces**
- **Kosher salt and pepper**
- **2 medium onions, thinly sliced**
- **4 garlic cloves, sliced**
- **One 12-oz. bottle pale ale**
- **1½ cups chicken stock or low-sodium broth**
- **2 oz. Spanish chorizo, cut into ¼-inch dice**
- **2 thyme sprigs**
- **1 sage sprig**
- **2 lbs. red potatoes, peeled and sliced ¼ inch thick**
- **2 Granny Smith apples, peeled and cut into ½-inch pieces**
- **1 large egg beaten with 1 tsp. water**

1. Make the pastry In a medium saucepan, combine the lard, butter and mustard with 1½ cups of water. Bring to a boil, then simmer over moderate heat until the butter and lard are melted, 3 minutes. In a large bowl, whisk the 4½ cups of flour with the salt. Stir in the lard mixture until a shaggy dough forms, then turn the dough out onto a lightly floured work surface and knead until smooth, about 5 minutes. Cut the dough in half and shape into disks. Wrap the disks in plastic and refrigerate until well chilled, about 2 hours.

2. Make the filling In a large saucepan, melt the butter in the oil. Season the pork with salt and pepper, add to the saucepan and cook over moderately high heat, turning occasionally, until browned, about 8 minutes. Add the onions and garlic and cook, stirring occasionally, until softened and lightly browned, about 5 minutes. Add the ale, stock, chorizo, thyme and sage and bring to a boil. Simmer over low heat until the pork is tender, about 1 hour. Using a slotted spoon, transfer the pork to a bowl. Discard the thyme and sage sprigs.

3. In a medium saucepan, cover the potatoes with water and bring to a boil. Add a generous pinch of salt and cook over moderate heat until just tender, about 8 minutes. Drain well. In a bowl, mash one-quarter of the potatoes with a fork. Stir the mashed potatoes into the braising liquid and bring to a boil. Lower the heat to moderate and simmer until reduced to 2 cups, about 7 minutes. Return the pork to the saucepan and season the filling with salt and pepper. Let cool completely.

4. Preheat the oven to 400°. On a floured work surface, roll out 1 disk of dough to a 12-inch round, a scant ¼ inch thick. Ease the dough into a 10-inch cast-iron skillet and up the side. Roll out the second disk of dough to a 12-inch round. Transfer to a wax paper–lined baking sheet and refrigerate. Spread half of the sliced potatoes in the skillet in an even layer. Cover with half of the pork filling and top with half of the apples. Repeat the layering with the remaining potatoes, pork filling and apples. Cover with the top crust and trim the overhang to 1 inch. Press the crust rims together, pinch to seal and tuck the dough into the skillet.

5. Brush the pie with the beaten egg and sprinkle with salt and pepper. Cut a hole or 4 small slits in the top to vent the steam. Bake in the center of the oven for 30 minutes. Lower the oven temperature to 375° and bake the pie for 40 to 45 minutes longer, until the juices are bubbling and the crust is golden brown. Transfer the skillet to a rack and let the pie cool for at least 30 minutes. Cut into wedges and serve. —*Marte Marie Forsberg*

WINE Earthy, herbal red: 2012 Russiz Superiore Cabernet Franc.

Cheater Chorizo Burgers

Total **30 min**; Serves **4**

1½ lbs. ground pork
2½ Tbsp. distilled white vinegar
1 Tbsp. hot paprika
2 garlic cloves, minced
2 tsp. chile powder
1 tsp. ground cumin
1 tsp. dried oregano
  Kosher salt and pepper
4 brioche hamburger buns, split and toasted
  Ketchup, Bibb lettuce and sliced yellow tomato, for serving

1. In a bowl, using a fork, gently stir the pork with the vinegar, paprika, garlic, chile powder, cumin, oregano, 1 teaspoon of salt and ¾ teaspoon of pepper. Using 2 lids from 1-quart takeout containers, press the mixture into 4 patties. Transfer to a plate.

2. Light a grill or heat a grill pan. Season the patties lightly with salt and pepper and grill over moderately high heat, turning once, until cooked through, about 8 minutes. Transfer the burgers to the buns, top with ketchup, lettuce and tomato and serve. —*Justin Chapple*

Double-Pea Sauté with Ground Pork

Total **30 min**; Serves **4 to 6**

2 Tbsp. canola oil
½ lb. ground pork
2 Tbsp. minced peeled fresh ginger
2 Tbsp. minced garlic
½ lb. snap peas
½ lb. fresh shelled or thawed frozen peas
2 Tbsp. fresh lime juice
1 cup chopped basil
  Kosher salt and pepper

In a large nonstick skillet, heat the oil. Add the pork, ginger and garlic and stir-fry over moderately high heat until the pork is browned, about 2 minutes. Stir in the snap peas and shelled peas and stir-fry until crisp-tender, about 3 minutes. Stir in the lime juice and basil, season with salt and pepper and serve. —*Kay Chun*

WINE Medium-bodied, herb-scented white: 2014 Dürnberg Alte Reben Grüner Veltliner.

Grilled Mushrooms and Sausages with Pimentón Vinaigrette

Total **40 min**; Serves **6**

Griddled wild mushrooms are the stars of this Catalan-inspired dish dressed with a smoky, garlicky vinaigrette.

½ cup plus 3 Tbsp. extra-virgin olive oil, plus more for brushing
2 lbs. mixed wild mushrooms, such as hen-of-the-woods, cremini and chanterelles, cut into large pieces
  Kosher salt and pepper
1½ lbs. mixed sausages, such as soft Spanish chorizo and Italian pork sausage
3 Tbsp. sherry vinegar
3 garlic cloves, minced
1½ tsp. pimentón
4 oz. frisée, torn into large pieces (4 cups)
  Crusty bread, for serving

1. Heat a griddle or 2 large cast-iron skillets and lightly brush with olive oil. In a large bowl, toss the mushrooms with 3 tablespoons of the olive oil and season with salt and pepper. Cook the mushrooms and sausages on the griddle over moderate heat, turning occasionally, until golden and cooked through, about 10 minutes for the mushrooms and 10 to 15 minutes for the sausages.

2. Meanwhile, in a small bowl, whisk the remaining ½ cup of olive oil with the vinegar, garlic and pimentón. Season the vinaigrette with salt and pepper.

3. Transfer the cooked mushrooms to the large bowl. Add the frisée and ¼ cup of the pimentón vinaigrette and toss to coat. Mound the salad on a platter, arrange the sausages alongside and spoon ¼ cup of the vinaigrette on top. Serve with crusty bread, passing the remaining vinaigrette at the table. —*Kay Chun*

WINE Crisp, berry-inflected Spanish sparkling rosé: 2012 Raventós i Blanc De Nit.

Stewed Sweet Sausages in Fennel-Tomato Sauce

Active **30 min**; Total **1 hr 30 min**; Serves **8**

A big pot of simmering red sauce makes New York City chef April Bloomfield think of the home kitchen of her former boss Ruth Rogers, of London's River Café. This is Bloomfield's version of the sauce, with sausage and large pieces of fresh fennel. "I just love slow-cooked fennel," she says. "It gives the dish a nice, soft creaminess with the slightly bouncy sausage."

¼ cup extra-virgin olive oil
12 sweet Italian sausages (4½ lbs.)
3 fennel bulbs—trimmed, each bulb cut into 8 wedges, fronds chopped
1 medium onion, chopped
4 garlic cloves, minced
½ tsp. fennel seeds, crushed
  Kosher salt
  One 28-oz. can San Marzano whole tomatoes, crushed by hand, juices reserved
1 cup dry white wine
3 pequin chiles (see Note) or 2 chiles de árbol
  Creamy polenta, for serving

1. In a large enameled cast-iron casserole, heat the olive oil. Add half of the sausages and cook over moderate heat, turning, until browned all over, 5 minutes. Transfer to a plate; repeat with the remaining sausages.

2. Add the fennel wedges to the casserole and cook over moderate heat, stirring, until golden, about 5 minutes. Add the onion, garlic, fennel seeds and 1 teaspoon of salt and cook, stirring, until the fennel is lightly browned, about 3 minutes. Add the tomatoes and their juices, the wine and chiles. Tuck the sausages into the sauce, cover and cook over low heat for 15 minutes. Uncover and simmer until the sausages are cooked through and the sauce is thickened, about 45 minutes longer. Garnish the stew with fennel fronds and serve over polenta. —*April Bloomfield*

NOTE Small, spicy dried red Mexican pequin chiles are available at Latin American markets and specialty food stores.

WINE Vivid Sicilian red: 2013 Tami Frappato.

MEATBALLS IN TOMATO
SAUCE; CRUSHED YUKON
GOLD POTATOES WITH
LEMON (RECIPE, P. 237)

Meatballs in Tomato Sauce

Active **1 hr 30 min**; Total **2 hr**; Serves **4 to 6**

Daniel Holzman of New York City's Meatball Shop simmers his meatballs in the tomato sauce without searing them first. "Searing creates a lot of flavor, but you lose a certain subtlety," he says.

TOMATO SAUCE

- ½ cup extra-virgin olive oil
- 1 onion, coarsely chopped (1 cup)
- 2 carrots, sliced ¾ inch thick (¾ cup)
- 3 large garlic cloves, crushed
- 2 Tbsp. tomato paste
- 1 bay leaf
- 6 oregano sprigs

  Two 28-oz. cans whole peeled San Marzano tomatoes with their juices, crushed by hand

  Pinch of crushed red pepper

  Kosher salt

MEATBALLS

- ¾ lb. ground pork
- ¾ lb. ground chuck
- ¾ lb. ground veal
- ½ cup Italian-style dry breadcrumbs (2½ oz.)
- ¼ cup freshly grated Pecorino Romano cheese (1 oz.)
- 2 tsp. kosher salt
- 2 large eggs
- ½ cup minced onion
- ½ cup chopped parsley
- 1 Tbsp. chopped oregano
- ¼ tsp. crushed red pepper
- ½ tsp. ground fennel

  Freshly grated Grana Padano cheese, for serving

1. Make the tomato sauce In a large ovenproof saucepan, heat the olive oil. Add the onion, carrots and garlic and cook over moderate heat, stirring occasionally, until the onion is softened and translucent, about 8 minutes. Stir in the tomato paste and cook until lightly caramelized, about 3 minutes. Add the bay leaf, oregano, tomatoes and crushed red pepper and bring to a simmer. Cook over moderately low heat, stirring occasionally, until slightly thickened, 15 minutes. Season with salt and keep at a bare simmer.

2. Meanwhile, make the meatballs Preheat the oven to 400°. In a large bowl, combine all of the ingredients except the Grana Padano and mix by hand until well incorporated. Using a 1½-ounce ice cream scoop (3 tablespoons), scoop 24 meatballs (1½ inches in diameter) and roll into neat balls.

3. Add the meatballs to the simmering tomato sauce and bring to a boil. Braise in the oven until firm and cooked through, about 30 minutes. Discard the bay leaf and oregano sprigs. Serve the meatballs and sauce with Grana Padano on the side. —*Daniel Holzman*

WINE Concentrated, medium-bodied Italian red: 2013 Giuseppe Cortese Langhe Nebbiolo.

Quinoa-Pork Meatballs

Active **20 min**; Total **50 min**; Serves **4**

- ⅓ cup black or white quinoa, rinsed and drained
- 1 lb. ground pork
- 2 large eggs, beaten
- 1 tsp. kosher salt
- 1 tsp. pepper
- ½ tsp. freshly grated nutmeg
- 2 Tbsp. canola oil
- 2 cups jarred marinara sauce
- 3 basil sprigs

1. In a medium saucepan of boiling water, cook the quinoa until tender, about 10 minutes. Drain and return the quinoa to the pan. Cover and let stand for 10 minutes; fluff with a fork. Spread the quinoa on a baking sheet and let cool to room temperature.

2. In a large bowl, combine the quinoa, pork, eggs, salt, pepper and nutmeg. Mix well and form into 12 meatballs.

3. In a large cast-iron skillet, heat the oil. Add the meatballs and cook over moderate heat, turning, until browned, about 8 minutes. Stir in the marinara sauce and basil and bring to a simmer. Cover and cook over low heat until the meatballs are cooked through, 7 to 8 minutes, then serve. —*Kay Chun*

MAKE AHEAD The meatballs can be prepared through Step 2 and refrigerated for up to 4 hours.

WINE Earthy, medium-bodied red: 2010 Au Bon Climat Los Alamos Pinot Noir.

Pork-and-Ricotta Meatballs in Parmesan Broth

Active **30 min**; Total **50 min**; Serves **6**

The meatballs in this fast and easy dish from F&W's Kay Chun are incredibly tender thanks to a generous amount of fresh ricotta mixed with the meat.

- 1 cup fresh ricotta (8 oz.)
- ¼ cup grated Parmigiano-Reggiano cheese, plus more for garnish
- 1 large egg
- ½ cup dry breadcrumbs
- ½ tsp. freshly grated nutmeg

  Kosher salt and pepper

- 1¼ lbs. ground pork
- 2 Tbsp. extra-virgin olive oil
- 1 quart low-sodium chicken broth

  One 3-by-1-inch piece of Parmigiano-Reggiano cheese

- 1 cup thawed frozen peas
- 2 cups baby spinach

  Egg noodles, for serving

1. In a large bowl, stir the ricotta and ¼ cup of grated Parmigiano with the egg, breadcrumbs, nutmeg, 1 teaspoon salt, ½ teaspoon pepper and ¼ cup of water. Add the pork and combine. Form into 12 meatballs.

2. In a large enameled cast-iron casserole, heat the olive oil. Add the meatballs and cook over moderate heat, turning, until golden all over, about 10 minutes. Stir in the broth and the piece of cheese. Cover and simmer gently over moderate heat, stirring occasionally, until the meatballs are cooked through and the broth is slightly reduced, about 20 minutes. Stir in the peas and spinach, season with salt and pepper and simmer until the peas are warmed through.

3. In shallow bowls, spoon the meatballs and broth over egg noodles. Garnish with grated Parmigiano and serve. —*Kay Chun*

WINE Rich, yellow apple–scented Chardonnay: 2013 Banshee.

Food52 test kitchen manager Allison Bruns Buford prepares smoked porter–braised short ribs (recipe, p. 194). "They're great for a party because they can be made ahead," she says.

BEEF, LAMB & MORE

PEPPER-CRUSTED
PRIME RIB ROAST
Recipe, page 202

Hunting Cabin Steak

Total **40 min plus overnight marinating**
Serves **4**

- 2 cups dry red wine
- 2 Tbsp. sugar
- 6 whole cloves
- 6 juniper berries, crushed
  Two 3-inch cinnamon sticks
- 1 tsp. finely grated orange zest
- 1 tsp. finely grated lemon zest plus 1 Tbsp. fresh lemon juice
- ½ tsp. freshly grated nutmeg
  Two 1-lb. bone-in rib eye steaks (about 1 inch thick)
- ¼ cup extra-virgin olive oil
  Kosher salt and pepper
- ½ lb. chanterelle mushrooms
  Chopped parsley and flaky sea salt, for garnish

1. In a medium saucepan, combine the wine and sugar and bring to a simmer. Cook for 5 minutes, stirring to dissolve the sugar. Remove the pan from the heat and stir in the cloves, juniper berries, cinnamon sticks, orange zest, lemon zest and nutmeg. Let cool completely.

2. In a resealable plastic bag or shallow baking dish, combine the steaks with the cooled marinade and refrigerate overnight.

3. Light a grill. Remove the steaks from the marinade and pat dry; discard the marinade. Rub the steaks with 2 tablespoons of the oil; season with salt and pepper. Grill over moderate heat, turning once, until nicely charred and an instant-read thermometer inserted in the center registers 125° for medium-rare, 10 to 12 minutes. Let rest for 10 minutes on a platter.

4. In a large skillet, heat the remaining 2 tablespoons of oil. Add the chanterelles and season with salt and pepper. Cook over moderately high heat, stirring, until golden, about 3 minutes. Stir in the lemon juice. Spoon the mushrooms over the steaks, garnish with parsley and sea salt and serve. —*Jon Shook and Vinny Dotolo*

WINE Fragrant, concentrated Umbrian red: 2008 Paolo Bea Rosso de Véo Sagrantino.

Tomahawk Steaks with Charred Tomato Charmoula

Active **50 min;** Total **1 hr 30 min;** Serves **6**

Tomahawk steaks are so-called because of their resemblance to the Native American axe. California chef Duskie Estes serves the impressive on-the-bone steaks with a North African–inspired spiced-tomato topping seasoned with fresh herbs, cumin, coriander and lemon.

- Two 2½-lb. tomahawk rib eye steaks
  Kosher salt and pepper
- 6 plum tomatoes, cored and halved lengthwise
  Extra-virgin olive oil
- 1½ tsp. each cumin and coriander seeds
- ½ cup each minced parsley and cilantro
- 1 tsp. finely grated lemon zest plus 3 Tbsp. fresh lemon juice
- 1½ tsp. sweet paprika
- ⅛ tsp. cayenne

1. Season the steaks generously with salt and pepper and let stand at room temperature for 45 minutes.

2. Meanwhile, light a grill. Brush the tomatoes with olive oil and season with salt and pepper. Grill over high heat, turning once, until lightly charred, about 8 minutes. Transfer to a work surface to cool, then cut into ½-inch dice and transfer to a bowl.

3. In a small skillet, toast the cumin and coriander seeds over moderately high heat, tossing, until fragrant, about 2 minutes. Transfer to a mortar or spice grinder and let cool, then grind into a powder. Add the spices and ½ cup of olive oil to the tomatoes along with the parsley, cilantro, lemon zest, lemon juice, paprika and cayenne. Season the charmoula with salt and pepper.

4. Grill the steaks over moderate heat, turning occasionally, until an instant-read thermometer inserted in the thickest part registers 130°, about 35 minutes. Remove from the heat and let rest for 10 minutes.

5. Carve the steaks off the bone, then thickly slice the meat against the grain. Transfer to a platter, spoon the charmoula on top and serve. —*Duskie Estes*

WINE Lively, cherry-scented Sonoma Pinot Noir: 2013 Senses.

Tri-Tip Steak with Grilled Scallion, Ginger and Cilantro Relish

Total **50 min;** Serves **4**

F&W's Kay Chun tranforms an inexpensive but flavorful steak with a bold relish of spicy charred scallions and just-grated ginger.

- One 1½-lb. tri-tip steak
- 18 large scallions, 2 thinly sliced
- 2 Tbsp. canola oil, plus more for brushing
  Kosher salt and pepper
- 1 cup chopped cilantro
- 2 red Thai chiles, minced
- 2 Tbsp. fresh lime juice
- 2 Tbsp. finely grated peeled fresh ginger, plus more for garnish

1. Light a grill. On a baking sheet, rub the steak and 16 whole scallions with the 2 tablespoons of oil; season with salt and pepper.

2. Oil the grill grate. Grill the steak for 20 to 25 minutes, turning occasionally, until an instant-read thermometer inserted in the center registers 125° for medium-rare. Transfer the steak to a cutting board and let rest for 15 minutes.

3. Meanwhile, grill the whole scallions over moderate heat, turning, until lightly charred and tender, about 3 minutes. Transfer 8 of the scallions to a platter. Chop the rest and transfer to a bowl; let cool. Add the sliced raw scallions, cilantro, chiles, lime juice and 2 tablespoons of ginger; mix well.

4. Thinly slice the steak across the grain and arrange on the platter. Spoon the scallion relish on the steak and garnish with freshly grated ginger. —*Kay Chun*

WINE Bold Chilean Syrah: 2013 Kingston Family Lucero.

Wok-Seared Steak Mah-Jongg with Shishito Peppers

⏲ Total **35 min**; Serves **4 to 6**

- ¼ cup plus 1 tsp. canola oil
- 1 lb. shishito peppers, stemmed
  Kosher salt and pepper
- 1 lb. filet mignon, New York strip or rib eye steak, cut into 1-inch pieces
- 1 Tbsp. potato starch or cornstarch
- 3 garlic cloves, minced
- 1 small shallot, minced
- 2 Tbsp. rice wine, vermouth or dry white wine
- 2 Tbsp. kecap manis (see Note) or 1 Tbsp. soy sauce mixed with 1 Tbsp. tomato paste
- 1 Tbsp. fresh lemon juice
- 1 tsp. toasted sesame seeds
- ½ tsp. toasted sesame oil
  Steamed rice, for serving

1. In a large skillet, heat 1 tablespoon of the canola oil. Add half of the shishito peppers and season with salt and pepper. Stir-fry over moderately high heat until crisp-tender and charred in spots, 4 to 5 minutes. Transfer to a large bowl. Repeat with 1 tablespoon of the oil, the remaining shishitos and more salt and pepper.

2. In a medium bowl, season the steak with salt and pepper and toss with 1 teaspoon of the oil. Sprinkle with the potato starch and toss to coat. Heat the remaining 2 tablespoons of oil in the skillet, add the steak and stir-fry over moderately high heat until browned, 3 minutes. Add the steak to the shishitos.

3. Add the garlic and shallot to the skillet and cook over moderate heat, stirring, until golden, about 2 minutes. Add the rice wine, scraping up any browned bits on the bottom of the skillet. Add the kecap manis, steak and shishito peppers and stir-fry until nicely glazed, about 2 minutes. Stir in the lemon juice, sesame seeds and sesame oil and season with salt and pepper. Serve with steamed rice. —*George Chen*

NOTE Kecap manis is an Indonesian soy sauce that's slightly thick and sweet. Look for it at Asian markets or on amazon.com.

WINE Juicy, fruit-forward red: 2013 Tasca d'Almerita Lamùri Nero d'Avola.

Skirt Steak Quinoa Bowls with Ginger-Sesame Dressing

⏲ Total **30 min**; Serves **4**

- 1¼ cups red or white quinoa, rinsed and drained
- 1 head of Bibb lettuce, roughly torn
- 2 cups bean sprouts
- ¼ cup soy sauce
- 2 Tbsp. finely grated peeled fresh ginger
- 1 Tbsp. distilled white vinegar
- 3 Tbsp. toasted sesame oil
- 1 lb. skirt steak, sliced ¼ inch thick
- 2 Tbsp. minced garlic
  Kosher salt and pepper

1. In a medium saucepan of boiling water, cook the quinoa until tender, about 10 minutes. Drain and return the quinoa to the pan. Cover and let stand for 10 minutes; fluff with a fork.

2. Divide the quinoa, lettuce and bean sprouts among 4 bowls. In a small bowl, whisk the soy sauce, ginger, vinegar and 2 tablespoons of the sesame oil.

3. In a large skillet, heat the remaining 1 tablespoon of sesame oil. Add the steak and garlic and cook over high heat, stirring, until the steak is browned, about 2 minutes. Season with salt and pepper. Spoon the steak over the quinoa and serve with the ginger-sesame dressing. —*Kay Chun*

WINE Spiced, medium-bodied Spanish red: 2006 CVNE Viña Real Gran Reserva.

Grilled Rib Eye Steaks with Apple-Radish Vinaigrette

⏲ Total **30 min**; Serves **4**

- ⅓ cup extra-virgin olive oil, plus more for oiling and brushing
  Two 1-inch-thick boneless rib eye steaks (1½ lbs. total), at room temperature
  Kosher salt and pepper
- 3 Tbsp. Champagne vinegar
- ¼ cup minced radish
- ¼ cup minced crisp, sweet apple, such as Honeycrisp

1. Light a grill and oil the grate. Brush the steaks all over with olive oil and season generously with salt and pepper. Grill over moderately high heat, turning once, until medium-rare, 6 to 8 minutes. Transfer to a carving board and let rest for 5 minutes.

2. Meanwhile, in a medium bowl, mix the ⅓ cup of olive oil with the vinegar, radish and apple. Season the vinaigrette with salt and pepper. Carve the steaks against the grain and serve with the vinaigrette. —*Justin Chapple*

WINE Lively, fruity Spanish red: 2014 Lurra Garnacha.

Sirloin Strips with Arugula and Tomatoes

Active **25 min**; Total **1 hr 30 min**; Serves **6**

- 2 lbs. beef eye of round in 1 piece, frozen for 30 minutes
  Kosher salt
- ¼ cup extra-virgin olive oil
- 1 garlic clove, crushed
- 1 lb. cherry tomatoes, halved
- 2 Tbsp. balsamic vinegar
- 4 oz. arugula (4 cups)
  Shaved Grana Padano cheese, for garnish

1. Using a very sharp knife, thinly slice the beef ⅛ inch thick, then cut into ¾-inch-wide strips. In a medium bowl, toss the meat with ½ teaspoon of salt to coat. Let stand at room temperature for 30 minutes.

2. In a large skillet, heat 2 tablespoons of the oil. Add the garlic; cook over moderate heat, stirring, for 1 minute. Add the tomatoes and cook, stirring occasionally, until they soften and start to split open, about 3 minutes. Transfer to a medium bowl. Wipe out the skillet.

3. In the same skillet, heat the remaining 2 tablespoons of olive oil. Add the beef strips and cook over high heat, stirring occasionally, until browned in spots, about 1 minute. Stir in the vinegar and cook until no trace of pink remains, about 2 minutes longer. Transfer the meat and any juices to shallow bowls and top with the tomatoes and arugula. Garnish with cheese shavings and serve. —*Katie Parla*

WINE Dark-fruited southern Italian red: 2012 Terredora Di Paolo Aglianico.

FLANK STEAKS
WITH SHALLOT–
RED WINE SAUCE

Beet-Braised Short Ribs

Active **1 hr**; Total **4 hr**; Serves **8**

- 2 Tbsp. extra-virgin olive oil
- Eight 10- to 12-oz. English-cut beef short ribs
- Kosher salt and pepper
- 2 large red beets, peeled and cut into ½-inch dice
- 1 large yellow onion, chopped
- 4 large garlic cloves, chopped
- 4 thyme sprigs
- 2 bay leaves
- 2½ cups dry red wine
- One 16-oz. can diced San Marzano tomatoes
- ¼ cup ice wine vinegar or white wine vinegar
- 1 Tbsp. pickling spices
- 1 red onion, thinly sliced
- 3 lbs. parsnips, peeled and chopped into 1-inch pieces
- 6 Tbsp. cold unsalted butter, cut into tablespoons
- 1 cup half-and-half
- 1 cup crème fraîche
- 2 Tbsp. drained prepared horseradish

1. Preheat the oven to 325°. In a large enameled cast-iron casserole, heat the olive oil until shimmering. Season the short ribs with salt and pepper. Cook half of the ribs over moderately high heat, turning occasionally, until browned, about 10 minutes; transfer to a plate. Repeat with the remaining short ribs. Pour off all but 2 tablespoons of fat from the casserole.

2. Add the beets, yellow onion, garlic, thyme and bay leaves to the casserole. Season with salt and pepper and cook over moderate heat, stirring occasionally, until the vegetables are softened, about 10 minutes. Stir in the wine, scraping up any browned bits from the bottom of the casserole. Return the ribs to the pot, add the tomatoes and bring to a simmer. Cover and braise in the oven for about 3 hours, until the ribs are very tender. Discard the thyme sprigs and bay leaves and skim off as much fat as possible from the sauce.

3. Meanwhile, in a small saucepan, bring the ice wine vinegar and pickling spices to a boil over high heat; add the red onion. Remove from the heat and let stand, tossing occasionally, until tender, about 30 minutes.

4. In a large pot, cover the parsnips with 2 inches of cold water, season with salt and bring to a boil over high heat. Reduce the heat and simmer until tender, 15 to 20 minutes; drain and transfer to a food processor. Add the butter and pulse until coarsely pureed. With the machine on, drizzle in the half-and-half; puree until smooth. Season with salt and pepper.

5. In a small bowl, whisk the crème fraîche with the horseradish and season with salt and pepper. To serve, spoon the parsnip puree into shallow bowls. Top with the short ribs, beets, horseradish cream and pickled onion and serve. —*Erin French*

WINE Bold Washington state red blend: 2011 Hedges CMS.

Flank Steaks with Shallot–Red Wine Sauce

⏱ Total **30 min**; Serves **4**

- Two 12-oz. flank steaks, about ¾ inch thick
- Kosher salt and pepper
- 5 Tbsp. unsalted butter
- 1 Tbsp. extra-virgin olive oil
- 4 large shallots, thinly sliced
- ¾ cup dry red wine
- 2 Tbsp. balsamic vinegar
- 1 tsp. sugar

1. Season the steaks generously with salt and pepper. In a large cast-iron skillet, melt 2 tablespoons of the butter. Add the steaks and cook over high heat, turning once, until medium-rare, 6 minutes total. Transfer to a carving board and let rest for 10 minutes.

2. Meanwhile, in a medium saucepan, melt 2 tablespoons of the butter in the olive oil. Add the shallots and cook over moderate heat, stirring occasionally, until softened and lightly browned, about 8 minutes. Add the red wine, vinegar and sugar and simmer until reduced by half, 3 to 5 minutes. Remove from the heat and whisk in the remaining 1 tablespoon of butter. Season the sauce with salt and pepper.

3. Slice the steaks across the grain and serve with the sauce. —*Mimi Thorisson*

WINE Bright and lively Beaujolais: 2013 Georges Descombes Brouilly.

Vindaloo Flank Steak

Active **25 min**; Total **2 hr 45 min**; Serves **4**

In India, fiery vindaloo is a type of curry. At Boti Walla in Atlanta, chef Meherwan Irani turns vindaloo spices into a thick paste to marinate steak.

- 8 dried guajillo chiles, stemmed and wiped clean
- 1 tsp. cumin seeds
- 1 tsp. black peppercorns
- ¾ cup distilled white vinegar
- One 3-inch piece of fresh ginger (2 oz.), peeled and coarsely chopped
- 6 garlic cloves
- 1 small cinnamon stick
- 2 cloves
- Kosher salt and pepper
- One 1½-lb. flank steak
- Extra-virgin olive oil, for brushing
- Warm paratha or naan, yogurt and lime wedges, for serving

1. In a saucepan, toast the chiles, cumin seeds and peppercorns over moderate heat, turning the chiles, until pliable and the cumin is fragrant, 2 minutes. Add ¼ cup of water and the vinegar, ginger, garlic, cinnamon stick, cloves and 1 teaspoon of salt and bring just to a boil. Let stand off the heat until the chiles are soft, about 30 minutes. Discard the cinnamon stick.

2. Transfer the chile mixture to a blender and puree to a smooth paste. In a baking dish, spread the paste all over the steak and refrigerate for 1 to 6 hours. Let stand at room temperature for 45 minutes before grilling.

3. Light a grill and brush with oil. Scrape some of the marinade off the steak, then season the meat with salt and pepper. Grill over moderately high heat, turning, until lightly charred and an instant-read thermometer inserted in the thickest part registers 125°, 10 to 12 minutes. Transfer the steak to a carving board and let rest for 5 minutes. Thinly slice against the grain and serve with warm paratha, yogurt and lime wedges. —*Meherwan Irani*

WINE Spicy, berry-rich Spanish red: 2014 Alvaro Palacios Camins del Priorat.

Kalbi Ribs and Grilled Corn with Kalbi Butter

Active **30 min**; Total **1 hr**; Serves **6**

Chef Stephanie Izard's kalbi (Korean grilled beef short ribs) are a summer mainstay at Girl & the Goat in Chicago. Izard uses a zippy mix of olive oil, vinegar, fish sauce and chile paste to season both the ribs and crisp, charred grilled corn.

¾ cup malt vinegar

⅓ cup extra-virgin olive oil

3 Tbsp. sambal oelek

2 Tbsp. Asian fish sauce

3 garlic cloves

4 lbs. flanken-style beef short ribs (sliced ⅓ inch thick across the bones)

1 stick unsalted butter, softened

4 ears of corn, shucked and cut crosswise into thirds

Kosher salt

Charred Okra Relish (p. 362), for serving

1. In a food processor, puree the vinegar with the olive oil, sambal, fish sauce and garlic. Transfer ½ cup of the kalbi marinade to a bowl. On a large baking sheet, brush the ribs with the remaining marinade and let stand for 30 minutes to 1 hour.

2. Meanwhile, in the processor, pulse the butter until smooth. With the machine on, gradually add the reserved ½ cup of kalbi marinade. Scrape the kalbi butter into the bowl.

3. Light a grill. Brush the corn with kalbi butter and grill over moderately high heat, turning and brushing with more butter, until lightly charred, 5 to 7 minutes. Transfer to a large platter.

4. Season the ribs lightly with salt and grill over high heat, turning once, until nearly cooked through and lightly charred, 4 to 6 minutes. Transfer to the platter and serve with the okra relish. —*Stephanie Izard*

BEER Dark, malty brown ale: Dark Horse Boffo Brown.

Smoked Porter–Braised Beef Short Ribs

📷 PAGE 188

Active **1 hr 15 min**; Total **5 hr**; Serves **8**

Ten 8-oz. English-cut beef short ribs, patted dry

Kosher salt and pepper

2 Tbsp. grapeseed oil

4 Braeburn apples, cored and cut into ½-inch pieces

4 medium leeks, white and light green parts only, thinly sliced

1 fennel bulb—halved, cored and cut into ½-inch pieces

4 garlic cloves, chopped

1½ Tbsp. caraway seeds

3 Tbsp. all-purpose flour

1 quart chicken stock or low-sodium broth

Two 12-oz. bottles smoked porter

1 cup brewed coffee

2 Tbsp. Dijon mustard

6 thyme sprigs

2 bay leaves

2 Tbsp. unsalted butter

2 shallots, thinly sliced

1 Tbsp. packed light brown sugar

Chopped fresh parsley and Polenta Facile (p. 251), for serving

1. Preheat the oven to 325°. Season the ribs with salt and pepper. In a large enameled cast-iron casserole, heat 1 tablespoon of the oil. Add half of the ribs and cook over moderately high heat, turning occasionally, until browned all over, about 10 minutes. Transfer the ribs to a baking sheet. Repeat with the remaining oil and ribs.

2. Pour off all but 2 tablespoons of fat from the casserole. Add the apples, leeks, fennel, garlic, caraway and a generous pinch each of salt and pepper. Cook over moderate heat, stirring occasionally, until softened and just starting to brown, about 12 minutes. Stir in the flour and cook for 1 minute, then add the stock, beer, coffee, mustard, thyme and bay leaves and bring to a boil. Add the short ribs, cover and braise in the oven for about 2 hours and 30 minutes, until very tender. Let stand at room temperature for 1 hour.

3. Using a slotted spoon, transfer the short ribs to a platter and tent with foil. Strain the braising liquid through a fine sieve into a heatproof bowl, pressing on the solids; discard the solids. Skim the fat off the braising liquid.

4. Wipe out the casserole and melt the butter in it. Add the shallots and cook over moderate heat, stirring, until softened and browned, about 5 minutes. Add the sugar and cook until melted. Add the strained braising liquid and bring to a boil. Simmer over moderately high heat until reduced by one-third, about 7 minutes. Season the sauce with salt and pepper. Add the ribs to the sauce and simmer over moderate heat until heated through, about 3 minutes. Top with chopped parsley and serve with the polenta. —*Sara Grimes*

MAKE AHEAD The short ribs can be covered and refrigerated in the sauce for 3 days. Reheat gently before serving.

WINE Robust California Cabernet Sauvignon: 2012 Foxglove from Paso Robles.

Sweet-and-Spicy Grilled Beef Short Ribs

⏱ Total **45 min**; Serves **4**

¼ cup packed light brown sugar

1½ Tbsp. kosher salt

1 Tbsp. paprika

1 Tbsp. chili powder

1 tsp. each of garlic salt, dried oregano and black pepper

3¾ lbs. flanken-style beef short ribs, sliced ⅓ inch thick

Canola oil, for oiling the grate

Lemon wedges and coleslaw, for serving

1. In a medium bowl, mix the sugar, kosher salt, paprika, chili powder, garlic salt, oregano and pepper. Rub the mixture all over the short ribs and let stand for 20 minutes.

2. Light a grill and oil the grate. Grill the ribs over high heat, turning once, until nicely charred and nearly cooked through, about 6 minutes. Transfer to a platter and serve with lemon wedges and coleslaw. —*Justin Chapple*

MAKE AHEAD The spice rub can be stored in an airtight container for up to 1 month.

WINE Dark-berried, full-bodied Argentinean Malbec: 2013 Altos Las Hormigas.

SWEET-AND-
SPICY GRILLED
BEEF SHORT RIBS

GRILLED SKIRT STEAK
WITH SHISHITOS AND
CHARRED LEMON

Grilled Skirt Steak with Shishitos and Charred Lemon

Total **50 min** plus overnight marinating
Serves **4**

STEAK

¼ **cup each rosemary and thyme leaves**

¼ **cup minced shallot**

8 **garlic cloves**

6 **whole peppercorns**

1 **cup grapeseed oil**

1½ **lbs. skirt steak, cut into 2 equal pieces**

Kosher salt and pepper

SALAD

4 **oz. shishito peppers**

3 **Tbsp. extra-virgin olive oil**

Kosher salt and pepper

1 **lemon, halved**

4 **cups frisée (2½ oz.), coarsely torn**

4 **cups watercress (2 oz.), stemmed and coarsely torn**

¼ **cup chopped mint**

2 **celery ribs, thinly sliced on the diagonal, plus ½ cup celery leaves**

2 **oz. Stilton or other blue cheese, crumbled**

1. Prepare the steak In a blender, combine the herbs, shallot, garlic, peppercorns and oil; puree until smooth. Put the steak in a large resealable plastic bag. Pour the marinade over the steak, then seal the bag and turn to coat the meat. Refrigerate overnight.

2. Light a grill or heat a grill pan. Pat the steak dry and season with salt and pepper. Grill over moderate heat until medium-rare, about 3 minutes per side. Transfer the steak to a cutting board and let rest for 10 minutes. Leave the grill on.

3. Make the salad In a medium bowl, toss the shishitos with 1 tablespoon of the oil and season with salt and pepper. Grill the peppers until lightly charred all over, about 2 minutes. Grill the lemon halves cut side down until lightly charred, 5 minutes.

4. In a serving bowl, toss the grilled shishitos with the frisée, watercress, mint, celery and leaves and the remaining 2 tablespoons of olive oil. Squeeze 1 tablespoon of juice from a grilled lemon over the salad, season with salt and pepper and toss. Top with the cheese.

5. Thinly slice the steak across the grain. Serve with the salad and grilled lemon halves for squeezing over the steak.
—*Dave Beran*

WINE Peppery Malbec from Argentina: 2013 La Posta Paulucci.

Spiced Short Rib Tagine

Active **1 hr 10 min;** Total **4 hr;** Serves **6**

SHORT RIBS

½ **cup sliced almonds**

2 **Tbsp. extra-virgin olive oil**

4 **lbs. English-cut bone-in short ribs (3-inch pieces)**

Kosher salt and pepper

2 **carrots, chopped**

1 **onion, chopped**

1 **preserved lemon (see Note), pulp discarded and peel minced**

1 **orange, quartered**

1 **unpeeled head of garlic, halved crosswise**

3 **thyme sprigs**

2 **rosemary sprigs**

3 **bay leaves**

¼ **cup diced California dried apricots**

¼ **cup diced dried figs**

¼ **cup all-purpose flour**

2 **Tbsp. tomato paste**

1 **Tbsp. minced fresh ginger**

1 **Tbsp. ras el hanout (see Note)**

1 **Tbsp. sweet paprika**

1½ **cups unsweetened pomegranate juice**

2 **quarts chicken stock**

ACCOMPANIMENTS

1½ **cups instant couscous**

2 **Tbsp. extra-virgin olive oil**

Kosher salt and pepper

1 **tsp. ras el hanout**

6 **small radishes, halved**

6 **baby turnips, quartered**

1 **Tbsp. fresh lemon juice**

1 **Tbsp. honey**

1. Make the short ribs Preheat the oven to 350°. Toast the nuts in a pie plate until golden, 10 minutes. Leave the oven on.

2. In an enameled cast-iron casserole, heat the oil. Season the short ribs with salt and pepper. Working in 2 batches, brown the meat over moderately high heat, turning, about 5 minutes per batch. Transfer to a plate.

3. Add the carrots, onion, preserved lemon, orange, garlic, thyme, rosemary, bay leaves, apricots and figs to the casserole and cook over moderate heat, stirring occasionally, until the vegetables are golden, about 5 minutes. Stir in the flour, tomato paste, ginger, ras el hanout and paprika and cook, stirring, for 1 minute. Add the ribs, pomegranate juice and stock and bring to a boil. Cover and braise in the oven until the ribs are very tender, about 2 hours.

4. Using a slotted spoon, transfer the ribs to a plate; discard the bones. Strain the sauce, discarding the solids. Wipe out the casserole and pour in the sauce. Return the ribs to the casserole and simmer until slightly thickened, about 10 minutes. Skim off any fat and keep warm.

5. Make the accompaniments In a heatproof bowl, stir the couscous with 1 tablespoon of the oil and 1 teaspoon of salt. In a small saucepan, bring 1¾ cups of water to a boil with the ras el hanout. Stir the water into the couscous, cover with plastic wrap and let stand for 5 minutes. Fluff the couscous with a fork and keep warm.

6. Meanwhile, in a medium skillet, heat the remaining 1 tablespoon of oil. Add the radishes and turnips and cook over moderate heat, stirring, until golden and crisp-tender, about 5 minutes. Stir in the lemon juice and honey and season with salt and pepper.

7. Spoon the couscous onto plates. Top with the short ribs and garnish with the almonds. Spoon the radishes and turnips alongside the meat and serve the sauce on the side.
—*Lior Lev Sercarz*

NOTE Preserved lemons and the North African spice mix ras el hanout are available at specialty food stores and from kalustyans.com.

WINE Bright, cherry-scented, medium-bodied California Grenache: 2013 Birichino Besson Vineyard.

Strip Loin Steaks with Garlic-Sake Sauce

⏱ Total **45 min**; Serves **4 to 6**

Los Angeles chef Kuniko Yagi drizzles these seared steaks with an intense, garlicky pan sauce sweetened with mirin and bits of carrot.

- **2 Tbsp.** extra-virgin olive oil
- **Four 12-oz.** strip loin steaks
- Kosher salt and pepper
- **2 Tbsp.** finely grated garlic
- **¼ cup** finely grated onion
- **¼ cup** finely grated carrot
- **3 Tbsp.** low-sodium soy sauce
- **3 Tbsp.** sake
- **3 Tbsp.** mirin

1. Preheat the oven to 425°. In a large cast-iron skillet, heat the oil. Season the steaks with salt and pepper. Cook 2 of the steaks over moderately high heat, turning once, until browned on both sides, about 5 minutes. Transfer to a plate and repeat with the remaining 2 steaks. Return all 4 to the skillet and roast in the oven for about 8 minutes, until an instant-read thermometer inserted in the thickest part of a steak registers 125° for medium-rare. Transfer the steaks to a cutting board; let rest for 10 minutes.

2. Pour off all but 3 tablespoons of fat from the skillet. Add the garlic and cook over moderate heat, stirring, until fragrant, 30 seconds. Add the remaining ingredients and cook, stirring, until the sauce is slightly reduced and thickened, about 2 minutes. Thinly slice the steaks against the grain, top with the sauce and serve. —*Kuniko Yagi*

SERVE WITH Steamed white rice.

WINE Bright, earthy Portuguese red: 2011 Prazo de Roriz.

Strip Steak Frites with Béarnaise Butter

Total **1 hr 15 min** plus overnight soaking Serves **4**

This brilliant take on steak frites is a specialty of New York City chef Andrew Carmellini. He tops seared strip steaks with a butter infused with tarragon, shallots and vinegar—key ingredients in béarnaise sauce—and serves them with tangy fries made with vinegar-brined potatoes.

FRITES

- **4** baking potatoes, peeled
- **¼ cup** fine sea salt
- **¼ cup** distilled white vinegar
- Canola oil, for frying

BÉARNAISE BUTTER

- **¼ cup** minced shallots
- **¼ cup** dry white wine
- **1½ Tbsp.** tarragon vinegar
- **2** sticks unsalted butter, at room temperature
- **¼ cup** minced tarragon
- **1 Tbsp.** minced parsley
- **1 Tbsp.** minced chervil (optional)
- Kosher salt and pepper

STEAK

- **Four 8-oz.** dry-aged New York strip steaks, cut ¾ inch thick, at room temperature
- Kosher salt and pepper
- **2 Tbsp.** canola oil

1. Make the frites Put the peeled potatoes in a bowl of cold water. Slice them lengthwise ¼ inch thick, then cut lengthwise into ¼-inch-thick fries. Rinse in cold water until the water runs clear. Refrigerate overnight in cold water.

2. In a large pot, bring 1 gallon of water to a boil. Stir in the salt and vinegar. Drain the potatoes and add them to the boiling water. Return to a gentle boil and cook for 3 minutes. Drain the potatoes well, then spread them in a single layer on paper towels. Pat thoroughly dry and let cool.

3. Line 2 baking sheets with paper towels. In a large enameled cast-iron casserole, heat 2 inches of oil to 365°. Working in batches, fry the potatoes for 1 minute, stirring gently so they don't stick together. Using a slotted spoon, transfer the fries to the paper towels to cool.

4. Make the béarnaise butter In a medium saucepan, combine the shallots, wine and vinegar and cook over moderate heat until all of the liquid has evaporated, about 5 minutes. Scrape the shallots into a medium bowl. Add the butter and beat with a hand mixer until creamy. Fold in the herbs and season with salt and pepper.

5. Make the steaks Season the steaks with salt and pepper. In a large cast-iron skillet, heat the oil. Cook 2 of the steaks over moderately high heat, turning once, until browned and medium-rare, 3 to 4 minutes per side. Transfer to plates. Repeat with the remaining 2 steaks. Let rest for 5 minutes.

6. Meanwhile, heat the oil in the casserole to 400°. In 2 batches, fry the potatoes, stirring occasionally, until golden and crisp, about 2 minutes. Drain briefly on paper towels. Season with salt. Top the steaks with some of the béarnaise butter and serve immediately with the fries and the remaining béarnaise butter. —*Andrew Carmellini*

MAKE AHEAD The béarnaise butter can be refrigerated for up to 1 week or frozen for 1 month.

WINE Cassis-scented, full-bodied Bordeaux: 2011 Chateau Fonplegade St-Emilion.

STRIP STEAK FRITES
WITH BÉARNAISE BUTTER

BACON-AND-
KIMCHI BURGERS

Bacon-and-Kimchi Burgers

⏱ Total **30 min;** Serves **4**

Vermont chef Wesley Genovart makes his over-the-top, Shake Shack–inspired burger with two thin stacked patties, thick-cut bacon, cabbage kimchi and a spicy home-made sauce.

- ¼ cup sambal oelek (Indonesian chile sauce)
- ¼ cup mayonnaise
- ¼ cup ketchup
- 4 slices of thick-cut bacon
- 1¼ lbs. ground beef chuck
  Kosher salt
- 4 slices of American cheese
- 4 potato buns, toasted
- 1 cup chopped drained kimchi (6 oz.)

1. In a small bowl, combine the sambal with the mayonnaise and ketchup and mix well.

2. Light a grill or heat a grill pan. Grill the bacon over moderate heat, turning, until golden and crisp, about 5 minutes. Drain on paper towels.

3. Form the beef into eight ¼-inch-thick burgers and season with salt. Grill over high heat, turning, until browned, 1 minute per side. Make 4 stacks of 2 burgers each on the grill and spoon 1 tablespoon of the sambal mayo over each stack. Top with the cheese, cover and grill over high heat just until the cheese is melted, about 1 minute.

4. Spread the remaining sambal mayo on the bottom buns. Top with the burgers, bacon and kimchi, close and serve. *—Wesley Genovart*

BEER Hoppy but balanced New England IPA: Harpoon.

MAD GENIUS TIP
Shaping Patties

To form perfect patties that cook evenly and look stellar, mound 6 ounces of ground meat on a plastic takeout lid, invert another lid on top, then press down to flatten.

Bloody Mary Burgers

⏱ Total **30 min;** Serves **4**

- 1½ lbs. ground sirloin
- 3 Tbsp. prepared horseradish, drained
- 3 Tbsp. tomato paste
- 2 tsp. hot sauce
- 2 tsp. Worcestershire sauce
- 1½ tsp. celery seeds
  Kosher salt and pepper
- 4 brioche hamburger buns, split and toasted
  Mayonnaise, red leaf lettuce, sliced tomato and American cheese, for serving

1. In a bowl, using a fork, gently stir the ground sirloin with the horseradish, tomato paste, hot sauce, Worcestershire, celery seeds and 1 teaspoon each of salt and pepper. Using 2 plastic lids from 1-quart take-out containers, press the beef mixture into 4 patties. Transfer to a plate.

2. Light a grill or heat a grill pan. Season the patties lightly with salt and pepper and grill over moderate heat, turning once, until medium-rare within, 8 to 10 minutes. Transfer the burgers to the buns, top with mayonnaise, lettuce, tomato and cheese and serve. *—Justin Chapple*

BEER Refreshing, hoppy pilsner: Sixpoint Crisp.

Steak Tacos with Pineapple

⏱ Total **45 min;** Serves **4**

- 3 Tbsp. soy sauce
- 1 Tbsp. finely grated garlic
- 1 Tbsp. finely grated peeled fresh ginger
- 1½ lbs. skirt steak, cut into 5-inch lengths
  Kosher salt and pepper
  Warm corn tortillas, diced fresh pineapple, thinly sliced red onion and cilantro leaves, for serving

1. In a small bowl, whisk the soy sauce with the garlic and ginger. Brush the mixture all over the steak and season lightly with salt and pepper. Let stand for 20 minutes.

2. Heat a large cast-iron skillet. Add the steak and cook over high heat, turning once, until charred on the outside and medium-rare within, about 6 minutes. Transfer to a carving board and let rest for 5 minutes.

Carve the steak against the grain and serve in warm corn tortillas with diced pineapple, sliced red onion and cilantro leaves. *—Justin Chapple*

BEER Toasty, chocolaty brown ale: Smutty-nose Old Brown Dog.

Picadillo Tacos

⏱ Total **40 min;** Serves **4 to 6**

- ½ cup sliced almonds
- 3 Tbsp. canola oil
- 1 onion, finely chopped
- 1 jalapeño, finely chopped
- 3 large garlic cloves, sliced
- 2 tsp. ground cinnamon
- 2 tsp. ground cumin
- 2 tsp. ground coriander
- ¼ tsp. ground cloves
- 1 lb. ground beef chuck
- 2 cups tomato puree
- ½ cup golden raisins
- 2 Tbsp. fresh lime juice
  Kosher salt and pepper
  Warm corn tortillas, shredded lettuce, chopped onion, pinto beans, grated Cotija cheese, salsa and lime wedges, for serving

1. In a large skillet, toast the almonds over low heat, stirring, until golden, 3 to 5 minutes. Transfer to a small bowl.

2. In the same skillet, heat 2 tablespoons of the canola oil. Add the onion, jalapeño and garlic and cook over moderately high heat, stirring occasionally, until the onion is golden, about 5 minutes. Add the cinnamon, cumin, coriander and cloves and cook, stirring, until fragrant, 1 minute. Add the remaining 1 tablespoon of oil and the ground beef and cook over moderate heat, breaking up the meat with a wooden spoon, until browned, about 3 minutes. Stir in the tomato puree and raisins. Simmer until thick, 7 to 8 minutes. Add the lime juice and season the picadillo with salt and pepper. Stir in the almonds.

3. Serve the picadillo in corn tortillas, passing shredded lettuce, chopped onion, pinto beans, grated cheese, salsa and lime wedges at the table. *—Jenn Louis*

BEER Crisp, malty ale: Full Sail Brewing Co. Amber.

Manti with Tomato Butter and Yogurt

Active **1 hr 30 min;** Total **3 hr;** Serves **6**

These classic boiled Turkish dumplings are filled with tasty ground beef and served swimming in two sauces: smoky tomato butter and garlicky yogurt.

DOUGH

- **1 cup plus 2 Tbsp. all-purpose flour, plus more for dusting**
- **1 large egg**
- **⅛ tsp. kosher salt**

MEAT FILLING

- **½ lb. ground beef**
- **1 small onion, grated**
- **3 Tbsp. minced parsley**
- **1 tsp. kosher salt**
- **¼ tsp. pepper**

YOGURT SAUCE

- **1 cup Greek yogurt**
- **½ tsp. finely grated garlic**
- **Kosher salt**

TOMATO-BUTTER SAUCE

- **4 Tbsp. unsalted butter**
- **2 Tbsp. tomato sauce**
- **1 tsp. paprika**
- **Dried mint and Aleppo pepper, for garnish**

1. Make the dough In a medium bowl, combine the flour, egg and salt with 5 tablespoons of water; mix with a wooden spoon until a dough forms. On a lightly floured work surface, knead the dough until smooth, about 5 minutes. Clean the bowl and return the dough to it. Cover with plastic wrap and let rest for 1½ hours.

2. Make the meat filling In a medium bowl, combine all of the ingredients and mix well.

3. Make the yogurt sauce In a small bowl, combine the yogurt and garlic and season with salt. Mix well and refrigerate.

4. Make the tomato-butter sauce In a small saucepan, melt the butter over low heat. Stir in the tomato sauce and paprika and keep warm.

5. Lightly dust a baking sheet with flour. Bring a large pot of salted water to a boil.

6. On a lightly floured work surface, using a lightly floured rolling pin, roll out the dough 1/16 inch thick. Cut the dough into 2-inch squares. Spoon ½ teaspoon of the filling in the center of each square. To form the manti, fold the dough over the filling to form a triangle; press the edges together to seal. Transfer the manti to the prepared baking sheet.

7. In a large pot of boiling water, boil the manti until tender and cooked through, about 5 minutes. Using a slotted spoon, transfer to bowls. Top with the yogurt sauce and warm butter sauce, sprinkle with dried mint and Aleppo pepper and serve. *—Scott Conant*

Roast Beef 101 with Winter Vegetables

Total **1 hr;** Serves **4 to 6**

- **1½ lbs. rutabaga, peeled and cut into 1-inch pieces**
- **½ lb. carrots, cut into 1-inch pieces**
- **3 garlic cloves, crushed**
- **2 Tbsp. extra-virgin olive oil**
- **Kosher salt and pepper**
- **One 2¼-lb. beef tri-tip or coulotte roast**
- **2 Tbsp. unsalted butter**
- **1 shallot, thinly sliced**
- **1 cup dry red wine**
- **1 tsp. cornstarch mixed with 1 Tbsp. water**

1. Preheat the oven to 425°. On a large rimmed baking sheet, toss the rutabaga with the carrots, garlic and olive oil. Season with salt and pepper. Roast the vegetables for 35 minutes, until tender and browned in spots. Transfer to a platter; keep warm.

2. Meanwhile, season the roast with salt and pepper. In a large cast-iron skillet, melt the butter over moderately high heat. Add the roast and brown it all over, about 6 minutes. Roast the meat in the oven for 20 to 25 minutes, until an instant-read thermometer inserted in the thickest part registers 120°. Transfer the roast to a carving board; let rest for 10 minutes.

3. Pour off all but 2 tablespoons of fat from the skillet. Add the shallot and cook over moderate heat until browned. Add the red wine, bring to a boil and simmer until reduced by half. Return the sauce to a boil and whisk in the cornstarch slurry. Cook over moderately high heat until thickened. Season with salt and pepper.

4. Thinly slice the roast across the grain and serve with the red wine sauce and roasted vegetables. *—Ian Knauer*

WINE Robust and fruity South Australian Shiraz: 2011 The Hedonist.

Pepper-Crusted Prime Rib Roast

PAGE 189

Active **15 min;** Total **4 hr 30 min;** Serves **12**

- **One 9- to 10-lb. prime rib roast**
- **2 Tbsp. kosher salt**
- **¼ cup multicolor whole peppercorns**
- **1 guajillo chile, stemmed and chopped**
- **2 Tbsp. rosemary leaves**
- **¼ cup Dijon mustard**
- **2 Tbsp. all-purpose flour**
- **2 Tbsp. soy sauce**
- **2 Tbsp. Worcestershire sauce**
- **4 garlic cloves, minced**
- **6 cups low-sodium beef broth**

1. Season the roast with the salt and let stand at room temperature for 1 hour.

2. In a spice grinder, grind the peppercorns, guajillo chile and rosemary until coarse. Transfer to a medium bowl. Add all of the remaining ingredients except the broth and mix well.

3. Preheat the oven to 400°. Rub the pepper mix all over the roast. Place the roast on a rack set in a roasting pan. Add 2 cups of the broth to the pan and roast for 30 minutes, until the meat is well browned. Add 2 more cups of the broth and loosely tent the roast with foil. Reduce the oven temperature to 350°. Roast for about 2½ hours, until an instant-read thermometer registers 115°; add the remaining 2 cups of broth halfway through. Set the roast on a cutting board to rest for about 30 minutes (the center of the roast will register at 125° for medium-rare).

4. Strain the pan juices into a small saucepan. Skim off as much fat as possible and bring to a simmer. Carve the roast and serve with the pan jus. *—Marcela Valladolid*

WINE Peppery California Cabernet: 2011 Chateau St. Jean Alexander Valley.

Roasted Dry-Aged Rib of Beef with Creamed Greens

Active **1 hr**; Total **3 hr 30 min**
Serves **10 to 12**

Christina Lecki, chef at The Breslin in New York City, makes a quick and easy compound butter with parsley, marjoram and peppercorns to melt over her wonderfully tender beef rib roast.

RIB ROAST

    One 10-lb. beef rib roast, chine bone removed

2 Tbsp. extra-virgin olive oil

    Kosher salt and pepper

2 cups chicken stock or low-sodium broth

2 rosemary sprigs

5 thyme sprigs

MARJORAM BUTTER

6 Tbsp. unsalted butter, at room temperature

¼ cup chopped parsley

2 Tbsp. chopped brined green peppercorns

2 Tbsp. chopped marjoram

1 Tbsp. chopped thyme

½ tsp. finely grated garlic

½ tsp. kosher salt

½ tsp. pepper

CREAMED ESCAROLE AND SPINACH

¼ cup extra-virgin olive oil

2 shallots, minced

4 anchovy fillets in oil, drained and chopped

1 Tbsp. finely chopped garlic

4 bunches of escarole (2 lbs.), trimmed and chopped (24 cups)

3 cups heavy cream

4 bunches of curly spinach (2 lbs.), stemmed (20 cups)

1 tsp. finely grated lemon zest plus 2 Tbsp. fresh lemon juice

¼ tsp. crushed red pepper

    Kosher salt and black pepper

1. Make the rib roast Preheat the oven to 450°. Place the roast fat side up on a rack set in a roasting pan. Rub all over with the olive oil and season with salt and pepper. Add the stock and the rosemary and thyme sprigs to the pan. Roast for 30 minutes, until well browned. Reduce the oven temperature to 350° and roast the meat for about 2½ hours longer, until an instant-read thermometer inserted in the center of the roast registers 125° for medium-rare. Transfer to a cutting board and let rest for 30 minutes.

2. Meanwhile, make the marjoram butter In a small bowl, combine all of the ingredients and mix well. Let the butter stand at room temperature.

3. Meanwhile, make the creamed escarole and spinach In a pot, heat the olive oil. Add the shallots, anchovies and garlic and cook over moderate heat, stirring, until the anchovies dissolve, about 2 minutes. In batches, stir in the escarole until wilted, about 5 minutes. Add the heavy cream and bring to a boil. Simmer briskly until the cream is slightly reduced, about 10 minutes. Add the spinach in batches, stirring, until wilted. Cook, stirring occasionally, until the greens are very tender and the cream is reduced and very thick, about 30 minutes longer. Stir in the lemon zest, lemon juice and crushed red pepper and season with salt and black pepper.

4. Spread the marjoram butter all over the warm roast. Cut the roast off the bone, then thinly slice. Serve with the creamed escarole and spinach. —*Christina Lecki*

MAKE AHEAD The marjoram butter can be refrigerated for up to 2 days; bring to room temperature before using. The creamed escarole and spinach can be refrigerated overnight and reheated before serving.

WINE Herb-scented, black currant–inflected Cabernet Franc: 2012 Charles Joguet Les Petites Roches Chinon.

Fez-Style Roast Lamb Shoulder

Active **10 min**; Total **3 hr 45 min**; Serves **8**

At major celebrations, Moroccans often serve spice-rubbed whole lamb that's been cooked for hours on a spit. Tara Stevens, who runs a cooking school in Fez, created this simplified version: She rubs lamb shoulder with a garlicky cumin-ginger butter, then roasts it until supertender.

¼ tsp. saffron threads

1 stick unsalted butter, at room temperature

10 garlic cloves, crushed

1 Tbsp. ground cumin, plus more for serving

1 Tbsp. ground coriander

1 tsp. ground turmeric

1 tsp. ground ginger

    One 5-lb. bone-in lamb shoulder, fat scored at ½-inch intervals

    Kosher salt

1 cup dry rosé wine or water

    Harissa, for serving

1. Preheat the oven to 425°. In a small skillet, toast the saffron over low heat just until fragrant, 1 to 2 minutes. Transfer the saffron to a small bowl and crumble between your fingers. Add the butter, garlic, the 1 tablespoon of cumin, the coriander, turmeric and ginger and mix well.

2. Set the lamb in a large baking dish fat side up and rub all over with the spiced butter. Season with salt and roast for about 30 minutes, until the meat is golden brown. Reduce the oven temperature to 325°.

3. Add the rosé to the baking dish, cover with foil and roast for about 3 hours longer, basting occasionally, until the lamb is falling-off-the-bone tender. Transfer to a cutting board and let rest for 10 minutes. Carve and serve with harissa and cumin for dipping. —*Tara Stevens*

WINE Bold, spiced Sicilian Nero d'Avola Valle dell'Acate: 2012 Case Ibidini.

Grilled Lamb Skewers with Sweet Pickles

Total **40 min plus 18 hr marinating**
Serves **6**

LAMB

¼ cup cilantro leaves
¼ cup parsley leaves
3 garlic cloves
3 bay leaves
2 chiles de árbol
2 Tbsp. fresh lemon juice
2 Tbsp. sweet pimentón
1 Tbsp. plus 1 tsp. garam masala
1 Tbsp. plus 1 tsp. dried thyme
2 tsp. kosher salt, plus more
   for seasoning
1½ tsp. pepper
1 cup canola oil, plus more
   for the grate
2 lbs. trimmed lamb shoulder,
   cut into 1½-inch cubes

PICKLES

1 hothouse cucumber, thinly
   sliced on a mandoline
½ medium sweet onion, very thinly
   sliced on a mandoline (1 cup)
½ cup sugar
2 tsp. kosher salt
¾ cup sherry vinegar
16 wooden skewers, soaked for 2 hours

1. Marinate the lamb In a blender, combine all of the ingredients except the lamb and puree until smooth. Transfer to a large bowl or resealable plastic bag, add the lamb and turn to coat. Marinate in the refrigerator for 18 to 24 hours.

2. Meanwhile, make the pickles In a large bowl, toss the cucumber and onion. In a saucepan, combine the sugar and salt with ¾ cup of water; bring to a simmer, stirring to dissolve the sugar and salt. Remove from the heat and stir in the vinegar; let cool slightly. Pour the warm brine over the cucumber and onion; let cool to room temperature, then refrigerate overnight.

3. Light a grill and oil the grate. Remove the lamb from the marinade and thread onto the skewers; season lightly with salt. Grill, turning, until lightly charred and medium within, 6 to 7 minutes total. Transfer the lamb to a platter; serve with the pickles.
—*Katie Button*

MAKE AHEAD The pickles can be drained and refrigerated for up to 3 days.

WINE Cherry-inflected, medium-bodied red Rioja: 2010 CVNE Viña Real Crianza.

Lamb Gyro Dumplings with Tzatziki

Total **1 hr 10 min**; Makes **30**

In a superdelicious mash-up of cuisines, Chicago chef Mike Sheerin packs gyro-inspired lamb into dumplings he serves with the Greek yogurt dip tzatziki. He makes the dumpling wrappers from scratch, but store-bought gyoza wrappers are a good substitute.

½ cup Greek yogurt
½ English cucumber, grated on a
   box grater and squeezed dry
1 tsp. finely grated lemon zest
   plus 2 Tbsp. fresh lemon juice
1 Tbsp. chopped dill, plus more
   for garnish
⅛ tsp. cayenne
   Kosher salt and pepper
1 lb. ground lamb
1 Tbsp. canola oil
2 tsp. onion powder
1 tsp. garlic powder
1 tsp. dried mint
1 tsp. dried oregano
1 garlic clove, minced
30 small round gyoza wrappers

1. In a medium bowl, whisk the yogurt with the cucumber, lemon zest, lemon juice, the 1 tablespoon of chopped dill and the cayenne. Season the tzatziki with salt and pepper. Cover and refrigerate until well chilled, about 20 minutes.

2. Meanwhile, in a large bowl, combine the lamb with the oil, onion powder, garlic powder, mint, oregano, garlic, 2 teaspoons of salt and 1 teaspoon of pepper and mix well.

3. On a work surface, brush the rims of 5 gyoza wrappers with water and spoon 1 tablespoon of the filling into the center of each. Fold the wrappers over to form half-moons. Seal the edges, pressing out any air, and crimp decoratively. Transfer the dumplings to a parchment paper–lined baking sheet; keep them covered with a moist paper towel. Repeat with the remaining wrappers and filling.

4. Fill a wok or large skillet with 2 inches of water and bring to a boil. Working in batches, arrange the dumplings in a double-tiered bamboo steamer lined with parchment paper. Set the steamer over the boiling water, cover and steam the dumplings until the filling is cooked through and firm, 6 to 8 minutes. Transfer the dumplings to a platter and garnish with chopped dill. Serve with the tzatziki. —*Mike Sheerin*

BEER Hoppy, slightly tangy Belgian pale ale: Orval.

Rosemary-Garlic Lamb Chops with Pimentón and Mint

Active **25 min**; Total **2 hr 25 min**; Serves **4**

L.A. chef Nancy Silverton adores the grilled, herb-flecked lamb chops *scottadito* ("burnt fingers") served at the restaurant she frequents whenever she's in Panicale, Italy. She tweaks the recipe by garnishing the lamb with smoky pimentón de la Vera and little mint leaves.

½ cup rosemary leaves
8 garlic cloves
   Kosher salt and pepper
½ cup extra-virgin olive oil, plus more
   for drizzling
12 baby lamb chops (about 3 oz. each)
¼ cup small mint leaves and a large
   pinch of pimentón de la Vera,
   for garnish

1. In a blender, pulse the rosemary and garlic with a pinch each of salt and pepper until coarsely chopped. With the machine on, gradually add the ½ cup of olive oil until the rosemary and garlic are finely chopped. Scrape the mixture into a large baking dish and add the lamb chops. Turn the chops to coat and refrigerate for at least 2 hours or overnight.

2. Light a grill or heat a grill pan. Season the lamb chops with salt and pepper. Grill over high heat, turning once, until nicely charred outside and medium-rare within, about 6 minutes. Transfer the lamb to a platter and let rest for 5 minutes. Garnish with the mint leaves and pimentón, top with a drizzle of olive oil and serve immediately.
—*Nancy Silverton*

WINE Dense, powerful Sagrantino: 2007 Paolo Bea Pagliaro Secco.

LAMB GYRO
DUMPLINGS
WITH TZATZIKI

THIN GRILLED LAMB CHOPS WITH
LEMON (OPPOSITE); CORN ON
THE COB WITH PARSLEY BUTTER
(RECIPE, P. 230); TOMATO-FETA
SALAD WITH MINT (RECIPE, P. 49)

Grilled Lamb with Pickled Eggplant Salad and Herbed Yogurt

Active **1 hr**; Total **1 hr 45 min plus 8 hr marinating**; Serves **4**

At Otium in L.A., chef Timothy Hollingsworth grills garlic-marinated lamb chops over almond wood, but the chops are also great simply seared on a charcoal grill or even in a grill pan.

LAMB

- ½ cup extra-virgin olive oil
- ¼ cup fresh lemon juice
- 1 Tbsp. minced garlic
- 1 Tbsp. minced rosemary
- 1 Tbsp. minced thyme
- 12 baby lamb chops (3 lbs.)
  Kosher salt and pepper

YOGURT SAUCE

- 1 cup whole-milk yogurt
- 1 tsp. finely grated lemon zest plus 1½ Tbsp. fresh lemon juice
- 1½ tsp. finely chopped thyme
- 1½ tsp. finely chopped rosemary
  Kosher salt and pepper

SALAD

- 1 cup Champagne vinegar
- ⅓ cup sugar
- ¼ cup fresh orange juice
  Two 12-oz. Japanese or Chinese eggplants, cut into ½-inch dice
- 1 English cucumber, chopped
- ¾ cup pitted mixed marinated olives
- 2 cups baby arugula
  Kosher salt and pepper

1. Marinate the lamb In a baking dish, whisk the olive oil with the lemon juice, garlic, rosemary and thyme. Add the lamb and turn to coat. Cover and refrigerate for 8 hours or overnight, turning occasionally. Bring the lamb to room temperature before grilling.

2. Make the yogurt sauce In a medium bowl, whisk the yogurt with the lemon zest, lemon juice, thyme and rosemary. Season the sauce with salt and pepper.

3. Make the salad In a medium saucepan, combine the vinegar with the sugar, orange juice and 1 cup of water; bring to a boil over moderately high heat. Add the eggplant and cook for 2 minutes. Off the heat, let the eggplant cool completely in the liquid, about 45 minutes. Drain well.

4. Light a grill or heat a grill pan. Remove the lamb from the marinade and season with salt and pepper. Grill over high heat, turning once, until charred outside and medium-rare within, about 6 minutes total. Transfer the chops to plates and let rest for 5 minutes.

5. In a serving bowl, toss the drained pickled eggplant with the cucumber, olives and arugula. Season the eggplant salad with salt and pepper. Serve the lamb with the salad, passing the yogurt sauce at the table. —*Timothy Hollingsworth*

MAKE AHEAD The pickled eggplant can be refrigerated for up to 3 days.

WINE Spicy, lightly smoky, full-bodied Shiraz: 2013 Paringa.

Thin Grilled Lamb Chops with Lemon

🕐 Total **30 min**; Serves **4 to 6**

New York City chef April Bloomfield's trick for juicy lamb chops is to pound them so thin they cook in a flash, which keeps them moist on the grill.

- 12 lamb rib chops (2¼ lbs.), frenched (have your butcher do this)
  Kosher salt
  Lemon wedges, for serving

1. On a work surface, wrap each lamb chop in 3 layers of plastic. Using a meat mallet or small saucepan, pound each chop to a ½-inch thickness.

2. Light a grill or heat a grill pan over high heat. Season the lamb chops all over with salt. Grill over high heat until nicely charred on the bottom, about 2 minutes. Flip the chops and cook until medium-rare within, 1 to 2 minutes longer. Transfer to a platter and serve with lemon wedges. —*April Bloomfield*

WINE Herb-inflected, red-berried southern French red: 2013 Mas de Gourgonnier Les Baux de Provence.

Roast Leg of Lamb with Hemp Seed Pesto

Active **45 min**; Total **4 hr 15 min plus overnight marinating**; Serves **8 to 10**

High-protein hemp seeds add nutty flavor to the pesto that accompanies this delectable yogurt-glazed lamb.

LAMB

- ½ cup full-fat plain Greek yogurt
- 6 garlic cloves, minced
- 3 Tbsp. fresh lemon juice
- 2 Tbsp. minced rosemary
- 2 Tbsp. extra-virgin olive oil
  Kosher salt and pepper
  One 6-lb. whole bone-in leg of lamb, excess fat trimmed
  Lemon wedges, for serving

PESTO

- 1¾ cups each lightly packed basil and parsley leaves
- 2 garlic cloves, crushed
- 1 Tbsp. fresh lemon juice
  Kosher salt and pepper
- ½ cup extra-virgin olive oil
- ½ cup hulled hemp seeds

1. Prepare the lamb In a bowl, whisk the yogurt with the garlic, lemon juice, rosemary, olive oil and 1 tablespoon each of salt and pepper. Rub the mixture all over the lamb and set on a large rimmed baking sheet. Cover with plastic wrap and refrigerate overnight. Let the lamb stand at room temperature for 1 hour before roasting.

2. Preheat the oven to 375°. Season the lamb lightly with salt and pepper and roast for about 1 hour and 50 minutes, until an instant-read thermometer inserted in the thickest part of the meat registers 140°. Transfer to a carving board and let rest for 30 minutes.

3. Make the pesto In a food processor, pulse the basil, parsley, garlic and lemon juice with a pinch of salt until minced. With the machine on, gradually add the olive oil until incorporated. Scrape the pesto into a bowl and stir in the hemp seeds. Season with salt and pepper. Carve the lamb and serve with the pesto and lemon wedges. —*Michael Schwartz*

WINE Berry-rich Spanish Garnacha: 2012 Joan d'Anguera.

Herbed Leg of Lamb with Olive Butter and Roasted Tomatoes

Active **1 hr;** Total **3 hr 30 min plus overnight marinating;** Serves **6 to 8**

- ⅓ **cup coarsely chopped shallots**
- ½ **cup crushed garlic cloves**
- ⅓ **cup each thyme leaves, parsley leaves and chopped rosemary**
- 3 **Tbsp. Dijon mustard**
- ⅓ **cup plus ¼ cup extra-virgin olive oil**
- 1 **stick plus 2 Tbsp. unsalted butter, at room temperature**
  One 5-lb. well-trimmed boned and butterflied leg of lamb
  Kosher salt and pepper
- 2 **lbs. cherry tomatoes**
- 2 **thyme sprigs**
  Chunky Olive Butter (recipe follows), for serving

1. In a blender or food processor, combine the shallots, garlic, thyme, parsley, rosemary, mustard and ⅓ cup of the olive oil; blend until smooth. Transfer to a bowl and stir in the butter.

2. Arrange the lamb fat side down on a rack set over a rimmed baking sheet. Spread the herb butter all over the lamb, leaving a 1-inch border. Refrigerate until the butter is semifirm, 30 minutes. Roll up the lamb with the butter inside and tie securely with kitchen twine at 1-inch intervals. Cover and refrigerate overnight.

3. Preheat the oven to 400°. Rub the lamb with 2 tablespoons of the oil and season with salt and pepper. Roast until an instant-read thermometer inserted in the thickest part registers 130° for medium-rare, about 1 hour and 45 minutes. Transfer the lamb to a cutting board and let rest for 20 minutes. Leave the oven on.

4. On a rimmed baking sheet, toss the tomatoes with the remaining 2 tablespoons of olive oil and the thyme sprigs and season with salt and pepper. Roast for 20 minutes, stirring, until softened.

5. Discard the strings and thinly slice the lamb. Serve with the roasted tomatoes and olive butter. —*Dave Beran*

WINE Dense, savory Côtes du Rhône: 2013 Éric Texier Brézème.

CHUNKY OLIVE BUTTER
⟳ Total **10 min;** Makes **about 1½ cups**

- 1 **stick plus 4 Tbsp. unsalted butter, at room temperature**
- 1 **cup pitted and chopped Picholine or Niçoise olives**
- ¼ **cup Dijon mustard**
- ¼ **cup chopped parsley**
  Kosher salt and pepper

In a medium bowl, combine the butter with the olives, mustard and parsley and season with salt and pepper. —*DB*

MAKE AHEAD The olive butter can be refrigerated for up to 1 week; bring to room temperature before serving.

Grilled Butterflied Leg of Lamb with Ancho-Huckleberry Sauce

Active **45 min;** Total **1 hr 15 min;** Serves **4**

This dish from Ari Weiswasser, chef-owner of Glen Ellen Star in Sonoma, is all about the sauce: It has just the right amounts of heat, spice and sweetness to highlight the pure lamb flavor of the simply grilled cut.

- 2 **oz. ancho chiles, stemmed and seeded**
  Boiling water
- 1 **Tbsp. extra-virgin olive oil**
- ¼ **cup minced Spanish onion**
- 2 **garlic cloves, minced**
  Kosher salt and pepper
- ⅛ **tsp. ground cumin**
- ⅛ **tsp. cinnamon**
- ⅛ **tsp. ground cloves**
- ⅛ **tsp. ground allspice**
- ⅛ **tsp. ground oregano**
- 2 **Tbsp. toasted sesame seeds**
- 2 **Tbsp. plain dry breadcrumbs**
- ½ **oz. unsweetened chocolate, finely chopped**
- 1 **Tbsp. sugar**
- ¼ **cup crushed tomatoes**
- ¼ **cup chicken stock**
- ⅓ **cup huckleberry or currant jam**
- 1 **Tbsp. aged balsamic vinegar**
  One 2-lb. butterflied leg of lamb
  Canola oil, for brushing

1. In a heatproof bowl, cover the chiles with boiling water and let stand until softened, 20 minutes. Drain the chiles, reserving ½ cup of the soaking liquid. In a blender, puree the chiles with the reserved soaking liquid until smooth. Strain the puree through a fine sieve.

2. In a medium saucepan, heat the olive oil. Add the onion, garlic and a pinch of salt and cook over moderately high heat, stirring occasionally, until the onion is softened, about 4 minutes. Add the cumin, cinnamon, cloves, allspice and oregano and cook, stirring, until fragrant, about 1 minute. Stir in the chile puree, sesame seeds, breadcrumbs, chocolate and sugar and bring to a boil. Stir in the tomatoes, chicken stock, jam and vinegar and bring just to a simmer. Season the sauce with salt and keep warm.

3. Light a grill or heat a grill pan. Brush the lamb with canola oil and season generously with salt and pepper. Grill over high heat, turning once, until lightly charred, about 5 minutes. Reduce the heat to moderate and grill until an instant-read thermometer inserted in the thickest part of the meat registers 135° for medium-rare or 140° for medium, about 20 minutes total. Transfer the lamb to a carving board and let rest for 10 minutes. Carve across the grain and serve with the warm ancho-huckleberry sauce. —*Ari Weiswasser*

MAKE AHEAD The sauce can be refrigerated for up to 1 week.

WINE Peppery, dark-berried Sonoma Zinfandel: 2013 Ravenswood Estate.

Curried Goat with Apricot-Ginger Chutney

Active **1 hr**; Total **6 hr plus 24 hr marinating**
Serves **6 to 8**

New York chef Adam Schop's brothy version of this Jamaican classic is lighter than most. He starts by marinating pieces of the tender goat forequarter with spices, aromatics and yogurt for at least 24 hours. The stew is usually made with water, but Schop uses vegetable stock to amp up the flavor.

MARINATED GOAT

10 **scallions, quartered crosswise**
½ **medium onion, finely chopped**
   One 2½-inch piece of fresh ginger, finely chopped
½ **cup finely chopped cilantro**
⅓ **cup plain yogurt**
¼ **cup plus 2 Tbsp. West Indian curry powder (see Note)**
¼ **cup ground coriander**
3 **Tbsp. garam masala**
3 **Tbsp. vegetable oil**
4 **lbs. meaty, well-trimmed goat forequarter, cut into 2½-inch pieces (see Note)**

GOAT STEW

   Kosher salt and pepper
¼ **cup vegetable oil**
3 **quarts vegetable stock**
10 **scallions, coarsely chopped**
1 **medium red pepper, coarsely chopped**
1 **medium red onion, coarsely chopped**
1 **large carrot, coarsely chopped**
10 **thyme sprigs**
1 **Scotch bonnet or habanero chile, stemmed and halved lengthwise**
1 **cup frozen peas**
   Apricot-Ginger Chutney (recipe follows) or Rice and Peas (p. 245), for serving

1. Marinate the goat In a food processor, combine all of the ingredients except the goat pieces and pulse until finely chopped. In a large bowl, rub the marinade into the meat. Cover with plastic wrap and refrigerate for 24 to 36 hours.

2. Make the stew Wipe the marinade off the goat; season with salt and pepper. In a large enameled cast-iron casserole, heat the oil. Working in batches, brown the goat on all sides over moderate heat, 10 minutes per batch; transfer to a plate.

3. Pour off the fat in the casserole and return all of the goat to it. Add the vegetable stock and bring to a boil, scraping up any browned bits on the bottom of the casserole. Reduce the heat to moderate and simmer uncovered for 3 hours, skimming as necessary. Cover the casserole and continue cooking until the goat is tender, about 1½ hours longer.

4. Add the scallions, red pepper, red onion, carrot, thyme and chile and simmer uncovered until the goat is very tender and the vegetables are softened, about 30 minutes. Stir in the peas and simmer for 5 minutes. Discard the thyme sprigs and skim off the fat. Season the stew with salt and pepper and serve with Apricot-Ginger Chutney and warm roti or naan, or Rice and Peas. —*Adam Schop*

NOTE West Indian curry powder usually contains allspice, which Indian blends often don't, and it's usually quite yellow, thanks to a large amount of turmeric. It's available at spice shops and kalustyans.com. Goat forequarter includes the neck, shoulder and shank. Ask your butcher to cut the bone-in meat into 2½-inch pieces.

WINE Spicy, red berry–dense Côtes du Rhône: 2013 Jean-Luc Colombo Les Abeilles.

APRICOT-GINGER CHUTNEY

Total **30 min**; Makes **1 cup**

This intensely gingery condiment is a sweet and spicy foil for the curry. When fresh apricots become available, feel free to dice some up and stir them in.

¾ **cup packed light brown sugar**
¾ **cup plus 2 Tbsp. red wine vinegar**
2 **large shallots, minced (1 cup)**
4 **oz. fresh ginger, peeled and minced (¾ cup)**
¼ **cup plus 2 Tbsp. apricot nectar**
12 **dried apricots, minced (½ cup)**
1 **Tbsp. thyme leaves**
2 **Tbsp. finely chopped fresh mint**
   Kosher salt

In a medium saucepan, cook the brown sugar over moderate heat, stirring occasionally, until evenly melted and caramelized, 6 to 8 minutes. Pour in the vinegar and stir until the caramel dissolves. Stir in the shallots, ginger, apricot nectar, dried apricots and thyme. Cook over moderately high heat until the shallots and dried apricots are tender, about 8 minutes longer. Transfer the chutney to a small bowl. Stir in the mint and season with salt. Let cool to room temperature before serving. —*AS*

MAKE AHEAD The chutney can be refrigerated for up to a week. Bring to room temperature before serving.

Lamb and Grilled Squash with Serrano Chile

Active **20 min**; Total **35 min**; Serves **4**

1 **lb. trimmed lamb shoulder, cut into 1½-inch pieces**
2 **small summer squash (zucchini and/or yellow squash), cut into 2-inch pieces**
2 **Tbsp. Asian fish sauce**
2 **Tbsp. distilled white vinegar**
¼ **cup canola oil**
   Thinly sliced serrano chile and chopped cilantro, for garnish
   Lime wedges, for serving

Light a grill. In a large bowl, toss the lamb and squash with the fish sauce, vinegar and oil. Let stand for 15 minutes. Grill the lamb and squash over moderate heat, turning, until the lamb is medium within, about 10 minutes. Transfer to plates. Garnish with the chile and cilantro and serve with lime wedges. —*Kay Chun*

WINE Juicy, floral South African Chenin Blanc: 2014 Indaba.

At her backyard grilling party, Chicago chef Stephanie Izard translates her favorite restaurant dishes into simple home recipes, like charred broccoli with blue cheese dressing (recipe, p. 224).

VEGETABLES

ROASTED LEMON
BROCCOLI WITH TAHINI-
YOGURT SAUCE
Recipe, page 224

WARM GREEN BEANS
AND LETTUCE IN
ANCHOVY BUTTER

Blistered Green Beans with XO Sauce

Active **30 min**; Total **1 hr 15 min**
Serves **4 (makes about 1½ cups sauce)**

Chez Pim blogger Pim Techamuanvivit makes her own version of the Hong Kong–style condiment XO sauce. The briny, funky flavors transform basic green beans.

½ **cup small dried shrimp (see Note)**

⅓ **cup dried scallops (see Note)**

2 **cups boiling water**

¼ **cup diced country ham or prosciutto (½ oz.)**

8 **garlic cloves**

1 **medium shallot, coarsely chopped**

One 1½-inch piece of fresh ginger, peeled and sliced

2 **Tbsp. soy sauce**

1½ **tsp. crushed red pepper**

1½ **tsp. sugar**

1¼ **cups rice bran, grapeseed or canola oil**

1 **lb. green beans**

Kosher salt and black pepper

Lemon wedges, for serving

1. In a small heatproof bowl, cover the dried shrimp and scallops with the boiling water and let stand until softened, about 15 minutes. Drain well.

2. In a mini food processor, combine the shrimp, scallops and ham with the garlic, shallot, ginger, soy sauce, crushed red pepper and sugar. Pulse until minced. Scrape the mixture into a small saucepan and stir in 1 cup of the oil. Bring to a boil over moderately high heat; reduce the heat to a simmer and cook until the solids are dark golden and fragrant, about 30 minutes. Remove the XO sauce from the heat and let cool to room temperature.

3. Heat a large wok or skillet over high heat for 5 minutes. Drizzle in the remaining ¼ cup of oil, add the green beans and cook for 2 to 3 minutes, tossing every 30 seconds; the beans are done when they're tender and blistered in spots. Drain off the oil. Stir in ¼ cup of the XO sauce; toss until the beans are evenly coated. Season with salt and pepper and transfer to a platter. Serve with lemon wedges. —*Pim Techamuanvivit*

NOTE Dried shrimp and dried scallops are available at Asian markets.

Warm Green Beans and Lettuce in Anchovy Butter

Total **30 min**; Serves **4**

Jasmine and Melissa Hemsley, the sisters behind the Hemsley + Hemsley wellness blog, like cooking skillet-tossed lettuce and green beans in anchovy butter. "I could eat this for breakfast, lunch and dinner," says Jasmine. "When vegetables are served this way, there's no need to feel like, 'Oh, greens, I have to eat them.'"

4 **Tbsp. unsalted butter**

1 **lb. green beans, trimmed**

6 **oil-packed anchovy fillets, drained and chopped**

2 **garlic cloves, minced**

4 **heads of Little Gem or baby romaine lettuce, quartered lengthwise**

2 **Tbsp. fresh lemon juice, plus lemon wedges for serving**

Sea salt and pepper

1 **scallion, thinly sliced**

Chopped pistachios and extra-virgin olive oil, for garnish

1. In a large skillet, melt 3 tablespoons of the butter. Add the green beans, anchovies and garlic and cook over moderate heat, stirring occasionally, until the beans are tender, about 5 minutes. Transfer the beans to a large plate.

2. Add the remaining 1 tablespoon of butter and the lettuce to the skillet and cook, turning occasionally, until the lettuce is golden and crisp-tender, about 2 minutes. Add the green beans and lemon juice and season with salt and pepper; toss to coat. Transfer the beans and lettuce to a platter and top with the sliced scallion. Scatter with pistachios, drizzle with olive oil and serve warm with lemon wedges.
—*Jasmine and Melissa Hemsley*

Green Beans with Roasted Almond Crumble

Total **45 min**; Serves **12**

2 **cups (3 oz.) crustless white bread (½-inch pieces)**

¼ **cup extra-virgin olive oil**

Kosher salt and pepper

½ **cup finely chopped salted roasted almonds**

2 **lbs. green beans, trimmed**

¼ **tsp. finely grated orange zest plus 1 Tbsp. fresh orange juice**

2 **Tbsp. chopped tarragon**

2 **Tbsp. chopped basil**

1. Preheat the oven to 450°. On a baking sheet, toss the bread with 1 tablespoon of oil; season with salt and pepper. Bake for 8 minutes, until golden. Cool, then finely chop. Transfer to a bowl; stir in the almonds.

2. Meanwhile, on a rimmed baking sheet, toss the green beans with the remaining 3 tablespoons of oil and season with salt and pepper. Roast for 20 minutes, stirring occasionally, until lightly browned. Add the orange zest, orange juice, tarragon and basil and toss. Transfer the beans to a platter, top with the almond crumble and serve. —*Carla Hall*

Charred Green Beans with Apricots

Total **20 min**; Serves **4**

F&W's Justin Chapple adds sweet apricots to his fiery Thai-style green beans. Swap in peaches if apricots aren't available.

1½ **Tbsp. canola oil**

½ **lb. haricots verts**

3 **apricots—halved, pitted and cut into ¼-inch-thick wedges**

2 **Tbsp. fresh lime juice**

1 **Tbsp. Asian fish sauce**

1 **Thai chile, thinly sliced**

1 **cup mint leaves, chopped**

Kosher salt

In a large skillet, heat the oil until shimmering. Add the beans and cook over high heat until charred on the bottom, about 4 minutes. Remove from the heat and stir in the apricots, lime juice, fish sauce, chile and mint. Season with salt. Transfer to a platter and serve. —*Justin Chapple*

Cast-Iron-Grilled Romano Beans with Garlic Aioli

Active **45 min**; Total **1 hr 45 min**; Serves **6**

Chef Sarah Schafer makes these beans over the fire-pit grill at her cabin in Rockaway Beach, Oregon, and serves them right out of the skillet. Any other meaty, flat bean can be substituted for the romanos.

AIOLI

- 1 **small head of garlic, halved lengthwise**
- 6 **Tbsp. extra-virgin olive oil**
  Kosher salt and pepper
- 1 **large egg yolk**
- ½ **tsp. whole-grain mustard**
- 1 **Tbsp. Champagne vinegar**
- 2 **Tbsp. fresh lemon juice**
- ¼ **cup canola oil**
  Pinch of cayenne

BEANS

- 4 **oz. dry chorizo, diced**
- 4 **tsp. extra-virgin olive oil**
- 2 **lbs. romano beans**
- 2 **shallots, thinly sliced**
  Kosher salt and pepper
  Lemon wedges

1. Make the aioli Light a grill. On a sheet of foil, drizzle the garlic with 1 tablespoon of the olive oil and season with salt and pepper. Wrap tightly and grill over moderately high heat, turning, until tender, 50 minutes. Unwrap and let cool.

2. Squeeze the garlic cloves into a mini food processor. Add the egg yolk, mustard, vinegar and lemon juice; pulse to blend. With the machine on, slowly drizzle in the remaining olive oil and the canola oil until incorporated. Season the aioli with cayenne, salt and pepper.

3. Grill the beans In a large cast-iron skillet set on the grill, cook half of the chorizo in 2 teaspoons of the olive oil over moderate heat until softened. Add half of the beans and cook until lightly charred and tender, 12 minutes. Stir in half of the shallots and cook until golden, 3 minutes. Season with salt and pepper. Transfer to a platter and repeat with the remaining ingredients. Serve the beans with the aioli and lemon wedges. —*Sarah Schafer*

Warm Snap Peas with Ham and Tarragon Butter

Total **20 min**; Serves **4 to 6**

- ½ **lb. snap peas, halved lengthwise**
- ½ **lb. cooked ham, shredded**
- 3 **Tbsp. unsalted butter, at room temperature**
- 3 **Tbsp. chopped tarragon**
- 1 **Tbsp. fresh lemon juice**
  Kosher salt and pepper

In a steamer basket set over a saucepan of simmering water, steam the snap peas and ham until the peas are crisp-tender, 3 minutes. Transfer to a large bowl and add the butter, tarragon and lemon juice. Season with salt and pepper, mix well and serve. —*Kay Chun*

Grilled Zucchini with Ricotta and Pomegranate Molasses

Total **25 min**; Serves **6**

Grilled zucchini, a home-cook staple, is infinitely more interesting dressed with ricotta and pomegranate molasses.

- ¼ **cup pumpkin seeds**
- 2 **lbs. medium zucchini or yellow squash, quartered lengthwise**
- ¼ **cup extra-virgin olive oil**
  Kosher salt and pepper
- 1 **cup fresh ricotta cheese**
- ¼ **cup pomegranate molasses**
- 2 **Tbsp. loosely packed tarragon leaves, chopped**

1. In a small skillet, cook the pumpkin seeds over moderately low heat, stirring, until toasted, 3 to 5 minutes.

2. Light a grill. Toss the zucchini with the olive oil and season with salt and pepper. Grill the zucchini over high heat, turning once, until charred and just tender, about 7 minutes. Transfer to a work surface and cut into 1-inch pieces. Arrange on a platter and top with dollops of the ricotta and the toasted pumpkin seeds. Season with salt and pepper. Drizzle the zucchini with the pomegranate molasses, garnish with the chopped tarragon and serve. —*Timothy Hollingsworth*

WINE Lively, fruit-forward Sonoma Sauvignon Blanc: 2014 Hanna.

Pickled Green Beans

Total **15 min plus 2 hr cooling**
Makes **4 cups**

These pickled green beans, made with white wine vinegar and lots of dill, require just 15 minutes of hands-on work.

- ½ **cup white wine vinegar**
- 1 **tsp. fine sea salt**
- 1 **lb. green or purple wax beans, trimmed**
- 1 **cup coarsely chopped dill**

In a small saucepan, simmer the vinegar, ¼ cup of water and the salt, stirring, until the salt dissolves. Combine the beans and dill in a heatproof bowl; cover with the hot brine. Let cool to room temperature, about 2 hours. Serve at room temperature or chilled. —*Zakary Pelaccio*

MAKE AHEAD The pickled beans can be refrigerated in the brine for up to 1 week.

Blistered Snap Peas with Salami and Feta

Total **30 min**; Serves **4**

- 1 **lb. sugar snap peas, trimmed**
- 3 **Tbsp. extra-virgin olive oil**
  Kosher salt and pepper
- 1½ **Tbsp. sherry vinegar**
- 2 **cups baby arugula**
- 2 **oz. thinly sliced salami, cut into matchsticks**
- ½ **cup crumbled feta cheese (2 oz.)**

1. Light a grill. In a large bowl, toss the snap peas with 1 tablespoon of the oil and season with salt and pepper. Spread the snap peas on a perforated grill pan and grill over high heat until lightly charred on one side, 1 to 2 minutes. Return the snap peas to the bowl and toss with the vinegar and the remaining 2 tablespoons of oil; season with salt and pepper.

2. Mound the arugula in a shallow bowl and make a well in the middle. Mound the snap peas in the well and top with the salami and feta. Serve. —*Greg Denton and Gabrielle Quiñónez Denton*

NOTE The snap peas can also be blistered in a hot cast-iron skillet over high heat for 2 minutes.

BLISTERED SNAP
PEAS WITH
SALAMI AND FETA

CHICKEN-FAT-ROASTED
VEGETABLES
WITH GREMOLATA

Chicken-Fat-Roasted Vegetables with Gremolata

Active **20 min**; Total **1 hr**; Serves **4**

For extra flavor, bloggers Jasmine and Melissa Hemsley toss vegetables in chicken or duck fat before roasting, then top with a bright, lemony mix of parsley and minced garlic.

ROASTED VEGETABLES

- **2 red onions, quartered**
- **1 lb. carrots, peeled and halved lengthwise**
- **1 head of garlic, halved crosswise**
- **½ lb. cauliflower or Romanesco, cut into 1½-inch florets (2 cups)**
- **4 oz. brussels sprouts, quartered (1 cup)**
- **3 Tbsp. chicken or duck fat, melted (see Note)**
-    **Sea salt and pepper**

GREMOLATA

- **1 cup packed parsley leaves, finely chopped**
- **1 garlic clove, minced**
- **½ cup extra-virgin olive oil**
- **1 tsp. finely grated lemon zest**
- **2 Tbsp. fresh lemon juice**
-    **Sea salt and pepper**

1. Roast the vegetables Preheat the oven to 425°. Toss all of the ingredients on a baking sheet lined with parchment paper and season with salt and pepper. Roast for about 40 minutes, until the vegetables are tender and deep golden in spots; stir halfway through roasting.

2. Meanwhile, make the gremolata In a small bowl, combine all of the ingredients and season with salt and pepper.

3. Arrange the roasted vegetables on a platter, sprinkle with the gremolata and serve. —*Jasmine and Melissa Hemsley*

NOTE Chicken fat is sold at most supermarkets. Duck fat is available at specialty food shops and from dartagnan.com.

Vegetable Bagna Cauda with Dill Oil

Total **1 hr 30 min**; Serves **4**

PICKLED SHIITAKE MUSHROOMS

- **3 oz. shiitake mushroom caps, thinly sliced (2 cups)**
- **½ cup apple cider vinegar**
- **1 Tbsp. kosher salt**
- **1 Tbsp. sugar**

DILL OIL

- **3 cups chopped dill**
- **½ cup grapeseed oil**
-    **Kosher salt**

BAGNA CAUDA

-    **One 2-oz. can anchovies, drained**
- **3 garlic cloves, minced**
- **2 Tbsp. fresh lemon juice**
- **1½ sticks cold unsalted butter, cubed**
- **2 Tbsp. chopped dill**

VEGETABLES

- **1 yellow summer squash, quartered lengthwise**
- **½ hothouse cucumber, halved lengthwise**
- **4 large shallots, halved lengthwise**
- **2 Tbsp. canola oil**
-    **Kosher salt and pepper**
- **4 oz. thin green beans**
- **1 Tbsp. unsalted butter**
- **4 radishes, quartered**
- **1 cup halved cherry tomatoes (6 oz.)**
- **½ cup mixed herbs, such as parsley, tarragon and dill**

1. Pickle the shiitake mushrooms Place the shiitake caps in a small heatproof bowl. In a saucepan, bring the vinegar, salt, sugar and ½ cup of water to a simmer, stirring to dissolve the sugar, and pour over the mushrooms; let stand for 15 minutes. Drain and squeeze dry. Discard the brine.

2. Meanwhile, make the dill oil In a blender, puree the dill with the oil until smooth. Strain through a fine sieve into a small bowl and season with salt.

3. Make the bagna cauda In a small saucepan, cook the anchovies, garlic and lemon juice over low heat, stirring, until the anchovies dissolve, 5 minutes. Whisk in the butter a few cubes at a time. Stir in the dill. Cover; keep warm.

4. Prepare the vegetables Light a grill. In a large bowl, toss the squash, cucumber and shallots with the canola oil and season with salt and pepper. Grill over moderately high heat, turning, until the vegetables are lightly charred and crisp-tender: 5 minutes for the cucumber and shallots, 8 minutes for the squash. Transfer the vegetables to plates; add the mushrooms.

5. Meanwhile, in a saucepan of salted boiling water, blanch the green beans until crisp-tender, about 3 minutes. Drain and cool under cold water; pat dry.

6. In a large skillet, melt the butter. Add the green beans and radishes and cook over moderate heat until golden brown, about 3 minutes. Stir in the tomatoes and cook for 1 minute. Season with salt and pepper. Transfer to the plates with the vegetables. Drizzle some of the dill oil on top and garnish with the herbs. Serve with the bagna cauda and the remaining dill oil. —*Jim Christiansen*

SERVE WITH Crusty bread.

Hot and Sour Cucumbers

Total **30 min**; Serves **4**

- **2 Tbsp. toasted sesame oil**
- **2 garlic cloves, thinly sliced**
- **1 tsp. minced fresh ginger**
- **4 oz. shiitake mushrooms, stemmed and thinly sliced**
- **1 jalapeño, minced**
- **2 Tbsp. unseasoned rice vinegar**
- **1 Tbsp. light brown sugar**
- **1 hothouse cucumber, sliced ½ inch thick on the diagonal**
- **1½ tsp. fresh lemon juice**
-    **Kosher salt**

In a large nonstick skillet, heat the sesame oil. Add the garlic and ginger and cook over moderately high heat, stirring, until fragrant, 30 seconds. Add the mushrooms and jalapeño and cook, stirring, until the mushrooms start to soften, about 2 minutes. Stir in the vinegar, sugar, cucumber slices and 2 tablespoons of water and stir to coat in the sauce. Cover and cook over moderate heat, stirring occasionally, until the cucumbers are tender and the sauce is thickened, 5 to 7 minutes. Stir in the lemon juice and season with salt. Serve warm. —*Sasha Martin*

Sugar Snap Peas and Oyster Mushrooms in Sherried Cream

Total **30 min**; Serves **4**

"There's something about the sherry and the cream and the sautéed mushrooms that has the power to draw other ingredients in," says Ashley Christensen, the chef at Poole's Diner in Raleigh, North Carolina. In the summer, she makes her side dish with corn; in the winter months, she substitutes cauliflower. For the short time that she can get asparagus in early spring, she uses that. Then she moves on to the peas that are featured here. "This dish is a chameleon," Christensen says.

- ¼ cup canola oil
- ½ lb. oyster mushrooms, cut into 1-inch pieces
  Kosher salt
- 1 shallot, minced
- 1 lb. sugar snap peas, strings discarded, halved lengthwise on the diagonal
- ½ cup dry sherry
- ½ cup heavy cream
- 1 Tbsp. fresh lemon juice
  Finely grated lemon zest, for garnish

1. In a very large skillet, heat 2 tablespoons of the oil until shimmering. Add the mushrooms and a generous pinch of salt. Cook over moderately high heat, stirring occasionally, until the mushrooms are browned and crisp, about 7 minutes. Add the shallot and the remaining 2 tablespoons of oil and cook until the shallot is softened, about 2 minutes. Add the snap peas and cook, stirring, for 1 minute.

2. Add the sherry to the skillet and simmer until reduced by half, about 3 minutes. Add the cream and simmer until the mushrooms and snap peas are coated in a light sauce, about 3 minutes. Stir in the lemon juice and season with salt. Transfer to a platter, garnish with finely grated lemon zest and serve. —*Ashley Christensen*

Grilled Asparagus with Taramasalata

Active **30 min**; Total **1 hr 30 min plus 24 hr** to blend the flavors
Makes **about 2 cups**

Taramasalata is a Greek dip or spread made with salted fish roe, olive oil and bread (or sometimes potatoes). This lemony, creamy version is a perfect accompaniment for grilled asparagus.

- 2 cups cubed crustless country white bread (1 inch)
  Boiling water
- 1 tsp. finely grated lemon zest
- ¼ cup plus ½ Tbsp. fresh lemon juice
- 1 small shallot, minced
- 1 small garlic clove, minced
- ¼ cup (about 1 oz.) grated tarama (salted mullet roe)
  Kosher salt and pepper
- ¾ cup plus 2½ Tbsp. extra-virgin olive oil
- 2 lbs. medium asparagus, trimmed
- 1 cup mixed small herb leaves, such as parsley, chervil and chives

1. In a medium heatproof bowl, cover the bread with boiling water. Top with a small plate to keep the bread submerged and let stand for 1 hour. Drain and squeeze out the excess water.

2. In a food processor, combine the bread, lemon zest, ¼ cup of the lemon juice, the shallot, garlic, tarama and 1 teaspoon each of salt and pepper; puree until smooth. With the machine on, slowly drizzle in ¾ cup of the oil and puree until well blended. Transfer the taramasalata to a bowl, cover and refrigerate for 1 day.

3. Light a grill to moderately high. On a baking sheet, toss the asparagus with 2 tablespoons of the oil and season with salt and pepper. Grill, turning, until crisp-tender, 3 to 5 minutes. Transfer to a platter.

4. In a small bowl, combine the herbs and the remaining ½ tablespoon each of lemon juice and olive oil. Season with salt and pepper and toss to coat.

5. Serve the taramasalata with the grilled asparagus. Garnish with the herb salad and serve. —*Zoi Antonitsas*

Braised Eggplant with Garlic

Active **30 min**; Total **1 hr 30 min**; Serves **6**

Scott Conant, a judge on Food Network's *Chopped*, packs robust flavor in this make-ahead vegetarian main—an Ottoman-era palace dish—with onion, tomato, peppers and lots of garlic.

- 2 medium onions, finely chopped (2 cups)
- 1 medium tomato, finely chopped (1 cup)
- 6 garlic cloves, finely chopped
- 2 long green peppers, finely chopped
- ½ cup finely chopped parsley
- 1 tsp. sugar
  Kosher salt and pepper
- 6 Italian baby eggplants (2½ lbs.)
- 1 cup extra-virgin olive oil

1. In a medium bowl, combine the onions with the tomato, garlic, peppers, parsley, sugar and 2 teaspoons of salt. Using your hands, knead the mixture until it is softened and well blended.

2. Peel the eggplants lengthwise at ½-inch intervals to create stripes. On one half of each eggplant, make 4 lengthwise slits halfway through the flesh. Rub the eggplants all over and in the slits with ¼ cup of the olive oil and season them with salt and pepper.

3. Arrange the eggplants slit side up in an ovenproof baking dish just large enough to hold them in a single layer. Spoon the filling liberally into the slits; some will spill out. Drizzle the remaining ¾ cup of olive oil over the eggplants and add ½ cup of water to the baking dish. Cover and bake for about 1 hour, until the eggplants are completely tender. Serve warm or at room temperature. —*Scott Conant*

SERVE WITH Country bread.

MAKE AHEAD The finished dish can be refrigerated for up to 3 days.

Creamy Spinach and Garlic Confit Gratin

Active **45 min**; Total **1 hr 30 min**
Serves **6 to 8**

Confited garlic, slowly cooked in oil, permeates the cream sauce for this luscious side dish. The spinach is tossed with the cream, then topped with cheesy breadcrumbs before baking.

GARLIC CONFIT

4 large garlic cloves, peeled

1 cup canola oil

CREAM SAUCE

2 cups heavy cream

1½ Tbsp. arrowroot

⅛ tsp. freshly grated nutmeg

Kosher salt

SPINACH

Extra-virgin olive oil, for greasing

4 lbs. curly spinach, stemmed

Kosher salt

1 cup fresh breadcrumbs

¼ cup freshly grated Parmigiano-Reggiano cheese

1. Make the garlic confit In a small saucepan, cover the garlic cloves with water and bring to a boil. Drain and pat dry. Wipe out the saucepan. Add the garlic and canola oil and cook over very low heat until the garlic is softened and golden, 30 minutes. Drain in a sieve, reserving the oil for another use. Transfer the garlic to a blender.

2. Make the cream sauce In a small bowl, whisk 2 tablespoons of the cream with the arrowroot. In a medium saucepan, bring the remaining cream to a simmer. Whisk in the arrowroot mixture and cook over moderate heat, whisking, until the cream is thickened, about 2 minutes. Stir in the nutmeg and season with salt. Add the cream sauce to the blender and puree with the garlic until smooth.

3. Make the spinach Preheat the oven to 350°. Lightly oil a 1½-quart baking dish. Working in batches, blanch the spinach in a large pot of salted boiling water just until wilted, 1 minute. Using tongs, transfer to a colander. Squeeze out as much water from the spinach as possible. Using paper towels, blot any excess water. Coarsely chop the spinach and transfer to a large bowl (you should have 6 packed cups). Add the cream sauce and mix well. Season with salt. Spread the spinach in the prepared dish and top with the breadcrumbs and cheese. Bake for about 30 minutes, until the cheese is golden and the sauce is bubbling. Let stand for 10 minutes before serving. —*Shane McBride and Daniel Parilla*

Sautéed Spinach with Lemon-and-Garlic Olive Oil

Active **30 min**; Total **1 hr 35 min**
Serves **4 to 6**

"In every little restaurant in Umbria, there are sautéed greens on the menu," says famed Los Angeles chef Nancy Silverton. Here, she blanches spinach, then sautés it in garlic-spiked oil until all the leaves are thoroughly coated.

¾ cup extra-virgin olive oil

10 garlic cloves, thickly sliced lengthwise

2 dried chiles de árbol, broken in half

Kosher salt and freshly ground pepper

Thick strips of zest from 1 lemon

2½ lbs. spinach, cleaned, thick stems discarded

1. In a small saucepan, stir together the olive oil, garlic, chiles and 1 teaspoon of salt. Stir in the lemon zest. Bring the oil to a gentle simmer over low heat and cook until the garlic begins to brown slightly, about 15 minutes. Remove from the heat and let the oil infuse for 1 hour. Discard the chiles and lemon zest and reserve the garlic.

2. Meanwhile, in a large pot of salted boiling water, cook the spinach until bright green, 15 seconds. Using tongs, transfer the spinach to a bowl of ice water and let cool for 10 seconds. Drain the spinach in a colander, pressing down to remove all the water. Pat dry with paper towels.

3. Heat a large skillet. Add the spinach and cook over moderately high heat until beginning to sizzle. Add the garlic oil and toss until the spinach is hot, about 2 minutes. Transfer the spinach and reserved garlic to a colander set over a bowl to drain. Mound the spinach on a platter, season with salt and pepper and serve. —*Nancy Silverton*

Wilted Swiss Chard with Warm Piccata Vinaigrette

Total **40 min**; Serves **10 to 12**

¼ cup extra-virgin olive oil

¼ cup drained capers

¼ cup finely minced garlic

3 bunches of Swiss chard, stemmed, leaves coarsely chopped (24 cups)

¼ cup fresh lemon juice

¼ cup chopped parsley

Kosher salt and pepper

In a large pot, heat the olive oil. Add the capers and garlic and cook over moderate heat, stirring, until fragrant and golden, 3 minutes. In batches, stir in the chard until wilted. Add the lemon juice and parsley, season with salt and pepper and serve. —*Kay Chun*

Sautéed Collard Greens with Pepperoni

Total **45 min**; Serves **12**

Collards are often paired with bacon, but spicy pepperoni is a fun, tasty twist.

⅓ cup extra-virgin olive oil

6 oz. pepperoni, julienned

2 large shallots, thinly sliced

6 garlic cloves, thinly sliced

4 lbs. collard greens, stemmed and coarsely chopped

Kosher salt and pepper

3 Tbsp. fresh lemon juice

1. In a pot, heat the olive oil. Add the pepperoni, shallots and garlic and cook over moderately high heat, stirring, until the shallots are softened, 3 to 5 minutes. Add the collard greens in large handfuls, stirring and letting each handful wilt slightly before adding more.

2. When all of the collards have wilted, add ¼ cup of water and a generous pinch of salt. Cook over moderately high heat, stirring occasionally, until the greens are crisp-tender and most of the liquid has evaporated, about 10 minutes. Stir in the lemon juice and season with salt and pepper. Transfer to a bowl and serve. —*Justin Chapple*

Cauliflower Couscous with Cheesy Crumbs

Active **30 min**; Total **1 hr**; Serves **4 to 6**

Dave Beran, the chef at Chicago's Next, makes this "couscous" with crumbled cauliflower florets that he roasts so they're toasty and tender. He scatters Manchego-panko all over the finished dish.

COUSCOUS

- **2 heads of cauliflower (4 lbs.), cut into 1-inch florets**
- **6 Tbsp. extra-virgin olive oil**
  Kosher salt and pepper
- **½ cup panko**
- **¼ cup finely grated Manchego cheese**
- **2 tsp. finely chopped chives**
- **2 tsp. finely chopped parsley, plus parsley leaves for garnish**
- **2 tsp. minced shallot**
- **⅛ tsp. minced garlic**
- **⅛ tsp. finely grated lemon zest**

VINAIGRETTE

- **3 Tbsp. extra-virgin olive oil**
- **1½ Tbsp. fresh lemon juice**
  Kosher salt

1. Make the couscous Preheat the oven to 375°. In a food processor, working in batches, pulse the cauliflower until it resembles coarse couscous. Spread the cauliflower on 2 large rimmed baking sheets and drizzle with the oil. Season with salt and pepper and toss to coat. Roast for 40 minutes, stirring and shifting the pans halfway through, until golden and caramelized in spots. Let cool slightly, then scrape into a serving bowl.

2. Meanwhile, toast the panko in a pie plate until golden, 8 minutes. Let cool.

3. Make the vinaigrette In a small bowl, whisk the oil and lemon juice. Season with salt. Add to the cauliflower couscous and toss to coat. Season with salt and pepper.

4. In a bowl, toss the toasted panko with the Manchego, chives, chopped parsley, shallot, garlic and lemon zest and season with salt and pepper. Scatter the panko topping over the cauliflower, garnish with parsley leaves and serve. —*Dave Beran*

WINE Full-bodied Loire Valley Chenin Blanc: 2013 Château d'Epiré Cuvée Speciale.

Sautéed Collards and Cabbage with Gremolata

☺ Total **45 min**; Serves **12**

- **¾ cup finely chopped parsley**
- **1½ tsp. minced garlic plus 2 thinly sliced garlic cloves**
- **1 Tbsp. finely grated lemon zest plus ¼ cup fresh lemon juice**
- **½ cup plus 2 Tbsp. extra-virgin olive oil**
  Kosher salt and black pepper
- **4 shallots, halved and thinly sliced (¾ cup)**
- **1½ lbs. green cabbage, cored and sliced ¼ inch thick (9 cups)**
- **1½ lbs. collard greens, stems discarded, leaves sliced ¼ inch thick (12 cups)**
- **¾ tsp. crushed red pepper**

1. In a small bowl, combine the parsley, minced garlic, lemon zest, 3 tablespoons of the lemon juice and 6 tablespoons of the olive oil. Season the gremolata with salt and black pepper and mix well.

2. In a large pot, heat 2 tablespoons of the olive oil. Add the shallots and sliced garlic and cook over moderate heat, stirring occasionally, until light golden, about 5 minutes. Add the green cabbage, collard greens and the remaining 2 tablespoons of olive oil and season with salt and black pepper. Cook over moderately high heat, stirring, until the collards and cabbage are wilted and crisp-tender, 7 to 8 minutes. Stir in the crushed red pepper and the remaining 1 tablespoon of lemon juice. Transfer the greens to a platter, top with the gremolata and serve. —*Carla Hall*

MAKE AHEAD The gremolata can be made up to 3 hours ahead and kept covered at room temperature.

Creamed Kale

Active **40 min**; Total **1 hr 15 min**
Serves **10 to 12**

- **3½ lbs. Tuscan kale, 4 leaves left whole, the rest stemmed and chopped**
- **¼ cup plus 1 Tbsp. extra-virgin olive oil**
  Kosher salt and pepper
- **2 Tbsp. unsalted butter**
- **2 white onions, finely chopped**
- **1½ cups heavy cream**
- **1 Tbsp. honey**

1. Preheat the oven to 350°. On a large baking sheet, rub the whole kale leaves with 1 tablespoon of the olive oil and season with salt and pepper. Bake for about 15 minutes, until crispy. Let cool.

2. Meanwhile, in a large pot, melt the butter in the remaining ¼ cup of olive oil. Add the onions, season with salt and cook over moderately high heat, stirring occasionally, until softened and just starting to brown, 8 to 10 minutes. Add the chopped kale and cook, stirring occasionally, until wilted, about 5 minutes. Add the cream and honey and bring to a simmer. Cover and cook over moderate heat, stirring occasionally, until the kale is very tender and coated in a thick sauce, 35 to 40 minutes.

3. Transfer half of the creamed kale to a food processor and puree until nearly smooth. Stir the puree into the pot and season with salt and pepper. Transfer the creamed kale to a serving bowl. Top with the crispy kale leaves and serve.
—*Tyler Florence*

Cumin-and-Chile-Braised Collard Green Stems

☺ Total **30 min**; Serves **4 to 6**

- **3 Tbsp. extra-virgin olive oil**
- **2 small Fresno chiles, seeded and minced**
- **6 garlic cloves, thinly sliced**
- **1 Tbsp. cumin seeds**
- **1¾ lbs. collard green stems, cut into 1-inch lengths**
- **1 cup chicken stock or low-sodium broth**
- **2 Tbsp. unsalted butter**
  Kosher salt

In a large skillet, heat the oil. Add the chiles, garlic and cumin; cook over moderate heat, stirring, until fragrant, 1 minute. Add the collard stems and cook, stirring, until bright green, about 3 minutes. Add the stock. Cover and cook over moderately high heat, stirring occasionally, until the stems are tender, 10 minutes. Swirl in the butter, season with salt and serve.
—*Justin Chapple*

MAKE AHEAD The braised collard stems can be refrigerated overnight.

CUMIN-AND-CHILE-
BRAISED COLLARD
GREEN STEMS

ROASTED
CAULIFLOWER WITH
TAHINI SAUCE

Roasted Cauliflower with Tahini Sauce

Active **30 min**; Total **1 hr 10 min**; Serves **6**

Chef Duskie Estes of Zazu Kitchen + Farm in Sebastopol, California, rubs aromatic seasonings and tangy sumac all over heads of cauliflower, then roasts them whole.

CAULIFLOWER

- 2 Tbsp. chopped thyme
- 1 Tbsp. sumac
- 1½ tsp. grated lemon zest
- 1 tsp. sesame seeds
- 1 tsp. coriander seeds
- 1 tsp. fennel seeds
- ¼ tsp. ground allspice
- ¼ tsp. crushed red pepper
- 2 small heads of cauliflower (1¼ lbs. each), ½ inch trimmed off the bottoms
- 3 Tbsp. extra-virgin olive oil
  Kosher salt and black pepper

TAHINI SAUCE

- ⅓ cup tahini
- ⅓ cup fresh lemon juice
- 2 garlic cloves, crushed
- 1 tsp. pomegranate molasses
- ½ tsp. sumac
- ½ tsp. ground coriander
  Kosher salt
  Chopped parsley

1. Make the cauliflower Preheat the oven to 450°. In a spice grinder, grind the first 8 ingredients to a powder. Brush the cauliflower with the olive oil and season generously all over with salt and pepper. Set the cauliflower in a 9-by-13-inch baking dish and rub with the spice mix. Add 1½ cups of water to the dish. Roast for 1 hour, or until tender and browned; add more water if necessary.

2. Make the tahini sauce In a blender, combine the first 6 ingredients and puree until very smooth. Season with salt.

3. Serve the cauliflower whole or cut into thick slabs and arrange on a platter. Garnish with parsley and serve with the tahini sauce. —*Duskie Estes*

Roasted Cauliflower and Grapes

Active **15 min**; Total **45 min**; Serves **8**

- One 2-lb. head of cauliflower— halved, cored and cut into florets
- ½ lb. red grapes, stemmed and halved (1½ cups)
- 3 garlic cloves, minced
- 2 tsp. chopped rosemary
- ¼ cup extra-virgin olive oil
  Fine sea salt and pepper

Preheat the oven to 425°. On a rimmed baking sheet lined with foil, toss the cauliflower with the grapes, garlic, rosemary and olive oil and season with salt and pepper. Roast for about 30 minutes, until the cauliflower is tender and lightly caramelized in spots; stir halfway through. Transfer to a platter and serve warm. —*Amanda Paa*

Baked Onions with Fennel Bread Crumbs

Active **30 min**; Total **2 hr**; Serves **4 to 6**

- 3 medium onions, peeled and halved lengthwise, root ends left intact
- 2 Tbsp. extra-virgin olive oil, plus more for brushing
  Kosher salt
- ½ cup chicken stock
- 6 bay leaves, preferably fresh
- 1 tsp. fennel seeds
- ¼ cup panko
- 1½ tsp. minced sage

1. Preheat the oven to 425°. Brush the onion halves with olive oil, season with salt and arrange cut side down in an ovenproof medium skillet. Add the chicken stock and scatter the bay leaves around the onions. Cover tightly with foil and bake for about 1½ hours, until the onions are very tender.

2. Meanwhile, in a small skillet, toast the fennel seeds over moderate heat until fragrant, about 3 minutes. Transfer to a work surface and let cool, then coarsely crush the seeds. Transfer to a small bowl, add the panko, sage and the 2 tablespoons of olive oil and toss. Season with salt.

3. Carefully turn the onions cut side up in the skillet. Spoon the fennel bread crumbs on top and bake for about 15 minutes longer, until the crumbs are lightly browned and crisp. Discard the bay leaves and serve the onions hot or warm. —*Nancy Silverton*

Aioli-Glazed Charred Broccoli

Total **30 min**; Serves **8**

These aioli-coated florets get bubbly and browned under the broiler or on a grill, almost like instant broccoli casserole. Be sure to serve the dish piping hot.

- 1 cup mayonnaise
- 3 Tbsp. extra-virgin olive oil
- 2 Tbsp. fresh lemon juice
- 1 small garlic clove, finely grated
  Kosher salt and pepper
- 2¾ lbs. broccoli (3 medium heads), cut into florets, stems reserved for another use

1. Preheat the broiler and position a rack 8 inches from the heat. In a large bowl, whisk the mayonnaise with the olive oil, lemon juice and garlic and season generously with salt and pepper. Add the broccoli florets and toss to coat.

2. Spread half of the broccoli on a large rimmed baking sheet and broil for about 7 minutes, until lightly charred and the edges are crisp. Transfer the charred broccoli to a platter and repeat with the remaining broccoli. Serve right away. —*Helene Henderson*

Brussels Sprouts with Sausage and Cumin

Total **15 min**; Serves **2**

- 2 Tbsp. extra-virgin olive oil
- 14 brussels sprouts (10 oz.), trimmed and halved
  Kosher salt and pepper
- 6 oz. sweet Italian sausage (2 links), casings removed
- 1 tsp. dried oregano
- 1 tsp. ground cumin
- ¼ cup fresh orange juice
- 1 tsp. honey

In a large nonstick skillet, heat the olive oil. Add the brussels sprouts and season with salt and pepper. Cover and cook over moderately high heat, stirring once, until golden, 4 minutes. Add the sausage, oregano and cumin. Cover and cook, stirring occasionally, until the brussels sprouts are caramelized and tender and the sausage is cooked through, 3 minutes longer. Stir in the orange juice and honey to coat the sprouts. Transfer to plates and serve warm. —*Ana Sortun*

Apple Cider–Braised Cabbage

Active **30 min**; Total **1 hr**; Serves **4 to 6**

Star chef Tom Colicchio uses both apple cider and apple cider vinegar to braise cabbage, so it's fruity and tangy. His recipe is super-versatile: You can make it with red cabbage instead of green and serve it with a huge array of proteins, from seared scallops or fish to roast pork or chicken.

- **2** Tbsp. extra-virgin olive oil
- **One 1½-lb.** head of green cabbage, cut through the core into 6 wedges
- **½** cup chopped bacon (2 oz.)
- **1** medium onion, halved through the core and thinly sliced lengthwise

  Kosher salt and pepper
- **½** cup apple cider vinegar
- **2** cups apple cider
- **1** Tbsp. unsalted butter

1. In a large, deep skillet, heat the olive oil until shimmering. Add the cabbage wedges cut side down and cook over moderate heat, turning once, until browned, 6 to 8 minutes total. Transfer to a plate.

2. Add the bacon to the skillet and cook over moderate heat, stirring occasionally, until rendered but not crisp, about 5 minutes. Add the onion and a generous pinch of salt and cook, stirring occasionally, until softened and just starting to brown, about 10 minutes. Stir in the vinegar and simmer over moderately high heat until reduced by half, about 3 minutes. Add the cider and bring to a boil. Nestle the cabbage wedges in the skillet, cover and braise over moderately low heat, turning once, until tender, about 20 minutes. Using a slotted spoon or spatula, transfer the cabbage to a platter and tent with foil.

3. Boil the sauce over moderately high heat, stirring occasionally, until slightly thickened, about 5 minutes. Remove the skillet from the heat and swirl in the butter. Season the sauce with salt and pepper, spoon over the braised cabbage and serve.
—*Tom Colicchio*

SERVE WITH Seared scallops or roast fish.

MAKE AHEAD The cabbage can be prepared through Step 2 and refrigerated overnight in the braising liquid. Let return to room temperature before finishing.

Roasted Lemon Broccoli with Tahini-Yogurt Sauce

📷 PAGE 211

⏱ Total **35 min**; Serves **4**

Tara Duggan, author of *Root-to-Stalk Cooking,* is a master of cooking all parts of vegetables. She uses both the broccoli stalk and the florets for this spicy, tangy recipe.

- **1½** lbs. broccoli—stalk trimmed and peeled, head cut into large florets
- **1** lemon, sliced into ⅛-inch-thick rounds
- **3** Tbsp. extra-virgin olive oil
- **¼** tsp. crushed red pepper, plus more for garnish

  Kosher salt
- **1** tsp. sesame seeds
- **½** cup plain Greek yogurt
- **2** Tbsp. tahini
- **1** Tbsp. fresh lemon juice
- **1** garlic clove, minced

  Flaky sea salt, for garnish

1. Preheat the oven to 450°. Slice the broccoli stalk crosswise and the florets lengthwise ¼ inch thick; transfer to a rimmed baking sheet. Add the sliced lemon, olive oil and the ¼ teaspoon of crushed red pepper and season with kosher salt; toss to coat. Roast for about 10 minutes, until lightly browned. Stir in the sesame seeds and roast until the broccoli is tender, about 10 minutes longer.

2. Meanwhile, in a small bowl, whisk the yogurt with the tahini, lemon juice and garlic and season with kosher salt. Spread the yogurt sauce on a platter and top with the broccoli. Garnish with sea salt and crushed red pepper and serve warm.
—*Tara Duggan*

Charred Broccoli with Blue Cheese Dressing and Spiced Crispies

Total **50 min**; Serves **6**

DRESSING

- **⅓** cup heavy cream

  Pinch of crushed red pepper

  Pinch of dark brown sugar
- **3** oz. smoked or Maytag blue cheese, crumbled (see Note)
- **⅓** cup sour cream

  Kosher salt

BROCCOLI

- **2** lbs. broccoli, cut into 1½-inch florets with stems
- **¼** cup unseasoned rice vinegar
- **1½** Tbsp. harissa
- **½** tsp. finely grated lemon zest plus 1½ Tbsp. fresh lemon juice
- **1½** Tbsp. soy sauce
- **1** Tbsp. Dijon mustard
- **1½** tsp. Sriracha
- **½** cup extra-virgin olive oil
- **⅓** cup minced shallots

  Kosher salt and pepper
- **2** Tbsp. unsalted butter
- **1** cup Rice Krispies cereal

1. Make the dressing In a small saucepan, warm the heavy cream until hot. Whisk in the crushed red pepper, sugar and one-third of the blue cheese until melted. Let cool completely, then whisk in the sour cream and the remaining cheese. Season the dressing with salt.

2. Prepare the broccoli In a large saucepan of salted boiling water, blanch the broccoli until crisp-tender, about 2 minutes. Drain well and spread on a large baking sheet to cool.

3. In a blender, combine the vinegar, harissa, lemon zest and juice, soy sauce, mustard and Sriracha and puree. With the blender on, gradually add the olive oil until incorporated. Transfer the vinaigrette to a medium bowl and stir in the shallots. Season with salt and pepper.

4. In a medium skillet, melt the butter. Add the cereal and 1½ teaspoons of the harissa vinaigrette and cook over moderately high heat, stirring, until lightly browned, about 3 minutes. Season with salt and transfer to a paper towel–lined plate to drain.

5. Light a grill or heat a grill pan. In a large bowl, toss the broccoli with half of the remaining vinaigrette and season with salt. Grill the broccoli over moderately high heat, turning occasionally, until lightly charred all over, about 5 minutes. Transfer to a plate.

6. Spread the blue cheese dressing on a platter and scatter the broccoli on top. Garnish with the spiced crispies and serve, passing the remaining harissa vinaigrette at the table. —*Stephanie Izard*

NOTE Izard likes Rogue Creamery Smokey Blue Cheese (roguecreamery.com).

MAKE AHEAD The blue cheese dressing can be refrigerated overnight.

BEER Funky farmhouse ale: Boulevard Brewing Tank 7.

Grilled Garlic and Vegetables
Total **45 min;** Serves **8**

- 2 heads of garlic, halved crosswise
- ¼ cup plus 2 Tbsp. extra-virgin olive oil, plus more for drizzling
- 1 lb. small young carrots, scrubbed
- 1 lb. spring onions, halved lengthwise
- ½ lb. haricots verts, trimmed
  Kosher salt and pepper
  Red wine vinegar, for drizzling
  Torn basil leaves, for garnish

1. Light a grill. Arrange the garlic halves cut side up on a sheet of foil and drizzle with 2 tablespoons of the olive oil. Wrap tightly.

2. In a large bowl, toss the carrots, spring onions and haricots verts with the remaining ¼ cup of olive oil and season with salt and pepper. Grill the garlic packet, turning occasionally, until the garlic is tender when pierced, 30 minutes. After 15 minutes, arrange the vegetables in a perforated grill pan; cook until tender and lightly charred, 3 minutes for the haricots verts, 10 minutes for the spring onions and 15 minutes for the carrots. Transfer to a platter.

3. Unwrap the garlic and let cool slightly. Squeeze the cloves out of the skins and scatter over the vegetables. Drizzle with olive oil and vinegar and garnish with basil. —*Zakary Pelaccio*

Grilled Pickled Carrots with Charmoula and Almonds
Active **40 min;** Total **1 hr 15 min;** Serves **4**

- 1 Tbsp. whole black peppercorns
- 3 cups white balsamic vinegar
  Kosher salt and freshly ground pepper
- 1 lb. baby carrots with tops—halved lengthwise and trimmed, 1 cup lightly packed chopped tops reserved
- 1½ tsp. cumin seeds
- 1½ cups lightly packed parsley leaves
- ½ cup lightly packed cilantro leaves
- 1 red Thai chile—stemmed, seeded and coarsely chopped
- 1 garlic clove
- 2 cubes (1 oz.) ice
- ¼ cup tahini
- ¼ cup fresh lemon juice
- 2 Tbsp. extra-virgin olive oil
- ⅓ cup roasted whole natural almonds, finely chopped

1. In a medium saucepan, toast the black peppercorns over moderately high heat, swirling the pan, until fragrant, about 3 minutes. Add the vinegar, 1½ cups of water and 2 tablespoons of kosher salt and bring to a boil. Remove from the heat and stir in the carrots. Let stand for at least 1 hour or up to 1 day.

2. Meanwhile, in a small skillet, toast the cumin seeds over moderately high heat, swirling the pan often, until fragrant, about 2 minutes. Pour the seeds into a blender. Add ½ cup of the parsley leaves, the chopped carrot tops, cilantro leaves, chile, garlic and ice. Blend into a coarse paste, then drizzle in the tahini and puree until a smooth sauce forms. Stir in the lemon juice and ¼ cup of water and season the charmoula sauce with salt and pepper.

3. Drain the carrots and discard the brine, or save it to use again. Pat the carrots dry and toss them with 1 tablespoon of the olive oil. Light a grill or heat a cast-iron grill pan. Add the carrots and grill over high heat until crisp-tender and grill marks appear, about 8 minutes. Transfer the carrots to a plate and let cool to room temperature.

4. Pour all but 2 tablespoons of the charmoula onto a platter and scatter the grilled carrots over the sauce. In a bowl, toss the remaining 1 cup of parsley leaves with the reserved 2 tablespoons of charmoula and the remaining 1 tablespoon of olive oil and scatter over the carrots. Sprinkle with the chopped almonds and serve. —*Johnny Clark and Beverly Kim*

Caramelized Endives and Leeks with Smoked Mozzarella
Total **30 min;** Serves **4**

- 1 Tbsp. unsalted butter
- 2 Tbsp. extra-virgin olive oil
- 3 leeks (1½ lbs.), white and light green parts only, halved lengthwise
  Kosher salt and pepper
- 3 endives (1 lb.), halved lengthwise
- 3 garlic cloves, sliced
- 5 thyme sprigs, plus thyme leaves for garnish
- 1 cup low-sodium chicken broth
- ¾ cup coarsely shredded smoked mozzarella cheese

1. Preheat the broiler and position a rack 6 inches from the heat.

2. In a large, deep ovenproof skillet, melt the butter in 1 tablespoon of the olive oil. Add the leeks, season with salt and pepper and cook over moderate heat, turning, until golden, about 5 minutes. Add the remaining 1 tablespoon of olive oil along with the endives, garlic and thyme sprigs and cook, turning, until the endives are golden, about 3 minutes. Add the broth and bring to a simmer. Cover and cook, stirring occasionally, until the vegetables are almost tender, about 5 minutes. Uncover and cook until almost all of the broth has evaporated, about 3 minutes.

3. Discard the thyme sprigs. Sprinkle the cheese over the endives and leeks. Broil for 2 to 3 minutes, until the cheese melts. Garnish with thyme leaves and serve warm. —*Kay Chun*

Roasted Winter Vegetables with Saffron Couscous

Total **50 min**; Serves **4 to 6**

In her class at New Jersey's Heirloom Kitchen, chef Rachel Nichols puts a twist on the traditional North African way of serving couscous by roasting vegetables in the oven instead of simmering them on the stove. This concentrates the vegetables' flavors and brings out their sweetness.

½ lb. sunchokes, scrubbed and cut into 2-inch pieces

3 small carrots, cut crosswise into 2-inch lengths

3 small parsnips, cut into 1½-inch pieces

2 medium sweet potatoes, peeled and cut into 1½-inch pieces

4 shallots, halved lengthwise

¼ cup extra-virgin olive oil

2 tsp. finely grated lemon zest

¼ tsp. ground ginger

¼ tsp. ground cinnamon

¼ tsp. ground turmeric

¼ tsp. crushed red pepper

   Kosher salt

½ cup dried currants

1 bay leaf

1 cup couscous

2 Tbsp. unsalted butter

⅛ tsp. saffron threads

   Chopped cilantro and pistachios, for garnish

1. Preheat the oven to 400°. On a large rimmed baking sheet, toss the sunchokes, carrots, parsnips, sweet potatoes, shallots, olive oil, lemon zest, ginger, cinnamon, turmeric and crushed red pepper. Season generously with salt. Roast the vegetables for about 30 minutes, until tender and browned in spots.

2. Stir 1 cup of water into the vegetables and scatter the currants and bay leaf on top. Roast for about 10 more minutes, until the currants are plump and the vegetables are saucy. Discard the bay leaf.

3. Meanwhile, put the couscous in a large heatproof bowl. In a small saucepan, bring 1¼ cups of water to a boil with the butter. Remove from the heat, add the saffron and a generous pinch of salt and let stand for 5 minutes. Bring the water back to a boil and pour it over the couscous. Cover the bowl with plastic wrap and let stand for 10 minutes. Fluff the couscous with a fork and season with salt.

4. Transfer the couscous to plates and spoon the roasted vegetables and their juices on top. Garnish with chopped cilantro and pistachios and serve.
—*Rachel Nichols*

WINE Fruit-forward Oregon Pinot Noir: 2013 Evening Land Willamette Valley.

Roasted Beets with Beet Green Salsa Verde

Active **30 min**; Total **1 hr 30 min**
Serves **10 to 12**

2¼ lbs. small or medium beets, scrubbed

1 lb. fresh ricotta cheese

   Sea salt and pepper

½ cup extra-virgin olive oil

¼ cup sherry vinegar

2 cups beet greens, halved lengthwise and very thinly sliced crosswise into ribbons

½ cup minced beet green stems

½ red onion, finely chopped

½ cup chopped dill, plus sprigs for garnish

½ cup pomegranate seeds

1. Preheat the oven to 400°. Wrap the beets in foil and transfer to a rimmed baking sheet. Bake for about 1 hour, until tender when pierced. Unwrap and let cool.

2. Spread the ricotta on a platter. Cut the beets into chunks and arrange on the cheese. Season lightly with sea salt.

3. In a medium bowl, whisk the oil with the vinegar. Add the beet greens and stems, the onion and chopped dill and mix well. Season the salsa verde with sea salt and pepper and spoon over the beets. Scatter the pomegranate seeds on top, garnish with dill sprigs and serve. —*Tyler Florence*

MAKE AHEAD The roasted beets can be refrigerated for up to 2 days. Return to room temperature before serving.

Roasted Beets with Salted Yogurt and Herbs

Active **15 min**; Total **1 hr 45 min**; Serves **6**

Baltimore chef Spike Gjerde is a huge fan of the small-batch, unrefined salt from J.Q. Dickinson Salt-Works (jqdsalt.com). In fact, it's the only salt he uses at Woodberry Kitchen. He shows it off with this simple dish, combining it with yogurt, olive oil and herbs to make a fresh and pretty sauce for beets.

12 small beets with 1 inch of stem (1½ lbs.), scrubbed but not peeled

3 Tbsp. extra-virgin olive oil, plus more for drizzling

   Flaky salt

1 Tbsp. apple cider vinegar

1 cup full-fat Greek yogurt

½ cup packed mixed herbs, leaves and shoots, such as dill, lovage, chervil, and young beet and radish greens

1. Preheat the oven to 350°. In a large baking dish, toss the beets with the 3 tablespoons of olive oil and 1 teaspoon of salt. Roast for about 1½ hours, until the beets are tender. Transfer the beets to a plate. Add the vinegar to the baking dish and stir with a wooden spoon, lifting up any browned bits. Scrape the vinegar mixture into a small bowl. Once the beets are cool enough to handle, slip off the skins and cut into wedges.

2. In a small bowl, season the yogurt with salt. Dollop the salted yogurt onto plates. Top with the beet wedges and herbs and drizzle with the vinegar mixture. Season with salt, drizzle with olive oil and serve immediately. —*Spike Gjerde*

MAKE AHEAD Step 1 can be completed 2 days in advance. Refrigerate the beets and vinegar mixture separately.

ROASTED BEETS
WITH SALTED
YOGURT AND HERBS

ROASTED WINTER
SQUASH WITH
VANILLA BUTTER

Roasted Winter Squash with Vanilla Butter

Active **20 min**; Total **45 min**
Serves **6 to 8**

Fragrant vanilla-bean butter does double duty here—it both flavors the squash and softens the skin during roasting. The greater the variety of winter squash you use, the more interesting the dish will be.

- **4 Tbsp. unsalted butter, at room temperature**
- **½ vanilla bean—split lengthwise, seeds scraped, pod reserved**
- **4 lbs. mixed squash, such as kabocha, Delicata and Red Kuri—scrubbed, seeded and sliced ½ inch thick**
- **3 sage sprigs plus 24 small sage leaves**
- **Kosher salt and pepper**
- **¼ cup extra-virgin olive oil**

1. Preheat the oven to 425°. In a small saucepan, combine the butter and vanilla bean and seeds and cook over moderately low heat, stirring occasionally, until the butter is deeply browned and has a nutty aroma, about 5 minutes. Discard the vanilla bean.

2. On a baking sheet, drizzle the squash and sage sprigs with the vanilla browned butter, season with salt and pepper and toss to coat. Roast for about 25 minutes, turning once, until the squash is golden in spots and tender. Arrange on a platter. Discard the sage sprigs.

3. In a small saucepan, heat the olive oil. In batches, fry the sage leaves over moderate heat, stirring, until crisp, about 2 minutes. Using a slotted spoon, transfer the sage to a paper towel–lined plate to drain. Scatter the fried sage over the squash and serve. —Kay Chun

Roasted Squash with Tamarind-Chile Glaze and Crispy Quinoa

Total **1 hr 15 min**; Serves **4**

- **One 2-lb. butternut squash, halved lengthwise and seeded**
- **3 Tbsp. canola oil**
- **Kosher salt and pepper**
- **⅓ cup quinoa, rinsed and drained**
- **¼ cup tamarind pulp with seeds**
- **1 garlic clove, minced**
- **1 red Thai chile, thinly sliced**
- **¾ tsp. ground annatto**
- **1 Tbsp. light brown sugar**
- **1 Tbsp. fresh lime juice**
- **1 cup baby arugula leaves**

1. Preheat the oven to 425°. Line a baking sheet with aluminum foil. Rub the cut sides of the squash with 1 tablespoon of the canola oil and season with salt and pepper. Set the squash cut side down on the prepared sheet and roast for about 45 minutes, until tender and caramelized. Scoop out the squash in 4 large pieces and transfer to plates; keep warm.

2. Meanwhile, in a small saucepan of boiling water, cook the quinoa until tender, about 10 minutes. Drain, then return the quinoa to the saucepan. Cover and let steam for 10 minutes. Scrape the quinoa onto a baking sheet in an even layer and let cool to room temperature.

3. Reduce the oven temperature to 375°. Drizzle the cooled quinoa with 1 tablespoon of the oil and season with salt and pepper; toss to coat and spread in an even layer. Toast in the oven for about 15 minutes, until golden and crisp. Let cool completely.

4. In a small saucepan, combine the tamarind pulp with ¼ cup of water and cook over low heat, mashing the tamarind until it breaks down and dissolves, 2 minutes. Strain the tamarind through a fine sieve, pushing on the seeds; discard the solids.

5. In a small skillet, heat the remaining 1 tablespoon of oil. Add the garlic, chile and annatto and cook over moderate heat, stirring, until fragrant, 1 minute. Add the tamarind, sugar and ½ cup of water and cook, stirring, until thickened to a glaze, about 3 minutes. Stir in ½ tablespoon of the lime juice and season with salt.

6. In a small bowl, toss the arugula with the remaining ½ tablespoon of lime juice and season with salt. Spoon some of the tamarind glaze over the squash and top with the crispy quinoa. Garnish with the arugula and serve. —CJ Jacobson

MAKE AHEAD The glaze can be refrigerated overnight and rewarmed before serving.

Roasted Acorn Squash with Garlic Butter and Burrata

Active **30 min**; Total **1 hr**; Serves **4**

Chicago chef Dave Beran created this wonderfully indulgent vegetarian dish of roasted sweet squash topped with just-melted burrata and a baby greens salad. "Squash is rich," Beran says, "especially with brown butter and cheese. I like the little salad—it's a mini palate cleanser."

- **4 Tbsp. unsalted butter, melted**
- **1 Tbsp. minced shallot**
- **1 garlic clove, minced**
- **½ tsp. thyme leaves**
- **Kosher salt and pepper**
- **Two 1½-lb. acorn squash, halved lengthwise, seeds discarded**
- **2 Tbsp. extra-virgin olive oil**
- **1 Tbsp. aged balsamic vinegar**
- **4 cups baby greens (2 oz.)**
- **¼ small red onion, thinly sliced and rinsed under cold water**
- **One ½-lb. ball of burrata**
- **Cracked black pepper and flaky sea salt, for garnish**

1. Preheat the oven to 425°. In a small bowl, combine the butter, shallot, garlic and thyme and season with salt and pepper. Season the squash halves with salt and pepper and set on a foil-lined baking sheet. Drizzle with the garlic butter and roast for about 30 minutes, until the squash is golden and tender. Transfer to plates.

2. In a large bowl, whisk the oil and vinegar and season with salt and pepper. Add the baby greens and red onion and toss to coat. Cut the burrata into 4 pieces. Top each squash half with burrata and salad, garnish with cracked pepper and sea salt and serve warm. —Dave Beran

WINE Focused, concentrated Sonoma Coast Chardonnay: 2013 Red Car.

Caramelized Vegetables with Dijon Butter

Active **40 min**; Total **1 hr 20 min**; Serves **12**

Carrots, fennel and beets get a double dose of mustard butter: first, to bake in the flavor before roasting, and again at the very end, for a rich, pungent finish.

- 1 stick unsalted butter, at room temperature
- 3 Tbsp. Dijon mustard
- 1 Tbsp. coriander seeds, crushed in a mortar
  Kosher salt and pepper
- 1½ lbs. carrots, scrubbed and halved lengthwise
- 3 fennel bulbs (1½ lbs.), cut into 1-inch-thick wedges
- 1½ lbs. beets, peeled and cut into 1-inch-thick wedges
- 2 Tbsp. chopped dill

1. Preheat the oven to 425°. In a bowl, mix 6 tablespoons of the butter with 2 tablespoons of the mustard and the coriander. Season with salt and pepper.

2. On a large rimmed baking sheet, combine the carrots and fennel. On another large rimmed baking sheet, arrange the beets. Dollop the Dijon butter over all of the vegetables and season with salt and pepper. Toss and rub to evenly coat the vegetables. Roast for about 40 minutes, stirring occasionally and rotating the sheets halfway through, until the vegetables are tender and caramelized.

3. Meanwhile, in a small bowl, mix the remaining 2 tablespoons of butter and 1 tablespoon of mustard. Dollop the butter over the warm vegetables and toss to evenly coat. Transfer the vegetables to a serving platter and garnish with the dill. —*Kay Chun*

Roasted Squash with Crispy Bulgur Crumbs

Active **30 min**; Total **50 min**; Serves **8**

- One 2-lb. kabocha squash— scrubbed, halved, seeded and cut into 1-inch wedges
- 5 Tbsp. extra-virgin olive oil
  Kosher salt and pepper
- ½ cup medium-grade bulgur
- 1 Tbsp. coriander seeds, crushed
- 2 scallions, thinly sliced

1. Preheat the oven to 450°. On a baking sheet, toss the squash with 3 tablespoons of the olive oil and season with salt and pepper. Roast for about 20 minutes, until tender. Transfer to a platter.

2. Meanwhile, in a medium saucepan of boiling water, cook the bulgur until tender, about 10 minutes. Drain and pat dry.

3. In a skillet, heat the remaining 2 tablespoons of oil. Add the bulgur and cook over moderate heat, stirring, until golden and crunchy, about 12 minutes. Stir in the coriander seeds. Sprinkle the bulgur over the squash and garnish with the scallions. —*Kay Chun*

Squash Gratin

Active **15 min**; Total **45 min**; Serves **6**

This gratin from F&W's Kay Chun features long spears of summer squash topped with panko and cheese and baked until tender and crisp.

- 2 Tbsp. extra-virgin olive oil, plus more for greasing
- 4 medium summer squash (zucchini and/or yellow squash), sliced lengthwise ⅛ inch thick
- 3 garlic cloves, sliced
  Kosher salt and pepper
- 1 cup panko
- 3 oz. Gruyère cheese, shredded (1 cup)

Preheat the oven to 450°. Grease a 2-quart ovenproof baking dish. In a large bowl, combine the squash, garlic and 2 tablespoons of oil; season with salt and pepper and toss. Arrange the squash in the prepared dish and bake for 20 minutes, until tender. Sprinkle with the panko and cheese and bake for 10 minutes longer, until golden and crisp on top. —*Kay Chun*

Grilled Corn with Jerk Mayo and Coconut

Total **40 min**; Serves **8**

Fresh green jerk made with scallions and raw Scotch bonnet flavors the mayo slathered on grilled corn.

- 1 Scotch bonnet chile, stemmed and seeded
- 6 scallions, chopped
- ½ medium onion, chopped
- 2 garlic cloves
- 2¼ tsp. thyme leaves
- 10 whole allspice berries
- 1½ tsp. kosher salt
- 1 cup mayonnaise
- 8 ears of corn, shucked
- 1 cup sweetened shredded coconut
- 2 limes, quartered

1. Light a grill or heat a grill pan. In a food processor, combine the chile, scallions, onion, garlic, thyme, allspice and salt and puree until smooth. Whisk ½ cup of this fresh jerk sauce into the mayonnaise; reserve the rest for another use.

2. Grill the corn over moderate heat until lightly charred, 12 to 15 minutes. Spread the jerk mayo all over the corn; transfer to a platter. Shower the corn with the coconut and serve with lime wedges. —*Adam Schop*

Corn on the Cob with Parsley Butter and Parmesan

PAGE 206

Total **30 min**; Serves **4 to 6**

April Bloomfield, the chef at New York City's Spotted Pig, boils corn in the husk to make removing the fine silk easier, then serves it with cheese and herb butter.

- 1 stick unsalted butter, softened
- 1 cup lightly packed parsley leaves
- 1 garlic clove, chopped
  Kosher salt
  4 to 6 ears of corn, in the husk
  Maldon salt
  Grated Parmigiano-Reggiano cheese, for sprinkling
  Lemon wedges, for serving

1. Bring a pot of water to a boil. Meanwhile, in a food processor, pulse the butter with the parsley and garlic until the butter is whipped and the parsley is very finely chopped; scrape down the bowl as needed. Transfer the parsley butter to a small bowl and season with kosher salt.

2. Add the corn and a generous pinch of kosher salt to the boiling water and cook for 8 minutes. Using tongs, transfer the corn to a rack and let cool slightly.

3. Slice off the bottoms of the corn and slide off the husks. Generously brush the parsley butter all over the corn and sprinkle with Maldon salt and cheese. Serve with lemon wedges. —*April Bloomfield*

Roasted Peppers with Garlicky Breadcrumbs
Total **40 min**; Serves **6**

- 8 mixed bell peppers (3½ lbs.)
- 3 oz. day-old country bread, crusts cut off, bread cubed
- 4 garlic cloves, thinly sliced
- ¼ cup extra-virgin olive oil
  Kosher salt and pepper
  Basil leaves, for garnish

1. Roast the peppers directly over a gas flame or under the broiler, turning occasionally, until charred all over, about 10 minutes. Transfer the peppers to a large bowl, cover tightly with plastic wrap and let steam for 15 minutes.

2. Meanwhile, in a food processor, pulse the bread until it is finely chopped. Add the garlic and pulse until breadcrumbs form; you should have about 1½ cups. In a large nonstick skillet, heat 2 tablespoons of the olive oil. Add the breadcrumbs and cook over moderately low heat, stirring, until golden and crisp, 5 minutes. Transfer the breadcrumbs to a paper towel–lined plate and season with salt. Wipe out the skillet.

3. Peel and seed the peppers, then cut them into ½-inch strips. Heat the remaining 2 tablespoons of olive oil in the skillet. Add the peppers and cook over moderate heat, stirring occasionally, until tender, about 8 minutes. Season with salt and pepper. Transfer the peppers to a large bowl or platter and garnish with basil. Serve the breadcrumb topping on the side, for sprinkling. —*Mimi Thorisson*

Wild Mushrooms with Garlic Butter
Total **30 min**; Serves **4**

- 4 Tbsp. unsalted butter, at room temperature
- 1 garlic clove, minced
- 2 Tbsp. chopped parsley
- 1½ lbs. mixed mushrooms, such as hen-of-the-woods and stemmed shiitake, cut into large pieces
- ¼ cup extra-virgin olive oil
- 1 tsp. thyme leaves
  Kosher salt and pepper
- ¼ cup chopped mixed herbs, such as chives and tarragon, for garnish

Preheat the oven to 450°. In a bowl, combine the butter, garlic and parsley. Spread the mushrooms on 2 rimmed baking sheets, toss with the oil and thyme and season with salt and pepper. Roast for about 15 minutes, stirring, until golden and tender. Toss the mushrooms with the garlic butter; season with salt and pepper. Scrape onto a platter, garnish with the herbs and serve warm. —*Rich Torrisi*

Mixed Mushroom–and–Cheese Quesadillas
Total **45 min**; Makes **6**

- ¼ cup corn oil
- ½ cup finely chopped white onion
- 3 large garlic cloves, minced
- 1 red jalapeño or Fresno chile, minced
- 12 oz. mixed oyster and white mushrooms, trimmed and very coarsely chopped
  Kosher salt
- 2 Tbsp. finely chopped epazote or 1 tsp. chopped oregano
  Six 8-inch Corn Tortillas (p. 182) or 12 fresh corn tortillas
- 9 oz. Oaxaca or Monterey Jack cheese, shredded (3 cups)

1. In a large skillet, heat the oil until shimmering. Add the onion, garlic and chile and cook over moderately high heat, stirring, until just softened, about 2 minutes. Add the mushrooms and a generous pinch of salt and cook, stirring occasionally, until tender and browned, about 10 minutes. Remove from the heat and stir in the epazote. Season with salt.

2. Heat a large cast-iron griddle over moderately high heat. Add 3 tortillas to the griddle and top each one with ½ cup of the cheese and ⅓ cup of the mushrooms. Cook until the cheese just starts to melt, about 2 minutes. Using a spatula, fold the tortillas in half, pressing lightly to form quesadillas. Cook, flipping once, until the tortillas are browned in spots and the cheese is melted, 2 to 3 minutes longer. Transfer to a work surface. Repeat with the remaining tortillas, cheese and mushrooms. Cut the quesadillas into wedges and serve. —*Enrique Olvera*

SERVE WITH Red salsa or Olvera's Salsa Verde (p. 182).

BEER Toasty, malty Mexican amber ale: Dos Equis Amber.

Chickpeas with Eggs and Mustard Greens
Total **30 min**; Serves **6**

- 6 large eggs
  Kosher salt and pepper
- ¼ cup extra-virgin olive oil
- 4 shallots, thinly sliced
- 6 garlic cloves, thinly sliced
- 1 Fresno chile, seeded and thinly sliced
  Two 15-oz. cans chickpeas, rinsed and drained
- 2½ cups chicken stock or low-sodium broth
- 4 oz. mustard greens, stemmed, leaves torn

1. Preheat the oven to 350°. Pour 1 tablespoon of water into 6 cups of a 12-cup muffin tin. Crack an egg into each of the 6 water-filled cups and season with salt and pepper. Bake the eggs for 13 to 15 minutes, until the whites are just firm and the yolks are still runny. Using a slotted spoon, immediately transfer the eggs to a plate.

2. Meanwhile, in a large skillet, heat the olive oil. Add the shallots, garlic and chile and cook over moderate heat until softened, about 5 minutes. Stir in the chickpeas and stock and bring to a boil. Add the mustard greens and cook until just wilted, 3 minutes. Season with salt and pepper. Ladle into 6 bowls and top with the eggs. —*Justin Chapple*

Ratatouille Tart

Active **50 min**; Total **4 hr**; Serves **6**

PASTRY

- 1 **stick plus 2 Tbsp. unsalted butter, at room temperature**
- 2 **Tbsp. whole milk**
- 1 **Tbsp. sugar**
- 1 **large egg yolk**
- 1¼ **cups all-purpose flour**

RATATOUILLE

- ½ **cup extra-virgin olive oil**
- 1 **small onion, cut into ½-inch dice**
- 1 **large Japanese eggplant, quartered lengthwise and sliced ⅓ inch thick**
  Kosher salt and pepper
- 2 **small red peppers, cut into ¾-inch dice**
- 1 **zucchini, quartered lengthwise and sliced ⅓ inch thick**
  One 8-oz. can crushed tomatoes
- 2 **Tbsp. chopped oregano**
- 1 **tsp. red wine vinegar**

1. Make the pastry In a large bowl, beat the butter with the milk, sugar and egg yolk until smooth. Add the flour and beat at low speed until the dough starts to come together. Pat the dough into a disk and wrap in plastic. Refrigerate for 1 hour.

2. On a lightly floured surface, using a lightly floured rolling pin, roll out the dough to a 12-inch round. Place in a fluted 9-inch tart pan with a removable bottom; trim the overhang. Refrigerate until firm, 1 hour.

3. Preheat the oven to 375°. Line the dough with parchment paper and fill with pie weights. Bake for about 30 minutes, until set. Remove the weights and parchment paper and bake until golden brown, 8 to 10 minutes longer. Transfer the tart shell to a rack and let cool to room temperature, about 1 hour.

4. Meanwhile, make the ratatouille In a large saucepan, heat 2 tablespoons of the olive oil. Add the onion and cook over moderate heat until softened. Add the eggplant and 3 tablespoons of the olive oil, season with salt and pepper and cook, stirring occasionally, until starting to soften, about 3 minutes. Add the red peppers, zucchini and the remaining 3 tablespoons of olive oil and cook until softened, 7 minutes. Stir in the tomatoes and oregano and cook until

the vegetables are tender and the sauce is thick, 20 minutes. Stir in the vinegar. Season with salt and pepper and let cool. Spoon the ratatouille into the tart shell and serve. —*Wade Moises and Koren Grieveson*

WINE Medium-bodied, juicy Beaujolais: 2013 Jean-Marc Burgaud Côte du Py.

Rice-and-Meat-Stuffed Zucchini and Green Peppers

Active **45 min**; Total **1 hr 30 min**; Serves **6**

- 6 **small cubanelle peppers (1 lb.)— stemmed, cored and seeded**
- 3 **medium zucchini (1½ lbs.), halved crosswise and seedy flesh scooped out with a melon baller**
  Kosher salt and pepper
- 12 **oz. ground beef chuck**
- 1 **medium onion, finely chopped**
- 1 **medium tomato, finely chopped**
- ½ **cup long-grain white rice**
- ¼ **cup finely chopped parsley**
- 2 **Tbsp. extra-virgin olive oil**
- 2 **tsp. thyme leaves**
- 2 **Tbsp. tomato paste**
- ¾ **cup Greek yogurt**
- ½ **tsp. finely grated garlic**
  Aleppo pepper, for sprinkling

1. Season the peppers and zucchini inside and out with salt and pepper and arrange them snugly, hollow side up, in a medium saucepan.

2. In a medium bowl, combine the beef, onion, tomato, rice, parsley, olive oil, thyme, 2 teaspoons of salt and 1 teaspoon of pepper and mix well. Spoon the filling into the peppers and zucchini.

3. In a small bowl, whisk the tomato paste with 1 cup of water; pour the mixture around the vegetables in the saucepan and bring to a simmer. Cover and cook over moderately low heat until the vegetables are tender and the filling is cooked through, about 25 minutes.

4. In another small bowl, stir the yogurt with the garlic. Transfer the stuffed vegetables to a platter and drizzle with some of the sauce from the pan. Spoon the yogurt on top, sprinkle with Aleppo pepper and serve. —*Scott Conant*

WINE Robustly fruity southern Italian rosé: 2014 Rosa del Golfo Rosato.

Rice-Stuffed Tomatoes with Currants and Pine Nuts

Active **35 min**; Total **2 hr**; Makes **8**

- 8 **medium tomatoes**
  Kosher salt and pepper
- ⅓ **cup pine nuts**
- 2 **Tbsp. extra-virgin olive oil, plus more for drizzling**
- 1 **large onion, finely chopped**
- ½ **cup long-grain white rice**
- 1 **Tbsp. tomato paste**
- ⅓ **cup currants**
- 1 **cup parsley, chopped**
  Plain dry breadcrumbs, for sprinkling

1. Cut the tops off the tomatoes and, using a spoon, scoop the seeds and pulp into a food processor; puree until smooth. Season the insides of the tomatoes with salt and pepper and arrange cut side up in a large ovenproof skillet.

2. In another large skillet, toast the pine nuts over moderate heat, shaking the pan, until lightly browned, about 5 minutes. Transfer to a plate.

3. In the same skillet, heat the 2 tablespoons of olive oil until shimmering. Add the onion and a generous pinch of salt and cook over moderately high heat, stirring occasionally, until softened, about 5 minutes. Add the rice and cook, stirring, until opaque, about 2 minutes. Stir in the pureed tomato, the tomato paste and ½ cup of water and bring to a boil. Cover and simmer over moderately low heat, stirring occasionally, until the rice is tender, about 15 minutes. Stir in the currants and pine nuts and simmer for 3 minutes. Stir in the parsley; season with salt and pepper.

4. Preheat the oven to 350°. Spoon the filling into the tomatoes. Sprinkle a thin layer of breadcrumbs on top and drizzle with olive oil. Bake for about 50 minutes, until tender and the tops are browned. Let stand for at least 5 minutes, then serve warm or at room temperature. —*Stelios Trilyrakis*

MAKE AHEAD The uncooked stuffed tomatoes can be refrigerated overnight. Bring to room temperature before baking.

WINE Bright, red-berry-scented Greek rosé: 2013 Gai'a 14-18h.

RATATOUILLE TART

New York City chef Marco Canora focuses on whole grains to create deeply satisfying dishes like risotto-style farro with short ribs (recipe, p. 252).

POTATOES, BEANS & GRAINS

POMMES PUREE
Recipe, page 237

Fried Pickled Potatoes with Harissa Tahini

Total **45 min plus overnight pickling**
Serves **4**

Philadelphia chef Michael Solomonov pickles sliced fingerlings in leftover pickle brine so they're flavor-packed through and through before frying them.

- **3 Yukon Gold potatoes (¾ lb.), peeled and sliced ¼ inch thick**
- **2 cups brine from Cauliflower-Heart Pickles (p. 362) or other jarred pickles**
- **3 garlic cloves**
- **3 Tbsp. fresh lemon juice**
  Kosher salt
- **½ cup tahini**
  Pinch of ground cumin
- **¼ cup harissa**
  Canola oil, for frying

1. In a medium bowl, cover the sliced potatoes with the pickle brine and refrigerate overnight.

2. In a food processor, combine the garlic, lemon juice and ¾ teaspoon of salt and pulse until a coarse puree forms. Let stand for 10 minutes. Strain through a fine sieve set over a small bowl. Stir in the tahini, cumin and 3 tablespoons of water until smooth, then stir in the harissa and ½ tablespoon of the pickle brine. Season the harissa tahini with salt.

3. Drain the potatoes and pat dry with paper towels. In a nonstick skillet, heat a thin layer of oil. Working in batches, fry the potatoes in a single layer over moderately high heat, turning occasionally, until lightly browned and tender, about 5 minutes per batch. Drain and serve with the harissa tahini. —*Michael Solomonov*

Grilled Red Potato and Pickled Chile Salad

⏱ Active **20 min**; Total **45 min**; Serves **8**

- **2 lbs. medium red potatoes**
- **2 small red onions, sliced into ½-inch-thick rings**
- **½ cup extra-virgin olive oil, plus more for drizzling**
  Kosher salt and pepper
  Dried oregano
- **½ cup Sweet Pickled Fresno Chiles (recipe follows), plus 2 Tbsp. brine**
  Chopped parsley, for garnish

1. In a large saucepan of salted boiling water, cook the potatoes until just tender, about 20 minutes. Drain and cool; halve the potatoes.

2. Light a grill. In a large bowl, toss the potatoes and onions with the ½ cup of olive oil and season with salt and pepper. Grill over moderate heat, turning, until the onions are tender and the potatoes are golden and crispy, about 3 minutes for the onions and 10 minutes for the potatoes. Transfer the onions and potatoes to a platter and season with salt, pepper and oregano. Top with the pickled chiles and drizzle with olive oil and the brine. Garnish with chopped parsley and serve warm.
—*Jon Shook and Vinny Dotolo*

SWEET PICKLED FRESNO CHILES

Total **20 min plus 2 hr cooling**
Makes **2 cups**

These sweet and spicy chiles are fabulous in the potato salad above, and they're also great on sandwiches or pasta. If you can't find Fresno chiles, use jalapeños (preferably red).

- **6 oz. Fresno chiles (about 8 medium), sliced crosswise into rings**
- **4 garlic cloves, crushed**
- **1 tsp. mustard seeds**
- **1 tsp. coriander seeds**
- **¼ tsp. fennel seeds**
- **¼ tsp. whole black peppercorns**
- **1¼ cups distilled white vinegar**
- **½ cup sugar**
- **2 Tbsp. kosher salt**

1. Pack the chiles and garlic in a 1-quart heatproof jar.

2. In a small saucepan, toast the mustard seeds, coriander seeds, fennel seeds and peppercorns over low heat, stirring, until very fragrant, about 3 minutes. Add the vinegar, sugar, salt and 1 cup of water and bring to a simmer. Cook for 5 minutes, stirring to dissolve the sugar and salt. Pour the hot brine over the chiles and garlic and let cool to room temperature, about 2 hours. Serve immediately or refrigerate in the brine. —*JS and VD*

MAKE AHEAD The pickled chiles can be refrigerated in the brine for up to 3 days.

BUILD YOUR OWN SALAD
Potato Salad

TOSS BOILED POTATOES WITH ONE FLAVOR COMBINATION

1. Kale, roasted garlic, pecorino, oregano, crushed red pepper	**4.** Feta, sautéed leeks, hard-boiled eggs, tarragon
2. Endive, roast pancetta, shaved pecorino, arugula, basil	**5.** Charred vegetables, cilantro, cracked coriander
3. White anchovies, green olives, red onion, toasted almonds, Espelette pepper	**6.** Yogurt, cabbage, white onion, caraway seeds, orange zest

DRESS WITH

Lemon Vinaigrette
Makes ½ cup

In a small bowl, combine 2 Tbsp. minced **shallots** with ½ tsp. finely grated **lemon zest**, 3 Tbsp. **fresh lemon juice**, 1 Tbsp. **Champagne vinegar** and ½ tsp. chopped **thyme**. Whisk in ¼ cup **extra-virgin olive oil** and season with **kosher salt** and **pepper**. —*Paul Kahan*

Ham-and-Potato Salad

Active **30 min**; Total **50 min**; Serves **6**

1½ lbs. fingerling potatoes
    Kosher salt and pepper
1 cup mayonnaise
3 hard-cooked large egg yolks, mashed with a fork
1½ Tbsp. minced cornichons
1 Tbsp. minced shallot
1 Tbsp. prepared horseradish
    Pinch of cayenne
¼ cup plus ½ Tbsp. extra-virgin olive oil
2½ Tbsp. red wine vinegar
    One ½-lb. piece of smoked ham, cut into bite-size pieces
½ English cucumber, chopped
4 cups mesclun (2 oz.)
    Pickled okra, halved lengthwise, for garnish

1. In a medium saucepan, cover the potatoes with water and bring to a boil. Add a generous pinch of salt and simmer over moderate heat until tender, about 20 minutes. Drain and let cool slightly, then cut in half lengthwise.

2. In a medium bowl, whisk the mayonnaise with the egg yolks, cornichons, shallot, horseradish, cayenne, ¼ cup of the olive oil and 2 tablespoons of the vinegar. Season the dressing with salt and pepper.

3. In a large bowl, toss the potatoes with half of the dressing. Fold in the ham and cucumber and season with salt and pepper. Transfer the salad to plates or a platter.

4. In another bowl, toss the mesclun with the remaining ½ tablespoon each of olive oil and vinegar and season with salt and pepper. Arrange on top of and around the ham-and-potato salad. Garnish with pickled okra and serve, passing additional dressing at the table. —José Andrés

WINE Berry-rich sparkling rosé cava: 2011 Llopart Brut Rosé.

Crushed Yukon Gold Potatoes with Lemon

PAGE 186

Active **15 min**; Total **40 min**; Serves **6**

3 lbs. large Yukon Gold potatoes, quartered
2 Tbsp. kosher salt, plus more for seasoning
¾ cup extra-virgin olive oil
2 Tbsp. fresh lemon juice
¼ cup chopped parsley

In a large saucepan, cover the potatoes with cold water, add the 2 tablespoons of salt and bring to a simmer. Cook over moderate heat until the potatoes are tender, about 20 minutes. Drain in a colander and let stand for 3 minutes to dry out. Return the potatoes to the saucepan and add the olive oil, lemon juice and parsley. Season with salt and mix and crush gently with a wooden spoon. Transfer to a bowl and serve. —Daniel Holzman

Mashed Potatoes with Parmesan Cream

Active **30 min**; Total **1 hr**; Serves **12**

For the fluffiest mashed potatoes, be sure to put them through a ricer while they're still warm.

6 lbs. large Yukon Gold potatoes— scrubbed, peeled and cut into large chunks
    Kosher salt and pepper
1½ sticks unsalted butter
1½ cups heavy cream
1½ cups whole milk
1¼ cups freshly grated Parmigiano-Reggiano cheese

1. In a pot, cover the potatoes with water; bring to a boil. Add a generous pinch of salt and simmer over moderate heat until tender, 20 minutes. Drain.

2. Meanwhile, in a medium saucepan, combine the butter, cream and milk; bring to a simmer. Add the cheese and let stand for 1 minute; whisk until smooth.

3. Pass the warm potatoes through a ricer into the pot. Fold in the Parmesan cream. Season generously with salt and pepper and serve. —Justin Chapple

Pommes Puree

PAGE 235

Active **20 min**; Total **1 hr**; Serves **4 to 6**

3 lbs. Yukon Gold potatoes
    Kosher salt
3 thyme sprigs
3 garlic cloves, crushed
3 sticks unsalted butter, cut into tablespoons
1 cup heavy cream, warmed

1. In a large saucepan, cover the potatoes with cold water and season generously with salt. Add the thyme and garlic, bring to a simmer and cook until tender, about 40 minutes. Drain well. Let the potatoes cool, then slip off and discard the skins.

2. Using a ricer and working over a large bowl, rice the potatoes with half of the butter. Strain through a fine sieve into a large saucepan, pushing them through with a sturdy rubber spatula. Mix in the remaining butter and the heavy cream. Season with salt and serve. —Rich Torrisi

Buttery Pumpkin Mashed Potatoes

Total **40 min**; Serves **10 to 12**

4 lbs. large Yukon Gold potatoes, peeled and cut into 1-inch cubes
    Kosher salt and pepper
1½ sticks unsalted butter
2 cups whole milk
1½ cups pumpkin puree

1. In a large saucepan, cover the potatoes with water and bring to a boil. Add a generous pinch of salt and simmer over moderate heat until tender, about 20 minutes. Drain well.

2. In the same saucepan, melt the butter in the milk over moderate heat, then add the pumpkin puree. Press the potatoes through a ricer into a large bowl and mix in the pumpkin mixture. Season with salt and pepper and serve. —Justin Chapple

MAKE AHEAD The pumpkin mashed potatoes can be refrigerated for up to 3 days. Reheat gently before serving.

Ombré Potato and Root Vegetable Gratin

Active **45 min**; Total **3 hr**; Serves **12**

Unsalted butter, for greasing

2 **cups heavy cream**

3 **garlic cloves, minced**

1 **small shallot, minced**

½ **tsp. freshly grated nutmeg**

1½ **tsp. kosher salt**

½ **tsp. pepper**

1¾ **cups freshly grated Parmigiano-Reggiano cheese (5 oz.)**

1 **lb. red beets, peeled and sliced on a mandoline ¹⁄₁₆ inch thick**

1 **lb. sweet potatoes or garnet yams, peeled and sliced on a mandoline ¹⁄₁₆ inch thick**

1 **lb. Yukon Gold potatoes, peeled and sliced on a mandoline ¹⁄₁₆ inch thick**

1 **lb. turnips, peeled and sliced on a mandoline ¹⁄₁₆ inch thick**

1. Preheat the oven to 375°. Lightly butter a 9-by-13-inch baking dish. In a medium bowl, whisk the cream with the garlic, shallot, nutmeg, salt and pepper. Stir in 1 cup of the grated cheese.

2. In a large bowl, gently toss the beets with one-fourth of the cream mixture. Arrange the beets in the baking dish in an even layer, overlapping them slightly. Scrape any remaining cream from the bowl over the beets. Repeat this process with the sweet potatoes, Yukon Golds and turnips, using one-fourth of the cream mixture for each vegetable. Press a sheet of parchment paper on top of the turnips, then cover the dish tightly with foil.

3. Bake the gratin for about 1½ hours, until the vegetables are tender. Uncover and top with the remaining ¾ cup of cheese. Bake for about 15 minutes longer, until golden on top. Transfer the gratin to a rack and let cool for at least 15 minutes before serving. —*Carla Hall*

MAKE AHEAD The gratin can be refrigerated overnight. Reheat gently.

Loaded Sweet Potatoes with Chorizo and Pomegranate

Active **40 min**; Total **1 hr 15 min**; Serves **4**

At Central Standard in Austin's South Congress Hotel, chef Michael Paley tweaks steakhouse conventions by topping a baked sweet potato with spicy chorizo and fresh pomegranate seeds.

Four 12-oz. sweet potatoes, scrubbed

3 **Tbsp. extra-virgin olive oil, plus more for drizzling**

Maldon salt

½ **lb. fresh chorizo, casings removed**

3 **cipollini onions, thinly sliced (½ cup)**

1 **Fresno chile, thinly sliced**

1 **Tbsp. minced garlic**

¼ **cup pure pomegranate juice**

¼ **cup chopped cilantro, plus leaves for garnish**

Kosher salt and pepper

Crème fraîche, sliced avocado, pomegranate seeds and finely grated lime zest, for topping

Lime wedges, for serving

1. Preheat the oven to 350°. Set each sweet potato on a sheet of foil. Drizzle with olive oil and season with Maldon salt. Wrap the potatoes in the foil and transfer to a baking sheet. Bake until tender, about 1 hour.

2. Meanwhile, in a large skillet, heat the 3 tablespoons of olive oil until shimmering. Add the chorizo and cook over moderately high heat, breaking up the meat with a wooden spoon, until nearly cooked through, about 5 minutes. Add the onions, chile and garlic and cook, stirring occasionally, until the chorizo is cooked through and the onions are softened, 3 to 5 minutes longer. Add the pomegranate juice and cook until nearly absorbed, 1 to 2 minutes. Stir in the chopped cilantro and season with kosher salt and pepper.

3. Unwrap the sweet potatoes and arrange on a platter. Cut a lengthwise slit in the top of each one and fluff the insides with a fork. Season with kosher salt and pepper and fill with the chorizo mixture. Top each sweet potato with crème fraîche, sliced avocado, pomegranate seeds, grated lime zest and cilantro leaves. Serve right away, with lime wedges. —*Michael Paley*

Grilled Potato Salad with Mustard Seeds

Total **50 min**; Serves **6**

Grilling sliced potatoes in butter in a foil pack gives them an amazing crust; tossing them in a tangy mustard seed vinaigrette infuses them with fantastic flavor.

4 **large Kennebec or baking potatoes, cut into ½-inch-thick rounds**

Kosher salt and pepper

1 **stick unsalted butter**

3 **Tbsp. seasoned rice vinegar**

2 **Tbsp. mustard seeds**

¼ **cup sherry vinegar**

2 **tsp. pure maple syrup**

2 **tsp. fresh lemon juice**

¼ **cup rice bran oil or canola oil**

2 **celery ribs, thinly sliced**

4 **scallions, thinly sliced**

1. In a large saucepan, cover the potato rounds with water and bring to a boil. Add a generous pinch of salt and simmer over moderate heat until the potatoes are tender but not falling apart, about 12 minutes. Drain the potatoes and transfer to a baking sheet to cool.

2. Light a grill or heat a grill pan. Lay 2 large sheets of heavy-duty foil on a work surface. Fold up the edges to form a ½-inch rim and pinch the corners together to seal. Transfer the foil to the grill and melt the butter on it. Add the potatoes in a single layer and grill over moderate heat until browned on the bottom, 12 to 15 minutes.

3. Meanwhile, in a small saucepan, bring the rice vinegar just to a boil. Add the mustard seeds and let cool completely. Whisk in the sherry vinegar, maple syrup, lemon juice and rice bran oil. Season the dressing with salt and pepper.

4. Transfer the potatoes to a large bowl. Add the celery, scallions and dressing and gently toss to coat. Season with salt and pepper and toss again. Serve right away. —*Stephanie Izard*

GRILLED POTATO
SALAD WITH
MUSTARD SEEDS

Sweet Potatoes with Toasted Marshmallow Swirls

Active **1 hr**; Total **2 hr**; Serves **10 to 12**

- 6 **medium sweet potatoes (4 lbs.), scrubbed but not peeled**
- **Extra-virgin olive oil**
- **Sea salt**
- 1 **cup pecans**
- 1 **cup fresh orange juice**
- ¾ **cup honey**
- ¾ **cup packed light brown sugar**
- ¾ **cup granulated sugar**
- ½ **cup light corn syrup**
- 2 **large egg whites**
- ¼ **tsp. cream of tartar**

1. Preheat the oven to 400°. Prick the potatoes all over with a fork and put them on a rimmed baking sheet. Brush with olive oil and season with salt. Bake the potatoes for about 1 hour, until tender.

2. Meanwhile, spread the pecans in a pie plate and toast in the oven until golden and fragrant, about 7 minutes. Let cool, then coarsely chop.

3. In a medium saucepan, combine the orange juice, honey and brown sugar and bring just to a boil, stirring to dissolve the sugar. Let the honey syrup cool.

4. In another medium saucepan, combine the granulated sugar with the corn syrup and ¼ cup of water and cook over moderate heat, stirring occasionally, until the sugar syrup registers 240° on a candy thermometer.

5. In a stand mixer fitted with the whisk, beat the egg whites with the cream of tartar at medium speed until soft peaks form. Turn the machine to medium-high and drizzle the hot sugar syrup into the egg whites in a very thin stream down the side of the bowl; beat until stiff peaks form and the marshmallow is cool. Scrape the marshmallow into a pastry bag fitted with a medium straight tip.

6. Cut off and discard the ends of the warm potatoes, then cut them crosswise into 2- to 3-inch sections. Arrange on a platter. Spoon some of the honey syrup over the potatoes and on the platter. Pipe the marshmallow onto the potatoes and, using a kitchen torch, lightly toast the tops. Alternatively, you can pipe the marshmallow onto a greased foiled-lined baking sheet and broil, then use a cake spatula to transfer onto each sweet potato section. Sprinkle the pecans over the top and serve. —*Tyler Florence*

MAKE AHEAD The honey syrup can be refrigerated overnight. Bring to room temperature before using. The roasted potatoes can be refrigerated overnight and reheated before proceeding.

Mushroom Risotto

Total **1 hr**; Serves **6**

The whipped cream in this risotto improbably makes the dish a little frothy and lighter tasting.

- 1 **stick plus 2 Tbsp. unsalted butter**
- ½ **lb. maitake or oyster mushrooms, broken into large clusters or pieces**
- ¼ **cup plus 2 Tbsp. minced shallots**
- 1 **tsp. minced garlic**
- **Kosher salt**
- ½ **cup heavy cream**
- ¼ **cup grapeseed oil**
- 1 **cup arborio rice (7 oz.)**
- 1 **cup dry vermouth**
- 1 **cup dry white wine**
- 4½ **cups hot water**
- 1 **Tbsp. fresh lemon juice**
- ¾ **cup freshly grated Parmigiano-Reggiano cheese**
- **Thyme, finely grated lemon zest and cracked black pepper, for garnish**

1. In a small saucepan, melt 4 tablespoons of the butter. Cook over moderate heat until deep golden, 4 to 5 minutes. Keep the browned butter warm.

2. In a medium skillet, melt 4 tablespoons of the butter. Add the mushrooms, 2 tablespoons of the shallots and the garlic and season with salt. Cook over moderately high heat, stirring occasionally, until the mushrooms are golden and tender, 3 to 4 minutes. Transfer to a plate and keep warm.

3. In a bowl, beat the heavy cream until soft peaks form; refrigerate.

4. In a medium saucepan, heat the grapeseed oil. Add the remaining ¼ cup of shallots and cook over moderate heat, stirring occasionally, until translucent, about 2 minutes. Add the rice and cook, stirring, for 2 minutes. Add the vermouth and cook until almost evaporated, then stir in the wine and cook until almost evaporated, about 2 minutes. Add ½ cup of the hot water and cook, stirring constantly, until the liquid is absorbed, about 2 minutes. Continue stirring in hot water, ½ cup at a time, until it is almost absorbed before adding more. The risotto is done when the rice is just al dente, about 18 minutes total. Stir in the lemon juice, grated cheese and the remaining 2 tablespoons of butter.

5. Fold the whipped cream into the risotto and bring to a simmer for 30 seconds; the risotto should be thick and frothy. Season with salt. Spoon the risotto into bowls and drizzle with the browned butter. Top with the caramelized mushrooms, garnish with thyme, grated lemon zest and cracked pepper and serve at once. —*Dave Beran*

WINE Herb-scented, earthy Piedmont red: 2010 Produttori del Barbaresco.

Coconut Rice Salad

Active **10 min**; Total **40 min**; Serves **4**

- 1 **cup jasmine rice**
- 2 **cups unsweetened coconut milk**
- 1 **Tbsp. sugar**
- **Kosher salt**
- 2 **cups shredded cooked chicken**
- 2 **small Kirby cucumbers, chopped**
- 1 **Tbsp. canola oil**
- **Chopped scallions, for garnish**

In a large saucepan, combine the rice, coconut milk, sugar and ½ teaspoon of salt and bring to a boil. Cover and cook over low heat until the rice is tender and all of the coconut milk is absorbed, about 20 minutes. Remove from the heat and let the rice stand for 10 minutes. Transfer to a large bowl and stir in the chicken, cucumbers and oil. Season with salt, garnish with scallions and serve. —*Kay Chun*

WINE Zesty, medium-bodied Australian Riesling: 2014 Pewsey Vale.

Chicken Rice Pilaf

Active **25 min**; Total **1 hr**; Serves **6**

Asha Gomez, the chef at Spice to Table in Atlanta, calls her chicken pilaf a "one-dish wonder." You can change up the spices here, adding a little cinnamon or ginger in place of the star anise, for instance.

- ¼ **cup ghee (see Note)**
- 1 **large onion, halved and thinly sliced**
- 6 **cardamom pods, cracked**
- 3 **star anise**
  Kosher salt
- 6 **garlic cloves, minced**
- 1½ **tsp. turmeric powder**
- 1 **lb. skinless, boneless chicken breasts, cut into ¾-inch dice**
- 2¼ **cups chicken stock or low-sodium broth**
- 1½ **cups basmati rice**
  Golden or green raisins, chopped cilantro and chopped toasted almonds, for garnish

1. In a large saucepan, heat the ghee. Add the onion, cardamom, star anise and a big pinch of salt and cook over moderately high heat, stirring, until the onion is softened and browned, 8 to 10 minutes. Add the garlic and turmeric and cook, stirring, until fragrant, 2 minutes. Add the chicken and cook over moderate heat for 4 minutes, stirring to coat it with the aromatics.

2. Add the stock to the pan and bring to a boil over moderately high heat. Stir in the rice and return to a boil, then cover and simmer over low heat until the water is absorbed and the rice is tender, about 15 minutes. Remove from the heat and let steam, covered, for 15 minutes.

3. Fluff the pilaf with a fork and season with salt. Transfer to a bowl, discarding the cardamom and star anise. Garnish with raisins, chopped cilantro and chopped toasted almonds and serve. —*Asha Gomez*

NOTE The Indian cooking fat ghee is available at specialty food stores, Whole Foods and amazon.com. Alternatively, you can make it by slowly heating butter and skimming off the milk solids on top.

WINE Apricot-scented, full-bodied Rhône white: 2013 Domaine le Garrigon Visan Côtes du Rhône Blanc.

Baked Shrimp Risotto

Active **10 min**; Total **30 min**; Serves **4**

- 2 **Tbsp. extra-virgin olive oil**
- 5 **garlic cloves, thinly sliced**
- 1 **cup arborio rice**
- 3½ **cups low-sodium chicken broth**
- ½ **cup freshly grated Parmigiano-Reggiano cheese, plus more for garnish**
- 20 **cooked shelled large shrimp**
- 1 **Tbsp. unsalted butter**
- 1 **Tbsp. fresh lemon juice**
  Kosher salt
  Pesto, for serving

Preheat the oven to 400°. In a medium enameled cast-iron casserole, heat the oil. Add the garlic and rice; cook over moderate heat, stirring, until very fragrant, 2 minutes. Stir in the broth and bring to a boil. Cover and bake for 20 minutes, until the rice is tender. Stir in the ½ cup of cheese, the shrimp, butter and lemon juice; season with salt. Serve, drizzled with pesto and garnished with cheese. —*Kay Chun*

WINE Lemony coastal Italian white: 2013 Bisson Vermentino Vignerta.

Sweet Brown Rice Risotto with Kale and Cremini

Active **45 min**; Total **1 hr 15 min**
Serves **6 to 8**

"Despite its name, sweet brown rice isn't sweet," says Marco Canora, chef at Hearth in Manhattan. Instead, this glutinous rice resembles whole-grain sushi rice.

- 1 **quart mushroom broth**
- 1 **quart vegetable broth**
- ¼ **cup extra-virgin olive oil, plus more for drizzling**
- 10 **oz. cremini mushrooms, thinly sliced**
  Fine sea salt and pepper
- ¾ **lb. Tuscan kale, stemmed, leaves chopped into ½-inch pieces**
- 2 **Tbsp. unsalted butter**
- 1 **yellow onion, minced**
- 2 **cups sweet brown rice (see Note)**
- 1 **cup dry white wine**
- 1 **Tbsp. chopped thyme**
- ⅓ **cup freshly grated Parmigiano-Reggiano cheese, plus more for serving**

1. In a large saucepan, combine the mushroom and vegetable broths and bring to a simmer; keep warm.

2. In a large enameled cast-iron casserole, heat 1 tablespoon of the olive oil. Add the mushrooms, season with salt and pepper and cook over moderately high heat, stirring occasionally, until golden, about 5 minutes. Transfer to a bowl.

3. Add 1 tablespoon of the olive oil to the casserole. Add the kale and cook over moderate heat until wilted, 3 minutes. Add the kale to the mushrooms.

4. In the casserole, melt 1 tablespoon of the butter in the remaining 2 tablespoons of olive oil. Add the onion, season with salt and pepper and cook over moderate heat until softened, about 5 minutes. Add the rice and stir until coated with oil and lightly toasted, 2 minutes. Add the wine and cook, stirring, until evaporated. Add 2 cups of the hot broth, cover partially and cook, stirring occasionally, until most of the broth has been absorbed, 10 minutes. Repeat with another 2 cups of broth.

5. Add 3 cups of the broth, 1 cup at a time, and cook, stirring often, until it is mostly absorbed between additions, about 15 minutes total. Add the last cup of broth, the mushrooms, kale, thyme, ⅓ cup of cheese and the remaining 1 tablespoon of butter. Cook, stirring, until the risotto is creamy. Season with salt and pepper. Drizzle with oil and serve with cheese. —*Marco Canora*

NOTE Sweet brown rice is available at Asian markets and online from bobsredmill.com.

WINE Juicy, versatile Italian red: 2013 Vigneti del Sole Montepulciano d'Abruzzo.

JEWELED RICE PILAF
WITH CARROTS

Jeweled Rice Pilaf with Carrots

Active **25 min**; Total **1 hr**; Serves **6**

F&W's Kay Chun replaces the dried fruits that traditionally bejewel this golden and aromatic Persian rice dish with roasted multihued carrots. Toasted angel hair pasta adds fantastic texture.

½ cup sliced almonds

1 lb. carrots, preferably in a mix of colors, peeled and sliced ¼ inch thick

3 Tbsp. extra-virgin olive oil
    Kosher salt and pepper

2 leeks, white and light green parts only, thinly sliced

2½ oz. angel hair pasta, broken into 2-inch pieces (1 cup)

2 cups basmati rice
    Pinch of saffron threads
    One 3-inch cinnamon stick

3¾ cups low-sodium chicken broth

3 Tbsp. fresh lemon juice, plus lemon wedges for serving

½ cup chopped pitted Picholine olives

¼ cup chopped parsley

1. Preheat the oven to 450°. Spread the almonds in a pie plate. On a rimmed baking sheet, toss the carrots with 1 tablespoon of the olive oil and season with salt and pepper. Roast the carrots until golden and tender, about 15 minutes. While the carrots are cooking, toast the almonds until golden, 3 to 4 minutes; let cool.

2. Meanwhile, in a large enameled cast-iron casserole, heat the remaining 2 tablespoons of oil. Add the leeks and angel hair pasta, season with salt and pepper and cook over moderate heat, stirring frequently, until golden, 5 minutes. Stir in the rice, saffron and cinnamon stick and cook, stirring, until the rice is golden, 3 minutes. Stir in the broth and bring to a simmer.

3. Cover the rice and cook over low heat until all of the broth has been absorbed, about 25 minutes. Remove the pan from the heat and let stand, covered, for 10 minutes.

4. Fluff the rice and stir in the carrots, toasted almonds, lemon juice, olives and parsley. Transfer the rice to a bowl and serve with lemon wedges. —*Kay Chun*

MAKE AHEAD The rice can be refrigerated overnight and rewarmed before serving.

Forbidden Black Rice with Ginger and Cardamom

Active **15 min**; Total **1 hr**; Serves **8 to 10**

This chewy, rich-tasting black rice dish from chef Akasha Richmond is fragrant with spices and aromatics.

2 Tbsp. ghee (see Note)

1 large shallot, thinly sliced

2 Tbsp. minced peeled fresh ginger

2 cups forbidden black rice (14 oz.), rinsed and drained (see Note)

1 Tbsp. green cardamom pods, cracked
    Sea salt
    Thinly sliced scallions, for garnish

In a medium saucepan, heat the ghee. Add the shallot and ginger and cook over moderate heat, stirring occasionally, until softened and lightly browned, about 5 minutes. Stir in the rice and cardamom and cook, stirring, for 2 minutes. Add 3 cups of water and a generous pinch of sea salt and bring to a boil. Cover and cook over low heat until the rice is tender and the water is absorbed, about 30 minutes. Remove from the heat and let steam for 15 minutes. Fluff the rice with a fork and season with salt. Transfer to a serving bowl, garnish with sliced scallions and serve. —*Akasha Richmond*

NOTE Ghee is a type of clarified butter. Forbidden rice is a nutty-tasting black rice from China. Both ghee and forbidden rice are available at specialty markets, Whole Foods and amazon.com. You can also make ghee by slowly heating butter and skimming off the milk solids on top.

Brown Basmati Rice with Coconut and Turmeric

Active **10 min**; Total **1 hr**; Serves **8 to 10**

2 cups brown basmati rice (12 oz.), rinsed and drained

1 cup unsweetened coconut milk
    One 2-inch piece of fresh turmeric, peeled and finely grated (1 Tbsp.)
    Kosher salt
    Mint leaves, for garnish

In a medium saucepan, combine the rice with 2 cups of water and the coconut milk, turmeric and a generous pinch of salt. Bring to a boil, cover and cook over low heat until the rice is tender and the liquid has been absorbed, 35 to 40 minutes. Remove from the heat and let steam for 15 minutes. Fluff the rice with a fork and season with salt. Transfer to a serving bowl, garnish with mint leaves and serve. —*Akasha Richmond*

RECIPE IMPROV

Jeweled Rice Pilaf

The pilaf at far left is fabulous as a side dish but can be transformed into a main course with just a few simple additions. F&W's **Kay Chun** shares three terrific ways to change it up:

THINK SPANISH For a paella hack, fold in steamed mussels, sautéed shrimp and diced chorizo during the last five minutes of cooking.

THINK BRUNCH Top the cooked rice with sunny-side-up eggs, drizzle with harissa olive oil and serve with grilled lamb merguez.

THINK HEARTY Add golden raisins and diced dried fruit. Fold in sautéed lamb or chicken and serve with yogurt and harissa.

Angry Pig Fried Rice

Active **30 min**; Total **1 hr**; Serves **4**

At Kings County Imperial in Brooklyn, chefs Josh Grinker and Tracy Jane Young make this version of fried rice using spicy pork jerky, a.k.a. "angry pig." Here, they substitute smoky bacon for the jerky and add chile-garlic sauce to bump up the heat. Their favorite store-bought sauce is Lan Chi Chili Paste with Garlic, available at Chinese markets and amazon.com.

- 1 cup jasmine rice
- ¾ tsp. whole Sichuan peppercorns
- 6 slices of bacon (5 oz.), chopped into 1-inch pieces
- 3 large eggs, beaten
  Kosher salt
- 1 Tbsp. finely chopped peeled fresh ginger
- ½ cup chopped scallions, plus more for garnish
- 4 oz. snow peas, thinly sliced on the diagonal (1⅔ cups)
- 5 oz. Asian-flavored marinated baked tofu, cut into ¼-inch dice (1 cup)
- 1½ tsp. chile-garlic sauce, plus more for serving
- 1 Tbsp. distilled white vinegar
- ½ tsp. toasted sesame oil
  Black pepper

1. In a medium saucepan, combine the rice with 1½ cups of water and bring to a boil. Cover, reduce the heat to low and cook until all of the liquid is absorbed and the rice is tender, about 20 minutes. Remove the pan from the heat and let stand, covered, for 10 minutes. Fluff the rice with a fork and spread out on a baking sheet to cool completely.

2. Meanwhile, in a small skillet, toast the Sichuan peppercorns over moderately low heat, stirring, until fragrant, 2 minutes. Let cool, then finely grind in a spice grinder.

3. In a large nonstick skillet, cook the bacon over moderate heat, stirring occasionally, until golden and crisp, about 5 minutes. Using a slotted spoon, transfer to a paper towel–lined plate to drain. Reserve 5 tablespoons of the bacon fat (if you don't have enough, use canola oil to get to 5 tablespoons); discard any remaining fat. Wipe out the skillet.

4. Heat 1 tablespoon of the reserved bacon fat in the skillet. Add the eggs, season with salt and cook over moderate heat, stirring constantly, until scrambled, about 30 seconds. Scrape the eggs into a small bowl.

5. Add 2 tablespoons of the bacon fat to the skillet along with the ginger and ½ cup of scallions and cook until softened, 1 minute. Stir in the snow peas and tofu and cook until the snow peas are crisp-tender, about 2 minutes. Add the remaining 2 tablespoons of bacon fat along with the 1½ teaspoons of chile sauce, the ground Sichuan peppercorns and the vinegar. Add the rice and cook, stirring, until combined and the rice is hot, about 2 minutes. Stir in the bacon, eggs and sesame oil and season with salt and pepper. Transfer the rice to a bowl, garnish with scallions and serve with chile sauce. —*Josh Grinker and Tracy Jane Young*

BEER Crisp, hoppy pilsner: Left Hand Brewing Polestar.

Indian Fried Rice with Chickpeas and Spinach

Total **20 min**; Serves **4**

F&W's Kay Chun creates a fast vegetarian one-bowl meal by stir-frying cooked rice with chickpeas, spinach and fragrant ginger and cumin.

- 3 Tbsp. canola oil
- 1 shallot, thinly sliced
- 1 Tbsp. minced peeled fresh ginger
- 1 tsp. cumin seeds
- 4 cups steamed basmati rice
  One 14½-oz. can chickpeas, rinsed
- 4 cups curly spinach
  Kosher salt and pepper
  Lemon wedges, for serving

In a large nonstick skillet, heat the oil. Add the shallot and ginger and cook over moderate heat, stirring occasionally, until the shallot is golden, about 3 minutes. Add the cumin, rice, chickpeas and spinach and cook, stirring, until the spinach is wilted, about 3 minutes. Season with salt and pepper. Serve with lemon wedges. —*Kay Chun*

WINE Peach-inflected, spicy Rhône white: 2014 Chateau de Campuget Blanc.

Arborio Rice Salad

Active **45 min**; Total **1 hr**; Serves **6**

Simple cold dishes like this rice salad are very popular in Rome in the summer. Katie Parla, the Rome-based blogger behind Parla Food, says any combination of meat, cheese and vegetables works here.

- 1½ cups arborio rice, rinsed and drained
- 1 cup fresh or thawed frozen peas (5 oz.)
- 3 large eggs
- 5 oz. scamorza or smoked mozzarella cheese, cut into ½-inch pieces (1 cup)
- 5 oz. mortadella, cut into ½-inch pieces (1 cup)
- 4 oz. cherry tomatoes, quartered (¾ cup)
- 1 Tbsp. chopped capers
  One 5-oz. can good-quality oil-packed tuna, drained and flaked
- 4 drained canned or thawed frozen artichoke hearts, thinly sliced lengthwise
- ½ cup chopped pitted kalamata olives (4 oz.)
- ⅓ cup chopped celery leaves
- ⅓ cup chopped basil
- 6 Tbsp. extra-virgin olive oil
- ¼ cup fresh lemon juice
  Kosher salt and pepper

1. Cook the rice in a large saucepan of salted boiling water until al dente, about 18 minutes. Add the peas and cook for 1 minute, then drain. Rinse the rice and peas under cold water to stop the cooking. Drain very well and transfer to a large bowl.

2. Meanwhile, in a saucepan, cover the eggs with water and bring to a boil. Remove from the heat, cover and let stand for 10 minutes. Drain, then cool the eggs under running water. Peel and quarter the eggs.

3. Add all of the remaining ingredients, except the eggs, to the rice in the bowl and mix well. Garnish the salad with the eggs, season with salt and pepper and serve. —*Katie Parla*

WINE Medium-bodied Tuscan white: 2013 Bibi Graetz Casamatta Bianco.

Rice and Peas

Active **25 min**; Total **2 hr plus overnight soaking**; Makes **12 cups**

The name for this typical Jamaican side dish is a bit of a misnomer, as the peas in the title are, in fact, kidney beans.

BEANS

- **2 cups dried kidney beans, soaked overnight and drained**
- **⅓ cup unsweetened coconut milk**
- **¼ cup unsweetened coconut cream**
- **14 thyme sprigs**
- **½ medium onion, finely chopped**
- **6 scallions, thinly sliced**
- **1½ tsp. kosher salt**
- **¼ tsp. ground allspice**

RICE

- **2 cups parboiled white rice**
- **1 cup unsweetened coconut milk**
- **½ cup finely chopped onion**
- **3 scallions, thinly sliced**
- **2 garlic cloves, minced**
- **2¼ tsp. kosher salt**

1. Prepare the beans In a large enameled cast iron casserole, combine the beans with the coconut milk, coconut cream, thyme sprigs, onion, scallions, salt and allspice. Add enough water to cover the beans by 2 inches and bring to a boil. Cover, reduce the heat to low and simmer until tender, about 1 hour. Drain the beans; discard the thyme sprigs.

2. Prepare the rice In a medium pot, combine the parboiled rice, coconut milk, onion, scallions, garlic, salt and 3¾ cups of water. Bring to a boil. Reduce the heat to moderately low, cover and simmer for 10 minutes.

3. Stir 4 cups of the drained beans into the rice. (Save the remaining 2 cups for another use.) Cover and cook for 10 minutes, then uncover and cook for 5 minutes longer. Fluff the rice and peas with a fork and serve. —*Adam Schop*

MAKE AHEAD The rice and peas can be refrigerated for up to 3 days. Reheat and fluff before serving.

Rice Congee with Pork Meatballs

⏱ Total **45 min**; Serves **4 to 6**

- **½ lb. ground pork**
- **2 Tbsp. Asian fish sauce, plus more for serving**
- **1 Tbsp. soy sauce**
- **Freshly ground white pepper**
- **8 cups chicken stock or low-sodium broth**
- **1 cup jasmine rice**
- **1 lemongrass stalk, cut into three 3-inch pieces and crushed**
- **5 dried Thai bird chiles, stemmed, or 1 Tbsp. crushed dried Thai chile**
- **¼ cup vegetable oil**
- **5 garlic cloves, thinly sliced**
- **1 serrano chile, seeded and minced**
- **¼ cup distilled white vinegar**
- **½ tsp. sugar**
- **Lime wedges, sliced scallions and chopped cilantro, for serving**

1. In a medium bowl, combine the pork with the 2 tablespoons of fish sauce, the soy sauce and a pinch of white pepper. Let stand for 10 to 30 minutes.

2. In a large enameled cast-iron casserole, combine the chicken stock, rice and lemongrass and bring to a boil over moderately high heat. Reduce the heat to low, cover partially and simmer until the rice is soft, about 25 minutes. Discard the lemongrass.

3. Meanwhile, in a small skillet, toast the dried chiles over moderate heat until lightly browned and fragrant, about 3 minutes. Transfer to a spice grinder and grind to a coarse powder; some seeds will remain. Transfer to a bowl and wipe out the skillet.

4. Heat the oil in the skillet. Add the garlic and cook over low heat until caramelized, about 10 minutes. Scrape the garlic oil into a small bowl. In another small bowl, combine the serrano, vinegar and sugar and stir until the sugar is dissolved.

5. Using a small ice cream scoop, make generous 1-inch meatballs with the ground pork. Drop into the rice and broth in the casserole. Cover and simmer over moderately high heat, stirring occasionally, until the meatballs are cooked through, about 10 minutes.

6. Ladle the congee into bowls. Serve with little bowls of the toasted chiles, fried garlic oil, chile vinegar, lime wedges, scallions, cilantro, white pepper and fish sauce. —*James Syhabout*

MAKE AHEAD The uncooked meatballs can be refrigerated overnight.

WINE Vibrant South African Chenin Blanc: 2014 Ken Forrester Petit.

Arroz Verde with Grilled Vegetables

Total **1 hr**; Serves **4 to 6**

The beauty of this simple dish is that the rice simmers in a bright salsa verde, absorbing all of its terrific flavor.

- **2 poblano chiles**
- **1 cup cilantro leaves plus 2 Tbsp. chopped cilantro**
- **½ cup minced white onion**
- **1 jalapeño, chopped**
- **2 garlic cloves**
- **Kosher salt**
- **1 Tbsp. vegetable oil**
- **1 cup long-grain white rice**
- **Grilled vegetables and grated Cotija cheese, for serving**

1. Roast the poblanos over a gas flame or under the broiler, turning, until charred all over. Transfer to a bowl, cover tightly with plastic wrap and let cool. Peel, stem and seed the poblanos, then chop them.

2. In a blender, combine the cup of cilantro leaves with the onion, jalapeño, garlic, chopped poblanos and ½ cup of water and puree until nearly smooth. Season the salsa verde with salt.

3. In a medium skillet, heat the oil. Add the rice and cook over moderately high heat, stirring, until opaque, 2 minutes. Add the salsa verde and cook, stirring, until the rice is coated. Stir in 2 cups of water, season with salt and bring to a boil. Cover and simmer over low heat until the rice is tender and the liquid is absorbed, 25 to 30 minutes. Remove from the heat and let stand, covered, for 15 minutes.

4. Fluff the rice with a fork and fold in the 2 tablespoons of chopped cilantro. Serve the rice topped with grilled vegetables and sprinkled with Cotija cheese. —*Deborah Schneider*

VEGETABLE QUINOA
BOWL WITH GARLIC
YOGURT

Vegetable Quinoa Bowls with Garlic Yogurt

Active **45 min**; Total **2 hr**; Serves **4 to 6**

- 1 head of garlic, halved crosswise
- ½ cup extra-virgin olive oil, plus more for drizzling
  Kosher salt and white pepper
- ¾ cup yogurt
- 1½ cups quinoa, rinsed and drained
- ¼ cup fresh lemon juice
- 2 tsp. honey
- ½ lb. green beans, cut into 1-inch pieces
- ½ lb. asparagus, cut into 1-inch pieces
- ½ lb. curly spinach (10 cups)
- 1½ cups thawed frozen peas
  Torn Bibb lettuce, diced cucumber, sliced avocado, sliced pickled ramps and kale chips, for serving

1. Preheat the oven to 350°. Arrange the garlic cut side up on a sheet of foil and drizzle with oil. Season with salt and white pepper and wrap it in the foil. Roast for about 1 hour, until very soft. Let cool, then squeeze the garlic cloves into a bowl and mash them to a paste. Whisk in the yogurt and season with salt and white pepper.

2. Meanwhile, in a large saucepan of salted boiling water, cook the quinoa until tender, about 10 minutes. Drain well and spread on a large baking sheet to cool.

3. In a medium bowl, whisk the ½ cup of olive oil with the lemon juice and honey. Season the lemon dressing with salt and white pepper.

4. Rinse out the saucepan. Fill it with water and bring to a boil. Add a generous pinch of salt along with the green beans, asparagus, spinach and peas and cook over high heat until the vegetables are crisp-tender, 1 to 2 minutes. Drain well.

5. Transfer the cooled quinoa to bowls and top with the warm vegetables. Top with lettuce, cucumber, avocado, pickled ramps and kale chips. Pass the lemon dressing and garlic yogurt at the table. —*José Andrés*

MAKE AHEAD The garlic yogurt and lemon dressing can be refrigerated for up to 3 days.

WINE Fresh northern Italian white: 2013 Alois Lageder Porer Pinot Grigio.

White Quinoa Grits with Shrimp and Mexican Grilled Corn

Total **1 hr 15 min**; Serves **4**

F&W Best New Chef 2015 Jonathan Brooks of Milktooth in Indianapolis puts a fun spin on buttery grits by making the dish with quinoa instead of cornmeal.

QUINOA GRITS

- 3 Tbsp. unsalted butter
- 2 small leeks, white and light green parts only, thinly sliced
- 2 garlic cloves, minced
- 4 cups chicken stock or low-sodium broth
- 1 cup white quinoa, rinsed and drained
  Kosher salt and pepper

SHRIMP AND CORN

- 2 Tbsp. extra-virgin olive oil
- ¼ cup pumpkin seeds
- 3 ears of corn, shucked
- 6 basil leaves, torn
- ½ cup chopped cilantro
- ¼ cup sliced scallions
  Kosher salt and pepper
- 1 Tbsp. unsalted butter
- 8 extra-large shrimp (1 lb.), peeled and deveined, heads left on
  Chile powder and crumbled Cotija cheese, for garnish
  Lime wedges, for serving

1. Make the grits In a medium saucepan, melt 1 tablespoon of the butter. Add the leeks and garlic and cook over moderate heat, stirring occasionally, until softened, about 5 minutes. Add the stock and bring to a boil. Whisk in the quinoa and cook, stirring occasionally, until tender and porridge-like, about 25 minutes. Stir in the remaining 2 tablespoons of butter and season with salt and pepper; keep warm.

2. Make the shrimp and corn In a large cast-iron skillet, heat 1 tablespoon of the olive oil until shimmering. Add the pumpkin seeds and cook over moderate heat, stirring, until golden, 2 minutes. Transfer to a paper towel–lined plate; let cool.

3. Wipe out the skillet. Add the corn and cook over moderately high heat, turning, until charred, 10 to 12 minutes. Cut the kernels off the cobs and transfer to a large bowl. Stir in the basil, cilantro and scallions and season with salt and pepper.

4. Wipe out the skillet and melt the butter in the remaining 1 tablespoon of oil. Season the shrimp with salt and pepper and cook over moderate heat, turning once, until just cooked through, about 3 minutes.

5. Spoon the quinoa grits into shallow bowls and top with the grilled corn, shrimp and pumpkin seeds. Garnish with chile powder and Cotija cheese and serve with lime wedges. —*Jonathan Brooks*

MAKE AHEAD The grits can be refrigerated for up to 2 days. Thin with chicken stock or water if they are too thick.

WINE Medium-bodied Spanish white: 2014 Oro de Castilla Verdejo.

Quinoa Pilaf with Dates, Olives and Arugula

Total **30 min**; Serves **4**

- 1½ cups white or red quinoa (9 oz.), rinsed and drained
- ⅓ cup chopped pitted Medjool dates
- ⅓ cup chopped pitted green olives
- 1 cup baby arugula
- 2 Tbsp. extra-virgin olive oil
- 2 Tbsp. fresh lemon juice
- ¼ cup sliced scallions
  Kosher salt and pepper

1. In a medium saucepan of boiling water, cook the quinoa until tender, about 10 minutes. Drain and return the quinoa to the pan. Cover and let stand for 10 minutes; fluff with a fork.

2. In a large bowl, toss the quinoa with the dates, olives, arugula, olive oil, lemon juice and scallions. Season with salt and pepper. Serve chilled or at room temperature. —*Kay Chun*

Quinoa with Yogurt and Sprouts

Active **45 min;** Total **1 hr;** Serves **6**

F&W Best New Chef 2015 Bryce Shuman of Betony in New York City combines three healthy ingredients (quinoa, yogurt and sprouts) in a dish that feels indulgent.

- 1 **cup quinoa, rinsed**
  Canola oil, for frying
  Kosher salt
- 3 **Tbsp. lemon olive oil**
- 2 **Tbsp. fresh lemon juice**
- 2 **Tbsp. minced shallot**
- 2 **Tbsp. minced chives**
- 1 **cup Greek yogurt**
  Extra-virgin olive oil, for drizzling
- 1½ **cups mixed radish and clover sprouts**

1. In a medium saucepan of salted boiling water, cook the quinoa until tender, about 10 minutes. Drain well and spread on a baking sheet. Let stand, stirring occasionally, until very dry, about 30 minutes.

2. Set a fine sieve over a heatproof bowl. In a medium skillet, heat ¼ inch of canola oil. Add half of the quinoa and fry over moderate heat, stirring, until the sizzling subsides and the quinoa is crisp, 1 to 2 minutes; drain in the sieve and spread on paper towels. Season with salt.

3. In a medium bowl, toss the cooked and crisped quinoa with the lemon oil, lemon juice, shallot and chives; season with salt.

4. Spread the yogurt on plates. Drizzle with olive oil and sprinkle with salt. Top with the quinoa and sprouts and serve.
—*Bryce Shuman*

WINE Focused, lively white Burgundy: 2013 Patrick Piuze Terroir de Chablis.

Warm Barley and Caramelized Mushroom Salad

Active **30 min;** Total **1 hr;** Serves **8 to 10**

- 2 **cups pearled barley**
- ½ **cup plus 2 Tbsp. extra-virgin olive oil**
- 2 **lbs. mixed mushrooms, stemmed and cut into bite-size pieces**
- 2 **tsp. chopped sage**
- ¼ **cup fresh lemon juice**
  Kosher salt and pepper

1. In a medium saucepan of boiling water, cook the barley until tender, about 30 minutes. Drain and transfer to a large bowl.

2. In a large skillet, heat 2 tablespoons of the olive oil. Add one-third of the mushrooms and cook over high heat, stirring, until golden brown, about 5 minutes. Transfer to the large bowl. Repeat in 2 more batches with 4 tablespoons of the oil and the remaining mushrooms. Add the sage, lemon juice and the remaining ¼ cup of oil to the bowl; season with salt and pepper, toss to coat and serve. —*Kay Chun*

MAKE AHEAD The salad can be kept at room temperature for up to 3 hours.

Five Healthy Food Swaps

Marco Canora, chef and author of *A Good Food Day*, reveals the simple substitutions that help him avoid everything from creeping weight gain to gout.

	BREAKFAST smart swap	
BREAKFAST CEREAL "Low in protein and fiber, it leaves you limp and hungry two hours later."		**STEEL-CUT OATS** "The fiber will keep you fuller longer, so you'll get to lunch without needing a snack."
CHEF'S SALAD "Sliced deli meats are pumped with salt, antibiotics, all that crap."	*LUNCH* smart swap	**GRAIN SALAD** "A no-brainer swap. You're getting fiber and nutrients, and it's lower in calories."
PROTEIN BAR "As a general rule, avoid foods that have colorful wrappers and bar codes."	*SNACK* smart swap	**LIME-ROASTED CASHEWS** "Toss raw nuts with lime juice and zest, add a pinch of curry powder and roast."
WHITE-FLOUR PASTA "Refined carbs cause blood sugar to spike, then drastically dip."	*DINNER* smart swap	**SPELT PASTA** "This intact-grain pasta made with an ancient strain of wheat balances carbs with protein."
BROWNIES FROM A BOXED MIX "Their jarringly sweet, artificial taste doesn't do it for me anymore."	*DESSERT* smart swap	**HOME-BAKED BROWNIES** "Now I make brownies with gluten-free hazelnut meal."

WARM BARLEY AND
CARAMELIZED
MUSHROOM SALAD

DIY Salad » Barley

The duo behind San Francisco's Rich Table, **EVAN AND SARAH RICH,** share their recipe for a tart and savory white soy vinaigrette to dress four amazing variations on barley salad.

Shiro Shoyu Vinaigrette
Makes 1¼ cups

In a medium bowl, whisk ½ cup **fresh lemon juice,** ½ cup **extra-virgin olive oil,** ¼ cup **shiro shoyu (white soy sauce)** or **low-sodium soy sauce** and ¼ cup minced **shallot** until well incorporated. Season with **kosher salt.**

PAN-ROASTED
SALMON
+
MARINATED
ARTICHOKES
+
RED ONION
+
CILANTRO

ROASTED
RADISHES
+
RAW RADISH
GREENS

ROASTED ACORN
SQUASH
+
GOAT CHEESE
+
MINT

Toss this tangy vinaigrette with cooked barley (whole-grain hulled or polished pearl) and any of the ingredient combinations here.

BROCCOLI RABE
+
CRISPY GARLIC
+
CHILE OIL
+
LEMON ZEST

Farro Tabbouleh with Burst Tomatoes

Active **20 min**; Total **1 hr**; Serves **4**

Top Chef judge Gail Simmons chars cut limes on the grill to make the smoky dressing for her riff on classic tabbouleh.

- 1 **pint cherry or grape tomatoes**
- 2 **garlic cloves**
- ¼ **cup plus 2 Tbsp. extra-virgin olive oil, plus more for brushing**
  Kosher salt and pepper
- 1½ **cups farro**
- 3 **limes, halved crosswise**
- 1 **shallot, finely chopped**
- 1 **Persian cucumber, finely chopped**
- 2 **cups arugula, chopped**
- 1 **cup parsley, finely chopped**
- ½ **cup mint, finely chopped**

1. Preheat the oven to 400°. On a foil-lined baking sheet, toss the tomatoes with the garlic and 2 tablespoons of the olive oil and season with salt and pepper. Roast for about 25 minutes, stirring occasionally, until the tomatoes are golden and some have burst. Transfer the baking sheet to a rack to cool. Chop the garlic.

2. Meanwhile, in a large saucepan of salted boiling water, cook the farro until tender, 12 to 15 minutes. Drain well.

3. Heat a grill pan. Brush the cut sides of the limes with oil and arrange them cut side down on the pan. Cook over moderately high heat, rotating occasionally, until charred, about 5 minutes. When the limes are cool enough to handle, squeeze them into a large bowl (you should have about ¼ cup of juice). Add the shallot and chopped garlic and gradually whisk in the remaining ¼ cup of olive oil until well blended. Season with salt and pepper. Add the farro, cucumber, arugula, parsley and mint and mix well; season with salt and pepper. Fold in the tomatoes and serve. —*Gail Simmons*

Whole-Grain Stuffing with Mustard Greens, Mushrooms and Fontina

Active **1 hr**; Total **2 hr 30 min**; Serves **12**

This stuffing is substantial enough to double as a vegetarian main dish; just substitute mushroom broth or water for the chicken stock.

- 4 **Tbsp. unsalted butter, plus more for greasing**
- 1 **cup farro**
- 1 **lb. whole-wheat bread, crusts removed, bread cut into 1-inch dice (8 cups)**
- ¼ **cup extra-virgin olive oil**
- 3 **leeks, light green and white parts only, thinly sliced**
- 6 **garlic cloves, finely chopped**
- 1 **lb. mustard greens, stemmed and coarsely chopped (12 packed cups)**
  Kosher salt and pepper
- 1 **lb. cremini mushrooms, quartered**
- 1½ **cups chicken stock or low-sodium broth**
- 1 **Tbsp. fresh lemon juice**
- 3 **large eggs, beaten**
- 3 **scallions, thinly sliced**
- 2 **cups shredded Italian Fontina cheese (6 oz.)**

1. Preheat the oven to 400°. Butter a 4-quart baking dish.

2. In a medium saucepan of salted boiling water, cook the farro until al dente, about 20 minutes. Drain well; transfer to a very large bowl.

3. Meanwhile, spread the bread on a large baking sheet and toast until golden and crisp, about 15 minutes. Transfer to the bowl with the farro.

4. In a large nonstick skillet, melt 2 tablespoons of the butter in 2 tablespoons of the olive oil. Add the leeks and garlic and cook over moderate heat, stirring occasionally, until softened, about 8 minutes. Stir in the mustard greens in batches and cook until wilted. Season with salt and pepper. Add the vegetables to the bowl.

5. In the same skillet, melt 1 tablespoon of the butter in 1 tablespoon of the olive oil. Add half of the mushrooms and season with salt and pepper. Cook over moderately high heat, stirring, until golden, about 3 minutes. Transfer to the bowl. Repeat with the remaining 1 tablespoon of butter, 1 tablespoon of oil and mushrooms.

6. Add the stock, lemon juice, eggs, scallions and 1 cup of the cheese to the bowl and mix well. Transfer the stuffing to the prepared baking dish and cover with foil. Bake for 40 minutes. Scatter the remaining cheese on top and bake uncovered for 25 to 30 minutes longer, until golden. —*Kay Chun*

MAKE AHEAD The assembled stuffing can be covered and refrigerated overnight.

Polenta Facile

Active **10 min**; Total **1 hr 45 min**; Serves **8**

The cooking method used here is great because you can leave the polenta pretty much unattended; in fact, the longer and more slowly it cooks, the better it is. Food52 executive editor Kristen Miglore adapted this recipe from *The Food of Southern Italy* by Carlo Middione.

- 2 **quarts water**
- 1 **Tbsp. kosher salt**
- 2 **cups polenta (not instant)**

1. Set a large heatproof bowl over a saucepan of simmering water; the bowl should be snug and its bottom should be submerged in 1 inch of water.

2. In another saucepan, bring the 2 quarts of water to a boil. Add the salt. Pour the water into the large bowl, then pour in the polenta in a slow stream while whisking constantly in one direction. Cook over moderate heat, whisking frequently, until the polenta thickens, about 5 minutes. Reduce the heat to low, cover the bowl and cook the polenta until tender and thick, about 1½ hours, stirring every 30 minutes. Scrape the polenta into a bowl and serve. —*Kristen Miglore*

MAKE AHEAD The cooked polenta can be refrigerated for up to 3 days. Reheat, adding water if it seems too thick.

Short Rib Farrotto with Carrots and Parsnips

Active **1 hr**; Total **1 hr 30 min**; Serves **6**

Farro is a chewy, earthy emmer wheat that's grown in Tuscany. For this dish, choose whole (unpearled) farro, which is the most intact form of the grain, including the nutritious bran and germ. Cooked risotto-style, as it is here, the grain releases its starch into the broth, making it creamy.

- 1 **quart low-sodium beef broth**
- 3 **Tbsp. extra-virgin olive oil**
- 2 **lbs. well-trimmed boneless grass-fed beef short ribs, cut into ½-inch pieces**
   Fine sea salt and pepper
- 2 **thyme sprigs plus 1 Tbsp. finely chopped thyme**
- 2 **garlic cloves, crushed**
- 8 **cipollini onions (¾ lb.), peeled and quartered**
- 1 **large carrot, cut into ½-inch pieces**
- 1 **large parsnip, cut into ½-inch pieces**
- 1½ **cups (9 oz.) unpearled farro**
- 1 **cup dry red wine**
- 1 **Tbsp. unsalted butter**
- ¼ **cup freshly grated Parmigiano-Reggiano cheese, plus more for serving**

1. In a medium saucepan, combine the beef broth with ½ cup of water and bring to a simmer over high heat. Remove from the heat, cover and keep warm.

2. In a large enameled cast-iron casserole, heat 2 tablespoons of the olive oil. Season the short ribs with salt and pepper. Add half of the short ribs to the casserole, spreading the pieces out, and cook over moderately high heat, turning occasionally, until browned, about 5 minutes. Using a slotted spoon, transfer the browned meat to a plate. Repeat with the remaining short ribs.

3. Add the remaining 1 tablespoon of olive oil to the casserole. Add the thyme sprigs, garlic, onions, carrot and parsnip and season with salt and pepper. Cook over moderate heat, stirring, until the vegetables are lightly browned, about 5 minutes. Stir in the farro and the browned short ribs. Add the wine and cook until evaporated, stirring and scraping the bottom of the casserole, about 2 minutes. Add 1 cup of the warm broth, cover partially and cook over moderately low heat for 15 minutes, stirring occasionally. Repeat this process twice, adding 1 cup of warm broth each time and cooking for about 15 minutes between additions, stirring occasionally.

4. Increase the heat to high. Add the remaining 1 cup of warm broth, ½ cup at a time and stirring constantly, allowing it to be absorbed before adding more. Cook the farrotto until creamy and the farro is al dente, about 5 minutes longer. Remove the casserole from the heat and discard the thyme sprigs. Stir in the butter, chopped thyme and the ¼ cup of grated Parmigiano. Season the farrotto with salt and pepper and serve hot, passing additional Parmigiano at the table. —*Marco Canora*

MAKE AHEAD The farrotto can be refrigerated for up to 2 days. Reheat gently, adding broth or water as necessary.

WINE Bold, cherry-rich Tuscan red: 2011 Fontodi Chianti Classico.

Snap Pea Falafel Salad

Total **20 min**; Serves **4 to 6**

- ¼ **cup extra-virgin olive oil**
- 2 **Tbsp. fresh lemon juice**
- 1 **tsp. cumin seeds, crushed**
- 1 **garlic clove, minced**
- ½ **lb. snap peas, chopped**
- 1 **tomato, chopped**
- 2 **scallions, thinly sliced**
- 1 **cup canned chickpeas**
- ⅓ **cup chopped parsley**
- 3 **cups cooked bulgur**
   Kosher salt and pepper

In a large bowl, whisk the olive oil with the lemon juice, cumin seeds and garlic. Add the snap peas, tomato, scallions, chickpeas, parsley and bulgur and season with salt and pepper. Mix well. —*Kay Chun*

Turkish Tabbouleh

Active **30 min**; Total **4 hr 30 min**; Serves **8**

This Turkish tabbouleh from Sasha Martin, the blogger behind Global Table Adventure, includes tomato paste and harissa. It's a spicier, richer-tasting version of the healthy, vegetable-rich dish.

- 2 **cups (12 oz.) medium-grade bulgur**
- ¼ **cup extra-virgin olive oil**
- 3 **Tbsp. tomato paste**
- 2 **Tbsp. fresh lemon juice**
- 1 **Tbsp. harissa**
   Kosher salt
- 2 **cups boiling water**
- 2 **tomatoes, cut into ¼-inch dice**
- ⅓ **cup finely chopped red onion**
- ½ **hothouse cucumber, cut into ¼-inch dice**
- 1 **yellow bell pepper, seeded and cut into ¼-inch dice**
- 1 **cup chopped parsley**
- ½ **cup thinly sliced scallions**
- ½ **cup chopped mint**

1. In a large heatproof bowl, combine the bulgur, olive oil, tomato paste, lemon juice and harissa and season with salt. Mix well, then stir in the boiling water. Add the remaining ingredients except the mint and mix well. Cover and refrigerate until the bulgur is tender, about 4 hours.

2. Season the tabbouleh with salt and stir in the mint. Transfer to a platter and serve. —*Sasha Martin*

MAKE AHEAD The tabbouleh can be refrigerated overnight.

Warm Lentils with Smoked Trout and Poached Eggs

Total **30 min**; Serves **6**

Justin Chapple, star of F&W's Mad Genius Tips videos, uses the oven to poach up to 12 eggs at a time. His clever technique: He cracks each egg into a muffin tin with a little bit of water in the cups.

1½ cups green lentils

8 oz. boneless smoked trout fillet, skin removed, trout broken up into large flakes

5 oz. baby spinach

⅓ cup snipped chives

¼ cup fresh lemon juice

3 Tbsp. extra-virgin olive oil

Kosher salt and pepper

6 large eggs

1. Preheat the oven to 350°. In a medium saucepan, cover the lentils with water and bring to a boil. Simmer over moderate heat until tender, about 20 minutes. Drain well and transfer to a large bowl. Fold in the trout, spinach, chives, lemon juice and olive oil and season with salt and pepper.

2. Pour 1 tablespoon of water into 6 cups of a 12-cup muffin tin. Crack an egg into each of the 6 water-filled cups and season with salt and pepper. Bake the eggs for 13 to 15 minutes, until the whites are just firm and the yolks are still runny. Spoon the lentil salad onto plates. Using a slotted spoon, immediately transfer the eggs to the plates and serve. —*Justin Chapple*

WINE Zesty, crisp Muscadet: 2013 Michel Delhommeau Harmonie.

Red Lentil Dal with Coconut Milk and Kale

Active **30 min**; Total **1 hr**; Serves **6**

These creamy, superflavorful lentils are served with vibrant toppings: spice-cooked onions, sliced red chiles and cilantro.

3 Tbsp. coconut oil

1 tsp. cumin seeds

1 tsp. fennel seeds

1 tsp. ground turmeric

2 onions, halved and thinly sliced

3 garlic cloves, finely chopped

2 Tbsp. finely chopped fresh ginger

2 small fresh red chiles, thinly sliced

1 quart chicken stock or broth

One 14-oz. can unsweetened coconut milk

2 cups red lentils, picked over (13 oz.)

2 Tbsp. chopped cilantro stems, plus chopped leaves for garnish

½ lb. kale, stemmed and leaves coarsely chopped (4 cups)

1½ tsp. fresh lemon juice, plus lemon wedges for serving

Sea salt and pepper

1. In a large saucepan, heat 1 tablespoon of the coconut oil. Add the cumin, fennel and turmeric and cook over moderate heat, stirring constantly, until fragrant, about 1 minute. Stir in the remaining 2 tablespoons of coconut oil and the onions and cook, stirring occasionally, until softened, 6 to 7 minutes. Add the garlic, ginger and half of the sliced chiles and cook, stirring, for 1 minute. Spoon half of the spiced onion mixture into a small bowl and reserve.

2. Add the chicken stock, coconut milk, red lentils and cilantro stems to the saucepan and bring to a simmer. Cook over moderately low heat, stirring occasionally, until the lentils are tender, about 20 minutes. Add the kale and cook until tender, about 5 minutes. Stir in the lemon juice and season with salt and pepper.

3. Spoon the dal into bowls. Top with the reserved onion mixture and the remaining sliced chiles. Garnish with chopped cilantro and serve with lemon wedges. —*Jasmine and Melissa Hemsley*

WINE Juicy Loire Valley Chenin Blanc: 2013 Vincent Raimbault Bel Air Vouvray Sec.

Red Lentil Dal with Mustard Seeds

Active **35 min**; Total **1 hr**; Serves **8 to 10**

L.A. chef Akasha Richmond makes this fragrant, soothing lentil dal to eat with rice, but it's equally delicious on its own.

4 cups red lentils (1½ lbs.), picked over

2 bay leaves

1 tsp. ground turmeric

¼ cup ghee (see Note on p. 241)

1½ Tbsp. brown mustard seeds

2 tsp. cumin seeds

1 large onion, minced

¼ cup minced peeled fresh ginger

One 28-oz. can whole peeled tomatoes, drained and chopped

1 serrano chile, minced

2 tsp. ground coriander

Kosher salt and pepper

Yogurt and chopped cilantro, cucumber and tomato, for serving

1. In a large cast-iron casserole, combine the red lentils with the bay leaves, turmeric and 12 cups of water and bring to a boil. Simmer over moderate heat, stirring frequently, until the lentils break down to a thick puree, about 40 minutes. Discard the bay leaves.

2. Meanwhile, in a large skillet, heat the ghee. Add the mustard and cumin seeds and cook over moderately high heat, stirring, until the seeds start to pop, about 1 minute. Add the onion and ginger and cook, stirring occasionally, until the onion is softened and lightly browned, about 8 minutes. Stir in the tomatoes, chile and coriander and cook until the tomatoes just start to break down, about 5 minutes. Season the tomato mixture with salt and pepper.

3. Stir the tomato mixture into the dal and cook over moderate heat for 10 minutes, stirring occasionally. Season with salt and pepper. Serve with yogurt and chopped cilantro, cucumber and tomato. —*Akasha Richmond*

MAKE AHEAD The dal can be refrigerated for 3 days. Reheat gently.

Black Bean Tamales with Cheese and Ancho Adobo

Active **1 hr**; Total **2 hr 45 min**; Serves **4**

ANCHO ADOBO

- **1½** oz. ancho chiles—stemmed, seeded and broken into small pieces
- **1** Tbsp. minced white onion
- **1** minced garlic clove
- **1** Tbsp. distilled white vinegar
- **½** tsp. kosher salt

TAMALES

- **12** dried cornhusks
- **1¾** cups masa harina, preferably Bob's Red Mill
- **3½** oz. lard, softened
- **¾** cup canned black beans, rinsed and drained
- **¼** cup chopped cilantro
- **¼** cup chopped epazote or 1 Tbsp. chopped oregano
- **1** Tbsp. thinly sliced scallion
- **2** tsp. kosher salt
- **¾** cup grated queso canasta or Monterey Jack cheese, plus more for serving

1. Make the ancho adobo In a small heat-proof bowl, cover the anchos with boiling water; let stand until softened, 15 minutes. Drain, discarding the soaking liquid. In a food processor, combine the anchos, onion, garlic, vinegar and salt; puree until smooth. Transfer to a small bowl.

2. Make the tamales In a large bowl, cover the cornhusks with hot water. Weigh down the husks with a plate and let stand until softened, about 30 minutes. Drain and pat dry with paper towels.

3. Meanwhile, in the bowl of a stand mixer fitted with the paddle, combine the masa with 1 cup plus 2 tablespoons of water. Beat at low speed until a dough forms, 2 minutes. Add the lard, beans, herbs, scallion and salt and beat, scraping down the side of the bowl, until the mixture is well blended and light in texture, 5 minutes.

4. For each tamale, spoon ¼ cup of the masa in the center of a cornhusk and top with 1 tablespoon of grated cheese and 1 teaspoon of ancho adobo. Roll the husks up and over the filling to make compact cylinders, folding in the sides as you go. Tie the tamales with kitchen string.

5. Arrange the tamales in a steamer basket and set it over a pot of boiling water. Cover and steam until firm, about 1 hour. Remove the steamer basket and let the tamales stand for 15 minutes. Serve with grated cheese and the remaining adobo.
—*Enrique Olvera*

MAKE AHEAD The ancho adobo can be refrigerated for up to 1 week. The uncooked tamales can be frozen for up to 1 month.

WINE Juicy, medium-bodied Spanish red: 2013 Altovinum Evodia Garnacha.

Kurdish White Beans with Tomatoes and Dried Lime

Active **15 min**; Total **1 hr 30 min plus overnight soaking**; Serves **4**

In Iraqi Kurdistan, there's a category of simmered dishes called shley that are spiced with cumin and turmeric and usually include tomato. Cookbook author Naomi Duguid learned to make this shley from a cook near the Iranian border. Dried lime provides the aroma and nuance that make the pot of beans special. It's available at Middle Eastern markets and online from kalustyans.com.

- **1½** cups dried navy beans, soaked overnight
  Kosher salt
- **2** Tbsp. extra-virgin olive oil
- **1** tsp. ground cumin
- **¼** tsp. ground turmeric
- **½** cup crushed tomatoes
- **1** dried lime, pierced in several places
  Feta, bread and fresh herbs and greens, such as parsley, watercress and scallions, for serving

1. Drain the beans. In a large saucepan, cover the beans with water and bring to a boil. Simmer gently until tender, 35 to 40 minutes. Off the heat, add a generous pinch of salt and let stand for 5 minutes, then drain.

2. Heat the oil in the saucepan. Add the cumin and turmeric and stir for 1 minute. Add the beans, tomatoes, dried lime and 1½ cups of water. Bring to a boil, cover partially and simmer for 25 minutes. Discard the lime and season the beans with salt. Serve with feta, bread and fresh herbs and greens. —*Naomi Duguid*

Stewed White Beans with Green Chile and Herbs

Active **20 min**; Total **1 hr 20 min plus overnight soaking**; Serves **6**

This recipe was inspired by a dish Fez cooking teacher Tara Stevens had in Marrakech. There, the stewed beans were made with chile powder; Stevens uses a chopped green chile instead to add fresh flavor. The beans are a great all-purpose side, particularly good with lamb chops.

- **1** lb. dried cannellini beans, soaked overnight and drained
- **2** Tbsp. extra-virgin olive oil, plus more for drizzling
- **1** medium onion, finely chopped
- **1** celery rib, finely chopped
- **3** garlic cloves, finely chopped
- **3** bay leaves
- **1** large poblano chile, seeded and finely chopped
  Kosher salt and pepper
- **½** cup dry vermouth or dry white wine
- **⅓** cup chopped mixed herbs, such as dill, tarragon and mint, for garnish

1. In a large saucepan, cover the beans with 2 inches of water and bring to a simmer. Cook over moderate heat, stirring occasionally, until the beans are tender, 30 to 40 minutes. Drain, reserving 1 cup of the cooking water.

2. Wipe out the saucepan and heat the 2 tablespoons of olive oil. Add the onion, celery, garlic, bay leaves and chile. Cook over moderate heat, stirring occasionally, until softened, 8 to 10 minutes. Discard the bay leaves and season with salt and pepper. Return the beans and the reserved cooking water to the saucepan. Stir in the vermouth and cook for 15 minutes, stirring occasionally, to meld the flavors. Season with salt and pepper. Spoon the beans into bowls and top with the chopped herbs. Drizzle with olive oil and serve warm.
—*Tara Stevens*

STEWED WHITE
BEANS WITH GREEN
CHILE AND HERBS

At Jon & Vinny's in L.A., chefs Jon Shook (left) and Vinny Dotolo crank out stellar wood-fired pies. They top their Supreme Pizza with mortadella and mustard greens (recipe, p. 266).

BREADS, SANDWICHES & PIZZAS

SCALLOP-AND-
BACON PIZZA
Recipe, page 267

GARLIC KNOTS WITH
FRIZZLED HERBS

Garlic Knots with Frizzled Herbs

Active **25 min**; Total **1 hr**; Serves **4 to 6**

Prepared pizza dough makes these tender pull-apart rolls easy to assemble. Brush them with garlic-infused butter as soon as they come out of the oven.

- **6 Tbsp. extra-virgin olive oil, plus more for greasing and brushing**
- **One 1-lb. ball of pizza dough, thawed if frozen**
- **Canola oil, for frying**
- **6 thyme sprigs**
- **6 small rosemary sprigs**
- **6 Tbsp. unsalted butter**
- **8 garlic cloves, thinly sliced**
- **¼ cup finely chopped parsley**
- **Kosher salt**

1. Preheat the oven to 450° and grease an 8-inch cast-iron skillet with olive oil. Cut the pizza dough into 8 wedges. Stretch each wedge slightly and gently tie into a loose knot, then transfer to the prepared skillet. Lightly brush the knots with olive oil. Cover with plastic wrap and let stand at room temperature for 20 minutes.

2. Remove the plastic and bake the knots for 20 to 25 minutes, until they are puffed and browned.

3. Meanwhile, in a medium saucepan, heat ¼ inch of canola oil until shimmering. Add the thyme sprigs and fry over moderately high heat until crisp, about 1 minute. Transfer to paper towels to drain. Add the rosemary sprigs to the hot oil and fry until crisp, about 1 minute; drain on paper towels.

4. Pour off the canola oil and wipe out the saucepan. Add the butter and 6 tablespoons of olive oil and cook until the butter is melted. Add the garlic and cook over moderate heat until lightly browned and crisp, 3 to 5 minutes. Stir in the parsley and season with salt. Brush the garlic butter all over the hot knots, top with the frizzled herbs and serve. —*Justin Chapple*

MAKE AHEAD The frizzled herbs can be stored at room temperature overnight.

Buttery Butternut Squash Rolls

Active **45 min**; Total **4 hr 30 min**; Makes **36**

- **1¼ cups whole milk**
- **½ cup butternut squash puree (see Note)**
- **2 Tbsp. sugar**
- **One 1-oz. packet active dry yeast**
- **1 large egg, beaten**
- **4¼ cups all-purpose flour, plus more for dusting**
- **2½ tsp. table salt**
- **1 stick unsalted butter, cut into tablespoons, plus 6 Tbsp. melted butter**
- **Canola oil, for greasing**

1. In a small saucepan, combine the milk, squash puree and sugar and cook over low heat, whisking, until the milk is lukewarm and the sugar is dissolved. Remove the pan from the heat. Whisk in the yeast and egg; let stand until foamy, 10 minutes.

2. In a stand mixer fitted with the paddle, beat the 4¼ cups of flour and the salt at low speed just to combine. With the machine on, slowly add the milk mixture and beat until incorporated, about 1 minute. Beat in 1 tablespoon of the butter until it's completely incorporated; scrape down the side of the bowl. Add the remaining 7 tablespoons of butter, 1 tablespoon at a time. Beat the dough until well combined, about 2 minutes.

3. Fit the mixer with the dough hook. Knead the dough at medium speed until smooth, occasionally scraping down the side of the bowl and dusting with 1 to 2 tablespoons of flour if the dough sticks, about 5 minutes. Transfer the dough to a lightly oiled bowl, turn to coat with oil and cover with plastic wrap. Let stand in a warm place until doubled in bulk, about 2 hours.

4. Line 2 baking sheets with parchment paper. Gently press down on the dough; it should be tacky. Divide the dough into 36 equal pieces and cover with plastic wrap. Gently squeeze 1 piece of dough through your thumb and index finger to form a ball; pinch the bottom. Place the ball pinched side down on a prepared baking sheet. Repeat with the remaining pieces of dough, spacing the balls 1½ inches apart. Loosely cover the rolls with plastic wrap and let rest in a warm place until doubled in size, about 1 hour.

5. Preheat the oven to 400°. Brush the tops of the rolls with the melted butter. Bake for 15 to 18 minutes, until golden and cooked through, shifting the pans from top to bottom and front to back halfway through baking. Serve warm. —*Carla Hall*

NOTE To make the puree, boil 1 cup of 1-inch-diced butternut squash for 20 minutes, then drain and puree.

Cheddar-Jalapeño Biscuits

Active **30 min**; Total **1 hr 15 min**
Makes **about 14**

- **2¼ cups all-purpose flour**
- **2 Tbsp. sugar**
- **2½ tsp. baking powder**
- **½ tsp. baking soda**
- **½ tsp. kosher salt**
- **1 stick cold unsalted butter, cubed**
- **1 cup cold whole milk**
- **1 cup shredded aged cheddar cheese**
- **¼ cup finely chopped pickled jalapeños**
- **1 large egg, lightly beaten**

1. Line a baking sheet with parchment paper. In a large bowl, whisk the flour with the sugar, baking powder, baking soda and salt. Scatter the cubed butter over the dry ingredients and, using your fingers, pinch the butter into the flour until the mixture resembles very coarse crumbs, with some of the butter the size of small peas. Gently stir in the milk, cheddar and jalapeños just until a shaggy dough forms.

2. Turn the biscuit dough out onto a lightly floured work surface and knead gently just until it comes together. Pat the dough out to a ½-inch-thick rectangle. Using a 3-inch round biscuit cutter, stamp out 10 to 12 biscuits. Gently press the scraps together and stamp out more biscuits. Arrange on the prepared baking sheet and freeze for 30 minutes.

3. Preheat the oven to 375°. Brush the biscuits with the beaten egg and bake until golden brown, about 15 minutes. Serve hot or warm. —*Matthew DeMille*

MAKE AHEAD The unbaked biscuits can be transferred to a sturdy plastic bag and frozen for up to 1 week.

Fig-and-Rosemary Focaccia with Pecorino

Active **25 min**; Total **4 hr 20 min**; Serves **8**

New York City chef Marco Canora makes this focaccia with whole-wheat flour. He prefers freshly milled, small-batch versions like those from Cayuga Pure Organics (cporganics.com).

- ¾ **cup extra-virgin olive oil, plus more for greasing**
- 1½ **cups warm water**
- 2½ **tsp. active dry yeast**
- 1½ **tsp. sugar**
- 3¾ **cups whole-wheat flour**
- 2 **Tbsp. chopped rosemary**
  Fine sea salt
- 12 **plump dried Black Mission figs (5 oz.)**
  Boiling water
  Black pepper
- ½ **cup freshly grated Pecorino Romano cheese**

1. Grease the bottom of a large bowl with olive oil. Pour the warm water into the bowl of a stand mixer fitted with the dough hook. Evenly sprinkle the yeast and sugar over the water. Mix at low speed until combined, about 30 seconds. Add the flour, rosemary, ½ cup of the olive oil and 4 teaspoons of salt and mix at medium speed until a dough forms, about 5 minutes; it will be a little sticky. Form the dough into a ball and transfer to the greased bowl. Cover tightly with plastic wrap and let stand at room temperature until it doubles in bulk, about 2 hours.

2. Punch the dough down in the bowl and form it into a loose ball. Cover with plastic wrap and let stand at room temperature for 1 hour.

3. Meanwhile, in a small heatproof bowl, cover the figs with boiling water. Let stand until softened, 1 hour. Drain the figs and slice them ¼ inch thick.

4. Lightly grease a 9-by-13-inch rimmed baking sheet. Transfer the dough to the prepared sheet and, using your fingertips, press it out to fill the sheet. Cover with plastic wrap and let rise at room temperature for 30 minutes.

5. Preheat the oven to 375°. Arrange the fig slices all over the dough; gently press them in. Drizzle with 2 tablespoons of the olive oil and season with salt and pepper. Sprinkle the cheese over the top. Bake for 25 to 30 minutes, rotating the sheet halfway through, until golden and firm. Let cool slightly on a rack. Drizzle with the remaining 2 tablespoons of olive oil and serve warm or at room temperature.
—*Marco Canora*

Multilayered Walnut Bread

Active **30 min**; Total **3 hr**
Makes **one 10-inch loaf**

- 3 **cups plus 2 Tbsp. all-purpose flour**
- 1 **cup yogurt**
- ½ **cup canola oil**
- 1 **Tbsp. baking powder**
- 1½ **tsp. kosher salt**
- 1 **cup extra-virgin olive oil**
- 2½ **cups coarsely chopped walnuts (10 oz.)**
- 1 **large egg, beaten**
  Caraway seeds, for garnish

1. In a large bowl, combine the flour with the yogurt, canola oil, baking powder, salt and ½ cup of water. Mix with a wooden spoon until a soft dough forms. On a lightly floured work surface, knead the dough until smooth, about 5 minutes. Transfer the dough to a clean bowl, cover with a kitchen towel and let stand at room temperature for 1 hour.

2. Lightly grease a 10-inch round cake pan. Cut the dough into 4 equal pieces. Working with 1 piece at a time, on a lightly floured work surface and using a lightly floured rolling pin, roll out the dough to a 14-inch round. Transfer to a large rimmed baking sheet and brush the dough with ¼ cup of the olive oil. Scatter one-fourth of the walnuts on top in an even layer. Arrange another dough round on top and brush with ¼ cup of the oil; scatter one-fourth of the nuts on top. Repeat the layering with the remaining pieces of dough, olive oil and walnuts. Roll up tightly into a long log.

3. Transfer the log to the prepared cake pan, forming a big spiral. Press gently to flatten, then brush with the beaten egg and sprinkle with caraway seeds. Let stand for 20 minutes.

4. Preheat the oven to 350°. Bake the bread for 50 to 60 minutes, until golden and cooked through. Transfer to a rack to cool. Serve warm or at room temperature. —*Scott Conant*

MAKE AHEAD The bread can be stored in an airtight container at room temperature for up to 3 days.

Pain d'Épices

Active **20 min**; Total **2 hr**
Makes **one 9-by-4-inch loaf**

"This pain d'épices is a staple *goûter* (teatime) dish for my family," says French blogger Mimi Thorisson of her hearty, spiced bread. "When the kids come home from school, they devour a whole loaf."

- 4 **Tbsp. salted butter, melted and cooled, plus more for greasing**
- 1 **cup honey**
- 1 **tsp. ground cinnamon**
- 1 **tsp. ground ginger**
- ½ **tsp. ground cloves**
- ½ **tsp. freshly grated nutmeg**
  Pinch of saffron threads
- 1 **cup whole-wheat flour**
- ½ **cup all-purpose flour**
- ½ **cup buckwheat flour**
- 1 **tsp. baking powder**
- 1 **tsp. baking soda**

1. Preheat the oven to 400°. Lightly butter a 9-by-4-inch loaf pan.

2. In a small saucepan, combine the honey, cinnamon, ginger, cloves, nutmeg, saffron and ¾ cup of water and bring to a simmer, whisking until smooth. Remove from the heat and let stand for 15 minutes.

3. In a large bowl, whisk the three flours with the baking powder, baking soda and melted butter. Add the honey mixture and whisk until smooth. Scrape the batter into the prepared pan and bake for about 30 minutes, until the loaf is deeply browned and a cake tester inserted in the center comes out clean. Transfer the loaf to a rack and let cool to room temperature, about 1 hour. Unmold and serve. —*Mimi Thorisson*

MAKE AHEAD The loaf can be stored in an airtight container at room temperature for 3 days or refrigerated for 1 week.

DIY RYE BREAD

Master baker **LIONEL VATINET** of La Farm Bakery in Cary, North Carolina, shares his recipe for the ultra-crusty, extra-flavorful, Scandi-style rye bread his family loves.

Scandivanian Rye Bread

Active **35 min**; Total **5 hr 45 min**
Makes **one 9-by-5 inch loaf**

- ½ cup rye berries, rinsed and drained
- 5¼ cups warm water
- ½ cup millet, rinsed and drained
- 1 envelope (¼ oz.) active dry yeast
- 4 cups whole-grain rye flour
- 1 cup bread flour
- 2 Tbsp. fine sea salt
- 1¼ cups rolled oats
- Vegetable oil, for greasing

MAKE THE DOUGH

1. In a small saucepan, cover the rye berries with 2 cups of the water and bring to a boil. Simmer gently over moderately low heat until all of the water has been absorbed and the rye berries are al dente, about 40 minutes. Spread the rye berries on parchment paper and let cool completely.

2. Meanwhile, in another small saucepan, cover the millet with 1 cup of the water and bring to a boil. Reduce the heat to moderately low and simmer until all of the water has been absorbed and the millet is halfway to tender, about 12 minutes. Spread the millet on parchment paper and let cool completely.

3. In the bowl of a stand mixer fitted with the paddle, mix the yeast with the remaining 2¼ cups of water and let stand until foamy, 10 minutes. Add both of the flours and the salt and mix at low speed for 5 minutes. Increase the speed to medium and mix for 2 minutes. Mix in the cooled rye berries and millet along with ¾ cup of the rolled oats. Scrape the dough into a greased large bowl and cover with plastic wrap. Let stand in a warm spot until doubled, about 2 hours.

SHAPE AND BAKE THE BREAD

4. Scatter the remaining ½ cup of oats on a work surface and scrape the dough onto them. Roll the dough until coated with the oats, then pat into a large brick shape. Transfer the dough to a greased 9-by-5-inch loaf pan and cover with a damp kitchen towel. Let stand in a warm spot until slightly risen, about 1½ hours.

5. Preheat the oven to 450°. Bake the bread for 55 minutes to 1 hour, until lightly browned on top and an instant-read thermometer inserted in the center registers 200°. Transfer to a rack and let cool for 30 minutes. Unmold the bread and let cool completely.

MAKE AHEAD The bread can be kept wrapped in plastic at room temperature for up to 5 days.

BREAD-MAKING TUTORIAL

Vatinet uses heirloom whole-rye flour from Carolina Ground (carolinaground.com). Here's how he turns it into rye bread.

1
COOK THE GRAINS and then spread them out to cool to prevent gumminess.

2
MIX THE DOUGH INGREDIENTS, adding the cooled cooked whole grains at the end.

3
ROLL THE DOUGH in oats. As the bread bakes, the oat crust gets crisp.

4
UNMOLD AND COOL THE BREAD completely before slicing into the loaf.

PULL-APART
SALT-AND-PEPPER
BISCUITS

Pull-Apart Salt-and-Pepper Biscuits

Active **15 min**; Total **1 hr**; Makes **14**

2½ cups all-purpose flour

4 tsp. baking powder

1 Tbsp. freshly ground black pepper

1 tsp. kosher salt

1 stick plus 2 Tbsp. cold unsalted butter, cubed, plus melted butter for greasing and brushing

1¼ cups buttermilk

1. Preheat the oven to 350°. In a large bowl, whisk the flour with the baking powder, pepper and salt. Using your fingertips, blend in the cubed butter until pea-size pieces form. Stir in the buttermilk just until a dough forms. Pat the dough into a 1-inch-thick round.

2. Grease a 12-inch cast-iron skillet with melted butter. Using a 2-inch-round biscuit cutter, stamp out dough rounds and arrange them almost touching in the skillet. Gather and pat out the scraps and stamp out the last few biscuits. Brush the tops with melted butter and bake for 40 minutes, until golden. Transfer to a rack to cool slightly before serving. —*Kay Chun*

Spicy Thai Coconut Mini Biscuits

Active **20 min**; Total **40 min**
Makes **about 4 dozen**

2¾ cups all-purpose flour

4 tsp. baking powder

1 tsp. baking soda

1 tsp. kosher salt

1 stick plus 2 Tbsp. cold unsalted butter, cubed

1¼ cups unsweetened coconut milk

One 4-oz. jar Thai red curry paste

1. Preheat the oven to 350°. Line a baking sheet with parchment paper. In a large bowl, whisk the flour with the baking powder, baking soda and salt. Using your fingertips, blend in the butter until pea-size pieces form. Stir in the coconut milk and curry paste just until a dough forms.

2. On a lightly floured surface, pat the dough into a 7-inch square. Cut the dough into 1-inch square biscuits and transfer to the baking sheet. Bake for 20 minutes, until cooked through. Transfer to a rack to cool slightly before serving. —*Kay Chun*

Ten-Grain Porridge Bread

Active **1 hr**; Total **6 hr plus 2 days soaking and fermenting**
Makes **two 10-inch round loaves**

9 oz. Bob's Red Mill 10 Grain Hot Cereal (1¾ cups)

3½ cups all-purpose flour

¼ tsp. active dry yeast

4¼ cups bread flour

1 Tbsp. fine sea salt

1. In a large bowl, cover the cereal with 3 inches of water. Cover the bowl with cheesecloth or a kitchen towel and let stand at room temperature for 48 hours. Drain through a cheesecloth-lined sieve; reserve 1½ cups of the soaking water.

2. Meanwhile, in another large bowl, mix the all-purpose flour with the yeast and 1 cup of water until the dough starts to come together. Turn the dough out onto a work surface and knead until a smooth ball forms, about 3 minutes. Wipe out the bowl and return the dough to it. Cover the bowl with plastic wrap and refrigerate the dough for 48 hours. This is the pâte fermentée.

3. In the bowl of a stand mixer fitted with the dough hook, combine the bread flour, sea salt, pâte fermentée, reserved soaking water and 2 cups (1 pound) of the soaked cereal; there may be some soaked cereal left over. Knead at low speed until the dough starts to come together, about 3 minutes. Cover with a kitchen towel and let stand for 20 minutes. Knead again at low speed for 5 minutes, until the dough is moist and smooth. Transfer the dough to a lightly greased bowl, cover and let rise at room temperature until doubled in bulk, about 2 hours.

4. Line 2 large bowls with kitchen towels or dust generously with flour. Divide the dough into 2 equal pieces and form each into a ball. Set the balls seam side up in the prepared bowls. Cover with kitchen towels and let stand at room temperature until doubled in bulk, about 2 hours.

5. Preheat the oven to 450°. Line 2 baking sheets with parchment paper. Place another baking sheet on the bottom of the oven and pour in 2 cups of water. Turn the dough rounds out onto the prepared sheets and bake for about 40 minutes, rotating and shifting the sheets halfway through baking, until the loaves are deep golden and crisp. Transfer to a rack to cool. —*Zakary Pelaccio*

MAKE AHEAD The loaves can be stored in an airtight container overnight, then refrigerated for 1 week.

Mexican Street Corn Drop Biscuits

Active **25 min**; Total **1 hr 25 min**
Makes **about 3 dozen**

In a nod to Mexican street corn, F&W's Kay Chun packs these chunky biscuits with corn, cheese, cilantro and lime zest.

2½ cups all-purpose flour

4 tsp. baking powder

½ tsp. kosher salt

1 stick plus 2 Tbsp. cold unsalted butter, cubed

2 cups grated Cotija cheese (7 oz.)

2 cups corn kernels

½ cup chopped cilantro

1 tsp. finely grated lime zest

1¼ cups heavy cream

1. Preheat the oven to 350°. Line 2 baking sheets with parchment paper. In a large bowl, whisk the flour with the baking powder and salt. Using your fingertips, blend in the butter until pea-size pieces form. Stir in the cheese, corn, cilantro, lime zest and heavy cream just until a soft dough forms. Spoon heaping 2-tablespoon mounds of dough onto the prepared baking sheets about 1 inch apart. Refrigerate for 30 minutes.

2. Bake the biscuits for 30 minutes, until golden. Transfer to a rack to cool slightly before serving. —*Kay Chun*

MAKE AHEAD The biscuits can be stored in an airtight container at room temperature overnight and reheated before serving.

Corn-Studded Corn Muffins with Honey Mascarpone

Active **20 min**; Total **50 min**; Makes **12**

F&W's Justin Chapple keeps his corn muffins light and moist by using buttermilk in the batter.

- 1 **cup all-purpose flour**
- 1 **cup finely ground cornmeal**
- ½ **cup sugar**
- 1 **Tbsp. baking powder**
  Kosher salt
- 2 **large eggs**
- 1 **cup buttermilk, at room temperature**
- 1 **stick unsalted butter, melted**
- 1 **cup fresh corn kernels (from about 1½ ears)**
- ½ **cup mascarpone cheese**
- 1½ **Tbsp. honey**

1. Preheat the oven to 350° and line a 12-cup muffin tin with paper or foil liners. In a medium bowl, whisk the flour with the cornmeal, sugar, baking powder and 1 teaspoon of salt. In a large bowl, beat the eggs with the buttermilk and melted butter. Whisk in the dry ingredients, then fold in the corn kernels.

2. Spoon the batter into the prepared muffin cups. Bake for 15 to 18 minutes, until a toothpick inserted in the center of the muffins comes out clean. Let the muffins cool in the pan for 10 minutes, then turn them out onto a wire rack to cool completely.

3. In a small bowl, whisk the mascarpone with the honey and a pinch of salt. Serve with the muffins. —*Justin Chapple*

MAKE AHEAD The corn muffins can be stored in an airtight container for up to 3 days.

Salt-and-Pepper Butter Crackers with Pimento Cheese

Active **1 hr**; Total **2 hr 45 min**; Serves **12**

TV chef Carla Hall makes her own buttery, crisp crackers to serve with her version of the classic Southern cheese spread.

CRACKERS

- 2 **cups all-purpose flour, plus more for dusting**
- 2 **cups whole-wheat pastry flour**
- 2 **Tbsp. baking powder**
- 2 **Tbsp. sugar**
- 1½ **tsp. table salt**
  Pepper
- 10 **Tbsp. unsalted butter, cubed and chilled, plus 3 Tbsp. melted butter**
- 6 **Tbsp. canola oil**
- ⅔ **cup plus 2 Tbsp. cold water**

PIMENTO CHEESE

- 2 **garlic cloves, crushed**
- 1 **jarred roasted red bell pepper, chopped**
- 8 **oz. sharp cheddar cheese, shredded (2 cups)**
- 8 **oz. Monterey Jack cheese, shredded (2 cups)**
- 4 **oz. cream cheese, at room temperature**
- ½ **cup mayonnaise**
- 1 **tsp. cayenne**
- 1 **tsp. kosher salt**

1. Make the crackers In a food processor, pulse both flours with the baking powder, sugar, table salt and ¼ teaspoon of pepper. Add the cubed butter and the oil and pulse until the mixture resembles coarse meal. Add the water and pulse just until the dough comes together. Transfer to a lightly floured work surface and knead several times. Divide the dough in half and form into two 1-inch-thick squares. Wrap in plastic and refrigerate for 1 hour.

2. Line 2 baking sheets with parchment paper. On a lightly floured work surface, using a lightly floured rolling pin, roll out 1 piece of dough to an ⅛-inch-thick square. Using a fluted pastry cutter, cut the dough into twenty-four 2½-inch squares. Arrange the crackers on the prepared baking sheets, spaced ½ inch apart. Poke 4 rows of holes in the center of each cracker. Freeze the crackers until firm, 30 minutes.

3. Preheat the oven to 400°. Brush the crackers with half of the melted butter; sprinkle with pepper. Bake for 12 to 15 minutes, shifting the pans halfway through. Transfer the crackers to a rack to cool. Repeat Steps 2 and 3 with the remaining cracker dough.

4. Meanwhile, make the pimento cheese In a food processor, pulse the garlic until finely chopped. Add all of the remaining ingredients and pulse until well blended. Scrape the pimento cheese into a large bowl and refrigerate for at least 1 hour before serving with the crackers. —*Carla Hall*

MAKE AHEAD The pimento cheese can be refrigerated for 1 week. The crackers can be kept in an airtight container overnight.

SALT-AND-PEPPER
BUTTER CRACKERS WITH
PIMENTO CHEESE

Leek-and-Scallion Fry Breads

Active **1 hr**; Total **1 hr 30 min**; Makes **6**

Malin Elmlid, the Berlin-based founder of The Bread Exchange barter site and blog, learned to make these crispy Afghani fry breads on a trip to Kabul. She serves them with a bright cilantro-walnut sauce for dipping.

  2 cups all-purpose flour
     Kosher salt and pepper
 ¾ cup warm water
  2 medium leeks, white and light green parts only, halved lengthwise and cut crosswise 1 inch thick
1½ Tbsp. extra-virgin olive oil
  6 scallions, chopped
1½ cups lightly packed cilantro leaves
 ⅓ cup walnuts
  3 Tbsp. fresh lime juice
  1 Tbsp. honey
  1 garlic clove
     Vegetable oil, for frying

1. Preheat the oven to 400°. In a large bowl, whisk the flour with 1½ teaspoons of salt. Make a well in the center of the flour and pour in the warm water. Using a fork, mix the water into the flour until a stiff, shaggy dough starts to come together. Turn the dough out onto a work surface and knead until smooth, about 10 minutes. Wrap the dough in plastic and let rest at room temperature for 30 minutes.

2. Meanwhile, on a large baking sheet, toss the leeks with the olive oil and season with salt and pepper. Bake for 30 to 35 minutes, stirring once or twice, until the leeks are lightly charred and tender. Let cool, then toss the leeks with the scallions and season with salt and pepper.

3. In a food processor, puree the cilantro with the walnuts, lime juice, honey and garlic until smooth. Generously season the sauce with salt and pepper.

4. Cut the dough into 6 pieces and roll into balls. On a lightly floured work surface, roll out the balls to 6-inch rounds, a scant ⅛ inch thick. Spoon 2 packed tablespoons of the leek-scallion filling on half of each round. Brush the edges with water, then fold the dough over to form half-moons. Flatten the breads to press out the air and pinch the edges to seal.

5. In a large saucepan, heat 2 inches of vegetable oil to 350°. In 2 batches, fry the breads until browned and crisp, about 5 minutes per batch. Transfer the fry breads to paper towels and sprinkle with salt. Serve warm with the cilantro sauce.
—*Malin Elmlid*

Armenian Beef Flatbreads with Garlicky Yogurt

Total **30 min**; Serves **4**

  4 flat pita breads
 ¼ lb. ground beef
 ½ small white onion, grated
 ½ small red bell pepper, minced
  1 tsp. tomato paste
  2 Tbsp. chopped unsalted pistachios
  2 Tbsp. chopped parsley
 ½ tsp. ground cumin
 ¼ tsp. dried oregano
 ⅛ tsp. allspice
  4 garlic cloves, minced
     Kosher salt
 ½ cup plain Greek yogurt
  1 tsp. fresh lemon juice
     Pickled vegetables, for serving

1. Preheat the oven to 425°. Arrange the pita breads on a parchment paper–lined baking sheet. In a medium bowl, combine the ground beef, onion, bell pepper, tomato paste, pistachios, parsley, cumin, oregano, allspice, half of the garlic and ¼ teaspoon of salt. Spread the meat mixture on the pitas in an even layer and bake for about 8 minutes, until the meat is browned in spots and cooked through.

2. In a small bowl, mix the yogurt with the lemon juice and remaining garlic. Season with salt. Serve the flatbreads with the garlicky yogurt and pickled vegetables.
—*Ana Sortun*

WINE Lively, earthy southern French red: 2013 Château Massiac Les Sentinelles Minervois Rouge.

The Supreme Pizza

Active **25 min**; Total **40 min**
Serves **6 to 8**

This is one of the star pizzas at Jon & Vinny's in Los Angeles. Chefs Jon Shook and Vinny Dotolo top the wood-fired pie with provolone, mortadella, mozzarella and mustard greens. For their sauce, they use excellent Bianco DiNapoli canned tomatoes from California.

     All-purpose flour, for dusting
     Two 8-oz. balls of pizza dough, thawed if frozen
 ¼ cup extra-virgin olive oil, plus more for brushing
 ⅔ cup crushed tomatoes
  1 packed cup coarsely chopped mustard greens
  1 cup shredded provolone piccante cheese (3 oz.)
  4 thin slices of mortadella (3 oz.), chopped into 1-inch pieces
 ¼ small red onion, thinly sliced
  3 oz. fresh mozzarella cheese, thinly sliced
  1 Tbsp. crushed red pepper
     Grated Grana Padano cheese, for garnish

1. Preheat the oven to 475°. On a lightly floured work surface, using a lightly floured rolling pin, roll out each ball of dough to a 10-inch round. Transfer each round to a separate baking sheet. Brush the dough with olive oil, then spread the crushed tomatoes on top, leaving a ½-inch border. Top with the mustard greens, provolone, mortadella, onion and mozzarella. Bake on the middle and bottom racks of the oven for about 15 minutes, shifting the sheets halfway through baking, until golden brown and cooked through.

2. In a small bowl, stir the crushed red pepper with the ¼ cup of olive oil. Drizzle the pizzas with some of the red pepper oil and garnish with Grana Padano. Pass the remaining red pepper oil at the table.
—*Jon Shook and Vinny Dotolo*

WINE Full-bodied Napa white: 2013 Forlorn Hope Sihaya Ribolla Gialla.

Tomato, Zucchini and Salami Pizzas

Active **50 min**; Total **2 hr 45 min**
Makes **two 12-inch pizzas**

DOUGH

1½ Tbsp. extra-virgin olive oil, plus more for greasing

¾ cup warm water

¾ tsp. active dry yeast

2½ cups all-purpose flour, plus more for dusting

Kosher salt

SAUCE

1 Tbsp. extra-virgin olive oil

1 small onion, finely chopped

3 garlic cloves, finely chopped

One 15-oz. can diced tomatoes

1 cup tomato puree

Pinch of crushed red pepper

Pinch of sugar

10 large basil leaves, torn

Kosher salt and black pepper

PIZZAS

8 slices of provolone cheese (6 oz.)

20 thin slices of spicy salami (4 oz.)

½ lb. baby zucchini with flowers (flowers optional)—zucchini thinly sliced, flowers halved lengthwise and pistils snipped off

½ lb. cherry tomatoes

Kosher salt and pepper

Dried oregano and extra-virgin olive oil, for serving

1. Make the dough Grease a large bowl with olive oil. In a small bowl, whisk the water with the yeast and let stand until foamy, about 5 minutes. In another large bowl, whisk the 2½ cups of flour with the salt. Make a well in the center of the flour and pour in the yeast mixture and the 1½ tablespoons of olive oil. Stir with a fork until the dough just starts to come together. Turn the dough out onto a generously floured work surface and knead until very smooth, about 5 minutes. Transfer the dough to the greased bowl, cover with plastic wrap and let rise in a warm place until doubled in bulk, about 1 hour.

2. Meanwhile, make the sauce In a large saucepan, heat the olive oil. Add the onion and garlic and cook over moderate heat, stirring occasionally, until just softened, about 4 minutes. Add the diced tomatoes, tomato puree, crushed red pepper, sugar and basil and bring to a boil. Simmer over moderately low heat, stirring occasionally, until thickened and reduced to 2 cups, about 18 minutes. Season the sauce with salt and black pepper.

3. Make the pizzas Preheat the oven to 450° for at least 30 minutes. Grease a large rimmed baking sheet. Cut the pizza dough into 2 pieces. On a lightly floured work surface, roll or stretch out 1 piece of the dough to a 12-inch round; transfer to the prepared baking sheet. Spread half of the sauce over the dough and top with half of the cheese, salami, zucchini and tomatoes. Season with salt and pepper. Bake the pizza for 15 to 18 minutes, until the crust is browned. Garnish with dried oregano and a drizzle of olive oil. Repeat with the remaining dough and toppings. Serve hot. —*Katie Quinn Davies*

WINE Fruity, refreshing Italian sparkling wine: NV Drusian Brut Prosecco.

Scallop-and-Bacon Pizza

📷 PAGE 257

⏱ Active **20 min**; Total **40 min**; Serves **4**

A quick-to-make garlicky béchamel stands in for crème fraîche and cheese in this luxurious white pizza.

3 garlic cloves, crushed

¼ cup plus 2 Tbsp. extra-virgin olive oil, plus more for drizzling

¼ cup all-purpose flour, plus more for dusting

1½ cups whole milk

¼ cup freshly grated Parmigiano-Reggiano cheese

2 Tbsp. fresh lemon juice

Kosher salt and pepper

Cornmeal, for dusting

1 lb. pizza dough

4 slices of thick-cut bacon (5 oz.)

4 sea scallops (5 oz.), sliced crosswise ¼ inch thick

1 cup baby arugula

1. Preheat the oven to 475°. In a medium saucepan, cook the garlic in ¼ cup of the olive oil over moderately low heat until it starts to sizzle, about 3 minutes. Whisk in the ¼ cup of flour until smooth and cook, whisking, until light golden, about 3 minutes. Slowly whisk in the milk and cook, whisking, until the béchamel is smooth and thickened, 2 to 3 minutes. Whisk in the cheese. Stir in 1 tablespoon of the lemon juice and season with salt and pepper. Transfer the béchamel to a small bowl. Discard the garlic.

2. Lightly dust a baking sheet with cornmeal. On a lightly floured work surface, using a lightly floured rolling pin, roll out the dough to a 12-inch round. Transfer to the prepared baking sheet. Brush the remaining 2 tablespoons of olive oil all over the dough and spread the béchamel evenly on top, leaving a 1-inch border around the edge. Bake on the bottom rack of the oven for about 18 minutes, until the dough is almost cooked through.

3. Meanwhile, in a medium nonstick skillet, cook the bacon slices over moderate heat, turning, until golden and crisp, 7 to 8 minutes. Transfer the bacon to paper towels to drain, then chop it.

4. Top the pizza with the scallops and drizzle with olive oil. Bake for about 3 minutes, until the béchamel is golden and bubbling and the scallops are just opaque.

5. In a small bowl, toss the arugula with the remaining 1 tablespoon of lemon juice. Top the pizza with the bacon and arugula and serve hot. —*Kay Chun*

WINE Succulent, pear-scented Chenin Blanc: 2014 A.A. Badenhorst Secateurs.

GRILLED PIZZA WITH
GREENS AND EGGS

Grilled Pizza with Greens and Eggs

Total **45 min;** Serves **4**

New York floral designer Sarah Ryhanen tops her easy grilled pizza with fresh ricotta, eggs and spigarello, a leafy green that tastes like broccoli—she says it's like eating green velvet. Spigarello is available at farmers' markets and from some green-grocers; Tuscan kale is a fine substitute.

- 1 Tbsp. extra-virgin olive oil, plus more for brushing and drizzling
- 6 oz. spigarello, chopped
- 2 garlic cloves, minced
- 1 tsp. crushed red pepper
  Kosher salt and black pepper
- 1 lb. store-bought pizza dough, thawed if frozen
- 1 cup fresh ricotta cheese
- 4 large eggs
  Grated pecorino cheese, for serving

1. In a large skillet, heat the 1 tablespoon of olive oil. Add the spigarello, garlic and crushed red pepper and cook over moderately high heat, stirring, until the spigarello is just wilted, about 3 minutes. Season with salt and black pepper.

2. Light a grill. On a lightly floured work surface, stretch the pizza dough out to a 15-inch-long oval and brush with olive oil. Oil the hot grill grate. Drape the dough on the grate oiled side down. Grill over moderately high heat until marks appear on the bottom and the dough is slightly puffed, about 3 minutes. Turn the dough over onto a lightly floured cookie sheet and brush with olive oil. Dollop the ricotta over the dough, leaving a 1-inch border. Scatter the spigarello on top. Crack 1 egg into a small bowl, then carefully slide it onto the pizza. Repeat with the remaining 3 eggs. Season the pizza with salt and pepper.

3. Slide the pizza back onto the grill. Close the grill and cook over moderate heat until the crust is browned and the egg whites are firm, about 5 minutes. Transfer the pizza to a carving board. Top with grated pecorino, drizzle with olive oil, cut into pieces and serve. —*Sarah Ryhanen*

WINE Lively, slightly herbal Italian white: 2013 ColleStefano Verdicchio di Matelica.

Alsatian Pizza

Active **30 min;** Total **1 hr**
Serves **8 to 10 as an appetizer**

This Canadian twist on a traditional Alsatian tarte flambée is topped with cheddar and smoky speck (a cured meat similar to prosciutto).

- 1 lb. pizza dough
  All-purpose flour, for dusting
- ⅔ cup crème fraîche
  Kosher salt and pepper
  Freshly grated nutmeg
- ⅔ cup shredded aged cheddar cheese
- 4 oz. thinly sliced speck
- 1 medium Vidalia onion, thinly sliced (1⅓ cups)

1. Set a pizza stone on the bottom rack of the oven and preheat to 500° for 30 minutes.

2. Cut the pizza dough in half and roll into balls. On a lightly floured surface, roll out each ball of dough to an 11-inch round. Transfer each round to a sheet of parchment paper. Spread half of the crème fraîche over 1 dough round and season with salt, pepper and nutmeg. Top with half of the cheddar, speck and onion. Slide the parchment paper onto the hot pizza stone and bake until the pizza is crisp, about 10 minutes. Transfer to a work surface, cut into wedges and serve hot. Repeat with the remaining dough round and toppings. —*David Mattachioni*

WINE Minerally white Alsace blend: 2013 Marcel Deiss Alsace Blanc.

Époisses Grilled Cheese and Pepper Jelly Sandwiches

Total **25 min;** Makes **4**

- ½ cup pecan halves
- 1 Tbsp. canola oil
- 1 tsp. kosher salt
- 4 Tbsp. unsalted butter, softened
  Eight ½-inch-thick slices of sourdough bread
- 4 Tbsp. hot pepper jelly
- 1 chilled round of Époisses cheese (8.8 oz.), cut into ¼-inch slices

1. Preheat the oven to 350°. In a pie pan, toss the pecans with the oil and salt. Bake for 8 minutes, or until toasted. Let the pecans cool, then coarsely chop.

2. Spread ½ tablespoon of butter on one side of each slice of bread. Spread ½ table-spoon of pepper jelly on the other side of each slice. Arrange the Époisses on the jelly side of 4 slices of bread and top with the pecans. Cover each sandwich with another slice of bread, butter side facing out.

3. Heat a large cast-iron skillet over moderate heat. Add 2 sandwiches and grill for about 4 minutes. Flip the sandwiches and cook until golden brown on the bottom and the cheese is melted, 4 minutes more. Transfer to a work surface and cook the remaining 2 sandwiches. —*Vivian Howard*

Tuna Banh Mi

Total **20 min;** Serves **4**

- 15 oz. tuna in olive oil, drained
- ¼ cup fresh lime juice
- 2 Tbsp. Asian fish sauce
- 1 jalapeño, minced
  Kosher salt and pepper
  One 24- to 32-inch soft baguette, split and toasted
  Mayonnaise, mint leaves, julienned carrots and sliced dill pickles, for serving

In a medium bowl, toss the tuna with the lime juice, fish sauce and jalapeño. Season with salt and pepper. Spread the cut sides of the baguette with mayonnaise and fill with the tuna salad, mint, carrots and pickles. Close, cut into 4 sandwiches and serve. —*Justin Chapple*

BEER Fresh, grassy India pale ale: Founder's All Day IPA.

Chicken Caesar Sandwiches with Garlic Dressing

Active **45 min**; Total **2 hr 30 min**; Makes **4**

- ½ cup plus 3 Tbsp. extra-virgin olive oil
- 2 Tbsp. fresh lemon juice plus 2 lemons halved crosswise
- 2 Tbsp. finely chopped rosemary
- 1 garlic clove, minced, plus 1 head of garlic, halved crosswise
- 8 skinless, boneless chicken thighs (2½ lbs.)
- 1 slice of white sandwich bread, cut into ¼-inch dice
- ½ cup crème fraîche
- ¼ cup freshly grated Parmigiano-Reggiano cheese
- 5 oil-packed anchovy fillets, minced
   Kosher salt and pepper
- 8 romaine lettuce leaves
- 4 brioche buns, split and toasted
- 2 Tbsp. large capers, rinsed

1. In a large bowl, stir 2 tablespoons of the olive oil with the lemon juice, rosemary and minced garlic. Add the chicken thighs, turn to coat and cover with plastic wrap. Refrigerate for at least 2 hours or overnight.

2. Preheat the oven to 425°. Wrap the head of garlic in foil, then set on a foil-lined baking sheet and bake for 40 minutes. Arrange the lemon halves cut side down on the baking sheet and bake for 10 minutes more. In a small bowl, toss the bread cubes with 1 tablespoon of the olive oil and spread on the baking sheet; bake until toasted, about 8 minutes. Let the garlic, lemon halves and croutons cool for 5 minutes.

3. To make the dressing, squeeze the garlic cloves from their skins into a small bowl and mash until smooth. Squeeze the flesh from the roasted lemons into the bowl and add any juices from the baking sheet. Add the remaining ½ cup of olive oil, the crème fraîche, cheese and anchovies and stir until smooth. Season with salt and pepper.

4. Light a grill or heat a grill pan over moderately high heat. Season the chicken thighs with salt and pepper and grill, turning once, until cooked through, 12 to 14 minutes. Transfer the chicken to a plate and let rest for 10 minutes.

5. To serve, arrange 2 romaine leaves on the bottom half of each toasted bun. Top each with 2 chicken thighs. Spoon the dressing generously over the chicken and then sprinkle the croutons and capers on top. Close the sandwiches and serve immediately with more dressing on the side. —*Bill or Beak*

WINE Bold, lemony Sonoma County Chardonnay: 2013 Lioco.

California BLTs

Total **45 min**; Serves **4**

To ensure that there's bacon in every bite of his BLT, F&W's Justin Chapple weaves uncooked strips of bacon into a tight lattice, then bakes until crisp.

- 12 slices of bacon, halved crosswise
- ½ cup mayonnaise
- 1 Tbsp. finely chopped tarragon
- 1 Tbsp. fresh lemon juice
   Kosher salt and pepper
- 8 slices of multigrain sandwich bread, toasted
- 1 Hass avocado—peeled, pitted and sliced
- 2 Persian cucumbers, thinly sliced on the diagonal
- 1 medium tomato, thinly sliced
- 4 small Bibb lettuce leaves
- ½ cup mixed sprouts, such as radish, sunflower and alfalfa

1. Preheat the oven to 400°. Line a large rimmed baking sheet with parchment paper or foil. For each lattice, weave 6 strips of bacon, 3 in each direction, on the prepared baking sheet.

2. Set an ovenproof rack upside down on the bacon to keep it flat. Bake for 15 to 20 minutes, until browned and crisp. Remove the rack, then transfer the bacon lattices to paper towels to drain.

3. Meanwhile, in a small bowl, whisk the mayonnaise with the tarragon and lemon juice. Season with salt and pepper.

4. Spread the tarragon mayonnaise on each slice of toast. Arrange the sliced avocado, cucumbers and tomato on 4 slices of the toast and sprinkle with salt and pepper. Top with the bacon lattices, Bibb leaves and sprouts. Close the sandwiches and serve. —*Justin Chapple*

Chicken-Cashew Tea Sandwiches with Shallot Gremolata

Total **25 min**; Serves **2 to 4**

A piquant mix of shallots, lemon zest and herbs punches up these chicken salad sandwiches. Rinsing the shallots before mixing them into the gremolata softens their oniony flavor.

- ¾ cup diced cooked chicken breast
- ¼ cup extra-virgin olive oil
- ¼ cup mayonnaise
- ¼ cup Champagne grapes or quartered small green grapes
- 3 Tbsp. finely chopped roasted cashews
- 2 tsp. minced chives, plus chopped chives for garnish
- 1 tsp. fresh lemon juice
- 3 Tbsp. minced shallots, rinsed and drained
- 1 Tbsp. minced chervil
   Kosher salt and pepper
   Finely grated zest of ½ lemon
- 2 slices of rye bread

1. In a medium bowl, mix the chicken, olive oil, mayonnaise, grapes, cashews, minced chives, lemon juice and two-thirds each of the shallots and chervil; season with salt and pepper. In a small bowl, mix the remaining shallots and chervil with the lemon zest.

2. Spread the chicken salad on the rye bread and cut the sandwiches into halves or quarters. Sprinkle the gremolata on top, garnish with chopped chives and serve. —*Ben Mims*

Tea Sandwiches » 3 Ways

Smoked Salmon and Preserved Lemon Tea Sandwiches
Serves 2 to 4

In a skillet, toast 1 tsp. **mustard seeds** over moderately high heat, 2 minutes. In a bowl, whisk ¼ cup **fromage blanc** with the mustard seeds, 1½ Tbsp. minced **preserved lemon**, 1 tsp. minced brined **green peppercorns**, ½ tsp. **dry mustard powder**, ¼ tsp. **smoked paprika** and a pinch of crushed **saffron threads**. Season with **salt** and **pepper**. Arrange 4 slices of **smoked salmon** on 2 slices of crustless **buckwheat** or **spelt bread**. Cut and top with a dollop of the fromage blanc and a few **cilantro leaves**. –*Ben Mims*

Radish Tea Sandwiches with Miso Yogurt
Serves 2 to 4

In a bowl, mix ½ cup **fat-free plain Greek yogurt** with 1½ Tbsp. **white miso**. Spread on 4 small crustless slices of **pumpernickel bread**. Thinly slice 8 **radishes** and arrange on the bread. Garnish with **radish sprouts** and toasted **sesame seeds**. –*Justin Chapple*

Spicy Avocado and Pea Tea Sandwiches
Serves 2 to 4

In a bowl, whisk 2 Tbsp. **canola oil** with the finely grated **zest of** ½ **lime**, 1 Tbsp. **fresh lime juice**, 1 tsp. chopped **mint**, ½ tsp. chopped **tarragon** and 1 minced seeded **red Thai chile**. Stir in half of a diced **Hass avocado**, season with **salt** and **pepper** and let stand for 10 minutes. Mash one-third of the marinated avocado on 4 small slices of **whole-grain bread**. Stir 2 Tbsp. of thawed **frozen peas** into the remaining avocado and spoon on top of the sandwiches. Garnish with chopped **mint** and **tarragon**. –*Ben Mims*

PROVENÇAL TUNA
SANDWICHES WITH
FENNEL MAYO

Provençal Tuna Sandwiches with Fennel Mayo

⏱ Total **40 min;** Makes **4**

- 2 tsp. fennel seeds
- ¾ cup mayonnaise
- ¼ cup crème fraîche
- 1 garlic clove, finely chopped
- 1 medium fennel bulb, shaved paper-thin, plus 2 Tbsp. chopped fronds
- 1 Tbsp. finely grated lemon zest plus 3 Tbsp. fresh lemon juice
  - Kosher salt and black pepper
- ¼ cup finely chopped red onion
- ¼ cup pitted Niçoise olives, chopped
- 2 Tbsp. capers, chopped
- 1 tsp. crushed red pepper
  - Two 6-oz. jars tuna packed in olive oil, drained and flaked
- 2 Tbsp. extra-virgin olive oil
- 1 baguette, halved lengthwise
- 2 cups arugula (2 oz.)
- 2 medium tomatoes, thinly sliced
- ½ English cucumber, thinly sliced
- 12 white anchovy fillets

1. In a small skillet, toast the fennel seeds over moderately low heat until golden, 3 minutes. Finely crush them in a mortar.

2. In a food processor, mix the fennel seeds with the mayonnaise, crème fraîche, garlic, fennel fronds, 2 teaspoons of the lemon zest and 1 tablespoon of the lemon juice; puree. Season with salt and black pepper.

3. In a bowl, mix the onion, olives, capers, crushed red pepper and the remaining 1 teaspoon of lemon zest and 2 tablespoons of lemon juice. Fold in the tuna and olive oil.

4. Spread the fennel mayo on the cut sides of the baguette. Arrange the arugula on the bottom baguette and top with the shaved fennel and the tuna. Layer the tomatoes, cucumber and anchovies on top. Close the baguette and cut into 4 sandwiches. —*Curtis Stone*

MAKE AHEAD The fennel mayonnaise can be refrigerated for 3 days. The sandwiches can be wrapped in parchment paper and kept in the fridge for 4 hours.

WINE Strawberry- and herb-scented Provençal rosé: 2014 Les Valentines.

Shrimp and Chorizo Tortas

⏱ Total **30 min;** Serves **4**

- 2 Tbsp. canola oil
- ¾ lb. shelled and deveined medium shrimp
- ½ lb. fresh Mexican chorizo, casing removed and meat crumbled
- ¾ cup finely chopped red onion
- 1 garlic clove, minced
- 2 Tbsp. fresh lime juice
  - Kosher salt and pepper
  - Toasted kaiser rolls, mayonnaise, lettuce and thinly sliced tomato and avocado, for serving.

In a large skillet, heat the oil. Add the shrimp, chorizo, onion and garlic and cook over high heat, stirring occasionally, until browned and the shrimp and chorizo are cooked through, about 8 minutes. Stir in the lime juice and 2 tablespoons of water and season with salt and pepper. Serve on toasted kaiser rolls with mayonnaise, lettuce and sliced tomato and avocado. —*Justin Chapple*

WINE Robust, full-bodied rosé: 2014 Edmunds St. John Bone Jolly.

Salmon Sandwiches with Bacon and Apple-Horseradish Mayo

⏱ Total **40 min;** Serves **4**

- ½ cup mayonnaise
- ½ cup finely chopped Granny Smith apple
- 3 Tbsp. drained prepared horseradish
  - Kosher salt and pepper
- 8 slices of bacon
- 1 Tbsp. canola oil
  - Four 5- to 6-oz. skinless center-cut salmon fillets
- 4 brioche burger buns, split and toasted
- 4 lettuce leaves

1. In a small bowl, whisk the mayonnaise with the apple and horseradish. Season the mayo with salt and pepper.

2. In a large nonstick skillet, cook the bacon over moderate heat, turning occasionally, until browned and crisp, 5 to 7 minutes. Transfer to paper towels to drain.

3. Wipe out the skillet and heat the oil in it. Season the salmon with salt and pepper and cook over moderately high heat, turning once, until just cooked through, 6 to 8 minutes.

4. Spread the apple-horseradish mayonnaise on the buns and top with the salmon, bacon and lettuce. Close the sandwiches and serve. —*Justin Chapple*

Lobster Salad Sandwiches on Brioche

Active **45 min;** Total **1 hr 15 min;** Serves **4**

Chef Anne Quatrano of Dub's Fish Camp in Atlanta is a huge lobster roll fan. Between the two major styles of lobster rolls—served warm with butter or cold mixed with mayonnaise—she advocates for the creamy mayo version. She also butters the rolls generously before toasting.

- Three 1¼-lb. live lobsters
- ¼ cup mayonnaise
- 1 celery rib, finely chopped
- 1 Tbsp. fresh lemon juice
- 1 tsp. minced tarragon
  - Salt and pepper
- 4 brioche burger buns, split
  - Softened butter, for brushing

1. Plunge the lobsters head first into a large pot of boiling water and cook until they turn bright red, about 10 minutes. Using tongs, transfer the lobsters to an ice bath to cool completely.

2. Twist off the bodies of the lobsters from the tails. Using scissors, cut along the underside of the tail shells and remove the meat. Halve the lobster tails, discarding the dark intestinal veins. Remove the meat from the claws and knuckles. In a medium bowl, stir the mayonnaise with the celery, lemon juice and tarragon. Cut all of the lobster meat into bite-size pieces and add to the bowl; season with salt and pepper and mix well. Refrigerate until chilled.

3. Heat a griddle. Brush the cut sides of the buns with butter and grill until toasted. Fill with the lobster salad and serve. —*Anne Quatrano*

WINE Citrusy, medium-bodied Austrian Grüner Veltliner: 2014 Högl Schön Federspiel.

Beet-Bean Cheeseburgers

Active **1 hr 15 min**; Total **2 hr 15 min**
Serves **4**

This stellar veggie burger, created by Dan Barber for his WastED pop-up at Blue Hill in New York City, has a lot of ingredients; each one adds to the taste and texture and makes the recipe exceptional.

BURGERS

- **3 cups** (not packed) beet pulp (from juicing 1½ lbs. beets)
- **2 cups** (not packed) carrot pulp (from juicing ¾ lb. carrots)
- **4 oz.** small white mushrooms, quartered
- **½ cup** canned kidney beans, rinsed and drained
- **2 oz.** firm tofu, cut into ¼-inch dice
- **1 Tbsp.** canola oil
- **¼ cup** cooked spelt or barley
- **¾ cup** (not packed) celery pulp (from juicing ¾ lb. celery ribs)
- **3** large eggs, beaten
- **½ cup** finely chopped roasted almonds
- **½ cup** freshly grated Parmigiano-Reggiano cheese
- **2 Tbsp.** plain dry breadcrumbs
- **2 tsp.** minced garlic
- **2 Tbsp.** white miso
- **1 tsp.** low-sodium soy sauce
- **½ tsp.** Worcestershire sauce
- **2 tsp.** kosher salt
- **¼ tsp.** pepper
- Few dashes of Tabasco

TO FINISH

- **2 Tbsp.** unsalted butter, at room temperature
- **4** hamburger buns, split
- **2 Tbsp.** canola oil
- **4** slices of Swiss cheese
- Lettuce, sliced tomato and stone-ground mustard, for serving

1. Make the burgers Preheat the oven to 375°. Spread the beet pulp evenly on a parchment paper–lined rimmed baking sheet. Spread the carrot pulp evenly on a second parchment-lined baking sheet. Roast for about 30 minutes, stirring occasionally, until the pulp is dry and browned in spots. Scrape into a bowl and let cool completely. Leave the oven on.

2. On the rimmed baking sheet, toss the mushrooms with the kidney beans, tofu and canola oil. Spread the mixture in an even layer and roast for 30 minutes, stirring occasionally, until browned and dry.

3. In a food processor, pulse the spelt until finely chopped; scrape into a large bowl. Add the mushroom mixture to the processor and pulse until finely chopped; add to the bowl. Add the roasted beet and carrot pulp, the celery pulp and all of the remaining burger ingredients and mix well. Pack the mixture into four ½-inch-thick burgers.

4. Finish the burgers Heat a grill pan. Spread the butter on the buns and toast cut side down over moderate heat until golden, about 2 minutes. Transfer the buns to a plate.

5. Brush the grill pan with oil and heat. Add the burgers and cook over moderate heat, turning once, until nicely charred, about 6 minutes. Top each burger with a slice of cheese, cover and cook until the cheese is melted, about 2 minutes longer. Set the burgers on the buns. Top with lettuce and tomato, spread mustard on the top buns and serve. —*Dan Barber*

WINE Spiced, black cherry–scented Oregon Pinot Noir: 2014 Mouton Noir O.P.P.

Italian Grinders with Garlic Aioli

⏱ Total **45 min**; Serves **4**

- **2** large egg yolks
- **1½ Tbsp.** fresh lemon juice
- **2** garlic cloves, minced
- **⅓ cup** vegetable oil
- **¾ cup** extra-virgin olive oil
- Kosher salt and pepper
- Four 8-inch light hoagie rolls, split lengthwise
- **¼ cup** chopped pickled hot cherry peppers
- **12** thin slices of mortadella
- **16** thin slices of Genoa salami
- **8** thin slices of prosciutto cotto
- **12** thin slices of provolone cheese
- **3** tomatoes, thinly sliced
- **1 tsp.** dried oregano
- **2 cups** finely shredded iceberg lettuce
- **¼ cup** red wine vinegar

1. Preheat the oven to 375°. In a bowl, whisk the egg yolks with the lemon juice and

garlic. Very gradually whisk in drops of the vegetable oil until starting to thicken, then gradually whisk in the remaining vegetable oil and ½ cup of the olive oil until thick. Season the aioli with salt and pepper.

2. Bake the closed hoagie rolls for 3 minutes, until warm. Spread the aioli on the cut sides. Top the bottom halves with the peppers, meats and cheese. Bake for 5 minutes, until the cheese melts. Top with the tomatoes and oregano and season with salt and pepper. Pile the lettuce on top, drizzle on the vinegar and remaining ¼ cup of olive oil and serve. —*Todd Ginsberg*

BEER Toasty, lightly hoppy English-style brown ale: SweetWater Georgia Brown.

Soppressata Sandwiches with Tomato Jam and Camembert

Active **20 min**; Total **3 hr 15 min**; Makes **4**

TOMATO JAM

- **8** medium tomatoes (3½ lbs.), cut into 6 wedges each
- **6 Tbsp.** extra-virgin olive oil
- **6** thyme sprigs
- **5** garlic cloves, crushed
- **2 tsp.** kosher salt
- **2 tsp.** sugar

SANDWICHES

- **8** slices of sourdough bread, cut from a round loaf
- Extra-virgin olive oil, for drizzling
- **8 oz.** sliced soppressata
- **6 oz.** chilled Camembert cheese, thinly sliced
- **4 cups** torn frisée

1. Make the tomato jam Preheat the oven to 325°. Line a rimmed baking sheet with foil. Combine all of the ingredients on the foil and toss to coat the tomato wedges. Bake for about 3 hours, stirring occasionally, until the tomatoes are deeply caramelized. Discard the thyme and garlic; let cool.

2. Make the sandwiches Arrange the bread on a baking sheet and drizzle with olive oil. Toast until golden, about 8 minutes. Spread some of the tomato jam on half of the toasts and top with the soppressata, cheese and frisée. Close the sandwiches and serve. —*Wesley Genovart*

BEER Sour golden Belgian ale: Backacre Golden Ale.

DIY SPIRALIZED HOT DOGS

JUSTIN CHAPPLE, star of F&W's Mad Genius Tips videos, reveals his crazy-smart method for spiral-cutting hot dogs using a sharp knife and a wooden skewer. This trick ensures that the hot dogs crisp up and cook evenly, and can hold more of his bold toppings.

Cutting hot dogs into a spiral isn't just fun–it makes the hot dog better, because it gets crispier on the grill and condiments like relish and mustard fall into the meaty grooves. To start, insert a skewer lengthwise through the center of each hot dog. With a small knife, cut at an angle all the way down to the skewer while rolling the hot dog away from you. (The skewer prevents the knife from cutting all the way through the meat.) Slide the hot dog off the skewer and stretch out the spirals. The hot dog is now ready to grill.

HOT DOG TOPPINGS

1. Chicago-Style Salsa

In a bowl, toss 1 finely chopped **Persian cucumber** with ½ cup **celery leaves**, ½ cup quartered **cherry tomatoes**, ¼ cup thinly sliced **peperoncini**, ¼ cup thinly sliced **red onion**, ¼ cup **sweet pickle relish** and 2 Tbsp. **olive oil**. Season with **salt** and **pepper**; serve on **hot dogs**.

2. Apricot Mostarda

In a saucepan, combine ½ cup each of **apple cider vinegar** and **water** with 1 cup chopped **dried apricots**, 2 Tbsp. **sugar**, 1 minced **shallot** and 1 minced **garlic clove**. Bring to a boil, then simmer over moderate heat, stirring occasionally, until the apricots are soft and coated in a light syrup, 7 to 10 minutes. Stir in 2 Tbsp. **whole-grain mustard** and 1 Tbsp. **Dijon mustard**. Season with **salt** and let cool; serve on **hot dogs**.

3. Pickled Pepper Slaw

In a bowl, toss 1 cup sliced **sweet and/or hot pickled peppers** with ½ cup shredded **romaine**, 2 Tbsp. **olive oil** and ¼ cup each chopped **parsley** and **dill**. Season with **salt** and **pepper**; serve on **hot dogs**.

STEP-BY-STEP

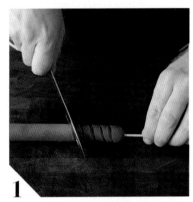

SLICE Cut at an angle while rolling the hot dog away from you.

STRETCH Remove the skewer, stretch out the spirals, then grill the hot dog.

GARNISH Spiralized hot dogs have lots of crevices that you can fill with chunky condiments like salsa, relish, chopped onions and pickled peppers.

BLACK BEAN AND
SHIITAKE BURGER

Black Bean and Shiitake Burgers

Active **45 min;** Total **1 hr 30 min;** Serves **6**

- 1 oz. dried shiitake mushroom caps (about 12)
  Boiling water
- 1½ cups lightly packed parsley leaves
- 1 large shallot, chopped
- 3 garlic cloves, chopped
- ½ tsp. finely grated lemon zest plus 3 Tbsp. fresh lemon juice
- 1 tsp. soy sauce
- 1 tsp. agave nectar
- ½ cup textured vegetable protein (see Note)
  Two 15-oz. cans black beans, drained and rinsed
- 2 Tbsp. flaxseed meal
- 2 tsp. kosher salt
  Oil, for grilling
- 6 brioche buns, split and toasted
  Banana Pepper Mustard (recipe follows), mayonnaise, lettuce and tomato, for serving

1. In a medium heatproof bowl, cover the shiitake caps with boiling water and let stand until softened, about 25 minutes. Drain well, then coarsely chop and transfer to a food processor. Add the parsley, shallot, garlic, lemon zest and lemon juice and pulse until the parsley is finely chopped.

2. Meanwhile, in another medium heatproof bowl, combine ½ cup plus 2 tablespoons of boiling water with the soy sauce and agave. Stir in the TVP and let stand until rehydrated and tender, about 15 minutes. Stir in the shiitake-parsley mixture, black beans, flax meal and salt. Using a fork, lightly mash half of the beans against the side of the bowl and stir to combine.

3. Using moistened hands, form the mixture into six ¾-inch-thick patties; pack tight. Transfer to a parchment paper–lined baking sheet.

4. Light a grill or heat a grill pan; oil the grate or the pan. Grill the burgers over moderately high heat until charred on the bottom, about 5 minutes. Using a spatula, carefully flip the patties and cook until lightly charred and heated through, 3 to 5 minutes longer. Serve the burgers on the buns with the Banana Pepper Mustard, mayonnaise, lettuce and tomato.
—*Tim Byres*

NOTE Textured vegetable protein (TVP) is available at large supermarkets and specialty food shops; look for the Bob's Red Mill brand.

WINE Fragrant, medium-bodied Sonoma Pinot Noir: 2013 Banshee Sonoma County.

BANANA PEPPER MUSTARD

Active **30 min;** Total **1 hr;** Makes **1¼ cups**

- ¼ lb. yellow banana peppers— stemmed, seeded and chopped
- ½ yellow bell pepper, seeded
- ½ small yellow onion, finely chopped
- 2 Tbsp. minced peeled fresh ginger
- ⅓ cup water
- ¼ cup apple cider vinegar
- 1½ tsp. sugar
- ⅛ tsp. ground turmeric
- ½ cup plus 2 Tbsp. Dijon mustard
  Kosher salt

In a medium saucepan, combine everything except the mustard and salt and bring to a boil. Simmer over moderate heat until the peppers and onion are soft, about 5 minutes. Transfer to a blender and puree until very smooth. Add the Dijon and puree until just incorporated. Season the mustard with salt. Transfer to a bowl and let cool completely, then refrigerate until well chilled, about 30 minutes. —*TB*

Kentucky Hot Brown

Active **30 min;** Total **1 hr 10 min**
Makes **8 sandwiches**

The Hot Brown originated in 1926 at the Brown Hotel in Louisville, Kentucky. Chef Bobby Flay adapted the open-face hot turkey sandwich for his New York City bistro, Bar Americain.

SAUCE

- **2¼ cups whole milk**
- 2 Tbsp. unsalted butter
- 2 Tbsp. all-purpose flour
- 2 cups shredded sharp white cheddar cheese (6 oz.)
- ¼ cup freshly grated Parmigiano-Reggiano cheese
  Pinch of freshly grated nutmeg
  Few dashes of hot sauce
  Kosher salt and pepper

SANDWICHES

- 16 slices of thick-cut bacon
- 2 tomatoes, cut into eight ¼-inch-thick slices
- 1 Tbsp. canola oil
  Kosher salt and pepper
  Eight ½-inch-thick slices of day-old white sandwich bread
- 4 Tbsp. unsalted butter, cut into pieces
- 2 lbs. roast turkey breast, sliced ¼ inch thick
- 1½ cups shredded sharp white cheddar cheese (4½ oz.)
- ½ cup freshly grated Parmigiano-Reggiano cheese
  Chopped chives and chopped parsley, for garnish

1. Make the sauce In a small saucepan, bring the milk to a simmer. In a medium saucepan, melt the butter. Add the flour to the butter and whisk over moderate heat for 1 minute. Gradually whisk in the hot milk and bring to a boil. Cook, whisking, until thickened, about 5 minutes. Remove the pan from the heat and whisk in both cheeses until melted. Stir in the nutmeg and hot sauce and season with salt and pepper.

2. Make the sandwiches Preheat the oven to 425°. Arrange the bacon on a rack set over a baking sheet. Cook until golden and crisp, about 30 minutes.

3. Preheat the broiler. Arrange the tomato slices on a baking sheet, drizzle with the canola oil and season with salt and pepper. Broil 6 inches from the heat until lightly charred, 1 to 2 minutes per side; keep warm.

4. Arrange the bread on a foil-lined baking sheet and spread each slice with ½ tablespoon of the butter; season with salt and pepper. Broil until lightly toasted, about 2 minutes. Flip the bread and toast for 1 minute. Top each toast with some turkey and a slice of tomato. Spoon the sauce on top and sprinkle on both cheeses. Broil until the cheese is melted and golden brown, 2 to 3 minutes. Transfer the sandwiches to plates and top with the bacon. Garnish with chopped chives and parsley and serve hot. —*Bobby Flay*

At Milktooth in Indianapolis, F&W Best New Chef 2015 Jonathan Brooks brilliantly redefines brunch with dishes like Red Cabbage and Fried Mortadella Okonomiyaki (recipe, p. 285).

BREAKFAST & BRUNCH

CREAMY STEEL-CUT OATS
WITH DRIED CHERRIES
AND ALMONDS
Recipe, page 296

OPEN-FACE OMELET
WITH SPICY FETA AND
ESCAROLE

Open-Face Omelets with Spicy Feta and Escarole

⟳ Total **20 min**; Serves **2**

Chef Ana Sortun of Oleana in Cambridge, Massachusetts, is a vegetable genius. Here she tops Middle Eastern–style omelets with a delicious mix of escarole and feta seasoned with scallion and jalapeño.

- 1½ Tbsp. za'atar (see Note)
- 2 Tbsp. plus 2 tsp. extra-virgin olive oil
- 3 oz. sheep-milk feta cheese, crumbled (½ cup)
- 1 scallion, white part only, finely chopped
- ½ jalapeño, minced
- 3 large eggs
- 2 tsp. all-purpose flour
- ¼ tsp. kosher salt
- 3 cups shredded escarole
  Pepper

1. In a small bowl, mix the za'atar with 2 tablespoons of the oil. In another bowl, mash the feta, scallion and jalapeño with 1 tablespoon of water until smooth.

2. In a small nonstick skillet, heat 1 teaspoon of the olive oil. In a bowl, beat the eggs with the flour, salt and 1 tablespoon of water (it's OK if a few lumps remain). Pour half the mixture into the skillet and swirl the pan to form a thin omelet. Sprinkle half the escarole and half the feta mixture evenly over the eggs; cook over moderately low heat until the escarole starts to wilt, the feta melts and the omelet is just cooked through, about 3 minutes. Slide the omelet onto a plate and season with pepper. Repeat with the remaining oil, eggs, escarole and feta mixture.

3. Drizzle the za'atar oil over the omelets and serve. —*Ana Sortun*

NOTE If the Middle Eastern spice blend za'atar is unavailable, stir 2 tablespoons of olive oil with 1 teaspoon each of sesame seeds and dried oregano.

WINE Zesty, light-bodied Spanish white: 2014 Doniene Gorrondona Txakoli.

Baked Spring Vegetable Omelet with Goat Cheese and Mint

Active **30 min**; Total **1 hr 45 min**
Serves **4 to 6**

Tara Stevens, who runs a little cooking school called The Courtyard Kitchen at Dar Namir in Fez, Morocco, created this recipe on the spur of the moment. "It was a way to use up a fridge full of eggs, goat cheese and mint the night before my family went on vacation," she says. "I always have mint in the fridge because my housekeeper, Rachida, thinks it's appalling if I don't."

- 2 Tbsp. extra-virgin olive oil, plus more for greasing
- ¾ lb. asparagus, cut into 1-inch pieces
- 1 medium white onion, thinly sliced
- 2 zucchini, thinly sliced
  Kosher salt and pepper
- ¾ cup thawed frozen peas
- 8 oz. goat cheese, crumbled
- 2 Tbsp. chopped mint
- 12 large eggs

1. Preheat the oven to 350°. Coat a 2½-quart baking dish with olive oil. In a medium saucepan of salted boiling water, blanch the asparagus until crisp-tender, about 2 minutes. Drain and cool under cold running water; drain well.

2. Meanwhile, in a large skillet, heat the 2 tablespoons of oil. Add the onion and zucchini and season with salt and pepper. Cook over moderate heat, stirring, until softened, 8 to 10 minutes. Stir in the peas and asparagus until heated through. Transfer the vegetables to a paper towel–lined plate to drain and let cool slightly. Spread the vegetables in the prepared baking dish. Scatter the goat cheese and mint on top.

3. In a bowl, beat the eggs until light and fluffy, about 3 minutes. Pour the eggs over the vegetables and bake for 40 to 45 minutes, until golden and set. Let cool for 30 minutes, then serve. —*Tara Stevens*

WINE Lively, crisp Pinot Grigio: 2014 Riff.

Fines Herbes Omelet

⟳ Total **10 min**; Serves **2**

Master chef Jacques Pépin vigorously stirs his eggs with a fork while they're cooking to lighten them and form small curds for a soft, creamy omelet.

- 5 large eggs
- 2 Tbsp. minced parsley
- 1 Tbsp. minced tarragon
- 1 Tbsp. minced chives
- ¼ tsp. kosher salt
- ¼ tsp. pepper
- 1 Tbsp. unsalted butter
- 1½ tsp. canola oil

In a medium bowl, beat the eggs with the parsley, tarragon, chives, salt and pepper until light. In a 10-inch nonstick skillet, heat the butter and oil until the butter begins to foam. Add the eggs and cook over moderate heat, shaking the pan and stirring constantly with a fork, until tiny curds form and the eggs begin to set. Stop stirring and allow the eggs to cook undisturbed for 1 minute. Shake the skillet to loosen the omelet and, using a rubber spatula, fold one-third of the omelet over the center. Tilt the skillet and turn the omelet out onto a large plate, folding it over itself as you release it from the pan. Cut the omelet in half and serve immediately.
—*Jacques Pépin*

WINE Creamy, fruit-forward Chardonnay-based Champagne: NV Pierre Gimonnet 1er Cru Blanc de Blancs.

CHEF TIP
Cracking Eggs

"Jacques Pépin taught me to crack eggs on a flat surface. Hitting them against the edge of a bowl makes it more likely you'll get shell fragments in your food."

–*Greg Richie*, Soco, Orlando, Florida

Quinoa-Dill Omelet with Feta

⏲ Total **30 min**; Serves **2**

¼ cup red or black quinoa, rinsed and drained

1 Tbsp. unsalted butter

6 large eggs

Kosher salt

¼ cup crumbled feta cheese

2 Tbsp. chopped dill

1. In a medium saucepan of boiling water, cook the quinoa until tender, about 10 minutes. Drain and return the quinoa to the pan. Cover and let stand for 10 minutes; fluff with a fork. Spread on a baking sheet and let cool to room temperature.

2. In a 9-inch nonstick skillet, melt the butter. In a medium bowl, beat the eggs with the quinoa and season with salt. Cook the eggs over moderately low heat, stirring, until almost set, 4 to 5 minutes. Top evenly with the cheese and dill and cook without stirring until set. Fold the omelet in half and serve hot. —*Kay Chun*

Open-Face Egg and Griddled Ham Breakfast Sandwiches

⏲ Total **30 min**; Makes **12**

1 dozen large eggs

Kosher salt and pepper

6 oz. thinly sliced baked ham

1 cup chopped mixed herbs, such as parsley, tarragon and chives

1 Tbsp. fresh lemon juice

6 slider buns, split and lightly toasted

1. Preheat the oven to 350°. Pour 1 tablespoon of water into each cup of a 12-cup muffin tin. Crack an egg into each cup and season with salt and pepper. Bake the eggs for 13 to 15 minutes, until the whites are just firm and the yolks are still runny. Using a slotted spoon, immediately transfer the eggs to a plate.

2. Meanwhile, in a medium skillet, cook the ham over moderate heat, turning, until hot, about 2 minutes. In a small bowl, toss the herbs with the lemon juice and season with salt and pepper.

3. Arrange the split buns cut side up on a platter. Top with the ham, eggs and herbs. Serve open-face. —*Justin Chapple*

Phoenicia Diner's Breakfast Skillet

⏲ Total **10 min**; Serves **1**

The Phoenicia Diner in Phoenicia, New York, has an impressive list of "skillets" on its breakfast menu. This creamy scramble studded with smoked trout serves one, but it can be easily doubled or quadrupled.

½ Tbsp. unsalted butter

3 large eggs, beaten

2 oz. flaked smoked trout (⅓ cup)

1 Tbsp. crème fraîche

1 Tbsp. finely grated Parmigiano-Reggiano cheese

1 Tbsp. snipped chives, plus more for garnish

Kosher salt

Toast, for serving

In a small cast-iron skillet, heat the butter until it starts to foam. Add the eggs, trout, crème fraîche, Parmigiano-Reggiano, the 1 tablespoon of chives and a generous pinch of salt and cook over moderate heat, shaking the pan and stirring gently with a spatula, until small curds form and the eggs are just set, about 4 minutes. Garnish with snipped chives and serve with toast. —*Melchor Rosas*

Tostada Chilaquiles

Total **1 hr**; Serves **4**

4 lbs. tomatillos, husked and rinsed

1 large jalapeño, stemmed

2 cups packed chopped cilantro leaves and stems, plus small sprigs for garnish

¼ cup garlic cloves

Kosher salt and pepper

¼ cup canola oil

1 small onion, thinly sliced

Twelve 6-inch tostadas

4 large eggs

One 15-oz. can black beans—rinsed, drained, warmed and seasoned with salt

Sliced radishes, sliced jalapeños and crumbled queso fresco, for garnish

1. In a large saucepan, combine the tomatillos and jalapeño with 8 cups of water. Bring to a boil, then simmer over moderate heat, stirring, until the tomatillos are very soft but not falling apart, about 15 minutes. Using a slotted spoon, transfer the tomatillos and jalapeño to a blender. Add 1 cup of the cooking liquid to the blender. Add the chopped cilantro and garlic cloves and puree until smooth. Season the salsa with salt and pepper. Discard the remaining cooking liquid.

2. In a large skillet, heat 2 tablespoons of the oil. Add the onion and cook over moderate heat, stirring occasionally, until golden, 7 to 8 minutes. Stir in the tomatillo salsa and simmer for 5 minutes. Dip 1 tostada at a time in the tomatillo salsa, turning, until some of the salsa is absorbed but the tostada still holds its shape, about 15 seconds. Transfer the tostada to a large plate; repeat with the remaining tostadas. Transfer the remaining salsa to a bowl.

3. In a large nonstick skillet, heat the remaining 2 tablespoons of oil. Crack the eggs into the skillet and cook sunny-side up over moderate heat, 3 to 4 minutes.

4. Place 1 tostada on each of 4 plates. Spoon some of the beans on top and cover with another tostada. Repeat with the remaining beans and 4 remaining tostadas. Top each stack with a fried egg. Garnish with the radishes, jalapeños, queso fresco and cilantro sprigs and serve with the remaining salsa. —*Christina Nguyen*

MAKE AHEAD The salsa can be refrigerated for 2 days; reheat before using.

WINE Crisp, zesty Sauvignon Blanc: 2014 Groth Napa Valley.

TOSTADA
CHILAQUILES

Brussels Sprout Frittata

⏲ Total **30 min;** Serves **6**

- 2 Tbsp. extra-virgin olive oil
- ½ lb. brussels sprouts, thinly sliced (about 3 cups)
- 1 small baking potato, peeled and sliced ¼ inch thick
- 1 small red onion, halved and thinly sliced
  Kosher salt and pepper
- 10 large eggs, beaten
- 1 tsp. smoked paprika
  Thinly sliced scallions, for garnish
  Hot sauce, for serving

Preheat the oven to 375°. In a large oven-proof nonstick skillet, heat the olive oil. Add the brussels sprouts, potato and onion and season with salt and pepper. Cover and cook over moderate heat, stirring occasionally, until the vegetables are golden and tender, about 10 minutes. Stir in the eggs and paprika and transfer to the oven. Bake for 10 minutes, or until set. Garnish with scallions and serve with hot sauce.
—*Kay Chun*

Mushroom Tortilla

⏲ Total **30 min;** Serves **4**

- 6 Tbsp. extra-virgin olive oil, preferably Spanish, plus more for brushing
- ½ small red onion, thinly sliced
  Kosher salt and pepper
- ¾ lb. cremini mushrooms, cut into ½-inch pieces
- ¼ cup coarsely chopped flat-leaf parsley, plus more for garnish
- 8 large eggs

1. In a 10-inch nonstick skillet, heat the 6 tablespoons of olive oil. Add the onion and a generous pinch of salt and pepper. Cook over moderate heat, stirring occasionally, until softened, about 5 minutes. Add the mushrooms and season with salt and pepper. Cook over moderately high heat, stirring occasionally, until the mushrooms are tender and golden, about 7 minutes. Stir in the ¼ cup of parsley.

2. In a large bowl, beat the eggs with a generous pinch of salt and pepper. Pour the eggs into the skillet and cook over moderate heat, gently stirring and lifting the tortilla, until the edge is set and the center is still loose, about 7 minutes. Put a large, flat plate on top of the skillet and carefully invert the tortilla onto the plate. Slide the tortilla back into the skillet and cook until the center is set, 1 to 2 minutes longer. Slide onto a serving plate, brush with olive oil and garnish with parsley. Serve right away. —*José Andrés*

MAKE AHEAD The tortilla can be kept at room temperature for up to 3 hours.

WINE Lightly herbal Albariño: 2014 Lícia.

Five-Herb Frittata with Prosciutto and Parmesan

⏲ Total **15 min;** Serves **2**

Nancy Silverton, famed chef of the Mozza restaurant empire in L.A. and beyond, has strong opinions about frittatas. She prefers them to be creamy like scrambled eggs, with a variety of toppings, such as prosciutto, cheese and fresh herbs. Serve this frittata for brunch or, as Silverton does, as a side dish at dinner parties, allowing guests to cut wedges at the table.

- 4 large eggs
- ½ tsp. kosher salt
- 1 Tbsp. each finely chopped mint, parsley and chives
- 1 tsp. each finely chopped oregano and thyme
- 1½ Tbsp. unsalted butter
- ½ oz. prosciutto, torn (2 slices)
  Coarsely ground black pepper
  Parmigiano-Reggiano cheese shavings, for serving

1. In a medium bowl, beat the eggs with the salt and 2 teaspoons of water. Beat in the mint, parsley, chives, oregano and thyme.

2. In a 10-inch nonstick skillet, melt the butter. Add the eggs and cook over moderately low heat, without stirring, until just beginning to set at the edge, about 3 minutes. Using a spatula, lift the edge and tilt the pan so the egg mixture can seep underneath. Continue to cook, lifting the frittata and tilting the pan occasionally, until the frittata is just set and creamy on top, 3 to 5 minutes longer. Scatter the prosciutto over the frittata and slide it onto a plate. Garnish with coarsely ground pepper and shaved Parmigiano and serve right away.
—*Nancy Silverton*

Potato Peel Tortilla with Garlicky Aioli

⏲ Total **40 min;** Serves **6**

- ½ cup plus 2 Tbsp. extra-virgin olive oil
- 1 onion, thinly sliced
- 4 cups scrubbed potato peels, chopped into 2-inch pieces
- 6 garlic cloves—3 finely chopped and 3 finely grated
- 4 scallions, chopped (1 cup)
- 1 dozen large eggs
- ½ tsp. pimentón de la Vera, plus more for sprinkling
  Kosher salt and pepper
- ⅓ cup mayonnaise
- 1 Tbsp. fresh lemon juice

1. Preheat the oven to 450°. In a large ovenproof nonstick skillet, heat ¼ cup of the olive oil. Add the onion, potato peels, chopped garlic and ¾ cup of the scallions and cook over moderate heat, stirring occasionally, until golden and crispy in spots, about 10 minutes.

2. In a medium bowl, beat the eggs with the ½ teaspoon of pimentón and add to the skillet. Season with salt and pepper and cook over moderately low heat, stirring frequently, until the eggs begin to set around the edge, 3 to 4 minutes. Transfer the skillet to the oven and bake the tortilla for 6 to 8 minutes, until just set.

3. Meanwhile, in a small bowl, whisk the mayonnaise with the grated garlic, lemon juice and the remaining 6 tablespoons of olive oil; season with salt and pepper.

4. Invert the tortilla onto a large plate. Garnish with the remaining ¼ cup of scallions and a sprinkling of pimentón and serve with the aioli. —*Kay Chun*

MAKE AHEAD The aioli can be refrigerated for up to 3 days.

WINE Minerally northern Italian Pinot Grigio: 2013 Livio Felluga.

Bacon, Egg and Crispy Bread Stir-Fry

Total **40 min**; Serves **4**

This one-skillet dish is a great way to use up leftover bread crusts. Toast and crumble them, then stir-fry until crisp and chewy.

- **6** oz. rustic whole-wheat bread crusts, torn into 2-inch pieces
- **4** large eggs
  Kosher salt
- **¼** cup canola oil
- **4** slices of bacon, finely chopped
- **2** Tbsp. finely chopped peeled fresh ginger
- **2** Tbsp. minced garlic
- **1** cup chopped scallions, plus more for garnish
- **2** Tbsp. fresh lime juice, plus lime wedges for serving
- **1½** Tbsp. soy sauce
  Sambal oelek or other Asian chile paste, for serving

1. Preheat the oven to 400°. Spread the bread crusts on a large rimmed baking sheet and bake for about 7 minutes, until lightly golden and just crisp. Let cool slightly, then break into ½-inch pieces.

2. In a medium bowl, beat the eggs with a pinch of salt. In a large skillet, heat 1 tablespoon of the canola oil. Add the eggs and cook over moderately high heat until lightly browned, about 2 minutes. Fold the eggs over and cook until just set throughout, about 1 minute longer. Transfer to a plate and cut into ½-inch pieces.

3. In the skillet, heat the remaining 3 tablespoons of oil. Add the bacon and stir-fry over high heat until lightly browned but not crisp, about 3 minutes. Add the ginger and garlic and stir-fry until fragrant, about 1 minute. Add the bread pieces and ¼ cup of water and stir-fry over moderately high heat until slightly softened, about 5 minutes. Stir in the 1 cup of scallions, the lime juice and soy sauce and stir-fry for 1 minute. Stir in the eggs and season with salt. Garnish with scallions and serve with sambal and lime wedges. —*Justin Chapple*

WINE Citrusy, dry Australian Riesling: 2014 Jim Barry The Lodge Hill.

Red Cabbage and Fried Mortadella Okonomiyaki

Total **45 min**; Serves **4**

- **4** oz. fresh or frozen udon noodles
- **2** slices of bacon
- **3** large eggs
- **¾** cup prepared dashi or chicken broth
- **¾** cup all-purpose flour
- **½** tsp. kosher salt
- **2** Tbsp. unsalted butter
- **¼** lb. mortadella, diced
- **¾** cup finely shredded red cabbage
- **2** Tbsp. shredded carrot
  Kewpie mayonnaise, Sriracha, hoisin sauce, sliced scallions and furikake seasoning, for serving

1. In a medium saucepan of boiling water, cook the udon noodles until tender, about 1 minute. Drain. Cut the noodles in half.

2. Preheat the oven to 350°. In a 10-inch ovenproof nonstick skillet, cook the bacon over moderately high heat until browned and crisp, about 5 minutes. Transfer to paper towels to drain, then coarsely chop.

3. In a medium bowl, beat 2 eggs with the dashi. Whisk in the flour and salt just until a batter forms.

4. In the skillet, melt 1½ tablespoons of the butter. Add the mortadella and stir-fry over moderately high heat until lightly browned, about 2 minutes. Add the cabbage and carrot and stir-fry until just wilted, about 1 minute. Stir in the udon and pour the batter into the skillet. Cook until the okonomiyaki is browned on the bottom and set around the edge, about 6 minutes. Transfer to the oven and bake for about 7 minutes, until the okonomiyaki is cooked through.

5. Meanwhile, in a small skillet, melt the remaining ½ tablespoon of butter. Crack the remaining 1 egg into the skillet and cook over moderate heat until the white is firm and the yolk is runny, 3 to 5 minutes.

6. Invert the okonomiyaki onto a platter. Top with the fried egg and chopped bacon. Drizzle with Kewpie, Sriracha and hoisin, garnish with sliced scallions and furikake and serve. —*Jonathan Brooks*

Vegetable Toad-in-the-Hole

Active **35 min**; Total **1 hr 10 min**; Serves **4**

- **2** large eggs
- **¾** cup whole milk
- **¾** cup all-purpose flour
- **2** Tbsp. plus 1 tsp. whole-grain mustard
- **3** Tbsp. vegetable oil
  Sea salt and pepper
- **2** small carrots, cut into 2-inch lengths
- **2** Tbsp. unsalted butter
- **1** medium onion, cut into ½-inch-thick wedges
- **2** garlic cloves, sliced
- **2** oz. haricots verts
- **1** cup halved cherry tomatoes
- **1** Tbsp. finely chopped basil
- **½** tsp. finely chopped thyme
- **½** tsp. finely chopped rosemary

1. In a medium bowl, beat the eggs with the milk, flour, 2 tablespoons of the mustard, 1 tablespoon of the oil and a generous pinch of salt. Let the batter stand for 15 minutes.

2. Preheat the oven to 400°. Set a steamer basket in a medium saucepan filled with 1 inch of water. Add the carrots, cover and steam over high heat until just tender, about 4 minutes.

3. Add the remaining 2 tablespoons of oil to a 9-inch-square baking pan and heat in the oven for 10 minutes.

4. Meanwhile, in a large skillet, melt the butter. Add the onion, garlic and a generous pinch of salt and cook over moderately high heat, stirring, until the onion just starts to soften, 3 minutes. Add the haricots verts and cook, stirring, until the onion is lightly browned and the beans are just softened, 3 to 4 minutes. Add the carrots, tomatoes, herbs and the remaining 1 teaspoon of mustard and cook, stirring, until hot, 1 minute. Season the vegetables with salt and pepper.

5. Pour the batter evenly into the hot pan and scatter the vegetable mixture on top. Bake for 30 to 35 minutes, until puffed and lightly browned. Cut into squares and serve. —*Marte Marie Forsberg*

LOADED POTATO
WAFFLES

Loaded Potato Waffles

⏱ Total **40 min**; Serves **4**

Justin Chapple, star of F&W's Mad Genius Tips videos, uses his waffle iron for extra-crispy hash brown–potato pancake mash-ups. He loads this potato waffle like a baked potato: with cheddar, bacon, sour cream and chives.

- 2 lbs. baking potatoes—peeled, coarsely shredded and squeezed dry
- 2 large eggs, lightly beaten
- 3 Tbsp. all-purpose flour
- 1½ tsp. kosher salt
- 1 tsp. baking powder
- ¾ cup shredded extra-sharp yellow cheddar cheese, plus more for topping
- 3 Tbsp. melted unsalted butter, plus more for brushing
- ½ cup crumbled cooked bacon, plus more for topping
- ⅓ cup chopped chives, plus more for topping
  Sour cream, for topping

1. Heat an 8-inch waffle iron and preheat the oven to 200°. In a large bowl, mix the potatoes with the eggs, flour, salt, baking powder, ¾ cup of cheese and 3 tablespoons of butter. Fold in the ½ cup of bacon and the ⅓ cup of chives.

2. Brush the waffle iron with melted butter and spread one-fourth of the potato mixture onto it. Close and cook on high until the waffle is golden and crisp, 5 to 7 minutes. Transfer to a rack in the oven to keep warm. Repeat with the remaining potato mixture. Serve the waffles topped with sour cream, crumbled bacon, cheddar and chopped chives. —*Justin Chapple*

NOTE These waffles can be made in a Belgian waffle maker to serve 3: Spoon one-third of the mixture onto the iron instead of one-fourth.

Waffled Potato Blini with Smoked Salmon

⏱ Total **40 min**; Serves **4**

Cooking shredded potatoes in a waffle iron creates potato waffles that are crunchy on the outside and moist within. These elevated potato waffles are topped with smoked salmon, sour cream and dill.

- 2 lbs. baking potatoes—peeled, coarsely shredded and squeezed dry
- 1 medium onion, shredded
- 2 large eggs, lightly beaten
- 3 Tbsp. all-purpose flour
- 1½ tsp. kosher salt
- 1 tsp. baking powder
- 2 Tbsp. chopped dill, plus more for garnish
- 3 Tbsp. melted unsalted butter, plus more for brushing
  Smoked salmon and sour cream, for serving

1. Heat an 8-inch waffle iron and preheat the oven to 200°. In a large bowl, mix the potatoes with the onion, eggs, flour, salt, baking powder, the 2 tablespoons of dill and 3 tablespoons of butter.

2. Brush the waffle iron with melted butter and spread one-fourth of the potato mixture onto it. Close and cook on high until the blini is golden and crisp, 5 to 7 minutes. Transfer to a rack in the oven to keep warm. Repeat with the remaining potato mixture. Serve the blini topped with smoked salmon, sour cream and dill. —*Justin Chapple*

NOTE These waffles can be made in a Belgian waffle maker to serve 3: Spoon one-third of the mixture onto the iron instead of one-fourth.

Spicy Chicken-and-Sausage Hash

⏱ Total **45 min**; Serves **6**

- ¼ cup canola oil
- ½ lb. baby Yukon Gold potatoes, chopped
- 1 yellow onion, thinly sliced
- 2 yellow bell peppers, thinly sliced
  Kosher salt and pepper
- ½ lb. skinless, boneless chicken, cut into 1-inch pieces
- ½ lb. breakfast sausages, casings removed
  One 14½-oz. can chopped tomatoes
- 3 garlic cloves, minced
- 1 Tbsp. Worcestershire sauce
- 1 Tbsp. hot sauce
- ½ Tbsp. prepared horseradish
  Biscuits, for serving

1. In a large cast-iron or nonstick skillet, heat 2 tablespoons of the oil. Add the potatoes and cook over moderately high heat, stirring occasionally, until softened and golden, 7 to 8 minutes. Using a slotted spoon, transfer the potatoes to a plate.

2. Add the remaining 2 tablespoons of oil to the skillet. Add the onion and bell peppers, season with salt and pepper and cook over moderate heat, stirring occasionally, until tender and lightly browned, about 8 minutes. Add the chicken and sausage and cook until browned, about 5 minutes. Stir in the tomatoes, garlic, Worcestershire sauce, hot sauce and horseradish and cook until the sauce is thickened, about 5 minutes. Stir in the potatoes until warmed through. Season with salt and pepper and serve with biscuits. —*Colby Garrelts*

WINE Juicy, medium-bodied red: 2013 Domaine Les Hautes Noëlles Hého Rouge.

Cheese, Ale and Potato Pie

Active **45 min**; Total **2 hr 30 min**
Serves **8 to 10**

To make this incredible savory pie, Claire Ptak, owner of the cult Violet Bakery in London, mixes potatoes with an ale-spiked cheese sauce. You can use any kind of ale—light or dark.

- **Two 14-oz. packages all-butter puff pastry, chilled**
- **2¼ lbs. medium Yukon Gold potatoes**
- **Kosher salt and pepper**
- **¾ cup ale, such as Bass**
- **1 cup plus 2 Tbsp. heavy cream**
- **15 oz. sharp cheddar cheese, shredded (5 cups)**
- **3 large egg yolks, plus 1 large egg lightly beaten**
- **1½ Tbsp. Worcestershire sauce**
- **1½ tsp. Dijon mustard**

1. On a lightly floured work surface, roll out each puff pastry sheet to a 10-by-14-inch rectangle. Stack the pastry sheets on a cookie sheet with a piece of parchment paper between them. Refrigerate until chilled.

2. In a large saucepan, cover the potatoes with 1 inch of water. Add salt, bring to a boil and cook over moderately high heat until the potatoes are just tender, about 15 minutes. Drain and cool under running water. Pat the potatoes dry, then peel and quarter them. Gently crush with your hand or a wooden spoon.

3. In a medium saucepan, boil the ale over high heat until reduced to ⅓ cup, about 5 minutes. Add the cream and cook, whisking, until reduced to ¾ cup, about 5 minutes. Add the cheese and cook over moderate heat, stirring constantly, until the sauce is smooth, about 3 minutes. Remove from the heat and whisk in the egg yolks, Worcestershire and mustard. Season the sauce with salt and pepper and let cool. Carefully stir in the crushed potatoes and season again with salt and pepper.

4. Arrange 1 chilled puff pastry sheet on a rimmed baking sheet lined with parchment paper and brush with some of the beaten egg. Spread the potato filling on top, leaving a ½-inch border all around. Top with the second sheet of puff pastry and press the edges together to seal; crimp decoratively. Brush the top of the pie with more of the beaten egg and cut a few slits for venting. Refrigerate until firm, at least 30 minutes.

5. Preheat the oven to 400°. Bake the pie for 25 minutes. Reduce the oven temperature to 350°, rotate the baking sheet and bake until the pastry is browned and the filling is bubbling, 25 to 30 minutes longer. Let cool slightly before serving. —*Claire Ptak*

BEER Balanced, malty English bitter: Wells Bombardier.

Buttermilk Pancakes with Quince-and-Cranberry Compote

Total **1 hr**; Serves **4**

COMPOTE

- **1 quince—peeled, cored and cut into ¼-inch dice**
- **⅓ cup granulated sugar**
- **½ tsp. kosher salt**
- **1 cinnamon stick**
- **2 Gala apples, peeled and cut into ¼-inch dice**
- **⅓ cup fresh or thawed frozen cranberries**
- **2 tsp. honey**
- **Finely grated zest and juice of ½ lemon**

PANCAKES

- **1½ cups all-purpose flour**
- **1½ Tbsp. baking powder**
- **½ tsp. kosher salt**
- **2 large eggs**
- **1½ cups buttermilk**
- **3 Tbsp. unsalted butter, melted, plus 4 Tbsp. cold unsalted butter, cut into tablespoons**
- **¼ cup confectioners' sugar**
- **Pure maple syrup, for serving**

1. Make the compote In a saucepan, combine the quince with the sugar, salt, cinnamon stick and ⅓ cup of water. Bring to a simmer and cook over moderately low heat for 5 minutes. Stir in the apples, cranberries, honey and lemon zest and juice and cook, stirring, until the fruit is tender but not broken down, 5 minutes. Let cool.

2. Make the pancakes In a medium bowl, whisk the flour, baking powder and salt. In a large bowl, beat the eggs with a hand mixer until pale yellow and doubled in volume, 4 minutes. Beat in the buttermilk, then beat in the melted butter. Using a rubber spatula, fold in the dry ingredients.

3. Heat a large nonstick skillet. Swirl 1 tablespoon of the cold butter around the pan until melted and foamy. Using a small measuring cup, scoop three 4-inch pancakes into the skillet. Cook over moderate heat until golden brown on the bottom and bubbles appear on the surface, 1 to 2 minutes. Flip the pancakes and cook until golden on the bottom, 1 to 2 minutes more. Transfer to a baking sheet and keep warm. Repeat with the remaining butter and batter.

4. Stack the pancakes on plates and top with the compote. Dust with the confectioners' sugar and serve with maple syrup. —*Amanda Freitag*

Lemony Apricot Clafoutis

Active **15 min**; Total **1 hr**; Serves **4**

- **3 large eggs**
- **½ cup granulated sugar**
- **½ cup half-and-half**
- **3 Tbsp. all-purpose flour**
- **1½ Tbsp. finely grated lemon zest (from 1 lemon)**
- **¾ tsp. kosher salt**
- **4 apricots—halved, pitted and cut into wedges**
- **Confectioners' sugar, for dusting**

Preheat the oven to 350°. In a large bowl, beat the eggs with the granulated sugar, half-and-half, flour, lemon zest and salt until very smooth. Pour the batter into a 1-quart gratin dish or a 9-inch ceramic pie plate and arrange the apricots on top. Bake for about 30 minutes, until the custard is just set. Let stand for 10 minutes, then dust with confectioners' sugar and serve. —*Justin Chapple*

BUTTERMILK PANCAKES
WITH QUINCE-AND-
CRANBERRY COMPOTE

BLUEBERRY
DUTCH BABY

Blueberry Dutch Baby

Total **30 min**; Serves **4**

Cookbook author Ben Mims uses pomegranate juice to sweeten the batter for this light and berry-rich pancake.

- ¾ cup all-purpose flour
- ½ cup whole milk
- ¼ cup pomegranate juice
- 3 large eggs
- 6 Tbsp. salted butter
- 1 cup blueberries
- Confectioners' sugar, for dusting

Preheat the oven to 425°. In a large bowl, whisk the flour with the milk, pomegranate juice and eggs until blended. In a 12-inch ovenproof skillet, melt the butter over high heat until foamy. Pour in the batter and sprinkle on the blueberries. Transfer the skillet to the oven and bake for 20 minutes, until the pancake is golden brown. Dust with confectioners' sugar and serve immediately. —*Ben Mims*

Cardamom-Vanilla Biscuits

Active **20 min**; Total **1 hr**; Makes **12**

F&W's Kay Chun slices the dough for these fragrant, scone-like biscuits into wedges, so you can make them without a biscuit cutter. She serves the biscuits with fresh fruit and whipped cream.

- 2½ cups all-purpose flour
- ½ cup sugar
- 1 Tbsp. baking powder
- ¾ tsp. ground cardamom
- ½ tsp. kosher salt
- 1 stick plus 2 Tbsp. cold unsalted butter, cubed
- 1¼ cups heavy cream
- 1 tsp. pure vanilla extract

1. Preheat the oven to 350°. Line a baking sheet with parchment paper. In a large bowl, whisk the flour with the sugar, baking powder, cardamom and salt. Using your fingertips, blend in the butter until pea-size pieces form. Stir in the heavy cream and vanilla just until a dough forms. Pat the dough into a 1-inch-thick round, about 9 inches in diameter. Cut into 12 equal wedges.

2. Transfer the wedges to the prepared sheet and bake for 40 minutes, until golden. Transfer the biscuits to a rack to cool slightly before serving. —*Kay Chun*

MAKE AHEAD The biscuits can be stored in an airtight container at room temperature overnight and reheated before serving.

Sugared Lemon-Rosemary Scones

Active **20 min**; Total **1 hr 45 min**; Makes **8**

- 2¼ cups all-purpose flour, plus more for dusting
- ⅓ cup sugar, plus more for sprinkling
- 2 Tbsp. finely chopped fresh rosemary
- 1 Tbsp. baking powder
- ¾ tsp. kosher salt
- Finely grated zest of 1 lemon
- 1½ sticks cold unsalted butter, cubed
- ¾ cup heavy cream, plus more for brushing

1. In a food processor, pulse the 2¼ cups of flour with the ⅓ cup of sugar, the rosemary, baking powder, salt and lemon zest. Add the butter and pulse until the mixture resembles coarse meal, with some pea-size pieces of butter still visible. Transfer to a large bowl and stir in the ¾ cup of cream until a shaggy dough forms. Turn the dough out onto a lightly floured work surface and gently knead just until it comes together. Gently roll the dough into a 14-inch log, wrap in plastic and refrigerate for 1 hour, or until firm.

2. Preheat the oven to 375° and line a baking sheet with parchment paper. Slice the log into 8 rounds and transfer to the baking sheet. Brush the scones with cream and sprinkle generously with sugar. Bake for 22 to 25 minutes, until the scones are golden. Let cool slightly before serving. —*Erin French*

MAKE AHEAD The recipe can be prepared through Step 1 and refrigerated overnight.

Ginger-Molasses Scones

Active **20 min**; Total **45 min**; Makes **8**

Whole-wheat flour and molasses give these scones a rich and hearty flavor.

- 2 cups all-purpose flour
- 1½ cups whole-wheat flour
- 1 Tbsp. baking powder
- 1 tsp. ground ginger
- ½ tsp. ground cinnamon
- ¼ tsp. ground cloves
- ¼ tsp. kosher salt
- 1 stick plus 6 Tbsp. cold unsalted butter, cut into small cubes
- ¾ cup crème fraîche
- 5 Tbsp. unsulfured molasses
- 1 Tbsp. honey, plus more for serving
- 1 tsp. finely grated orange zest
- ¼ cup turbinado sugar, plus more for sprinkling
- 1 cup candied ginger (4 oz.), finely chopped
- 1 large egg, lightly beaten
- Softened unsalted butter, for serving

1. Preheat the oven to 400°. In a food processor, combine the flours, baking powder, ground ginger, cinnamon, cloves and salt; pulse to combine. Add the butter and pulse until pea-size crumbs form.

2. In a medium bowl, whisk the crème fraîche with the molasses, the 1 tablespoon of honey, the grated orange zest and the ¼ cup of sugar. Add the molasses mixture to the food processor along with the candied ginger. Pulse until the dough just comes together, 30 seconds. Transfer to a lightly floured work surface and pat into a 12-by-4-inch rectangle, about 1 inch thick. Divide the dough into 4 equal rectangles, then cut each rectangle into 2 triangles.

3. Arrange the scones on a parchment paper–lined baking sheet and brush generously with the beaten egg. Sprinkle with sugar. Bake the scones until golden brown and slightly firm, 20 to 25 minutes. Serve warm with butter and honey. —*Claire Ptak*

MAKE AHEAD The unbaked scones can be wrapped in plastic and frozen for up to 1 month. Bake from frozen, allowing a little extra baking time.

DIY CROISSANTS

Baker **ERICA SKOLNIK** of Frenchie's in Washington, DC, simplifies the method for making light and flaky croissants. Here, she gives a hands-on lesson for anyone who wants to tackle this iconic French pastry.

Croissants

Active **1 hr 15 min**; Total **10 hr plus 2 overnight restings**; Makes **18**

SPONGE

- 1¼ cups all-purpose flour
- ⅔ cup water, at room temperature
- One ¼-oz. package active dry yeast

DOUGH

- Extra-virgin olive oil, for greasing
- 1¾ cups plus 1 Tbsp. whole milk
- 3 cups all-purpose flour
- 3 cups bread flour
- ⅓ cup plus 1 Tbsp. sugar
- 1½ Tbsp. kosher salt
- Two ¼-oz. packages active dry yeast
- 5 sticks (1¼ lbs.) cold unsalted European-style butter (82% butterfat), such as Plugrá
- 2 large eggs

1. Make the sponge In a medium bowl, combine the flour, water and yeast and mix well with a wooden spoon. Cover with plastic wrap and refrigerate overnight.

2. Make the dough Let the sponge stand at room temperature for 30 minutes. Lightly grease a large bowl with olive oil.

3. In a small saucepan, heat the milk until lukewarm. In the bowl of a stand mixer fitted with the dough hook, combine both flours with the sugar, salt and yeast. Scrape in the sponge. At low speed, drizzle in the milk and mix just until the dough comes together. Let stand for 10 minutes.

4. Knead the dough at low speed until it forms a ball, about 3 minutes. Transfer to the prepared bowl, cover with plastic wrap and let stand at room temperature for 30 minutes. Punch down and refrigerate the dough for 3 hours.

5. Meanwhile, on a sheet of parchment paper, arrange the sticks of butter side by side so they touch. Cover with another sheet of parchment. Using a rolling pin, pound the butter flat and roll out to a 10-by-12-inch rectangle. Refrigerate until ready to use.

6. Remove the butter from the refrigerator and let stand at room temperature for about 10 minutes, until soft and pliable—the butter should yield gently when you press it with your finger and hold the indent, like a ripe avocado. On a lightly floured surface, using a lightly floured rolling pin, roll out the dough to a 12-by-28-inch rectangle. If the dough springs back, cover it with a kitchen towel and let rest for 5 minutes before rolling. Arrange the butter in the center of the dough so the short sides are parallel. Fold over the 2 short sides of the dough so they meet in the center; pinch together to seal. Pinch the long sides of the dough together to completely seal in the butter. Turn the dough so that a long side is facing you and roll out to a 12-by-28-inch rectangle. Starting from the bottom, fold the dough into thirds like a letter. Brush off any excess flour and wrap the dough in plastic. Chill until firm but pliable, about 1 hour.

7. Arrange the dough on a lightly floured surface with a short side facing you. Using a lightly floured rolling pin, roll out the dough to a 12-by-28-inch rectangle. Fold into thirds like a letter, wrap in plastic and freeze overnight. Before baking, let

PREP THE DOUGH

1

ADD WARM MILK and the yeasty "sponge" to the dry ingredients. Mix to make an elastic dough.

2

SHAPE THE BUTTER by pounding it flat, then rolling it into a rectangle between sheets of parchment paper.

3

FOLD THE DOUGH over the rectangle of butter, then pinch the seams together to form a sealed package.

4

DO THE FIRST TURN Roll out the dough into a large rectangle, then fold into thirds like a letter.

thaw in the refrigerator until semi-firm and pliable, about 3 hours.

8. Line 3 baking sheets with parchment paper. On a lightly floured surface, using a lightly floured rolling pin, roll out the layered dough to a 13-by-36-inch rectangle. Using a pizza cutter or sharp knife, cut the dough crosswise to form nine 13-by-4-inch strips. Halve each strip lengthwise on the diagonal to make 18 long triangles. Starting at the short side, roll each triangle into a crescent shape. Arrange the croissants on the prepared sheets, tip side down and spaced 3 inches apart. Cover loosely with plastic wrap and let rise at room temperature until doubled in size, 1 to 2 hours.

9. Preheat the oven to 400°. In a small bowl, beat the eggs with 1 tablespoon of water. Brush the croissants with the egg wash and bake until deep golden brown and crisp, 20 to 23 minutes. Transfer the croissants to a rack to cool.

MAKE AHEAD The baked croissants can be frozen for up to 1 month. Reheat in a 350° oven until warm and crisp.

BIGGER, BETTER CROISSANTS
Skolnik makes her croissants larger than the classic kind. "There are more layers to unravel," she says. "People feel like they're getting something special."

CROISSANT-SHAPING TUTORIAL

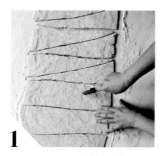

1 CUT THE DOUGH Roll out the layered dough; cut into wide strips, then cut in half diagonally to make long triangles.

2 FORM THE CROISSANTS Starting at the short side of each triangle, roll the dough to create a crescent shape.

3 GLAZE WITH AN EGG WASH For a shiny, burnished look, brush with a mixture of egg and water just before baking.

DATE SCONES WITH
FLEUR DE SEL
WHIPPED BUTTER

Date Scones with Fleur de Sel Whipped Butter

Active **20 min;** Total **1 hr 30 min plus cooling;** Makes **8**

The breakfast menu at Jon & Vinny's in L.A. is heavy on homey baked goods like these scones. The salty whipped butter is fabulous with the sugary dates.

BUTTER

- 1 **stick unsalted butter, at room temperature**
- ½ **Tbsp. fleur de sel**

SCONES

- 2¼ **cups all-purpose flour, plus more for dusting**
- ¼ **cup granulated sugar**
- 1½ **Tbsp. baking powder**
- ¼ **tsp. kosher salt**
- 4 **Tbsp. cold unsalted butter, cubed**
- 1 **cup chopped pitted dates**
- 1½ **cups heavy cream, plus more for brushing**

  Turbinado sugar, for sprinkling

  Jam, for serving

1. Make the butter In a medium bowl, beat the butter with the fleur de sel until fluffy, about 3 minutes.

2. Make the scones Line a baking sheet with parchment paper. In a large bowl, sift the 2¼ cups of flour with the granulated sugar, baking powder and salt. Using your fingertips, rub the butter into the flour mixture until it resembles coarse crumbs. Add the dates and toss to coat in flour. Drizzle in the 1½ cups of cream and stir until a dough forms. Cover with plastic wrap and let stand for 10 minutes.

3. Turn the dough out onto a lightly floured work surface and knead gently until it comes together. Pat the dough into a 5-by-10-inch rectangle. Cut into 8 equal squares and arrange on the prepared sheet. Refrigerate for 30 minutes.

4. Preheat the oven to 375°. Brush the tops of the scones with cream and sprinkle with turbinado sugar. Bake for about 25 minutes, until golden. Transfer the scones to a rack to cool completely. Serve with the salted whipped butter and jam.
—*Jon Shook and Vinny Dotolo*

Pumpkin-Chai Muffins

Active **15 min;** Total **45 min plus cooling** Makes **12**

- 1 **stick unsalted butter**
- 1 **Tbsp. crushed chai tea (from 4 bags)**
- 2 **large eggs**
- 1 **cup sugar**
- 1 **cup pumpkin puree**
- 1⅓ **cups all-purpose flour**
- 1¼ **tsp. baking soda**
- ½ **tsp. kosher salt**
- 1½ **cups chopped walnuts**

1. Preheat the oven to 350° and line a 12-cup muffin pan with paper or foil liners. In a small saucepan, melt the butter with the chai tea. In a large bowl, whisk the eggs with the sugar, pumpkin puree and chai butter until smooth. Whisk in the flour, baking soda and salt until incorporated.

2. Scoop the batter into the muffin cups and top with the walnuts. Bake for 20 to 25 minutes, until a toothpick inserted in the center of a muffin comes out clean. Transfer the muffins to a rack to cool completely before serving. —*Justin Chapple*

Garlic Pain Perdu

Total **30 min;** Serves **4**

- 4 **large eggs**
- 2 **cups milk**
- 3 **large garlic cloves, finely grated**
- 1½ **tsp. kosher salt**
- 1 **tsp. finely chopped thyme**
- ½ **tsp. pepper**

  Eight 1-inch-thick slices of soft white French or Italian bread

  Unsalted butter, for brushing

1. In a large baking dish, beat the eggs with the milk, garlic, salt, thyme and pepper. Add half the bread and let soak for 5 minutes, turning once.

2. Meanwhile, preheat a cast-iron griddle or skillet over moderately high heat; brush with butter. Remove the bread from the egg mixture, allowing the excess to drip off. Add the soaked bread to the griddle and cook, turning once, until golden and cooked through, 4 minutes. Transfer to a platter; keep warm. Butter the griddle again and repeat with the remaining bread. —*Mimi Thorisson*

Sour Cream Coffee Cake Muffins

Active **30 min;** Total **1 hr 5 min;** Makes **18**

Two Old Tarts was a super-popular farmers' market stand in New York's Catskill Mountains before becoming a brick-and-mortar bakery and café. It's famous for the sour cream coffee cake sold at the pastry counter; this is a muffin version.

- 1 **cup pecans**
- 1 **cup packed dark brown sugar**
- 1½ **tsp. cinnamon**
- 1 **stick plus 2 Tbsp. unsalted butter, softened**
- 1¾ **cups all-purpose flour**
- 1 **tsp. baking powder**
- ½ **tsp. baking soda**
- ½ **tsp. kosher salt**
- 1 **cup granulated sugar**
- 3 **large eggs**
- 1 **cup sour cream**
- 1½ **tsp. pure vanilla extract**

1. Preheat the oven to 400° and line 18 muffin cups with paper or foil liners. Spread the pecans in a pie plate and toast in the oven until fragrant and lightly browned, about 8 minutes. Let cool completely.

2. In a food processor, combine the pecans with the brown sugar, cinnamon and 4 tablespoons of the butter and pulse until the pecans are finely ground and the crumb topping resembles wet sand.

3. In a medium bowl, whisk the flour with the baking powder, baking soda and salt. In a large bowl, using a hand mixer, beat the remaining 6 tablespoons of butter with the granulated sugar at medium speed until fluffy, 1 to 2 minutes. Beat in the eggs 1 at a time until incorporated, then beat in the sour cream, vanilla and 2 tablespoons of water. Beat in the dry ingredients.

4. Spoon half of the batter into the prepared muffin cups and sprinkle with one-third of the crumb topping. Top with the remaining batter and sprinkle the remaining crumb topping evenly over the batter. Bake for about 25 minutes, until the tops are browned and a toothpick inserted in the center of a muffin comes out clean. Transfer the muffins to a rack to cool for 10 minutes. Serve warm or at room temperature.
—*Scott Finley and John Schulman*

Spiced Rice Breakfast Porridge

⏱ Active **10 min;** Total **40 min;** Serves **4**

In this hearty porridge from F&W's Kay Chun, steel-cut oats and brown rice come together under a buttery, sweet topping of caramelized bananas.

- **1 cup steel-cut oats (not quick-cooking)**
- **½ cup short-grain brown rice (not quick-cooking)**
- **One 3-inch cinnamon stick**
- **⅓ cup plus 2 Tbsp. turbinado sugar**
- **½ tsp. kosher salt**
- **2 Tbsp. unsalted butter**
- **2 bananas, peeled and halved lengthwise**
- **Roasted chopped almonds and heavy cream, for serving**

1. In a medium saucepan, combine 4 cups of water with the oats, rice, cinnamon stick, ⅓ cup of the sugar and the salt; bring to a simmer. Cover and cook over low heat, stirring occasionally, until tender and thickened, about 30 minutes. Discard the cinnamon stick.

2. Meanwhile, in a nonstick skillet, melt the butter. Press the remaining 2 tablespoons of sugar on the cut sides of the bananas. Cook sugar side down over moderately high heat until caramelized, about 2 minutes. Top the porridge with the bananas. Serve with chopped almonds and cream. —*Kay Chun*

Creamy Steel-Cut Oats with Dried Cherries and Almonds

📷 PAGE 279

⏱ Total **30 min;** Serves **4 to 6**

Steel-cut oats are simply chopped whole oats; they're super-nutritious and have a great chew. Marco Canora, chef at Hearth in New York City and author of *A Good Food Day,* likes to simmer the oats in whole milk or cream and almond milk with sweet spices for a breakfast with staying power.

- **½ cup dried sour cherries**
- **1 cup whole milk or cream**
- **1 cup unsweetened, unflavored almond milk**
- **1 cup steel-cut oats**
- **1 tsp. cinnamon**
- **1 tsp. ground ginger**
- **¼ tsp. ground allspice**
- **Kosher salt**
- **1 Tbsp. pure maple syrup, plus more for drizzling**
- **¼ cup sliced almonds, plus more for topping**

1. In a small bowl, cover the dried sour cherries with warm water and let stand until plumped and softened, about 15 minutes. Drain the cherries and discard the soaking water.

2. Meanwhile, in a medium saucepan, combine the whole milk, almond milk and 1 cup of water and bring to a boil. Stir in the oats, cinnamon, ginger, allspice and ¼ teaspoon of salt. Cover and cook over low heat, stirring occasionally, until the oats are al dente and the porridge is creamy, 20 minutes.

3. Stir in the cherries, 1 tablespoon of maple syrup and ¼ cup of almonds and season with salt. Serve topped with more maple syrup and almonds. —*Marco Canora*

MAKE AHEAD The porridge can be refrigerated for up to 2 days. Reheat gently with more milk or cream to loosen as necessary.

Oatmeal with Strawberries, Toasted Walnuts and Skyr

⏱ Total **15 min;** Serves **2**

Grød, a stall in Copenhagen's Torvehallerne market, specializes in porridge, with flavors that change seasonally. This lovely berry version is especially good because it's not too sweet: There's no added sugar.

- **½ cup walnuts**
- **1½ cups rolled oats (about 5 oz.)**
- **1½ cups milk**
- **Pinch of kosher salt**
- **6 strawberries, hulled and sliced**
- **2 Tbsp. skyr (Icelandic yogurt) or Greek yogurt**

1. Heat a medium saucepan. Add the walnuts and cook over moderately high heat, tossing, until toasted and fragrant, about 2 minutes. Transfer to a cutting board and coarsely chop. Wipe out the saucepan.

2. Combine the oats, milk and salt with 1½ cups of water in the saucepan and bring to a boil. Reduce the heat to moderately low and simmer, stirring often, until thickened, 7 to 8 minutes.

3. Spoon the oatmeal into bowls and sprinkle with the toasted walnuts. Top with the sliced strawberries and skyr and serve. —*Lasse Andersen*

Wunderkind blogger and cookbook author Kamran Siddiqi sometimes tries up to 80 versions while perfecting desserts like banoffee pie layered with dulce de leche (recipe, p. 308).

TARTS, PIES & FRUIT DESSERTS

PISTACHIO PAVLOVA
WITH RHUBARB CREAM
Recipe, page 318

BLUEBERRY PIE
WITH RYE CRUST

Blueberry Pie with Rye Crust

Active **1 hr**; Total **4 hr plus 5 hr cooling**
Makes **one 9-inch pie**

CRUST

- **1¼ cups all-purpose flour**
- **1 cup dark rye flour**
- **1½ tsp. kosher salt**
- **1 stick plus 6 Tbsp. cold unsalted butter, cubed**
- **⅔ cup ice water**

FILLING

- **1 vanilla bean, split lengthwise, seeds scraped**
- **¾ cup granulated sugar**
- **½ tsp. kosher salt**
- **2 lbs. blueberries (6 cups)**
- **½ cup all-purpose flour**
- **1 Tbsp. finely grated lemon zest plus 2 Tbsp. fresh lemon juice**
- **1 large egg beaten with 2 tsp. water**
- **Turbinado sugar, for sprinkling**

1. Make the crust In a food processor, pulse both flours with the salt to mix. Add the butter and pulse until it is the size of small peas. Sprinkle the water over the flour and pulse just until a dough starts to form. Turn the dough out onto a work surface, gather up any crumbs and knead gently until the dough comes together. Cut the dough in half and pat each piece into a disk. Wrap the disks in plastic and refrigerate until well chilled, about 1 hour.

2. On a lightly floured work surface, roll out 1 disk of dough to a 12-inch round. Ease the dough into a 9-inch glass pie plate and trim the overhang to ½ inch. Freeze for 15 minutes.

3. Prepare the filling In a large bowl, rub the vanilla seeds into the granulated sugar and salt. Add the blueberries, flour, lemon zest and lemon juice and toss well. Scrape the filling into the pie crust.

4. On a lightly floured work surface, roll out the remaining disk of dough to a 12-inch round. Using three sizes of small round cutters, stamp out decorative holes in the dough, leaving a 2-inch border. Lay the dough over the filling and trim the overhang to ½ inch. Press the overhang together to seal, then fold it under itself. Freeze the pie for 1 hour.

5. Preheat the oven to 375°. Brush the pie with the egg wash and sprinkle with turbinado sugar. Bake for about 1 hour and 15 minutes, until the filling is bubbling and the crust is browned; cover the edge of the pie with foil if it browns too quickly. Let the pie cool completely before serving, at least 5 hours or overnight. —*Justin Chapple*

Strawberry Slab Pie

Active **30 min**; Total **3 hr plus cooling**
Serves **6**

A slab pie is a shallow pie made in a baking sheet or pan. This one from Boston's Joanne Chang has a perfectly buttery crust and a sweet jammy filling.

PASTRY

- **2 cups all-purpose flour, plus more for dusting**
- **4 tsp. granulated sugar**
- **1 tsp. kosher salt**
- **2 sticks plus 2 Tbsp. unsalted butter, cut into tablespoons and chilled**
- **2 large egg yolks**
- **¼ cup cold whole milk**
- **Baking spray**

PIE

- **1½ lbs. strawberries, hulled and quartered (4 cups)**
- **1 cup granulated sugar**
- **¼ cup cornstarch**
- **½ tsp. finely grated orange zest**
- **¼ tsp. kosher salt**
- **1 large egg, beaten**
- **3 Tbsp. sanding or turbinado sugar**

1. Make the pastry In a stand mixer fitted with the paddle, combine the 2 cups of flour, the sugar and salt and mix at low speed. Add the butter and mix at medium speed until almost incorporated, with some pecan-size pieces remaining, about 1 minute. In a small bowl, whisk the egg yolks with the milk. With the machine on, drizzle the egg mixture into the flour mixture and mix until the pastry just starts to come together, about 30 seconds; it will be crumbly. Scrape the pastry onto a lightly floured work surface and gather it together. Using the heel of your hand, smear the pastry against the work surface to work in the butter. Form the pastry into a 1-inch-thick disk, cover in plastic wrap and refrigerate until firm, at least 1 hour.

2. Preheat the oven to 350°. Grease an 8-inch-square baking pan with baking spray and line with parchment paper, leaving 3 inches of overhang on all sides.

3. Cut one-third of the pastry off the disk. On a lightly floured surface, using a lightly floured rolling pin, roll out the smaller piece of pastry to an 8-inch square; transfer to a parchment paper–lined baking sheet and refrigerate. Roll out the larger piece of pastry to a 12-inch square, about ¼ inch thick. Ease the pastry into the prepared pan, pressing it into the corners and up the sides; trim the excess pastry, leaving no overhang. Line the pastry with parchment paper and fill with pie weights. Bake for about 30 minutes, until just pale golden and set. Remove the pie weights and parchment paper. Transfer the pan to a rack and let the crust cool completely.

4. Make the pie In a medium bowl, toss the strawberries with the granulated sugar, cornstarch, orange zest and salt. Spread the filling in the pastry crust. Cover with the chilled piece of pastry crust, gently pressing it down around the edges. Brush the top with the beaten egg and sprinkle with the sanding sugar. Using a sharp paring knife, make six 2-inch-long slits in the top pastry. Bake for about 50 minutes, until the crust is deep golden. Transfer the pan to a rack to cool, at least 3 hours. Carefully lift the pie out of the pan and transfer to a platter before serving. —*Joanne Chang*

Mountain Rose Apple Pie

Active **1 hr 15 min;** Total **3 hr 15 min plus cooling; Makes one 9-inch pie**

Pastry chef Rebecca Masson of Houston's Fluff Bake Bar adds layers of flavor to her desserts, and also obsesses over texture: "I do not like toothless apple pie," she declares. Here, Masson tops her dense and delicious apple pie with a thick mound of buttery crumble.

CRUST

1½ cups all-purpose flour, plus more for dusting

1 Tbsp. granulated sugar

½ tsp. kosher salt

1½ sticks unsalted butter, cubed and chilled

¼ cup ice water

2 tsp. distilled white vinegar

TOPPING

1½ cups all-purpose flour

1 cup old-fashioned rolled oats

1 cup packed dark brown sugar

Pinch of kosher salt

2 sticks cold unsalted butter, cubed

FILLING

3 lbs. Mountain Rose or Granny Smith apples—peeled, cored and cut into ⅓-inch-thick wedges

3 Tbsp. all-purpose flour

1½ Tbsp. fresh lemon juice

1½ tsp. ground cinnamon

½ tsp. ground cloves

½ tsp. freshly grated nutmeg

½ tsp. kosher salt

1. Make the crust In a food processor, pulse the 1½ cups of flour with the granulated sugar and salt. Add the butter and pulse until the mixture resembles coarse meal with some pea-size pieces remaining. Sprinkle the ice water and vinegar on top and pulse until evenly moistened. Turn the dough out onto a work surface, gather up any crumbs and form into a ball. Flatten into a disk, wrap in plastic and refrigerate until firm, about 1 hour.

2. Preheat the oven to 400°. On a floured work surface, roll out the dough to a 14-inch round, a scant ¼ inch thick. Ease the dough into a 9-inch deep-dish glass pie plate and trim the overhang to 2 inches. Fold the overhanging dough under itself to form a ½-inch-high rim; crimp decoratively. Freeze the crust for 15 minutes.

3. Meanwhile, make the topping In a stand mixer fitted with the paddle, mix the flour with the oats, brown sugar and salt at low speed. With the machine at medium speed, gradually beat in the butter. Transfer to a bowl and press into clumps. Cover and refrigerate until firm, about 15 minutes.

4. Make the filling In a large bowl, toss the apples with the flour, lemon juice, cinnamon, cloves, nutmeg and salt. Spread the apple mixture in the crust and set the pie on a large rimmed baking sheet. Bake the pie for about 25 minutes, until the crust is just starting to brown.

5. Remove the pie from the oven and gently pack the crumb topping onto the apples. Bake for 30 minutes longer, until the topping is golden and the pie is just starting to bubble. Let cool completely on a rack before serving. —*Rebecca Masson*

Blueberry Hand Pies

Active **45 min;** Total **2 hr 15 min; Makes 16**

These crisp, berry-filled mini pies can be frozen (unbaked) for 2 weeks and popped in the oven 25 minutes before serving.

DOUGH

2 cups all-purpose flour, plus more for rolling

½ cup confectioners' sugar

½ tsp. fine sea salt

1½ sticks cold unsalted butter, cubed

1 large egg yolk

¼ cup ice water

FILLING

2 cups blueberries

⅓ cup granulated sugar

2 Tbsp. all-purpose flour

2 Tbsp. fresh lemon juice

¼ tsp. fine sea salt

¼ tsp. ground cinnamon

1 large egg beaten with 1 tsp. water

Turbinado sugar, for sprinkling

1. Make the dough In a large bowl, whisk the 2 cups of flour with the confectioners' sugar and salt. Cut in the butter using a pastry cutter or 2 knives until the mixture resembles coarse meal with some pea-size pieces of butter remaining. Using a wooden spoon, stir in the egg yolk and water until a shaggy dough forms. Turn the dough out onto a work surface and knead gently until smooth. Cut the dough in half and shape into 2 disks. Wrap the disks in plastic and refrigerate until chilled, about 1 hour.

2. Meanwhile, make the filling In a medium bowl, toss the blueberries with the granulated sugar, flour, lemon juice, salt and cinnamon.

3. On a lightly floured work surface, roll out 1 disk of dough to a 16-by-9-inch rectangle, about ⅛ inch thick. Using a 4-inch plate as a guide, cut out 8 rounds from the dough. Spoon 2 tablespoons of the filling into the center of a dough round and fold the dough over to form a half-moon. Press the edge to seal, then crimp decoratively. Transfer the hand pie to a parchment paper–lined baking sheet. Repeat with all of the remaining dough and filling; space the pies 1 inch apart. Refrigerate the hand pies until well chilled, about 30 minutes.

4. Preheat the oven to 400°. Brush the hand pies with the beaten egg and sprinkle with turbinado sugar. Bake for 15 to 18 minutes, until golden; some of the juices will spill out. Let cool slightly. Serve warm or at room temperature. —*Kamran Siddiqi*

BLUEBERRY

BUTTERMILK
EGGNOG PIE

Buttermilk Eggnog Pie

Active **30 min;** Total **3 hr 45 min plus cooling;** Serves **12**

TV chef Carla Hall makes her sweet Southern buttermilk pie with rum and lots of nutmeg, giving it the flavor of eggnog.

CRUST

- **1 cup all-purpose flour, plus more for rolling**
- **1½ tsp. sugar**
- **½ tsp. table salt**
- **1 stick cold unsalted butter, cut into ½-inch cubes**
- **2 Tbsp. ice water**

FILLING

- **1½ cups sugar**
- **1 Tbsp. all-purpose flour**
- **2 tsp. freshly grated nutmeg**
- **½ tsp. kosher salt**
- **3 large eggs, at room temperature**
- **5 Tbsp. unsalted butter, melted and cooled**
- **1 cup buttermilk, at room temperature**
- **1 Tbsp. dark rum**
- **1 tsp. pure vanilla extract**

1. Make the crust In a medium bowl, whisk the 1 cup of flour with the sugar and salt. Add the butter and, using your fingertips, rub it into the flour until the mixture resembles coarse meal with some pea-size pieces remaining. Stir in the ice water just until the dough comes together. Form the dough into a ball, then flatten it into a 1-inch-thick disk. Wrap in plastic and refrigerate until firm, at least 1 hour or up to 1 day.

2. On a lightly floured work surface, using a lightly floured rolling pin, roll out the dough to a 12-inch round. Ease the dough into a 9-inch pie plate and tuck any overhang under itself. Crimp decoratively. Freeze until firm, about 30 minutes.

3. Preheat the oven to 425°. Line the dough with parchment paper, then fill with pie weights or dried beans. Bake for about 25 minutes, just until the dough is set. Remove the parchment paper and weights; bake for 8 to 10 minutes longer, until light golden. Transfer the crust to a rack to cool slightly, about 10 minutes. Reduce the oven temperature to 375°.

4. Make the filling In a large bowl, whisk the sugar with the flour, nutmeg and salt. Whisk in the eggs 1 at a time. While whisking constantly, slowly drizzle in the melted butter followed by the buttermilk, rum and vanilla. Pour the filling into the warm crust. Bake for 15 minutes, then reduce the oven temperature to 350° and bake for about 40 minutes longer, until the custard is just set at the edge and slightly jiggly in the center. Transfer the pie to a rack and let cool completely. Serve at room temperature or chilled. —*Carla Hall*

MAKE AHEAD The baked and cooled pie can be refrigerated overnight.

Pumpkin and White Chocolate Mousse Pie

Active **45 min;** Total **3 hr 30 min** Makes **one 9-inch pie**

This reimagined pumpkin pie from Mr. Holmes Bakehouse in San Francisco has an ethereal mousse filling and a stellar graham cracker crust made with macadamia nuts.

CRUST

- **¼ cup macadamia nuts**
- **10 whole graham crackers, broken into small pieces**
- **7 Tbsp. unsalted butter, melted**
- **¼ cup light brown sugar**
- **1 Tbsp. fine cornmeal**
- **¾ tsp. ground cinnamon**
- **¼ tsp. grated nutmeg**
- **¼ tsp. kosher salt**

PUMPKIN FILLING

- **1 Tbsp. unflavored powdered gelatin**
- **3½ oz. white chocolate, finely chopped**
- **2 large egg yolks**
- **¼ cup granulated sugar**
- **1 cup heavy cream**
- **1 small bay leaf**
- **One 2-inch cinnamon stick**
- **2 pinches of ground allspice**
- **1 pinch of grated nutmeg**
- **½ tsp. pure vanilla extract**
- **1½ cups pumpkin puree**
- **½ tsp. kosher salt**

1. Make the crust Preheat the oven to 325°. Toast the macadamias on a pie plate for 15 minutes, until golden. Let cool.

2. In a food processor, pulse the graham crackers until finely ground; transfer to a medium bowl. In the processor, pulse the macadamias until finely ground; add to the bowl. Add all of the remaining ingredients to the bowl and mix well. Press the crust over the bottom and up the side of a 9-inch pie plate. Bake for about 20 minutes, until set. Transfer to a rack and let cool.

3. Meanwhile, make the filling In a small bowl, sprinkle the gelatin over ⅓ cup of water; let stand for 5 minutes. Place the white chocolate in a large bowl.

4. In a medium bowl, whisk the egg yolks with the granulated sugar. In a small saucepan, simmer ¾ cup of the heavy cream with the bay leaf, cinnamon stick, allspice, nutmeg and vanilla for 1 minute. Discard the cinnamon stick and bay leaf. While whisking constantly, slowly drizzle the heavy cream mixture into the egg mixture. Whisk in the gelatin mixture. Immediately pour the hot egg mixture over the white chocolate; let stand for 1 minute, then whisk until smooth. Whisk in the pumpkin puree and salt until incorporated. Refrigerate until cold, about 1 hour.

5. In a small bowl, whisk the remaining ¼ cup of heavy cream until soft peaks form; fold into the pumpkin filling until incorporated. Scrape the filling into the baked crust and spread in an even layer. Cover and refrigerate for 1 hour before serving. —*Mr. Holmes Bakehouse*

Coconut Cream Pie

Active **1 hr 10 min**; Total **4 hr 10 min**
Makes **one 9-inch pie**

Kierin Baldwin, the pastry chef at Locanda Verde in New York City, is a self-proclaimed pie geek. Here, she adds coconut to every part of her fluffy pie: the crust, the fillling and the topping.

FILLING

1½ cups unsweetened coconut milk
1 tsp. unflavored powdered gelatin
2 cups heavy cream
⅓ cup granulated sugar
1½ Tbsp. corn syrup
½ tsp. kosher salt
1 vanilla bean—split lengthwise, seeds scraped, pod reserved
2½ Tbsp. cornstarch mixed with 2 Tbsp. water
2 Tbsp. unsalted butter
¼ cup plus 2 Tbsp. sweetened cream of coconut, such as Coco Lopez

CRUST

3 cups Nilla Wafer cookies, crushed (1 cup packed)
½ cup sweetened shredded coconut
1 Tbsp. all-purpose flour
1 Tbsp. granulated sugar
1 Tbsp. turbinado sugar
½ tsp. kosher salt
5 Tbsp. unsalted butter, melted
Toasted coconut flakes, for garnish

1. Make the filling In a small bowl, whisk ¼ cup of the coconut milk with the gelatin. In a medium saucepan, combine the remaining 1¼ cups of coconut milk with ½ cup of the heavy cream. Add the sugar, corn syrup, ¼ teaspoon of the salt and the vanilla bean and seeds; bring just to a simmer over moderately high heat. Whisk in the cornstarch mixture and bring to a boil, then simmer, whisking constantly, until thickened, about 3 minutes. Remove from the heat and whisk in the gelatin mixture until dissolved, then whisk in the butter and ¼ cup of the cream of coconut. Strain the filling through a fine sieve into a heatproof bowl; discard the vanilla bean. Press a sheet of plastic wrap directly on the surface of the filling and let cool, then refrigerate until well chilled, about 1 hour.

2. Meanwhile, make the crust Preheat the oven to 325°. In a food processor, pulse the cookies with all of the remaining ingredients except the toasted coconut. Transfer the crumbs to a 9-inch metal pie plate. Press the crumbs evenly over the bottom and up the side of the pie plate, forming a ¼-inch edge over the rim of the plate. Bake the crust for 10 to 12 minutes, rotating halfway through baking, until dry and lightly browned. Let cool.

3. In a large bowl, using a hand mixer, beat the remaining 1½ cups of heavy cream, 2 tablespoons of cream of coconut and ¼ teaspoon of salt until firm. Fold one-third of the whipped cream into the filling until no streaks remain. Spread the filling in the crust. Mound the remaining whipped cream on top and refrigerate the pie for at least 2 hours. Garnish with toasted coconut before serving.
—*Kierin Baldwin*

MAKE AHEAD The finished pie can be refrigerated overnight.

Custard Phyllo Pie with Almonds and Pistachios

Active **35 min**; Total **3 hr 15 min plus cooling**; Serves **8**

For this unusual open-face pie, pastry chef Ghaya Oliveira of Daniel in New York City layers buttered phyllo with nuts, then drenches the crust with lemon syrup and fills it with custard.

1 cup plus 2 Tbsp. sugar
1½ Tbsp. cornstarch
¼ tsp. kosher salt
1 large egg yolk
1½ cups plus 2 Tbsp. whole milk
½ vanilla bean—split lengthwise, seeds scraped, pod reserved
1 cup raw almonds
¾ cup raw pistachios
1 stick unsalted butter, melted
10 sheets of phyllo dough
2 Tbsp. fresh lemon juice

1. In a medium saucepan, whisk 2 tablespoons of the sugar with the cornstarch and salt. Whisk in the egg yolk, then whisk in the milk and vanilla bean and seeds. Bring to a simmer over moderately high heat, whisking constantly, and cook until a loose custard forms, about 3 minutes. Strain into a bowl and press a sheet of plastic wrap directly onto the surface of the custard. Let cool, then refrigerate until chilled, at least 2 hours.

2. Preheat the oven to 350°. Toast the almonds and pistachios on a rimmed baking sheet for about 8 minutes, stirring occasionally, until lightly browned. Transfer to a rack to cool; coarsely chop the nuts. Leave the oven on.

3. Butter a 9-inch pie plate. Set 1 sheet of phyllo on a work surface and brush the top with some of the melted butter. Arrange the buttered phyllo in the pie plate and sprinkle with 2 tablespoons of the nuts. Repeat the process with the remaining phyllo sheets and melted butter, and more of the nuts; reserve the remaining nuts.

4. Poke holes through and around the phyllo layers with a fork. Using scissors, trim the overhanging dough. Bake for about 25 minutes, until the phyllo is golden brown and crisp, rotating the pie plate halfway through baking. Place the plate on a rack set over a foil-lined rimmed baking sheet.

5. Meanwhile, in a small saucepan, stir the remaining 1 cup of sugar with ¾ cup of water and the lemon juice. Bring to a boil over high heat and cook until the syrup thickens slightly, about 4 minutes. Slowly drizzle the syrup all over the phyllo crust, including the edge. Let cool completely.

6. To serve, pour half of the custard into the crust and sprinkle the reserved nuts on top. Serve the pie sliced into wedges with the remaining custard on the side.
—*Ghaya Oliveira*

MAKE AHEAD The pie can be prepared through Step 4 one day ahead: Refrigerate the custard; let the nuts and phyllo crust stand at room temperature.

Lazy Mary's Lemon Tart

Active **30 min**; Total **3 hr 50 min plus 6 hr cooling**; Makes **one 9-inch tart**

A whole Meyer lemon goes into this improbably delicious tart—just toss it in the blender with the other filling ingredients.

PASTRY DOUGH

- **1¾ cups plus 2 Tbsp. all-purpose flour, plus more for dusting**
- **⅓ cup plus 3 Tbsp. confectioners' sugar**
- **¾ tsp. kosher salt**
- **⅓ cup plus 3 Tbsp. chilled lard or vegetable shortening**
- **2 Tbsp. unsalted butter, cubed and chilled**
- **¼ cup plus 2 Tbsp. ice water**

FILLING

- **1 large Meyer lemon, chopped**
- **1½ cups superfine sugar**
- **1 stick unsalted butter, at room temperature**
- **1 tsp. pure vanilla extract**
- **4 large eggs**

1. Make the dough Into a medium bowl, sift the flour with the confectioners' sugar and salt. Using your fingertips, rub half of the lard into the flour mixture until it resembles coarse meal. Rub the remaining lard and the butter into the flour mixture until pea-size pieces remain. Sprinkle with the ice water and mix with a fork until the dough comes together. On a lightly floured work surface, pat the dough into a 1-inch-thick disk. Wrap with plastic and chill until firm, about 1 hour.

2. On a lightly floured work surface and using a lightly floured rolling pin, roll out the dough to a 14-inch circle, about ⅛ inch thick. Ease the dough into a 9-inch fluted tart pan with a removable bottom (2 inches deep) and trim the overhang. Prick the dough all over with a fork and freeze until firm, 1 hour.

3. Preheat the oven to 375°. Line the frozen pie shell with parchment paper and fill with pie weights or dried beans. Bake for 25 minutes, until the edge is lightly golden. Remove the paper and bake for 15 minutes longer, until the shell is golden. Transfer to a rack and let cool completely, 3 hours.

4. Make the filling Preheat the oven to 350°. In a blender, combine the Meyer lemon, superfine sugar, butter, vanilla and eggs and puree until smooth. Pour the mixture into the tart shell. Bake for 40 minutes, until the filling is set. Transfer the tart to a rack and let cool to room temperature, 3 hours. Serve at room temperature or chilled. —*Mary Constant*

MAKE AHEAD The dough can be prepared through Step 1 and refrigerated overnight, or prepared through Step 2 and frozen for up to 1 month. The finished tart can be wrapped and refrigerated for 2 days.

Portuguese Custard Tarts

Active **1 hr**; Total **2 hr 30 min** Makes **12 small tarts**

Beth Kirby of the Local Milk blog says that in Portugal, pastéis de nata (egg tarts) are a touristy snack—but that didn't stop her from eating them everywhere, even at the airport. This superlight version is the best one of all, she says.

PASTRY

- **1¼ cups all-purpose flour, plus more for dusting**
- **Pinch of kosher salt**
- **1 stick plus 5 Tbsp. cold unsalted butter, cubed**
- **⅓ cup ice water**

CUSTARD

- **3 Tbsp. all-purpose flour**
- **1 cup whole milk**
- **¾ cup granulated sugar**
- **One 3-inch cinnamon stick**
- **Two 2-inch strips of lemon zest**
- **¼ cup heavy cream**
- **6 large egg yolks**
- **Confectioners' sugar and cinnamon, for dusting**

1. Make the pastry In a large bowl, whisk the 1¼ cups of flour with the salt. Scatter the butter on top. Using a pastry cutter or 2 knives, cut the butter into the flour until the mixture resembles coarse meal, with some pea-size pieces remaining. Stir in the water until the dough just comes together. Scrape the dough out onto a floured work surface, gather up any crumbs and pat the dough into a rectangle. Dust with flour and roll into a 6-by-9-inch rectangle. Brush off any visible flour. Fold one short side of the

dough into the center and dust off any flour. Fold the other short side on top, like you would fold a letter. Turn the dough 90 degrees, so the folds are facing you. Roll out the dough again to a 6-by-9-inch rectangle and fold like a letter again; this is 2 turns. Repeat the rolling and folding 4 more times for a total of 6 turns. Wrap the dough in plastic and refrigerate until well chilled, about 1 hour.

2. Meanwhile, make the custard In a large bowl, whisk the flour with ¼ cup of the milk. In a microwave-safe bowl, microwave the remaining ¾ cup of milk on high until hot, about 30 seconds. Gradually whisk the hot milk into the flour mixture.

3. In a small saucepan, combine the granulated sugar with ½ cup plus 2 tablespoons of water, the cinnamon stick and lemon zest. Bring to a boil over high heat, stirring to dissolve the sugar. Simmer over moderately high heat until the temperature reaches 220° on a candy thermometer, about 12 minutes; discard the cinnamon stick and lemon zest. Gradually whisk the hot syrup into the milk mixture, then whisk in the heavy cream and egg yolks. Let cool completely.

4. Preheat the oven to 450°. On a floured work surface, roll out the pastry to a 14-by-6-inch rectangle, about ¼ inch thick. Brush off any excess flour and, starting at a long side, tightly roll up the pastry into a log. Using a sharp knife, cut the log crosswise into 12 pieces. Lay each piece cut side down on a work surface and gently flatten it with your palm, then roll out to a 4-inch round. Ease each round into 1 cup of a 12-cup muffin pan. Refrigerate until the pastry cups are firm, about 20 minutes.

5. Spoon the custard into the chilled pastry cups. Bake for 18 to 20 minutes, until the crusts are browned and the custard is set. Let cool for 15 minutes. Transfer the tarts to a platter and dust with confectioners' sugar and cinnamon. Serve warm or at room temperature. —*Beth Kirby*

MAKE AHEAD The custard and unbaked pastry cups can be refrigerated separately overnight. The tarts can be baked up to 6 hours ahead and kept at room temperature.

Cherry Jam–and–Ricotta Tart

Active **45 min;** Total **2 hr 30 min plus
overnight chilling;** Serves **8**

"Romans are masters at using 'the fifth
quarter,' things that are usually discarded—
like ricotta, a by-product of making pecorino
cheese," says Rachel Roddy, a Rome-based
blogger and author of *My Kitchen in Rome*.
She adds lushness to this spectacular dou-
ble-crust tart with a thick layer of fresh
ricotta.

**2¼ cups all-purpose flour, plus more
for rolling**

**10 Tbsp. cold unsalted butter, cubed,
plus more for greasing**

¾ cup superfine sugar

1 tsp. finely grated lemon zest

Pinch of kosher salt

4 large eggs plus 1 large egg yolk

1 lb. fresh ricotta cheese (2 cups)

**One 13-oz. jar cherry or sour cherry
jam (1¼ cups)**

Whipped cream, for serving

1. In a medium bowl, combine the 2¼ cups
of flour and cubed butter. Using your fingertips, rub the butter into the flour until
the mixture resembles fine breadcrumbs.
Stir in ½ cup of the sugar, the lemon zest
and salt. In a small bowl, beat 2 of the eggs;
add to the flour mixture and stir with a
wooden spoon until a dough starts to come
together. Knead with your hands just until
a dough forms. Divide the dough into a
one-third piece and a two-thirds piece; pat
each piece into a 1-inch-thick disk and wrap
in plastic. Refrigerate for at least 1 hour
or overnight.

2. Preheat the oven to 350°. Lightly
butter a 9-inch fluted tart pan. In a small
bowl, whisk the ricotta with 1 egg, the
egg yolk and the remaining ¼ cup of sugar
until blended.

3. On a lightly floured surface, using a
lightly floured rolling pin, roll out the larger
piece of dough to a 12-inch round about
⅛ inch thick. Ease the dough into the prepared tart pan and trim off the excess;
prick the bottom of the dough all over with
a fork. Spread the jam in an even layer over
the bottom of the tart, then spread the
ricotta mixture evenly on top of the jam.

4. Roll out the remaining piece of dough
to a 10-inch round. Using a sharp knife, cut
the pastry into strips of different widths
and arrange on top of the ricotta, leaving
space between the strips and pressing
them to adhere to the rim of the pan.

5. In a small bowl, beat the remaining egg
and brush onto the pastry strips. Bake the
tart in the center of the oven for about
50 minutes, until the crust is golden and
the filling is set. Transfer to a rack and
let cool to room temperature. Cover and
refrigerate overnight. Serve chilled, with
whipped cream. —*Rachel Roddy*

MAKE AHEAD The tart can be refrigerated
for up to 2 days.

Banoffee Pie

Active **45 min;** Total **6 hr 30 min**
Makes **one 9-inch pie**

Banoffee pie is a classic English dessert
made with bananas, toffee and cream.
Blogger and cookbook author Kamran Siddiqi puts his spin on the recipe by using
dulce de leche in the filling and spreading
the crust with a layer of dark chocolate
to prevent it from getting soggy.

**1¼ cups all-purpose flour, plus more
for rolling**

¼ cup confectioners' sugar

½ tsp. fine sea salt

**2 sticks plus 2 Tbsp. cold
unsalted butter, cubed**

3 Tbsp. cold water

1 large egg yolk

½ cup packed dark brown sugar

1 cup dulce de leche

**One 3½-oz. dark chocolate bar,
finely chopped**

3 large bananas, thinly sliced

1 cup heavy cream

1. In a large bowl, whisk the 1¼ cups of flour
with the confectioners' sugar and salt.
Using a pastry blender or 2 knives, cut in
1 stick plus 2 tablespoons of the butter
until the mixture resembles coarse meal
with some pea-size pieces of butter
remaining. Stir in the cold water and egg
yolk until the dough just comes together.
Scrape the dough out onto a work surface
and pat into a disk. Wrap the dough in
plastic and refrigerate for 1 hour.

2. Preheat the oven to 350°. On a lightly
floured work surface, roll out the dough to
a 12-inch round, a scant ¼ inch thick. Ease
the dough into a 9-inch pie plate. Trim the
overhang to 1 inch and fold it under itself.
Crimp the edge and freeze until firm, about
15 minutes.

3. Line the crust with parchment paper and
fill with pie weights or dried beans. Bake for
about 20 minutes, until the crust is barely
set. Remove the parchment and pie weights
and bake for 20 to 25 minutes longer, until
the crust is lightly browned; prick the bottom of the crust lightly to deflate it if it puffs
up. Let cool.

4. In a medium saucepan, combine the
remaining 1 stick of butter with the brown
sugar and cook over moderate heat until
the sugar is melted, about 5 minutes.
Remove from the heat. Stir in the dulce de
leche until smooth. Let the filling cool.

5. Meanwhile, in a microwave-safe medium
bowl, microwave the chopped chocolate
on high power in 10-second intervals until
melted. Spread the chocolate over the
cooled crust and freeze until firm, about
10 minutes.

6. Spread the dulce de leche filling over
the chocolate and top with the sliced
bananas. In a large bowl, using a hand
mixer, beat the cream until firm. Pile the
whipped cream on the pie and refrigerate
for at least 3 hours, until the filling is set.
Cut into wedges and serve.
—*Kamran Siddiqi*

BANOFFEE PIE

CRANBERRY-WALNUT TART
WITH BUCKWHEAT CRUST

Cranberry-Walnut Tart with Buckwheat Crust

Active **30 min**; Total **2 hr 30 min**
Makes **one 14-inch tart**

For this gorgeous tart, pastry chef Claire Ptak of London's Violet Bakery fills a cookie-like crust with walnut frangipane and glistening cranberries.

DOUGH

- 1 cup buckwheat flour
- 1 Tbsp. tapioca flour
- 1 stick plus 2 Tbsp. cold unsalted butter, cubed, plus more for greasing
- 1 tsp. kosher salt
- 2 large egg yolks, plus 1 large egg lightly beaten

FRANGIPANE

- ½ cup walnut halves
- ¼ cup sugar
- ½ stick unsalted butter, softened
- 1 large egg
- 1 Tbsp. tapioca flour
- 1 Tbsp. heavy cream
- 1 Tbsp. Grand Marnier
  Finely grated zest of 1 clementine or small orange
  Pinch of kosher salt

TOPPING

- 2 cups fresh or thawed frozen cranberries
- ¼ cup sugar
- 3 Tbsp. fresh clementine or orange juice

1. Make the dough In a food processor, pulse the two flours with the butter and salt until the mixture is the texture of wet sand. Add the egg yolks and 1 tablespoon of water and pulse until the dough just comes together in a ball. Transfer to a work surface and pat into a 3-by-6-inch rectangle. Wrap in plastic and refrigerate until firm, at least 30 minutes.

2. Butter a 4-by-14-inch fluted rectangular tart pan with a removable bottom. Set the dough between 2 sheets of plastic wrap; roll out to a 6-by-16-inch rectangle. Discard the top sheet of plastic wrap and invert the dough into the prepared pan. Gently press into the corners and up the sides of the pan. Discard the plastic wrap and trim the overhanging dough flush with the rim. Refrigerate until firm, at least 15 minutes.

3. Preheat the oven to 375°. Line the tart shell with parchment paper and fill with pie weights or dried beans. Bake for 15 minutes. Remove the parchment and pie weights and brush the tart shell with the beaten egg. Bake for about 5 more minutes, until set. Let cool slightly. Reduce the oven temperature to 350°.

4. Meanwhile, make the frangipane In a food processor, combine the walnuts and sugar; process until finely chopped. Add the butter, egg, tapioca flour, cream, Grand Marnier, clementine zest and salt and pulse until smooth. Scrape the frangipane into a bowl; chill until firm, 30 minutes.

5. Make the topping In a food processor, combine the cranberries, sugar and clementine juice and pulse just until the cranberries begin to break up.

6. Spread the frangipane in the tart shell and top with the cranberries. Set the tart on a rimmed baking sheet and bake, rotating once, until the frangipane is puffed and lightly browned at the edges, 30 to 35 minutes. Transfer to a rack and let cool. Unmold and serve. —*Claire Ptak*

SERVE WITH Greek yogurt.

Apple and Pear Galette with Walnut Streusel

Active **45 min**; Total **2 hr 45 min plus cooling**; Serves **12**

Free-form galettes are simpler to make than pies. Using unpeeled apples and pears adds texture and flavor while cutting down on time and ingredient waste.

CRUST

- 2 cups all-purpose flour, plus more for rolling
- ¾ tsp. kosher salt
- 1½ sticks cold unsalted butter, cubed
- ½ cup ice water

STREUSEL

- ⅔ cup walnuts
- ½ cup all-purpose flour
- ½ cup packed light brown sugar
- ½ tsp. kosher salt
- 6 Tbsp. cold unsalted butter, cubed

FILLING

- 2 Granny Smith apples—halved, cored and thinly sliced lengthwise
- 2 firm Bartlett pears—halved, cored and sliced lengthwise ¼ inch thick
- ¼ cup granulated sugar, plus more for sprinkling
- ¼ tsp. kosher salt
- 2 tsp. fresh lemon juice
- 1 large egg beaten with 1 tsp. water
  Confectioners' sugar, for dusting (optional)

1. Make the crust In a food processor, pulse the 2 cups of flour with the salt. Add the butter and pulse until the pieces are the size of small peas. Sprinkle the water on top and pulse until the dough just comes together. Turn the dough out onto a work surface, gather up any crumbs and pat into a disk. Wrap in plastic and refrigerate until well chilled, 1 hour.

2. Meanwhile, make the streusel Preheat the oven to 400°. Spread the walnuts in a pie plate and bake for about 8 minutes, until lightly browned. Let cool, then chop.

3. In a medium bowl, whisk the flour with the brown sugar and salt. Add the butter and, using your fingers, pinch it into the dry ingredients until the mixture resembles coarse meal. Add the walnuts and pinch the streusel into clumps. Refrigerate until chilled, about 15 minutes.

4. Make the filling Line a rimmed baking sheet with parchment paper. In a large bowl, toss the apples with the pears, ¼ cup of granulated sugar, the salt and lemon juice. On a lightly floured work surface, roll out the dough to a 19-by-13-inch oval. Ease the dough onto the prepared baking sheet. Mound the filling in the center of the oval, leaving a 2-inch border. Sprinkle the streusel evenly over the fruit and fold the edge of the dough up and over the filling.

5. Brush the crust with the egg wash and sprinkle evenly with granulated sugar. Bake the galette for 45 to 50 minutes, until the fruit is tender and the streusel and crust are golden brown. Let the galette cool. Dust with confectioners' sugar, if using, before serving. —*Justin Chapple*

Walnut Galette with Bourbon-Vanilla Custard Sauce

Active **1 hr**; Total **2 hr 30 min plus cooling**
Serves **8**

Maine chef Erin French makes a superflaky crust for this rustic tart and bakes it with a sticky-crunchy walnut filling that's not too sweet. On the side, she serves a luscious custard sauce spiked with bourbon.

CRUST

1¼ cups all-purpose flour, plus more for rolling

½ tsp. kosher salt

1 stick plus 2 Tbsp. cold unsalted butter, cubed

¼ cup ice water

FILLING

2 cups walnut halves

4 Tbsp. unsalted butter

½ cup light brown sugar

½ cup light corn syrup

1 tsp. pure vanilla extract

½ tsp. finely grated orange zest

Kosher salt

2 large eggs, lightly beaten

1 Tbsp. granulated sugar

CUSTARD SAUCE

¾ cup heavy cream

¾ cup whole milk

½ vanilla bean—split lengthwise, seeds scraped, pod reserved

3 large egg yolks

3 Tbsp. granulated sugar

2 tsp. bourbon

Pure maple syrup and Maldon sea salt, for serving

1. Make the crust In a food processor, pulse the 1¼ cups of flour with the salt. Add the butter and pulse until the mixture resembles coarse meal with some pea-size pieces of butter still visible. Sprinkle in the ice water and pulse until the dough starts to come together; you should still see small pieces of butter. Scrape the dough out onto a work surface and pat into a disk. Wrap in plastic and refrigerate until chilled, at least 1 hour or up to 3 days.

2. On a lightly floured work surface, roll out the dough to a 14-inch round. Transfer to a 10-inch springform pan and press in gently; it should reach halfway up the side. Refrigerate for 20 minutes, or until firm.

3. Make the filling Preheat the oven to 375°. Spread the walnuts in the chilled crust. In a medium saucepan, melt the butter over low heat. Add the brown sugar and corn syrup and stir until dissolved. Add the vanilla, orange zest and a pinch of salt. Whisk in the eggs. Pour the filling over the walnuts, then fold the dough over the filling in an overlapping pattern. Sprinkle the crust with the granulated sugar. Bake the galette for 40 minutes, until the filling is set and the crust is golden brown. Transfer to a rack and let cool completely.

4. Meanwhile, make the custard sauce In a medium saucepan, combine the cream, milk and vanilla bean and seeds and bring to a simmer over moderate heat. Remove from the heat, cover and let steep for 20 minutes. Discard the vanilla bean.

5. Set a heatproof medium bowl over a bowl of ice water. Return the cream mixture to a simmer and remove from the heat. In another medium bowl, whisk the egg yolks with the sugar until pale; slowly whisk in the hot cream. Pour the mixture into the saucepan and cook the custard sauce over moderate heat for 1 to 2 minutes, stirring constantly and scraping the bottom and side of the saucepan, until thickened. Pour the sauce into the bowl set over ice water and let cool completely, stirring occasionally. Stir in the bourbon and refrigerate.

6. Unmold the galette and transfer it to a plate. Drizzle with maple syrup and sprinkle with sea salt. Serve with the custard sauce. —*Erin French*

MAKE AHEAD The galette can be kept at room temperature for up to 2 days. The custard can be refrigerated for up to 3 days.

Fig and Frangipane Galettes

Active **1 hr**; Total **2 hr 30 min plus cooling**
Makes **six 4-inch galettes**

Frangipane (almond paste) adds flavor and richness to these moist, free-form tarts.

DOUGH

2 cups plus 2 Tbsp. all-purpose flour, plus more for dusting

1 Tbsp. granulated sugar

1 tsp. fine salt

2 sticks cold unsalted butter

½ cup ice water

FRANGIPANE

5 oz. almond paste

3 Tbsp. unsalted butter, softened

2 Tbsp. all-purpose flour

1 tsp. finely grated lemon zest

Pinch of fine salt

2 large eggs

½ cup apricot preserves

11 fresh Black Mission figs, stemmed and quartered

¼ cup turbinado sugar

1. Make the dough In a large bowl, whisk the flour with the sugar and salt. Using the large holes on a box grater, grate the butter over the flour. Gently toss the butter with the flour to mix. Sprinkle on the water and stir with a wooden spoon until the dough just starts to come together. Turn the dough out onto a lightly floured work surface and gather any crumbs. Gently flatten the dough with your hands and fold in half; repeat the flattening and folding 2 more times. Pat the dough into a disk, wrap it in plastic and refrigerate until chilled, about 30 minutes.

2. Preheat the oven to 375°. Line 2 large rimmed baking sheets with parchment paper. Divide the dough into 6 equal pieces and form into balls. On a lightly floured work surface, roll out each ball to a 6-inch round. Transfer the rounds to the baking sheets and refrigerate for 15 minutes.

3. Meanwhile, make the frangipane In a food processor, combine the almond paste with the butter, flour, lemon zest, salt and 1 egg. Pulse until smooth.

4. Spread the apricot preserves on the pastry rounds, leaving a 1-inch border around the edges. Spread the frangipane over the preserves and arrange the figs decoratively on top. Fold the pastry up and over the fruit. Beat the remaining egg with 1 tablespoon of water and brush some of the egg wash on the pastry rims; sprinkle with the turbinado sugar.

5. Bake the galettes for 40 to 45 minutes, rotating the baking sheets halfway through, until the crusts are browned and the frangipane is puffed. Let cool before serving. —*Gesine Bullock-Prado*

Lemon-Buttermilk Pudding

📷 BACK COVER

Active **20 min;** Total **4 hr;** Serves **6**

- 4 large egg yolks
- 6 Tbsp. sugar
- 1½ Tbsp. cornstarch
- ½ tsp. kosher salt
- 1½ cups heavy cream
- ½ cup buttermilk
- 1 tsp. pure vanilla extract
- ½ tsp. finely grated lemon zest plus 1 Tbsp. fresh lemon juice
- 1 cup unsweetened whipped cream
  Fresh berries, for serving

1. In a heatproof medium bowl, whisk the egg yolks with the sugar, cornstarch and salt until well blended.

2. In a medium saucepan, combine the heavy cream, buttermilk and vanilla and bring to a simmer. While whisking constantly, slowly drizzle ¼ cup of the hot cream mixture into the egg yolk mixture. Slowly whisk in the remaining cream mixture. Return the pudding to the saucepan and cook over moderately low heat, whisking occasionally, until thickened, about 7 minutes. Scrape the pudding into a medium bowl and whisk in the lemon zest and lemon juice. Press a sheet of plastic wrap directly on the surface of the pudding and let cool to room temperature, about 45 minutes. Refrigerate until cold, about 3 hours.

3. Swirl the whipped cream into the pudding. Serve in bowls topped with berries. —*Cheryl Day*

Peach Crisp with Brown Butter Crumble

Active **30 min;** Total **1 hr 45 min;** Serves **6**

PEACH CRISP

- Unsalted butter, for greasing
- 2 lbs. ripe peaches, pitted and cut into ¼-inch-thick wedges
- ¼ cup plus 2 Tbsp. sugar
- 3 Tbsp. fresh lemon juice
- 1 Tbsp. cornstarch
  Pinch of kosher salt

BROWN BUTTER CRUMBLE

- 1 cup all-purpose flour
- ½ cup quick-cooking oats
- ½ cup granulated sugar
- ¼ cup turbinado sugar
- 2 Tbsp. dark brown sugar
- ½ tsp. kosher salt
- ¼ tsp. ground cinnamon
- 1 stick unsalted butter, cut into tablespoons
  Vanilla ice cream, for serving

1. Make the crisp Preheat the oven to 350°. Butter a 2-quart baking dish. In a large bowl, toss the peaches with the sugar and lemon juice. Cover and let stand at room temperature for about 30 minutes, stirring occasionally, until the sugar dissolves and the peaches have released some of their juices. Drain the peaches in a colander set over a small saucepan, then return them to the bowl.

2. Add ¼ cup of water and the cornstarch to the peach juices and bring to a simmer. Cook, whisking constantly, until thickened and translucent, about 1 minute. Add the thickened juices and the salt to the peaches and toss to coat. Scrape into the prepared baking dish.

3. Meanwhile, make the brown butter crumble In a medium bowl, whisk the flour with the oats, the 3 sugars, the salt and cinnamon. In a small saucepan, cook the butter over moderately low heat, stirring, until deep golden and nutty-smelling, about 8 minutes. Scrape the butter and any browned bits at the bottom of the pan into the flour mixture and stir until well combined.

4. Press the topping into small clumps and scatter over the peaches. Bake for 50 to 60 minutes, until the crisp is golden and bubbling. Transfer to a rack and let stand for 15 minutes before serving with vanilla ice cream. —*Kierin Baldwin*

Lemon Soufflé Pudding Cakes

Active **30 min;** Total **1 hr;** Serves **6**

Maggie Harrison, winemaker for Antica Terra in Oregon's Willamette Valley, makes these decadent cakes with sweet, aromatic Meyer lemons and tangy buttermilk. The cakes are excellent either warm or cold.

- Softened butter, for greasing
- ½ cup plus 2 Tbsp. sugar
- 3 large eggs, separated
- ¼ cup all-purpose flour
- ¼ cup fresh lemon juice
- 1 Tbsp. finely grated Meyer lemon zest plus ¼ cup fresh Meyer lemon juice
- ½ cup full-fat buttermilk
- 6 Tbsp. whole milk
- ¼ tsp. fine salt
  Whipped cream, for serving

1. Preheat the oven to 350°. Butter six 6-ounce ramekins and set them in a baking dish.

2. In a large bowl, whisk ½ cup of the sugar with the egg yolks, flour, lemon juice and Meyer lemon zest and juice. Whisk in the buttermilk and whole milk.

3. In another bowl, using a hand mixer, beat the egg whites with the salt until frothy. Gradually beat in the remaining 2 tablespoons of sugar at medium-high speed; beat until medium-firm peaks form. Whisk one-third of the beaten whites into the lemon mixture, then fold in the rest; the batter will be thin.

4. Spoon the batter into the ramekins. Add enough hot water to the dish to reach halfway up the sides of the ramekins. Bake the cakes for 30 to 35 minutes, until puffed. Serve warm or cold, with whipped cream. —*Maggie Harrison*

Strawberry Mousse with Strawberry Salad

Total **30 min plus 1 hr chilling**; Serves **4**

STRAWBERRY MOUSSE

- **8 oz. ripe strawberries, hulled and halved**
- **1 Tbsp. powdered unflavored gelatin**
- **2 cups heavy cream**
- **½ cup sugar**
- **2 cups mascarpone**
- **1 vanilla bean, split lengthwise, seeds scraped**

STRAWBERRY SALAD

- **1 lb. ripe strawberries, hulled and sliced crosswise**
- **2 Tbsp. sugar**
- **2 tsp. finely grated lime zest**

1. Make the mousse In a food processor, puree the strawberries until smooth; you should have 1 cup. Scrape the puree into a small bowl.

2. In another small bowl, sprinkle the gelatin over ¼ cup of the cream and let stand for 5 minutes.

3. In a small saucepan, stir ¼ cup of the cream with the sugar over moderate heat until the sugar dissolves. Whisk in the gelatin mixture until dissolved; remove from the heat.

4. In a large bowl, combine the mascarpone and vanilla seeds. Using a hand mixer, beat the mascarpone at medium speed until thickened, about 3 minutes. With the mixer on, slowly drizzle in the gelatin mixture and beat for 1 minute. Fold in the strawberry puree.

5. In a large bowl, beat the remaining 1½ cups of heavy cream at medium speed until stiff peaks form. Fold the whipped cream into the mousse and spoon into bowls. Refrigerate until well chilled, at least 1 hour.

6. Meanwhile, make the strawberry salad In a medium bowl, toss the strawberries with the sugar and lime zest. Let macerate at room temperature for 20 minutes.

7. Spoon the strawberry salad and juices over the mousse and serve.
—*Dominic Quirke*

MAKE AHEAD The strawberry mousse can be refrigerated overnight.

Blueberry Cheesecake Mousse

Active **30 min**; Total **1 hr**; Serves **6**

- **1 cup blueberries, plus more for garnish**
- **½ cup sugar**
- **1 tsp. kosher salt**
- **1 cup sour cream**
- **8 oz. cream cheese, softened**
- **1 cup chilled heavy cream**
- **Chopped pistachios, for garnish**

1. In a small saucepan, mash the 1 cup of blueberries with the sugar and salt and bring to a simmer over moderate heat. Cook, stirring, until jammy, 10 minutes. Remove from the heat and scrape the jam into a food processor. Let cool completely.

2. Add the sour cream and cream cheese to the food processor and puree with the jam until smooth. In a large bowl, beat the heavy cream to soft peaks. Fold in the berry cream until blended. Spoon the mousse into glasses and sprinkle with chopped pistachios and blueberries.
—*Ben Mims*

Russian Cream with Strawberries

Total **30 min plus overnight chilling** Serves **8**

- **1 cup sugar**
- **Two ¼-oz. envelopes unflavored gelatin**
- **2¼ cups sour cream**
- **6 Tbsp. plus 1½ tsp. pure maple syrup**
- **1½ cups heavy cream**
- **1 cup red wine vinegar**
- **8 oz. strawberries, hulled and thinly sliced**

1. In a medium saucepan, combine the sugar and gelatin. Stir in ¾ cup of cold water and let stand for 5 minutes to soften the gelatin.

2. In a large bowl, whisk the sour cream with 1½ teaspoons of the maple syrup.

3. Bring the sugar-gelatin mixture to a boil, stirring constantly, until the sugar and gelatin dissolve. Remove the pan from the heat and whisk in the heavy cream until frothy on top. While whisking constantly, slowly drizzle the heavy cream mixture into the sour cream; whisk until fully incorporated. Divide the cream among eight 6-ounce ramekins and refrigerate overnight.

4. Meanwhile, in a small saucepan, combine the vinegar and the remaining 6 tablespoons of maple syrup and bring to a simmer. Cook until thickened and reduced to ½ cup, 15 to 20 minutes. Let the maple gastrique cool to room temperature and refrigerate.

5. To serve, top the Russian cream with the strawberries and drizzle with some of the maple gastrique. —*Zakary Pelaccio*

MAKE AHEAD The Russian cream can be refrigerated for up to 2 days.

Winter Fruit Salad in Ginger-Lime Syrup

Total **35 min**; Serves **6**

- **¼ cup pure maple syrup**
- **One 3-inch piece of fresh ginger, peeled and thinly sliced**
- **2 Tbsp. fresh lime juice**
- **3 clementines or mandarins**
- **2 blood oranges**
- **1 grapefruit**
- **1 Fuyu persimmon**
- **1 Asian pear**
- **1 red pear**
- **1 cup pomegranate seeds**
- **2 Tbsp. finely chopped mint**
- **Hemp seeds, for garnish**

1. In a small saucepan, bring the maple syrup and 1 tablespoon of water to a simmer with the ginger over moderately high heat. Remove from the heat and let steep for 15 minutes. Pick out and discard the ginger. Stir the lime juice into the syrup; let cool completely.

2. Meanwhile, using a sharp knife, peel all of the citrus fruits and cut off all of the bitter white pith. Working over a serving bowl, cut in between the membranes to release the sections. Squeeze the membranes over the bowl to catch all of the juices; discard the membranes.

3. Core the persimmon and both pears and then cut them into thin slices. Arrange the slices in the bowl with the citrus and top with the pomegranate seeds. Drizzle the fruit salad with the ginger-lime syrup, sprinkle with the mint and hemp seeds and serve immediately. —*Sara Forte*

STRAWBERRY MOUSSE WITH
STRAWBERRY SALAD

ORANGES IN RUM
AND CARAMEL

Oranges in Rum and Caramel

Total **30 min**; Serves **8**

- 8 navel oranges
- ¼ cup dark rum
- 1 cup sugar

1. Finely grate the zest of 2 of the oranges. Using a very sharp knife, peel all of the oranges, carefully removing all of the bitter white pith. Slice the oranges into ¼-inch-thick rounds and arrange them in a large, shallow bowl. Drizzle the rum over the oranges and sprinkle the zest on top.

2. In a large saucepan, spread the sugar in an even layer. Warm over moderate heat, without stirring, until the sugar starts to melt around the edge, about 3 minutes. Reduce the heat to low and shake the pan to mix the dry sugar and melted sugar. Continue to cook over low heat, swirling the pan frequently, until all of the sugar is melted and a dark amber caramel forms. Drizzle the caramel in long, thin lines over the oranges. Let the caramel cool, then serve. —*Alice Medrich*

Honeydew Granita

Active **30 min**; Total **3 hr 30 min**; Serves **8**

- One 5¼-lb. honeydew melon, rind removed, melon seeded and cut into chunks
- 3 Tbsp. sugar
- 2 Tbsp. fresh lime juice
- Kosher salt
- Mint leaves, for garnish

1. In a blender, working in batches, pulse the melon to a coarse puree. Strain through a fine sieve into another bowl, pressing very lightly on the pulp; discard the pulp. You should have 3 cups of juice.

2. In a small bowl, whisk the sugar with 3 tablespoons hot water until dissolved. Stir the sugar syrup into the melon juice along with the lime juice and a generous pinch of salt. Pour the mixture into a 9-by-13-inch metal or glass baking dish and freeze for 1 hour. Using a fork, scrape the granita to form fluffy ice. Continue to freeze and scrape every 30 minutes until the granita is frozen and fluffy, about 2 hours.

3. Fluff the granita with a fork. Scoop into small glasses, garnish with mint and serve right away. —*Ellen Bennett*

Burnt Strawberry Tamales

Active **45 min**; Total **2 hr 45 min plus overnight macerating**; Makes **8**

F&W Best New Chef 2015 Carlos Salgado of Taco María in Costa Mesa, California, makes these fantastic dessert tamales by charring strawberries in a skillet, then mixing them into a buttery masa filling.

- 2¾ cups evaporated cane sugar (see Note)
- 1 lb. strawberries, hulled
- 8 large dried cornhusks
- Boiling water
- 1¾ cup Bob's Red Mill masa harina
- 2 sticks unsalted butter, preferably cultured, at room temperature
- 2 tsp. baking powder
- ½ tsp. kosher salt
- 1 vanilla bean—split lengthwise, seeds scraped, pod reserved for later use
- Eight 10-inch squares of thin sandwich paper, moistened
- Vanilla ice cream or whipped cream with lime zest, for serving

1. In a medium saucepan, combine ¾ cup of the sugar with ¾ cup of water and bring to a simmer, stirring, until the sugar is dissolved. Transfer the syrup to a large bowl and let cool completely.

2. Heat a large cast-iron skillet over moderately high heat. When very hot, carefully add the strawberries, hulled side down, in a single layer and cook, undisturbed, until blackened, about 8 minutes. Transfer the strawberries to the cooled syrup. Cover and refrigerate overnight.

3. Drain the burnt strawberries and reserve the syrup for cocktails. In a medium saucepan, combine the strawberries and 1½ cups of the sugar and bring to a simmer. Cook, mashing the strawberries and stirring until the sugar is dissolved and the mixture is thickened, about 8 minutes. Let cool completely.

4. In a large heatproof bowl, cover the cornhusks with enough boiling water to completely submerge them; weigh them down with a plate. Cover and let stand for 15 minutes. Drain well; pat dry with paper towels.

5. In a medium bowl, combine the masa harina with 1 cup plus 2 tablespoons of water and mix until a dough forms.

6. In a stand mixer fitted with the paddle, beat the butter with the remaining ½ cup of sugar at medium-high speed until whipped and smooth, about 3 minutes. Beat in the baking powder, salt and vanilla seeds. Scrape the butter mixture into a bowl.

7. Add the masa dough to the stand mixer and beat until light and fluffy, about 3 minutes. Beat in 1 cup of the cooled strawberry mixture, ⅓ cup at a time and scraping down the bowl, until incorporated. Beat in the whipped butter in 3 additions, scraping down the bowl, until smooth. Refrigerate for 30 minutes.

8. Lay 1 cornhusk smooth side up on a work surface and spoon ½ cup of the tamale dough in the center. Roll the husk around the dough to make a compact cylinder, folding in the sides as you roll. Tie the tamale with kitchen string and wrap it tightly in a sheet of the sandwich paper. Repeat to form 7 more tamales.

9. Arrange the tamales in a steamer set over a pot of simmering water. Cover and steam until firm, 90 minutes. Let rest for 15 minutes before serving. Serve warm or at room temperature with the remaining burnt strawberry jam and ice cream or whipped cream. —*Carlos Salgado*

NOTE Evaporated cane sugar is a less processed form of cane sugar. Look for it at health food stores.

MAKE AHEAD The uncooked tamales can be frozen for 2 weeks; steam from frozen. The cooked tamales can be refrigerated for 2 days and rewarmed to serve. The jam can be refrigerated for 2 days.

Coconut-Lime Ice Pops

Active **10 min**; Total **2 hr 10 min**
Makes **10 to 12**

- Two 14-ounce cans unsweetened coconut milk
- ½ cup sugar
- Finely grated zest of 1 lime plus ½ cup fresh lime juice

In a blender, puree the coconut milk with the sugar and lime zest and juice. Pour through a fine strainer into a large measuring cup, then pour into 10 to 12 ice-pop molds. Freeze until set, at least 2 hours or up to 1 week. —*Rick Bayless*

Pistachio Pavlova with Rhubarb Cream

📷 PAGE 299

Active **40 min**; Total **3 hr 15 min plus cooling**; Serves **8**

Baker Gesine Bullock-Prado puts a spring spin on traditional pavlova by folding pistachios into the crisp-chewy meringue and mixing tangy rhubarb and strawberries into the cream that's piled on top.

PAVLOVA

- **1 cup chopped unsalted pistachios**
- **2 Tbsp. cornstarch**
- **5 large egg whites, at room temperature**
- **½ tsp. kosher salt**
- **1 tsp. distilled white vinegar**
- **1½ cups sugar**

RHUBARB CREAM

- **4 oz. rhubarb, chopped into 1-inch pieces (1 cup)**
- **¼ cup sugar**
- **½ tsp. finely grated lemon zest plus 3 Tbsp. fresh lemon juice**
- **1 cup hulled and quartered strawberries, plus ½ cup small strawberries for garnish**
- **1 tsp. vanilla bean paste or pure vanilla extract**
- **1½ cups heavy cream, chilled**
- **½ cup mascarpone cheese, chilled**
- **¼ cup chopped unsalted pistachios, for garnish**

1. Make the pavlova Preheat the oven to 350°. Line a baking sheet with parchment paper. In a small bowl, toss the pistachios with the cornstarch.

2. In a stand mixer fitted with the whisk, beat the egg whites with the salt at high speed until foamy, 2 minutes. Beat in the vinegar, then beat in the sugar, 1 tablespoon at a time, and continue beating until the whites are glossy and stiff peaks form, 8 to 10 minutes. Gently fold in the pistachio mixture. Using a large spoon, dollop the meringue onto the prepared sheet and spread into a 10-inch round with a slight indentation in the center. Lower the oven temperature to 225° and bake the meringue for about 1½ hours, until crisp but still chewy on the inside. Turn the oven off; let the meringue rest in the oven for 1 hour. Transfer to a rack and let cool.

3. Meanwhile, make the rhubarb cream In a small saucepan, simmer the rhubarb, sugar, lemon zest and lemon juice over moderate heat, stirring and mashing the rhubarb with the back of a wooden spoon, until the sugar is dissolved and the rhubarb breaks down, about 5 minutes. Remove the saucepan from the heat and stir in the quartered strawberries and vanilla bean paste. Let cool completely.

4. In a large bowl, using a hand mixer, beat the cream with the mascarpone at medium speed until moderately firm, about 3 minutes. Stir ¼ cup of the whipped cream into the cooled rhubarb, then fold the mixture into the remaining whipped cream. Spoon into the center of the meringue. Garnish with the small strawberries and chopped pistachios and serve.
—Gesine Bullock-Prado

Fruity Caipirinha Jelly

Total **25 min plus overnight chilling** Serves **4**

Spanish star chef Jordi Roca laces this fruit-packed jelly with the Brazilian spirit called cachaça. The dessert is like a spoonable cocktail.

- **¾ tsp. unflavored gelatin**
- **½ cup sugar**
- **½ cup cachaça**
- **½ cup finely diced apricot**
- **½ cup finely diced mango**
- **½ cup finely diced strawberries**
- **½ cup finely diced peeled apple**
- **4 fresh lychees—peeled, pitted and quartered**
- **1 Tbsp. finely shredded mint leaves**
- **Zest of 1 lime**

1. In a small saucepan, sprinkle the gelatin over 1¼ cups of cold water and let soften for 5 minutes. Add the sugar. Stir over moderately high heat until the sugar and gelatin are completely dissolved; do not boil. Remove from the heat and stir in the cachaça. Transfer to a heatproof bowl, cover with plastic wrap and refrigerate until the jelly is set, at least 8 hours or overnight.

2. Gently fold in the fruit, mint and lime zest. Spoon into chilled glasses and serve.
—Jordi Roca

Halvah Parfait with Figs and Spiced Crumble

Active **1 hr**; Total **5 hr**; Serves **6 to 8**

PARFAIT

- **1½ cups plus 2 Tbsp. heavy cream**
- **4 large egg yolks**
- **¾ cup granulated sugar**
- **1½ cups plus 2 Tbsp. lebneh**
- **2 cups shredded halvah (5 oz.)**

CRUMBLE

- **1 tsp. Sichuan peppercorns**
- **½ cup plus ⅓ cup all-purpose flour**
- **½ cup plus 3 Tbsp. almond meal**
- **½ cup plus ⅓ cup confectioners' sugar**
- **2 Tbsp. granulated sugar**
- **2 Tbsp. light brown sugar**
- **¾ tsp. ground cinnamon**
- **¼ tsp. kosher salt**
- **1 stick cold salted butter, cubed**

DATE PUREE

- **8 oz. pitted Medjool dates, chopped**
- **¾ cup ruby port wine**

SPICED FIGS

- **1 Tbsp. extra-virgin olive oil**
- **12 fresh or dried Black Mission figs, halved lengthwise**
- **3 Tbsp. honey**
- **1 tsp. ground cardamom**
- **1 tsp. ground ginger**
- **1 tsp. ground coriander**
- **¼ cup dry sherry**
- **2 tsp. sherry vinegar**
- **Vanilla ice cream, for serving**

1. Make the parfait In a small saucepan, bring the cream just to a simmer. In a large bowl, using a hand mixer, beat the egg yolks with the sugar until thickened and pale yellow, about 3 minutes. Beating constantly, slowly drizzle in the hot cream until well blended. Continue beating until the mixture is lightened and lukewarm, about 8 minutes. Beat in the lebneh and halvah at low speed until well blended, about 2 minutes. Evenly spread the mixture in a 9-inch-square metal pan lined with plastic wrap; freeze until firm, at least 4 hours.

2. Make the crumble Preheat the oven to 350°. In a spice grinder, finely grind the Sichuan peppercorns. Transfer to a large bowl and mix in all of the remaining dry ingredients, then beat in the butter until the mixture forms small pebbles. Spread the peppercorn crumble on a parchment-lined rimmed baking sheet and bake for 15 minutes, stirring a few times, until golden. Let cool.

3. Make the date puree In a small sauce-pan, combine the dates and port and bring to a simmer. Cook over moderate heat, stirring, until the dates break down, 5 to 7 minutes. Transfer to a food processor and puree until smooth. Scrape into a bowl.

4. Make the spiced figs In a nonstick skil-let, heat the oil. Add the figs cut side down and cook over moderately low heat, turn-ing once, until golden on both sides, about 4 minutes. Add the honey, cardamom, gin-ger and coriander and cook, stirring, until lightly caramelized, about 2 minutes. Add the sherry and vinegar and cook, stirring, until the liquid thickens, 3 minutes. Trans-fer to a bowl to cool.

5. Cut the halvah parfait into 6 or 8 squares or rounds. Spoon the date puree onto plates. Top with the halvah squares and spiced figs. Sprinkle with the crumble and serve with ice cream. —*Lior Lev Sercarz*

Riesling-Poached Peaches with Tarragon and Salted Sour Cream

Total **30 min plus chilling**; Serves **4**

2½ cups semidry Riesling

¼ cup sugar

½ vanilla bean, split, seeds scraped

5 tarragon sprigs

4 ripe but firm freestone peaches, halved and pitted

⅔ cup sour cream

Kosher salt

1. In a medium saucepan, combine the wine, sugar, vanilla bean and seeds and 1 tarragon sprig and bring just to a boil. Add the peach halves and simmer over moder-ate heat, turning occasionally, until tender, about 10 minutes. Let cool completely, then refrigerate until chilled, at least 1 hour.

2. In a medium bowl, whisk the sour cream with a big pinch of salt. Dollop the cream in bowls and top with the peach halves and some of their poaching liquid. Garnish each plate with a tarragon sprig and serve. —*Justin Chapple*

Cranberry and Almond Meringue Roulade

Active **45 min**; Total **2 hr 30 min** Serves **8 to 10**

L.A. chef Helene Henderson adores cran-berries, which remind her of her native Sweden. She serves them here with a light, soft meringue rolled around fluffy whipped cream.

2 cups fresh or thawed frozen cranberries

1¾ cups sugar

Vegetable oil, for brushing

4 large egg whites

1 cup sliced almonds

1 cup heavy cream

2 Tbsp. crème fraîche

1. Preheat the oven to 375°. In a saucepan, bring the cranberries, 1 cup of water and 1 cup of the sugar to a boil. Simmer over moderate heat, stirring, until the cranber-ries start to burst, 5 to 7 minutes. Let cool.

2. Brush a foil-lined rimmed baking sheet with oil. In a stand mixer, whisk the egg whites at medium-high speed to soft peaks. Beat in the remaining ¾ cup of sugar at high speed until the whites are stiff, 3 min-utes. Spread the meringue on the baking sheet in a ½-inch-thick rectangle. Top with the almonds and bake in the center of the oven for 15 minutes, until springy. Slide the meringue and foil onto a rack; let cool completely.

3. Beat the heavy cream and crème fraîche at medium speed until soft peaks form.

4. Cover the meringue with a sheet of foil and top with a baking sheet. Invert the meringue onto a work surface and remove the rack and top layer of foil. With a long side facing you, spread the cream over the meringue, leaving a 2-inch border. Using a slotted spoon, scatter the cranberries on top; reserve the syrup. Starting at the long side nearest you, carefully roll up the meringue. Transfer to a platter and refrigerate until chilled, at least 1 hour or up to 5 hours. Using a serrated knife, cut the roulade into slices and serve, passing the reserved syrup at the table.
—*Helene Henderson*

Sticky Drunken Pears

Active **10 min**; Total **1 hr 20 min**; Serves **8**

These pears are covered in a sweet wine syrup that becomes a wonderful glaze as they bake.

8 firm Bosc pears, stems attached

2 Tbsp. fresh lemon juice

3 cups sweet wine, such as Muscat de Beaumes-de-Venise

Strips of zest from 1 lemon

1 vanilla bean, split, seeds scraped

1 medium cinnamon stick

1 cup turbinado sugar

Whipped crème fraîche, for serving

1. Preheat the oven to 400°. In a 9-inch-square baking dish, arrange the pears stem end up, leaving space between them. Mix the lemon juice with the sweet wine and pour over the pears. Add the lemon zest, vanilla bean and seeds and cinnamon stick to the baking dish and sprinkle the sugar over the pears. Bake, basting every 15 minutes, until the pears are softened and starting to burst slightly, about 45 min-utes. Let cool for 10 minutes.

2. Using a slotted spoon, transfer the pears to a serving dish. Pour the syrup into a small saucepan. Cook over moderately high heat until reduced by one-third, 12 to 15 minutes; pour over the pears and serve with whipped crème fraîche. —*Claire Ptak*

Caramelized Figs with Pistachios and Vanilla Ice Cream

Total **20 min**; Serves **4**

¼ cup pistachios

12 fresh, firm figs, halved lengthwise

Honey, for brushing

Vanilla ice cream, for serving

1. Preheat the oven to 425°. Spread the pis-tachios in a pie plate and toast for about 5 minutes, until golden. Let cool slightly, then coarsely chop.

2. Brush the cut sides of the figs with honey. Heat a large nonstick skillet until hot. Working in 2 batches, cook the figs cut side down over moderately high heat until lightly caramelized, 30 seconds to 1 minute. Transfer the figs to a plate and top with the toasted pistachios. Serve warm, with ice cream. —*Kristen Kish*

At Dominique Ansel Kitchen in New York City, the star pastry chef Dominique Ansel makes desserts like extra-creamy chocolate mousse (recipe, p. 347).

CAKES, COOKIES & MORE

PORTER BUNDT CAKE
WITH WHISKEY-
CARAMEL SAUCE
Recipe, page 332

CARAMEL LAYER
CAKE

Caramel Layer Cake

Active **1 hr**; Total **1 hr 45 min** plus cooling
Serves **16 to 20**

Nashville pastry chef Lisa Donovan's sweet, fudge-like caramel frosting is key to this excellent cake, which is adapted from a recipe by the pioneering Southern chef Edna Lewis. Be ready to frost the cake as soon as you're done beating the frosting in the stand mixer or it will harden.

- 2 sticks unsalted butter, softened, plus more for greasing
- 4 cups all-purpose flour, plus more for dusting
- 2 Tbsp. baking powder
- 2 tsp. kosher salt
- ½ tsp. baking soda
- 2½ cups sugar
- 1 vanilla bean, split lengthwise, seeds scraped
- 4 large eggs
- 3 cups buttermilk
- Caramel Frosting (recipe follows)

1. Preheat the oven to 350°. Butter and flour two 10-inch round cake pans and line the bottoms with parchment paper. In a large bowl, whisk the flour, baking powder, salt and baking soda. In a stand mixer fitted with the paddle, beat the 2 sticks of butter with the sugar and vanilla seeds at medium speed until fluffy, 3 minutes. Beat in the eggs 1 at a time until incorporated, then beat until very pale and billowy, 3 minutes. At low speed, alternately beat in the dry ingredients and buttermilk until just combined.

2. Divide the batter between the pans. Bake for 35 minutes, until the cakes are golden and a toothpick inserted in the centers comes out clean. Transfer to a rack; let cool in the pans for 30 minutes. Unmold the cakes, peel off the parchment and let cool. Place 1 cake layer on a cake stand or serving platter.

3. Working quickly, scrape about 1 cup of the Caramel Frosting onto the cake on the stand and spread it to the edge. Top with the second cake layer. Pour the remaining frosting on top; quickly spread it over and around the cake to cover completely. Let the frosting cool for at least 2 hours before serving. —*Lisa Donovan*

CARAMEL FROSTING

Total **25 min**; Makes **about 3 cups**

- 3 sticks unsalted butter
- 3 cups sugar
- 1½ cups buttermilk
- 1 Tbsp. baking soda
- 1 tsp. pure vanilla extract

In a large, heavy-bottomed saucepan, melt the butter over moderately high heat. Stir in the sugar, buttermilk and baking soda. Cook, stirring constantly, until the mixture foams up and then subsides, 5 to 7 minutes. Continue cooking, stirring steadily, until the caramel mixture is very dark brown and reaches 240° on a candy thermometer, about 10 minutes. Carefully pour the mixture into the bowl of a stand mixer fitted with the paddle, add the vanilla and beat at low speed for 3 minutes, until thickened but still pourable. Use the frosting immediately. —*LD*

Plum Upside-Down Cake

Active **40 min**; Total **2 hr 15 min**
Makes **one 9-inch cake**

This pretty plum cake from pastry chef Joanne Chang of Flour Bakery + Café in Boston and Cambridge is moist and buttery, with plenty of sweet and tangy caramelized plums on top.

PLUMS

- ¾ cup sugar
- 2 Tbsp. unsalted butter, softened
- 1½ lbs. medium plums (about 6), pitted and cut into ½-inch-thick wedges

CAKE

- ½ cup crème fraîche
- 2 Tbsp. whole milk
- 2 tsp. pure vanilla extract
- 1½ cups all-purpose flour
- ⅔ cup sugar
- 1 tsp. baking powder
- ½ tsp. baking soda
- ½ tsp. salt
- 1½ sticks unsalted butter, softened
- 2 large eggs, beaten
- Whipped cream, for serving

1. Prepare the plums Preheat the oven to 350°. In a small saucepan, combine the sugar and ⅓ cup of water and bring to a boil without stirring. Cook over high heat, washing down the side of the saucepan with a wet pastry brush, until an amber caramel forms, 5 to 7 minutes. Remove from the heat and whisk in the butter. Immediately pour the caramel into a 9-inch (2 inches deep) metal cake pan. Carefully arrange the plum wedges in the caramel in concentric circles.

2. Make the cake In a small bowl, whisk the crème fraîche with the milk and vanilla. In a large bowl, using a hand mixer, mix the flour with the sugar, baking powder, baking soda and salt. At low speed, beat in the butter until the mixture resembles moist crumbs, about 30 seconds. Beat in the eggs at low speed until incorporated, then beat the batter at medium-high speed until light and fluffy, about 1 minute; scrape down the side of the bowl. At medium speed, beat in the crème fraîche mixture until smooth, about 30 seconds. Scrape the batter over the plums and gently spread in an even layer.

3. Bake the cake in the center of the oven for 55 to 60 minutes, until golden and springy. Let cool in the pan on a rack for 30 minutes, then invert the cake onto a serving plate. Cut into wedges and serve warm or at room temperature with whipped cream. —*Joanne Chang*

MAKE AHEAD The cake can be stored in an airtight container overnight.

Chocolate Ice Cube Cake

Active **1 hr**; Total **2 hr 30 min plus 1 hr chilling**; Makes **one 9-by-13-inch cake**

For her blog, Global Table Adventure, Sasha Martin cooked a recipe from every country in the world. Her entry for Serbia was this striking dessert: a light chocolate sponge cake soaked in orange blossom syrup and topped with vanilla custard and chocolate.

CUSTARD

- **3** cups whole milk
- **⅔** cup sugar
- **1** vanilla bean—split lengthwise, seeds scraped, pod reserved
- **⅔** cup all-purpose flour
- **2** sticks unsalted butter, cut into tablespoons, at room temperature

CAKE

- Unsalted butter, for greasing
- **⅓** cup unsweetened cocoa powder
- **⅓** cup all-purpose flour
- **½** tsp. baking powder
- **6** large egg whites
- **⅓** cup sugar
- **6** large egg yolks, beaten

SYRUP

- **1** cup sugar
- **¾** tsp. orange blossom or rose water (optional)

CHOCOLATE TOPPING

- **8** oz. semisweet chocolate, finely chopped
- **⅓** cup vegetable oil

1. Make the custard In a saucepan, combine the milk, sugar and vanilla bean and seeds and bring to a simmer. Cook over moderate heat, stirring, until the sugar dissolves. In a blender, combine the flour and half of the hot milk mixture (but not the vanilla bean) and puree until smooth. Add the flour-milk mixture to the milk in the saucepan and cook over moderately low heat, whisking frequently, until thickened, about 8 minutes. Strain the custard into a medium bowl; discard the vanilla bean. Let cool until warm, then whisk in the butter a few pieces at a time. Press a piece of plastic wrap on the surface of the custard and chill for about 1 hour, or until firm.

2. Meanwhile, make the cake Preheat the oven to 350°. Butter a 9-by-13-inch cake pan. In a medium bowl, whisk the cocoa powder with the flour and baking powder. In a stand mixer fitted with the whisk, beat the egg whites at medium-high speed until foamy, 2 minutes. With the machine on, add the sugar 1 tablespoon at a time and beat until the whites are glossy and stiff, 8 to 10 minutes. Fold in the egg yolks, then fold in the dry ingredients. Scrape the batter into the prepared pan and smooth the surface. Bake for about 25 minutes, until a cake tester inserted in the center comes out clean. Transfer the cake to a rack to cool slightly.

3. Meanwhile, make the syrup In a medium saucepan, combine the sugar, orange blossom water, if using, and 1 cup of water and bring to a simmer. Cook over moderate heat, stirring, until the sugar dissolves, about 2 minutes. Let the syrup cool to room temperature.

4. Using a fork or skewer, poke holes all over the top of the cake. Pour the syrup evenly over the warm cake. Let stand until the cake is completely cool, about 1 hour. Run a sharp knife around the edge of the cake and invert it onto a rectangular platter.

5. Make the chocolate topping In a medium heatproof bowl set over a saucepan of simmering water, melt the chocolate, about 2 minutes. Remove the bowl from the pan and whisk in the oil. Let the chocolate topping cool completely.

6. Using an offset spatula or the back of a spoon, spread the custard in an even layer all over the top of the cake. Carefully pour the chocolate on top of the custard and spread in an even layer. Chill until the chocolate sets, about 1 hour. Serve cold.
—*Sasha Martin*

Gluten-Free Chocolate-Chile Cakes

Active **30 min**; Total **4 hr plus 24 hr draining**; Makes **12 cupcakes**

These fudgy flourless chocolate cakes have a surprise ingredient: beets. The tangy yogurt frosting coupled with a little heat from cayenne and crushed pepper makes them fun to eat.

- **2** cups full-fat plain probiotic yogurt
- **2** Tbsp. honey
- **1** Tbsp. plus ½ tsp. pure vanilla extract
- **½** lb. Medjool dates, pitted
- **5** oz. cooked beets, chopped (2 cups)
- **4** Tbsp. unsalted butter, melted and cooled
- **½** tsp. tamari (optional)
- **½** tsp. baking soda
- **½** cup unsweetened cocoa powder
- **1** tsp. cinnamon
- **⅛** tsp. cayenne
- Pinch of sea salt
- **3** large eggs
- Grated dark chocolate and crushed red pepper, for garnish

1. Line a sieve with cheesecloth and place it over a bowl. Add the yogurt, cover with plastic wrap and refrigerate for 24 hours to drain until thick. Transfer the yogurt to a medium bowl and stir in the honey and ½ teaspoon of the vanilla; refrigerate.

2. Preheat the oven to 350°. Line 12 muffin cups with paper liners. In a food processor, combine the dates, beets, butter, tamari (if using), baking soda and the remaining 1 tablespoon of vanilla and puree until smooth. Scrape down the side of the bowl. Add the cocoa powder, cinnamon, cayenne, salt and eggs and puree until well blended and smooth.

3. Spoon the batter into the muffin cups and bake until a cake tester inserted in the center of a cake comes out clean, about 30 minutes. Transfer the cakes to a rack to cool completely, then refrigerate them until cold, at least 3 hours or overnight.

4. Peel the paper liners off the cakes. Dollop the yogurt frosting on top of the cakes; garnish with grated chocolate and crushed red pepper. Serve cold.
—*Jasmine and Melissa Hemsley*

GLUTEN-FREE
CHOCOLATE-CHILE
CAKES

Black-and-White Cupcakes

Active **40 min**; Total **1 hr 30 min**; Makes **12**

CUPCAKES

- 1 **cup all-purpose flour**
- ⅓ **cup unsweetened cocoa powder**
- ½ **tsp. baking powder**
- ½ **tsp. kosher salt**
- ¼ **tsp. baking soda**
- 6 **Tbsp. unsalted butter, softened**
- ¾ **cup granulated sugar**
- 2 **large eggs**
- ½ **cup sour cream**
- 2½ **tsp. pure vanilla extract**

FROSTING

- 2 **sticks unsalted butter, softened**
- 4 **cups confectioners' sugar**
- 2 **tsp. pure vanilla extract**
- ½ **tsp. kosher salt**
- 4 **Tbsp. milk**
- ½ **cup unsweetened cocoa powder**

1. Make the cupcakes Preheat the oven to 350° and line a 12-cup muffin pan with paper liners. In a medium bowl, whisk the flour with the cocoa powder, baking powder, salt and baking soda. In a large bowl, using a hand mixer, beat the butter with the granulated sugar at medium-high speed until fluffy. Beat in the eggs 1 at a time, then beat in the sour cream and vanilla until smooth. At low speed, beat in the dry ingredients. Scoop the batter into the lined muffin cups.

2. Bake the cupcakes in the center of the oven for about 17 minutes, until springy and a toothpick inserted in the centers comes out clean. Let cool slightly in the pan, then transfer to a rack to cool completely.

3. Meanwhile, make the frosting In a large bowl, using a hand mixer, beat the butter at medium speed until smooth. Add the confectioners' sugar, vanilla, salt and 2 tablespoons of the milk and beat at low speed just until combined, then beat at medium speed until smooth. Scrape half of the vanilla frosting into a medium bowl. Add the cocoa powder and the remaining 2 tablespoons of milk to the frosting in the large bowl and beat at low speed until fully incorporated.

4. Lay a large sheet of plastic wrap on a work surface with the long side facing you. Using a small spatula, spread the vanilla frosting in a 3-inch-wide strip down the center of the plastic wrap. Spread the chocolate frosting in a 3-inch-wide strip alongside the vanilla. Using the plastic, fold the chocolate frosting over the vanilla, twisting one end of the plastic to seal. Pull the twisted end of the plastic through a pastry bag fitted with a large star tip and cut off the protruding plastic at the tip. Refrigerate the frosting until barely firm, about 15 minutes. Pipe onto the cupcakes and serve. —*Justin Chapple*

Triple-Layer Sour Cream Chocolate Cake

Active **1 hr 15 min**; Total **2 hr 45 min**
Serves **12**

CAKE

- **Unsalted butter, for greasing**
- 3 **cups cake flour, plus more for dusting**
- 9 **oz. unsweetened chocolate, finely chopped**
- 2 **cups hot brewed coffee**
- 1 **Tbsp. pure vanilla extract**
- 4 **large eggs, at room temperature**
- 1 **cup canola oil**
- 1 **cup sour cream, at room temperature**
- 3 **cups sugar**
- 1½ **tsp. baking soda**
- 1 **tsp. ground cinnamon**
- 1 **tsp. fine sea salt**

GANACHE

- 1½ **cups heavy cream**
- 1½ **sticks unsalted butter, cut into 1-inch pieces**
- ½ **cup sugar**
- ½ **tsp. fine sea salt**
- 1½ **lbs. semisweet chocolate, finely chopped**
- ⅓ **cup hot brewed coffee**
- 1½ **tsp. pure vanilla extract**
- **Sugared cranberries, for garnish (see Note)**

1. Make the cake Preheat the oven to 350° and position the racks in the center and lower thirds. Butter three 9-by-2-inch round cake pans and line with parchment paper. Butter the paper and dust the pans with flour, tapping out the excess.

2. In a medium bowl, combine the chocolate with the coffee and vanilla and let stand for 2 minutes, then stir until the chocolate is melted. In another medium bowl, whisk the eggs with the oil until pale yellow, then whisk in the sour cream. Gradually whisk in the melted chocolate mixture until smooth.

3. In a stand mixer fitted with the paddle, combine the 3 cups of flour with the sugar, baking soda, cinnamon and salt and mix well. At medium speed, beat in the wet ingredients in 3 batches until just incorporated. Scrape down the bowl and beat until the batter is smooth.

4. Pour the batter evenly into the prepared cake pans. Gently tap the pans on the counter to release any air bubbles. Bake for about 35 minutes, until a toothpick inserted in the center of each cake comes out clean; shift the pans halfway through baking. Let the cakes cool completely, then carefully invert onto a rack and peel off the parchment.

5. Meanwhile, make the ganache In a medium saucepan, bring the cream, butter, sugar and salt just to a simmer over moderate heat, stirring to dissolve the sugar. Remove from the heat and add the chocolate. Let stand for 2 minutes, then stir until smooth. Stir in the coffee and vanilla. Let the ganache cool completely, stirring occasionally.

6. Transfer 1 cake to a plate. Spoon one-fourth of the ganache on top and spread in an even layer. Top with another cake and one-fourth of the ganache. Cover with the third cake and spread the remaining ganache over the top and side of the cake; decoratively swirl the ganache on top. Top the cake with sugared cranberries, cut into wedges and serve.
—*Cheryl and Griffith Day*

NOTE Toss fresh cranberries in simple syrup, drain and chill. Roll the cranberries in sugar and spread on a plate; chill for about 1 hour before serving.

Skillet Graham Cake with Peaches and Blueberries

Active **1 hr;** Total **3 hr 30 min;** Serves **10**

Instead of cooking this cake on a grill, you can bake it in a 300° oven for the same amount of time.

STREUSEL

- ¾ cup graham cracker crumbs
- ¾ cup all-purpose flour
- ½ cup light brown sugar
- 1 stick unsalted butter, softened
- ½ tsp. kosher salt

FRUIT

- 3 large peaches, each cut into 1-inch wedges
- ¾ cup blueberries
- ½ cup granulated sugar
- 3 Tbsp. fresh lemon juice
- 1 Tbsp. cornstarch
- 1 Tbsp. unsalted butter

CAKE

- 1½ cups all-purpose flour
- ½ cup whole-wheat flour
- ½ cup fine graham cracker crumbs
- 2 tsp. baking powder
- 1½ tsp. kosher salt
- 1 stick plus 3 Tbsp. unsalted butter, softened
- 1¼ cups light brown sugar
- ¼ cup granulated sugar
- 3 Tbsp. honey
- 4 large eggs
- 1¼ cups buttermilk
- ⅓ cup canola oil
- 1 Tbsp. pure vanilla extract
  Vanilla ice cream, for serving

1. Make the streusel In a stand mixer fitted with the paddle, beat all of the ingredients together at medium speed until crumbs form. Transfer the crumbs to a bowl and press into clumps. Refrigerate until chilled, about 15 minutes.

2. Meanwhile, prepare the fruit Set up a gas grill for indirect grilling, then heat to 300°. In a medium bowl, toss the peaches with the blueberries, sugar, lemon juice and cornstarch. In a 12-inch cast-iron skillet, melt the butter over low heat. Remove from the heat. Scrape the fruit and any juices into the skillet.

3. Make the cake In a medium bowl, whisk both flours with the graham cracker crumbs, baking powder and salt. In a stand mixer fitted with the paddle, beat the butter with both sugars and the honey at medium speed until fluffy. Beat in the eggs 1 at a time, then beat in the buttermilk, oil and vanilla. Scrape down the side of the bowl and beat in the dry ingredients until just smooth. Spread the batter in the skillet in an even layer. Scatter the streusel evenly on top.

4. Set the skillet on the grill over indirect heat. Close the grill and bake for about 1 hour and 30 minutes, rotating the skillet every 20 minutes, until a toothpick inserted in the cake comes out clean; keep an eye on the heat to maintain the grill temperature. Let the cake cool for 1 hour. Cut into wedges and serve with vanilla ice cream. —*Stephanie Izard*

Orange and Olive Oil Cake

Active **30 min;** Total **1 hr 15 min plus cooling;** Makes **one 10-inch cake**

- Unsalted butter, for greasing
- 2 cups self-rising flour, plus more for dusting
- 4 large eggs
- 1 cup granulated sugar
- 2 Tbsp. finely grated orange zest
- ½ tsp. kosher salt
- 1 cup fresh orange juice
- 1 cup extra-virgin olive oil
  Confectioners' sugar, for dusting

1. Preheat the oven to 350°. Line the bottom of a 10-inch cake pan with parchment paper. Butter the paper and the side of the pan and dust with flour.

2. In a large bowl, using a hand mixer, beat the eggs with the granulated sugar, orange zest and salt. In a medium bowl, combine the orange juice and olive oil. At low speed, gradually beat the orange juice mixture into the egg mixture. Beat in the 2 cups of flour in 3 additions until a smooth batter forms.

3. Scrape the batter into the prepared pan and bake for 45 to 50 minutes, until the cake is golden and a toothpick inserted in the center comes out clean. Let the cake cool completely; unmold and discard the paper. Dust with confectioners' sugar and serve. —*Danai Kindeli*

Almond-Coconut Orange Cake

Active **40 min;** Total **2 hr 45 min;** Serves **12**

Alice Quillet and Anna Trattles, chef-bakers at Le Bal Café in Paris, pack their macaroon-like cake with coconut and flavor it with pureed oranges.

- Unsalted butter, for greasing
- 1½ lbs. blood oranges or navel oranges, scrubbed
- 6 large eggs
- 2¾ cups granulated sugar
- 5 cups unsweetened shredded coconut (9 oz.)
- 3 cups almond flour
- 1 tsp. baking powder
- ½ cup sliced almonds
- 2 cups heavy cream
- 2 Tbsp. confectioners' sugar
- ¼ cup apricot jam melted with 1 tsp. water

1. Preheat the oven to 350°. Brush a 10-inch springform pan with butter. Line the bottom of the pan with parchment paper and butter the paper.

2. Put the oranges in a microwave-safe bowl; add enough water to reach halfway up the side. Cover partially with plastic wrap. Microwave on high power, turning the oranges every 3 minutes, until very soft, about 15 minutes; drain. Quarter the oranges, discarding any seeds. In a food processor, puree until smooth, 2 to 3 minutes.

3. In a large bowl, beat the eggs with the granulated sugar. Whisk in 1½ cups of the orange puree. Using a spatula, fold in the coconut, almond flour and baking powder. Scrape the mixture into the prepared pan and smooth the top. Sprinkle the sliced almonds over the cake and bake until a toothpick inserted in the center comes out with a few moist crumbs attached, about 45 minutes. Let cool slightly on a rack.

4. In a bowl, whip the cream with the confectioners' sugar and fold in the remaining ¼ cup of orange puree.

5. Brush the melted jam over the warm cake and let cool. Unmold the cake and serve with the orange whipped cream. —*Alice Quillet and Anna Trattles*

GRAPEFRUIT
CORNMEAL CAKE

Grapefruit Cornmeal Cake

Active **40 min;** Total **2 hr 30 min;** Serves **12**

CAKE

1½ **sticks unsalted butter, melted and cooled, plus more for greasing**

1½ **cups all-purpose flour**

½ **cup medium-grind cornmeal**

1½ **cups granulated sugar**

2 **tsp. baking powder**

½ **tsp. kosher salt**

3 **large eggs**

1 **Tbsp. finely grated grapefruit zest plus ¼ cup fresh grapefruit juice**

GLAZE

2 **cups confectioners' sugar, sifted**

¼ **cup poppy seeds**

¼ **cup fresh grapefruit juice**

1. Make the cake Preheat the oven to 350°. Butter a 9-inch cake pan. Line the bottom with parchment paper and butter the paper.

2. In a medium bowl, whisk the flour with the cornmeal, granulated sugar, baking powder and salt. In another medium bowl, whisk the melted butter with the eggs, grapefruit zest and grapefruit juice. While whisking constantly, add the butter mixture to the flour mixture in a slow, steady stream. Whisk until well blended. Scrape the batter into the prepared pan and bake for about 40 minutes, until golden and a cake tester inserted in the center comes out clean.

3. Transfer the cake to a rack to cool for 10 minutes. Run a sharp paring knife around the edge of the cake, then invert it onto the rack. Peel off the parchment paper. Carefully flip the cake right side up and set the rack over a baking sheet. Let cool until warm, about 30 minutes.

4. Meanwhile, make the glaze In a medium bowl, mix the confectioners' sugar and poppy seeds. While whisking constantly, slowly drizzle in the grapefruit juice until a smooth, thick glaze forms. Pour the glaze all over the top of the warm cake and spread evenly over the top and side. Let stand until set, about 30 minutes. *—Kay Chun*

MAKE AHEAD The cake can be stored in an airtight container at room temperature for up to 3 days.

Almond Cake with Mixed Berries

Active **30 min;** Total **1 hr 40 min plus cooling;** Makes **one 9-inch cake**

At her cooking school, The Courtyard Kitchen at Dar Namir in Fez, Morocco, Tara Stevens bakes berries into this dense, moist cake that she tops with even more fruit. Students eat it for breakfast; it's so popular that she usually has to make extra.

Baking spray

1 **lb. blanched almond flour (2¼ cups)**

2 **tsp. baking powder**

Pinch of kosher salt

1 **lb. mixed raspberries, blueberries and strawberries, or pitted fresh cherries**

6 **large eggs**

1 **cup granulated sugar**

1 **tsp. rose water (optional)**

Confectioners' sugar, for dusting

Crème fraîche, for serving

1. Preheat the oven to 325°. Lightly coat a 9-inch springform cake pan with baking spray and line the bottom with parchment.

2. In a medium bowl, whisk the almond flour with the baking powder and salt. Set aside one-third of the berries in a small bowl for garnish.

3. In a large bowl, using a hand mixer, beat the eggs with the granulated sugar and rose water, if using, at medium-high speed until very thick and glossy, about 12 minutes. Fold in the almond flour mixture and the remaining berries in 3 alternating batches, ending with the almond flour, just until blended. Scrape the batter into the prepared pan and smooth the surface.

4. Bake the cake for about 55 minutes, until a tester inserted in the center comes out clean. Transfer to a rack and let cool for 10 minutes. Unmold the cake and let cool completely.

5. Top the cake with the reserved berries and dust with confectioners' sugar. Serve with crème fraîche. *—Tara Stevens*

Pistachio Cake with Orange Cream and Lavender Honey

Active **30 min;** Total **1 hr plus cooling** Serves **8 to 10**

This extra-nutty cake, inspired by one from Food Network star Anne Burrell, gets a double dose of pistachio flavor from chopped nuts and creamy pistachio paste (available from kingarthurflour.com).

1½ **sticks unsalted butter, at room temperature, plus more for greasing**

1½ **cups all-purpose flour, plus more for dusting**

1¼ **cups unsalted pistachios (7 oz.)**

1 **tsp. baking powder**

¼ **tsp. kosher salt**

1 **cup plus 1 tsp. sugar**

½ **cup (5 oz.) pistachio paste**

1 **tsp. pure vanilla extract**

3 **large eggs**

½ **cup mascarpone**

¼ **cup sour cream**

½ **tsp. finely grated orange zest**

Chopped candied oranges and lavender honey, for garnish

1. Preheat the oven to 325°. Butter and flour a 9-inch cake pan. In a food processor, pulse the pistachios until finely chopped. In a medium bowl, whisk the 1½ cups of flour with the baking powder and salt. In a large bowl, combine the 1½ sticks of butter, 1 cup of the sugar, the pistachio paste and vanilla. Using a hand mixer, beat the butter mixture at medium speed until fluffy, about 3 minutes. Beat in the eggs 1 at a time, then beat in the flour mixture at low speed just until incorporated. Fold in 1 cup of the chopped pistachios. Spread the batter in the prepared pan and bake for about 35 minutes, until a cake tester inserted in the center comes out clean. Transfer the cake to a rack to cool completely, about 2 hours.

2. In a small bowl, whisk the mascarpone with the sour cream, the remaining 1 teaspoon of sugar and the orange zest. Cut the pistachio cake into wedges and serve with a big dollop of the orange cream, candied orange and a drizzle of lavender honey. Garnish the slices with the remaining chopped pistachios and serve. *—Koren Grieveson*

Sticky Toffee Pudding Cake

Active **45 min**; Total **1 hr 30 min**
Makes **one 10-inch cake**

Rich and buttery, this killer sticky toffee cake soaks up great flavor from a brandy-spiked caramel sauce.

CAKE

1½ **cups chopped pitted dates (9 oz.)**
 1 **tsp. baking soda**
1½ **cups all-purpose flour**
 1 **tsp. baking powder**
 ½ **tsp. kosher salt**
 4 **Tbsp. unsalted butter,
   at room temperature**
 1 **cup granulated sugar**
 2 **large eggs**
 1 **tsp. pure vanilla extract**

SAUCE

1¼ **cups dark brown sugar**
 1 **stick unsalted butter, cubed**
 ½ **cup heavy cream**
 2 **tsp. brandy**
 1 **tsp. pure vanilla extract**
 ½ **tsp. kosher salt**

1. Make the cake Preheat the oven to 350°. Coat a 10-inch round cake pan with nonstick spray and line with parchment paper. In a saucepan, cover the dates with 1 cup of water; bring to a boil. Remove the pan from the heat and whisk in the baking soda; it will foam up. Let cool slightly.

2. In a medium bowl, sift the flour with the baking powder and salt. In a stand mixer fitted with the paddle, beat the butter with the granulated sugar at medium speed until light and fluffy, 1 to 2 minutes. Beat in the eggs and vanilla. In 2 alternating batches, beat in the dry ingredients and the date mixture until just incorporated. Scrape the batter into the prepared pan and bake until a toothpick inserted in the center comes out clean, 35 to 40 minutes. Let the cake cool in the pan for 10 minutes.

3. Meanwhile, make the sauce In a medium saucepan, bring the brown sugar, butter and heavy cream to a boil over moderate heat, whisking to dissolve the sugar. Simmer over moderately low heat, whisking, for 2 minutes. Remove from the heat; whisk in the brandy, vanilla and salt. Keep warm.

4. Turn the cake out onto a rack and peel off the parchment. Carefully return the cake, top side down, to the pan. Using a skewer, poke 15 to 20 holes in it. Pour half of the warm sauce over the cake and let stand until absorbed, about 5 minutes. Invert onto a platter and poke another 15 to 20 holes in the top. Pour the remaining sauce over the top. Serve warm.
—Abigail Quinn

Party Cake with Whipped Cream and Raspberries

Active **30 min**
Total **1 hr 30 min plus overnight resting**
Makes **one 9-inch-square cake**

1½ **sticks unsalted butter, softened,
   plus more for greasing**
2¾ **cups all-purpose flour**
1¼ **cups granulated sugar**
 1 **Tbsp. baking powder**
 ½ **tsp. fine sea salt**
 ¾ **cup whole milk, at room temperature**
 3 **large eggs, at room temperature**
 2 **tsp. pure vanilla extract**
 ½ **cup heavy cream**
 1 **Tbsp. confectioners' sugar**
 2 **Tbsp. seedless raspberry jam mixed
   with 1 tsp. hot water**
   Raspberries, for garnish

1. Preheat the oven to 350°. Line a 9-inch-square baking pan with foil; allow 2 inches of overhang on two sides. Butter the foil.

2. In a large bowl, using a hand mixer at low speed, mix the flour, granulated sugar, baking powder and salt. Add the 1½ sticks of butter, milk, eggs and vanilla and beat at medium speed until smooth, 1 to 2 minutes. Spread the batter in the pan and bake for about 45 minutes, until a toothpick inserted in the cake comes out clean. Let cool on a rack, then cover with foil and let stand at room temperature overnight.

3. In a large bowl, using a hand mixer, beat the cream with the confectioners' sugar at high speed until firm, 1 to 2 minutes. Unmold the cake; peel off the foil. Spread the raspberry jam over the cake and top with the whipped cream. Garnish with raspberries and serve. *—Kamran Siddiqi*

Sweet Semolina Cake with Rose Water

Active **30 min**; Total **3 hr**
Makes **one 8-inch cake**

This easy and quick-to-make Middle Eastern semolina cake from blogger Sasha Martin is dense but moist. She recommends serving it with a hefty dollop of whipped cream and a strong cup of tea.

CAKE

 ¼ **cup ghee (clarified butter), melted,
   plus more for greasing**
 3 **cups (17 oz.) fine durum semolina**
1¼ **cups sugar**
 1 **Tbsp. baking powder**
 1 **tsp. rose water**
   Slivered almonds, for garnish

SYRUP

 ½ **cup sugar**
 1 **Tbsp. fresh lemon juice**
 ¼ **tsp. rose water**
   Whipped cream, for serving

1. Make the cake Grease an 8-inch round cake pan. In a large bowl, combine all of the ingredients except the almonds. Add 1¼ cups of warm water and mix with a wooden spoon until a thick batter forms. Scrape the batter into the prepared pan and let rest at room temperature until set and semi-firm, about 30 minutes.

2. Preheat the oven to 325°. Using the tip of a sharp paring knife, score the top of the cake in a diamond pattern, cutting ¼ inch deep into the cake. Place a few almond slivers in each diamond, pressing gently to help them adhere. Bake the cake until golden and a cake tester inserted in the center comes out clean, 45 minutes. Transfer to a rack and let cool for 30 minutes.

3. Meanwhile, make the syrup In a small saucepan, combine the sugar, lemon juice, rose water and ½ cup of water and bring to a simmer. Cook over moderate heat, stirring, until the sugar dissolves, about 2 minutes. Let cool.

4. Using a sharp paring knife, cut the cake along the score lines all the way to the bottom of the pan. Pour the syrup evenly all over the cake. Let the cake stand for at least 1 hour or overnight to absorb the syrup. Serve with whipped cream.
—Sasha Martin

SWEET SEMOLINA
CAKE WITH
ROSE WATER

Porter Bundt Cake with Whiskey-Caramel Sauce

📷 PAGE 321

Active **1 hr**; Total **1 hr 50 min**; Serves **8 to 10**

CAKE

- **1½ cups porter**
- **1 cup unsulfured molasses**
- **1½ tsp. baking soda**
- **¼ cup pure maple syrup**
- **1½ sticks unsalted butter, softened, plus more for greasing**
- **3 cups all-purpose flour, plus more for dusting**
- **1½ tsp. baking powder**
- **¾ tsp. ground cinnamon**
- **½ tsp. freshly grated nutmeg**
- **¼ tsp. fine sea salt**
- **⅓ cup cocoa nibs**
- **½ cup packed light brown sugar**
- **½ cup granulated sugar**
- **3 large eggs**

SAUCE

- **1 cup granulated sugar**
- **¼ cup heavy cream**
- **¼ cup whiskey**

1. Make the cake Preheat the oven to 350°. In a large saucepan, whisk 1 cup of the porter with the molasses and bring just to a boil. Remove from the heat, stir in the baking soda and let cool completely.

2. In a medium saucepan, whisk the maple syrup with the remaining ½ cup of porter and bring to a boil. Reduce the heat and simmer, stirring occasionally, until reduced by half and syrupy, about 20 minutes. Let cool completely.

3. Meanwhile, butter a 10-inch Bundt pan and dust with flour; shake off the excess. In a large bowl, whisk the 3 cups of flour with the baking powder, cinnamon, nutmeg, salt and cocoa nibs. In a stand mixer fitted with the whisk, beat the 1½ sticks of butter with the brown and granulated sugars at medium speed until fluffy. Beat in the eggs, 1 at a time, until just incorporated. At low speed, beat in the cooled porter-molasses mixture, then gradually beat in the dry ingredients.

4. Scrape the batter into the prepared pan and smooth the surface. Bake in the center of the oven for about 50 minutes, until a toothpick inserted in the center of the cake comes out clean. Let cool for 15 minutes. Invert the warm cake onto a rack and brush with the cooled porter-syrup mixture.

5. Make the sauce In a medium saucepan, combine the sugar with ¼ cup of water and bring to a boil. Cook over moderately high heat, without stirring, until an amber caramel forms. Remove from the heat and whisk in the cream and whiskey. Cook over low heat for 1 minute. Let cool slightly.

6. Cut the cake into wedges and serve, passing the warm whiskey caramel at the table. —*Courtney Contos*

No-Bake Bananas Foster Cheesecake

Active **1 hr**; Total **4 hr**; Serves **10 to 12**

Star chef Tyler Florence sets his mousse-like cheesecake in the fridge, then tops it with sweet and boozy bananas.

CHEESECAKE

- **Baking spray**
- **1½ cups sugar**
- **1 packet unflavored powdered gelatin**
- **1 cup hot water**
- **3 cups fresh ricotta cheese (about 1½ lbs.)**
- **8 oz. cream cheese, at room temperature**
- **1 tsp. finely grated lemon zest plus 3 Tbsp. fresh lemon juice**
- **½ tsp. pure vanilla extract**
- **24 whole graham crackers (1 lb.), broken up**
- **¼ tsp. ground cinnamon**
- **4 Tbsp. unsalted butter, softened**

BANANAS FOSTER

- **4 Tbsp. unsalted butter**
- **1 cup sugar**
- **½ tsp. ground cinnamon**
- **Pinch of ground allspice**
- **Pinch of kosher salt**
- **¼ cup amaretto**
- **¼ cup dark rum**
- **4 ripe bananas, sliced ⅓ inch thick**

1. Make the cheesecake Coat a 2½-quart glass bowl with nonstick spray and line with plastic wrap, allowing 6 inches of overhang all around.

2. In a medium bowl, whisk ½ cup of the sugar with the gelatin. Stir in the hot water and let stand for 3 minutes, then whisk to dissolve the sugar and gelatin.

3. In a stand mixer fitted with the paddle, beat the ricotta with the cream cheese at medium speed until smooth. With the machine on, gradually beat in the gelatin mixture, then beat in the lemon zest, lemon juice and vanilla. Scrape the cheesecake mixture into the prepared bowl and cover with the overhanging plastic. Refrigerate until nearly set, about 1 hour.

4. Meanwhile, in a food processor, pulse the graham crackers with the cinnamon until fine crumbs form. Transfer to a heatproof medium bowl.

5. In a medium saucepan, combine the remaining 1 cup of sugar with ½ cup of water and cook over moderate heat until it reaches 330° on a candy thermometer, 5 to 7 minutes. Remove from the heat and whisk in the butter. Immediately pour over the graham cracker crumbs and stir quickly until evenly moistened; clumps will form.

6. Uncover the cheesecake and sprinkle the graham cracker mixture evenly on top; pack it gently onto the surface of the cake. Cover and refrigerate until the cake is completely set, at least 2 hours or overnight.

7. Make the bananas Foster In a large saucepan, melt the butter with the sugar. Cook over moderate heat, swirling the pan, until a very light caramel forms, 5 to 7 minutes. Stir in the cinnamon, allspice and salt and cook, swirling, for 30 seconds. Add the amaretto and rum and, very carefully, using a long-handled match, ignite the alcohol. When the flame subsides, stir in the bananas. Let cool.

8. Unwrap the cake and carefully invert onto a rimmed serving plate. Spoon the bananas Foster over the top and serve right away. —*Tyler Florence*

No-Bake White Chocolate Cheesecake with Strawberries

Active **45 min**; Total **4 hr**
Makes **one 9-inch cake**

CRUST

1½ cups graham cracker crumbs (7 oz.)
  1 stick unsalted butter, melted
¼ cup granulated sugar
½ tsp. pure vanilla extract
    Pinch of fine sea salt

FILLING

  7 oz. white chocolate, finely chopped
  1 lb. cream cheese,
    at room temperature
  1 cup confectioners' sugar
1½ tsp. vanilla bean paste or 1 tsp.
    pure vanilla extract
¼ tsp. finely grated orange zest
¼ tsp. finely grated lemon zest
  1 cup heavy cream
  3 Tbsp. strawberry jam
    mixed with 1 tsp. hot water
    Quartered strawberries, for garnish

1. Make the crust In a medium bowl, mix the graham cracker crumbs with the butter, sugar, vanilla and salt until evenly moistened. Press the crumbs over the bottom of a 9-inch round springform pan. Freeze until firm, about 20 minutes.

2. Meanwhile, make the filling In a microwave-safe bowl, microwave the white chocolate on high power in 10-second intervals until just melted. Let cool slightly.

3. In a stand mixer fitted with the paddle, beat the cream cheese with the confectioners' sugar, vanilla bean paste and orange and lemon zests until smooth. Gradually beat in the white chocolate. Scrape the mixture into a large bowl.

4. Wipe out the bowl of the stand mixer and add the cream to it. Attach the whisk and beat the cream at high speed until firm peaks form. Stir one-third of the whipped cream into the cream cheese mixture, then fold in the remaining whipped cream until no streaks remain. Spread the cheesecake filling over the chilled crust in an even layer. Cover with foil and refrigerate for at least 3 hours or overnight.

5. Unmold the cheesecake. Top with the strawberry jam, garnish with quartered strawberries and serve. —*Kamran Siddiqi*

Pralinella Icebox Cakes

Active **1 hr**; Total **2 hr plus overnight setting**
Serves **10**

For this outrageous chocolate and nut dessert, L.A. chef Courtney McBroom layers crisp cookies with a creamy Nutella filling, then garnishes the stacks with candied pecans.

CAKES

  1 cup pecans (4 oz.)
  1 stick plus 6 Tbsp. unsalted butter,
    softened
½ cup plus 2 Tbsp. light brown sugar
¼ cup plus 2 Tbsp. granulated sugar
¾ tsp. pure vanilla extract
  2 cups all-purpose flour
  6 Tbsp. unsweetened cocoa powder
¼ tsp. baking soda
¾ tsp. kosher salt
  3 Tbsp. whole milk

FILLING

  2 cups heavy cream
  1 cup Nutella
    Chopped candied pecans,
    for garnish

1. Make the cakes Preheat the oven to 350°. Spread the pecans in a pie plate and toast until golden, 8 to 10 minutes. Let cool, then very coarsely chop.

2. In a large bowl, beat the butter with both sugars and the vanilla until fluffy. In a medium bowl, whisk the flour with the cocoa powder, baking soda and salt. Beat the dry ingredients and the milk into the butter mixture in 3 alternating batches; beat in the pecans until just incorporated. On a work surface, divide the dough into 2 pieces. Roll each piece to a 5½-inch log, about 2¼ inches in diameter. Wrap the logs in plastic and refrigerate until firm, 1 hour.

3. Preheat the oven to 325°. Line 2 large baking sheets with parchment paper. Remove 1 log of dough from the plastic. Using a thin knife, cut the log crosswise into ¼-inch-thick slices and arrange on the baking sheets. One log should yield 20 cookies.

4. Bake the cookies for 12 to 15 minutes, until just firm. Let cool for 5 minutes, then transfer to a rack to cool. Let the baking sheets cool, then repeat Steps 3 and 4 with the second log of dough.

5. Make the filling In a medium bowl, beat the cream and Nutella until stiff. For each cake stack, set a cookie on a platter and top with 1 tablespoon of the filling. Top with another cookie and another 1 tablespoon of filling. Repeat to make 2 more layers. Repeat with the remaining cookies and filling to make 9 more stacks. Tent the platter with plastic wrap and refrigerate the cakes overnight. Garnish with candied pecans before serving. —*Courtney McBroom*

MAKE AHEAD The cakes can be stored in an airtight container for 3 days.

Date and Almond Fudge with Sesame and Coconut

Active **20 min**; Total **1 hr 20 min**
Makes **about 5 dozen 1-inch squares**

Melissa and Jasmine Hemsley, the sisters behind the wellness blog Hemsley + Hemsley, make this minimalist vegan recipe with two healthy fats, coconut oil and roasted almond butter.

14 oz. pitted Medjool dates (2 cups),
    plus sliced dates for garnish
  1 cup roasted almond butter
¼ cup extra-virgin coconut oil
½ tsp. pure vanilla extract
    Flaky sea salt, sesame seeds and
    unsweetened shredded coconut,
    for garnish

1. Line an 8-inch square baking dish with parchment paper, leaving 1 inch of overhang. In a food processor, combine the 2 cups of dates with the almond butter, coconut oil and vanilla and puree until a smooth paste forms. Scrape the mixture into the prepared pan and, using your fingertips or a spatula, press it into an even layer. Garnish with sliced dates, flaky sea salt, sesame seeds and shredded coconut, pressing gently to help them adhere. Refrigerate until firm, about 1 hour.

2. Cut the fudge into 1-inch squares and serve cold.
—*Jasmine and Melissa Hemsley*

CHOCOLATE-PEANUT
BUTTER SWISS ROLLS

Chocolate–Peanut Butter Swiss Rolls

Active **1 hr**; Total **3 hr 30 min**; Makes **12**

Tiffany MacIsaac of Washington, DC's Buttercream Bakeshop describes her take on Ho Hos as "perfect little packages of rich, rich chocolate and peanut butter."

CAKE

    Baking spray
  2 cups granulated sugar
  1 cup all-purpose flour
  2 Tbsp. unsweetened cocoa powder
  1½ tsp. baking soda
  ½ tsp. baking powder
  ¼ tsp. kosher salt
  2 large eggs
  ½ cup whole milk
  2 Tbsp. unsalted butter
  1 tsp. pure vanilla extract
  1 tsp. ground instant espresso

PEANUT BUTTER FILLING

  1½ sticks unsalted butter, at room temperature
  ⅓ cup confectioners' sugar, sifted
  ½ cup creamy peanut butter
  ⅛ tsp. kosher salt
  1 Tbsp. whole milk
  ½ tsp. pure vanilla extract

GANACHE

  9 oz. bittersweet chocolate, finely chopped
  1½ Tbsp. unsalted butter, at room temperature
  3 Tbsp. light corn syrup
     Pinch of kosher salt
  1 cup plus 2 Tbsp. heavy cream
     Flaky sea salt or chopped peanuts, for garnish

1. Make the cake Preheat the oven to 325°. Liberally grease a large rimmed baking sheet with baking spray. Line the sheet with parchment paper and liberally grease the paper.

2. In a large bowl, sift the granulated sugar, flour, cocoa powder, baking soda, baking powder and salt. In a medium bowl, whisk the eggs with the milk.

3. In a small saucepan, combine the butter, vanilla and espresso powder with ½ cup of water and bring to a simmer, stirring to dissolve the espresso. Drizzle the hot mixture over the dry ingredients. Add the egg mixture and whisk until smooth. Scrape the batter onto the prepared sheet and spread in an even layer. Bake for about 20 minutes, until set and a cake tester inserted in the center of the cake comes out clean (the cake will look wet). Transfer the sheet to a rack and let cool.

4. Meanwhile, make the peanut butter filling In a medium bowl, using a hand mixer, beat the butter with the confectioners' sugar at medium speed until light, about 2 minutes. Beat in the peanut butter and salt, scraping down the bowl as necessary. Beat in the milk and vanilla.

5. Line a large baking sheet with parchment paper and generously grease it with baking spray. Invert the cooled cake onto the prepared sheet. Peel the parchment paper off the cake; it will be sticky. Cut the cake in half lengthwise, then crosswise. Spread the filling all over the cake pieces, leaving a ¼-inch border all around the sides. Roll up the cakes lengthwise (the parchment will come off easily) to form 4 logs. Refrigerate for 1 hour.

6. Make the ganache In a bowl, combine the chocolate, butter, corn syrup and salt. In a small saucepan, bring the cream to a simmer. Pour the hot cream over the chocolate mixture and whisk until smooth. Let cool.

7. Line another large baking sheet with parchment paper. Cut each cake log into 3 equal pieces. Working with 1 piece at a time and using a fork or skewer, dip the logs into the ganache to coat all over, letting the excess drip off. Transfer the cakes to the prepared sheet and sprinkle with flaky salt or peanuts. Freeze until firm, about 1 hour, before serving.
—*Tiffany MacIsaac*

Honey-Walnut Bars

Active **30 min**; Total **1 hr plus cooling** Makes **24**

SHORTBREAD

  1½ sticks cold unsalted butter, cut into ½-inch dice
  1½ cups all-purpose flour
  ⅓ cup granulated sugar
  ½ tsp. flaky sea salt, such as Maldon

WALNUT CARAMEL

  1½ sticks unsalted butter, softened
  ½ cup honey
  ½ cup light brown sugar
  ¼ cup dark brown sugar
  1 tsp. kosher salt
  1 tsp. flaky sea salt
  1 tsp. pure vanilla extract
  ½ cup heavy cream
  1 cup walnut halves plus 1 cup coarsely chopped walnuts

1. Make the shortbread Preheat the oven to 350°. Line a 9-by-13-inch pan with parchment paper, allowing 1 inch of overhang on the long sides. In the bowl of a stand mixer fitted with the paddle, mix the butter with the flour, sugar and salt at medium speed until a crumbly dough forms, about 6 minutes. Press the dough into the bottom of the prepared pan in an even layer. Refrigerate for 20 minutes.

2. Bake the shortbread for 25 minutes, until golden brown; rotate the pan from front to back halfway through baking. Transfer to a rack and let cool completely.

3. Meanwhile, make the walnut caramel In a medium saucepan, melt the butter over moderate heat. Whisk in the honey, both sugars and salts and the vanilla. Cook, stirring occasionally, until the caramel reaches 220° on a candy thermometer, 2 to 3 minutes. Carefully add the cream and cook until the mixture reaches 238°, 3 to 4 minutes. Stir in all of the walnuts and cook until fragrant and toasty and slightly thickened, about 3 minutes longer.

4. Pour the walnut caramel over the shortbread and let cool completely. Using the parchment paper, lift onto a cutting board. Cut into bars and serve. —*Mindy Segal*

MAKE AHEAD The bars can be refrigerated for up to 5 days.

HOMEMADE CANDY

Mirracole Morsels in Kingston, Washington, makes peanut butter candy squares that are as flaky as the inside of a Butterfinger bar. Essential to the recipe, according to owner **NICOLE HALEY,** are the best, freshest peanuts you can find and the aerating power of baking soda to achieve the light, layered texture.

Miracle Peanut Butter Crunch

Total **20 min plus cooling**
Makes **about 3 dozen candies**

- 1 **cup sugar**
- ¾ **cup light corn syrup**
- 1 **Tbsp. unsalted butter**
- 1½ **cups natural peanut butter**
- 1 **cup coarsely chopped roasted peanuts**
- ¾ **tsp. kosher salt**
- ¾ **tsp. pure vanilla extract**
- ½ **tsp. baking soda**

1. Line a 9-inch-square pan with foil. In a medium saucepan, stir the sugar with the corn syrup and 2 tablespoons of water. Add the butter and bring to a boil over high heat, stirring to dissolve the sugar. Attach a candy thermometer to the pan and cook over moderately high heat until the caramel reaches 285°, about 10 minutes.

2. Meanwhile, in a large heatproof microwave-safe bowl, combine the peanut butter with the peanuts and salt. Heat the peanut butter mixture in the microwave at high power for about 1½ minutes, until melted and hot. Stir well.

3. In a small bowl, whisk the vanilla with the baking soda. As soon as the caramel reaches 285°, carefully stir in the baking soda mixture; the caramel will foam and bubble up.

4. Immediately pour the caramel into the melted peanut butter mixture and, using a heatproof spatula, fold together as quickly as possible. You want the mixtures to be combined but not homogenized; the candy will come together very fast.

5. Immediately scrape the hot candy into the prepared pan and press into a flat, even layer. Let cool completely. Peel off the foil and cut the candy into squares.

MAKE AHEAD Cut or uncut, the candy can be stored in an airtight container at room temperature for up to 2 weeks.

STEP-BY-STEP

1

START THE CARAMEL In a saucepan, boil sugar with light corn syrup, water and unsalted butter.

2

MAKE THE PEANUT MIXTURE Add chopped peanuts and salt to peanut butter, then mix until fully blended.

3

MELT THE PEANUT MIXTURE Microwave at high power until hot to the touch.

4

FINISH THE CARAMEL When it reaches 285°, aerate by stirring in the baking soda–vanilla mixture.

5

MAKE THE CANDY Using a heatproof spatula, fold the hot caramel into the hot peanut butter mixture.

6

SHAPE THE CANDY Scrape into a foil-lined pan and smooth the surface, pressing down with the spatula.

Salted Caramel–Filled Fudge Brownies

Active **30 min;** Total **1 hr 15 min plus cooling;** Makes **12**

CARAMEL

1¼ cups sugar

¾ cup heavy cream

4 Tbsp. unsalted butter

1½ tsp. flaky sea salt

BROWNIES

2 sticks unsalted butter, plus more for greasing

10 oz. bittersweet chocolate, finely chopped

1½ cups sugar

¼ cup unsweetened cocoa powder

2 tsp. pure vanilla extract

½ tsp. kosher salt

3 large eggs, chilled

1 cup all-purpose flour

1. Make the caramel In a medium saucepan, cook the sugar with 3 tablespoons of water over moderate heat, swirling the pan frequently, until a dark amber caramel forms. Slowly drizzle in the cream, then whisk in the butter and sea salt. Transfer the caramel to a small bowl and refrigerate until thickened, about 2 hours.

2. Make the brownies Preheat the oven to 325°. Lightly butter a 9-by-13-inch metal baking pan. Melt the 2 sticks of butter in a heatproof medium bowl set over (not in) a saucepan of simmering water. Add the chopped chocolate, the sugar, cocoa powder, vanilla and salt and stir until smooth. Remove the bowl from the heat and whisk in the eggs. Add the flour and stir until just incorporated. Scrape the batter into the prepared pan and bake the brownies for about 40 minutes, until a tester inserted in the center comes out with a few moist crumbs attached. Transfer the pan to a rack and let cool completely.

3. Invert the brownies onto a cutting board and cut in half to form 2 rectangles. Spread the chilled caramel over 1 rectangle, then top with the other rectangle. Cut into 12 bars and serve. —*Anya von Bremzen*

MAKE AHEAD The caramel can be refrigerated for 2 weeks. The brownies can be refrigerated for 3 days or frozen for 1 month.

Chocolate-Peppermint Brownies

Active **15 min;** Total **45 min plus 2 hr cooling;** Makes **24**

Pastry chef Claire Ptak of London's Violet Bakery stirs peppermint extract into her rich brownie batter and also tops the brownies with candy cane pieces. If you can't find candy canes, use striped peppermint candies.

2 sticks unsalted butter, cut into small pieces, plus more for greasing

1 lb. bittersweet chocolate, chopped

2 tsp. pure peppermint extract

4 large eggs

1¾ cups packed light brown sugar

¾ cup all-purpose flour

1 tsp. fine sea salt

4 candy canes, crushed (⅓ cup)

1. Preheat the oven to 350°. Butter a 9-by-13-inch baking pan and line with parchment paper; allow 2 inches of overhang on the long sides.

2. In a heatproof bowl, combine two-thirds of the chopped chocolate with the 2 sticks of butter. Set the bowl over a pot of simmering water and stir until melted. Scrape the chocolate into another bowl and let cool slightly. Add the remaining chopped chocolate and the peppermint extract to the heatproof bowl and melt over the simmering water; remove from the heat and let cool slightly.

3. In a medium bowl, whisk the eggs with the brown sugar until combined. Whisk in the chocolate-butter mixture until glossy and thick. Sprinkle the flour and salt into the bowl and stir until just incorporated. Spread the brownie batter in the prepared baking pan. Dollop the peppermint chocolate onto the brownie batter and swirl in with a table knife.

4. Bake the brownies in the center of the oven for 15 minutes. Sprinkle the crushed candy canes on top and bake for 10 to 15 minutes longer, until the edges are set and a toothpick inserted in the center comes out with a few moist crumbs. Let the brownies cool in the pan for at least 2 hours. Cut into squares and serve. —*Claire Ptak*

Salt-and-Pepper Sandwich Cookies with Strawberry-Lemonade Jam

Active **1 hr;** Total **1 hr 30 min plus 4 hr chilling;** Makes **18**

JAM

1 lb. strawberries, hulled and coarsely chopped

1 Tbsp. finely grated lemon zest plus 2 Tbsp. fresh lemon juice

1½ Tbsp. rice wine vinegar

½ tsp. kosher salt

Pinch of freshly ground pepper

2 Tbsp. Ball Low or No-Sugar Needed Pectin

¾ cup sugar

COOKIES

4 cups all-purpose flour

2 Tbsp. kosher salt

4 tsp. freshly ground pepper

1 tsp. baking powder

½ tsp. baking soda

1 lb. (4 sticks) unsalted butter, softened

3 cups sugar

2 large eggs

1. Make the jam In a medium bowl, mash half of the strawberries with a potato masher. In a medium saucepan, whisk the mashed and chopped strawberries with the lemon zest and juice, the vinegar, salt, pepper and ⅓ cup of water. Sprinkle the pectin evenly on top, then whisk until incorporated. Bring the mixture to a rolling boil over high heat. Whisk in the sugar, return to a boil and cook over high heat until the sugar dissolves, about 1 minute. Remove from the heat and skim off any foam. Let the jam cool. Scrape into a bowl, cover with plastic wrap and refrigerate for at least 4 hours or overnight.

2. Make the cookies In a large bowl, whisk the flour with the salt, pepper, baking powder and baking soda until evenly combined. In a stand mixer fitted with the paddle, beat the butter and sugar at medium speed until light and fluffy, about 3 minutes. Beat in the eggs 1 at a time until incorporated. Add the dry ingredients and beat at low speed until just combined.

3. Preheat the oven to 375°. Using a 1½-ounce ice cream scoop or a soup spoon and working in 2 batches, scoop the dough into 1½-inch balls and arrange at least 3 inches apart on 2 parchment paper–lined baking sheets. Bake the cookies for 12 to 14 minutes, until set at the edges and lightly browned; rotate the baking sheets from top to bottom and front to back halfway through baking. Let the cookies cool for 10 minutes, then transfer to a rack to cool completely.

4. To serve, spread 1 heaping tablespoon of the strawberry jam on one side of half the cookies. Sandwich with the remaining cookies and serve. —*Christina Tosi*

S'mores Bars with Marshmallow Meringue

Active **50 min;** Total **2 hr;** Makes **12**

CRUST

- **3 cups graham cracker crumbs (12 oz.)**
- **1½ sticks unsalted butter, melted**
- **2 Tbsp. packed light brown sugar**
- **¼ tsp. fine sea salt**

BROWNIE FILLING

- **1 stick cold unsalted butter, cubed**
- **4 oz. unsweetened chocolate, chopped**
- **1¼ cups granulated sugar**
- **2 tsp. pure vanilla extract**
- **¼ tsp. fine sea salt**
- **2 large eggs, at room temperature**
- **½ cup all-purpose flour**

MERINGUE

- **3 large egg whites**
- **¾ cup granulated sugar**
- **½ tsp. pure vanilla extract**
- **¼ tsp. cream of tartar**

1. Make the crust Preheat the oven to 350°. Line a 9-inch-square baking pan with foil, allowing 2 inches of overhang on two sides. In a medium bowl, using a fork, mix all of the ingredients until evenly moistened. Press the crumbs evenly into the bottom of the prepared pan. Bake for 8 to 10 minutes, just until lightly browned. Let cool completely. Leave the oven on.

2. Make the filling In a heatproof medium bowl set over a saucepan of simmering water, melt the butter with the chocolate over moderate heat, stirring occasionally, until smooth, about 5 minutes. Remove

from the heat and whisk in the sugar, vanilla and salt. Whisk in the eggs until smooth, then stir in the flour until just incorporated. Spread the batter evenly over the cooled crust. Bake for about 25 minutes, until the edges are set but the center is still slightly jiggly. Transfer to a rack and let cool completely.

3. Make the meringue Preheat the broiler. In a heatproof medium bowl set over a saucepan of simmering water, whisk the egg whites with the sugar until the whites are warm and the sugar is dissolved, about 3 minutes. Transfer the egg whites to the bowl of a stand mixer fitted with the whisk. Add the vanilla and cream of tartar and beat at medium speed until firm. Increase the speed to high and beat the meringue until stiff and glossy, 5 to 7 minutes.

4. Mound the meringue on top of the filling, swirling it decoratively. Broil the meringue 8 inches from the heat until lightly browned at the tips, about 1 minute. Cut into bars and serve. —*Cheryl and Griffith Day*

Crispy Quinoa Brittle

Active **20 min;** Total **1 hr;** Makes **1 pound**

- **1 cup quinoa, rinsed**
- **2 Tbsp. canola oil**
- **1½ cups sugar**
- **½ tsp. baking soda**
- **2 Tbsp. toasted sesame seeds**

1. Preheat the oven to 350°. Cook the quinoa in a saucepan of boiling water until al dente, about 10 minutes. Drain and spread on a large baking sheet; let cool to room temperature.

2. Drizzle the quinoa with the oil and toss to coat. Bake for 30 minutes, until crisp.

3. In a medium saucepan, cook the sugar over moderately low heat, stirring occasionally, until a deep amber caramel forms, about 8 minutes. Stir in the baking soda, then stir in the quinoa and sesame seeds. Immediately scrape the mixture onto the baking sheet and, working quickly, spread it as thinly as possible. Let cool completely. —*Kay Chun*

Chocolate Sandwich Cookies

Active **30 min;** Total **2 hr 45 min;** Makes **16**

These sandwich cookies get their pleasantly bitter, intense chocolate flavor from extra-dark or black cocoa powder. The recipe is from Gillian Shaw of Black Jet Baking Company in San Francisco, adapted from Thomas Keller's cookbook *Ad Hoc at Home.*

COOKIES

- **1½ cups all-purpose flour**
- **1 cup Guittard unsweetened cocoa powder or King Arthur black cocoa**
- **¾ cup sugar**
- **2 tsp. kosher salt**
- **½ tsp. baking soda**
- **2 sticks cold unsalted butter, cut into cubes**

FILLING

- **2 sticks unsalted butter, at room temperature**
- **1½ tsp. salt**
- **3 cups confectioners' sugar**
- **1½ tsp. pure vanilla extract**
- **1½ tsp. whole milk**

1. Make the cookies In a stand mixer fitted with the paddle, mix the flour, cocoa, sugar, salt and baking soda. Add the butter and mix at low speed until the dough is sandy, about 10 minutes. Transfer the dough to a sheet of parchment paper, cover with another sheet of parchment paper and roll out ¼ inch thick. Transfer to a cookie sheet and refrigerate until completely chilled, about 1 hour, or freeze.

2. Preheat the oven to 350°. Stamp out cookies using a 1½-inch round cutter and place them on 2 parchment-lined baking sheets 2 inches apart. Bake 1 sheet at a time for about 12 minutes, until slightly firm. Transfer to a rack to cool completely.

3. Meanwhile, make the filling In a large bowl, cream the butter with the salt. Add the confectioners' sugar, vanilla and milk and beat until light and fluffy. Transfer the filling to a piping bag fitted with a round medium tip.

4. Pipe a mound of filling on the underside of half of the cookies. Top with the remaining cookies and press lightly. Refrigerate until the filling has firmed up, about 1 hour. —*Gillian Shaw*

MATCHA TEA
CAKE COOKIES

Matcha Tea Cake Cookies

Active **30 min**; Total **1 hr**; Makes **24**

Oil makes these delicate cookies moist and cake-like; matcha tea powder gives them a light, toasty flavor and lovely green color. Look for matcha at Asian markets and stores like Whole Foods.

- **2 cups all-purpose flour**
- **2 tsp. baking powder**
- **½ tsp. kosher salt**
- **⅛ tsp. ground cardamom**
- **¾ cup granulated sugar**
- **⅔ cup canola oil**
- **2 large eggs**
- **½ tsp. pure vanilla extract**
- **¼ tsp. pure almond extract**
- **2 Tbsp. plus 1 tsp. matcha tea powder**
- **¼ cup confectioners' sugar**

1. In a medium bowl, whisk the flour with the baking powder, salt and cardamom. In another bowl, whisk the granulated sugar with the oil, eggs and vanilla and almond extracts. In a small bowl, stir 2 tablespoons of the matcha powder with 2 tablespoons of water, then stir into the wet ingredients. Stir the wet ingredients into the flour mixture just until combined.

2. Using a 1-ounce ice cream scoop or 2 tablespoons, scoop 1-inch balls of dough at least 2 inches apart onto 2 baking sheets lined with parchment paper. Refrigerate for at least 20 minutes.

3. Preheat the oven to 350°. Bake the cookies for about 10 minutes, until set at the edges and very lightly browned on the bottoms. Let the cookies cool for 10 minutes, then transfer them to a rack to cool completely.

4. Arrange the cookies on 1 baking sheet. In a sieve, combine the confectioners' sugar with the remaining 1 teaspoon of matcha. Dust over the cookies and serve. —*Ben Mims*

Basler Leckerli

Active **1 hr**; Total **1 hr 30 min**
Makes **48 bars**

These classic German spiced bars are great to make ahead; in fact, they get tastier and more tender the longer they sit.

- **¾ cup honey**
- **⅓ cup plus 1 Tbsp. granulated sugar**
- **¼ tsp. kosher salt**
- **2 cups all-purpose flour**
- **1½ tsp. baking powder**
- **1 large egg, lightly beaten**
- **⅔ cup blanched almonds, finely chopped**
- **½ cup finely chopped candied orange peel**
- **¼ cup finely chopped candied citron peel**
- **1 Tbsp. finely grated orange zest**
- **1½ tsp. finely grated lemon zest**
- **1½ tsp. ground cinnamon**
- **⅛ tsp. ground cloves**
- **⅛ tsp. freshly grated nutmeg**
- **¼ cup confectioners' sugar**

1. In a small saucepan, combine the honey with the granulated sugar and salt. Cook over moderate heat, stirring occasionally, until the honey and sugar are melted and beginning to simmer, about 3 minutes. Transfer to a large heatproof bowl and let cool slightly, about 20 minutes.

2. Preheat the oven to 350° and line a large rimmed baking sheet with parchment paper. In a small bowl, sift the flour with the baking powder. Using a sturdy spatula or wooden spoon, stir the egg into the honey mixture. Stir in the almonds, candied orange and citron peels, orange and lemon zests, cinnamon, cloves and nutmeg, then stir in the sifted flour.

3. Scrape the dough onto the prepared baking sheet and, with floured hands, press into a 12-by-9-inch rectangle, about ¼ inch thick. Bake for about 20 minutes, rotating the baking sheet halfway through, until golden and puffy.

4. Meanwhile, in a small saucepan, combine the confectioners' sugar with 2 tablespoons of water and bring to a boil over moderately high heat. Boil the syrup until it begins to thicken, about 5 minutes. Keep the glaze warm.

5. As soon as the leckerli is done, brush the surface with the hot glaze. While it's still hot, carefully slide the parchment onto a work surface. Using a sharp knife, trim the edges of the rectangle and cut the leckerli into 2-by-1-inch bars. Let cool before serving. —*Luisa Weiss (From* My Berlin Kitchen *by Luisa Weiss, published on August 27, 2013, by Penguin, an imprint of Penguin Publishing Group, a division of Penguin Random House LLC. Copyright © by Luisa Weiss, 2012.)*

MAKE AHEAD The bars can be stored at room temperature in an airtight container with half an apple for up to 2 months. Swap out the apple once a week.

Forgotten Cookies

Active **20 min**; Total **8 hr 30 min**; Makes **18**

This Southern classic is so named because the cookies sit in the oven overnight to develop their wonderful crispy-chewy texture.

- **2 large egg whites**
- **½ tsp. cream of tartar**
- **¾ cup sugar**
- **½ tsp. vanilla bean paste**
- **¼ tsp. ground cardamom**
- **¾ cup bittersweet chocolate chips**
- **¾ cup chopped toasted pecans**
- **¼ cup dried cherries**
- **Coarse sea salt**

1. Preheat the oven to 350°. In a stand mixer fitted with the whisk, beat the egg whites with the cream of tartar at medium speed until soft peaks form, 1 to 2 minutes. With the machine on, gradually add the sugar. Add the vanilla bean paste and cardamom and beat at high speed until stiff peaks form, about 3 minutes. Using a spatula, scrape down the side and bottom of the bowl and fold in the chocolate chips, pecans and cherries.

2. Using 2 spoons, drop 2-inch balls of the meringue mixture onto a large foil-lined baking sheet. Sprinkle the cookies with sea salt and bake for 5 minutes. Turn the oven off and leave the cookies in for at least 8 hours or overnight before serving. —*Sarah Grueneberg*

Crispy Florentine Cookie Stacks with Ricotta

Total **1 hr 15 min plus cooling; Serves 6**

Sandy D'Amato of Good Stock Farm cooking school in Hatfield, Massachusetts, creates a deconstructed version of cannoli by topping crisp, lacy florentine cookies with a mix of ricotta, chocolate chips and Grand Marnier–soaked dried cherries. These light cookies are easier to make than cannoli shells because they don't require frying or piping.

COOKIES

2½ Tbsp. minced dried sour cherries
1 tsp. Grand Marnier
3 Tbsp. unsalted butter
¼ cup granulated sugar
¼ cup dark corn syrup
1 tsp. finely grated orange zest
1 tsp. finely grated lemon zest
¼ tsp. kosher salt
1¾ cups sliced almonds (7 oz.)
¼ cup packed all-purpose flour

FILLING

¼ cup dried sour cherries, finely chopped
1 Tbsp. Grand Marnier
¾ cup fresh ricotta cheese
½ cup mascarpone cheese
1 Tbsp. heavy cream
½ tsp. vanilla bean paste or pure vanilla extract
Pinch of kosher salt
3 Tbsp. confectioners' sugar, plus more for dusting
¼ cup bittersweet chocolate chips, finely chopped

1. Make the cookies Preheat the oven to 375°. Line 2 baking sheets with silicone mats or parchment paper. In a small bowl, toss the minced sour cherries with the Grand Marnier and let stand for 10 minutes.

2. In a large bowl set over a saucepan of simmering water, combine the butter with the granulated sugar, corn syrup, orange and lemon zests and salt. Cook over moderate heat, whisking, until the butter melts and the sugar is dissolved, about 5 minutes. Fold in the almonds and macerated cherries, then fold in the flour.

3. Spoon nine 2-teaspoon-size mounds onto each baking sheet and spread them into 1½-inch rounds. Bake the florentines for 13 to 15 minutes, until deep golden brown. Let cool completely on the sheets.

4. Meanwhile, make the filling In a small bowl, toss the cherries with the Grand Marnier; let stand for 10 minutes. In a medium bowl, blend the ricotta with the mascarpone, heavy cream, vanilla bean paste, salt and the 3 tablespoons of confectioners' sugar. Fold in the chocolate chips and soaked cherries.

5. For each stack, set a cookie on a plate and top with 2 tablespoons of the ricotta filling. Top with another cookie, another 2 tablespoons of filling and a final cookie. Repeat with the remaining cookies and filling to make 5 more stacks. Dust the stacks with confectioners' sugar and serve. —*Sandy D'Amato*

MAKE AHEAD The crispy florentine cookies can be stored in an airtight container overnight.

Hausfreunde

Active **50 min**; Total **3 hr**
Makes **24 sandwich cookies**

These German chocolate-dipped almond-apricot sandwich cookies are somewhat labor-intensive but well worth the effort.

2 cups all-purpose flour
¼ cup plus 1 Tbsp. granulated sugar
¼ tsp. kosher salt
1½ sticks cold unsalted butter, cubed
1 large egg, beaten
½ tsp. pure vanilla extract
About ½ cup apricot jam
7 oz. almond paste
¾ cup confectioners' sugar
5 oz. bittersweet chocolate, chopped
24 walnut halves, toasted

1. In a food processor, pulse the flour with the granulated sugar and salt. Add the butter and pulse until the mixture resembles coarse meal with some pea-size pieces remaining. Add the egg and vanilla and pulse until the dough just comes together. Scrape out onto a work surface and pat into a disk. Wrap in plastic and refrigerate until chilled, about 1 hour.

2. Preheat the oven to 350° and line 2 large rimmed baking sheets with parchment paper. On a lightly floured work surface, roll out the dough ¼ inch thick. Using a 2-inch round cookie cutter, stamp out cookies as close together as possible; transfer to the prepared baking sheets. Gather the scraps, reroll and stamp out more cookies. You should have a total of 48 cookies.

3. Bake the cookies for about 20 minutes, until golden; rotate the baking sheets from top to bottom and front to back halfway through baking. Transfer to a rack to cool.

4. In a small saucepan, warm the jam over moderate heat, stirring, until runny, about 3 minutes. Brush a thin layer of jam on 24 of the cookies and top with the remaining cookies.

5. In a medium bowl, combine the almond paste with the confectioners' sugar and knead until blended. Roll out the almond paste ⅛ inch thick between 2 sheets of parchment paper. Using a 2-inch round cookie cutter, stamp out 24 rounds. Brush the top of each cookie sandwich with another thin layer of jam and top with the rounds of almond paste.

6. In a microwave-safe bowl, heat the chocolate at high power in 30-second bursts until just melted. Stir until smooth. Dip the top of each sandwich cookie in the chocolate, just enough to coat the almond paste; transfer to the baking sheet. Top each cookie with a walnut half. Let the chocolate set before serving. —*Luisa Weiss*

MAKE AHEAD The cookies can be stored at room temperature in an airtight container between wax paper for up to 5 days.

Haselnussmakronen

Active **45 min**; Total **1 hr**
Makes **about 30 cookies**

Luisa Weiss, the author of *My Berlin Kitchen*, says that this no-fuss German Christmas cookie is one of her favorites. "No complicated doughs that need to ripen for weeks, no rolling or cutting. You just throw the dough together, heat up some jam and you're almost there."

- **1½ cups whole hazelnuts**
- **2 large egg whites**
- **¼ tsp. kosher salt**
- **¾ cup sugar**
- **½ cup raspberry jam**

1. Preheat the oven to 400° and line 2 large rimmed baking sheets with parchment paper.

2. Spread the hazelnuts in a pie plate and toast until the skins split and the nuts are fragrant, about 10 minutes. Transfer to a clean kitchen towel and rub together to release the skins. Let the hazelnuts cool completely.

3. In a food processor, pulse the hazelnuts until finely chopped. In a medium bowl, using a hand mixer, beat the egg whites with the salt at medium speed until foamy, 2 minutes. Gradually add the sugar and continue beating until soft peaks form when the beaters are lifted, 5 to 7 minutes. Fold in the hazelnuts.

4. Using a 1-ounce ice cream scoop or a soup spoon, scoop 1½-inch rounds of the batter onto the prepared baking sheets, about 1 inch apart. Bake the cookies for 11 to 13 minutes, until fragrant and lightly browned; rotate the baking sheets from top to bottom and front to back halfway through baking. Remove the cookies from the oven and, while they're still hot, carefully make an indentation in the center of each with the back of a teaspoon.

5. In a small saucepan, boil the raspberry jam for 30 seconds, until slightly thickened. Carefully spoon about 1 teaspoon of the hot jam into the center of each cookie. Let the jam set and the cookies cool completely before serving. *—Luisa Weiss*

MAKE AHEAD The cookies can be stored at room temperature in an airtight container between wax paper for up to 4 days.

Cranberry-Lime Shortbread Cookies with Lime Curd

Active **1 hr**; Total **3 hr 30 min**
Makes **about 36**

LIME CURD

- **6 Tbsp. unsalted butter, at room temperature**
- **1 cup granulated sugar**
- **2 large eggs plus 2 large egg yolks**
- **½ cup fresh lime juice**
- **2 Tbsp. fresh lemon juice**
- **⅛ tsp. kosher salt**

SHORTBREAD COOKIES

- **2 cups all-purpose flour**
- **1 Tbsp. finely grated lime zest (from about 2 limes)**
- **1 tsp. kosher salt**
- **2 sticks unsalted butter, at room temperature**
- **¾ cup confectioners' sugar**
- **2 tsp. pure vanilla extract**
- **¾ cup coarsely chopped dried cranberries**

1. Make the lime curd In a medium bowl, using a hand mixer, beat the butter with the granulated sugar at medium speed until light and fluffy, about 3 minutes. With the machine on, beat in the eggs and egg yolks 1 at a time. Beat in the lime juice, lemon juice and salt; the mixture will curdle. Scrape the curd mixture into a medium saucepan and cook over moderately low heat, stirring constantly, until it's thickened and reaches 180° on an instant-read thermometer, about 10 minutes. Strain the curd through a fine sieve into a medium bowl. Press a sheet of plastic wrap directly on the surface of the curd and refrigerate until firm, at least 3 hours or overnight.

2. Meanwhile, make the cookies Line 2 baking sheets with parchment paper. In a medium bowl, whisk the flour with the lime zest and salt. In another medium bowl, using a hand mixer, beat the butter with the confectioners' sugar at medium speed until light and fluffy, about 3 minutes. Beat in the vanilla, then beat in the dry ingredients just until combined. Stir in the cranberries. On a lightly floured surface, roll out the dough ¼ inch thick, then cut into 2-inch squares and transfer to the baking sheets. Refrigerate for 1 hour.

3. Preheat the oven to 350°. Bake the cookies for about 20 minutes, shifting the pans halfway through baking, until golden. Transfer the cookies to a rack and let cool. Serve with the lime curd. *—Jodi Elliott*

Toasted Chickpea Shortbread Squares

Total **1 hr 15 min**; Makes **30**

Ghaya Oliveira, pastry chef at Daniel in New York City, makes these Tunisian cookies, known as ghraiba, with toasted chickpea flour. They have a lovely crumbly texture and a deep nuttiness.

- **2 cups chickpea flour**
- **1 cup confectioners' sugar**
- **½ cup all-purpose flour**
- **1½ sticks unsalted butter**
- **½ tsp. kosher salt**

1. Preheat the oven to 350°. Spread the chickpea flour on a rimmed baking sheet and toast for about 15 minutes, stirring occasionally, until lightly browned. Reduce the oven temperature to 325°.

2. Meanwhile, sift the sugar and all-purpose flour into the bowl of a stand mixer. Carefully sift in the hot chickpea flour.

3. In a medium saucepan, bring the butter just to a boil with the salt. Turn the mixer to its next-to-lowest speed and slowly drizzle the hot butter into the flour mixture. Continue beating the dough at this speed until it forms a solid ball, about 20 minutes.

4. Scrape the dough out onto a sheet of parchment paper and cover with another sheet of parchment paper. Roll out the dough into a ¾-inch-thick rectangle. Peel off the top layer of parchment paper, transfer the dough to a baking sheet and refrigerate until firm, about 20 minutes.

5. Line another baking sheet with parchment paper. Cut the dough into 1-inch squares and arrange at least 1 inch apart on the lined baking sheets. Bake for about 10 minutes, until the squares are lightly browned at the edges; rotate the baking sheets from front to back and top to bottom halfway through baking. Transfer the shortbreads to a rack and let cool to room temperature before serving.
—Ghaya Oliveira

Chocolate–and–Pinot Noir S'mores Puddings

Active **45 min**; Total **2 hr 45 min**; Serves **6**

An intense Pinot Noir syrup flavors these chocolaty, meringue-topped puddings.

PUDDINGS

1½ cups Pinot Noir

1 cup sugar

1 cup whole milk

¾ cup heavy cream

4 large egg yolks

1 lb. dark chocolate, finely chopped

1 Tbsp. butter, softened

MERINGUE

3 large egg whites

½ cup sugar

Pinch of cream of tartar

Espresso Shortbreads (at right), for serving

1. Make the puddings In a medium saucepan, combine the wine and sugar and bring to a boil. Simmer over moderately high heat until reduced to 1 cup, about 18 minutes.

2. In another small saucepan, bring the milk and cream to a boil. In a large bowl, beat the egg yolks. Gradually beat in the hot cream. Add the chocolate and butter; let stand for 2 minutes, then stir until smooth. Stir in half of the wine syrup. Pour the pudding into six 6- to 8-ounce heatproof glass jars or glasses. Refrigerate for at least 2 hours or overnight.

3. Make the meringue In the bowl of a stand mixer set over a saucepan of simmering water, whisk the egg whites with the sugar and cream of tartar until warm and the sugar is dissolved, 3 to 5 minutes. Let cool slightly. In the mixer, beat the whites at medium-high speed until firm, glossy peaks form, about 2 minutes.

4. Scrape the meringue into a pastry bag fitted with a large star tip and pipe it onto the puddings. Using a kitchen torch, brown the meringue. Serve with the shortbreads and remaining wine syrup. —*Duskie Estes*

NOTE If you don't have a torch, pipe the meringues onto a foil-lined baking sheet. Broil 6 inches from the heat until lightly browned, about 1 minute. Using a small spatula, set the meringues on the puddings just before serving.

Semolina Budino

Active **35 min**; Total **1 hr 10 min**
Serves **12**

Nashville pastry chef and writer Lisa Donovan says this not-too-sweet Italian pudding recalls one of her favorite recipes, spoon bread, from M.F. K. Fisher's classic *How to Cook a Wolf.*

4 Tbsp. unsalted butter, melted, plus more for greasing

5 cups whole milk

¾ cup honey

⅛ tsp. kosher salt

1 cup semolina

3 large egg yolks

2 large egg whites

Roasted pears and sweetened mascarpone, for serving

1. Preheat the oven to 350°. Butter twelve 4-ounce ramekins and arrange them on a baking sheet.

2. In a medium saucepan, warm the milk with the honey and salt over low heat, stirring, just until the honey dissolves. Slowly whisk in the semolina. Cook, whisking constantly, until the mixture thickens to a porridge consistency, 8 to 10 minutes. Remove from the heat and whisk in the 4 tablespoons of melted butter.

3. In a heatproof medium bowl, whisk the egg yolks. While whisking constantly, slowly drizzle in 2 cups of the semolina pudding and whisk until incorporated. Whisk in the remaining pudding.

4. In a medium bowl, beat the egg whites until medium-stiff peaks form. Fold the whites into the pudding.

5. Spoon the semolina pudding into the prepared ramekins. Bake until golden and set, about 30 minutes. Serve warm with roasted pears and sweetened mascarpone. —*Lisa Donovan*

Espresso Shortbreads

Active **30 min**; Total **1 hr 15 min plus cooling**; Makes **about 20**

5 Tbsp. unsalted butter, softened

2 Tbsp. confectioners' sugar

1 Tbsp. granulated sugar

¾ cup all-purpose flour

1 tsp. instant espresso powder

⅛ tsp. kosher salt

Turbinado sugar, for sprinkling

1. Preheat the oven to 350° and line a large baking sheet with parchment paper. In a stand mixer fitted with the paddle, beat the butter with the confectioners' and granulated sugars until fluffy. Add the flour, espresso powder and salt and beat until just combined. Scrape the dough onto a work surface and pat into a disk. Wrap in plastic and refrigerate until just firm, about 30 minutes.

2. On a lightly floured work surface, roll out the dough ⅛ inch thick. Using a 2½-inch round cookie cutter, stamp out cookies and transfer them to the prepared baking sheet. Sprinkle with turbinado sugar. Bake until the cookies are just firm to the touch and golden at the edges, 15 to 18 minutes; rotate the baking sheet halfway through baking. Let the cookies cool on the baking sheet for 5 minutes, then transfer them to a rack to cool completely. —*Duskie Estes*

Semolina Pudding

🙂 Active **20 min**; Total **40 min**; Serves **6**

1 cup fine semolina

1 stick unsalted butter

¼ cup pine nuts

1¼ cups plus 1 Tbsp. sugar

1¼ cups whole milk

¼ cup chopped walnuts

Ground cinnamon, for sprinkling

In a medium saucepan, cook the semolina, butter and pine nuts over moderate heat, stirring, until the pine nuts are golden, about 5 minutes. Add 1¼ cups of the sugar, the milk and 1¼ cups of water and bring to a simmer. Cover and cook over low heat, stirring occasionally, until very thick, 10 minutes. Sprinkle the remaining sugar on top, cover and let stand until warm, 10 minutes. Serve in bowls topped with the walnuts and cinnamon. —*Scott Conant*

DOUBLE-CHOCOLATE
SOUFFLÉS

Double-Chocolate Soufflés

⏱ Total **45 min**; Serves **8**

Mimi Thorisson, author of *A Kitchen in France*, makes her soufflé doubly chocolaty by using bittersweet chocolate with 70 percent or more cocoa, as well as unsweetened cocoa powder.

- **2 Tbsp. unsalted butter, plus more for greasing**
- **½ cup sugar, plus more for dusting**
- **6 oz. bittersweet chocolate (70%), finely chopped**
- **¼ tsp. kosher salt**
- **¾ cup plus 2 Tbsp. milk**
- **2 Tbsp. unsweetened cocoa powder**
- **6 large eggs, separated**

1. Preheat the oven to 400°. Grease eight 10-ounce ramekins with butter and dust with sugar, tapping out the excess; set on a rimmed baking sheet.

2. In a large bowl set over a saucepan of simmering water, melt the bittersweet chocolate with the 2 tablespoons of butter and the kosher salt, stirring a few times. In another medium saucepan, bring the milk just to a simmer over moderate heat. Whisk in the cocoa powder, then whisk in the melted chocolate.

3. In a large bowl, beat the egg yolks. Gradually whisk in the chocolate mixture until smooth. In another large bowl, using a hand mixer, beat the egg whites at high speed until medium peaks form, about 2 minutes. Gradually beat in the ½ cup of sugar and continue beating until the whites form stiff peaks, 2 to 3 minutes.

4. Carefully fold the egg whites into the chocolate mixture until no streaks remain. Spoon the soufflé into the prepared ramekins and bake in the center of the oven until risen, about 15 minutes. Serve right away. —*Mimi Thorisson*

WINE Orange-scented Sauternes: 2011 Carmes de Rieussec.

Milk Chocolate Mousse with Brown Butter Shortbread and Roasted Strawberries

Active **1 hr**; Total **1 hr 30 min**; Serves **6 to 8**

"Berries with cream is a surefire hit," says chef Eli Kirshtein of The Luminary in Atlanta's Krog Street Market. "We go one step further by adding milk chocolate to the cream and making it into a mousse."

SHORTBREAD

- **1 stick plus 6 Tbsp. unsalted butter**
- **½ cup dark brown sugar**
- **1½ cups all-purpose flour**
- **½ tsp. kosher salt**

MOUSSE AND STRAWBERRIES

- **1¾ cups heavy cream**
- **10 oz. milk chocolate, finely chopped Kosher salt**
- **1 quart strawberries, hulled and halved**
- **¼ cup granulated sugar**

1. Make the shortbread Preheat the oven to 350°. In a medium saucepan, cook the butter over moderate heat, stirring, until fragrant and the solids turn dark golden, 5 to 7 minutes. Let cool.

2. Line a large rimmed baking sheet with parchment paper. In a stand mixer fitted with the paddle, beat the browned butter with the brown sugar until smooth. Beat in the flour and salt. Scrape the mixture onto the prepared baking sheet and spread into a 9-by-12-inch rectangle. Bake for 12 to 15 minutes, until just set. Using a knife, score the shortbread into 12 squares. Let cool, then cut into squares.

3. Meanwhile, prepare the mousse and strawberries In a medium saucepan, bring the cream just to a simmer over moderate heat. Remove from the heat and add the chocolate and a pinch of salt. Let stand for 2 minutes, then stir until the chocolate is melted. Let cool completely, then refrigerate until well chilled, about 30 minutes.

4. Pour the chocolate cream into a stand mixer fitted with the whisk. Beat at medium-high speed until thick and smooth; do not overbeat. Refrigerate the chocolate mousse for 30 minutes.

5. Reheat the oven to 350°. On a rimmed baking sheet, toss the strawberries with the sugar and a pinch of salt. Roast for about 10 minutes, until the strawberries are just softened and starting to release their juices. Transfer to a bowl and let cool completely. Serve the mousse with the shortbread and roasted strawberries. —*Eli Kirshtein*

Extra-Creamy Chocolate Mousse

📷 PAGE 320

⏱ Total **40 min**; Serves **10 to 12**

- **1 cup sugar**
- **3 large egg whites, at room temperature**
- **14 oz. bittersweet chocolate, preferably 70%, finely chopped**
- **1 cup whole milk**
- **2 cups cold heavy cream**

1. In a small saucepan, combine the sugar with ¼ cup of water and bring to a boil over moderately high heat. Cook, without stirring, until the syrup reaches 250° on a candy thermometer, 4 to 6 minutes.

2. Meanwhile, in a stand mixer fitted with the whisk, beat the egg whites at medium-high speed until soft peaks form. With the mixer on, gradually pour in the hot syrup in a steady stream and beat at high speed until the whites are stiff, 2 to 3 minutes. Cover the meringue with plastic wrap and let stand at room temperature.

3. Put the chocolate in a heatproof bowl. In a small saucepan, heat the milk just to a simmer. Pour the milk over the chocolate and let stand for 1 minute, then stir until smooth and let cool.

4. In a medium bowl, beat the cream to soft peaks. Reserve ½ cup of the whipped cream for serving.

5. Scoop half of the meringue into a bowl (reserve the rest for another use). Whisk in the remaining whipped cream.

6. Warm the chocolate mixture in a bowl set over a pan of simmering water, stirring, until just melted. Pour the chocolate over the meringue and quickly fold it in. Spoon the mousse into glasses, swirl in the reserved whipped cream and serve. —*Dominique Ansel*

MAKE AHEAD The meringue can be refrigerated overnight. The chocolate can stand at room temperature overnight, covered with plastic wrap.

Eton Mess

Active **1 hr**; Total **5 hr 15 min**; Serves **8**

Named for the iconic English boarding school where it originated, Eton Mess is a multitextured dessert featuring strawberries, meringue and whipped cream. This modern version adds pink peppercorns to the meringue and cardamom to the whipped cream, and baked rhubarb compote swaps in for the fresh strawberries.

CARDAMOM CREAM

- **2¼ cups heavy cream**
- **1 Tbsp. sugar**
- **10 cardamom pods, cracked**

PINK PEPPERCORN MERINGUE

- **¼ vanilla bean, split lengthwise, seeds scraped**
- **½ cup superfine sugar**
- **2½ tsp. cornstarch**
- **3 large egg whites**
- **Pinch of kosher salt**
- **1 Tbsp. pink peppercorns, coarsely ground**

RHUBARB COMPOTE

- **½ vanilla bean, split lengthwise, seeds scraped**
- **¾ cup sugar**
- **2 lbs. rhubarb, cut into ¾-inch pieces**
- **¼ cup Grand Marnier**
- **¼ tsp. kosher salt**
- **Cocoa nibs, for sprinkling**

1. Make the cardamom cream In a medium saucepan, combine the cream, sugar and cardamom and bring just to a simmer. Remove from the heat, cover and let stand for 1 hour. Strain the cream through a fine sieve into a large bowl. Cover and refrigerate for 4 hours.

2. Meanwhile, make the meringue Preheat the oven to 200° and line a large baking sheet with parchment paper. In a small bowl, rub the vanilla seeds into the sugar and stir in the cornstarch. In a stand mixer fitted with the whisk, beat the egg whites with the salt at medium-high speed to soft peaks. Gradually beat in the vanilla sugar, then beat at high speed until the whites are stiff, about 3 minutes. Fold in the pink peppercorns.

3. Spread the meringue on the prepared baking sheet in a ¼-inch-thick layer. Bake in the center of the oven for about 2 hours and 30 minutes, until very lightly colored and crisp. Let cool completely, then break into bite-size pieces.

4. Make the compote Preheat the oven to 325°. In a 9-by-13-inch baking dish, rub the vanilla bean and seeds into the sugar. Add the rhubarb, Grand Marnier and salt and toss to coat. Let the rhubarb macerate for 15 minutes.

5. Tightly cover the baking dish with foil and bake for 30 minutes, until the rhubarb is soft but not falling apart. Let cool slightly. Discard the vanilla bean.

6. Drain the rhubarb in a sieve set over a medium saucepan. Bring the juices to a boil, then simmer over moderately high heat until syrupy, about 5 minutes. Fold the rhubarb into the syrup and let cool completely. Refrigerate the compote until slightly chilled, 45 minutes.

7. Whip the cardamom cream at medium-high speed until firm peaks form.

8. Layer the rhubarb compote, cardamom whipped cream and meringue on plates or in glasses. Sprinkle with cocoa nibs and serve. —*Brandi Henderson*

Cornhusk Meringues with Corn Mousse

Active **1 hr**; Total **2 hr plus cooling**; Serves **4**

This beloved and much-Instagrammed dessert—meringues flavored with charred cornhusk powder and filled with a luscious, sweet corn cream—is the signature dish at chef Enrique Olvera's New York City restaurant, Cosme.

MERINGUES

- **4 dried cornhusks (½ oz.)**
- **2 large egg whites**
- **½ cup sugar**

MOUSSE

- **1½ cups fresh corn kernels (from 3 ears)**
- **1 Tbsp. sugar**
- **⅛ tsp. kosher salt**
- **1 cup heavy cream**
- **¼ cup mascarpone**

1. Make the meringues Preheat the oven to 450°. Spread the husks on a large baking sheet; bake for 8 to 10 minutes, until lightly browned. Reduce the oven temperature to 200°.

2. Break the husks into small pieces. Transfer to a spice grinder in batches and grind to a powder. Sift the husk powder through a fine sieve.

3. In a stand mixer fitted with the whisk, beat the egg whites until soft peaks form. With the mixer on, gradually beat in the sugar until medium peaks form. Add 2½ tablespoons of the husk powder; beat at medium-high speed until stiff.

4. Transfer the meringue to a pastry bag fitted with a ¾-inch round tip. Pipe four 3-inch rounds of meringue onto a parchment paper–lined baking sheet. Bake for about 1 hour and 10 minutes, until the meringues are set and sound hollow when lightly tapped on the bottom. Let cool completely, at least 2 hours.

5. Meanwhile, make the mousse In a skillet, combine the corn, sugar, salt and ¾ cup of the cream and bring just to a boil. Simmer over moderate heat, stirring, until the corn is tender, 5 minutes. Transfer to a blender and puree until smooth. Strain the puree through a fine sieve, pressing on the solids. Let cool completely, then whisk in the mascarpone.

6. In a bowl, beat the remaining ¼ cup of cream until stiff. Fold into the corn mixture until no streaks remain.

7. Transfer the meringues to plates and gently crack open with a table knife. Spoon the corn mousse into the meringues and sprinkle with the remaining husk powder. Serve right away. —*Enrique Olvera*

MAKE AHEAD The meringues can be stored in an airtight container overnight. The mousse can be prepared through Step 5 and refrigerated overnight.

CORNHUSK
MERINGUE WITH
CORN MOUSSE

Grilled Chocolate Sandwiches with Caramel Sauce

Total **45 min;** Serves **6**

DARK CHOCOLATE GANACHE

- 4½ oz. semisweet chocolate chips (⅔ cup)
- 4½ oz. 70% dark chocolate, finely chopped (1 cup)
- ¾ cup heavy cream
- ¼ cup unsweetened cocoa powder
- 1 Tbsp. sugar
- ¼ tsp. kosher salt

CARAMEL SAUCE

- 1 cup heavy cream
- ¾ cup sugar
- 2 tsp. unsalted butter, at room temperature
- ½ tsp. kosher salt

SANDWICHES

- Twelve ¼-inch-thick slices of white country bread
- 4 Tbsp. unsalted butter, melted

1. Make the ganache In a heatproof medium bowl, combine both chocolates. In a medium saucepan with a candy thermometer attached, combine the cream, cocoa powder, sugar and salt. Cook over moderately low heat, whisking frequently, until the mixture is smooth and thick and registers 165° on the thermometer, 3 to 5 minutes. Pour the cream mixture over the chocolate and stir until smooth. Let cool to room temperature.

2. Meanwhile, make the caramel sauce In a small saucepan, warm the cream. In a medium saucepan, spread the sugar in an even layer. Cook over moderate heat, without stirring, until the sugar starts to melt around the edge, about 3 minutes. Reduce the heat to low and shake the pan to incorporate the dry sugar into the melted sugar. Continue to cook over low heat, swirling the pan frequently, until a light amber caramel forms, about 3 minutes longer. Slowly drizzle in the warm cream. Cook over moderate heat, whisking occasionally, until the caramel is smooth, about 3 minutes. Whisk in the butter and salt. Transfer the caramel to a small bowl and let cool until warm.

3. Make the sandwiches Spread ¼ cup of the ganache onto 6 slices of bread. Top with the remaining 6 slices of bread and butter both sides.

4. Heat a large nonstick skillet. Place 3 sandwiches in the skillet and cook over moderate heat until golden and crisp and the ganache is melted, about 2 minutes per side. Transfer the sandwiches to a platter. Repeat with the remaining sandwiches. Serve the sandwiches with the caramel dipping sauce. —*Autumn Martin*

MAKE AHEAD The ganache and caramel can be refrigerated separately for 3 days. Bring to room temperature before using.

Lemon Curd Toasts with Coconut

Active **45 min;** Total **3 hr;** Makes **about 24**

- 3 large eggs
- 1½ cups sugar
- 3 Tbsp. finely grated lemon zest plus ⅔ cup fresh lemon juice
- ¼ cup extra-virgin olive oil
- ¼ cup chopped cocoa butter (see Note)
  - Baguette toasts, for serving
  - Fresh blackberries and toasted coconut flakes or chips, for garnish

1. In a medium bowl, whisk the eggs with ¾ cup of the sugar until combined. In a small saucepan, warm the lemon zest, lemon juice, olive oil, cocoa butter and the remaining ¾ cup of sugar over moderate heat, stirring to dissolve the sugar. While whisking constantly, slowly drizzle half of the lemon juice mixture into the eggs. Add the egg mixture to the saucepan and cook the curd over moderately low heat, stirring constantly, until thickened and a candy thermometer inserted in the curd registers 186°, about 12 minutes.

2. Strain the curd through a fine sieve into a blender. Puree until lightened, about 1 minute. Scrape into a bowl. Press a sheet of plastic wrap directly on the curd and let cool to room temperature. Refrigerate until cold and set, about 2 hours.

3. Spread the lemon curd on the toasts and top with blackberries. Garnish with toasted coconut and serve. —*William Werner*

NOTE Cocoa butter is available at natural food shops, Whole Foods and amazon.com.

MAKE AHEAD The lemon curd can be refrigerated for up to 1 week.

Yuzu Kosho Cashew Butter Toasts

Active **1 hr 30 min;** Total **3 hr**
Makes **about 24**

CANDIED MANDARINS

- 1 cup sugar
- 4 mandarins (10 oz.), scrubbed and sliced crosswise ⅛ inch thick
- 1 vanilla bean—split lengthwise, seeds scraped, pod reserved

YUZU KOSHO CASHEW BUTTER

- 2½ cups cashews (about 1 lb.)
- 3 Tbsp. sugar
- 2 tsp. kosher salt
- 1 Tbsp. red yuzu kosho (see Note)
- ⅓ cup canola oil
  - Pumpernickel bread toasts, for serving
  - Pure grade B maple syrup, for drizzling

1. Make the candied mandarins In a medium saucepan, combine the sugar with 1½ cups of water and bring to a bare simmer, stirring to dissolve the sugar. Add the mandarins and vanilla seeds and pod and cook over low heat, stirring occasionally, until the mandarins are softened and slightly translucent, about 1 hour and 15 minutes. Remove the pan from the heat; discard the vanilla pod. Let the mandarins cool in the syrup, about 1 hour.

2. Meanwhile, make the yuzu kosho cashew butter Preheat the oven to 350°. Spread the cashews on a baking sheet and toast for about 20 minutes, until deep golden. Transfer the sheet to a rack and let the cashews cool completely.

3. In a food processor, pulse the cashews until finely chopped. Add the sugar, salt and yuzu kosho. With the machine on, slowly drizzle in the oil until well blended. Scrape into a medium bowl.

4. Spread the yuzu kosho cashew butter on the toasts and drizzle lightly with maple syrup. Top with the drained candied mandarins and serve. —*William Werner*

NOTE Red yuzu kosho is made with yuzu zest (from the sour citrus fruit), red chiles and salt. It's spicy and packed with citrus flavor. Look for it at Asian markets and on amazon.com.

Whipped Vanilla Ganache Toasts with Pear and Pomegranate

Active **45 min**; Total **3 hr 15 min**
Makes **about 24**

POACHED PEARS

1 vanilla bean—split lengthwise, seeds scraped, pod reserved

2 cups sugar

Five 3-inch-long pieces of lemon zest

4 Forelle pears (1 lb.)—peeled, halved lengthwise and cored

WHIPPED VANILLA GANACHE

3 oz. white chocolate, chopped

1¼ cups heavy cream

½ Tbsp. light corn syrup

¼ tsp. vanilla bean paste or ½ vanilla bean, split lengthwise, seeds scraped

Pain de mie bread toasts, for serving (see Note)

Pomegranate seeds, for garnish

1. Poach the pears In a medium saucepan, combine the vanilla seeds and pod with the sugar, 2½ cups of water and 3 pieces of the lemon zest. Bring to a simmer, stirring to dissolve the sugar. Remove the pan from the heat and let steep for 30 minutes. Strain the syrup through a fine sieve. Return the syrup to the saucepan and let cool completely.

2. Add the pears and the remaining 2 pieces of lemon zest to the syrup and bring to a bare simmer. Cook over moderately low heat, turning occasionally, until the pears are just tender, about 20 minutes. Remove the saucepan from the heat and let cool to room temperature. Cover and refrigerate until chilled, about 2 hours.

3. Meanwhile, make the whipped vanilla ganache Place the white chocolate in a heatproof medium bowl. In a small saucepan, combine ½ cup of the heavy cream with the corn syrup and vanilla bean paste and bring to a boil. Pour the hot cream over the chocolate and let stand for 1 minute, then whisk until smooth; transfer to a blender. With the machine on, slowly drizzle in the remaining ¾ cup of heavy cream until smooth. Scrape the vanilla ganache into a large bowl and chill until it is very cold, about 2 hours.

4. Using a hand mixer, beat the chilled ganache at medium speed until soft peaks form, about 2 minutes. Spread the whipped ganache on the toasts. Slice the pears into thin wedges; arrange on top. Garnish with pomegranate seeds and serve. —William Werner

NOTE Pain de mie is sliced packaged white bread that's available at bakeries.

Coffee-Caramel-Jam Toasts

Active **1 hr**; Total **2 hr 15 min plus overnight steeping**; Makes **about 24**

COFFEE-CARAMEL JAM

½ cup crushed coffee beans

1¼ cups heavy cream

1 cup whole milk

1 cup sugar

1 Tbsp. light corn syrup

2 tsp. instant espresso

⅛ tsp. fine sea salt

CHOCOLATE CRUMBLE

¾ cup all-purpose flour

¾ cup almond flour

½ cup sugar

¼ cup unsweetened cocoa powder

¼ tsp. fine sea salt

1 stick cold unsalted butter, cubed

Dark rye toasts, for serving

1. Make the jam Preheat the oven to 350°. Spread the coffee beans on a baking sheet and toast for 10 minutes, until fragrant. Transfer to a large bowl. Stir in the heavy cream and milk, cover and let steep in the refrigerator overnight.

2. Strain the coffee cream through a fine sieve, pressing on the solids; you should have 2 cups. In a large saucepan, cook the sugar over moderate heat, stirring occasionally, until a light amber caramel forms, about 5 minutes. Slowly add the coffee cream; be careful, as it will boil vigorously. Add the corn syrup, espresso and sea salt and bring to a simmer; the caramel will harden but will dissolve as it simmers. Cook over moderately low heat, stirring, until a candy thermometer inserted in the caramel jam registers 210°, about 12 minutes. Carefully transfer the jam to a blender and puree until smooth and shiny. Scrape into a medium bowl and let cool to room temperature.

3. Meanwhile, make the crumble In a medium bowl, whisk the all-purpose flour with the almond flour, sugar, cocoa powder and sea salt. Using your fingers, rub in the butter until coarse crumbs form. Spread the crumbs in an even layer on a parchment paper–lined baking sheet and refrigerate until firm, about 1 hour.

4. Preheat the oven to 350°. Bake the crumble for about 18 minutes, until golden. Transfer to a rack to cool completely.

5. Spread some coffee-caramel jam on the toasts. Sprinkle the chocolate crumbles on one half of each toast; press gently to help them adhere. —William Werner

MAKE AHEAD The jam can be refrigerated for up to 1 week. Serve at room temperature. The baked crumble can be stored in an airtight container for 1 week or frozen for 1 month.

Pumpkin Parfaits

Active **45 min**; Total **1 hr 45 min**; Serves **12**

Two 15-oz. cans pumpkin puree

1 tsp. pumpkin pie spice

¼ tsp. kosher salt

4 cups mascarpone cheese

2½ cups confectioners' sugar

2 cups heavy cream

1½ cups crushed chocolate wafer cookies (6 oz.)

1. In a large bowl, using a hand mixer, beat the pumpkin puree with the pie spice, salt, 2 cups of the mascarpone and 1½ cups of the confectioners' sugar until thick.

2. In another large bowl, beat the heavy cream with the remaining 2 cups of mascarpone and 1 cup of confectioners' sugar until soft peaks form.

3. Spoon half of the pumpkin mixture into 12 glasses and top with half of the mascarpone mixture and half of the crushed wafers. Repeat the layering once more. Refrigerate until well chilled, at least 1 hour, before serving. —Justin Chapple

MAKE AHEAD The parfaits can be refrigerated for up to 2 days.

MAPLE SEMIFREDDO
WITH CANDIED
PECANS

Maple Semifreddo with Candied Pecans

Active **45 min**; Total **5 hr 15 min**; Serves **6**

- ½ cup pure maple syrup, preferably grade B
- ½ vanilla bean—split lengthwise, seeds scraped, pod reserved
- 1¾ cups heavy cream
- 1 large egg plus 4 large egg yolks
- ¾ tsp. kosher salt
- ¼ cup maple sugar
- 1 cup candied pecans

1. Fill a large bowl with ice water. In a medium saucepan, combine the maple syrup with the vanilla bean and seeds and bring to a boil. Cook over moderate heat, stirring occasionally, until extremely fragrant, chocolate brown in color and thickened, 3 to 5 minutes. Remove the saucepan from the heat. Whisking constantly, slowly drizzle in the cream. Scrape the maple cream into a medium metal bowl and set it in the ice bath; stir occasionally until very cold, about 30 minutes. Discard the vanilla bean. Refrigerate the maple cream.

2. Meanwhile, in a stand mixer fitted with the whisk, beat the egg, egg yolks and salt at medium speed until the mixture is light and fluffy, about 3 minutes.

3. In a small saucepan with a candy thermometer attached, combine the maple sugar with 1 tablespoon of water and bring to a boil. Cook over moderate heat, swirling the pan occasionally, until the syrup is very foamy and reaches 235°. With the mixer at low speed, slowly drizzle the hot syrup down one side of the egg mixture and beat until the side of the bowl is cool to the touch, about 5 minutes.

4. Using a hand mixer, beat the chilled maple cream at medium speed until firm. Fold the maple cream into the egg mixture. Scrape the semifreddo into a 9-by-13-inch baking pan in an even layer. Freeze until firm, about 4 hours or overnight.

5. Serve the maple semifreddo in tall glasses layered with the candied pecans. —*Kierin Baldwin*

MAKE AHEAD The semifreddo can be covered with plastic wrap and frozen for up to 1 week.

Creamy Mocha Ice Pops

Total **25 min plus 6 hr chilling and freezing**; Makes **10**

These chocolate-and-coffee ice pops are from Debi Mazar and her husband, Gabriele Corcos, hosts of *Extra Virgin* on the Cooking Channel. They give the pops a silky, ice cream–like texture by folding whipped cream into the coffee-infused chocolate before molding and freezing.

- 2½ oz. dark chocolate, finely chopped
- ½ cup plus 1 Tbsp. sugar
- ½ cup ground medium-roast coffee (3 oz.)
- 1 cup heavy cream
- Chopped toasted hazelnuts (optional)

1. Line a sieve with cheesecloth. Put the chocolate in a heatproof bowl. In a medium saucepan, combine ½ cup of the sugar with the coffee and 1¾ cups of water and bring to a boil. Simmer over low heat for 4 minutes, stirring. Strain the coffee over the chocolate; whisk until melted. Let cool, then refrigerate for at least 2 hours or overnight.

2. In a medium bowl, using a hand mixer, beat the cream with the remaining 1 tablespoon of sugar at medium speed until soft peaks form. Whisk the chilled mocha mixture until smooth, then fold in the whipped cream. Pour the mocha mixture into 10 ice pop molds and freeze for at least 4 hours. If using hazelnuts, press the frozen ice pops into the chopped nuts and return to the freezer for at least 30 minutes before serving. —*Debi Mazar and Gabriele Corcos*

Brownie Cake Sundaes with Pecan–Ice Cream Balls

Active **25 min**; Total **1 hr 40 min**; Serves **4**

Instead of making brownies in one big pan, Atlanta chef Ford Fry bakes them in muffin cups, so each one has the perfect ratio of crusty exterior to fudgy interior.

- ¾ cup all-purpose flour
- ¼ cup unsweetened cocoa powder
- Kosher salt
- 4 large eggs
- 1 large egg yolk
- 1 Tbsp. pure vanilla extract
- 1 stick unsalted butter, at room temperature
- 8 oz. bittersweet chocolate, chopped
- 1½ cups sugar
- 8 oz. pecans (2 cups)
- 1 Tbsp. canola oil
- 1 pint vanilla ice cream
- Warm hot fudge sauce and whipped cream, for serving

1. Preheat the oven to 325°. Spray a 12-cup muffin pan with nonstick baking spray or line with muffin liners. In a medium bowl, whisk the flour, cocoa and ½ teaspoon salt. In another medium bowl, whisk the eggs with the egg yolk and vanilla.

2. In a heatproof bowl set over a saucepan of simmering water, melt the butter and chopped chocolate over low heat. Remove from the heat; let cool for 10 minutes. Whisk in the sugar, then gradually whisk in the egg mixture. Stir in the dry ingredients.

3. Spoon the batter into the prepared muffin cups. Bake for about 28 minutes, rotating the pan halfway through, until a toothpick inserted in the center of a brownie comes out with just a few crumbs attached. Let the brownies cool in the pan for 10 minutes, then unmold onto a rack and let cool completely.

4. Meanwhile, on a large rimmed baking sheet, toss the pecans with the canola oil and 1½ teaspoons of salt. Roast for about 10 minutes, tossing occasionally, until lightly browned. Let cool, then coarsely chop.

5. Scoop 8 small balls of ice cream and roll them in the pecans. Transfer to 4 bowls; add a brownie, hot fudge sauce and whipped cream to each bowl and serve immediately. —*Ford Fry*

Salty, crunchy, tangy snacks—like popcorn and sesame pistachios, chile-toasted marcona almonds and spiced pickled beets (recipes, pp. 357, 358 and 363)—make up the new, updated relish plate.

SNACKS, CONDIMENTS & SAUCES

POTATO CHIPS
WITH WHIPPED
BEURRE BLANC
Recipe, page 357

TROUT SKIN CRISPS

Trout Skin Crisps

Active **15 min**; Total **3 hr 15 min**
Serves **4**

These smoky crisps can be served like crackers with toppings or dips, or crumbled on eggs or salads.

**Skins from 4 smoked
trout fillets**

**Kosher salt and/or
Old Bay seasoning**

Preheat the oven to 200°. Line a baking sheet with parchment paper. Scrape all the meat off the trout skins and pat dry with paper towels. Tear or cut the skins into large pieces. Arrange on the prepared sheet and bake until dry and crisp, about 3 hours. Season the crisps with salt and/or Old Bay and serve. —*Kay Chun*

WINE Brisk, citrusy Prosecco: NV Sommariva Brut.

Hurricane Popcorn

Total **10 min**; Makes **about 8 cups**

¼ cup canola oil

½ cup popcorn kernels

4 Tbsp. butter

2 Tbsp. furikake (see Note)

2 tsp. chili powder

¼ cup crushed wasabi peas, for serving

1. In a large pot, combine the canola oil and popcorn kernels. Cover and cook over moderate heat until the corn starts to pop. Cook, shaking the pot, until the popping stops, about 3 minutes. Remove the pot from the heat.

2. Stir the butter, furikake and chili powder into the popcorn. Transfer to a large bowl, top with the wasabi peas and serve.
—*Bob Tam*

NOTE Furikake, a seaweed-based seasoning from Japan, is available at Asian markets and many Whole Foods stores.

Potato Chips with Whipped Beurre Blanc

📷 PAGE 355

Active **20 min**; Total **1 hr 15 min**
Makes **about 3 cups beurre blanc**

2 cups dry white wine

¼ cup white wine vinegar

½ cup sliced shallots

1 garlic clove, crushed

3 parsley sprigs

1 thyme sprig

3 whole black peppercorns

1 tsp. fresh lemon juice

Kosher salt

1½ cups crème fraîche

Chopped chives, minced shallot and finely grated lemon zest, for garnish

Salt-and-vinegar potato chips, for serving

Celery Salt (recipe follows), for serving

1. In a medium saucepan, combine the wine, vinegar, sliced shallots, garlic, parsley, thyme and peppercorns and bring to a boil. Cook over moderate heat until reduced to ½ cup, about 20 minutes. Strain into a bowl. Stir in the lemon juice, season with salt and refrigerate until chilled.

2. Add the crème fraîche to the wine reduction and beat until soft peaks form, 1 to 2 minutes. Transfer the dip to a serving bowl; garnish with chives, shallot and grated lemon zest. Serve with potato chips and celery salt for sprinkling. —*Dave Beran*

CELERY SALT

Total **5 min**; Makes **about 2 tablespoons**

2 tsp. celery seeds

2 tsp. fennel seeds

1 tsp. piment d'Espelette

1 tsp. kosher salt

Pinch of freshly ground pepper

In a spice grinder, combine the celery seeds, fennel seeds and piment d'Espelette; pulse until a fine powder forms. Transfer to a small bowl and stir in the salt and pepper. —*DB*

Popcorn with Sesame-Glazed Pistachios

Active **15 min**; Total **30 min**
Makes **about 10 cups**

⅓ cup vegetable oil

½ cup popcorn kernels

Kosher salt

3 Tbsp. extra-virgin olive oil

2 Tbsp. sugar

2 Tbsp. toasted sesame seeds

2 tsp. soy sauce

½ tsp. garlic powder

2 cups shelled unsalted pistachios (8 oz.)

1. Preheat the oven to 350° and line a baking sheet with parchment paper. In a large saucepan, combine the vegetable oil and popcorn, cover and cook over moderate heat until the corn starts to pop. Cook, shaking the pan, until the popping stops, 3 to 5 minutes. Transfer the popcorn to a large bowl and season lightly with salt.

2. Wipe out the saucepan. Add the olive oil, sugar, sesame seeds, soy sauce, garlic powder and 2 teaspoons of salt and cook over moderate heat, stirring, until the sugar dissolves, about 3 minutes. Add the pistachios and cook, stirring, for 1 minute. Scrape the pistachios onto the prepared baking sheet and bake for about 10 minutes, until bubbling. Scrape the pistachio mixture into the popcorn and toss well. Let cool before serving. —*Martha Wiggins*

MAKE AHEAD The mix can be made early in the day and stored in an airtight container at room temperature.

Chile-Toasted Marcona Almonds

Total **15 min plus cooling**
Makes **3 cups**

- 2 **Tbsp. unsalted butter**
- 1 **Tbsp. minced garlic**
- 1 **tsp. crushed red pepper**
- 3 **cups roasted marcona almonds**
  Kosher salt and black pepper
- 1 **Tbsp. minced chives**

In a large skillet, melt the butter. Add the garlic and crushed red pepper and cook over moderate heat, stirring, until the garlic is softened, about 2 minutes. Add the almonds and cook, stirring occasionally, until coated and hot, about 2 minutes. Season with salt and black pepper. Let cool completely, stir in the chives and serve.
—*Martha Wiggins*

MAKE AHEAD The almonds can be stored at room temperature overnight; stir in the chives before serving.

Parmigiano-Reggiano Puffs

⏱ Total **5 min**

Justin Chapple, star of F&W's Mad Genius Tips videos, makes a delectable snack with Parmesan rinds: He pops them in the microwave until they get puffy and crisp.

Parmigiano-Reggiano cheese rinds, cut into ½-inch dice

On a microwave-safe plate, microwave the cheese rinds at high power until puffed and sizzling, 30 seconds to 1 minute. Transfer the cheese puffs to paper towels to drain. Serve hot. —*Justin Chapple*

Nori Granola

Active **20 min;** Total **1 hr plus cooling**
Makes **about 6 cups**

Heidi Swanson, the author of *Near & Far,* makes her crunchy, savory snacking granola with oats, cashews, fennel seeds and plenty of salty nori.

- ¼ **cup runny honey**
- ¼ **cup natural cane sugar**
- 3½ **cups rolled oats**
- 1½ **cups coarsely chopped raw cashews (6 oz.)**
- ¼ **cup sesame seeds**
- 2 **Tbsp. fennel seeds**
- 1 **Tbsp. shichimi togarashi (see Note)**
- ½ **tsp. black pepper**
  Five 8-inch-square sheets of nori, torn and crumbled into 1-inch pieces
- 1½ **tsp. fine sea salt**
- ¼ **cup extra-virgin olive oil**

1. Preheat the oven to 300°. In a small saucepan, combine the honey, sugar and 2 tablespoons of water. Cook over moderately high heat, stirring constantly, until the sugar dissolves and bubbles appear at the edge, about 5 minutes. Remove from the heat and let cool slightly.

2. In a large bowl, toss the oats with the cashews, sesame seeds, fennel seeds, shichimi togarashi, black pepper and nori. Drizzle with the honey mixture and sprinkle with the salt. Stir to coat the oats. Stir in the olive oil.

3. Line a large rimmed baking sheet with parchment paper. Spread the granola on the sheet in an even layer, getting as close to the edges as possible. Bake for about 35 minutes, stirring occasionally (especially at the edges), until the granola is golden brown. Transfer the pan to a rack and let cool completely before serving; the granola will crisp as it cools. —*Heidi Swanson*

NOTE Shichimi togarashi is a Japanese spice blend. It's available at specialty grocers and from amazon.com.

MAKE AHEAD The granola can be stored in an airtight container for up to 1 week.

Corn Dogs with Krab Relish

Total **1 hr;** Makes **12**

F&W Best New Chef 2015 Tim Maslow of Ribelle in Boston ingeniously incorporates fresh corn into the batter for his crispy corn dogs. He tops the dogs with a playful relish made of imitation crab, pickles and yellow mustard.

RELISH

- ½ **lb. imitation crab, diced**
- 1 **medium shallot, minced**
- 1 **medium-size sour dill pickle, seeded and minced**
- ¼ **cup chopped celery leaves**
- ¼ **cup chopped parsley**
- ½ **cup Kewpie mayonnaise**
- 1 **Tbsp. yellow mustard**
- 1 **tsp. togarashi**
  Kosher salt

CORN DOGS

- 3 **ears of corn, shucked**
  Vegetable or canola oil, for frying
- ¼ **cup white rice flour, plus more for dredging**
- ¼ **cup all-purpose flour**
- ½ **cup finely ground yellow cornmeal**
- ½ **tsp. baking powder**
- ½ **tsp. baking soda**
- 1 **tsp. kosher salt**
- 1½ **cups buttermilk**
- 12 **beef hot dogs**
  Twelve 8-inch wooden skewers

1. Make the relish In a medium bowl, combine all of the ingredients and season with salt. Mix well, cover and refrigerate.

2. Make the corn dogs On a work surface, cut the corn kernels off the cobs; using the sharp side of the knife, scrape the pulp off the cobs. You should have 1½ cups of kernels and pulp. Transfer the kernels and pulp to a blender and pulse to form a coarse puree.

3. Scrape the puree into a large nonstick skillet and cook over moderately high heat, stirring frequently, until thickened and reduced to 1 cup, about 5 minutes. Let cool.

4. In a heavy pot, heat 2 inches of oil to 350°. In a large bowl, whisk the ¼ cup of both flours with the cornmeal, baking powder, baking soda and salt. Stir in the corn puree and buttermilk. Skewer each hot dog lengthwise, leaving about 2 inches of wood exposed to use as a handle. Dredge each hot dog in rice flour, then dip in the batter and twirl to coat, letting the excess drip back into the bowl. Gradually lower each hot dog into the hot oil and fry until the batter is browned and crisp, 3 to 5 minutes (don't fry more than 4 at once). Drain the corn dogs on a paper towel–lined baking sheet. Serve with the krab relish.
—*Tim Maslow*

WINE Bold, cherry-rich Italian rosé: 2014 San Giovanni Il Chiaretto.

Blueberry Vinaigrette

Total **30 min**; Makes **½ cup**

A touch of adobo sauce in this blueberry vinaigrette adds a nice smoky flavor.

- ¼ cup blueberries
- 1 tsp. sugar
- 1 tsp. fresh lemon juice
- ¼ cup vegetable oil
- 1 Tbsp. balsamic vinegar
- 1 tsp. adobo sauce from a can of chipotles in adobo
- Kosher salt and pepper

1. In a small saucepan, mash the blueberries with the sugar and lemon juice and bring to a simmer over moderate heat. Cook, stirring, until thickened, about 8 minutes. Let cool slightly.

2. Scrape the blueberry mixture into a medium bowl and whisk in the oil, vinegar and adobo sauce. Season with salt and pepper. —*Ben Mims*

SERVE WITH Baby spinach and radishes.

MAKE AHEAD The vinaigrette can be refrigerated overnight.

Kale-Buttermilk Dressing for Roasted Vegetables

Total **25 min**; Makes **about 1 cup**

At San Francisco's Bar Tartine, co-chef Cortney Burns has a cult following for her brilliant vegetable dishes. Instead of adding raw kale leaves to a salad, here she uses cooked kale in a creamy dressing for roasted vegetables.

- ½ bunch green kale (4 oz.), stemmed, leaves torn into large pieces
- 1 garlic clove, crushed
- ½ small serrano chile with seeds, chopped
- 1 oil-packed anchovy fillet, drained
- ¼ cup plain whole-milk Greek yogurt
- 2 Tbsp. buttermilk
- ½ tsp. granulated onion powder
- ⅛ tsp. ground cumin
- 1 Tbsp. chopped dill, chives or parsley
- ½ tsp. fresh lemon juice
- ½ cup extra-virgin olive oil
- Kosher salt and pepper
- Roasted root vegetables (such as beets and sweet potatoes), for serving

1. In a medium saucepan, bring ¼ inch of water to a boil. Add the kale, cover and cook over moderate heat until wilted, 3 minutes. Drain the kale and let cool slightly, then squeeze dry.

2. In a food processor, combine the kale, garlic, serrano, anchovy, yogurt, buttermilk, onion powder, cumin, dill and lemon juice and pulse to combine. With the machine on, slowly drizzle in the olive oil until a thick dressing forms. Season with salt and pepper. Transfer the dressing to a small bowl and serve with roasted root vegetables. —*Cortney Burns*

MAKE AHEAD The dressing can be refrigerated for up to 3 days.

LocoL Dipping Sauce

Active **20 min**; Total **50 min** plus chilling
Makes **2¾ cups**

Chefs Daniel Patterson and Roy Choi are taking on the fast-food chains with their LocoL restaurants in L.A. and San Francisco. They serve their awesome tomato-based spicy sauce with everything from french fries and onion rings to hamburgers and chicken.

- ¼ cup vegetable oil
- 1 fennel bulb—halved, cored and finely chopped
- 3 garlic cloves, thinly sliced
- Kosher salt
- Two 28-oz. cans whole peeled tomatoes, crushed by hand and drained
- ¼ cup white wine vinegar
- ¼ cup gochujang (Korean chile paste)

In a large saucepan, heat the oil. Add the fennel, garlic and a pinch of salt and cook over moderate heat, stirring occasionally, until softened, 15 minutes. Add the tomatoes and vinegar and bring to a boil. Simmer over moderate heat, stirring frequently, until nearly all the liquid has evaporated, about 10 minutes. Transfer to a blender. Add the gochujang and puree until very smooth. Season with salt and let cool completely, then refrigerate until chilled. —*Roy Choi and Daniel Patterson*

Burnt-Pineapple Salsa

Total **20 min**; Makes **3 cups**

- 1 pineapple, peeled and cut into ½-inch-thick rounds
- ½ small red onion, minced
- 1 large jalapeño, minced
- 1 garlic clove, minced
- ¼ cup chopped cilantro
- 3 Tbsp. fresh lime juice
- Kosher salt and pepper
- Tortilla chips, for serving

In a large cast-iron skillet, working in batches, lightly char the pineapple over moderately high heat, about 5 minutes per side. Let cool, then chop and transfer to a bowl. Add the onion, jalapeño, garlic, cilantro and lime juice. Season with salt and pepper and serve with tortilla chips.
—*Michael Babcock*

Salsa Negra

⟳ Total **20 min**; Makes **1 cup**

At Taco María in Costa Mesa, California, F&W Best New Chef 2015 Carlos Salgado serves this smoky, spicy, rich salsa with grilled meats and cruciferous vegetables. He also uses it to spike rice and beans; you'll want to put it on everything.

- ¾ cup plus 2 Tbsp. grapeseed oil
- ¾ oz. chiles de árbol, stemmed
- ¾ oz. guajillo chiles (about 3)—stemmed, seeded and cut into pieces
- 10 black garlic cloves, peeled and minced (see Note)
- 10 fresh garlic cloves, minced
- 1 Tbsp. white wine vinegar
- 1 Tbsp. piloncillo (raw Mexican sugar) or packed light brown sugar
- ¾ tsp. cumin seeds
   Kosher salt

1. In a large saucepan, combine the oil and both chiles and cook over moderate heat, stirring frequently, until the chiles are fragrant and browned in spots, about 7 minutes. Remove from the heat and stir in both garlics along with the vinegar, sugar, cumin and 1 teaspoon of salt. Cover and let cool.

2. Transfer the chile mixture to a blender and pulse until a coarse paste forms. Season with salt. —*Carlos Salgado*

SERVE WITH Grilled chicken legs or steak.

NOTE Black garlic is available at Trader Joe's markets and from obisone.com.

MAKE AHEAD The salsa negra can be refrigerated for up to 5 days.

Smoky Pasilla-Tomatillo Sauce

⟳ Active **10 min**; Total **35 min**
Makes **2 cups**

This fruity, spicy sauce is made with pasilla de Oaxaca chiles, deeply smoky dried chiles that are hotter than chipotles. Serve the sauce with pan-seared or roast duck, lamb or pork.

- 2 large pasilla de Oaxaca chiles (½ oz.)—stemmed, seeded and wiped clean
- 2 large black pasilla chiles (½ oz.)—stemmed, seeded and wiped clean
- ½ lb. tomatillos—husked, rinsed and quartered
- ½ cup finely chopped white onion
- 3 large garlic cloves
- 2 Tbsp. packed dark brown sugar
- 1½ cups chicken stock or low-sodium broth
   Kosher salt

1. In a medium skillet, toast the chiles over moderate heat, turning occasionally, until pliable and blistered in spots, about 1 minute. Add the tomatillos, onion, garlic, brown sugar and chicken broth and bring to a boil. Cover partially and simmer over moderately low heat, stirring occasionally, until the vegetables are very soft, about 20 minutes.

2. Transfer the mixture to a blender and let cool slightly, then puree until smooth. Strain the sauce through a fine sieve and season with salt. Serve warm. —*Shelley Wiseman*

MAKE AHEAD The sauce can be refrigerated for up to 5 days.

Raw Oysters with Cava Mignonette

⟳ Total **5 min**; Makes **about ¾ cup**

- ½ cup chilled cava
- ¼ cup minced shallot
- 1 Tbsp. white wine vinegar
- ¼ tsp. freshly ground pepper
   Raw oysters on the half shell, for serving

In a small bowl, stir together all of the ingredients except the oysters. Serve the mignonette with the oysters.
—*Matt Jennings*

Green Mango with Dipping Sauce

⟳ Total **35 min**; Serves **4 to 6**

James Syhabout, chef at Hawker Fare in Oakland, California, makes a simple dipping sauce of chiles, shallot and pungent fish sauce. It's great with green mango—a combo known as *mak muang som klub jaew wan* in Lao—as well as ripe mango and pineapple.

- 2 Tbsp. raw sticky rice or jasmine rice
- 3 dried Thai bird chiles, stemmed, or 2 tsp. crushed dried Thai chiles
- ½ cup Asian fish sauce
- ¼ cup sugar
- 2 Tbsp. chopped shallot
- 1 fresh red Thai chile or other hot red chile, minced
- 2 large green (unripe) mangoes, peeled and cut into ½-inch slices
   Lime wedges, for serving

1. In a small skillet, toast the rice over moderate heat, shaking the pan frequently, until lightly browned and fragrant, about 10 minutes. Let cool slightly, then transfer to a spice grinder and coarsely grind. Sift to remove any big pieces; you should have 1 tablespoon.

2. Wipe out the skillet. Add the dried chiles and toast over moderate heat until browned in spots, about 3 minutes. Transfer to the spice grinder and grind to a coarse powder; some seeds will remain.

3. In a medium bowl, stir the fish sauce with the sugar until the sugar dissolves. Stir in the shallot, fresh chile and toasted rice powder. Add the dried chile powder, 1 teaspoon at a time, checking the heat as you go. Let the dipping sauce stand for 20 minutes. Transfer to a small bowl and serve with the mangoes and lime wedges.
—*James Syhabout*

GREEN MANGO WITH
DIPPING SAUCE

Cauliflower-Heart Pickles

Total **15 min** plus overnight pickling
Makes **2 pints**

- **2** cauliflower hearts (cores), cut into 1½-inch pieces
- **3** celery ribs, sliced 1 inch thick on the diagonal
- **2** carrots, sliced 1 inch thick on the diagonal
- **2** cups white wine vinegar
- **¼** cup kosher salt
- **¼** cup sugar
- **3** garlic cloves, smashed
- **3** cardamom pods, crushed
- **1** jalapeño, halved
- **1** tsp. ground turmeric

Pack the cauliflower, celery and carrots into two 1-pint jars. In a small saucepan, combine the vinegar with the salt, sugar and 1 cup of water and bring to a boil. Cook, stirring, until the salt and sugar dissolve, about 1 minute. Stir in the garlic, cardamom, jalapeño and turmeric. Pour the brine over the vegetables. Let cool to room temperature, then refrigerate overnight before serving. —*Michael Solomonov*

Charred Okra Relish

Total **20 min**; Serves **6**

- **1** poblano chile
- **1** lb. okra
    - Canola oil, for brushing
    - Kosher salt and pepper
- **1½** Tbsp. Asian fish sauce
- **1** Tbsp. minced shallot
- **½** Tbsp. malt vinegar

1. Light a grill. Grill the poblano, turning, until charred all over. Transfer to a bowl, cover tightly with plastic wrap and let cool. Peel, stem and seed the poblano, then cut into ¼-inch dice.

2. Brush the okra with oil and season with salt and pepper. Grill over high heat, turning, until lightly charred all over, 3 to 5 minutes. Let cool, then cut off the stems and slice the okra crosswise into ¼-inch rounds.

3. In a medium bowl, toss the okra with the poblano, fish sauce, shallot and vinegar. Season with salt and pepper and serve. —*Stephanie Izard*

Fresh Cabbage, Cucumber and Radish Kimchi

Active **30 min**; Total **5 hr 45 min**
Makes **12 cups**

In this simple, crunchy kimchi recipe, *Top Chef* Season 12 winner Mei Lin cuts the traditional fermentation process down to just five hours. Lin sometimes uses the kimchi to make a quick and healthy stew by simmering it in dashi with tofu.

- **1** large head of napa cabbage (3 lbs.)—halved lengthwise, cored and cut into 2-inch pieces
- **3** English cucumbers, sliced ⅓ inch thick
- **1¼** lbs. daikon, peeled and cut into ½-inch pieces
- **20** medium radishes, quartered
- **½** cup kosher salt
- **4** oz. fresh ginger, peeled and coarsely chopped (about ¾ cup)
- **½** cup gochugaru (Korean red chile flakes; see Note)
- **¼** cup plus 2 Tbsp. unseasoned rice vinegar
- **6** large garlic cloves, chopped (¼ cup)
- **3** Tbsp. hot sesame oil
- **3** Tbsp. fish sauce
- **2** scallions, chopped
- **¾** tsp. sugar

1. Put the cabbage, cucumbers, daikon and radishes in 4 separate bowls. Add 2 tablespoons of the kosher salt to each bowl and toss well to coat the vegetables. Let stand at room temperature for 1 hour.

2. Meanwhile, in a blender, combine all of the remaining ingredients and puree until almost smooth.

3. Drain the vegetables thoroughly and gently squeeze out any excess water. In a large bowl, toss all of the vegetables with the ginger-gochugaru dressing. Cover the kimchi and refrigerate at least 4 hours before serving. —*Mei Lin*

MAKE AHEAD The kimchi can be refrigerated for up to 2 weeks.

NOTE Gochugaru is available at Asian markets and stores like Whole Foods and online from amazon.com.

Spicy Quick-Pickled Radishes

Total **15 min** plus cooling; Makes **1 quart**

Pickling with dill, garlic and chiles tones down the radishes' harshness while making them nicely herbal and aromatic.

- **1** lb. radishes with fresh leafy greens, halved lengthwise
- **12** dill sprigs
- **1½** cups distilled white vinegar
- **5** garlic cloves, crushed
- **5** chiles de árbol, halved
- **3** Tbsp. kosher salt
- **1** Tbsp. sugar

1. Pack the radishes and dill into a heatproof 1-quart jar.

2. In a small saucepan, combine the vinegar, garlic, chiles, salt, sugar and ½ cup of water and bring to a boil, stirring to dissolve the sugar. Pour the hot brine over the radishes and let cool to room temperature. Serve at room temperature or chilled. —*Kay Chun*

MAKE AHEAD The pickled radishes can be refrigerated in the brine for up to 3 days.

CONDIMENT TIP

Alice Waters's Essentials

In her book *My Pantry*, the legendary chef teaches how to DIY the essentials for a global pantry.

ZA'ATAR Mix equal parts sumac, dried thyme and white sesame seeds. Measure the mixture and add an equal amount of sea salt.

HOT SAUCE Blend ½ cup Champagne vinegar, 2 Tbsp. piment d'Espelette and 1½ tsp. sea salt at high speed for 30 seconds. Refrigerate for up to 3 months.

CHILE-LIME SALT Mix 1 Tbsp. each of kosher salt and ground chile. Stir in the finely grated zest of 1 lime.

Spiced Pickled Beets

Active **30 min**; Total **2 hr plus overnight pickling**; Makes **6 cups**

- 3 lbs. medium beets
- Kosher salt
- 1½ cups apple cider vinegar
- 1½ cups sugar
- 3 bay leaves
- One 2-inch cinnamon stick
- 2 tsp. whole allspice berries
- 2 tsp. black peppercorns
- ¾ tsp. whole cloves

1. Preheat the oven to 375°. Put the beets in a large baking dish. Add 1 cup of water and a generous pinch of salt. Cover tightly with foil and bake for about 1 hour, until the beets are tender. Uncover and let cool. Peel the beets and cut them into ¾-inch wedges. Transfer to a large heatproof bowl.

2. In a medium saucepan, combine 1½ cups of water with the vinegar, sugar, bay leaves, cinnamon stick, allspice, peppercorns, cloves and 2 teaspoons of salt. Bring to a boil over high heat, then simmer over moderately low heat until reduced to 3 cups, about 12 minutes. Pour the liquid over the beets and let cool; refrigerate overnight. Drain the following day, before serving. —*Martha Wiggins*

Maraschino Blueberries

Active **20 min**; Total **2 days**; Makes **3½ cups**

- 1 tsp. kosher salt
- 2 cups warm water
- 2 cups blueberries
- 2 cups sugar
- 1 cup Chambord liqueur
- 1 Tbsp. fresh lemon juice

1. In a medium bowl, stir the salt into the water until dissolved. Stir in the blueberries and refrigerate overnight.

2. In a medium saucepan, bring the sugar, Chambord and lemon juice to a simmer over high heat, stirring to dissolve the sugar; remove from the heat. Drain and rinse the blueberries and add them to the saucepan. Transfer the blueberries and syrup to a jar and refrigerate for at least 24 hours before serving. —*Ben Mims*

SERVE WITH Ice cream or pancakes or in Manhattans and other cocktails.

Puddletown Pub Chutney

Active **20 min**; Total **1 hr 15 min plus cooling** Makes **3 cups**

This slow-simmered apple chutney is an homage to Oregon: Liz Cowan, who runs Portland's Three Little Figs jam company, uses Oakshire Brewing's Overcast Espresso Stout from Eugene, Oregon, and Walla Walla sweet onions. The result is a sweet-savory chutney that's fabulous with sharp cheddar and charcuterie.

- 4 Granny Smith apples—peeled, cored and cut into ⅓-inch dice (5 cups)
- 2 cups finely chopped sweet onion
- 12 oz. espresso stout beer
- 1 cup packed dark brown sugar
- ½ cup apple cider vinegar
- ½ cup brewed strong coffee, cooled
- ⅓ cup currants
- 2 bay leaves
- 2 Tbsp. unsulfured molasses
- 1½ tsp. yellow mustard seeds
- 1 tsp. brown mustard seeds
- 1 tsp. fine sea salt, plus more for seasoning
- ½ tsp. black pepper
- ¼ tsp. Chinese five-spice powder
- Pinch of freshly grated nutmeg
- 1½ Tbsp. Ball Low or No-Sugar Needed Pectin

1. In a large saucepan, combine all of the ingredients except the pectin and bring to a boil. Simmer over moderate heat, stirring occasionally, until the chutney is thickened and reduced to 3 cups, 45 to 50 minutes.

2. Bring the chutney back to a boil over high heat. Whisk in the pectin and simmer for 1 minute. Remove from the heat and let cool completely. Discard the bay leaves. Season the chutney with salt and transfer to glass jars. Serve at room temperature or slightly chilled. —*Liz Cowan*

Turkey Bouillon Cubes

Active **30 min**; Total **1 hr 20 min plus freezing**; Makes **12**

These supercharged cubes of stock are great to keep on hand for adding flavor to pasta dishes, thinning out sauces and enriching grain pilafs. If you don't have a turkey carcass, you can swap in two roast chicken carcasses.

- 2 Tbsp. canola oil
- Carcass of a 12-lb. turkey, cut into large pieces
- 1 head of garlic, halved
- 1 onion, chopped
- 2 carrots, chopped
- 1 tsp. whole black peppercorns
- 7 parsley stems plus 2 Tbsp. chopped parsley
- Kosher salt and pepper
- 2 Tbsp. chopped chives

In a large pot, heat the oil. Add the turkey carcass and cook over moderately high heat, stirring, until golden, 10 minutes. Add the garlic, onion, carrots, peppercorns and parsley stems and cook, stirring, for 5 minutes. Add 2 quarts of water. Bring to a boil, scraping up any browned bits. Simmer until reduced to 1½ cups, 40 minutes. Strain into a heatproof bowl and let cool. Season with salt and pepper and add the chopped parsley and chives. Pour into an ice cube tray and freeze. Once frozen solid, transfer to a sturdy resealable plastic bag. —*Kay Chun*

Espresso Dry Rub

Total **5 min**; Makes **about 4⅓ cups**

Joe Carroll makes stellar barbecue at Brooklyn's Fette Sau. This flavor-packed rub is the only one he uses—it's that good.

- 1½ cups packed dark brown sugar
- 1 cup kosher salt
- 1 cup ground espresso beans
- ¼ cup freshly ground black pepper
- ¼ cup garlic powder
- 2 Tbsp. each of ground cinnamon, cumin and cayenne

In a container, mix all of the ingredients. Cover and shake well. Store in a cool place for up to 2 months. —*Joe Carroll*

MISO CARAMEL
SAUCE

Miso Caramel Sauce

⏱ Total **15 min**; Makes **3 cups**

Miso gives this extraordinary 15-minute caramel a slightly salty, umami-rich flavor.

- 1½ **cups heavy cream**
- 6 **Tbsp. unsalted butter**
- 1½ **cups sugar**
- ⅓ **cup light corn syrup**
- ½ **cup white miso**
- ½ **tsp. pure vanilla extract**

1. In a small saucepan, combine the cream and butter and bring just to a simmer over moderate heat.

2. In a medium saucepan, mix the sugar, corn syrup and ¼ cup of water and cook over moderately high heat, without stirring, until the sugar is dissolved. Using a wet pastry brush, wash down any crystals from the side of the pan. Continue to cook, gently swirling the pan occasionally, until an amber caramel forms, about 5 minutes.

3. Remove the pan from the heat and whisk in the cream mixture; it will bubble up. When the bubbles subside, very carefully pour the hot caramel into a heatproof blender. With the blender on medium speed, gradually add spoonfuls of the miso until incorporated. Transfer to a bowl and let cool, then whisk in the vanilla. —*Jake Bickelhaupt*

SERVE WITH Vanilla ice cream.

Chocolate Double-Nut Butter

⏱ Total **20 min**; Makes **2 cups**

- 2 **cups walnuts, toasted**
- 1 **cup almonds, toasted**
- 1½ **cups semisweet chocolate chips (about 10 oz.)**
- 2 **tsp. salt**
  Toasted white bread and honey, for serving

In a food processor, grind the nuts until they start to turn into a paste, about 30 seconds. Scrape down the side and add the chocolate and salt. Puree until very smooth, about 3 minutes. For a thicker texture, freeze the spread for about 10 minutes. Serve on toasted bread, drizzled with honey. —*Zak Stern*

Hot Fudge Sauce

⏱ Total **30 min**; Makes **3 cups**

- 5 **oz. semisweet chocolate, coarsely chopped**
- 3 **oz. unsweetened chocolate, coarsely chopped**
- 6 **Tbsp. unsalted butter**
- 1 **cup plus 2 Tbsp. light corn syrup**
- ¾ **cup sugar**
- ¾ **tsp. kosher salt**
- 2 **tsp. pure vanilla extract**

1. In a medium heatproof bowl, combine both of the chocolates with the butter. Set the bowl over a medium saucepan of simmering water and stir until the chocolate and butter are melted and blended. Remove the bowl and set aside. Pour off the water.

2. In the same saucepan, combine the corn syrup, sugar, salt and 2 cups of water and bring to a boil over high heat. Reduce the heat to moderate and whisk in the melted chocolate. Cook, stirring occasionally, until the sauce is thick and shiny, 18 to 20 minutes. Remove from the heat and stir in the vanilla. Use immediately or let cool completely and refrigerate. Rewarm in a microwave before serving.
—*Annabelle Topacio and Ian Flores*

Strawberry Sauce

Total **20 min plus chilling**; Makes **3 cups**

In this ultra-fresh sauce for ice cream, Annabelle Topacio and Ian Flores, pastry chefs at San Francisco's Mr. and Mrs. Miscellaneous, cook the berries briefly with vanilla seeds.

- 2 **lbs. strawberries, hulled and quartered**
- 2 **cups sugar**
- ½ **tsp. finely grated lemon zest**
- 1 **vanilla bean, seeds scraped**

Combine all of the ingredients in a medium saucepan. Stir to coat the strawberries with sugar and bring to a boil over high heat. Reduce the heat to moderate and simmer, stirring occasionally, until the berries begin to break down and the sauce is thickened, 10 to 12 minutes. Remove from the heat and let cool completely, then refrigerate. Serve cold or at room temperature.
—*Annabelle Topacio and Ian Flores*

Wet Mixed Nuts

⏱ Total **30 min**; Makes **3 cups**

Golden syrup (treacle) and maple syrup give this elevated sundae garnish a complex sweetness.

- 1 **cup walnuts**
- ½ **cup pecans**
- ½ **cup blanched hazelnuts**
- ½ **cup pure maple syrup**
- ½ **cup Lyle's golden syrup**
- ½ **cup light corn syrup**
- ¼ **cup sugar**
- ½ **vanilla bean, seeds scraped**

1. Preheat the oven to 350°. Spread the walnuts, pecans and hazelnuts on a rimmed baking sheet and bake for 10 minutes, until toasted. Let cool, then coarsely chop.

2. In a medium saucepan, combine the three syrups with the sugar, vanilla seeds and ½ cup of water. Bring to a boil over high heat, then reduce the heat to moderate and simmer until thickened, about 8 minutes. Remove from the heat and stir in the chopped nuts. Let cool completely, then transfer to a container and refrigerate for up to 2 weeks. Serve at room temperature.
—*Annabelle Topacio and Ian Flores*

Fresh Pineapple Sauce

Total **20 min plus chilling**; Makes **3 cups**

This pineapple ice cream topping has a smart tweak: Campari, which adds a pleasant hint of bitterness.

- 2 **cups diced fresh pineapple**
- 2 **cups fresh pineapple juice**
- 1 **cup sugar**
- 1 **cup light corn syrup**
  Finely grated zest of 1 lemon plus 2 tsp. fresh lemon juice
- ½ **tsp. kosher salt**
- 2 **tsp. Campari**

In a medium saucepan, combine all of the ingredients except the Campari and bring to a boil over high heat. Reduce the heat to moderate and simmer for 5 minutes. Stir in the Campari and cook, stirring occasionally, until the sauce is thick and shiny, 10 minutes. Remove from the heat and let cool completely, then refrigerate. Serve cold.
—*Annabelle Topacio and Ian Flores*

Chocolate Shell

Total **15 min;** Makes **2 cups**

F&W's Justin Chapple makes his own version of Magic Shell, a sauce that quickly hardens when poured over cold things. Coconut oil adds extra flavor.

- 1 **lb. bittersweet chocolate, finely chopped**
- ½ **cup coconut oil**
  Kosher salt
  Ice cream, for serving

In a large microwave-safe bowl, melt the chopped chocolate with the coconut oil at high power in 20-second intervals, stirring between bursts. Stir in a generous pinch of salt and let stand at room temperature until cooled before pouring over ice cream. —*Justin Chapple*

Butterscotch Sauce

Total **15 min;** Makes **3 cups**

This easy, luscious butterscotch ice cream topping has just the right amount of salt and lemon juice to balance the sweetness.

- ¾ **cup packed dark brown sugar**
- ¾ **cup granulated sugar**
- 6 **Tbsp. Lyle's golden syrup (treacle)**
- 1¼ **tsp. kosher salt**
- 1 **stick unsalted butter, diced**
- 1 **cup plus 2 Tbsp. heavy cream, at room temperature**
- 1 **Tbsp. pure vanilla extract**
- ¾ **tsp. fresh lemon juice**

In a medium saucepan, combine both sugars with the syrup and salt. Cook over moderate heat, stirring occasionally, until the mixture is molten and beginning to bubble at the edge, 6 minutes. Simmer, stirring, for 1 minute, then stir in the butter. Attach a candy thermometer to the side of the pan and cook until the sauce reaches 240°, about 2 minutes. Carefully stir in the cream until incorporated and bring to a rolling boil. Remove from the heat and stir in the vanilla, lemon juice and 1½ tablespoons of water. Let cool completely, then transfer to a container and refrigerate. Serve warm or at room temperature. —*Annabelle Topacio and Ian Flores*

Honey-Nut-Oat Crumble Topping

Active **10 min;** Total **35 min plus cooling** Makes **4 cups**

This healthy, oat-based crumble is terrific with fruit, yogurt or ice cream, but it's also delicious for snacking.

- 1¼ **cups old-fashioned rolled oats (not instant or quick-cooking)**
- ¾ **cup whole-wheat flour**
- ½ **cup chopped walnuts**
- ½ **cup sliced almonds**
- 1¼ **tsp. ground cinnamon**
- ¼ **tsp. freshly grated nutmeg**
- ¾ **tsp. kosher salt**
- ½ **cup canola oil**
- ½ **cup honey**
- 1 **Tbsp. pure vanilla extract**
  Roasted or poached fruit or yogurt, for serving

1. Preheat the oven to 325°. In a large bowl, mix the oats with the flour, walnuts, almonds, cinnamon, nutmeg and salt. In a small bowl, whisk the oil with the honey and vanilla; drizzle over the crumb topping and mix until well coated.

2. Spread the crumble on a baking sheet in an even layer. Bake in the center of the oven for 25 to 30 minutes, stirring occasionally, until the crumble is golden brown. Transfer to a rack and let cool completely to crisp up, about 1 hour.

3. Spoon the crumble over roasted or poached fruit or yogurt. —*Joanne Chang*

MAKE AHEAD The crumble can be stored in an airtight container for up to 1 week.

Sweet and Savory Cranberry Conserva

Total **30 min;** Makes **3 cups**

- 2 **Tbsp. canola oil**
- 1 **large shallot, minced**
- 1 **garlic clove, minced**
- 1 **tsp. ground fennel**
- 1 **lb. fresh cranberries**
- 1 **cup packed light brown sugar**
- ¼ **cup unseasoned rice vinegar**
- 2 **Tbsp. whole-grain mustard**
- 2 **tsp. Dijon mustard**
  Kosher salt and pepper

In a medium saucepan, heat the oil. Add the shallot, garlic and fennel and cook over moderate heat, stirring, until softened, 3 minutes. Add ⅓ cup of water, the cranberries, sugar, vinegar and mustards and bring to a boil. Simmer over moderately high heat, stirring occasionally, until the cranberries are coated in a thick sauce, about 7 minutes. Season with salt and pepper. Scrape into a bowl and let cool; serve. —*Justin Chapple*

Molded Cranberry Sauce

Active **30 min;** Total **4 hr;** Serves **10 to 12**

Star chef Tyler Florence makes his not-too-sweet molded cranberry sauce with chunks of pineapple.

- 2 **lbs. fresh or frozen cranberries**
- 3 **cups sugar**
- 2 **cups finely chopped fresh pineapple (8 oz.)**
- 1 **Tbsp. finely grated orange zest**
- 1 **Tbsp. fresh lemon juice**
  Kosher salt and pepper
  Shaved celery, snipped chives and chopped toasted walnuts, for garnish

1. Line a 1½-quart glass bowl or mold with plastic wrap, allowing 4 inches of overhang all around.

2. Reserve ¼ cup of the cranberries for garnish. In a large saucepan, combine the rest of the cranberries with the sugar, pineapple, orange zest, lemon juice and ½ cup of water and bring to a boil. Cook over moderately low heat, stirring frequently, until the cranberries are broken down and the mixture is thick, 30 to 35 minutes. Season the sauce with salt and pepper.

3. Scrape the sauce into the prepared bowl and let cool for 30 minutes. Cover with the overhanging plastic. Refrigerate until the cranberry sauce is chilled and set, at least 3 hours or overnight.

4. Peel back the plastic and carefully invert the cranberry mold onto a plate; remove the plastic wrap. Garnish with the reserved cranberries, shaved celery, snipped chives and chopped walnuts and serve cold. —*Tyler Florence*

MAKE AHEAD The molded cranberry sauce can be refrigerated for up to 3 days.

Cranberry-Clementine Preserves

Total **45 min plus overnight macerating**
Makes **5 cups**

Elizabeth Madden of Rare Bird Preserves in Chicago puts cranberries to great use in this versatile recipe: Serve the relish with turkey, stir it into a cocktail or whisk it into a vinaigrette.

- ¾ **lb. clementines, unpeeled, thinly sliced crosswise and seeds discarded**
- ¾ **lb. fresh or frozen cranberries**
- 3 **cups sugar**
- 2 **Tbsp. fresh lemon juice**
  Fine salt
- ⅓ **cup warm water**
- ⅓ **cup warm apple juice**

1. In a food processor, pulse the clementines until coarsely chopped. Add the cranberries and pulse until the clementines are finely chopped and the cranberries are coarsely chopped. Transfer the fruit to a large nonreactive saucepan and stir in the sugar, lemon juice and a pinch of salt. Bring just to a boil, then simmer over moderate heat, stirring occasionally, until the sugar dissolves, about 5 minutes. Let cool completely, then cover the saucepan and refrigerate the fruit overnight.

2. Stir the water and apple juice into the fruit in the saucepan and bring to a boil over high heat. Reduce the heat to moderately high and boil, stirring occasionally, until the preserves are thickened slightly, about 12 minutes. Test the preserves: Spoon 1 tablespoon onto a chilled plate and refrigerate until it cools to room temperature, about 3 minutes; the preserves are ready when thickened slightly and a spoon dragged through them leaves a clear trail. If the preserves are too loose, continue simmering and test every 5 minutes. Let the preserves cool completely, then transfer to glass jars and refrigerate until chilled.
—Elizabeth Madden

Kiwi Jam

Total **40 min plus cooling;** Makes **6 cups**

California's kiwi season runs from October to May, which is when the fruit becomes fair game for Dafna Kory of Inna Jam. She sources all of her produce from within a 150-mile radius of her kitchen in Emeryville, California.

- 2½ **lbs. kiwis, peeled and cut into ½-inch pieces (5 cups)**
  Kosher salt
- 2 **cups sugar**
- ⅓ **cup plus ½ tsp. Ball Low or No-Sugar Needed Pectin**
- 3½ **Tbsp. fresh lemon juice**

1. In a medium saucepan, combine the kiwis, ½ cup of water and a pinch of salt and cook over moderate heat, stirring occasionally, until the kiwis start to release their juice, 3 to 5 minutes. Reduce the heat to moderately low, cover and cook, stirring occasionally, until the fruit is nearly submerged in juice, about 15 minutes.

2. Bring the fruit to a rolling boil. Add the sugar and boil over high heat, stirring, until the sugar dissolves, about 2 minutes. Whisk in the pectin and boil over high heat for 1 minute. Remove from the heat, stir in the lemon juice and skim off any foam. Transfer the jam to glass jars and let cool completely. *—Dafna Kory*

Grapefruit Marmalade with Smoked Salt

Total **35 min plus cooling;** Makes **7½ cups**

"I call this my gateway marmalade," says Laena McCarthy of Anarchy in a Jar, a small-batch preserves company in Brooklyn. "It's less bitter because it's made with the zest of the grapefruit without the pith." McCarthy adds a mild smoked salt to the marmalade, such as Maldon, so as not to overpower the sweet and aromatic grapefruit.

- 3 **cups sugar**
- 2 **tsp. mild smoked salt flakes**
- 2 **tsp. Pomona's Universal Pectin (see Note)**
- ½ **cup finely grated grapefruit zest (from 6 medium grapefruits)**
- 6 **cups strained fresh grapefruit juice (from 12 medium grapefruits)**
- 2 **Tbsp. fresh lemon juice**
- 1 **Tbsp. Pomona's calcium water (see Note)**

1. In a medium bowl, whisk the sugar with the smoked salt and pectin.

2. In a large saucepan, whisk the grapefruit zest with the grapefruit and lemon juices and the calcium water and bring to a boil. Gradually whisk in the sugar mixture and bring back to a boil over high heat, whisking, until the sugar dissolves, about 3 minutes. Remove from the heat and skim off any foam. Test the marmalade: Spoon 1 tablespoon onto a chilled plate and refrigerate until it cools to room temperature, about 3 minutes; the marmalade is ready when it is thickened slightly and a spoon dragged through it leaves a clear trail. If the marmalade is too loose, continue simmering and test every 5 minutes.

3. Pour the marmalade into glass jars and let cool completely. *—Laena McCarthy*

SERVE WITH Toast or crackers or stirred into a gin or bourbon cocktail.

NOTE Pomona's Universal Pectin is activated with calcium. A packet of calcium powder is included in each box—simply combine ¼ teaspoon of the powder with ¼ cup water to make the calcium water. The calcium water can be refrigerated for several months.

"You wouldn't think a comedian would be so precise, but Aziz measures every drink exactly," says L.A. chef Courtney McBroom about her boyfriend, Aziz Ansari. Their pool parties feature margaritas and bonbon root beer floats (recipe, p. 377).

DRINKS

MEADOW MOCKTAILS
Recipe, page 377

DARK SPARKLERS

Dark Sparklers

Active **10 min**; Total **30 min plus cooling**
Makes **16 drinks**

"I wanted to focus on very simple, three- or four-ingredient cocktails," says North Carolina chef Andrea Reusing about the drinks she serves at The Durham Hotel and its rooftop bar. Reusing uses peak-season black plums to give the syrup in this cocktail its striking hue. "I want a cashmere sweater in that color!" she says.

- **4 small black plums,
  quartered and pitted**
- **½ cup sugar**
- **2 tsp. black peppercorns**
- **2 tsp. fresh lemon juice**
- **½ tsp. kosher salt**
- **Chilled sparkling wine, for serving**

1. In a medium saucepan, combine the plums, sugar, peppercorns, lemon juice and salt with 2 cups of water and bring to a boil. Simmer over moderately low heat until the plums are very soft and the syrup is deep purple, about 20 minutes.

2. Strain the syrup through a fine sieve set over a bowl, pressing on the solids. You should have 2 cups. Let the syrup cool completely, then refrigerate until chilled.

3. For each cocktail, pour 1 ounce of syrup into a chilled flute and top with sparkling wine. —*Andrea Reusing*

MAKE AHEAD The black plum syrup can be refrigerated for 2 weeks.

Road Soda

Total **5 min**; Makes **1 drink**

- **1½ oz. honjozo sake, such as
  Kikusui Funaguchi**
- **1 oz. London dry gin**
- **¾ oz. fresh lemon juice**
- **¾ oz. simple syrup (see Note on p. 372)**
- **Ice**
- **1 lemon twist, for garnish**

In a cocktail shaker, combine the sake, gin, lemon juice and simple syrup. Fill the shaker with ice and shake well. Strain into a chilled cocktail glass and garnish with the lemon twist. —*Timothy Koenig*

Pomelder Prosecco Punch

Total **20 min plus 2 hr cooling**
Makes **12 drinks**

This sweet-tart punch gets a ton of flavor and a rosy tint from a syrup of pomegranate juice, fresh ginger and cardamom. St-Germain elderflower liqueur adds a fragrant sweetness.

- **2 cups pure pomegranate juice**
- **One 3-inch piece of fresh ginger,
  thinly sliced**
- **20 green cardamom pods, crushed**
- **1 chilled 750-ml bottle
  extra-dry Prosecco**
- **1 chilled 750-ml bottle
  sparkling pear juice**
- **½ cup St-Germain elderflower liqueur**
- **2 cups chilled club soda or
  sparkling water**
- **Ice**

1. In a medium saucepan, combine the pomegranate juice, ginger and cardamom and bring to a boil. Simmer briskly until reduced to 1¼ cups, about 10 minutes. Remove from the heat and let cool to room temperature. Strain the syrup into a bowl. Cover and refrigerate for 2 hours.

2. In a chilled pitcher or large punch bowl, combine the pomegranate syrup, Prosecco, sparkling pear juice, St-Germain and club soda and stir well. Serve the punch in chilled, ice-filled rocks glasses. —*Sara Grimes*

MAKE AHEAD The pomegranate syrup can be refrigerated for up to 2 weeks.

Pineapple-Sake Sangria
with Jalapeño

Active **15 min**; Total **1 hr 40 min**
Makes **8 drinks**

- **¾ cup sugar**
- **1 jalapeño, thinly sliced crosswise**
- **4½ cups pineapple juice**
- **One 750-ml bottle dry filtered sake**
- **Ice**
- **Pineapple slices and mint sprigs,
  for garnish**

1. In a small saucepan, bring ¾ cup of water to a boil with the sugar and jalapeño, stirring to dissolve the sugar. Let cool completely, then strain the syrup; discard the jalapeño.

2. In a large pitcher, combine the jalapeño syrup, pineapple juice and sake and stir well. Refrigerate until well chilled, about 1 hour. Serve the sangria in chilled, ice-filled tumblers, garnished with pineapple and mint. —*Helene Henderson*

MAKE AHEAD The sangria can be refrigerated overnight.

Sparkling Yuzu Gimlets

Total **15 min**; Makes **8 drinks**

Top Chef Season 12 winner Mei Lin makes her Asian-style vodka gimlet in a pitcher for easy entertaining.

- **2 Tbsp. sugar**
- **2 cups lightly packed mint leaves,
  plus small sprigs for garnish**
- **1½ cups lightly packed basil leaves,
  plus small sprigs for garnish**
- **1 cup thinly sliced English cucumber,
  plus 8 spears for garnish**
- **¼ cup plus 2 Tbsp. yuzu juice**
- **2 cups chilled vodka**
- **2¼ cups chilled sparkling water**
- **Ice**

In a small bowl, whisk the sugar with 2 tablespoons of hot water until dissolved. In a pitcher, muddle the mint and basil leaves with the sliced cucumber and the sugar syrup. Stir in the yuzu juice, vodka and sparkling water. Serve in chilled, ice-filled collins glasses garnished with small sprigs of mint and basil and a cucumber spear. —*Mei Lin*

Two Palms

⏱ Total **5 min**; Makes **1 drink**

Coconut water is the breakout beverage of the decade, but people were actually mixing it into cocktails back in the 1800s. Here, Nick Detrich of Cane & Table in New Orleans riffs on that tradition.

1 oz. London dry gin, such as Beefeater

½ oz. fresh lime juice

½ oz. simple syrup (see Note)

1 large egg white

Ice

1 oz. chilled coconut water

Pinch of freshly grated nutmeg, for garnish

In a cocktail shaker, combine the gin, lime juice, simple syrup and egg white. Shake vigorously. Fill the shaker with ice and shake again. Strain into a chilled coupe. Stir the coconut water into the cocktail and garnish with the grated nutmeg. —*Nick Detrich*

NOTE To make simple syrup, simmer equal parts of water and sugar over moderate heat, stirring, until the sugar dissolves. Let the syrup cool completely, then refrigerate for up to 1 month.

Negronis with Fresh Oregano

⏱ Total **10 min**; Makes **8 drinks**

To put his own spin on a classic Negroni, New York chef Zakary Pelaccio makes this extra-boozy version, doubling the usual amount of gin. He garnishes the cocktail with a sprig of oregano from his garden.

16 oz. Plymouth gin

8 oz. sweet vermouth

8 oz. Campari

Ice

8 oregano sprigs

In a large pitcher, combine the gin, vermouth and Campari and stir well; pour into 8 chilled, ice-filled rocks glasses. Garnish each drink with a sprig of oregano and serve. —*Zakary Pelaccio*

The Big Come-Up

⏱ Total **5 min**; Makes **1 drink**

This dry martini revamp from superstar Seattle chef Tom Douglas features Washington state ingredients, including bitters from Seattle's fantastic Scrappy's and Captive Spirits Big Gin, an assertive, high-proof gin.

2 oz. Captive Spirits Big Gin

1 oz. chilled Chateau Ste. Michelle Eroica Riesling

2 dashes of Scrappy's orange bitters

Ice

1 orange twist, for garnish

In a mixing glass, combine the gin, Riesling and bitters. Fill the glass with ice and stir well. Strain into a chilled cocktail glass and garnish with the orange twist. —*Tom Douglas*

Long Island Iced Coffee

⏱ Total **10 min**; Makes **1 drink**

To go with his brunch dishes at Milktooth in Indianapolis, F&W Best New Chef 2015 Jonathan Brooks makes this strong and delicious coffee version of the classic Long Island iced tea.

1¼ oz. Amaro Nardini

1 oz. St. George NOLA coffee liqueur

¾ oz. orgeat

½ oz. Fernet-Branca (bitter Italian digestif)

½ oz. vodka

½ oz. mezcal

¼ oz. rye whiskey

2 dashes of mole bitters

Ice cubes, plus crushed ice for serving

½ oz. half-and-half

2 Luxardo cherries, for garnish

In a cocktail shaker, combine the first 8 ingredients. Fill the shaker with ice and shake well. Strain into a tall glass filled with crushed ice. Top with the half-and-half, garnish with the cherries and serve. —*Jonathan Brooks*

Casa Santo Domingo

⏱ Total **5 min**; Makes **1 drink**

1 oz. aged dark rum

¼ oz. Cointreau

6 dashes of Angostura bitters

6 dashes of Peychaud's bitters

Ice

5 oz. chilled Champagne or Prosecco

1 orange twist, for garnish

In a cocktail shaker, combine the rum with the Cointreau and bitters. Add ice and shake well. Strain into a chilled flute and top with the Champagne. Garnish with the orange twist. —*Lynnette Marrero*

BARTENDING LESSON

Three Classic Gin Cocktails

These gin classics are easy enough for the novice home bartender. Simply combine the liquids in a shaker, fill with ice, stir (shake the gimlet) and garnish.

BITTER

NEGRONI
Equal parts gin, Campari and sweet vermouth; orange twist garnish

SPIRITUOUS

MARTINI
3 oz. gin + 1 oz. dry vermouth; olive or lemon twist garnish

TANGY

GIMLET
2 oz. gin + 1 oz. Rose's Lime Juice Cordial; lime wedge garnish

The Holy Trinidad

⏱ Total **5 min**; Makes **1 drink**

This rum drink is refreshing but strong—the kind of cocktail you want to unwind with after a long day.

- 1½ oz. aged Trinidadian dark rum
- ½ oz. Cynar (bitter, artichoke-flavored aperitif)
- ½ oz. amontillado sherry
- ½ oz. Cocchi Americano
  Dash of Angostura bitters
  Dash of orange bitters
  Ice
- 1 lemon twist and 1 orange twist, for garnish

In a mixing glass, combine the rum, Cynar, sherry, Cocchi Americano and both bitters. Fill the glass with ice and stir well. Strain into a chilled rocks glass. Pinch the citrus twists over the drink, add them to the glass and serve. —*Diego Sanchez-Maitret*

Mai Tai

⏱ Total **5 min**; Makes **1 drink**

Adding a splash of whiskey to this modern interpretation of the classic rum cocktail helps tone down the sweetness. A good-quality orgeat (almond syrup) makes a big difference; look for an artisanal version from Small Hand Foods.

- Ice cubes, plus crushed ice for serving
- 1½ oz. dark rum
- ¾ oz. orgeat
- ¾ oz. fresh lime juice
- ¾ oz. dry curaçao
- ¼ oz. whiskey
- 2 dashes of Angostura bitters
- 1 mint sprig, 1 strawberry and 1 orange twist, for garnish

Fill a cocktail shaker with ice cubes. Add all of the remaining ingredients except the crushed ice and garnishes and shake well. Strain into a rocks glass filled with crushed ice. Garnish with the mint sprig, strawberry and orange twist and serve.
—*Romée de Goriainoff*

Autumn Fruit Old-Fashioned

⏱ Total **10 min**; Makes **1 drink**

The base of this drink is an infused bourbon that makes excellent use of fruit scraps like citrus peels and apple and pear cores.

- ½ tsp. sugar
- 5 dashes of Angostura bitters
  Ice
- 2 oz. Autumn Fruit–Infused Bourbon (recipe follows)
- 1 orange twist, for garnish

In a chilled rocks glass, muddle the sugar with the bitters until a paste forms. Fill the glass with ice and stir in the infused bourbon and ½ ounce of water. Pinch the orange twist over the drink and add to the glass.
—*Kay Chun*

AUTUMN FRUIT–INFUSED BOURBON

Active **10 min**; Total **8 hr**
Makes **about 750 ml**

- Peel from 1 grapefruit
- Peels from 2 lemons
- 2 pear cores
- 2 apple cores
- One 750-ml bottle bourbon

Combine all of the ingredients in a large jar. Cover and let stand at room temperature for 8 to 12 hours. Strain the infused bourbon through a cheesecloth-lined fine sieve. Refrigerate for up to 1 month. —*KC*

SUPERHEALTHY DRINK

Turmeric Elixir

Makes 4 cups

In a blender, combine 1 cup **unsweetened coconut milk** with 2 Tbsp. **chopped fresh turmeric** and 1 tsp. each of **chopped fresh ginger**, **coconut oil** and **ground turmeric**. Blend at medium speed for 2 minutes. Pour into a saucepan and add 1½ cups each of **coconut water** and **almond milk**, 8 **green cardamom pods** and a pinch of **salt** and **pepper**. Bring to a simmer over moderate heat, then let steep off the heat for 10 minutes. Strain and reheat. Serve with raw honey if you like.
—*Amanda Michael*

Spiced Buttery Rum

Total **20 min plus 24 hr freezing**
Makes **about 750 ml**

This luscious buttered rum from tiki revivalist Paul McGee of Lost Lake cocktail bar in Chicago uses a technique called fat-washing. Try the rum in any classic cocktail.

- 10 allspice berries, crushed
  Eight 3-inch cinnamon sticks
- 1 stick unsalted butter
- 1 vanilla bean—split lengthwise, seeds scraped, pod reserved
  One 750-ml bottle light rum

In a skillet, lightly toast the allspice berries and cinnamon sticks over moderately low heat for about 5 minutes. Add the butter and vanilla bean and seeds and stir until the butter melts. Pour the butter into a jar and add the rum. Cover and freeze for 24 hours. Skim off the butter. Strain the rum through cheesecloth. Keep in the refrigerator for up to 2 weeks. —*Paul McGee*

Mott and Mulberry

⏱ Total **5 min**; Makes **1 drink**

Leo Robitschek, the star mixologist behind Manhattan's NoMad Bar, uses fresh apple cider and maple syrup in this perfect cold-weather cocktail.

- 1 oz. rye
- 1 oz. Luxardo Amaro Abano
- ¾ oz. apple cider
- ¼ oz. pure maple syrup
- ¼ oz. fresh lemon juice
  Ice
- 5 thin apple slices skewered on a pick, for garnish

In a cocktail shaker, combine the rye, amaro, cider, maple syrup and lemon juice. Fill the shaker with ice and shake well. Using a fine sieve as well as a cocktail strainer (preferably a Hawthorne), strain the cocktail into a chilled coupe. Garnish with the apple slices. —*Leo Robitschek*

DIY NUT MILKS

They're simple to make, astonishingly delicious and as good straight up as in dishes like a rich panna cotta. **TERESA PIRO,** founder of Can Can Cleanse in San Francisco, shares her recipes for homemade almond milk and mixed-nut milk that customers crave long after their cleanse is over.

Best-Ever Nut Milks

Active **20 min;** Total **1 hr 20 min plus overnight soaking;** Makes **3 cups almond milk or 4 cups mixed-nut milk**

Teresa Piro sweetens her nut milks naturally with dates or honey and uses vanilla and salt to bring out the nuts' richness. Choose a variety below, then follow the same two steps, at right.

ALMOND MILK

- 1 **cup raw almonds**
- 5 **cups filtered water, plus more for soaking**
- 4 **plump Medjool dates, pitted**
- ¼ **tsp. cinnamon**
- 2 **pinches of sea salt**

MIXED-NUT MILK

- 1 **cup raw hazelnuts**
- ½ **cup raw almonds**
- ½ **cup raw Brazil nuts**
- 1 **vanilla bean**
- 5 **cups filtered water, plus more for soaking**
- 2 **Tbsp. honey**
- ½ **tsp. sea salt**

SOAK THE NUTS

In a medium bowl, cover the nuts and vanilla bean (if applicable) with filtered water. Cover and let stand overnight at room temperature.

MAKE THE NUT MILK

Drain and rinse the nuts and vanilla bean (if applicable) and transfer to a blender. Add the 5 cups of water and all of the remaining ingredients to the blender and puree at high speed until very smooth, about 2 minutes. Line a fine sieve with cheesecloth and set it over a bowl. Pour in the nut milk and let drain for 30 minutes. Using a spatula, press on the solids to extract any remaining milk; discard the solids. Pour the nut milk into an airtight container and refrigerate until chilled, about 30 minutes. Stir or shake the milk before serving.

MAKE AHEAD The milk can be refrigerated for up to 4 days.

Mixed-Nut-Milk Panna Cotta
Total 30 min plus 2 hr chilling
Serves 6

In a bowl, sprinkle 2 tsp. **unflavored gelatin** over ½ cup **Mixed-Nut Milk** and let stand until softened, about 5 minutes. In a medium saucepan, combine 2½ cups **Mixed-Nut Milk** with ⅓ cup **sugar,** 2 Tbsp. **honey,** the seeds of ½ **vanilla bean** and a pinch of **salt.** Bring just to a simmer over moderately high heat. Remove from the heat and whisk in the gelatin mixture until dissolved. Lightly brush six ½-cup ramekins with **vegetable oil** and set them on a baking sheet. Carefully fill the ramekins with the panna cotta mixture and refrigerate until set, at least 2 hours or up to 2 days. Run a knife around each panna cotta and invert onto a plate. Top with crushed toasted **hazelnuts** and serve with ¼ cup **strawberry jam** whisked with 1 Tbsp. **water.**

STEP-BY-STEP

1 COVER the nuts with filtered water and then let them soak overnight at room temperature.

2 DRAIN and rinse the nuts. Puree in a blender with more filtered water and the flavoring ingredients.

3 POUR the pureed mixture through a cheesecloth-lined sieve, then let it sit and drain for 30 minutes.

4 PRESS on the solids with a spatula to make sure you extract all the liquid.

You can also make this jiggly panna cotta with almond milk for a more delicate and pure almond flavor.

Mixed-Nut Milk

Almond Milk

Mixed-Nut-Milk Panna Cotta

ANJOU PUNCH

Fennel Ridgecrests

⊙ Total **30 min**; Makes **4 drinks**

¼ cup strained fresh grapefruit juice

¼ cup superfine sugar

1 Tbsp. pear brandy

8 oz. fresh fennel juice, chilled

Ice

8 oz. chilled sparkling hard cider

Fennel fronds, for garnish

1. In a medium bowl, whisk the grapefruit juice with the sugar and brandy until the sugar is dissolved. Chill the grapefruit cordial for 15 minutes.

2. In a large measuring cup, stir the fennel juice with 2 ounces of the grapefruit cordial. Pour the drink into 4 tall ice-filled glasses and top with the cider. Garnish with fennel fronds and serve.
—*Chad Arnholt and Claire Sprouse*

MAKE AHEAD The grapefruit cordial can be refrigerated for up to 1 week.

Anjou Punch

⊙ Total **40 min**; Serves **12**

Three 3-inch cinnamon sticks, broken into pieces, plus whole cinnamon sticks for garnish

½ cup sugar

Crushed ice

Orange and lemon wheels

12 oz. Cognac

12 oz. Belle de Brillet (pear liqueur)

9 oz. fresh lemon juice

6 oz. triple sec

12 oz. chilled Champagne

1. In a small saucepan, cover the broken cinnamon sticks with 1 cup of water and bring to a boil. Simmer over moderately low heat until reduced by half. Stir in the sugar until dissolved. Let cool, then strain the cinnamon syrup through a fine sieve into a bowl; refrigerate until chilled.

2. Mound crushed ice in the middle of a large punch bowl. Using a long stirrer or spoon, slide orange and lemon wheels against the inside of the punch bowl, then push the crushed ice back to keep the fruit in place.

3. In a cocktail shaker, combine one-fourth each of the cinnamon syrup, Cognac, Belle de Brillet, lemon juice and triple sec; shake well. Add one-fourth of the Champagne and shake once, then add to the punch bowl. Repeat the shaking 3 more times with the remaining ingredients. Serve the punch in crushed-ice-filled glasses, garnished with cinnamon sticks and orange and lemon wheels. —*Leo Robitschek*

Meadow Mocktails

📷 PAGE 369

Total **20 min plus 2 hr steeping**
Makes **8 drinks**

Make this refreshing lavender-and-grapefruit spritzer in large batches for easy entertaining. To turn it into a cocktail, swap gin or vodka for some of the sparkling water (see Note).

LAVENDER SYRUP

1 cup sugar

¼ cup dried lavender flowers

MOCKTAILS

½ cup basil leaves

2 Tbsp. fresh lemon juice

11 oz. fresh grapefruit juice

¼ oz. Angostura bitters

40 oz. chilled sparkling water

Ice

Basil leaves, grapefruit slices and/or lavender flowers, for garnish

1. Make the lavender syrup In a medium saucepan, combine the sugar and lavender flowers with 1 cup of water and bring to a boil. Cook over moderate heat, stirring, until the sugar dissolves, about 3 minutes. Remove from the heat, cover and let steep for 2 hours. Strain the syrup through a fine sieve.

2. Make the mocktails In a mini food processor, pulse the basil with the lemon juice until minced. Scrape into a large pitcher. Stir in 11 ounces of the lavender syrup (any remaining syrup can be refrigerated for 2 weeks) and the grapefruit juice, bitters and sparkling water. Strain into ice-filled glasses, garnish with basil and serve.
—*Johanna Corman*

NOTE For a cocktail version of this drink, use 24 ounces of sparkling water plus 16 ounces of gin or vodka.

Elixir Bonbon Floats

Active **1 hr**; Total **2 hr 45 min**
Makes **8 to 10 drinks**

L.A. chef Courtney McBroom makes a fantastic version of homemade root beer for these playful floats served with ice cream bonbons.

ELIXIR

2 cups water

1¾ cups sugar

Three 2-inch pieces of orange peel

One 1-inch piece of fresh ginger, sliced

1 Tbsp. sassafras (see Note)

1 Tbsp. sarsaparilla (see Note)

½ cinnamon stick (1½ inches)

1 star anise

5 cloves

¼ tsp. kosher salt

½ tsp. pure vanilla extract

2½ cups cold sparkling water

BONBONS

12 oz. bittersweet chocolate (70%), finely chopped

½ cup coconut oil

1 pint vanilla ice cream

1. Make the elixir In a saucepan, combine everything except the vanilla and sparkling water and bring to a boil, stirring to dissolve the sugar. Let cool for 1 hour. Strain through a fine sieve and stir in the vanilla, then refrigerate until well chilled, 1 hour.

2. Make the bonbons In a microwave-safe bowl, melt the chocolate with the coconut oil on high power in 30-second bursts until nearly melted. Stir until melted and smooth. Let cool completely.

3. Using a 1-tablespoon scoop, scoop 30 ice cream balls onto wax-paper-lined plates and freeze until firm, 20 minutes. Using 2 spoons, dip 1 ice cream ball at a time in the cooled chocolate mixture and return to the plate. Freeze the bonbons until very firm.

4. For each drink, pour ¼ cup of the elixir into a chilled glass. Add 3 bonbons, top with ¼ cup of sparkling water and serve.
—*Courtney McBroom*

NOTE Sassafras and sarsaparilla are available at kalustyans.com.

ESCAROLE SALAD
WITH RED QUINOA
AND HAZELNUTS
Recipe, page 44

RECIPE INDEX

Page numbers in **bold** indicate photographs.

D

E

H

I

J

K

L

S

Roasted Squash with Tamarind-Chile Glaze and Crispy Quinoa, 229

Roasted Winter Squash with Vanilla Butter, **228,** 229

Roast Pork with Acorn Squash Romesco Puree, 177

Squash Gratin, 230

Vegetable Bagna Cauda with Dill Oil, 217

Winter Squash Soup with Kale and Fideos, **74,** 75

STARTERS. SEE ALSO DIPS & SPREADS

Apricot and Ricotta Tartines, 22

Bacony Tortillas with Melted Cheese and Crispy Mushrooms, 35

Baked Sweet Potato and Tempeh Empanadas, 32, **33**

Bruschetta with Peperonata, 19

Buffalo Mozzarella with Neat and Messy Roasted Tomatoes, **18,** 19

Carbonara Arancini, 25

Cheese Sables with Rosemary Salt, 28

Chicken and Cashew Dumplings, 36

Country Ham with Okra and Cheddar, 15

Crispy Summer Squash Pancakes, **14,** 15

Filipino Salad Crêpes, **30,** 31

Free-Form Autumn Vegetable Tart with Bacon Marmalade, 34

Grilled Escarole Toasts with Trout Roe, 22

Grilled Kale Toasts, 23

Ham-and-Cheese Puff Pastry Tart, **8,** 34

Herbed Chickpea Bruschetta, 22

Herbed Potato Chips, 11

Jamaican Greens-Stuffed Patties, 29

Marinated Olives with Orange, 11

Mini Spinach-and-Herb Pies, **24,** 25

Mixed Radishes with Yogurt Butter, 11

Olive, Chile and White Bean Crostini, 22

Open-Face Cheese Toasts with Broccoli Rabe Relish, 20, **21**

Oyster Mushroom and Truffle Croquettes, 28

Pan con Tomate with Garrotxa Cheese, 19

Pink Peppercorn and Fennel Gravlax, 26

Pork and Shrimp Dumplings, 37

Quick-Cured Salmon with Salmon Cracklings, 26, **27**

Quinoa Balls with Cauliflower and Cheese, 28

Roasted Shrimp Skewers with Fennel and Mustard Chimichurri, 31

Salt Cod Fritters with Curry Aioli, 15

Sea Scallop Lollipops, 29

Shrimp and Avocado Summer Rolls, 31

Smoked Whitefish Tartare with Herb Oil, 26

Spicy Mapo Tofu Dumplings, 37

Stuffed Grape Leaves, 35

Tomatoes Two Ways with Crab and Soppressata, 35

Tuna Briks, 29

Venezuelan Fresh Corn Cakes with Cheese, 32

Warm Tofu with Soy-Ginger Sauce, 23

White Anchovy Toasts with Parsnip Butter, 20

STEWS

Asian Beef Stew, 87

Autumn Oxtail Stew, 87

Brisket and Mushroom Stew, 86

Chicken Chile Verde, 153

Duck Confit and White Bean Stew, 85

Hunter's Chicken Stew, **84,** 85

Irish Lamb and Turnip Stew, 86

Monkfish Stew with Saffron Broth, **80,** 81

Smoky Mussel Stew, 81

Spring Beef Stew, 86

STRAWBERRIES

Almond Cake with Mixed Berries, 329

Burnt Strawberry Tamales, 317

Fruity Caipirinha Jelly, 318

Milk Chocolate Mousse with Brown Butter Shortbread and Roasted Strawberries, 347

No-Bake White Chocolate Cheesecake with Strawberries, 333

Oatmeal with Strawberries, Toasted Walnuts and Skyr, 296, **297**

Pistachio Pavlova with Rhubarb Cream, **299,** 318

Russian Cream with Strawberries, 314

Salt-and-Pepper Sandwich Cookies with Strawberry-Lemonade Jam, 338

Strawberry Mousse with Strawberry Salad, 314, **315**

Strawberry Sauce, 365

Strawberry Slab Pie, 301

Stuffing, Whole-Grain, with Mustard Greens, Mushrooms and Fontina, 251

SUNCHOKES

Chunky Artichoke and Sunchoke Soup, 69

Roasted Winter Vegetables with Saffron Couscous, 226

SUNFLOWER SEEDS

Broccoli Coleslaw with Bacon and Raisins, 54

Wedge Salad with Sunflower Tahini and Ranch Dressing, 43

SWEET POTATOES

Baked Sweet Potato and Tempeh Empanadas, 32, **33**

Loaded Sweet Potatoes with Chorizo and Pomegranate, 238

Ombré Potato and Root Vegetable Gratin, 238

Roasted Winter Vegetables with Saffron Couscous, 226

Sweet Potatoes with Toasted Marshmallow Swirls, 240

SWISS CHARD

Farro and White Bean Soup with Swiss Chard and Herb Oil, 72, **73**

Jamaican Greens-Stuffed Patties, 29

Spaghetti with Clams and Braised Greens, 93

Wilted Swiss Chard with Warm Piccata Vinaigrette, 219

T

TACOS

Chipotle Chicken Tacos, 150, **151**

Crispy Pork Belly Tacos with Pico de Gallo, 184

Double-Decker Dr Pepper Chicken Tacos, 157

Fish Tacos with Tomatillo-Jalapeño Salsa, 121

Grilled Salmon and Lentil Tacos with Spicy Pickled Onions, 114

Picadillo Tacos, 201

Salsa Verde Chicharrón Tacos, 182

Steak Tacos with Pineapple, 201

Tacos al Pastor, 178, **179**

TAHINI

Fried Pickled Potatoes with Harissa Tahini, 236

Grilled Pickled Carrots with Charmoula and Almonds, 225

Hake with Walnut Tahini and Carrot Tabbouleh, 117

Roasted Cauliflower with Tahini Sauce, **222,** 223

Roasted Lemon Broccoli with Tahini-Yogurt Sauce, **211,** 224

CONTRIBUTORS

RECIPES

LASSE ANDERSEN is the owner of Grød, a porridge restaurant with three locations in Copenhagen.

JOSÉ ANDRÉS, an F&W Chef-in-Residence, is the chef and owner of restaurants in Las Vegas, Washington, DC, Los Angeles, Miami Beach and Dorado, Puerto Rico. He has authored four cookbooks, including *Tapas* and *Made in Spain,* a companion to his PBS series of the same name.

RYAN ANGULO is the chef at French Louie and a co-owner and chef at Buttermilk Channel, both in Brooklyn.

DOMINIQUE ANSEL is the pastry chef and owner of Dominique Ansel Bakery and Dominique Ansel Kitchen, both in Manhattan. He is the author of *Dominique Ansel: The Secret Recipes.*

ZOI ANTONITSAS, an F&W Best New Chef 2015, is the chef at Westward in Seattle.

CHAD ARNHOLT is a bartender at Comstock Saloon and co-founder of the Tin Roof Drink Community, which develops drinks for The Perennial in San Francisco.

MICHAEL BABCOCK is the chef and co-owner of Welcome Diner and Welcome Chicken + Donuts, both in Phoenix.

CHARLEEN BADMAN is the chef and co-owner of FnB in Scottsdale, Arizona.

CORY BAHR, F&W's People's Best New Chef 2015, is the chef and co-owner of Cotton and Nonna in Monroe, Louisiana.

KIERIN BALDWIN is the pastry chef at Locanda Verde in New York City.

DAN BARBER, an F&W Best New Chef 2002, is the chef and co-owner of Blue Hill in New York City and Blue Hill at Stone Barns in Pocantico Hills, New York. He is the author of *The Third Plate.*

MARIO BATALI, an F&W Chef-in-Residence, is the chef and co-owner of more than a dozen restaurants in New York City, Las Vegas, L.A. and Singapore and a co-owner of Eataly, a market and restaurant complex in Manhattan and Chicago. He co-hosts *The Chew* and is the author of nine cookbooks; his most recent is *America Farm to Table.*

RICK BAYLESS is the chef and co-owner of several restaurants in the Chicago area and Philadelphia, including Topolobampo, Xoco and Frontera Grill. He hosts PBS's *Mexico—One Plate at a Time;* his most recent cookbook is *More Mexican Everyday.*

CAMILLE BECERRA is the former chef and co-owner of Navy in New York City. She is currently working on a cookbook.

ELLEN BENNETT is the founder of Hedley & Bennett, a handmade apron company.

DAVE BERAN, an F&W Best New Chef 2014, is a co-chef at Next in Chicago.

MICHELLE BERNSTEIN is the chef and co-owner of Cena by Michy in Miami.

JAKE BICKELHAUPT, an F&W Best New Chef 2015, is the chef and co-owner of 42 Grams in Chicago.

BILL OR BEAK is a street vendor specializing in sandwiches at Kerb and other markets in London.

APRIL BLOOMFIELD, an F&W Chef-in-Residence and Best New Chef 2007, is the chef and co-owner of The Spotted Pig, The Breslin, The John Dory Oyster Bar and Salvation Taco, all in New York City, and Tosca Cafe in San Francisco. She most recently authored the cookbook *A Girl and Her Greens.*

JONATHAN BROOKS, an F&W Best New Chef 2015, is the chef and co-owner of Milktooth in Indianapolis.

GESINE BULLOCK-PRADO is a pastry chef and cookbook author. Her most recent book is *Let Them Eat Cake.*

CORTNEY BURNS is a co-chef at Bar Tartine in San Francisco and co-author of *Bar Tartine: Techniques & Recipes.*

ANNE BURRELL is the host of Food Network's *Chef Wanted* and the author of two cookbooks; her most recent book is *Own Your Kitchen.*

KATIE BUTTON, an F&W Best New Chef 2015, is the chef and co-owner of Cúrate and Nightbell, both in Asheville, North Carolina. She is the author of *The Cúrate Cookbook.*

TIM BYRES is the chef and co-owner of Smoke, Chicken Scratch, Bar Belmont and The Foundry, all in Dallas, and the author of *Smoke: New Firewood Cooking.*

KATIE CALDESI is a co-owner of two restaurants and a cooking school in England. She has also co-authored a number of cookbooks, most recently *Rome: Centuries in an Italian Kitchen.*

MARCO CANORA is the chef and owner of Hearth, Fifty Paces and Brodo, all in New York City. He is also the author of *Salt to Taste* and *A Good Food Day.*

ANDREW CARMELLINI, an F&W Best New Chef 2000, is the co-owner of several restaurants in New York City, including Locanda Verde and Lafayette, and The Dutch Miami in Miami Beach. He is the co-author of *Urban Italian* and *American Flavor.*

JOE CARROLL is the chef and owner of Fette Sau and St. Anselm, both in Brooklyn. He is also a co-author of the cookbook *Feeding the Fire.*

JOANNE CHANG is the pastry chef and co-owner of Flour Bakery + Café, with locations in the Boston area, and a co-owner of Myers + Chang in Boston. She has written several cookbooks; her most recent is *Baking with Less Sugar.*

JUSTIN CHAPPLE is an F&W Test Kitchen senior editor and the talent behind the Mad Genius Tips videos on foodandwine.com.

GEORGE CHEN is the chef and co-owner of Eight Tables restaurant in the China Live food hall in San Francisco.

ROY CHOI, an F&W Best New Chef 2010, is the chef and co-owner of Kogi BBQ food trucks as well as several brick-and-mortar restaurants in the Los Angeles area. He is also the owner of Pot and Pot Lobby Bar and a co-owner of Commissary, all in The Line Hotel in L.A., and a co-founder of the LocoL fast-food restaurants in Los Angeles and San Francisco. He is the author of *L.A. Son.*

ASHLEY CHRISTENSEN is the chef and owner of Poole's Downtown Diner, Beasley's Chicken + Honey, Chuck's, Fox Liquor Bar, Joule Coffee and Death & Taxes, all in Raleigh, North Carolina.

JIM CHRISTIANSEN, an F&W Best New Chef 2015, is the chef and co-owner of Heyday in Minneapolis.

KAY CHUN is an F&W Test Kitchen senior editor.

JOHNNY CLARK is a co-chef and co-owner of Parachute in Chicago.

THIBAUT CLOCHET is the chef and owner of Le Vin Vivant in Nantes, France.

TOM COLICCHIO, the head judge on *Top Chef* and an F&W Best New Chef 1991, is the chef and owner of Crafted Hospitality, which includes Craft in Manhattan, Craftsteak in Las Vegas and Beachcraft in Miami.

NINA COMPTON is the chef and co-owner of Compère Lapin restaurant in The Old No. 77 Hotel in New Orleans.

SCOTT CONANT is the chef and owner of several restaurants, including Scarpetta in Miami, L.A. and Las Vegas. He is also a judge on Food Network's *Chopped* and the author of three cookbooks; his most recent is *The Scarpetta Cookbook.*

MATT CONROY is the chef at Little Prince in New York City.

MARY CONSTANT is a Food52 member and winemaker in Calistoga, California.

COURTNEY CONTOS is the owner of Chef Contos Kitchen & Store, a cooking school in Shelburne, Vermont.

GABRIELE CORCOS is a co-host with his wife, Debi Mazar, of *Extra Virgin* on the Cooking Channel. He and Mazar split their time between Tuscany and Brooklyn, where they own the shop and restaurant The Tuscan Gun.

JOHANNA CORMAN is a co-owner of Vena's Fizz House in Portland, Maine.

SUZANNE COUCH is a reggae singer, caterer and culinary consultant for Miss Lily's restaurant in New York City. She lives in Kingston, Jamaica.

LIZ COWAN is the owner of Three Little Figs jam company in Portland, Oregon.

GERARD CRAFT is the chef and owner of Niche Food Group, which includes Niche and Porano Pasta in St. Louis.

JOHNPAUL DAMATO is the chef at Compass Rose in Washington, DC.

SANDY D'AMATO, the former chef and owner of Sanford in Milwaukee, runs Good Stock Farm cooking school in Hatfield, Massachusetts.

AMÉLIE DARVAS is the chef and co-owner of Haï Kaï in Paris.

KATIE QUINN DAVIES is the Sydney-based blogger behind What Katie Ate. Her most recent cookbook is *What Katie Ate on the Weekend.*

CHERYL DAY and her husband, **GRIFFITH DAY,** are the owners of Back in the Day Bakery in Savannah, Georgia. They have co-authored two cookbooks, most recently *Back in the Day Bakery Made with Love.*

ROMÉE DE GORIAINOFF is a co-owner of the Experimental Cocktail Club, with locations in Paris, London and New York City; Grand Pigalle in New York City; and Experimental Beach in Ibiza.

MATTHEW DEMILLE is the chef at the Drake Devonshire Inn in Wellington, Ontario, Canada.

GREG DENTON and his wife, **GABRIELLE QUIÑÓNEZ DENTON,** F&W Best New Chefs 2014, are the chefs and owners of Ox Restaurant in Portland, Oregon.

NICK DETRICH is the bartender and co-owner of Cane & Table in New Orleans.

LISA DONOVAN is a writer and pastry chef in Nashville. She caters private events, teaches cooking classes and runs an online bakeshop called Buttermilk Road.

VINNY DOTOLO, an F&W Best New Chef 2009, is a co-chef and co-owner of Animal, Son of a Gun and Jon & Vinny's and a co-owner of Trois Mec and Petit Mec, all in Los Angeles.

TOM DOUGLAS is the chef and co-owner of numerous restaurants in Seattle. He is the author of several cookbooks and offers classes at Hot Stove Society, his cooking school in the Hotel Ändra.

TARA DUGGAN is a writer for the San Francisco *Chronicle* and the author of *Root-to-Stalk Cooking.*

NAOMI DUGUID is a Canadian food writer and photographer. Her most recent cookbook is *Burma: Rivers of Flavor.*

DANIEL EDDY is the chef at Rebelle in Manhattan.

JODI ELLIOTT is the pastry chef and owner of Bribery Bakery in Austin.

MALIN ELMLID is the Berlin-based founder of the barter site and blog The Bread Exchange. She is also the author of a book of the same name.

DUSKIE ESTES is a co-chef and co-owner of Zazu Kitchen + Farm and Black Pig Meat Co. in Sebastopol, California.

SUSAN FENIGER is a chef and restaurateur. She co-owns Mud Hen Tavern in Los Angeles; Border Grill in Las Vegas, Los Angeles and Santa Monica; and Border Grill Truck in L.A. She is a co-author of several cookbooks, including *Cooking with Too Hot Tamales* and *Susan Feniger's Street Food.*

SCOTT FINLEY is a co-baker and co-owner of Two Old Tarts café and bakery in Andes, New York.

BOBBY FLAY is the chef and co-owner of several restaurants in the US and Bahamas, among them Gato and Bar Americain in New York City, and the host of various cooking shows, including *Beat Bobby Flay.* He has written many cookbooks; his most recent is *Brunch at Bobby's.*

TYLER FLORENCE, the host of Food Network's *Tyler's Ultimate* and *The Great Food Truck Race,* is the owner of Wayfare Tavern in San Francisco and co-owner of El Paseo in Mill Valley, California. He is the author of several cookbooks; his most recent is *Inside the Test Kitchen.*

IAN FLORES is a pastry chef and co-owner of Mr. and Mrs. Miscellaneous in San Francisco.

MICHAEL FOJTASEK, an F&W Best New Chef 2015, is a co-chef and co-owner of Olamaie in Austin.

MARTE MARIE FORSBERG is a food and lifestyle photographer and home cook. Her blog is the Marte Marie Forsberg Food Journal.

SARA FORTE is the author of the Sprouted Kitchen blog and two Sprouted Kitchen cookbooks.

JEREMY FOX, an F&W Best New Chef 2008, is the chef at Rustic Canyon in Santa Monica, California.

AMANDA FREITAG is a judge on Food Network's *Chopped* and the host of *American Diner Revival.* She is also a co-author of the cookbook *The Chef Next Door* and a co-owner of Empire Diner in New York City.

ERIN FRENCH is the chef and owner of The Lost Kitchen in Freedom, Maine.

FORD FRY is the chef and owner of several Georgia restaurants, including The Optimist in Atlanta.

SHEA GALLANTE, an F&W Best New Chef 2005, is the chef at Chevalier restaurant in the Baccarat Hotel in New York City.

JOSH GALLIANO is a bread-production manager at Companion Bakery in St. Louis.

COLBY GARRELTS, an F&W Best New Chef 2005, is the chef and co-owner of Bluestem in Kansas City, Missouri, and Rye in Leawood, Kansas. He is a co-author of the cookbook *Made in America.*

WESLEY GENOVART is the chef and co-owner of SoLo Farm & Table in South Londonderry, Vermont.

TODD GINSBERG is the chef and co-owner of several restaurants in Atlanta, including Fred's Meat & Bread.

SPIKE GJERDE is the chef and co-owner of Woodberry Kitchen, Artifact Coffee, Shoo-Fly Diner and Parts and Labor, all in Baltimore.

ASHA GOMEZ is the chef and owner of the restaurant Spice to Table in Atlanta. She is a co-author of the forthcoming cookbook *My Two Souths.*

GERARDO GONZALEZ is the chef at El Rey Coffee Bar and Luncheonette in New York City.

KOREN GRIEVESON, an F&W Best New Chef 2008, is the chef at Resto in Manhattan.

BRAD GRIMES is the winemaker at Abreu Vineyards in Napa Valley.

SARA GRIMES is a Food52 member, a veterinarian and a home cook in Portland, Oregon.

JOSH GRINKER is the chef and co-owner of Kings County Imperial and co-chef and co-owner of Stone Park Café, both in Brooklyn.

SARAH GRUENEBERG is the chef and co-owner of Monteverde in Chicago.

NICOLE HALEY is the owner of Mirracole Morsels, a confectionery in Kingston, Washington.

CARLA HALL is a co-host of ABC's *The Chew;* the owner of Carla Hall Petite Cookies, an artisan cookie company; and co-owner of Carla Hall's Southern Kitchen, a restaurant in Brooklyn. She is a co-author of *Cooking with Love* and *Carla's Comfort Food.*

MAGGIE HARRISON is the winemaker and co-owner of Antica Terra winery in Dundee, Oregon.

JASMINE HEMSLEY and her sister **MELISSA HEMSLEY** are London-based nutritional consultants who created the wellness blog Hemsley + Hemsley. They co-authored *The Art of Eating Well.*

BRANDI HENDERSON is a co-founder and owner of The Pantry, a cooking school in Seattle.

HELENE HENDERSON is the chef and owner of Malibu Farm in Malibu, California.

JAMES HENRY is the former chef and co-owner of Bones in Paris.

TIMOTHY HOLLINGSWORTH is the chef and co-owner of Barrel & Ashes and Otium, both in Los Angeles.

DANIEL HOLZMAN is the chef and co-owner of The Meatball Shop restaurants in New York City. He is also a co-author of *The Meatball Shop Cookbook.*

VIVIAN HOWARD, the star of *A Chef's Life* on PBS, is the chef and co-owner of Chef & the Farmer in Kinston, North Carolina.

MEHERWAN IRANI is a chef and co-owner of Chai Pani Restaurant Group, which includes Boti Walla, a food stall in the Ponce City Market in Atlanta.

STEPHANIE IZARD, an F&W Best New Chef 2011 and *Top Chef* Season 4 winner, is the chef and co-owner of Girl & the Goat, Little Goat and the forthcoming Duck, Duck, Goat, all in Chicago.

CJ JACOBSON is the chef and co-owner of Girasol in Studio City, California, and the winner of *Top Chef Duels* in 2014.

MATT JENNINGS is the chef and co-owner of Townsman in Boston.

PAUL KAHAN, an F&W Best New Chef 2009, is the chef and co-owner of several restaurants in Chicago, including Blackbird, Publican and Dove's Luncheonette.

KIAN LAM KHO is the blogger behind Red Cook and the author of the cookbook *Phoenix Claws and Jade Trees.*

BEVERLY KIM, winner of *Top Chef* Season 9, is a co-chef and co-owner of Parachute in Chicago.

DANAI KINDELI manages Metohi Kindelis guesthouse on the Greek island of Crete.

BETH KIRBY is a Tennessee-based photographer, stylist, writer and recipe developer. Her blog is called Local Milk.

ELI KIRSHTEIN is the chef and co-owner of The Luminary in the Krog Street Market in Atlanta.

KRISTEN KISH, winner of *Top Chef* Season 10, is a chef based in Boston. She is a co-host of Travel Channel's *36 Hours.*

CHRIS KIYUNA is the chef and co-founder of The Perennial in San Francisco.

DAN KLUGER, an F&W Best New Chef 2012, is a former chef at ABC Kitchen in New York City. His forthcoming restaurant will open in early 2016.

IAN KNAUER is the founder of The Farm Cooking School in Stockton, New Jersey, and author of the cookbook *The Farm.*

TIMOTHY KOENIG is the manager of Yusho in Chicago.

DAFNA KORY is the owner of Inna Jam, a preserves company in Emeryville, California.

PHILIP KRAJECK is the chef and co-owner of Rolf and Daughters in Nashville.

EMERIL LAGASSE is the superstar chef and owner of numerous restaurants across the country, including Emeril's and NOLA in New Orleans. His most recent cookbook is *Emeril's Cooking with Power.*

SAL LAMBOGLIA is a co-chef and co-owner of Bar Primi in New York City.

RICHARD LANDAU is the chef and co-owner of Vedge and V Street, both in Philadelphia.

ALEX LARREA is the chef at Experimental Beach Ibiza on the Spanish island of Ibiza.

MIKE LATA is the chef and co-owner of FIG and The Ordinary, both in Charleston, South Carolina.

CHRISTINA LECKI is a chef at The Breslin in New York City.

SHU HAN LEE is a graphic designer and freelance food stylist and writer. She writes the blog Mummy, I Can Cook.

LUDO LEFEBVRE is the chef and co-owner of Petit Trois and Trois Mec and the chef and owner of LudoBird, all in Los Angeles.

TATIANA LEVHA is the chef and co-owner of Le Servan in Paris.

MARGARET LI and her siblings, **IRENE LI** and **ANDY LI,** are the chefs and owners of Mei Mei in Boston.

MEI LIN, winner of *Top Chef* Season 12, is a chef based in Los Angeles.

DONALD LINK is a co-chef and co-owner of several restaurants in New Orleans, including Herbsaint and Pêche. His newest restaurant, Cochon Butcher, is in Nashville and New Orleans. He is the author of *Real Cajun* and *Down South.*

JENN LOUIS, an F&W Best New Chef 2012, is the chef and co-owner of Lincoln Restaurant and Sunshine Tavern in Portland, Oregon, and the author of *Pasta by Hand.*

TIFFANY MACISAAC is the pastry chef and co-owner of Buttercream Bakeshop in Washington, DC.

ELIZABETH MADDEN is the founder of Rare Bird Preserves in Chicago.

EVELINA MAKRINAKI is the chef and co-owner of Pemptousia Taverna in Chaniá on the Greek island of Crete.

LYNNETTE MARRERO is a mixologist and co-founder of Speed Rack, an all-women bartending competition.

AUTUMN MARTIN is the chocolatier and owner of Hot Cakes Molten Chocolate Cakery in Seattle.

SASHA MARTIN is the author of the cookbook-memoir *Life from Scratch* and the blogger behind Global Table Adventure.

TIM MASLOW, an F&W Best New Chef 2015, is the chef at Strip-T's in Watertown and chef and owner of Ribelle in Brookline, Massachusetts.

REBECCA MASSON is the pastry chef and owner of Fluff Bake Bar in Houston.

DAVID MATTACHIONI is chef and owner of Mattachioni in Toronto.

ANNA MAY is a Food52 member who lives in West Dorset, England. Her blog is called Anna May, Everyday.

DEBI MAZAR is an actor and a co-host with her husband, Gabriele Corcos, of *Extra Virgin* on the Cooking Channel. She and Corcos split their time between Tuscany and Brooklyn, where they own the shop and restaurant The Tuscan Gun.

SHANE MCBRIDE is the chef at Balthazar and Schiller's Liquor Bar and a co-chef at Cherche Midi, all in New York City.

COURTNEY MCBROOM is a co-chef and co-owner of Large Marge catering company in Los Angeles.

LAENA MCCARTHY is the founder of the jam company Anarchy in a Jar in Brooklyn. She is the author of the cookbook *Jam On: The Craft of Canning Fruit.*

PAUL MCGEE is the beverage director of Land and Sea Dept. and a co-owner of Lost Lake cocktail bar, both in Chicago.

ALICE MEDRICH is the author of 11 cookbooks; her most recent is *Flavor Flours.*

PETER MEEHAN is the editor of *Lucky Peach* magazine and a co-author of several cookbooks, most recently *Lucky Peach Presents 101 Easy Asian Recipes.*

ORI MENASHE, an F&W Best New Chef 2015, is the chef and co-owner of Bestia in Los Angeles.

AMANDA MICHAEL is the chef and owner of Jane in San Francisco.

KRISTEN MIGLORE is the executive editor of the Food52 online community. She compiled the recipes in the *Food52 Genius Recipes* cookbook.

BEN MIMS is the author of *Sweet & Southern: Classic Desserts with a Twist.*

PREETI MISTRY is the chef and co-owner of Juhu Beach Club in Oakland, California.

WADE MOISES is the chef at Rosemary's in New York City.

BONNIE MORALES is the chef and co-owner of Kachka in Portland, Oregon.

MR. HOLMES BAKEHOUSE is a bakery in San Francisco.

SEAMUS MULLEN is the chef and co-owner of Tertulia in New York City and a judge on Food Network's *Chopped.* He is the author of *Seamus Mullen's Hero Food.*

NHI MUNDY is the chef and owner of the Bà & Me Vietnamese restaurants in Honesdale, Pennsylvania, and Callicoon, New York.

PAUL NANNI is the chef and co-owner of The Heron in Narrowsburg, New York.

CHRISTINA NGUYEN is the chef and co-owner of Hola Arepa in Minneapolis.

RACHEL NICHOLS is a chef at The Smile To Go in New York City and an instructor at Heirloom Kitchen cooking school in Old Bridge, New Jersey.

GRAE NONAS, an F&W Best New Chef 2015, is a co-chef at Olamaie in Austin.

GHAYA OLIVEIRA is the executive pastry chef at Daniel in New York City.

ENRIQUE OLVERA is the superstar chef behind Grupo Enrique Olvera, which includes the restaurants Cosme in New York City and Pujol in Mexico City. He is the author of the cookbook *Mexico from the Inside Out.*

AMANDA PAA is the author of the cookbook *Smitten with Squash* and the creator of the blog Heartbeet Kitchen.

MICHAEL PALEY is the chef at Central Standard and Café No Sé in the South Congress Hotel in Austin.

DANIEL PARILLA is a co-chef at Cherche Midi in New York City.

KATIE PARLA is a food and beverage educator and journalist based in Rome. Her blog is called Parla Food; her cookbook, *Tasting Rome,* will be released in early 2016.

DANIEL PATTERSON is the co-owner of Coi, Plum Bar, Haven and Alta CA, all in the San Francisco Bay Area. He is a co-founder of the LocoL fast-food restaurants in L.A. and San Francisco.

ZAKARY PELACCIO is a co-chef and co-owner of Fish & Game in Hudson, New York, and the author of the cookbook *Eat with Your Hands.*

JACQUES PÉPIN, master chef and F&W Chef-in-Residence, is the dean of special programs at Manhattan's International Culinary Center and the host of PBS's *Heart & Soul.* His most recent cookbook is *Jacques Pépin Heart & Soul in the Kitchen.*

TERESA PIRO is the founder of Can Can Cleanse in San Francisco.

CASSIE PIUMA is the chef and co-owner of Sarma in Somerville, Massachusetts.

NAOMI POMEROY, an F&W Best New Chef 2009, is the chef and co-owner of Beast in Portland, Oregon.

LUDOVIC POUZELGUES is the chef and owner of Lulu Rouget in Nantes, France.

CLAIRE PTAK is the pastry chef and owner of Violet Bakery in London. She is the author of *The Violet Bakery Cookbook.*

ANNE QUATRANO, an F&W Best New Chef 1995, is a co-chef and co-owner of several restaurants in Atlanta, including Bacchanalia. She is the author of *Summerland: Recipes for Celebrating with Summer Hospitality.*

PAUL QUI, an F&W Best New Chef 2014 and the winner of *Top Chef* Season 9, is the chef and co-owner of Qui and the food truck and restaurant group East Side King in Austin. He is also the chef and co-owner of Otoko in the South Congress Hotel in Austin.

ALICE QUILLET is a co-owner and chef-baker at Le Bal Café in Paris.

ABIGAIL QUINN is a co–pastry chef at Proof Bakeshop in Atlanta and Cakes & Ale in Decatur, Georgia.

DOMINIC QUIRKE is the chef and owner of Pickles Restaurant in Nantes, France.

TIM RATTRAY is the chef and co-owner of The Granary in San Antonio, Texas.

NATE READY is a master sommelier and winemaker in Oregon.

ANDREA REUSING is the chef and co-owner of Lantern in Chapel Hill and the chef at The Durham Hotel in Durham, North Carolina.

CONTRIBUTORS

ELLIOT REYNOLDS is the chef at The Hubb at Angeline's in Bloomfield, Ontario, Canada.

EVAN RICH and his wife, **SARAH RICH,** are the chefs and owners of Rich Table in San Francisco.

AKASHA RICHMOND is the chef and co-owner of Akasha and Sāmbār, both in Culver City, California.

ANDY RICKER is the chef and owner of the Pok Pok restaurants in Portland, Oregon, and Los Angeles, and the chef and co-owner of the Pok Pok restaurants in New York City. He is a co-author of the cookbook *Pok Pok*.

ERIC RIPERT is the chef and co-owner of Le Bernardin and Aldo Sohm Wine Bar in New York City and chef-adviser for Blue by Eric Ripert in Grand Cayman.

MORGAN ROBINSON is the chef at El Original in New York City.

LEO ROBITSCHEK is the bar director at NoMad Bar and Eleven Madison Park, both in Manhattan. He is the author of *The NoMad Cocktail Book,* part of the two-volume NoMad cookbook set.

JORDI ROCA is the pastry chef and co-owner of El Celler de Can Roca in Girona, Spain, and the author of *The Desserts of Jordi Roca*.

RACHEL RODDY is the blogger behind Rachel Eats and the author of *My Kitchen in Rome: Recipes and Notes on Italian Cooking*.

MELCHOR ROSAS is the chef at the Phoenicia Diner in Phoenicia, New York.

SLADE RUSHING is the chef at Brennan's in New Orleans.

SARAH RYHANEN is a floral designer and co-owner of Saipua, a flower and soap boutique in Brooklyn.

CARLOS SALGADO, an F&W Best New Chef 2015, is the chef and owner of Taco María in Costa Mesa, California.

AARÓN SÁNCHEZ is a guest judge on Food Network's *Chopped* and the author of *Simple Food, Big Flavor*.

DIEGO SANCHEZ-MAITRET is a cocktail caterer and consultant and the on-call mixologist for Spring Street Social Society in New York City.

SARAH SCHAFER is the chef at Irving Street Kitchen in Portland, Oregon.

DEBORAH SCHNEIDER is the chef and co-owner of Sol Cocina in Newport Beach, California, and the author of *Salsas and Moles*.

ADAM SCHOP is the chef at Miss Lily's and Miss Lily's 7A, both in Manhattan.

JOHN SCHULMAN is a co-baker and co-owner of Two Old Tarts café and bakery in Andes, New York.

MICHAEL SCHWARTZ is the chef and owner of numerous restaurants in Miami, including Michael's Genuine Food & Drink. He is the author of *Michael's Genuine Food: Down-to-Earth Cooking for People Who Love to Eat.*

MINDY SEGAL is the pastry chef and owner of Mindy's HotChocolate in Chicago. She is a co-author of the cookbook *Cookie Love*.

LIOR LEV SERCARZ is a chef and the owner of La Boîte, a spice blend company in New York City.

GILLIAN SHAW is the owner of Black Jet Baking Company in San Francisco.

ALON SHAYA is the chef and co-owner of Domenica and Shaya in New Orleans.

MIKE SHEERIN, an F&W Best New Chef 2010, is the chef at Embeya and the chef and co-owner of Packed, both in Chicago.

JULIA SHERMAN is a photographer and writer who shares her garden-centric recipes on the blog Salad for President.

DAI SHINOZUKA is the chef and co-owner of Les Enfants Rouges in Paris.

JON SHOOK, an F&W Best New Chef 2009, is a co-chef and co-owner of Animal, Son of a Gun and Jon & Vinny's and a co-owner of Trois Mec and Petit Mec, all in Los Angeles.

BRYCE SHUMAN, an F&W Best New Chef 2015, is the chef and co-owner of Betony in New York City.

KAMRAN SIDDIQI is the author of the cookbook *Hand Made Baking*. His blog is called The Sophisticated Gourmet.

NANCY SILVERTON, an F&W Best New Chef 1990, is the chef and co-owner of Osteria Mozza and Mozza2Go in Los Angeles and the owner of Chi Spacca, also in L.A., and Pizzeria Mozza, with locations in Los Angeles, Newport Beach and Singapore. She is the founder of La Brea Bakery and the author or co-author of nine books, including *Nancy Silverton's Pastries from the La Brea Bakery*.

GAIL SIMMONS is the F&W special projects director and a judge on *Top Chef.* She is the author of *Talking with My Mouth Full: My Life as a Professional Eater.*

JOSHUA SKENES is the chef and co-owner of Saison and the forthcoming Fat Noodle, both in San Francisco.

ERICA SKOLNIK is the baker and owner of Frenchie's in Washington, DC.

MICHAEL SOLOMONOV is the chef and co-owner of Zahav and a co-owner of Federal Donuts, Percy Street Barbecue, Dizengoff and Abe Fisher, all in Philadelphia. He is a co-author of *Zahav: A World of Israeli Cooking.*

ANA SORTUN is the chef and co-owner of Sofra and Oleana restaurants in Cambridge, Massachusetts. She is the author of the cookbook *Spice: Flavors of the Eastern Mediterranean*.

CLAIRE SPROUSE is a co-founder of the Tin Roof Drink Community, which develops drinks for The Perennial in San Francisco.

CARA STADLER, an F&W Best New Chef 2014, is the chef and co-owner of Tao Yuan in Brunswick, Maine, and Bao Bao Dumpling House in Portland, Maine.

MICHAEL STEBNER is the culinary director of the Sweetgreen chain of restaurants.

ZAK STERN is the owner of Zak the Baker, a café and bakery in Miami.

TARA STEVENS is a food writer, chef and cooking teacher at The Courtyard Kitchen at Dar Namir in Fez, Morocco. She is the author of *Clock Book: Recipes from a Modern Moroccan Kitchen.*

CURTIS STONE, host of Food Network's *Kitchen Inferno,* is the chef and owner of Maude in Los Angeles. His latest cookbook is *Good Food, Good Life.*

ETHAN STOWELL, an F&W Best New Chef 2008, is the chef and co-owner of several restaurants in Seattle, including Staple & Fancy, How to Cook a Wolf and Anchovies & Olives. He is a co-author of *Ethan Stowell's New Italian Kitchen.*

ALEX STUPAK, an F&W Best New Chef 2013, is the chef and co-owner of Empellón Cocina, Empellón Taqueria and Empellón Al Pastor in New York City. He is a co-author of *Tacos: Recipes and Provocations.*

HEIDI SWANSON is the creator of the blog 101 Cookbooks and author of several cookbooks, including *Near & Far: Recipes Inspired by Home and Travel.*

JAMES SYHABOUT, an F&W Best New Chef 2010, is the chef and owner of Commis and Hawker Fare and chef and co-owner of The Dock, all in Oakland, California.

MICHAEL SYMON, an F&W Best New Chef 1998 and winner of Food Network's *The Next Iron Chef* Season 1, is the chef and co-owner of Lola and Lolita in Cleveland, Roast in Detroit and B Spot in Detroit, Cleveland and Columbus, Ohio. He is a co-host of ABC's *The Chew* and the author or co-author of several books, including *Michael Symon's Carnivore.*

BOB TAM is the chef and co-owner of Bitter & Twisted Cocktail Parlour in Phoenix.

PIM TECHAMUANVIVIT is the blogger behind Chez Pim and the co-owner of Kin Khao in San Francisco.

MIMI THORISSON is the host of the French cooking show *La Table de Mimi,* author of *A Kitchen in France* and the blogger behind Manger. She holds cooking workshops in her home in St. Yzans de Médoc, France.

JENNIFER TOOMEY is the chef de cuisine at Milo & Olive in Santa Monica, California.

ANNABELLE TOPACIO is a pastry chef and co-owner of Mr. and Mrs. Miscellaneous in San Francisco.

RICH TORRISI, an F&W Best New Chef 2012, is a co-chef and co-owner of Dirty French, Parm, Santina and Sadelle's in New York City and Carbone in Las Vegas, New York City and Hong Kong.

CHRISTINA TOSI, a judge on *MasterChef* and *MasterChef Junior,* is the chef and co-owner of Momofuku Milk Bar bakery. Her most recent book is *Milk Bar Life.*

ANNA TRATTLES is a co-owner and chef-baker at Le Bal Café in Paris.

JERRY TRAUNFELD is the chef and co-owner of Lionhead and Poppy, both in Seattle.

STELIOS TRILYRAKIS is the chef and owner of Ntounias in Chaniá, on the Greek island of Crete.

YIANNIS TSIVOURAKIS is a chef at the Minoa Palace Hotel in Chaniá, on the Greek island of Crete.

MARCELA VALLADOLID is the host of Food Network's *Mexican Made Easy.* She is the author of two cookbooks, *Fresh Mexico* and *Mexican Made Easy.*

LIONEL VATINET is the master baker and owner of La Farm Bakery in Cary, North Carolina.

ANYA VON BREMZEN is the author of six cookbooks. Her memoir is *Mastering the Art of Soviet Cooking.*

DAVID WALTUCK is the chef and co-owner of Élan in New York City. He co-authored *Chanterelle* and *Staff Meals from Chanterelle.*

ALICE WATERS is the chef and owner of Chez Panisse in Berkeley, California, and the author of 12 books; her latest is *My Pantry.* She is the founder of The Edible Schoolyard Project, a nonprofit program that aims to get an "edible education" into public schools.

JOANNE WEIR is a chef, cooking teacher and the author of several cookbooks, most recently *Kitchen Gypsy.*

LUISA WEISS, author of *My Berlin Kitchen,* is the blogger behind The Wednesday Chef.

ARI WEISWASSER is the chef and co-owner of Glen Ellen Star in Sonoma.

ALEXA WEITZMAN is a cooking instructor at Heirloom Kitchen in Old Bridge, New Jersey. She is the author of the blog Sustainable Pantry.

WILLIAM WERNER is the pastry chef and co-owner of Craftsman and Wolves in San Francisco.

MARTHA WIGGINS is the chef at Sylvain in New Orleans.

SHELLEY WISEMAN is a teacher at The Farm Cooking School in Stockton, New Jersey. She is the author of two cookbooks, *Just Tacos* and *The Mexican Gourmet.*

ERLING WU-BOWER is the chef at Nico Osteria in Chicago.

KUNIKO YAGI is the former chef at Hinoki & the Bird in Los Angeles.

TRACY JANE YOUNG is a co-chef and co-owner of Kings County Imperial in Brooklyn.

IMAGES

CEDRIC ANGELES 4, 60, 168, 183

TARA FISHER 5, 17, 95, 108, 126, 127, 147, 261, 289, 292, 293, 297, 336, 337, 374, 375

NICOLE FRANZEN 10, 14, 39, 52, 66, 123, 164, 165, 186, 206, 215, 250, 268, 275, 278, 286, 299, 343, 352, 376

LUIS GARCIA 88

CHRISTINA HOLMES 107, 151, 158, 161, 189, 205, 211, 227, 246, 249, 262, 276, 280, 320, 322

NICHOLAS HOPPER 212, 216, 325

PER-ANDERS JORGENSEN 234

JOHN KERNICK 13, 21, 36, 37, 45, 46, 51, 56, 59, 67, 73, 134, 140, 162, 170, 210, 239, 354, 364, 368, back cover (pudding)

EVA KOLENKO 113, 116, 176, 195, 290

RYAN ROBERT MILLER 180

CHRIS PHILPOT 101

RICK POON 38, 104, 256, 294

CON POULOS Front cover, 9, 18, 27, 30, 33, 40, 65, 68, 74, 79, 82, 83, 89, 92, 99, 109, 110, 119, 120, 128, 133, 139, 141, 144, 148, 152, 155, 169, 175, 179, 196, 199, 200, 221, 228, 233, 235, 242, 255, 257, 258, 265, 271, 272, 279, 283, 300, 304, 310, 315, 321, 328, 331, 334, 340, 349, 355, 356, 361, 369, 370, 378, back cover (chicken and salad)

ANDREW PURCELL 96, 222

JAMES RANSOM 316

KAMRAN SIDDIQI 298, 303, 309

FREDRIKA STJÄRNE 55; **FREDRIKA STJÄRNE** and **JAMES RANSOM** 188

ODDUR THORISSON 6, 8, 80, 84, 192, 346

GUSTAV WIKING 24

MEASUREMENT GUIDE

BASIC MEASUREMENTS

GALLON	QUART	PINT	CUP	OUNCE	TBSP	TSP	DROPS
1 gal	4 qt	8 pt	16 c	128 fl oz			
½ gal	2 qt	4 pt	8 c	64 fl oz			
¼ gal	1 qt	2 pt	4 c	32 fl oz			
	½ qt	1 pt	2 c	16 fl oz			
	¼ qt	½ pt	1 c	8 fl oz	16 Tbsp		
			⅞ c	7 fl oz	14 Tbsp		
			¾ c	6 fl oz	12 Tbsp		
			⅔ c	5⅓ fl oz	10⅔ Tbsp		
			⅝ c	5 fl oz	10 Tbsp		
			½ c	4 fl oz	8 Tbsp		
			⅜ c	3 fl oz	6 Tbsp		
			⅓ c	2⅔ fl oz	5⅓ Tbsp	16 tsp	
			¼ c	2 fl oz	4 Tbsp	12 tsp	
			⅛ c	1 fl oz	2 Tbsp	6 tsp	
				½ fl oz	1 Tbsp	3 tsp	
					½ Tbsp	1½ tsp	
						1 tsp	60 drops
						½ tsp	30 drops

US TO METRIC CONVERSIONS

THE CONVERSIONS SHOWN HERE ARE APPROXIMATIONS. FOR MORE PRECISE CONVERSIONS, USE THE FORMULAS TO THE RIGHT.

VOLUME			WEIGHT			TEMPERATURE			CONVERSION FORMULAS
1 tsp	–	5 mL	1 oz	–	28 g	475°F	–	246°C	tsp × 4.929 = mL
1 Tbsp	=	15 mL	¼ lb (4 oz)	=	113 g	450°F	=	232°C	Tbsp × 14.787 = mL
1 fl oz	=	30 mL	½ lb (8 oz)	=	227 g	425°F	=	218°C	fl oz × 29.574 = mL
¼ c	=	59 mL	¾ lb (12 oz)	=	340 g	400°F	=	204°C	c × 236.588 = mL
½ c	=	118 mL	1 lb (16 oz)	=	½ kg	375°F	=	191°C	pt × 0.473 = L
¾ c	=	177 mL				350°F	=	177°C	qt × 0.946 = L
1 c	=	237 mL	**LENGTH**			325°F	=	163°C	oz × 28.35 = g
1 pt	=	½ L	1 in	=	2.5 cm	300°F	=	149°C	lb × 0.453 = kg
1 qt	=	1 L	5 in	=	12.7 cm	275°F	=	135°C	in × 2.54 = cm
1 gal	=	4.4 L	9 in	=	23 cm	250°F	=	121°C	(°F – 32) × 0.556 = °C